ESSAY 2

READING WITH

THE WRITER'S EYE

ESSAY 2
READING WITH
THE WRITER'S EYE

HANS P. GUTH
SAN JOSE STATE UNIVERSITY

RENÉE HAUSMANN SHEA
UNIVERSITY OF THE DISTRICT OF COLUMBIA

WADSWORTH PUBLISHING COMPANY
Belmont, California
A Division of Wadsworth, Inc.

English Editor:	John Strohmeier
Production Editor:	Leland Moss
Editorial Assistant:	Holly Allen
Managing Designer:	MaryEllen Podgorski
Text and Cover Design:	Vargas/Williams/Design
Print Buyer:	Barbara Britton
Copy Editor:	Noel Deeley
Compositor:	Boyer and Brass

Cover photograph by André Kertész, courtesy of the Estate of André Kertész ©.

Printed in the United States of America   50

1 2 3 4 5 6 7 8 9 10—91 90 89 88 87

ISBN 0-534-07872-9

Library of Congress Cataloging-in-Publication Data

Guth, Hans Paul, 1926–
   Essay 2: reading with the writer's eye.

   1. College readers.   2. English language—Rhetoric.
I. Shea, Renée Hausmann.   II. Title.   III. Title: Essay two.
PE1417.G87   1987   808'.0427   86-24625
ISBN 0-534-07872-9

PREFACE
To the Instructor

The aim of this book is to help students become better readers and writers. Virginia Woolf once said that the ideal reader is the "author's fellow-worker and accomplice." The ideal reader senses what the writer is trying to do, is willing to get into the spirit of a piece of writing, and responds to the signals that point the reader in the right direction. It is this kind of reader who is best equipped to profit from the work of successful fellow writers. This book encourages students to read with the writer's eye—to see in the finished piece of writing the author's footsteps, to become aware of how a successful piece of writing works.

What makes this book different from other "readers for writers"?

(1) *Essay 2* reprints lively, thought-provoking prose on topics that matter. Many of the writers in this book write on topics close to their hearts, dealing with subjects that the reader can take seriously. They have something to say and they say it well.

(2) *Essay 2* treats each selection as a meaningful whole. The focus throughout is on the *why and how* of writing. What is the author trying to say and how does the author do it? Rather than artificially separating purpose from meaning, or form from content, questions and guidelines in each unit focus on how forms and techniques serve the writer's purpose.

(3) The organization of *Essay 2* mirrors major dimensions of the writing process. The central part of the book ("Part Two: Patterns for Writing"), focusing on how writing takes shape, presents the familiar patterns of exposition: process, comparison and contrast, classification, cause and effect, definition, persuasion. But Part One ("Sources for Writing") asks the preliminary question of where writing comes from, what sets it in motion, what gives it substance. It explores the roots of writing in personal experience, alert observation, and our response to the opinions of others (experience, observation, points of view). Part Three ("Areas for Writing") takes the student writer "across the curriculum" and into actual "fields of writing": science, media, history. It looks at areas where writers write to inform, to evaluate, or to interpret the past.

(4) *Essay 2* helps teachers bridge the gap between professional writers and the student writer. Pointed guidelines in the "Writer's Guides" help students translate theory into practice. In candid interviews, authors talk about their own practice in writing and revision. Short student models complete each unit. A rich array of carefully worked-out writing assignments follows each essay.

The following are special features of this second edition:

- a new introduction, "Reading with a Purpose," guiding the student through the reading of a sample essay
- lively shorter new essays on timely topics (our threatened wildlife, women and pornography, math anxiety)
- larger representation of favorite authors: Annie Dillard, John McPhee, Garrison Keillor, Joan Didion, Kurt Vonnegut, Carl Sagan, Maxine Hong Kingston, Alice Walker, Ellen Goodman
- author interviews ("Writers on Writing") in which authors talk about writing and revision
- added "Overviews" in each section, specifying for each mode purpose, audience, and benefits for the writer
- student models at the end of each section (with both rough first draft and final revision included for one of these)
- streamlined apparatus with strengthened emphasis on purpose, structure, and audience
- new additional writing topics at the end of each section
- an instructor's manual offering an introduction to the use of model essays, capsule reviews of essays as well as sample responses to questions, additional "Writing Across the Curriculum" topics, and vocabulary reviews

This book is designed to help writing teachers teach by example as much as by precept, to help them nurture their students' gift for language, and to help their student writers succeed.

ACKNOWLEDGMENTS We are grateful to friends and critics of the book for many valuable suggestions. We especially acknowledge the advice of colleagues who reviewed the manuscript of the second edition at various stages: Professors Lester Adelsberg, Delgado Community College, West Bank Campus; Liz Anderson, Kirkwood Community College; Kathleen L. Bell, Old Dominion University; Amy Doerr, SUNY College at Buffalo; Eileen B. Evans, Western Michigan University; Joseph Harris, Parkland College; William Johnson, Augusta College; Patricia Maida, University of District of Columbia; Gratia Murphy, Youngstown State University; Nancy Walker, Southwest Missouri State University; and Peter Zoller, Wichita State University.

Hans P. Guth
Renée Hausmann Shea

CONTENTS

Introduction: Reading with a Purpose   1

What Makes Good Writing   1

Reading a Sample Essay   9

Reading and Writing   14

PART ONE

SOURCES FOR WRITING
17

1   PERSONAL EXPERIENCE: The Story with a Point   19

Writer's Guide 1: Writing from Experience   22

Prewriting Activities 1   25

Paragraph Practice 1   26

Maya Angelou, "Step Forward in the Car, Please"   28

A young black woman from the South takes on the Market Street Railway Company and overcomes the traditional barriers denying her employment.

Garrison Keillor, "Born Among the Born-Again"   34

In a small town in the rural Midwest, a boy growing up in a fundamentalist family rebels against "being different."

Writers on Writing: Garrison Keillor on Story-Telling   39

George Orwell, "Shooting an Elephant"   41

In this classic autobiographical essay, a central incident reveals to a young British police officer in colonial Burma the hollowness of the white man's colonial role.

Jade Snow Wong, "Fifth Chinese Daughter"   49

Like countless children of immigrant parents, a young girl in Chinatown has to chart her way between the old-country ways of home and the American ways of school and the outside world.

Student Model 1: Neal Lerner, "Sports Anyone?"   58

Additional Writing Topics 1   60

2 OBSERVATION: Seeing with Your Own Eyes 61

Writer's Guide 2: Writing from Observation 63

Prewriting Activities 2 67

Paragraph Practice 2 67

Leonard Michaels, "New York, New York" 69

On a return visit, an ex-New Yorker rediscovers the idyllic surface and the ugly underbelly of the city where he grew up.

Annie Dillard, "Looking Spring in the Eye" 72

A naturalist with a gift for taking a fresh look at the world around us reveals to our eyes the burgeoning life of a springtime pond, with its startling blend of grace and violence, of the beautiful and the grotesque.

N. Scott Momaday, "The Way to Rainy Mountain" 77

A gifted writer of native American (Kiowa) ancestry turns to early memories in search of a half-effaced heritage.

Gretel Ehrlich, "Wide Open Spaces" 84

A writer who goes to Wyoming in search of "new and unpopulated territory" discovers what it is like to live and work as a sheepherder in open country.

Writers on Writing: Gretel Ehrlich on Writing and Revising 92

Student Model 2: Joe Pollifrone, "A Day in the Life" 93

Additional Writing Topics 2 95

3 POINTS OF VIEW: Taking a Stand 97

Writer's Guide 3: Supporting a Thesis 99

Prewriting Activities 3 102

Paragraph Practice 3 103

Arthur Ashe, "A Black Athlete Looks at Education" 104

An outstanding black athlete asks young readers to look beyond the surface glamour of the athletic star system, encouraging young blacks to find role models other than athletes and entertainers.

Writers on Writing: Arthur Ashe on Professional Writers and Amateurs 106

Susan Jacoby, "Pornography and the First Amendment" 108

A "First Amendment junkie" asks women to look for alternatives to censorship in fighting pornography.

Writers on Writing: Susan Jacoby on Point of View 112

Charles McCabe, "Muggers and Morals"   114

A crusty newspaper columnist with strong opinions defends bystanders who roughed up a mugger against charges of vigilantism.

George Leonard, "Born to Run"   117

A prominent American journalist marshals an impressive array of anthropological, biological, and medical evidence to convince us that running is more than a fad.

Margaret Mead, "We Need Taboos on Sex at Work"   123

Looking at current remedies to problems of sexual harassment and sexual discrimination, a famous American anthropologist concludes that new laws and regulations alone will not be enough to change traditional patterns of behavior.

Student Model 3: Maureen Barney, "A Good Move" (First Draft and Revision)   129

Additional Writing Topics 3   132

PART TWO

PATTERNS FOR WRITING
135

4   PROCESS: How it Works   137

Writer's Guide 4: Tracing a Process   139
Prewriting Activities 4   143
Paragraph Practice 4   143

Marie De Santis, "The Last of the Wild Salmon"   144

A writer who worked for eight years as a commercial fisherwoman and captain of her own boat traces the life cycle of the wild salmon that are threatened by the destruction of their spawning grounds and replaced with artificially bred fish "no more suited to the stream than a poodle is to the woods."

John McPhee, "Oranges"   148

A lover of freshly squeezed orange juice (who has been called the "best nonfiction writer practicing today") traces the process that turns oranges into the frozen concentrate from which we make what now passes for orange juice.

Writers on Writing: An Editor on McPhee's Working Methods   154

Peter Meyer, "Land Rush"   156

In an article based on observation, interviews, and the patient sifting of stacks of documents, the author takes a critical look at the process that transforms rural neighborhoods into suburban developments in the name of progress.

Joan Didion, "Bureaucrats"   161

A witty, sharp-eyed observer of what is absurd in American life takes us behind the scenes of the traffic control center in Los Angeles to explain how things work and why they often don't.

Student Model 4: Catherine A. Russell, "Tree-Cutting, Country Style"   166

Additional Writing Topics 4   169

5   COMPARISON AND CONTRAST: Guiding Our Choices   170

Writer's Guide 5: Comparison and Contrast   172

Prewriting Activities 5   176

Paragraph Practice 5   177

Carolyn Lewis, "A Different Drummer"   178

A successful practitioner and teacher of broadcast journalism develops a contemporary version of a familiar topic: the contrast between life in the city and life in the country.

William Ouchi, "The Competitive Edge: Japanese and Americans"   182

A famous comparison of Japanese and American attitudes toward work reveals underlying differences between two societies that have become superficially very much alike.

Gloria Steinem, "Erotica and Pornography"   188

Taking on two terms likely to be confused in the heat of current argument, a leading American feminist works out a vital distinction designed to help us "untangle the lethal confusion of sex with violence."

Amy Gross, "The Appeal of the Androgynous Man"   194

Following the lead of current research into changing sex roles, the author sketches out the sensitive, caring, interesting alternative to the stereotypical steak-and-potatoes, whiskey-and-football, "all-man" man.

Writers on Writing: Amy Gross on Writing and Revising   198

Student Model 5: Mina Lunt, "L-Mode, R-Mode"   200

Additional Writing Topics 5   202

6 CLASSIFICATION: Sorting Things Out 204

Writer's Guide 6: Division and Classification 206

Prewriting Activities 6 210

Paragraph Practice 6 211

Jane Brody, "Three Kinds of Fatigue" 213

In order to help her readers understand and overcome fatigue, the author of a personal health column in the *New York Times* examines three major categories.

Ellen Goodman and Sam Keen, "Americans at Work: Three Portraits" 219

Three capsule portraits depict three types from the world of work: the corporate workaholic, the Supermom working mother, and the (intermittently) self-employed artisan who has dropped out of the rat race.

Judith Viorst, "Friends, Good Friends—and Such Good Friends" 226

A poet, journalist, and author of children's books sorts out the kinds of friends that play a role in her life.

Writers on Writing: Judith Viorst on the Influence of Reading 231

Marya Mannes, "Television: The Splitting Image" 233

An outspoken TV critic analyzes four major stereotypes that misrepresent American women in the "relentless sales procession" of American television.

Student Model 6: Sandra Bouslaugh, "New Options, New Attitudes" 240

Additional Writing Topics 6 242

7 ARGUMENT: Cause and Effect 244

Writer's Guide 7: Analyzing Causes and Effects 246

Prewriting Activities 7 250

Paragraph Practice 7 251

Sheila Tobias, "Who's Afraid of Math, and Why?" 252

Drawing on an impressive study of the subject, the author probes the causes of math anxiety. How can "math avoiders"—especially young women—avoid being left out in a society that worships science and technology?

Writers on Writing: Sheila Tobias on Math Anxiety and Writing Anxiety 259

Garrett Hardin, "Lifeboat Ethics"   261

Projecting our future on this crowded planet, an influential neoconservative writer rejects the sharing ethic implied in the spaceship metaphor in favor of the survival ethics of the lifeboat and explains why not all of us can be in the same boat.

Carl Sagan, "The Warming of the World"   269

In a classic example of an essay that takes us from a problem to its solution, a famous astrophysicist and television lecturer sounds a warning about the greenhouse effect that threatens to have a drastic impact on life on this planet.

Michael Novak, "The Family Out of Favor"   276

In a social climate hostile to lasting family ties, a writer speaking for the white ethnics looks back to the traditional family as a source of strength and essential moral values.

Student Model 7: Karen McLaughlin, "Stress: The Combat Zone"   282

Additional Writing Topics 7   284

8   DEFINITION: Drawing the Line   286

Writer's Guide 8: Writing to Define   288

Prewriting Activities 8   294

Paragraph Practice 8   296

Susannah Lessard, "The Real Conservatism"   297

Mapping out essential elements in a conservative outlook, the author helps us understand a general swing to the right in American life and politics.

Writers on Writing: Susannah Lessard on Choosing and Developing a Topic   299

Jane Howard, "In Search of the Good Family"   301

A journalist who became known for her books about the American scene gives new meaning to an old familiar term.

Ralph Nader, "A New Kind of Patriotism"   309

A crusading consumer advocate sets out in search of a new kind of patriotism to replace the "my-country-right-or-wrong" patriotism of past generations.

Richard Rodriguez, "Does America Still Exist?"   314

A prominent Mexican American writer looks beyond the surface contradictions of American society for clues for our common identity.

Student Model 8: Veda Anderson, "Reversing Discrimination" 319

Additional Writing Topics 8 321

9 PERSUASION: The Power of Words 323

Writer's Guide 9: The Strategies of Persuasion 325
Prewriting Activities 9 329
Paragraph Practice 9 331

George F. Will, "The Barbarity of Boxing" 332

One of America's best-known pundits takes on the audience that finds pleasure in a sport whose "crowning achievement is the infliction of serious trauma on the brain."

Fern Kupfer, "Institution Is Not a Dirty Word" 336

The parent of a severely brain-damaged child takes on the difficult task of changing the reader's mind on an emotion-laden subject.

Writers on Writing: Fern Kupfer on Writer and Audience 339

Kurt Vonnegut, Jr., "War Preparers Anonymous" 341

A novelist famous for his psychedelic fantasy, far-out humor, and turned-off antiestablishment satire uses a strategic analogy to help start a civilization hooked on war on the "long, hard trip back to sobriety."

Martin Luther King, Jr., "I Have a Dream" 345

In a famous speech, the leader of the civil rights movement mobilizes the aspirations of the black community and stirs the conscience of white Americans.

Student Model 9: Sally Finnegan, "Getting MADD" 350

Additional Writing Topics 9 352

PART THREE

AREAS FOR WRITING
355

10 SCIENCE WRITING: Writing to Inform 357

Writer's Guide 10: Writing to Inform 359
Prewriting Activities 10 362
Paragraph Practice 10 362

Lewis Thomas, "Ant City and Human Society"   364

A scientist who is the opposite of the narrow specialist makes us look at the behavior of "social animals" for the light it throws on our behavior and our problems as human beings. *(Comparison and contrast)*

Rachel Carson, "Our War Against Nature"   368

In this chapter from *Silent Spring*, a famous scientist and forerunner of the environmentalist movement delivers a classic indictment of our thoughtless abuse of our natural habitat and our genetic heritage. *(Cause and effect)*

Isaac Asimov, "Nuclear Fusion"   374

A prolific popularizer of scientific concepts explains what it will take for us to move beyond conventional nuclear energy to the age of nuclear fusion. *(Comparison and contrast)*

Writers on Writing: Isaac Asimov on Writing to Inform   379

Ed Edelson, "Smart Computers—Now They Speak Our Language"   382

A widely published science writer explores what is involved in teaching computers the mysteries of human language. *(Process)*

Writers on Writing: Ed Edelson on Using the Word Processor   389

Student Model 10: Dolores LaGuardia, "Talking to Apes"   390

Additional Writing Topics 10   391

11   MEDIA AND POPULAR CULTURE: Writing to Evaluate   393

Writer's Guide 11: Writing to Evaluate   395
Prewriting Activities 11   399
Paragraph Practice 11   401

Andy Rooney, "There's One Born Every Minute"   402

A well-known television commentator and syndicated columnist, who bills himself as a normal, ordinary person and "the all-American consumer," deals in his own fashion with the aggressive huckstering that is one of the petty annoyances of every day. *(Persuasion)*

Stanley Kauffman, "The Return of Rambo"   405

A widely read movie critic takes on one of the blockbuster successes on which the movie industry depends for survival, examining its subliminal message and the psychological needs of the audience the movie exploits. *(Thesis and support)*

Richard Harsham, "A Beeper for Violence"   409

A concerned observer looks for a way, short of censorship, to reduce the amount of violence in television programs for children. *(Persuasion)*

Tom Wolfe, "The Right Stuff"   413

Writing about the astronauts of Project Mercury, a leading chronicler of American popular culture takes us on the roller-coaster ride toward the "right stuff." *(Definition)*

Writers on Writing: Tom Wolfe on Fact and Fiction   419

Student Model 11: Anne Gelhaus, "Portraying Rape: Realism and Ratings"   420

Additional Writing Topics 11   422

12 WRITING ABOUT HISTORY: Interpreting the Past   423

Writer's Guide 12: Using and Documenting Sources   425

Prewriting Activities 12   429

Paragraph Practice 12   432

Larry Heinemann, "Tour of Duty"   433

A Vietnam veteran writes about a traumatic chapter in this country's history as an eyewitness who shares the "blunt and heartfelt bitterness" of those who "had been lied to and used by arrogant and selfish men." *(Personal experience)*

Writers on Writing: Larry Heinemann on the Process of Writing   438

Jonathan Schell, "What Happened at Hiroshima"   440

Challenging public apathy toward the threat of nuclear war, the author makes us listen to the testimony of survivors in order to force us "to confront head on the nuclear peril in which we all find ourselves." *(Persuasion)*

Alice Walker, "In Search of Our Mothers' Gardens"   450

A famous black novelist rediscovers the women who were her spiritual forebears. *(Personal experience)*

Barbara Tuchman, "Humanity's Better Moments"   460

A distinguished American historian who has written widely about war and calamity here takes stock of humanity's accomplishments in order to help counteract the prevailing modern pessimism about the future. *(Thesis and support)*

Student Model 12: J. Strum, "Growing Up Liberal"   469

Additional Writing Topics 12   470

13 CLASSIC ESSAYS: Prose and the Imagination   472

Writer's Guide 13: The Elements of Style   474

Prewriting Activities 13   478

Paragraph Practice 13   478

Maxine Hong Kingston, "The Woman Warrior"   480

Drawing on a rich fund of personal observation, family legend, and traditional tales, the daughter of Chinese immigrants writes with intense emotion about growing up as a girl in a patriarchal Chinese family in a country hostile to her people. *(Personal experience)*

E. B. White, "Once More to the Lake"   487

In this widely reprinted masterpiece, a famous essayist sets out to recapture the mood of childhood summers when "the sun shone endlessly, day after day." *(Observation)*

Jonathan Swift, "A Modest Proposal"   494

In a slashing satire aimed at the oppression of the Irish under British rule, the author of *Gulliver's Travels* proposes an outrageous imaginary scheme designed to shock his readers out of their complacency and arouse their sense of indignation. *(Persuasion)*

George Orwell, "Politics and the English Language"   503

Addressing readers tired of propaganda and doublespeak, the author of *1984* champions his conviction that if we get rid of bad verbal habits we "can think more clearly," and that to think clearly "is a necessary first step toward political regeneration." *(Classification)*

Student Model 13: D. Cossina, "A Good Neighbor"   515

Additional Writing Topics 13   517

THEMATIC CONTENTS

1 GROWING UP AMERICAN

Garrison Keillor, "Born Among the Born-Again"   34

Jade Snow Wong, "Fifth Chinese Daughter"   49

N. Scott Momaday, "The Way to Rainy Mountain"   77

Richard Rodriguez, "Does America Still Exist?"   314

Maureen Barney, "A Good Move" (student theme)   131

2 THE THREATENED WORLD OF NATURE

Marie De Santis, "The Last of the Wild Salmon"   144

Annie Dillard, "Looking Spring in the Eye"   72

Gretel Ehrlich, "Wide Open Spaces"   84

E. B. White, "Once More to the Lake"   487

3 WITH FAMILY AND FRIENDS

Jane Howard, "In Search of the Good Family"   301

Michael Novak, "The Family Out of Favor"   276

Judith Viorst, "Friends, Good Friends—and Such Good Friends"   226

Fern Kupfer, "Institution Is Not a Dirty Word"   336

4 AMERICANS AT WORK

Joe Pollifrone, "A Day in the Life" (student theme)   94

Catherine A. Russell, "Tree-Cutting, Country Style" (student theme)   167

Ellen Goodman and Sam Keen, "Americans at Work: Three Portraits"   219

Carolyn Lewis, "A Different Drummer"   178

William Ouchi, "The Competitive Edge: Japanese and Americans"   182

Mina Lunt, "L-Mode, R-Mode" (student theme)   200

5 SPORTS—BOON OR BANE?

Arthur Ashe, "A Black Athlete Looks at Education"   104

George Leonard, "Born to Run"   117
George F. Will, "The Barbarity of Boxing"   332
Neal Lerner, "Sports, Anyone?" (student theme)   58

6   SEX ROLES: TYPES AND STEREOTYPES

Marya Mannes, "Television: The Splitting Image"   233
Amy Gross, "The Appeal of the Androgynous Man"   194
Margaret Mead, "We Need Taboos on Sex at Work"   123
Sheila Tobias, "Who's Afraid of Math, and Why?"   252
Sandra Bouslaugh, "New Options, New Attitudes" (student theme)   240

7   MEDIA ALERT: ON SEX AND VIOLENCE

Richard Harsham, "A Beeper for Violence"   409
Susan Jacoby, "Pornography and the First Amendment"   108
Gloria Steinem, "Erotica and Pornography"   188
Anne Gelhaus, "Rape: Realism and Ratings" (student theme)   420

8   SELF AND SOCIETY

Leonard Michaels, "New York, New York"   69
Charles McCabe, "Muggers and Morals"   114
Sally Finnegan, "Getting MADD" (student theme)   350
Susannah Lessard, "The Real Conservatism"   297
Ralph Nader, "A New Kind of Patriotism"   309
George Orwell, "Politics and the English Language"   503

9   MEDIA WATCHERS AND POP CULTURE

Andy Rooney, "There's One Born Every Minute"   402
Stanley Kauffmann, "The Return of Rambo"   405
Tom Wolfe, "The Right Stuff"   413

10   THE PRICE OF PROGRESS

Joan Didion, "Bureaucrats"   161
John McPhee, "Oranges"   148
Peter Meyer, "Land Rush"   156
Rachel Carson, "Our War Against Nature"   368
Karen McLaughlin, "Stress: The Combat Zone" (student theme)   282

11   THE LEGACY OF RACE

Maya Angelou, "Step Forward in the Car, Please"   28
Maxine Hong Kingston, "The Woman Warrior"   480
Martin Luther King, Jr., "I Have a Dream"   345

Alice Walker, "In Search of Our Mothers' Gardens"   450
D. Cossina, "A Good Neighbor" (student theme)   513
Veda Anderson, "Reversing Discrimination" (student editorial)   319

12 THE WORLD OF SCIENCE
Jane Brody, "Three Kinds of Fatigue"   213
Carl Sagan, "The Warming of the World"   269
Lewis Thomas, "Ant City and Human Society"   364
Ed Edelson, "Smart Computers—Now They Speak Our Language"   382
Dolores LaGuardia, "Talking to Apes" (student theme)   390

13 THE BURDEN OF HISTORY
Larry Heinemann, "Tour of Duty"   433
Jonathan Schell, "What Happened at Hiroshima"   440
George Orwell, "Shooting an Elephant"   41
Jonathan Swift, "A Modest Proposal"   494
J. Strum, "Growing Up Liberal" (student theme)   469

14 THE UNCERTAIN FUTURE
Kurt Vonnegut, Jr., "War Preparers Anonymous"   341
Garrett Hardin, "Lifeboat Ethics"   261
Isaac Asimov, "Nuclear Fusion"   374
Barbara Tuchman, "Humanity's Better Moments"   460

INTRODUCTION
Reading with a Purpose

This book is designed to help you become a better writer. It will do so in two major ways. First, like any serious reading, the readings in this book will give you issues to confront, information to digest, and arguments to take into account. You will get involved in some topics that you already care about and discover others that before may have meant little to you. You will read about career choices, the quality of life, the fitness movement, protecting our wildlife, the vanishing traditional family, changing sex roles, street crime, the nature of friendship. To write on any of these topics, you need more than good intentions, and you need to move beyond familiar, ready-made ideas. Your reading will make you think. It will give you ammunition to use; it will alert you to arguments and counterarguments. It will make your writing more knowledgeable, less vulnerable, more confident.

However, this book will do more than ask you to read for information and ideas. It will ask you to read with the writer's eye: It will ask you to pay attention not only to the *what* of writing but also to the *why* and the *how*. How do successful writers work? How much can we learn from the finished product about the process that gave it shape?

WHAT MAKES GOOD WRITING

When you read the selections in this book, you will be asked to look for answers to the basic questions that help a reader see how a piece of writing works. These will be questions like the following:

- What is the writer's purpose?
- Who is the intended audience?

1

- What is the key issue or the major point?
- Where has the writer turned for material?
- How has the writer organized the material?
- What makes the writer's message effective or persuasive?

When we try to answer these questions, we try to reconstruct the writer's *agenda*. The writer had things to do: a topic to bring into focus, readers to consider, resources to mobilize, choices to make, problems to solve. When you are asked basic questions about a writer's agenda, look for answers like the following:

(1) *What is the writer's purpose?* What activates good writing—what sets it in motion? Much everyday writing serves an immediate, practical purpose. We may want instructions on how to program a VCR, use a computer, or bake our own bread. We may want advice on how to find decent day care or on how to overcome fatigue. Much writing serves a larger public purpose. A writer may set out to tell us how to relieve traffic congestion, what to do about the homeless, or how to reduce the amount of mindless, gory violence on TV.

In some of the most effective writing we encounter, we sense a strong personal commitment. Much vigorous writing is currently done by women who look at the conditions they encounter in the workplace. What obstacles do women find in professions that have been dominated by men? What can be done to break down the barriers in women's path? Much purposeful, committed writing results when an author feels the need to talk back. An Italian American educator may be writing to attack the "Godfather image" that persists in much movie and television fare. To talk back to the media stereotype that identifies organized crime with one particular ethnic group, the author may quote actual statistics compiled by crime commissions; he may attack the omission from textbooks and media accounts of such outstanding Italian Americans as William Paca, who signed the Declaration of Independence, or the explorer John Cabot, whose Italian name was Giovanni Caboto.

Often when we talk about a writer's purpose, we are really talking about a means to an end. We may say that a writer's purpose was to *describe*, or to *explain*, or to *compare*—but description or explanation or comparison is not an end in itself. A writer may describe the wild beauty of one of our last undammed rivers in order to make us respect unspoiled nature and make us help protect it. A writer may explain the nature of synthetic fuels or compare two kinds of rapid transit to help us make intelligent choices. Description, explanation, and comparison are not ends in themselves but writing strategies; they are part of the *tools* that serve a writer's purpose.

(2) *Who is the intended audience?* What are the background, the needs, and the values of the intended reader? Writing varies in how directly

it aims at a specific audience. Some writing is very personal. In autobiographical writing, we may write mainly to sort things out in our own minds, to come to terms with our own experience. A writer torn between the traditional values of immigrant parents and the Americanized world of school and work may be writing mainly to define for herself her own identity: "Who am I?" Such writing finds an audience because the search for identity and the need for a sense of belonging are part of the experience of many other people.

Other kinds of writing may be aimed directly at a specific target audience. A book on "corporate gamesmanship" may aim directly at young women planning a business career. It may try to show how much of the talk and the folkways of American management are borrowed from the world of team sports. It may trace patterns of competitiveness, teamwork, and camaraderie with which some young women may be less familiar than their male competitors.

Much of the writing in this collection of readings aims at a more general audience. It aims at the educated reader who cares (or should care) about topics that concern us as voters, workers, members of families, or more generally as human beings: job satisfaction, urban violence, the environment, the price we pay for progress, war and peace. Even when writing for a general audience, a writer must reckon with a great diversity of backgrounds, interests, and commitments. Readers may be conservative or liberal, for example; they may be suspicious of or friendly to business, excited or apathetic about the arts, bored with or entertained by commercial television. Writers need to decide whether to appeal mainly to readers with views similar to their own; they need to decide whether to confront, try to please, or risk alienating the less receptive reader.

(3) *What is the message?* What does the writer want the reader to know or think or do? When all is said, what is the reader supposed to remember? A serious piece of writing will often focus on one key question or raise one central issue. The writer takes a stand; we as readers are made to reconsider our own thinking on the subject. In a well-focused magazine article on a current topic, our attention as readers may be centered on a question like the following:

- Is the American work ethic a thing of the past?
- Are American parents too permissive?
- Is pornography a harmless outlet for sexual fantasies?
- What gives Japanese industry its competitive edge?
- Can drug-related violence be reduced by the decriminalizing of drugs?
- How do children cope with their parents' divorce?

Often a writer sums up the answer to such a key question early in an essay—sometimes in the very first sentence (sometimes in the title: "We

Need Taboos on Sex at Work"). The following are examples of statements that sum up an author's point of view. We call such a statement a *thesis*—an assertion designed to satisfy the reader who wants to know: "What is the point?" The thesis is the proposition that the rest of the essay or article will try to explain, support, or defend:

- Today's students are obsessed with jobs and careers.

- Today's ethnic minorities are proud of their separate heritage and at the same time often the most patriotic of Americans.

- Pornography distorts men's views of women, leaving men unable to form relationships based on mutual trust and respect.

A well-supported or well-argued thesis cannot be a superficial impression or an unexamined prejudice. It is the result of a process of investigation, of soul-searching. It is the result of the writer's thinking the matter through. In fact, for you as a fellow writer, the key question is: How did the author *arrive* at the thesis? What is it based on? What material did the author explore when formulating his or her point of view?

In much writing, the thesis or central idea appears at the end of a short introduction. It is then reinforced and developed as the rest of the essay takes shape. Putting the thesis "up front" satisfies readers who want to know from the beginning what they are asked to accept or believe. But a writer may also choose to raise a question and then make us *participate* in the search for the answer. The author may take us along, examining possible answers or taking us through the steps that lead to the right conclusion. Such writing requires patience on the part of the reader, and a firm sense of direction on the part of the writer. When well done, it can leave the reader with a lasting impression, with lasting conviction.

(4) *Where has the writer turned for material?* A good writer is an alert observer, a good listener, and a receptive reader. Good writing draws on a rich fund of first-hand observation, personal experience, and authoritative information. When challenged, a writer should be able to say: "This is not merely hearsay—I have taken a close look at the subject." In reading a well-developed essay, ask yourself: "What has this writer done to *work up* the subject?" How much is drawn from personal memory? How much represents first-hand investigation? What use does the writer make of authoritative sources—quoting people whose opinion we should respect, citing facts or figures from sources we feel we can trust?

The readings (and writing assignments) in this book start close to personal experience and first-hand observation. On what has happened in your own life, you are the foremost authority. A black or Hispanic student is likely to write about discrimination from a perspective that is hard to pick up from a book. Those who have lived through a bitter divorce (their parents' or their own) can write about family life as actors in the drama rather than as spectators. Part of our growth as writers is to learn to write with similar authority or with similar conviction when we move from our private history to more impersonal subjects or larger general issues.

What do writers do to generate a rich fund of material on the more objective general issues that go beyond their personal, private concerns? Many professional writers work from a combination of sources: personal memories, field trips, interviews, collections of press clippings, systematic exploration of books and articles on their subject. Sometimes the most influential book on a subject is by a writer who knows how to question and to listen—authors like Studs Terkel, who asked Americans how they felt about their work, or Robert Coles, who interviewed children involved first-hand in school desegregation. In studying a writer's work, look for the mix of personal anecdote, first-hand observation, telling statistics, summarized information, and strategically used quotation that gives weight to much substantial writing.

(5) *How has the writer organized the material?* What gives a piece of writing its shape? How has the writer brought the material under control? In well-organized writing, the writer has worked out a pattern that serves the purpose and that the reader can follow. The writer has a master plan that makes its parts fall into place. Effective writers make us feel early that they know where they are headed; they keep us moving in the right direction.

Some basic patterns of organization are relatively easy to outline or to chart. These include the tried-and-true strategies for organizing material: classification, comparison and contrast, tracing a process. Often the task we face in organizing our writing is to sort out a confusing collection of material into major categories. To help us find our way in a bookstore, the manager may set up one major section for serious imaginative literature— divided into categories such as poetry, drama, and fiction; another major section for entertainment literature or lighter reading—divided into categories such as science fiction, detective fiction, and fantasy; a third major section of "how-to" literature, including cookbooks, diet guides, exercise manuals, and the like. Often part of a writer's task is a similar job of classification. A writer investigating why people feel tired may set up three major kinds of fatigue:

I. Physical fatigue (the kind of normal, healthy tiredness that results from hard work or vigorous physical exercise)

II. Psychological fatigue (the kind of mental exhaustion that results from stress and worry)

III. Pathological fatigue (the kind of incapacitating fatigue that results from illness or depression)

The familiar basic patterns of organization are not ends in themselves; writers use and adapt them to help us find our way, to guide our choices, to help us move from a problem to a solution. For example, to help us understand the competitive edge of Japanese industry in world markets, a writer may set up a point-by-point comparison. The purpose of the comparison will be to help Americans develop strategies that will enable them to cope with the challenge. The overall plan might look like this:

Catching Up with Number One

I. The Japanese emphasis on group loyalty vs. the American emphasis on individual effort and reward

II. The Japanese flexibility in filling new needs vs. resistance to innovation by American unions and management

III. The Japanese eagerness to study the language and folkways of their American customers vs. the American ignorance of foreign languages and cultures

In the work of an effective writer, such patterns do not seem merely mechanical. Instead, they effectively take us from here to there; they carry us along by their own inner logic. For instance, a writer may want to introduce us to the idea that the two hemispheres of the brain are attuned to different tasks. She starts by dwelling on the functions of the left side of the brain, which tends to be literal, linear, analytical—taking things apart into their components, proceeding item by item, looking for direct logical connections. The more cut-and-dried this left-brain approach begins to sound, the more ready we will be for a section that will supply what is missing: an account of the right side of the brain as being more intuitive and more creative—seizing patterns as meaningful wholes, finding vital connections between things that to literal-minded people seem worlds apart.

Truly live writing is dynamic rather than static. Some of the most effective writing, rather than telling us (or bullying us), makes us think. A writer may make us look at different possible solutions to a problem—to eliminate the unworkable ones and to help us settle on the one that will do the job. A writer may make us look at different case histories to help us find a common denominator for a label like "the underclass" or "the new poor." A writer may involve us in the debate on decriminalizing hard drugs by weighing the pros and cons, helping us make up our own minds:

I. Advantages
  • Reducing the pressure on addicts to steal and rob to feed their habits
  • Reducing drug-related violence caused by suppliers fighting over a profitable "turf"
  • Keeping addicts out of prison

II. Disadvantages
- • Spread of addiction to much larger numbers
- • Harmful effects on family life
- • Harmful effects on job performance

As you chart such a pattern of organization, remember that it is the result of a process of sorting things out, of trying to fit them into place. An author may start with a first tentative plan, then adjust it (and sometimes drastically revise it) as necessary. Remember also that in a longer article, several major organizing strategies are likely to combine. For instance, an author may start with a brief history of the issue, taking up major steps in chronological order, following the order of events in time. Then the author may look at the different areas where the problem is currently most urgent, setting up major categories. Finally, the author may look at different possible solutions, eliminating those that raise false hopes and settling on the one that seems most promising.

(6) *What makes good writing effective?* People who write well seem to have a special gift for putting ideas into words. They know how to make clear what before was confusing or half-understood. Their writing is a pleasure to read, making us want to say "Well said! Well put!" We remember it when much else that we read or hear is forgotten; what they say is memorable, quotable:

A riot is the language of the unheard. (Martin Luther King, Jr.)

We have just religion enough to make us hate, but not enough to make us love one another. (Jonathan Swift)

Scientists have to be interested in things, not persons. (Marie Curie)

Learning from the example of other writers, you will extend your range of words; you will develop your ear for what makes a good sentence. You will develop your sense of *style*: You will develop your confidence and ease in making words serve your purpose. Here are some of the elements of style that you should watch for (and practice and imitate) as you study other writers' work:

EMPHASIS Emphasis makes what is important stand out. Effective writers know how to focus on a key idea and sum it up in pointed, memorable fashion. Readers tire of writers who *always* seem to be shouting, treating minor annoyances and major injustices in the same high-pitched tone of complaint. Readers tire equally of a monotonous low-key approach that makes it sound as though nothing would ever upset or excite or inspire the writer. We tend to trust writers who show that they can be calm or reasonable but who come on strong when something really matters:

> A society that thinks the choice between ways of living is just a choice between equally eligible "life-styles" turns universities into academic cafeterias offering junk food for the mind. (George F. Will)

Effective writers save the big, weighty words (*love, excellence, dehumanize*) for important occasions, so that they will not wear out. The author of a short article on how men's magazines dehumanize women saved this weighty charge for an emphatic conclusion—making it literally her last word on the subject:

> By turning women from people into fleshy objects and by teaching men to see and define us as such, men's magazines do not simply remove women's clothes. They remove our humanity. (Carol Lynn Mithers)

CONCRETE LANGUAGE Effective writers know how to bridge the gap between words and reality; they know how to use words to conjure up the world of sights and sounds and smells in which we live. Concrete language helps us visualize textures, shapes, and movements. Look at how the author of the following passage uses concrete words like *budge, drift, tumble,* and *surge* to help us imagine what she saw:

> Sheep shade up in the hot sun and won't *budge* until it cools. *Bunched* together now, and excited into a run by the storm, they *drift* across dry land, *tumbling* into draws like water and *surging* out again onto the rugged, *choppy* plateaus that are the building blocks of this state. (Gretel Ehrlich)

IMAGINATIVE COMPARISONS Effective writers use their imagination to make language come to life. They use imaginative comparisons to make us take a fresh look at what is familiar or to help us imagine the unfamiliar and strange. Here a writer with an exceptional gift for vivid imaginative language writes on the subject of self-respect:

> To be driven back upon oneself is an uneasy affair at best, *rather like trying to cross a border with borrowed credentials* . . . .

> To do without self-respect . . . is to be an unwilling audience of one to an *interminable documentary* that details one's failings, both real and imagined, with *fresh footage spliced in for every screening.* (Joan Didion)

We call such examples of figurative (as opposed to literal) language *similes* when the comparison is signaled by words such as *like* or *as if* or *as though.* We call the comparison a *metaphor* when the signal is left out, and when the writer talks about what he or she describes as if it were indeed something else ("more than a square mile of tomatoes—a shaggy, vegetable-green *rug* dappled with murky red dots"). Figurative language helps us dramatize what might have been lifeless or abstract. It brings color and movement into a writer's prose; it brings the right attitude and emotions into play.

SENTENCE STYLE Effective writers have an ear for the patterns and rhythms of the English sentence. They make full use of its varied resources. They know how to write the brief pointed sentence that neatly sums up a key idea:

> Nature made ferns for pure leaves, to show what she could do in that line. (Henry David Thoreau)

> Rage cannot be hidden; it can only be dissembled. (James Baldwin)

> Everyone is a moon and has a dark side which he never shows to anybody. (Mark Twain)

At the same time, effective writers know how to write the fully developed sentence that packs in telling detail, that makes effective use of repetition or contrast, and that we take in as a satisfying whole:

> It is about time we realize that many women make
> *better teachers than mothers,*
> *better actresses than wives,*
> *better diplomats than cooks.* (Marya Mannes)

Remember that the right word and the well-built sentence are sometimes the result of happy inspiration but more often the result of rewriting, of revision. A writer reworking a first draft has to be patient enough to search for the word with just the right shade of meaning or to clear away awkward, roundabout constructions.

READING A SAMPLE ESSAY

To learn from the example of other writers, you have to be a receptive reader. You have to provide a good audience—alert to the signals, ready to read the clues that a writer provides for the reader. Develop a strategy for sizing up and taking in another writer's work. Focus your attention at strategic points.

TITLE Effective titles serve a double function. One part of their job is to inform—to stake out the territory, to raise the issue. But an equally important part of their job is to beckon the reader—to invite (or to provoke), so that the writer can compete successfully with other claims on the reader's time. Often an effective title stakes out the topic, raises the issue, and suggests an agenda:

> Who's Afraid of Math, and Why?
> Stonehenge: Can It Be Saved?
> Corporate Gamesmanship for Women

Often a title sums up (or at least strongly hints at) the central idea of an article ("Superworkingmom or Superdrudge?"). At the same time, the title often sets the *tone*. It establishes the attitude of the author toward her subject and her audience. The tone may range from urgently concerned, to serious with an occasional lighter touch, to humorous with a serious undertone. (Note that for excerpts from longer pieces, as for some of the essays in this book, a title may have been chosen by an editor.)

INTRODUCTION The basic function of the introduction or "lead" is to raise the issue, to get the reader involved in the subject. True, the introduction may also do all kinds of preliminary spadework for the writer. It may fill in historical background; it may show the writer's personal qualifications (an eyewitness, researcher, or participant) for dealing with the topic. But often the most effective introduction is the kind of striking example that dramatizes the issue. Newsmagazines often effectively use the human-interest example as a "grabber": an account of a farmer's family watching their livestock and equipment auctioned off (to lead into an article on the decline of the family farm); the story of a teenage girl killed by a drunk driver (to lead into an article on new laws aimed at drunk drivers).

Look at introductory examples, anecdotes, or statistics to ask: What question are they designed to raise? What basic point do they illustrate?

THESIS Often an effective introduction leads directly to the author's main point, or *thesis*. A Hispanic writer going counter to the familiar melting-pot theory of American culture may take his stand early in the essay, after a brief introduction stressing the importance of *language* to a person's identity and culture:

> Loyal, productive, and effective Hispano citizens, proud of what they are and what they have to give, have more to offer their country than a de-hispanized, disoriented Anglo with a dark skin, mispronounced name, and a guilty conscience to boot. (Sabine R. Ulibarri)

A strong thesis provides direction for an essay as a whole. It provides the central claim that the writer's examples and evidence are designed to shore up. It provides the focus for the arguments and counterarguments that the writer may want to examine. Remember, however, that writers vary greatly in where (and how fully) they spell out a central thesis. A writer may raise a key question early but then take the reader along step by step to an answer spelled out at the end. On a subject that generates much heat— abortion, American policy in Central America—a writer may choose to stay close to widely accepted or hard-to-challenge facts and only gradually lead up to a controversial proposal or solution.

PREVIEW Look early in an essay for a preview or at least a strong hint of the author's program—of the strategy that will give shape to the essay as a whole. Ask yourself early: "Where are we headed?" Often the thesis of an essay will hint strongly at the overall pattern of organization. It may prepare us for an essay that first looks at the lifestyle of the crowded, fast-paced, anxiety-ridden city and then goes on to contrast it with the more leisurely, more neighborly lifestyle of the small town. We may gather from the introduction or the thesis (or both) that the author will first look at the glorified media image of American football and then go on to debunk it by looking at the harsh competitive realities behind the glamorous facade.

Effective writers know how to create the *expectations* that the rest of an article will satisfy. When they tell us that television commercials create stereotyped images of women (or of men), we will be prepared for an essay that takes a close look at several of the more damaging or more objectionable stereotypes. Effective writers prepare us for what is ahead by the way they approach the subject, by the way they set an essay in motion.

TRANSITIONS Look for the major signposts that keep a reader headed in the right direction. Transitions provide the bridge from one point to the next. A transition may be a word or phrase (*therefore, in the second place, furthermore*). However, a transition may be a whole sentence or a short paragraph ("These statistics, startling as they are, cover only one part of the problem. The true extent of the danger becomes clear only when we ....")

Look especially for the transitions that keep the basic architecture of an essay in view—the major stages of a process, the major categories an author has set up, the major causes that contribute to a problem:

"The first and most obvious reason is that ...."

"A second cause that has received much attention in recent years is that ...."

"Only recently have the media taken notice of a third and no less important cause ...."

Look especially for the transitions that mark major *turning points* in an argument. Look for the signals showing that an author is going from "on the one hand" to "on the other hand"; from "We have to admit that . . . ." to "Nevertheless, it is true that . . . ." In a pro-and-con argument, look for the signal that the author is going from the advantages to the disadvantages of a proposed change or reform.

CONCLUSION The conclusion is the author's last chance to make sure that a key point will be remembered or that a crucial argument will make a lasting impression. A fully developed argument may have had to take various detours through counterarguments to be weighed, misunderstandings to be cleared up. An effective conclusion is likely to reinforce the author's main point through an emphatic restatement (not just lame repetition), through a dramatic final example, or through a clinching supporting quotation from an impressive authority. Here is the parting shot of a writer arguing emphatically in favor of prison reform:

> . . . there must be a way in which humaneness can be applied instead of suppression. We hear so little of experiments in approval and sympathy; and we hear so much of the savage men made more savage by the savagery of society . . . by the savagery of what we call justice, and by that powerful weapon of the haves against the have-nots—Law and Order. (A. S. Neill)

The following short essay by a well-known columnist is a short piece of nonfiction prose that illustrates many of the features you are likely to find in longer, more elaborate pieces of writing. The author writes as a trend watcher; her purpose, as in much of her writing, is to help us understand current patterns as they take shape, to help us find our way in the everyday world. A columnist who has built up a steady following, she writes for an audience of mostly white-collar workers and professionals (a group from which most of the examples in her essay are taken). She draws her material from a familiar mix of sources: current observation, memories of the past, and informally quoted research.

Reading this essay with the writer's eye, look especially at how the early paragraphs bring the subject into focus and lead up to the thesis. Look at the kind of follow-through that is the hallmark of the experienced writer—material that explains the main point, illustrates it with a rich array of examples, clarifies it by contrast with the past, bolsters it with supporting testimony, and traces its ramifications. Look at the transitions that serve as signposts to the reader.

Ellen Goodman

We Are What We Do

INTRODUCTION:
examples that set up a
common pattern (a —
new meaning of the
word *community*)

I have a friend who is a member of the medical community. It does not say that, of course, on the stationery that bears her home address. This membership comes from her hospital work.

I have another friend who is a member of the computer community. This is a fairly new subdivision of our economy, and yet he finds his sense of place in it.

Other friends and acquaintances of mine are members of the academic community, or the business community, or the journalistic community. Though you cannot find these on any map, we know where we belong.

None of us, mind you, was born into these communities. Nor did we move into them, U-Hauling our possessions along with us. None has papers to prove we are card-carrying members of one such group or another. *Yet it seems that more and more of us are identified by work these days, rather than by street.*

THESIS:
spells out the meaning
of the introductory
examples (with
PREVIEW of the
basic contrast)

FOLLOW-UP:
contrast between
"then" and "now" is —
traced in detail

In the past, most Americans lived in neighborhoods. We were members of precincts or parishes or school districts. My dictionary still defines community first of all in geographic terms, as "a body of people who live in one place."

But today fewer of us do our living in that one place; more of us just use it for sleeping. Now we call our towns "bedroom suburbs," and many of us, without small children as icebreakers, would have trouble naming all the people on our street.

It's not that we are more isolated today. It's that many of us have transferred a chunk of our friendships, a major portion of our everyday social lives, from home to office. As more of our neighbors work away from home, the work place becomes our neighborhood.

The kaffeeklatsch of the '50s is the coffee break of the '80s. The water cooler, the hall, the elevator and the parking lot are the back fences of these neighborhoods. The people we have lunch with day after day are those who know the running saga of our mother's operations, our child's math grades, our frozen pipes and faulty transmissions.

FURTHER SUPPORT:

Supporting Testimony
(quoting research or
surveys)

We may be strangers at the supermarket that replaced the corner grocer, but we are known at the coffee shop in the lobby. We share with each other a cast of characters from the boss in the corner office to the crazy lady in Shipping, to the lovers in Marketing. It's not surprising that *when researchers ask Americans* what they like best about work, they say it is "the shmooze (chatter) factor." When they ask young mothers at home what they miss most about work, it is the people.

Concession
(anticipating reader's possible objections)

Not all the neighborhoods are empty, nor is every work place a friendly playground. Most of us have had mixed experiences in these environments. *Yet* as one woman told me recently, she knows more about the people she passes on the way to her desk than on her way around the block.

Extension
(change as part of a larger pattern)

Our new sense of community *hasn't just moved from house to office building.* The labels that we wear connect us with members from distant companies, cities and states. We assume that we have something "in common" with other teachers, nurses, city planners.

Clarifying Analogy
(parallel from history)

It's not unlike the experience of our immigrant grandparents. Many who came to this country still identified themselves as members of the Italian community, the Irish community, the Polish community. They sought out and assumed connections with people from the old country. Many of us have updated that experience. We have replaced ethnic identity with professional identity, the way we replaced neighborhoods with the work place.

This whole realignment of community is surely most obvious among the mobile professions. People who move from city to city seem to put roots down into their professions. In an age of specialists, they may have to search harder to find people who speak the same language.

CONCLUSION:
author's reservations
(possible problems resulting from the change)

I don't think that there is anything massively disruptive about this shifting sense of community. The continuing search for connection and shared enterprise is very human. *But I do feel uncomfortable with* our shifting identity. The balance has tipped and we seem increasingly dependent on work for our sense of self.

If our offices are our new neighborhoods, if our professional titles are our new ethnic tags, then how do we separate ourselves from our jobs? Self-worth isn't just something to measure in the marketplace. But in these new communities, it becomes harder and harder to tell who we are without saying what we do.

READING AND WRITING

When you read with the writer's eye, you are tracing the footsteps of a fellow writer. The introductions and the follow-up questions that go with the essays in this book will frequently "walk" you through an essay, showing you how it develops or takes shape. The materials in this book will have done their job if they help you adapt the strategies of other writers to your own ends, and if they help you write with a similar sense of purpose.

To profit from the study of this book, remember that the essays herein are the end result of a process. In producing a major piece of writing, a writer typically starts with a preliminary collection of notes, then produces one or more rough drafts, and then after final revision and editing turns out the finished version. The "Writer's Agenda" questions following each essay frequently include questions about the earlier stages of the process: To what *sources* did the writer turn for material? What *choices* did the writer make in giving shape and direction to the essay? In the "Writers on Writing" interviews, several of the authors talk about the process of *revision* that gives a first rough draft its final form. One of the student models (Unit 3) presents two versions of the same student paper: a first rough draft and a final revision. Learn to look at your own writing through the reader's eye: What can you do to clarify your purpose? How can you bring out your central point more strongly or more clearly? What material later in your paper might be more helpful earlier? What key points need additional explanation or examples? People who are important enough can sometimes hand over their first rough effort to a rewrite team or to an editor who licks it into shape. Effective writers have learned to do their own rewrites; they have learned to be their own editors and friendly critics.

PART

ONE

SOURCES

FOR

WRITING

Where does a writer start? Throughout this book, you will be asked to pay attention to the *purposes* that set writing in motion. To understand good writing, you have to ask frequently: What was this writer trying to do? What was the writer's agenda? Throughout this book, you will be asked to think about the writer's *audience*: Who is the intended reader? What kind of response does the writer expect? What kind of results is the writer trying to produce? Throughout this book, you will be asked to look at what gives writing *shape*: What overall plan helped the writer organize a selection? What strategy gives a piece of writing shape and direction?

However, in the early sections of this book, you will be asked to pay special attention to questions that loom large when you begin to write: Where does good writing come from? Where does a writer turn for material? What gives good writing substance? Good writing has its sources in the author's experience, observation, viewing, and reading. A good writer knows how to work up a subject—how to gather a rich fund of material to explore, to think about, to sort out, to pull into shape. The material you gather early on will supply the striking examples, the live incidents, and the clinching evidence that you will need to support the stand you take in a finished paper. A good writer has learned to pay attention, to take things in. A good writer is an alert observer and a responsive reader.

Part One of this book focuses on the resources that you should mobilize for your writing. It takes up in turn three major sources of material:

PERSONAL EXPERIENCE On what you have experienced and lived through, you are the best authority. Effective writers know how to relate general issues to their own experience—to what they themselves have witnessed and undergone.

OBSERVATION Effective writers have learned to look for themselves, to use their own eyes and ears. They know how to go beyond second-hand information and superficial impressions to take a closer look.

POINTS OF VIEW Much effective writing takes shape in the give-and-take of current discussion and debate. We take into account the opinions of others and the evidence they offer in support. We explore a range of views as we make up our own minds. Before we hold forth, we listen and we read.

1

PERSONAL EXPERIENCE

The Story with a Point

OVERVIEW

As a student in a composition class, you will be doing at least some writing that draws on your personal experience. Such writing is auto-biographical—you will be writing about your own life; about what you have experienced, witnessed and felt. Autobiographical writing is different from a diary that chronicles events from day to day. Effective autobiography takes stock; it soon focuses on what truly matters to the author. Although it tells the story of events from the writer's life, it tells a story with a point. Some of the strongest writing we read deals with an achievement, conflict, grievance, or loss that had a personal meaning for the author.

PURPOSE In writing from personal experience, we are close to some of the underlying motives that set much true writing in motion. A writer can get a personal satisfaction from telling the story of put-downs experienced at school or of a handicap overcome. People write to register a personal grievance, to justify important choices they have made, or to relive a conflict that has marked their personality. People write to talk back to a stereotype—to rebel against superficial cate-gories that put them in a box, against prejudices that hold them back.

AUDIENCE Some autobiographical writing aims at a special audi-ence that shares a common ethnic, religious, or professional identity.

An autobiographical article or book may prove especially inspiring to women or to Americans close to the immigrant experience. But much autobiographical writing is of general human interest; it appeals to the general reader. As general readers, we identify with writers in their search for identity or self-esteem, in their attempt to resolve divided loyalties.

BENEFITS FOR THE WRITER (1) Writing about your own experience, you can learn to write with greater confidence. On what you have witnessed and felt, *you* are the authority. You have a wealth of material—a varied procession of people and events that you can call back to mind. Learn to draw on personal experience as the most immediately available *source* of material for your writing.

(2) Writing about personal experience, you learn how to *organize* material. Experience-in-the-raw is one thing after another, one day at a time. But as we look back over what has happened to us or what has made us what we are, things fall into place. A pattern takes shape. One student wrote about being excluded from the glamorous world of the athletic elite in junior high school, being picked last for every sport. He then went on to a second phase in which he fanatically tried to become good in at least one sport (basketball), eventually succeeding—acquiring the nickname of a famous player, moving up to gym helper, and joining the "cool" crowd. He finally went on to a third phase—discovering in college the pleasure and rewards of joining in sports not for status but for their own sake. The paper put together in this fashion had a satisfying structure; it had a design that made it move purposefully through three meaningful stages to a satisfying conclusion.

(3) The use of material from personal experience is not limited to writing whose main purpose is autobiographical. Good writers know how to bring *ideas and issues* to life by drawing on what they have experienced in their own lives. Suppose a student writer asks whether too many Americans lack a real sense of belonging, moving too often from one place to another to take permanent roots. Sooner or later in her paper, we will expect her to talk about some of her own experiences—traumatic or otherwise—that involved "moving on." We want to see that the issue means more to her than theory or statistics. Whether you write about the vanishing family farm, the divorce rate, or the neglect of the elderly, your readers want to see that your topic means something to you personally as an eyewitness, participant, or concerned observer.

PERSONAL EXPERIENCE
Additional Reading

Larry Heinemann, Tour of Duty   (p. 433)
Alice Walker, In Search of Our Mothers' Gardens   (p. 450)
Maxine Hong Kingston, The Woman Warrior   (p. 480)
J. Strum (student theme), Growing Up Liberal   (p. 469)

WRITER'S GUIDE 1

Writing from Experience

The roots of much truly effective writing are in what the writers know for themselves. Much writing that is truly worth reading grows out of the writer's own experience. We sense that the subject matters to the writer personally. Theoretical arguments come to life when the examples or the evidence presented make us feel: "This is something this writer has lived through. This is close to the writer's own life."

Writing that takes a close look at the writer's personal experience is called **autobiography**. As you work up the material for an autobiographical paper, ask yourself questions like the following:

- Where are we?
- What people are involved?
- What happens?
- What feelings or emotions do the events bring into play?
- What does it all mean to you as the author?

Effective autobiographical writing creates a setting. It uses authentic detail to make places and people come to life before our eyes. It tells us how people act and what they say, and especially what they think and feel. The thoughts, feelings, and attitudes of the people involved play a major role. Autobiographical writing tells the story of events, but its central interest is in what the events meant to the writer.

In papers in which you draw on your personal experience, try to do justice to the five major dimensions of successful autobiographical writing:

(1) *Use vivid, authentic detail to recreate the setting.* Satisfy the readers who want to know: "Where are we?" In the autobiographical essays reprinted in this unit, setting plays a major role. They take us to places that helped shape the outlook or the personality of the author: the rural Midwest, the basement sweatshops of Chinatown in San Francisco, the wretched prisons and squalid "native" quarters of colonial Burma under British rule.

(2) *Make the people you write about real for the reader.* Satisfy the readers who want to know: "Who are these people?" The following capsule portrait from an autobiographical essay is packed with details about the author's father. It uses details that reveal character; we feel we are coming to know the father as a person:

> Six days a week he rose early, dressed, ate breakfast alone, put on his hat, and walked to his barbershop at 207 Henry Street on the Lower East Side of Manhattan, about half a mile from our apartment. He returned after dark. The

family ate dinner together on Sundays and Jewish holidays. Mainly he ate alone. I don't remember him staying home from work because of illness or bad weather. He took few vacations, but once we spent a week in Miami and he tried to enjoy himself, wading into the ocean, being brave, stepping, inch by inch, into the warm blue unpredictable immensity. Then he slipped.... He came up thrashing, struggling back to the beach on skinny white legs. "I nearly drowned," he said, very exhilarated. He never went into the water again. I think he preferred his barbershop to the natural world. He retired after thirty-five years, when his hands trembled too much for scissors and razors and angina made it impossible for him to stand up for long periods. Then he took walks in the neighborhood and carried a vial of whiskey in his shirt pocket. When pain stopped him in the street, he'd stand very still and sip his whiskey. A few times I stood beside him, as still as he, waiting for the pain to end, both of us speechless and frightened.   (Leonard Michaels, "My Father's Life," *Esquire*)

(3) *Give a dramatic account of key events.* Satisfy the readers who want to know: "What happened?" Select incidents that help us see how an issue arose in a concrete situation. If you write about an important conflict, show how it was acted out—in little incidents or in a major confrontation. If you want us to be aware of an important character trait, make it show in what the person did and said. Here is a revealing incident as told by a writer who knows how to dramatize everyday situations and events:

I forgot to give change to a middle-aged woman with bitter eyes. I charged her forty-five cents for a pound and a third of apples and she gave me half a dollar. Now she is demanding her nickel, and her eyes are narrower than the sides of dimes. She is a round-shouldered person, beaky and short—short-changed. In her stare at me, there is an entire judiciary system—accusation, trial, and conviction. "You give me my nickel, mister."
"I'm sorry. I forgot. Here is your nickel."
She does not believe my mistake a mistake. She walks away in a white huff. Now she stops, turns, glowers. She moves on. Twice more, as she departs from the market, she stops, turns, and stares angrily back. I watch her all the way to the curb.   (John McPhee, "Giving Good Weight")

(4) *Work out a pattern that the reader can follow.* When you trace a common theme through a series of related events, try to set up major *stages* that the reader can absorb and ponder. For instance, a student might be writing about her loneliness as a newcomer at a strange school, her struggle to become accepted by a small group of popular students, and finally her finding true friends outside the clique of "beautiful people." The reader will have a satisfying sense of meaningful forward movement if the paper clearly reflects these three major stages:

I. Life as an outsider
II. Trying to join the clique
III. Finding true friends

(5) *Do justice to feelings and attitudes.* Satisfy the readers who want to know: "How do these people think and feel?" In autobiographical writing, the external events are important, but just as important, or more so, is what happens in people's minds. Give a candid account of your own feelings and reactions. In the following passages, the author vividly recalls standards and feelings that were part of the spirit of her favorite sport:

> There were important by-products of playing field hockey. We always congratulated the loser on having played well. We congratulated the winner on her superb work, whether we thought she cheated, or had an advantage of age or experience. I am still anguished when I hear my Brooklyn-bred husband scream at the children over the Monopoly board: "Hurrah, I win—ha-ha, you lose." . . .
>
> I remember a girl named Karen with blood pouring down her face and onto her white middy blouse and a dark accusing hole where her front teeth had been. It is blurred in my mind whose stick was responsible, but I was close enough to feel guilt and fear and the excitement of both those emotions. It never occurred to me that a simple child's game, a ball playing, might not be worth a lifetime of false teeth. (Anne Roiphe, on field hockey, in *Ms.*)

(6) *Aim at a unifying overall point.* Satisfy the readers who want to know: "Why is this important?" If you focus on a single important event, spell out what it meant to you or what you learned from the experience. If you discuss related experiences, make your readers see the common thread. Have a central question or key issue arise early in the paper. Concentrate on a unifying theme or concern.

The following passage from an autobiographical essay spells out a theme that we encounter in much American autobiography: Millions of young Americans have grown up with immigrant parents whose goal was to have their children become "Americanized" and live out the dream of success that had brought the parents across the sea. The author's father, who had come to this country from Puerto Rico, constantly exhorted his children to become educated and not to "end up like me":

> "You're all going to get good educations and good jobs," he'd tell us day after day. He meant that we were not going to follow in his stumbling footsteps. . . . We had to avoid his mistakes from the beginning; otherwise we'd end up like him: paying for his sins in the hotel kitchen, and at night in bed, unable to sleep because—there was that job of his. Job? He'd been better off tending anemic chickens in the old home village. He was paying, but we weren't going to; we were going to collect, and that, he said, was the reward he wanted out of life. We told Mami we wanted to go back to the Island, but she said "Muy tarde," too late. We were americanos—not she, not Papi, but *we*, los hijos—and we'd just have to make the most of that situation. (Edward Rivera, "La Situación," *New York*)

Much autobiographical writing focuses from the beginning on things that really mattered to the writer. We then follow along as the author's conclusions take shape or as the meaning of what happened becomes clear. However, in a paper that aims at one major point, you may state your central idea as your thesis at the beginning of the paper. You then follow up by discussing in detail the experiences that were part of the same basic pattern. The following might be the introduction of an autobiographical student paper that is clearly focused on one major point:

Child Labor

THESIS   *Have I encountered the "work ethic"? I grew up with it.* To my family, work is a virtue, and play is a sin. My earliest memories of my mother include watching her work at a machine that punched holes in cards. For as long as I can remember, my father has been moonlighting and working on weekends. By the time I was in the fourth grade, my parents had me get up at six to deliver papers so I would learn "the value of a dollar."

To sum up: Autobiographical writing often appears under the heading of **narration**—it tells the story of events from the author's own life. But the central interest in autobiographical writing is in the *meaning* of the events. The key question for the writer is: "What have I learned from the experience? How has it affected me as a person?" Writing that draws directly on the author's personal experience often has a strength missing from more impersonal writing. People write with a special commitment when they try to make sense of what has happened to them, when they try to understand where they come from and who they are.

Prewriting Activities 1

1. Write a *personal résumé* that will introduce you to other people. Write a paragraph under each of the following headings:
   - Roots (family; place or places where you grew up)
   - Schooling (what kind of schools, best and worst subjects)
   - Interests (reading, hobbies, sports, activities)
   - Work (summer jobs, chores, regular employment)

   Include some factual information, but concentrate mostly on what mattered to you as a person.

2. What are some of your earliest memories of people other than your parents? Who are some of the people who mattered to you most during your childhood years or your first years of school? Do some *free writing* about one or

more of these people. Record events, images, or feelings as they come to mind. Write quickly, following the chain of associations as one remembered scene calls up another.

3. Start a *journal.* Two or three times a week, write about things that have happened, scenes you have observed, or people you have met. Record your candid impressions and reactions. Develop the habit of writing down in a rough preliminary form things that you might later use as material for more structured writing.

4. Use the following *discovery frame* to work up material for a paper that will deal with an especially meaningful or memorable event from your own experience. The event could be a quarrel, a brush with the law, a memorable confrontation, a happy encounter, an accident, a memorable experience with success or failure. For a preliminary collection of material, write responses to the kinds of questions that appear under the following five headings.

The Setting: Where did the event take place? What was the setting? What were some of the sights and sounds that helped create the atmosphere of the place? Re-create the place and the time for the reader.

The People: Who took part? What kind of people were they? How would the reader recognize them? How did they look, act, or talk? Provide capsule portraits of the key individuals involved.

The Situation: Why could things happen the way they did? What relationships, or what events in the past, led up to the present situation? Fill your readers in on any background that is important for them to know.

The Event: What actually happened? How did things come to a head? Give the high points of the action in vivid detail.

The Point: What was the meaning of the incident for you? What did you learn from the experience? Why, when you look back, does it seem important? What did the experience seem to show or to prove? Explain the point of the story or the meaning of the incident to your reader.

Paragraph Practice 1

Write a paragraph that brings someone you know (or knew) well to life for your readers. You might write about someone you especially admired, or disliked, or were puzzled by. Use vivid detail. Study and discuss the following *student-written paragraph* as a possible model:

Tell Us a Story

The most vivid image I have of my childhood is of my uncle reading stories to my brothers and sisters and me. He would call us into the living room, and we would trip over each other trying to get through the doorway. There he would be waiting. He was a big man, sitting high in a big chair. We would scatter around his feet, looking up into his dark, mysterious, slightly scary face. He would always wait until we settled down, and then he would break into a wide smile and pull a book out from behind his back. He read us most of Roald Dahl's books; our favorite was *Charlie and the Chocolate Factory* in which a young boy named Charlie and his grandfather go to a mysterious chocolate factory. Willy Wonka, the strange little chocolate magnate; Veronica, the fat spoiled rich kid; the boy who always dressed up as a cowboy; the gas-bubble room; the candy that turned around; the candy that whistled; and the candy that flew over air-waves were all parts of the story. I would get more and more excited, leaning forward as I waited for the next word. There was so much in that book. And my uncle knew how to make us laugh by acting out the story with giggles, grunts, groans, and grins. He controlled the whole setting, raising and lowering his voice, rocking back and forth, and waving his arms about. I felt close to him as he acted out my wildest fantasies, dreams, and desires. He created magic out of those words, taking me places I had always wanted to go.   (Vincent Piro)

BACKGROUND: Maya Angelou (born 1928) has become widely known during her career as dancer, actress, teacher, writer, director, and producer. In her autobiographical *I Know Why the Caged Bird Sings* (1970), she told the story of her growing up as a Southern black girl determined to "defy the odds." She was born in St. Louis and spent much of her childhood in Stamps, Arkansas, where she attended a segregated school and where her grandmother had a general merchandising store that at the same time served as a social center for the black people living there. Angelou became a successful dancer and actress, and she performed in the musical *Porgy and Bess* when it was sponsored by the State Department on a twenty-two-nation tour. She worked for a time with Martin Luther King, Jr., for the Southern Christian Leadership Conference. She has written plays and screenplays and directed a television series on Africa. She has traveled widely, and she wrote newspaper columns while living in Ghana and Egypt. Her later autobiographical books include *Gather Together in My Name* (1974) and *The Heart of a Woman* (1981). In the following selection from *I Know Why the Caged Bird Sings*, the author has left the South to live in California with her mother. The situation confronting her tests her determination to overcome the traditional barriers in a young black woman's path.

Maya Angelou

Step Forward in the Car, Please

GUIDE TO READING: This account, focused on a single autobiographical episode, follows a classic pattern of challenge and achievement. What was the author's goal? What were the obstacles in her path? How did she overcome them?

My room had all the cheeriness of a dungeon and the appeal of a tomb. It was going to be impossible to stay there, but leaving held no attraction for me, either. The answer came to me with the suddenness of a collision. I would go to work. Mother wouldn't be difficult to convince; after all, in school I was a year ahead of my grade and Mother was a firm believer in self-sufficiency. In fact, she'd be pleased to think that I had that much gumption, that much of her in my character. (She liked to speak of herself as the original "do-it-yourself girl.")

Once I had settled on getting a job, all that remained was to decide which kind of job I was most fitted for. My intellectual pride had kept me from selecting typing, shorthand, or filing as subjects in school, so office work was ruled out. War plants and shipyards demanded birth certificates, and mine would reveal me to be fifteen, and ineligible for work. So the well-paying defense jobs were also out. Women had replaced men on the streetcars as conductors and motormen, and the thought of sailing up and down the hills of San Francisco in a dark-blue uniform, with a money changer at my belt, caught my fancy.

Mother was as easy as I had anticipated. The world was moving so fast, so much money was being made, so many people were dying in Guam, and Germany, that hordes of strangers became good friends overnight. Life was cheap and death entirely free. How could she have the time to think about my academic career? 3

To her question of what I planned to do, I replied that I would get a job on the streetcars. She rejected the proposal with: "They don't accept colored people on the streetcars." 4

I would like to claim an immediate fury which was followed by the noble determination to break the restricting tradition. But the truth is, my first reaction was one of disappointment. I'd pictured myself, dressed in a neat blue serge suit, my money changer swinging jauntily at my waist, and a cheery smile for the passengers which would make their own work day brighter. 5

From disappointment, I gradually ascended the emotional ladder to haughty indignation, and finally to that state of stubbornness where the mind is locked like the jaws of an enraged bulldog. 6

I would go to work on the streetcars and wear a blue serge suit. Mother gave me her support with one of her usual terse asides, "That's what you want to do? Then nothing beats a trial but a failure. Give it everything you've got. I've told you many times, 'Can't Do is like Don't Care.' Neither of them has a home." 7

Translated, that meant there was nothing a person can't do, and there should be nothing a human being didn't care about. It was the most positive encouragement I could have hoped for. 8

In the offices of the Market Street Railway Company, the receptionist seemed as surprised to see me there as I was surprised to find the interior dingy and drab. Somehow I had expected waxed surfaces and carpeted floors. If I had met no resistance, I might have decided against working for such a poor-mouth-looking concern. As it was, I explained that I had come to see about a job. She asked, was I sent by an agency, and when I replied that I was not, she told me they were only accepting applicants from agencies. 9

The classified pages of the morning papers had listed advertisements for motorettes and conductorettes and I reminded her of that. She gave me a face full of astonishment that my suspicious nature would not accept. 10

"I am applying for the job listed in this morning's *Chronicle* and I'd like to be presented to your personnel manager." While I spoke in supercilious accents, and looked at the room as if I had an oil well in my own backyard, 11 my armpits were being pricked by millions of hot pointed needles. She saw her escape and dived into it.

"He's out. He's out for the day. You might call him tomorrow and if he's 12 in, I'm sure you can see him." Then she swiveled her chair around on its rusty screws and with that I was supposed to be dismissed.

"May I ask his name?" 13

She half turned, acting surprised to find me still there. 14

"His name? Whose name?" 15

"Your personnel manager." 16

We were firmly joined in the hypocrisy to play out the scene. 17

"The personnel manager? Oh, he's Mr. Cooper, but I'm not sure you'll 18 find him here tomorrow. He's ... Oh, but you can try."

"Thank you." 19

"You're welcome." 20

And I was out of the musty room and into the even mustier lobby. In 21 the street I saw the receptionist and myself going faithfully through paces that were stale with familiarity, although I had never encountered that kind of situation before and, probably, neither had she. We were like actors who, knowing the play by heart, were still able to cry afresh over the old tragedies and laugh spontaneously at the comic situations.

The miserable little encounter had nothing to do with me, the me of 22 me, any more than it had to do with that silly clerk. The incident was a recurring dream concocted years before by whites, and it eternally came back to haunt us all. The secretary and I were like people in a scene where, because of harm done by one ancestor to another, we were bound to duel to the death. (Also because the play must end somewhere.)

I went further than forgiving the clerk; I accepted her as a fellow 23 victim of the same puppeteer.

On the streetcar, I put my fare into the box and the conductorette 24 looked at me with the usual hard eyes of white contempt. "Move into the car, please move on in the car." She patted her money changer.

Her Southern nasal accent sliced my meditation and I looked deep 25 into my thoughts. All lies, all comfortable lies. The receptionist was not innocent and neither was I. The whole charade we had played out in that waiting room had to do with me, black, and her, white.

I wouldn't move into the streetcar but stood on the ledge over the 26 conductor, glaring. My mind shouted so energetically that the announcement made my veins stand out, and my mouth tighten into a prune.

I WOULD HAVE THE JOB. I WOULD BE A CONDUCTORETTE AND 27 SLING A FULL MONEY CHANGER FROM MY BELT. I WOULD.

The next three weeks were a honeycomb of determination with aper- 28 tures for the days to go in and out. The Negro organizations to whom I appealed for support bounced me back and forth like a shuttlecock on a badminton court. Why did I insist on that particular job? Openings were going begging that paid nearly twice the money. The minor officials with whom I was able to win an audience thought me mad. Possibly I was.

Downtown San Francisco became alien and cold, and the streets I had [29] loved in a personal familiarity were unknown lanes that twisted with malicious intent. My trips to the streetcar office were of the frequency of a person on salary. The struggle expanded. I was no longer in conflict only with the Market Street Railway but with the marble lobby of the building which housed its offices, and elevators and their operators.

During this period of strain Mother and I began our first steps on the [30] long path toward mutual adult admiration. She never asked for reports and I didn't offer any details. But every morning she made breakfast, gave me carfare and lunch money, as if I were going to work. She comprehended that in the struggle lies the joy. That I was no glory seeker was obvious to her, and that I had to exhaust every possibility before giving in was also clear.

On my way out of the house one morning she said, "Life is going to give [31] you just what you put in it. Put your whole heart in everything you do, and pray, then you can wait." Another time she reminded me that "God helps those who help themselves." She had a store of aphorisms which she dished out as the occasion demanded. Strangely, as bored as I was with clichés, her inflection gave them something new, and set me thinking for a little while at least. Later when asked how I got my job, I was never able to say exactly. I only knew that one day, which was tiresomely like all the others before it, I sat in the Railway office, waiting to be interviewed. The receptionist called me to her desk and shuffled a bundle of paper to me. They were job application forms. She said they had to be filed out in triplicate. I had little time to wonder if I had won or not, for the standard questions reminded me of the necessity for lying. How old was I? List my previous jobs, starting from the last held and go backward to the first. How much money did I earn, and why did I leave the position? Give two references (not relatives). I kept my face blank (an old art) and wrote quickly the fable of Marguerite Johnson, aged nineteen, former companion and driver for Mrs. Annie Henderson (a White Lady) in Stamps, Arkansas.

I was given blood tests, aptitude tests, and physical coordination tests, [32] then on a blissful day I was hired as the first Negro on the San Francisco streetcars.

Mother gave me the money to have my blue serge suit tailored, and I [33] learned to fill out work cards, operate the money changer and punch transfers. The time crowded together and at an End of Days I was swinging on the back of the rackety trolley, smiling sweetly and persuading my charges to "step forward in the car, please."

For one whole semester the streetcars and I shimmied up and scooted [34] down the sheer hills of San Francisco. I lost some of my need for the black ghetto's shielding-sponge quality, as I clanged and cleared my way down Market Street, with its honky-tonk homes for homeless sailors, past the quiet retreat of Golden Gate Park and along closed undwelled-in-looking dwellings of the Sunset District.

My work shifts were split so haphazardly that it was easy to believe ₃₅ that my superiors had chosen them maliciously. Upon mentioning my suspicions to Mother, she said,"Don't you worry about it. You ask for what you want, and you pay for what you get. And I'm going to show you that it ain't no trouble when you pack double."

She stayed awake to drive me out to the car barn at four-thirty in the ₃₆ mornings, or to pick me up when I was relieved just before dawn. Her awareness of life's perils convinced her that while I would be safe on the public conveyances, she "wasn't about to trust a taxi driver with her baby."

When the spring classes began, I resumed my commitment with ₃₇ formal education. I was so much wiser and older, so much more independent, with a bank account and clothes that I had bought for myself, that I was sure I had learned and earned the magic formula which would make me a part of the life my contemporaries led.

Not a bit of it. Within weeks, I realized that my schoolmates and I were ₃₈ on paths moving away from each other. They were concerned and excited over the approaching football games. They concentrated great interest on who was worthy of being student body president, and when the metal bands would be removed from their teeth, while I remembered conducting a streetcar in the uneven hours of the morning.

Using the Dictionary

Synonyms are often near-synonyms; they share common territory but differ in other ways. In each of the following pairs, what does the word used by the author *add* to the meaning of its synonym? 1. (prison) *dungeon* (1)   2. (self-confidence) *self-sufficiency* (1)   3. (unqualified) *ineligible* (2)   4. (anger) *indignation* (6) 5. (brief) *terse* (7)   6. (superior) *supercilious* (11)   7. (make up) *concoct* (22)   8. (acting) *charade* (25)   9. (strange) *alien* (29)   10. proverb *aphorism* (31)

The Writer's Agenda

In this selection, Angelou tells the story of an experience that brought into focus for her a major challenge she had to face and overcome. Answer the following questions about the major dimensions of her autobiographical narrative:

1. What is the author's *purpose*? What do you think made her write? (Is she "getting even"?)

2. Where does the *setting* become most real? Where or how does it play a role in the author's story?

3. How real do the *characters* become? Prepare capsule portraits of the three people involved in these events: the narrator, the receptionist, and the mother.

4. The *high point* of the narrative is the author's confrontation with the receptionist. Here and later, what do we learn about the excuses, roundabout ways, or subterfuges through which prejudice works?

5. Where does the author seem to you most candid, taking the readers into her confidence? Where does she reveal contradictory attitudes or *mixed feelings*?

6. How would you sum up what Angelou learned from this experience or what the experience meant to her? What is the *point* of her story?

For Discussion or Writing

7. How much in this narrative is objective fact; how much is subjective interpretation? What would be a factual summary of the events?

8. What is the *audience* today for the kind of writing that this selection represents?

9. Is the kind of discrimination that Angelou encountered a thing of the past? Or do similar patterns of discrimination exist in our society today? Have they perhaps taken a different form? (Draw on detailed evidence from your observation, experience, or reading.)

10. What were your own first encounters with prejudice? How did they shape your outlook? Conversely, have you or people close to you ever been in the role of the outsider? What did you learn from the experience? (Discuss a major incident or several major incidents and show what they meant to you.)

11. Part of growing up is facing limitations that hem us in, challenges that we try to meet, or situations that we find hard to change. Focus on one such limitation or challenge that has played a role in your own experience. Tell the story of how it has affected your life or shaped your outlook.

12. What was your first experience with success or failure?

Branching Out

13. Have you had any experience with efforts aimed at counteracting historical patterns of discrimination? For instance, have you had experience with busing, programs like Headstart, open admission, or equal opportunity efforts? Describe your experience and what you learned from it.

BACKGROUND: In his native Minnesota, Garrison Keillor (born 1942) built up a large, loyal following as the host of *A Prairie Home Companion*, a live radio show originating on Saturday evenings in St. Paul. Founder, host, and writer of the show, Keillor mixes nostalgia and humor in skits and monologues about small-town life in the rural Midwest. He has published many short pieces—true stories and fictionalized autobiography—in magazines like *The Atlantic* and *The New Yorker*; many of these were reprinted in a collection called *Happy to Be Here* in 1982. Much of Keillor's material deals with a fictional rural town with one café, one bar, two churches, one traffic light, a grain elevator, one-hundred-degree summer days and thirty-below winter nights. Keillor is a master of the kind of humor that puts earnest ideals and ordinary human weaknesses next to each other. ("In school and church," he says, "we were called to high ideals such as truth and honor by someone perched on truth and hollering for us to come on up, but the truth was that we fell always short.") The selection that follows is from *Lake Wobegon Days* (1985), a book that, in the words of one reviewer, inhabits the ground between fiction and autobiography.

Garrison Keillor

Born Among
the Born-Again

GUIDE TO READING: This selection focuses on a single strand in the author's upbringing: the small-town fundamentalism of his family. How does he get his readers to understand the nature and the spirit of his family's religious tradition? What use does he make of examples, explanation, contrast, and key incidents?

In a town where everyone was either Lutheran or Catholic, our family 1 was not and never had been. We were Sanctified Brethren, a sect so tiny that nobody but us and God knew about it, so when kids asked what I was, I just said Protestant. It was too much to explain, like having six toes. You would rather keep your shoes on.

Grandpa Cotten was once tempted toward Lutheranism by a preacher 2 who gave a rousing sermon on grace that Grandpa heard as a young man while taking Aunt Esther's dog home who had chased a Model T across town. He sat down on the church steps and listened to the voice boom out the open windows until he made up his mind to go in and unite with the truth, but he took one look from the vestibule and left. "He was dressed up like the Pope of Rome," said Grandpa, "and the altar and the paintings and the gold candlesticks—my gosh, it was just a big show. And he was reading the whole darn thing off a page, like an actor."

Jesus said, "Where two or three are gathered together in my name, 3 there am I in the midst of them," and the Brethren believed that was enough. We met in Uncle Al and Aunt Flo's bare living room, with plain folding chairs arranged facing in toward the middle. No clergyman in a black smock. No organ or piano, for that would make one person too prominent. No uphol- stery—it would lead to complacence. No picture of Jesus—He was in our Hearts. The faithful sat down at the appointed hour and waited for the Spirit to move one of them to speak or to pray or to give out a hymn from our Little Flock hymnal. No musical notation, for music must come from the heart and not off a page. We sang the texts to a tune that fit the meter, of the many tunes we all knew. The idea of reading a prayer was sacrilege to us—"If a man can't remember what he wants to say to God, let him sit down and think a little harder," Grandpa said.

"There's the Lord's Prayer," said Aunt Esther meekly. We were sitting 4 on the porch after Sunday dinner. Esther and Harvey were visiting from Minneapolis and had attended Lake Wobegon Lutheran, she having turned Lutheran when she married him, a subject that was never brought up in our family.

"You call that prayer? Sitting and reciting like a bunch of school- 5 children?"

Harvey cleared his throat and turned to me and smiled. "Speaking of 6 school, how are you doing?" he asked.

There was a lovely silence in the Brethren assembled on Sunday 7 morning as we waited for the Spirit. Either the Spirit was moving someone to speak who was taking his sweet time or else the Spirit was playing a wonderful joke on us and letting us sit, or perhaps silence was the point of it. We sat listening to rain on the roof, distant traffic, a radio playing from across the street, kids whizzing by on bikes, dogs barking, as we waited for the Spirit to inspire us. It was like sitting on the porch with your family, when nobody feels that they have to make talk. So quiet in church. Minutes drifted by in silence that was sweet to us. The old Regulator clock ticked, the rain stopped, and the room changed light as the sun broke through— shafts of brilliant sun through the windows and motes of dust falling through it—the smell of clean clothes and floor wax and wine and the fresh bread of Aunt Flo, which was Christ's body given for us. Jesus in our midst, who loved us. So peaceful; and we loved each other, too. I thought perhaps the Spirit was leading me to say that, but I was just a boy, and children were supposed to keep still.

And my affections were not pure. They were tainted with a sneaking 8 admiration of Catholics—Catholic Christmas, Easter, the Living Rosary, and the Blessing of the Animals, all magnificent. Everything we did was plain, but they were regal—especially the Feast Day of Saint Francis, which they did right out in the open, a feast for the eyes. Cows, horses, some pets, right on the church lawn. The turmoil, animals bellowing and barking and clucking and a cat scheming how to escape and suddenly leaping out of the girl's arms who was holding on tight, the cat dashing through the crowd, dogs straining at the leash, and the ocarina band of third graders playing a song, and the great calm of the sisters, and the flags, and the Knights of Columbus decked out in their handsome black suits—the whole thing was gorgeous. I stared at it until my eyes almost fell out, and then I wished it would go on much longer.

"Christians," my Uncle Al used to say, "do not go in for show," referring 9 to the Catholics. We were sanctified by the blood of the Lord; therefore we were saints, like Saint Francis, but we didn't go in for feasts or ceremonies, involving animals or not. We went in for sitting, all nineteen of us, in Uncle Al and Aunt Flo's living room on Sunday morning and having a plain meeting and singing hymns in our poor thin voices, while not far away the Catholics were whooping it up. I wasn't allowed inside Our Lady, of course, but if the Blessing of the Animals on the Feast Day of Saint Francis was any indication, Lord, I didn't know but what they had elephants in there and acrobats. I sat in our little group and envied them for the splendor and gorgeousness, as we tried to sing without even so much as a harmonica to give us the pitch. Hymns, Uncle Al said, didn't have to be sung perfect, because God looks on the heart, and if you are In The Spirit, then all praise is good.

The Brethren, also known as The Saints Gathered in the Name of 10 Christ Jesus, who met in the living room were all related to each other and raised in the Faith from infancy except Brother Mel, who was rescued from a life of drunkenness, saved as a brand from the burning, a drowning sailor, a sheep on the hillside, whose immense red nose testified to his previous condition. I envied his amazing story of how he came to be with us. Born to godly parents, Mel left home at fifteen and joined the Navy. He sailed to distant lands in a submarine and had exciting experiences while traveling the downward path, which led him finally to the Union Gospel Mission in Minneapolis, where he heard God's voice "as clear as my voice speaking to you." He was twenty-six, he slept under bridges and in abandoned buildings, he drank two quarts of white muscatel every day, and then God told him that he must be born again, and so he was, and became the new Mel, except for his nose.

Except for his nose, Mel Burgess looked like any forty-year-old 11 Brethren man: sober, preferring dark suits, soft-spoken, tending toward girth. His nose was what made you look twice: battered, swollen, very red with tiny purplish lines, it looked ancient and dead on his otherwise fairly handsome face, the souvenir of what he had been saved from, the "Before" of his "Before . . . and After" advertisement for being born again.

For me, there was nothing before. I was born among the born-again. 12 This living room so hushed, the Brethren in their customary places on folding chairs (the comfortable ones were put away on Sunday morning) around the end table draped with a white cloth and the glass of wine and loaf of bread (unsliced), was as familiar to me as my mother and father, before whom there was nobody. I had always been here.

I never saw the "Before" until the Sunday we drove to St. Cloud for 13 dinner and traipsed into a restaurant that a friend of Dad's had recommended, Phil's House of Good Food. The waitress pushed two tables together and we sat down and studied the menu. My mother blanched at the prices. A chicken dinner went for $2.50, the roast beef for $3.75. "It's a nice place," Dad said, multiplying the five of us times $2.50. "I'm not so hungry, I guess," he said. "Maybe I'll just have soup." We weren't restaurantgoers— "Why pay good money for food you could make better at home?" was Mother's philosophy—so we weren't at all sure about restaurant customs. For example, could a person who had been seated in a restaurant simply get up and walk out? Would it be proper? Would it be *legal*?

The waitress came and stood by Dad. "Can I get you something from 14 the bar?" she said. Dad blushed a deep red. The question seemed to imply that he looked like a drinker.

"No," he whispered, as if he were turning down her offer to take off her 15 clothes and dance on the table.

Then another waitress brought a tray of glasses to a table of four 16 couples next to us. "Martini," she said, setting the drink down, "whiskey sour, whiskey sour, Manhattan, whiskey sour, gin and tonic, martini, whiskey sour."

"Ma'am? Something from the bar?" Mother looked at her in disbelief. 17

Suddenly the room changed for us. Our waitress looked hardened, 18 rough, cheap; across the room a woman laughed obscenely, "Haw, haw, haw"; the man with her lit a cigarette and blew a cloud of smoke; a swearword drifted out from the kitchen like a whiff of urine; even the soft lighting seemed suggestive, diabolical. To be seen in such a place on the Lord's Day—*what had we done*?

"Ed," my mother said, rising. 19

"We can't stay. I'm sorry," Dad told the waitress. We all got up and put 20 on our coats. Everyone in the restaurant had a good long look at us. A bald little man in a filthy white shirt emerged from the kitchen, wiping his hands. "Folks? Something wrong?" he said.

"We're in the wrong place," Mother told him. Mother always told the 21 truth, or something close to it.

"This is *humiliating*," I said out on the sidewalk. "I feel like a *leper* or 22 something. Why do we always have to make such a big production out of everything? Why can't we be like regular people?"

She put her hand on my shoulder. "Be not conformed to this world," 23 she said. I knew the rest by heart: "...but be ye transformed by the renewing of your mind, that ye may prove what is that good and acceptable and perfect will of God."

"Where we gonna eat?" Phyllis asked. 24

"We'll find someplace reasonable," said Mother, and we walked six 25 blocks across the river and found a lunch counter and ate sloppy joes (called Maid-Rites) for fifteen cents apiece. They did not agree with us, and we were aware of them all afternoon through prayer meeting and Young People's.

Using the Dictionary

Check the following words: 1. *sanctified (9)*   2. *vestibule* (2)   3. *complacence* (3)   4. *notation* (3)   5. *sacrilege* (3)   6. *regal* (8)   7. *blanched (13)*   8. *diabolical* (18). Find several *informal* expressions that are in keeping with the half-serious, half-humorous tone of the selection.

The Writer's Agenda

Keillor writes as the insider who knows how to take us into his confidence and how to initiate us into the ways of his group. Answer the following questions about how the essay takes shape:

1. The introductory paragraph sounds the *keynote*; it brings the subject into focus and reveals the boy's basic attitude. What is that attitude?   ,

2. What were the basic or the distinctive beliefs of the Brethren? Point out some of the many different *examples* of their attitudes or beliefs.

3. For the boy, what was the attraction of the rival Catholic tradition? (Point out and discuss some of the many striking, rich details.) How does the *contrast* highlight the basic points the author makes about the Brethren?

4. Brother Mel's case illustrates an important and familiar dimension of the family's kind of religion. How?

5. The selection concludes with a climactic incident—an incident that becomes the *high point* and dramatizes the boy's feelings about his family in graphic detail. What makes the author's choice of this incident particularly effective? How does the incident take up and reinforce the unifying central point or unifying theme of the selection?

6. The author has a keen ear for how people talk. Cite and discuss several *quotations* that have the true ring—true to the setting, right for the people.

For Discussion or Writing

7. What is the role of the author's humor in this selection? (Point out and discuss some striking examples.) Is it his purpose to ridicule the Brethren? Is his humor the debunking kind of humor that undercuts or destroys?

8. Who would make the right kind of audience for this selection? What would you say to readers who find the selection offensive or irreligious?

9. If you were asked to speak in defense or in praise of the Brethren, what would you say? If you had grown up in the setting described in this selection, how would you have reacted?

10. Has the awareness of "being different" played a major role in your own life? Where and how? (On the whole, has it been a bad or a good experience?)

11. Have you ever been a member of a group that had its own distinctive standards, rituals, criteria for admission, or the like (for instance, scouts, fraternity or sorority, the army, a religious group)? What was the experience like? How did you react to it? Did it have a lasting effect on you as a person?

12. A sense of humor, or the lack of it, can make a big difference in people's lives. Can you show this statement to be true by writing about your own experience?

13. What was the dominant outlook or prevailing philosophy in your own bringing up? How did you react to it?

Branching Out

14. Have you ever felt the need to speak up in defense of a group considered different or alien in our society? Write an essay in defense of the group.

WRITERS ON WRITING

Garrison Keillor on Story-Telling

I started out telling true stories from my childhood, dressed them up as fiction, and then discovered Lake Wobegon as a place to set them so as to put more distance between them and the innocent persons I was talking about. . . .

There is a wonderful literature from the 19th century of the people who came out to the Midwest, starting in the 1830s, when my Unitarian Transcendentalists came out to Minnesota. These people were great letter-writers and journal-keepers, and some were even poets. They had so much fun recording their impressions that fiction never occurred to them. The first serious lies were not told in Minnesota until the Age of Elegance in the 1880s when comfortable, bored people developed a taste for fiction from faraway places. . . .

Radio was a way to get out from under the cold hand of the short story, as it was taught to me in college. Reading those magnificent exercises in prose by the greats—Katherine Mansfield, Flannery O'Connor, Cheever, Fitzgerald, Hemingway—you knew you couldn't do those things any better than they had already done them. But slipping into radio is like those people who got up and left Vermont and came to Minnesota. Vermont was crowded and hilly and rocky and as hard as you worked, you would never be as good as the people who were there a long time. But you came out to Minnesota and there was vast, virgin land. It was the same in radio. If you just stood up in front of a live microphone 10 years ago and started to tell a story—not reading, because that's literary, but telling the simplest kind of story— you were different. You could go off and be as sentimental as you please and just blurt things out. But if you were writing, you'd think about it twice. You'd think about it 15 times.

— From an interview in *USA Today*

When I was a boy, the storyteller in our family was my uncle Lew Powell, who was my great uncle, my grandma's brother, who died only a couple of years ago, at the age of 93. In a family that tended to be a little withdrawn, taciturn, my uncle Lew was the friendliest. He had been a salesman, and he liked to drive around and drop in on people. He would converse, ask how we were doing in school, but there would be a point when he would get launched, and we would try to launch him.

The period he talked about so well was about ten years on either side of the turn of the century. A beautiful time, I still think so. And I just wanted him to tell more and more and more. I wanted to know everything. What it looked and smelled like, what they ate and what they wore.

I remember Uncle Lew's stories not as coming to a point, really, but to a point of rest, a point of contemplation. As I got older, of course, life was becoming strange. I just looked to those stories of his, and to the history of the family, as giving a person some sense of place, that we were not just chips floating on the waves, that in some way we were meant to be here, and had a history. That we had standing.

— From an interview in *Time*

BACKGROUND: George Orwell (1903−50), whose real name was Eric Blair, was a British socialist widely admired as one of the great masters of modern expository prose. Many of his essays and books are autobiographical; others reflect his sharp-eyed observations of what was happening in the world around him. He wrote at a time in European history when print and radio often seemed dominated by tired clichés, blatant propaganda, and self-serving lies. Orwell went against the tide by writing as an honest witness, telling the truth as he knew it from his own experience. He had been born in India as the son of English parents; his early political education took place when he served with the British Imperial Police in Burma, a country to the east of India that was then, like India, a British colony. He later fought in the Spanish Civil War with the republican, or loyalist, forces opposing the armies of the future fascist dictator, Franco. Two of his novels have been read by millions around the world: *Animal Farm* (1946), a biting satirical attack on Russian communism under Stalin; and *1984* (1949), which predicted a joyless totalitarian society of the future where every move and thought of a citizen would be watched by Big Brother.

George Orwell

Shooting an

Elephant

GUIDE TO READING: This autobiographical essay takes an honest look at a *single central event* in order to explore its significance. As you read the essay, look for the answers to five basic questions: Where are we? What people are involved? What happens? What feelings or emotions do the events bring into play? What does it all mean to the author?

In Moulmein, in Lower Burma, I was hated by large numbers of people—the only time in my life that I have been important enough for this to happen to me. I was subdivisional police officer of the town, and in an aimless, petty kind of way anti-European feeling was very bitter. No one had the guts to raise a riot, but if a European woman went through the bazaars alone somebody would probably spit betel juice[1] over her dress. As a police officer I was an obvious target and was baited whenever it seemed safe to do so. When a nimble Burman tripped me up on the football field and the referee (another Burman) looked the other way, the crowd yelled with hideous laughter. This happened more than once. In the end the sneering

[1][The betel (bē′tl) palm was a tree whose nuts and leaves were chewed as a stimulant in some parts of Asia.]

yellow faces of young men that met me everywhere, the insults hooted after me when I was at a safe distance, got badly on my nerves. The young Buddhist priests were the worst of all. There were several thousands of them in the town and none of them seemed to have anything to do except stand on street corners and jeer at Europeans.

All this was perplexing and upsetting. For at that time I had already made up my mind that imperialism was an evil thing and the sooner I chucked up my job and got out of it the better. Theoretically—and secretly, of course—I was all for the Burmese and all against their oppressors, the British. As for the job I was doing, I hated it more bitterly than I can perhaps make clear. In a job like that you see the dirty work of Empire at close quarters. The wretched prisoners huddling in the stinking cages of the lockups, the gray, cowed faces of the long-term convicts, the scarred buttocks of the men who had been flogged with bamboos—all these oppressed me with an intolerable sense of guilt. But I could get nothing into perspective. I was young and ill-educated and I had had to think out my problems in the utter silence that is imposed on every Englishman in the East. I did not even know that the British Empire is dying, still less did I know that it is a great deal better than the younger empires that are going to supplant it. All I knew was that I was stuck between my hatred of the empire I served and my rage against the evil-spirited little beasts who tried to make my job impossible. With one part of my mind I thought of the British Raj[2] as an unbreakable tyranny, as something clamped down, *in saecula saeculorum*,[3] upon the will of prostrate peoples; with another part I thought that the greatest joy in the world would be to drive a bayonet into a Buddhist priest's guts. Feelings like these are the normal by-products of imperialism; ask any Anglo-Indian official, if you can catch him off duty.

One day something happened which in a roundabout way was enlightening. It was a tiny incident in itself, but it gave me a better glimpse than I had had before of the real nature of imperialism—the real motives for which despotic governments act. Early one morning the subinspector at a police station the other end of town rang me up on the phone and said that an elephant was ravaging the bazaar. Would I please come and do something about it? I did not know what I could do, but I wanted to see what was happening and I got onto a pony and started out. I took my rifle, an old .44 Winchester and much too small to kill an elephant, but I thought the noise might be useful *in terrorem*.[4] Various Burmans stopped me on the way and told me about the elephant's doings. It was not, of course, a wild elephant, but a tame one which had gone "must."[5] It had been chained up as tame elephants always are when their attack of "must" is due, but on the previous

2

3

---

[2] [Raj (räj) and rajah (rä′jə) are the words for "rule" and "ruler" in Hindi, one of the principal languages of India.]
[3] [a Latin phrase meaning "throughout the ages, forever and ever"]
[4] [a Latin phrase meaning "to cause fright"]
[5] [a phase of sexual excitement and destructive frenzy]

night it had broken its chain and escaped. Its mahout,[6] the only person who could manage it when it was in that state, had set out in pursuit, but he had taken the wrong direction and was now twelve hours' journey away, and in the morning the elephant had suddenly reappeared in the town. The Burmese population had no weapons and were quite helpless against it. It had already destroyed somebody's bamboo hut, killed a cow, and raided some fruit stalls and devoured the stock; also it had met the municipal rubbish van, and, when the driver jumped out and took to his heels, had turned the van over and inflicted violence upon it.

The Burmese subinspector and some Indian constables were waiting 4
for me in the quarter where the elephant had been seen. It was a very poor quarter, a labyrinth of squalid bamboo huts, thatched with palm leaf, winding all over a steep hillside. I remember that it was a cloudy stuffy morning at the beginning of the rains. We began questioning the people as to where the elephant had gone, and, as usual, failed to get any definite information. That is invariably the case in the East; a story always sounds clear enough at a distance, but the nearer you get to the scene of events the vaguer it becomes. Some of the people said that the elephant had gone in one direction, some said that he had gone in another, some professed not even to have heard of any elephant. I had almost made up my mind that the whole story was a pack of lies, when we heard yells a little distance away. There was a loud, scandalized cry of "Go away, child! Go away this instant!" and an old woman with a switch in her hand came round the corner of a hut, violently shooing away a crowd of naked children. Some more women followed, clicking their tongues and exclaiming; evidently there was something there that the children ought not to have seen. I rounded the hut and saw a man's dead body sprawling in the mud. He was an Indian, a Dravidian[7] coolie, almost naked, and he could not have been dead many minutes. The people said that the elephant had come suddenly upon him round the corner of the hut, caught him with its trunk, put its foot on his back, and ground him into the earth. This was the rainy season and the ground was soft, and his face had scored a trench a foot deep and a couple of yards long. He was lying on his belly with arms crucified and head sharply twisted to one side. His face was coated with mud, the eyes wide open, the teeth bared and grinning with an expression of unendurable agony. (Never tell me, by the way, that the dead look peaceful. Most of the corpses I have seen looked devilish.) The friction of the great beast's foot had stripped the skin from his back as neatly as one skins a rabbit. As soon as I saw the dead man I sent an orderly to a friend's house nearby to borrow an elephant rifle. I had already sent back the pony, not wanting it to go mad with fright and throw me if it smelled the elephant.

The orderly came back in a few minutes with a rifle and five cartridges, 5

[6][A mahout (mə hout') is a trainer and driver of an elephant used for work and transportation.]
[7][Dravidians were a major ethnic group in southern India.]

and meanwhile some Burmans had arrived and told us that the elephant was in the paddy fields below, only a few hundred yards away. As I started forward practically the whole population of the quarter flocked out of their houses and followed me. They had seen the rifle and were all shouting excitedly that I was going to shoot the elephant. They had not shown much interest in the elephant when he was merely ravaging their homes, but it was different now that he was going to be shot. It was a bit of fun to them, as it would be to an English crowd; besides, they wanted the meat. It made me vaguely uneasy. I had no intention of shooting the elephant—I had merely sent for the rifle to defend myself if necessary—and it is always unnerving to have a crowd following you. I marched down the hill, looking and feeling a fool, with the rifle over my shoulder and an ever-growing army of people jostling at my heels. At the bottom, when you got away from the huts, there was a metaled road and beyond that a miry waste of paddy fields a thousand yards across, not yet plowed but soggy from the first rains and dotted with coarse grass. The elephant was standing eighty yards from the road, his left side toward us. He took not the slightest notice of the crowd. He was tearing up bunches of grass, beating them against his knees to clean them, and stuffing them into his mouth.

I had halted on the road. As soon as I saw the elephant I knew with 6 perfect certainty that I ought not to shoot him. It is a serious matter to shoot a working elephant—it is comparable to destroying a huge and costly piece of machinery—and obviously one ought not to do it if it can possibly be avoided. And at that distance, peacefully eating, the elephant looked no more dangerous than a cow. I thought then and I think now that his attack of "must" was already passing off; in which case he would merely wander harmlessly about until the mahout came back and caught him. Moreover, I did not in the least want to shoot him. I decided that I would watch him for a little while to make sure that he did not turn savage again, and then go home.

But at that moment I glanced round at the crowd that had followed me. 7 It was an immense crowd, two thousand at the least and growing every minute. It blocked the road for a long distance on either side. I looked at the sea of yellow faces above the garish clothes—faces all happy and excited over this bit of fun, all certain that the elephant was going to be shot. They were watching me as they would watch a conjurer about to perform a trick. They did not like me, but with the magical rifle in my hands I was momentarily worth watching. And suddenly I realized that I should have to shoot the elephant after all. The people expected it of me and I had got to do it; I could feel their two thousand wills pressing me forward, irresistibly. And it was at this moment, as I stood there with the rifle in my hands, that I first grasped the hollowness, the futility of the white man's dominion in the East. Here was I, the white man with his gun, standing in front of the unarmed native crowd—seemingly the leading actor of the piece; but in reality I was only an absurd puppet pushed to and fro by the will of those yellow faces behind. I perceived in this moment that when the white man turns tyrant it is his own freedom that he destroys. He becomes a sort of hollow, posing dummy, the conventionalized figure of a sahib. For it is the condition of his rule that he shall spend his life in trying to impress the "natives" and so in every crisis he has got to do what the "natives" expect of him. He wears a mask, and his face grows to fit it. I had got to shoot the elephant. I had committed myself to doing it when I sent for the rifle. A sahib has got to act like a sahib; he has got to appear resolute, to know his own mind and do definite things. To come all that way, rifle in hand, with two thousand people marching at my heels, and then to trail feebly away, having done nothing— no, that was impossible. The crowd would laugh at me. And my whole life, every white man's life in the East, was one long struggle not to be laughed at.

But I did not want to shoot the elephant. I watched him beating his [8] bunch of grass against his knees, with that preoccupied grandmotherly air that elephants have. It seemed to me that it would be murder to shoot him. At that age I was not squeamish about killing animals, but I had never shot an elephant and never wanted to. (Somehow it always seems worse to kill a *large* animal.) Besides, there was the beast's owner to be considered. Alive, the elephant was worth at least a hundred pounds; dead, he would only be worth the value of his tusks—five pounds, possibly. But I had got to act quickly. I turned to some experienced-looking Burmans who had been there when we arrived, and asked them how the elephant had been behaving. They all said the same thing: he took no notice of you if you left him alone, but he might charge if you went too close to him.

It was perfectly clear to me what I ought to do. I ought to walk up to [9] within, say, twenty-five yards of the elephant and test his behavior. If he charged I could shoot; if he took no notice of me it would be safe to leave him until the mahout came back. But also I knew that I was going to do no such thing. I was a poor shot with a rifle and the ground was soft mud into which one would sink at every step. If the elephant charged and I missed him, I should have about as much chance as a toad under a steamroller. But even then I was not thinking particularly of my own skin, only the watchful yellow faces behind. For at that moment, with the crowd watching me, I was not afraid in the ordinary sense, as I would have been if I had been alone. A white man mustn't be frightened in front of "natives"; and so, in general, he isn't frightened. The sole thought in my mind was that if anything went wrong those two thousand Burmans would see me pursued, caught, trampled on, and reduced to a grinning corpse like that Indian up the hill. And if that happened it was quite probable that some of them would laugh. That would never do. There was only one alternative. I shoved the cartridges into the magazine and lay down on the road to get a better aim.

The crowd grew very still, and a deep, low, happy sigh, as of people [10] who see the theater curtain go up at last, breathed from innumerable throats. They were going to have their bit of fun after all. The rifle was a beautiful German thing with cross-hair sights. I did not then know that in shooting an elephant one should shoot to cut an imaginary bar running from earhole to earhole. I ought therefore, as the elephant was sideways on, to have aimed straight at his earhole; actually I aimed several inches in front of this, thinking the brain would be further forward.

When I pulled the trigger I did not hear the bang or feel the kick—one never does when a shot goes home—but I heard the devilish roar of glee that went up from the crowd. In that instant, in too short a time, one would have thought, even for the bullet to get there, a mysterious, terrible change had come over the elephant. He neither stirred nor fell, but every line of his body had altered. He looked suddenly stricken, shrunken, immensely old, as though the frightful impact of the bullet had paralyzed him without knocking him down. At last, after what seemed a long time—it might have been five seconds, I dare say—he sagged flabbily to his knees. His mouth slobbered. An enormous senility seemed to have settled upon him. One could have imagined him thousands of years old. I fired again into the same spot. At the second shot he did not collapse but climbed with desperate slowness to his feet and stood weakly upright, with legs sagging and head drooping. I fired a third time. That was the shot that did for him. You could see the agony of it jolt his whole body and knock the last remnant of strength from his legs. But in falling he seemed for a moment to rise, for as his hind legs collapsed beneath him he seemed to tower upwards like a huge rock toppling, his trunk reaching skyward like a tree. He trumpeted, for the first and only time. And then down he came, his belly toward me, with a crash that seemed to shake the ground even where I lay.

I got up. The Burmans were already racing past me across the mud. It was obvious that the elephant would never rise again, but he was not dead. He was breathing very rhythmically with long rattling gasps, his great mound of a side painfully rising and falling. His mouth was wide open—I could see far down into caverns of pale pink throat. I waited a long time for him to die, but his breathing did not weaken. Finally I fired my two remaining shots into the spot where I thought his heart must be. The thick blood welled out of him like red velvet, but still he did not die. His body did not even jerk when the shots hit him; the tortured breathing continued without a pause. He was dying, very slowly and in great agony, but in some world remote from me where not even a bullet could damage him further. I felt that I had got to put an end to that dreadful noise. It seemed dreadful to see the great beast lying there, powerless to move and yet powerless to die, and not even to be able to finish him. I sent back for my small rifle and poured shot after shot into his heart and down his throat. They seemed to make no impression. The tortured gasps continued as steadily as the ticking of a clock.

In the end I could not stand it any longer and went away. I heard later that it took him half an hour to die. Burmans were arriving with dahs[8] and

---

[8][large, heavy knives]

baskets even before I left, and I was told they had stripped his body almost to the bones by the afternoon.

Afterwards, of course, there were endless discussions about the shooting of the elephant. The owner was furious, but he was only an Indian and could do nothing. Besides, legally I had done the right thing, for a mad elephant has to be killed, like a mad dog, if its owner fails to control it. Among the Europeans opinion was divided. The older men said I was right, the younger men said it was a shame to shoot an elephant for killing a coolie, because an elephant was worth more than any Coringhee coolie. And afterwards I was very glad that the coolie had been killed; it put me legally in the right and it gave me a sufficient pretext for shooting the elephant. I often wondered whether any of the others grasped that I had done it solely to avoid looking like a fool.

Using the Dictionary

This essay uses a number of political terms as well as words that came into British English in the days of colonialism. What do the following words mean? From what language or region did they come into English?   1. *bazaar* (1)   2. *raj* (2)   3. *prostrate* (2)   4. *imperialism* (3)   5. *despotic* (3)   6. *constable* (4)   7. *coolie* (4)   8. *paddy* (5)   9. *dominion* (7)   10. *sahib* (7)

The Writer's Agenda

This essay is a classic example of autobiographical writing focused on one central event. Answer the following questions about the author's account of the event and about its meaning.

1. How do the two opening paragraphs *set the scene*? (Where are we? What do we learn about the people? What are the author's attitudes and feelings?) How does the opening sentence get the reader's attention?

2. What *events* lead up to the climactic shooting? What striking details help make the setting and the events real for the reader?

3. As we approach the climactic shooting, the author begins to focus on the *meaning* that the experience had for him. What were the contradictory thoughts and feelings that went through his mind? (What sentence or passage best sums up for you the central idea, thus serving as a possible thesis for the essay as a whole?)

4. We reach the dramatic high point or climax of the essay with the two paragraphs (11, 12) beginning "When I pulled the trigger . . . ." What is the keynote or *dominant impression* in the first of these two paragraphs? What is it in the second? In each paragraph, trace the network of closely related words and details that all reinforce the same dominant impression.

5. How does the author wind up the essay in his conclusion? Does he restate his main point? What added thoughts or considerations appear in the conclusion, and how are they related to the central thesis of the essay?

For Discussion or Writing

6. Representatives of colonial rule have often been accused of callousness, insensitivity, or condescension. They have been accused of being unable to understand or feel sympathy for the oppressed. How would you judge the author in the light of these charges?

7. A test of a writer's candor is the willingness to give a frank account of inner doubts, divided loyalties, and unflattering truths. What role do these play in the essay as a whole? How do they affect your view of the author as a person?

8. Is it common for people in authority to feel the need to keep up a facade or to keep up a front? Where have you observed or encountered something similar?

9. Great autobiography often reveals the divided loyalties or conflicts of conscience experienced by people faced with conflicting demands on their allegiance. Discuss one such conflict that you believe is especially meaningful to members of your generation.

10. We like to think of ourselves as being on the right side or serving the good cause. Have you ever felt you were on the wrong side or were serving the wrong cause? Describe your experience, and discuss what you learned from it.

11. Write an autobiographical essay modeled on Orwell's "Shooting an Elephant." Focus on a single major incident or event that had a special meaning for you as a person.

BACKGROUND: Jade Snow Wong was born in 1922 as the daughter of Chinese immigrants. She graduated from Mills College and worked for the Navy during World War II. Like millions of young Americans, she had to chart her way between the old-country ways of home and the American ways of school or neighborhood. The record of her search for identity is her book *Fifth Chinese Daughter*, about her growing up in the traditional Chinatown of San Francisco. Many Chinese immigrants of her parents' generation had come to the American West to work as laborers building the railroads or as restaurant and laundry workers in the towns. They often maintained the strong traditional family unit of their homeland. People sought protection and justice in a clan that included many of their close relatives. People honored their parents and their ancestors; the upkeep of their ancestors' graves in the distant homeland was an important duty. Children were taught obedience and filial respect—the respect of a dutiful, grateful son or daughter for the parents. The following excerpt from a longer essay follows a classic pattern of autobiography: The author traces the change from the unquestioning attitudes of childhood days to the first assertion of independence during adolescence. The essay comes to a head with the first open conflict between the adolescent daughter and her parents.

Jade Snow Wong

Fifth Chinese

Daughter

GUIDE TO READING: In reading the essay, pay special attention to how the contrast between two different styles of life takes shape. What are the cornerstones of the parents' traditional way of life? What are key differences between the parents' ways and more familiar American ways? What is the basic issue in the conflict between parents and daughter, and what is the outcome?

From infancy to my sixteenth year, I was reared according to nineteenth-century ideals of Chinese womanhood. I was never left alone, though it was not unusual for me to feel lonely, while surrounded by a family of seven others, and often by ten (including bachelor cousins) at meals.

My father (who enjoyed our calling him Daddy in English) was the unquestioned head of our household. He was not talkative, being preoccupied with his business affairs and with reading constantly otherwise. My mother was mistress of domestic affairs. Seldom did these two converse before their children, but we knew them to be a united front, and suspected that privately she both informed and influenced him about each child.

In order to support the family in America, Daddy tried various occupations—candy making, the ministry to which he was later ordained—but finally settled on manufacturing men's and children's denim garments. He leased sewing equipment, installed machines in a basement where rent was cheapest, and there he and his family lived and worked. There was no thought that dim, airless quarters were terrible conditions for living and working, or that child labor was unhealthful. The only goal was for all in the family to work, to save, and to become educated. It was possible, so it would be done.

My father, a meticulous bookkeeper, used only an abacus, a brush, ink, and Chinese ledgers. Because of his newly learned ideals, he pioneered for the right of women to work. Concerned that they have economic independence, but not with the long hours of industrial home work, he went to shy housewives' apartments and taught them sewing.

My earliest memories of companionship with my father were as his passenger in his red wheelbarrow, sharing space with the piles of blue-jean materials he was delivering to a worker's home. He must have been forty. He was lean, tall, inevitably wearing blue overalls, rolled shirt sleeves, and high black kid shoes. In his pockets were numerous keys, tools, and pens. On such deliveries, I noticed that he always managed time to show a mother how to sew a difficult seam, or to help her repair a machine, or just to chat.

I observed from birth that living and working were inseparable. My mother was short, sturdy, young looking, and took pride in her appearance. She was at her machine the minute housework was done, and she was the hardest-working seamstress, seldom pausing, working after I went to bed. The hum of sewing machines continued day and night, seven days a week. She knew that to have more than the four necessities, she must work and save. We knew that to overcome poverty, there were only two methods: working and education.

Having provided the setup for family industry, my father turned his attention to our education. Ninety-five percent of the population in his native China had been illiterate. He knew that American public schools would take care of our English, but he had to nurture our Chinese knowledge. Only the Cantonese tongue was ever spoken by him or my mother. When the two oldest girls arrived from China, the schools of Chinatown received only boys. My father tutored his daughters each morning before breakfast. In the midst of a foreign environment, he clung to a combination of the familiar old standards and what was permissible in the newly learned Christian ideals.

My eldest brother was born in America, the only boy for fourteen years, and after him three daughters—another older sister, myself, and my younger sister. Then my younger brother, Paul, was born. That older brother, Lincoln, was cherished in the best Chinese tradition. He had his own room; he kept a German shepherd as his pet; he was tutored by a Chinese scholar; he was sent to private school for American classes. As a male Wong, he would be responsible some day for the preservation of and pilgrimages to ancestral graves—his privileges were his birthright. We girls were content with the unusual opportunities of working and attending two schools. By day, I attended American public school near our home. From 5:00 P.M. to 8:00 P.M. on five weekdays and from 9:00 A.M. to 12 noon on Saturdays, I attended the Chinese school. Classes numbered twenty to thirty students, and were taught by educated Chinese from China. We studied poetry, calligraphy, philosophy, literature, history, correspondence, religion, all by exacting memorization.

Daddy emphasized memory development; he could still recite fluently 9 many lengthy lessons of his youth. Every evening after both schools, I'd sit by my father, often as he worked at his sewing machine, sing-songing my lessons above its hum. Sometimes I would stop to hold a light for him as he threaded the difficult holes of a specialty machine, such as one for bias bindings. After my Chinese lessons passed his approval, I was allowed to attend to American homework. I was made to feel luckier than other Chinese girls who didn't study Chinese, and also luckier than Western girls without a dual heritage.

There was little time for play, and toys were unknown to me. In any 10 spare time, I was supplied with embroidery and sewing for my mother. The Chinese New Year, which by the old lunar calendar would fall sometime in late January or early February of the Western Christian calendar, was the most special time of the year, for then the machines stopped for three days. Mother would clean our living quarters very thoroughly, decorate the sitting room with flowering branches and fresh oranges, and arrange candied fruits or salty melon seeds for callers. All of us would be dressed in bright new clothes, and relatives or close friends, who came to call, would give each of us a red paper packet containing a good luck coin—usually a quarter. I remember how my classmates would gleefully talk of *their* receipts. But my mother made us give our money to her, for she said that she needed it to reciprocate to others.

Yet there was little reason for unhappiness. I was never hungry. 11 Though we had no milk, there was all the rice we wanted. We had hot and cold running water—a rarity in Chinatown—as well as our own bathtub. Our sheets were pieced from dishtowels, but we had sheets. I was never neglected, for my mother and father were always at home. During school vacation periods, I was taught to operate many types of machines—tacking (for pockets), overlocking (for the raw edges of seams), buttonhole, double seaming; and I learned all the stages in producing a pair of jeans to its final inspection, folding, and tying in bundles of a dozen pairs by size, ready for pickup. Denim jeans are heavy—my shoulders ached often. My father set up a modest nickel-and-dime piecework reward for me, which he recorded in my own notebook, and paid me regularly.

My mother dutifully followed my father's leadership. She was ex- 12 tremely thrifty, but the thrifty need pennies to manage, and the old world had denied her those. Upon arrival in the new world of San Francisco, she accepted the elements her mate had selected to shape her new life: domestic duties, seamstress work in the factory-home, mothering each child in turn, church once a week, and occasional movies. Daddy frowned upon the community Chinese operas because of their very late hours (they did not finish till past midnight) and their mixed audiences.

Very early in my life, the manners of a traditional Chinese lady were 13 taught to me. How to hold a pair of chopsticks (palm up, not down); how to hold a bowl of rice (one thumb on top, not resting in an open palm); how to pass something to elders (with both hands, never one); how to pour tea into the tiny, handleless porcelain cups (seven-eighths full so that the top edge would be cool enough to hold); how to eat from a center serving dish (only the piece in front of your place; never pick around); not to talk at table, not to show up outside of one's room without being fully dressed; not to be late, ever; not to be too playful—in a hundred and one ways, we were molded to be trouble-free, unobtrusive, cooperative.

We were disciplined by first being told, and then by punishment if we 14 didn't remember. Punishment was instant and unceremonious. At the table, it came as a sudden whack from Daddy's chopsticks. Away from the table, punishment could be the elimination of a privilege or the blow on our legs from a bundle of cane switches.

Only Daddy and Oldest Brother were allowed individual idiosyncra- 15 sies. Daughters were all expected to be of one standard. To allow each one of many daughters to be different would have posed enormous problems of cost, energy, and attention. No one was shown physical affection. Such familiarity would have weakened my parents and endangered the one-answer authoritative system. One standard from past to present, whether in China or in San Francisco, was simpler to enforce. My parents never said "please" and "thank you" for any service or gift. In Chinese, both "please" and "thank you" can be literally translated as "I am not worthy" and naturally, no parent is going to say that about a service which should be their just due.

Traditional Chinese parents pit their children against a standard of 16 perfection without regard to personality, individual ambitions, tolerance for human error, or exposure to the changing social scene. It never occurred to that kind of parent to be friends with their children on common ground.

During the Depression, my mother and father needed even more hours 17 to work. Daddy had been shopping daily for groceries (we had no icebox) and my mother cooked. Now I was told to assume both those duties. My mother would give me fifty cents to buy enough fresh food for dinner and breakfast. In those years, twenty-five cents could buy a small chicken or three sanddabs, ten cents bought three bunches of green vegetables, and fifteen cents bought some meat to cook with these. After American school I rushed to the stores only a block or so away, returned and cleaned the foods, and cooked in a hurry in order to eat an early dinner and get to Chinese school on time. When I came home at 8:00 P.M., I took care of the dinner dishes before starting to do my homework. Saturdays and Sundays were for housecleaning and the family laundry, which I scrubbed on a board, using big galvanized buckets in our bathtub.

I had no sympathetic guidance as an eleven-year-old in my own reign [18] in the kitchen, which lasted for four years. I finished junior high school, started high school, and continued studying Chinese. With the small earnings from summer work in my father's basement factory (we moved back to the basement during the Depression), I bought materials to sew my own clothes. But the routine of keeping house only to be dutiful, to avoid tongue or physical lashings, became exasperating. The tiny space which was the room for three sisters was confining. After I graduated from Chinese evening school, I began to look for part-time paying jobs as a mother's helper. Those jobs varied from cleaning house to baking a cake, amusing a naughty child to ironing shirts, but wearying, exhausting as they were, they meant money earned for myself.

As I advanced in American high school and worked at those jobs, I was [19] gradually introduced to customs not of the Chinese world. American teachers were mostly kind. I remember my third-grade teacher's skipping me half a year. I remember my fourth-grade teacher—with whom I am still friendly. She was the first person to hold me to her physically and affectionately—because a baseball bat had been accidentally flung against my hand. I also remember that I was confused by being held, since physical comfort had not been offered by my parents. I remember my junior high school principal, who skipped me half a grade and commended me before the school assembly, to my great embarrassment.

In contrast, Chinese schoolteachers acted as extensions of Chinese [20] parental discipline. There was a formal "disciplinarian dean" to apply the cane to wayward boys, and girls were not exempt either. A whisper during chapel was sufficient provocation to be called to the dean's office. No humor was exchanged; no praise or affection expressed by the teachers. They presented the lessons, and we had to learn to memorize all the words, orally, before the class. Then followed the written test, word for word. Without an alphabet, the Chinese language requires exact memorization. No originality or deviation was permitted and grading was severe. One word wrong during an examination could reduce a grade by 10 percent. It was the principle of learning by punishment.

Interest and praise, physical or oral, were rewards peculiar to the [21] American world. Even employers who were paying me thanked me for a service or complimented me on a meal well cooked, and sometimes helped me with extra dishes. Chinese often said that "foreigners" talked too much about too many personal things. My father used to tell me to think three times before saying anything, and if I said nothing, no one would say I was stupid. I perceived a difference between two worlds.

By the time I was graduating from high school, my parents had done 22 their best to produce an intelligent, obedient daughter, who would know more than the average Chinatown girl and should do better than average at a conventional job, her earnings brought home to them in repayment for their years of child support. Then, they hoped, she would marry a nice Chinese boy and make him a good wife, as well as an above-average mother for his children. Chinese custom used to decree that families should "introduce" chosen partners to each other's children. The groom's family should pay handsomely to the bride's family for rearing a well-bred daughter. They should also pay all bills for a glorious wedding banquet for several hundred guests. Then the bride's family could consider their job done. Their daughter belonged to the groom's family and must henceforth seek permission from all persons in his home before returning to her parents for a visit.

But having been set upon a new path, I did not oblige my parents with 23 the expected conventional ending. At fifteen, I had moved away from home to work for room and board and a salary of twenty dollars per month. Having found that I could subsist independently, I thought it regrettable to terminate my education. Upon graduating from high school at the age of sixteen, I asked my parents to assist me in college expenses. I pleaded with my father, for his years of encouraging me to be above mediocrity in both Chinese and American studies had made me wish for some undefined but brighter future.

My father was briefly adamant. He must conserve his resources for my 24 oldest brother's medical training. Though I desired to continue on an above-average course, his material means were insufficient to support that ambition. He added that if I had the talent, I could provide for my own college education. When he had spoken, no discussion was expected. After his edict, no daughter questioned.

But this matter involved my whole future—it was not simply asking 25 for permission to go to a night church meeting (forbidden also). Though for years I had accepted the authority of the one I honored most, his decision that night embittered me as nothing ever had. My oldest brother had so many privileges, had incurred unusual expenses for luxuries which were taken for granted as his birthright, yet these were part of a system I had accepted. Now I suddenly wondered at my father's interpretation of the Christian code: was it intended to discriminate against a girl after all, or was it simply convenient for my father's economics and cultural prejudice? Did a daughter have any right to expect more than a fate of obedience, according to the old Chinese standard? As long as I could remember, I had been told that a female followed three men during her lifetime: as a girl, her father; as a wife, her husband; as an old woman, her son.

My indignation mounted against that tradition and I decided then that 26 my past could not determine my future. I knew that more education would prepare me for a different expectation than my other female schoolmates, few of whom were to complete a college degree. I, too, had my father's unshakable faith in the justice of God, and I shared his unconcern with popular opinion.

So I decided to enter junior college, now San Francisco's City College, because the fees were lowest. I lived at home and supported myself with an after-school job which required long hours of housework and cooking but paid me twenty dollars per month, of which I saved as much as possible. The thrills derived from reading and learning, in ways ranging from chemistry experiments to English compositions, from considering new ideas of sociology to the logic of Latin, convinced me that I had made a correct choice. I was kept in a state of perpetual mental excitement by new Western subjects and concepts and did not mind long hours of work and study. I also made new friends, which led to another painful incident with my parents, who had heretofore discouraged even girlhood friendships.

The college subject which had most jolted me was sociology. The instructor fired my mind with his interpretation of family relationships. As he explained to our class, it used to be an economic asset for American farming families to be large, since children were useful to perform agricultural chores. But this situation no longer applied and children should be regarded as individuals with their own rights. Unquestioning obedience should be replaced with parental understanding. So at sixteen, discontented as I was with my parents' apparent indifference to me, those words of my sociology professor gave voice to my sentiments. How old-fashioned was the dead-end attitude of my parents! How ignorant they were of modern thought and progress! The family unit had been China's strength for centuries, but it had also been her weakness, for corruption, nepotism, and greed were all justified in the name of the family's welfare. My new ideas festered; I longed to release them.

One afternoon on a Saturday, which was normally occupied with my housework job, I was unexpectedly released by my employer, who was departing for a country weekend. It was a rare joy to have free time and I wanted to enjoy myself for a change. There had been a Chinese-American boy who shared some classes with me. Sometimes we had found each other walking to the same 8:00 A.M. class. He was not a special boyfriend, but I had enjoyed talking to him and had confided in him some of my problems. Impulsively, I telephoned him. I knew I must be breaking rules, and I felt shy and scared. At the same time, I was excited at this newly found forwardness, with nothing more purposeful than to suggest another walk together.

He understood my awkwardness and shared my anticipation. He asked me to "dress up" for my first movie date. My clothes were limited but I changed to look more graceful in silk stockings and found a bright ribbon for my long black hair. Daddy watched, catching my mood, observing the dashing preparations. He asked me where I was going without his permission and with whom.

I refused to answer him. I thought of my rights! I thought he surely 31
would not try to understand. Thereupon Daddy thundered his displeasure
and forbade my departure.

I found a new courage as I heard my voice announce calmly that I was 32
no longer a child, and if I could work my way through college, I would
choose my own friends. It was my right as a person.

My mother heard the commotion and joined my father to face me; both 33
appeared shocked and incredulous. Daddy at once demanded the source of
this unfilial, non-Chinese theory. And when I quoted my college professor,
reminding him that he had always felt teachers should be revered, my father
denounced that professor as a foreigner who was disregarding the superior-
ity of our Chinese culture, with its sound family strength. My father did not
spare me; I was condemned as an ingrate for echoing dishonorable opinions
which should only be temporary whims, yet nonetheless inexcusable.

The scene was not yet over. I completed my proclamation to my 34
father, who had never allowed me to learn how to dance, by adding that I
was attending a movie, unchaperoned, with a boy I met at college.

My startled father was sure that my reputation would be subject to 35
whispered innuendos. I must be bent on disgracing the family name; I was
ruining my future, for surely I would yield to temptation. My mother under-
scored him by saying that I hadn't any notion of the problems endured by
parents of a young girl.

I would not give in. I reminded them that they and I were not in China, 36
that I wasn't going out with just anybody but someone I trusted! Daddy gave
a roar that no man could be trusted, but I devastated them in declaring that I
wished the freedom to find my own answers.

Both parents were thoroughly angered, scolded me for being shame- 37
less, and predicted that I would some day tell them I was wrong. But I dimly
perceived that they were conceding defeat and were perplexed at this
breakdown of their training. I was too old to beat and too bold to intimidate.

Using the Dictionary

What are the roots that help explain the following words from this essay? How does
a shared root help explain the word itself and the related words that follow?
1. *calligraphy—orthography, stenography, stenographer* (8)   2. *philosophy—
philanthrophy* (8)   3. *unobtrusive—intrusion, intruder* (13)   4. *exasperating—asperity* (18)   5. *deviation—deviate, deflect* (20)   6. *edict—verdict, indictment* (24)   7. *impulsive—compulsive, repulsive* (29)   8. *incredulous—incredible* (33)   9. *filial—affiliation* (33)   10. *ingrate—gratitude* (33)

The Writer's Agenda

To explain to herself the kind of person she is, the author of this essay weighs the
influence of her traditional Chinese parents and the influence of "Western," or

American, ways. Trace the major elements in her traditional upbringing and the role of new or different ideas.

1. Early in the essay, the author says, "I observed from birth that living and working were inseparable." Find the details that give substance to this statement. Describe the *attitudes toward work* that were an important part of the author's upbringing.

2. Where and what does Wong tell us about the *traditional relationship* between parents and children during her childhood years? (What was expected of children? What manners was the author taught? What were traditional ideas of discipline? What were traditional attitudes toward giving praise and toward displays of affection?)

3. The contrast between the traditional Chinese style of *education* and new or different American ways played a major part in the author's growing up. What were the traditional ways? Where and how did the author experience the new American ways?

4. Jade Snow Wong's parents had come from a *patriarchal society* where men had special privileges and where women played an inferior role. How did this tradition affect the author's life and that of her family? Where does she express her feelings about this tradition? (Had her parents moved *away* from the traditional definition of sex roles in any way?)

5. The high point, or **climax**, of this autobiographical narrative is the daughter's open defiance of her father's authority. What was the central issue? What were the thoughts that went through her mind? What strategy did she adopt during the confrontation with her parents, and what was the outcome?

6. What is the tone of the author as she looks back over her experiences? Would you call her bitter or resentful?

For Discussion or Writing

7. We often hear that the "work ethic" is part of the American tradition. Where have you encountered it, or where have you had a chance to observe it? Do you believe it is anchored in the experience of immigrants like Wong's parents?

8. Some people say that our society is overly permissive toward the young. To judge from your experience, how far has American society moved from the kind of parental authority and discipline that we observe in this essay?

9. A dual heritage or an exposure to two cultures is sometimes seen as a problem, sometimes as an asset. From what the author has told us about her life, would you conclude that in her case the experience was an asset or a liability? Defend your answer.

10. Where have you observed or experienced the meeting of two cultures or of two different ways of life? In your own family or among your friends, have you been able to see the encounter or the merging of different traditions? Show the contrast in two or three areas—manners, customs, attitudes toward work, or the like.

11. Focus on a situation or an experience in which you have seen two different traditions or ways of life come into conflict. Describe and explain the clash between two different ways of doing things or of looking at life.

12. Write an essay whose title begins "In Defense of . . . " Fill in the word *Permissiveness, Authority,* or *Discipline* to complete the title. Use material from your own first-hand observation and experience.

STUDENT MODEL 1

FOR READING: Study the following short selection as a possible model for writing of your own. How do you react to it overall? What makes it interesting or effective? Answer the following more specific questions:

1. (PURPOSE) What was the writer trying to do?
2. (AUDIENCE) What kind of reader would make a good reader for this selection?
3. (SOURCES) Where did the writer turn for material?
4. (THESIS) Does the selection have a central idea or unifying thesis?
5. (STRUCTURE) What is the author's overall plan or strategy?
6. (STYLE) What makes the piece effective or memorable (for instance, striking details, memorable phrases)?
7. (REVISION) What do you think the writer could or should have done differently?

Neal Lerner

Sports, Anyone?

As a child I had a marked disdain for sports. This was probably the result of my being very bad at them. While my grammar school peers played Pop Warner football and Little League baseball I went to art and music camp. This was no real problem until junior high school. There, adolescents were socially made or broken in gym class. It didn't matter if a student were an arsonist, a self-mutilator, or of subhuman mentality—people who were good at sports were cool. People who had the misfortune of having a pair of hands like masonry were seriously not cool. The male gym teachers reinforced this social dynamic by favoring the athletic elite, joking with them, calling them by their first names, or, for those with even greater social status, endowing them with nicknames.

The uncoordinated among us had only last or forgotten names, ill-fitting gym clothes, and black sneakers, not gym shoes. This macho world dominated the rest of school life. Status was attained in gym class and nowhere else. I could have spoken six languages, known Avogadro's number, and memorized the Magna Carta, but it didn't mean squat if I couldn't catch a pass, hit a baseball, or sink a basket.

I cowered my way through seventh grade, my self-confidence plummeting to new lows as I was picked last for every sport. That summer, mired in puberty, I grew a few inches and wondered how I would survive. One way was to become a fan of sports. If I couldn't play, at least I could watch. I attached myself to basketball—the New York Knicks and Willis Reed. I rooted hard, studied statistics daily, and learned about jump shots and layups. 3

By eighth grade my fanaticism included a tentative attempt at playing basketball. A backboard and rim tacked to a telephone pole in the cul-de-sac playground provided equipment. I shot baskets, imitating Walt "Clyde" Frazier and Earl "the Pearl" Monroe. I practiced constantly, the obsession of sports taking over. I grew a few more inches that year and discovered two things—I could jump high and, suddenly, I had coordination. I was a basketball player. 4

By winter of that year my new-found skills had manifested themselves in gym class. My basketball prowess enabled teams to pick me first or second. I even acquired a nickname, "Cesare," for Cesare Maniago, the goaltender of the Minnesota North Stars. I took up soccer by the next fall and joined the freshman team. But the real status leap occurred in ninth grade when I became a gym helper, assisting the gym teachers with the lowly seventh graders. 5

Since, I have graduated from basketball, soccer, and stickball in high school to volleyball, bicycling, and jogging in college. Today, I enjoy sports for the physical pleasure of doing something well with my body, of feeling healthy, of learning the limits of my physical capabilities. I have moved beyond the kind of jock mentality that knows sports only for winning, for dominating the other side, and for putting down those who don't perform. 6

For the seventh grade non-athlete, things have a way of evening out. As the years go by, the jocks get athletic scholarships, ruined knees, and jobs in the Sherwin-Williams store. The scrawny, thick-lensed kid grows up to be a scrawny, thick-lensed management type. But a curious development takes place. Both ends of society's athletic scale can be seen on Saturday, jogging around the circular track at their local high school, taking an occasional windsprint, treasuring their pair of Etonic running shoes—the great melting pot, at last. 7

FOR WRITING: Write about your experience in one of the roles you have played during your growing up. For instance, write about your career as an athlete, a churchgoer, an employee, a student, a son or daughter, a parent. Try to work out a pattern; try to show what you have learned or how you have grown.

ADDITIONAL WRITING TOPICS 1

Personal Experience

A. Write a piece titled "A Day in the Life of . . ." (fill in your name). Trace the highlights (or low points) of an ordinary day. Use this piece as a means of letting your readers see what kind of a life you lead and what kind of a person you are.

B. As you read over the following topics, which triggers a reaction or calls up memories? What material could you use? What might be your overall point? (How might you have to change or modify the topic to make it serve your purpose?) Be prepared to discuss one or more of these topics with your peers or with your instructor.

1. a happy (or an unhappy) childhood
2. breaking away
3. a turning point
4. my parents don't understand me
5. rebel with a cause
6. a family secret
7. a family quarrel
8. a relative we don't talk about
9. my substitute father (mother)
10. thinking thin
11. making friends
12. losing a friend
13. a secret dislike
14. my friend, my enemy
15. I want to be popular
16. the sweet taste of success
17. the bitter taste of defeat
18. a death in the family
19. not really a sister
20. overcoming a handicap
21. battling illness
22. first love
23. dreams and reality
24. being poor
25. a "home" is not a home
26. a victim's view of crime
27. the police, your friend and helper
28. no more ethnic jokes
29. growing up American
30. after the accident

2

OBSERVATION

Seeing with Your Own Eyes

OVERVIEW

Writing that records honest first-hand observation is called *description*. Descriptive writing is sometimes made to sound like a pastime or a luxury: When we have no urgent business to attend to, we may pause to read a description of the harsh beauty of the Big Sur coast, or an account of a train trip through India. But careful observation and effective description are more basic than that. A good writer is first of all a good observer. If you want to write effectively, you have to learn to notice things, to take things in. Weak writing is thin writing, full of generalities and clichés. Effective writing is done by people who have learned to look for themselves, who have learned to pay attention to the world around them.

PURPOSE Description, or writing based on close observation, re-creates for the reader the sights and sounds of a scene, the shape and texture of things, the way things and people look and move. Effective description makes writing real. Often it is not an end in itself: Not only in description, but also in argument and persuasion, the effective writer knows how to make places, things, and people graphic and vivid for the mind's eye.

AUDIENCE Some readers need accurate technical description of objects, machines, utensils, plants, or sites for practical purposes. Many other readers enjoy vivid, fresh description of places and people that satisfies their curiosity. Today especially, nature writers find a large, sympathetic following among those who love wildlife and unspoilt open spaces.

BENEFITS FOR THE WRITER (1) Honest first-hand observation is a basic *source* of material for your writing. Students sometimes feel that they have nothing to write about or nothing to say. One way to overcome this feeling is to ask yourself: "What is out there? What do I see? What do I hear?" An alert, open-eyed observer can always find an audience for a description of a memorable person, of a place that was a good place to be, or a place that was very different from what a travel folder might make us expect.

(2) Careful observation teaches us a respect for *detail*, for what is "out there." Our readers need to feel that our opinions are based on more than personal whim, hearsay, or superficial impressions. They need to see that what we think and feel is anchored in the world of observable fact. An article on American agribusiness will gain authenticity if the writer at some point takes us out at five in the morning to watch the giant harvesters rumbling across the tomato fields to start the day's work.

(3) Descriptive writing teaches us a respect for the *right word*— the specific, accurate word that calls up the right image and associations in the reader's mind.

OBSERVATION
Additional Reading

E. B. White, Once More to the Lake (p. 487)

WRITER'S GUIDE 2

Writing from Observation

Good writing is rooted in first-hand observation. Good writers have learned to look for themselves and to reach their own conclusions. They have learned to trust their own eyes and ears. When writing about places, people, and events, effective writers know how to move in for a closer look. They know how to describe a scene in such a way that we see it before our eyes.

As you study and practice writing based on observation, remember the following guidelines:

(1) *Bring in authentic first-hand detail.* Instead of calling something beautiful or interesting or colorful, *show* it to the reader. Provide the details that enable your readers to imagine themselves in your place as a first-hand observer at the scene. When we read a passage like the following about small towns in California, we know that the details do not come from a travel folder or a Chamber of Commerce brochure. We read about these places with the feeling: "She was there."

> Every so often along 99 between Bakersfield and Sacramento there is a town: Delano, Tulare, Fresno, Madera, Merced, Modesto, Stockton. Some of these towns are pretty big now, but they are all the same at heart, one- and two- and three-story buildings artlessly arranged, so that what appears to be the good dress shop stands beside a W. T. Grant store, so that the big Bank of America faces a Mexican movie house. *Dos Peliculas, Bingo Bingo Bingo.* Beyond the downtown (pronounced *down*town, with the Okie accent that now pervades Valley speech patterns) lie blocks of old frame houses—paint peeling, sidewalks cracking, their occasional leaded amber windows overlooking a Foster's Freeze or a five-minute car wash or a State Farm Insurance office; beyond those spread the shopping centers and miles of tract houses, pastel with redwood siding, the unmistakable signs of cheap building already blossoming on those houses which have survived the first rain.   (Joan Didion, *Slouching Towards Bethlehem*)

As we read this passage, we know that we can trust this writer to remember and bring in authentic detail: a hotel that still has tile floor in the dining room and dusty potted palms and big ceiling fans; the arched sign over the main street of a small town, saying "Water—Wealth, Contentment—Health."

(2) *Move in for a close look.* Every writer has to learn to focus on one thing at a time—to concentrate, to pay attention. Many things that are not superficially interesting *become* interesting when we bother to look. Here is

an expert at close observation writing about a twenty-five-cent goldfish. Note the many details that a less attentive observer would have overlooked:

> Ellery is a deep red-orange, darker than most goldfish. He steers short distances mainly with his slender red lateral fins; they seem to provide impetus for going backward, up, or down. It took me a few days to discover his ventral fins; they are completely transparent and all but invisible—dream fins. He also has a short anal fin, and a tail that is deeply notched and perfectly transparent at the two tapered tips. He can extend his mouth, so that it looks like a length of pipe; he can shift the angle of his eyes in his head so he can look before and behind himself, instead of simply out to his side. His belly, what there is of it, is white ventrally, and a patch of this white extends up his sides—the variegated Ellery. When he opens his gill slits he shows a thin crescent of silver where the flap overlapped—as though all his brightness were sunburn. (Annie Dillard, *Pilgrim at Tinker Creek*)

(3) *Make your details add up to an overall impression.* We tire of details that remain scattered or miscellaneous. We want things to fall into place; we want to see details become part of a larger picture. In effective description, well-chosen details help create a mood or set a scene that we will remember. Together, the details build a strong dominant impression. They are relevant to some overall result the writer is trying to achieve. The following sentences are from successive paragraphs of a chapter called "Flood"; the author is trying to impress on us the force and speed of the rain-swollen waters. Note the many words like *smash, hurtle, lurch, zip, stream,* and *pour* that reinforce the **dominant impression:**

> I look at the creek at my feet. It smashes under the bridge like a fist, but there is no end to its force; it hurtles down as far as I can see till it lurches round the bend, filling the valley. . . .

> The water arches where the bridge's supports at the banks prevent its enormous volume from going wide, forcing it to go high. . . .

> Everything imaginable is zipping by, almost too fast to see. . . . There are dolls, split wood and kindling, dead fledgling songbirds, bottles, whole bushes and trees, rakes and garden gloves. . . .

> The whole world is in flood, the land as well as the water. Water streams down the trunks of trees, drips from hat-brims, courses across roads. The whole earth seems to slide like sand down a chute; water pouring over the least slope leaves the grass flattened, silver side up, pointing downstream. . . . (Annie Dillard, *Pilgrim at Tinker Creek*)

In this example, the untamed energy of the floodwaters becomes the keynote that unifies the author's description. Try summing up the keynote or unifying central impression at the beginning of a paper. When the main point or central idea of a paper is summed up in one or two pointed sentences, we call it the **thesis** of a paper. Each of the following might serve as the thesis of a well-focused descriptive paper:

> THESIS: The beauty of nature is not just in sunsets and sweeping panoramas. *A camping trip gives us a chance to watch and enjoy the little things*—insects around a lantern, the frogs in a pond.

> THESIS: We often think of the vast gray ocean as bleak and lifeless. *A tide pool gives us a chance to look at a concentrated sample of busy, colorful ocean life.*

(4) *Set up a clear pattern for your readers to follow.* When you describe a scene, help your readers find their bearings. Effective description often follows a clear, consistent pattern in **space**. Suppose you are describing a city that is struggling to reverse the familiar pattern of urban blight. An overall scheme like the following will seem to have grown naturally out of the subject you describe:

A Tale of Three Cities

I. *Starting at the center*, we see the new financial and commercial downtown, with its banks and glossy shops and pedestrian malls.
II. *Moving away from the center*, we see the older neighborhoods around the core of the city, with their aging two-story frame houses and vacant lots and old-style alleys.
III. *Following the expressways farther out*, we see the suburban ring of tract houses with their two-car garages and trimmed lawns.

Often effective description brings movement into a static scene by combining spatial order with **chronological** order—a clear sequence in time. A pattern like the following combines spatial and chronological order:

Once More to the Lake

I. Approaching the lake on the hillside trail
II. Exploring the lakeside
III. Canoeing to the island in the center of the lake
IV. Returning to shore for the campfire as night falls

(5) *Find the right word.* Effective description uses fresh, specific language that makes the things being described take shape before our eyes. A passage like the following uses simple and unpretentious words that carry accurate information and bring the right picture to the reader's mind:

> I handed the man a quarter, and he handed me a *knotted plastic bag bouncing with water* in which a green plant floated and the goldfish swam. This fish, two bits' worth, has *a coiled gut, a spine radiating fine bones*, and a brain.   (Annie Dillard, *Pilgrim at Tinker Creek*)

Look at the way the author uses the words *bouncing, coiled,* and *radiating*: Each is the right word for what the author wants us to see; these are highly "visual" words. Words that are exceptionally effective in calling up sights, sounds, smells, and other sense impressions are **concrete** words. *Lurch, veer,* and *stir* are more concrete than the colorless general word *move. Hover, soar,* and *swoop* are more concrete than *fly. Caw, twitter,* and *trill* are concrete words for the sounds of birds; *hum, whir, clunk,* and *wheeze* are concrete words for noises made by machines. The more general and colorless words give us only a fuzzy general picture. Concrete words help writers make us see what they saw and hear what they heard.

(6) *Bring the reader's imagination into play.* A writer with an active imagination can help revive our blunted senses and make us notice the color and life in the world around us. Imaginative comparisons help us go beyond the literal resources of language; they help us verbalize impressions and feelings that are hard to put into words. Look at the comparisons that help bring the following description of a laundromat to life:

> A middle-aged man whose clothes are in a small washing machine is standing in front of it reading a sports column in the *News*, but most of the other patrons who are between putting-in and taking-out chores seem to be mesmerized by the *kaleidoscopic activity inside the machines.* In one washing machine, a few striped sheets and pillowcases are spinning, creating a dizzying optical effect. In another, *a lively clothes dance is taking place— three or four white shirts jitterbugging with six or eight pairs of gray socks.* In a third, the clothes, temporarily obscured by a flurry of soapsuds, still cast a spell over their owner, who doesn't take her eyes off the round glass window in the front of the machine. The clothes in the dryers—here a few towels, there some men's work pants—seem to be *free-falling, like sky divers drifting down to earth.*   (Susan Sheehan, "Laundromat," *The New Yorker*)

To sum up: Writing becomes real to us and holds our attention when it was done by a writer with open eyes and quick ears. In books about writing, description is sometimes treated as a somewhat optional aid to other kinds of writing. It is treated as a supporting device that makes explanation or argument more vivid or more understandable. But in the training of an effective writer, writing from observation plays a more fundamental role: It takes us to one of the basic sources of writing. A good writer is more receptive and more observant than other people. A good writer takes in things that others overlook.

Prewriting Activities 2

1. Take a close look at a scene, taking notes on the place and the people. Be the *camera eye*—do a series of vignettes or snapshots of a scene like the following: a busy downtown intersection, a hub of campus life, a hometown scene, a skid row, a thoroughfare in the big city. What did you see? What did you hear? Include telling details; record your candid impressions. (Some of your entries may be sentence length, some paragraph length.)

2. Practice packing a sentence with details from close first-hand observation. For *sentence practice*, write two or more sentences in each of the following three categories. Study the student-written examples before writing your own sentences:

(a sentence providing a *capsule portrait* of a person)

a. A girl with thick glasses and jet-black, long, straight hair was reading a worn, thick literature book in her math class.
b. A bald, elderly man with tuning forks, brushes, and a wrench in the back pocket of his baggy old pants hit a sour "C" octave on our antique piano as I walked into the living room.

(a sentence summing up the *atmosphere of a place*)

c. The self-service station has a sullen cashier sitting behind dark glass in a burglarproof, bulletproof cubicle with "Pay before pumping gas" posted all over it.
d. The gym was filled with the sounds of bouncing basketballs, squeaking tennis shoes, grunting players, and a constantly criticizing coach.

(a sentence giving *details first* and then going on to a general label)

e. The slow rumble of the ball rolling down the alley; the loud crash as the pins are scattered in every direction; the "Yippee" from the thrower of the ball as he realizes he has got a strike: this is a bowling alley.
f. The white acoustical tile, the floor-to-ceiling mirror, the high-backed piano, and the thick door with a double-plate glass window: this is a musicians' practice room.

3. For *sentence practice*, write four or five sentences, each making us visualize a person, an object, a scene, or an event by presenting a vivid *imaginative comparison*. Study the following examples before writing your own sentences:

a. On the site of the new building, a crane extends upward into the sky, *like a giraffe reaching for green leaves at the top of the tree.*
b. The great fantastic arch of the Delaware River bridge loomed ahead of me *like a preposterous giant's toy.*
c. The candidate *surfed* to the speaker's table *on a nice wave of applause.*

Paragraph Practice 2

Write a paragraph about a place that you know or remember well. For instance, write about a room in your childhood home, a schoolroom, a restaurant kitchen, a hospital room. Use vivid, characteristic detail. Give your readers a feeling for how it felt to be there. Study and discuss the following student-written paragraph as a possible model:

Grandma's Cactuses

When I think of Sundays at Grandma's house, I remember the noise and confusion, but mostly I remember Grandma's cactuses. Grandma Matchko loved cactuses, and she had them lined up along every windowsill in the house—in the kitchen, the living room, the bathroom, the dining room, and in her bedroom. There the cactuses all stood—like tiny retired soldiers, all whiskery and wiry, nodding their heads toward the sun. No matter where we went in her home, no matter where we tried to sit, we were always pricked unexpectedly by one of her miniature barbed-wire friends. Everyone in our family hated those cactuses, including me. I never escaped a visit to her house without taking an elbowful or fingerful of cactus splinters home with me. We always tried bringing Grandma other plants, but she never watered them and they died. "I like cactus," she'd say. "They don't need lots of fussin', and they don't bother nobody if you just leave 'em alone."   (Diane McBurnie)

BACKGROUND: Leonard Michaels was born in 1933 in New York City. He grew up on the Lower East Side and graduated from New York University. After graduate work in the Midwest, he went to California to teach and became a professor of English at the University of California at Berkeley. He has published several volumes of short stories, including *Going Places* (1969) and *I Would Have Saved Them If I Could* (1975). In the words of one reviewer, Michaels's short fiction takes his readers to the "surrealistic cityscape of modern fiction, where people are obsessed by sex and violence"; his themes include alienation, indifference, terror, the radicalism of the sixties, and the Holocaust. Michaels wrote the following short piece after a return visit to New York City.

Leonard Michaels

New York,

New York

GUIDE TO READING: What is the author's overall strategy in approaching his subject? What details does he select, and to what purposes does he put them? What overall impression takes shape as he fits striking, revealing details into a pattern?

My mother has four rooms with a balcony on the 16th floor of the 1 Seward Park Project. Her windows look onto Grand Street and East Broadway. The park lies between these streets. Daylong it's wild with kids and pigeons. People sit on the benches under the trees, gossiping, watching the crowd that strolls by—mommas and babies, gangs of adolescents, women with shopping bags, men with newspapers. Nameless elements enter the park at night.

From my mother's balcony I could see the neighborhood where I grew 2 up. The schools, the library, the stores, and many of the buildings are still there, but formerly Jewish streets are now Puerto Rican. The Forward Building is owned by Chinese investors. I could also follow the skyline, beginning at the Empire State Building, going west and south until stopped by the new, twin towers of the World Trade Center. They stand shoulder to shoulder like huge rectangular thugs.

I'd take morning coffee on the balcony when the sky was clear. 3 Sometimes, it looked almost pure: and the complexity of Manhattan, downtown to midtown, seemed to strike up to the sky in one dazzling voice from a vast field of streets. Directly below, in the park, a group of men and women occasionally practiced the slow, dreamy motions of Chinese calisthenics. Kids always arrived early and started basketball games. Beyond the park the streets were soon quick and squeezed with traffic. Noise increased all day and then sirens became frequent—fire engines, police cars, ambulances—announcing the supernatural agonies of nighttime Manhattan.

My first night was buried in a hot, kosher meal of meats. Wrong for this 4 African August, but correct for my psychological climate. I was home, the place I came from, to which mail is addressed "New York, New York," as if to the essence of the essence.

We sat in it after dinner—mother, wife, kids—sweating and familial, a 5 body above the war, planning what to do. In fact, they planned. I was here on business and I'd already decided the important thing. I would not go even once into the subway. I wouldn't see trains decorated by sacred hysteria, or guns who pace from car to car to protect me from sudden death between stations, and I wouldn't read the sign that advises you to hurry into the front car if nobody is smiling.

Kafka, my favorite writer, loved the noise in the Paris Metro.[1] He loved 6 the sense of mysterious passage and the freedom from speech. Our subway is a different story; it is all about raging harassment through dingy, lunatic channels.

But I went into the subway. Taxis were expensive, they were too slow 7 and they were also much too fast. The first one I rode in hit 40 m.p.h. near Chatham Square when a pothole received us and spit us out into the blazing emphysema. I glanced back. Apparently, the divider line had been painted into and out of the hole.

The next day, riding the F train, feeling like a Kafka, I witnessed an 8 argument. One man wanted doors shut between cars and another didn't. It was hot and miserable in the train, but if he wanted the doors shut that seemed no reason to rise up against him full of dangerous threats. They stood eyeball to eyeball.

The night before we left New York, I couldn't sleep. I was on the 9 balcony very early. The morning was cool. The city lay in quiet, hazy, blue light. When I glanced down into the park, I saw the body of a woman, lying on a bench. The police had roped off the area and thrown a sheet over her. She seemed to be naked. That evening I phoned my mother from California. She told me some facts: 26 years old; a heroin addict; she'd been stabbed. Then, in a sad apologetic tone, she said, "It has never happened before." She meant never in that park. She meant it is possible to mourn and to feel responsible for strangers.

Sirens, taxis, arguments—does New York have a coherent idea? A 10 woman said to me, "Where anything is possible, everything is equivalent. New York is the only place I feel alive."

[1][Franz Kafka (1883–1924), German-speaking, Jewish author who lived in Prague, wrote the great classics of modern alienation: *The Trial* and *The Castle*. His novels chronicle the struggle for survival of the unwanted, anonymous individual, ground down by a huge, impersonal bureaucracy, living in a world beyond rational control.]

Using the Dictionary

Check the following if necessary: 1. *calisthenics* (3)   2. *essence* (4)   3. *hysteria* (5)   4. *Metro* (6)   5. *lunatic* (6)   6. *emphysema* (7)

The Writer's Agenda

The author selects telling details to make the sights and sounds of the city real for us and to make us share his feelings about the place. Answer the following questions:

1. If you had to sum up in one sentence or two the author's attitude toward his native city, what would you say?

2. This piece works with a basic contrast between the city during the day and the city at night. What are some of the graphic details that shape our initial impression or surface view of the city during the day?

3. What are early hints of the ugly underbelly or the flip side of the city? What striking details and symbolic incidents bring it fully into view?

4. How does the author treat the climactic final incident, and why? (Does he treat it sensationally, matter-of-factly, sentimentally?)

5. Michaels hints at the mystique, perpetuated by many New Yorkers, of New York as a very special place. Where and how?

For Discussion or Writing

6. Does Michaels's view of the city seem to you biased or unfair? (Defend your answer.)

7. Give your readers your own first-hand view of the city, or of a small town, or of a place in the country. Aim at a unifying overall impression.

8. Report on a visit to a place that to you seems symbolic of contemporary American life: the modern shopping mall, an airport, a bus depot, a subway station, a modern office building. Include striking, telling details; make your readers share in your feelings about the place.

9. Contrast the two faces of a place: night and day, welcoming and hostile, old-fashioned and modern, or the like.

BACKGROUND: Annie Dillard (born 1945) has an uncanny gift for making us take a fresh look at the natural world. She grew up in Pittsburgh, Pennsylvania, and attended Hollins College. She has worked as a contributing editor for *Harper's Magazine* and as a columnist for the Wilderness Society. She has published in periodicals including *Harper's*, *The Atlantic*, *Sports Illustrated*, *The Christian Science Monitor*, and *Cosmopolitan*. The following selection is from her best-known book, *Pilgrim at Tinker Creek*, which was published in 1974 and won a Pulitzer Prize. This book is a year's record of observations of the natural world around her house by Tinker Creek, in the Roanoke Valley of Virginia. She records both "nature's facts" and the thoughts they inspire as she ponders nature's mysteries. She says of herself, "I am no scientist . . . I am a wanderer with a background in theology and a penchant for quirky facts." In the following selection, as in much of her other writing, she reveals to our jaded eyes the burgeoning life around us, with its startling blend of grace and violence, of the beautiful and the grotesque.

Annie Dillard

Looking Spring
in the Eye

GUIDE TO READING: This selection was written by an author who knows how to take a fresh look, who uses her own eyes and ears. What did she see and hear? How does she make the sights and sounds she takes in real for her readers?

On an evening in late May, a moist wind from Carvin's Cove shoots down the gap between Tinker and Brushy mountains, tears along Carvin's Creek valley, and buffets my face as I stand by the duck pond. The surface of the duck pond doesn't budge. The algal layer is a rigid plating; if the wind blew hard enough, I imagine it might audibly creak. On warm days in February the primitive plants start creeping over the pond, filamentous green and blue-green algae in sopping strands. From a sunlit shallow edge they green and spread, thickening throughout the water like bright gelatin. When they smother the whole pond they block sunlight, strangle respiration, and snarl creatures in hopeless tangles. Dragonfly nymphs, for instance, are easily able to shed a leg or two to escape a tight spot, but even dragonfly nymphs get stuck in the algae strands and starve.

Several times I've seen a frog trapped under the algae. I would be staring at the pond when the green muck by my feet would suddenly leap into the air and then subside. It looked as though it had been jabbed from underneath by a broom handle. Then it would leap again, somewhere else, a jumping green flare, absolutely silently—this is a very disconcerting way to spend an evening. The frog would always find an open place at last, and break successfully onto the top of the heap, trailing long green slime from its back, and emitting a hollow sound like a pipe thrown into a cavern. Tonight I walked around the pond scaring frogs; a couple of them jumped off, going, in effect, eek, and most grunted, and the pond was still. But one big frog, bright green like a poster-paint frog, didn't jump, so I waved my arm and stamped to scare it, and it jumped suddenly, and I jumped, and then everything in the pond jumped, and I laughed and laughed.

There is a muscular energy in sunlight corresponding to the spiritual energy of wind. On a sunny day, sun's energy on a square acre of land or pond can equal 4500 horsepower. These "horses" heave in every direction, like slaves building pyramids, and fashion, from the bottom up, a new and sturdy world.

The pond is popping with life. Midges are swarming over the center, and the edges are clotted with the jellied egg masses of snails. One spring I saw a snapping turtle lumber from the pond to lay her eggs. Now a green heron picks around in the pondweed and bladderwort; two muskrats at the shallow end are stockpiling cattails. Diatoms, which are algae that look under a microscope like crystals, multiply so fast you can practically watch a submersed green leaf transform into a brown fuzz. In the plankton, single-cell algae, screw fungi, bacteria, and water mold abound. Insect larvae and nymphs carry on their eating business everywhere in the pond. Stillwater caddises, alderfly larvae, and damselfly and dragonfly nymphs stalk on the bottom debris; mayfly nymphs hide in the weeds, mosquito larvae wriggle near the surface, and red-tailed maggots stick their breathing tubes up from between decayed leaves along the shore. Also at the pond's muddy edges it is easy to see the tiny red tubifex worms and bloodworms; the convulsive jerking of hundreds and hundreds together catches my eye.

Once, when the pond was younger and the algae had not yet taken over, I saw an amazing creature. At first all I saw was a slender motion. Then I saw that it was a wormlike creature swimming in the water with a strong, whiplike thrust, and it was two feet long. It was also slender as a thread. It looked like an inked line someone was nervously drawing over and over. Later I learned that it was a horsehair worm. The larvae of horsehair worms live as parasites in land insects; the aquatic adults can get to be a yard long. I don't know how it gets from the insect to the pond, or from the pond to the insect, for that matter, or why on earth it needs such an extreme shape. If the one I saw had been so much as an inch longer or a shave thinner, I doubt if I would ever have come back.

The plankton bloom is what interests me. The plankton animals are all those microscopic drifting animals that so staggeringly outnumber us. In the spring they are said to "bloom," like so many poppies. There may be five times as many of these teeming creatures in spring as in summer. Among them are the protozoans—amoebae and other rhizopods, and millions of various flagellates and ciliates; gelatinous moss animalcules or byrozoans;

rotifers—which wheel around either free or in colonies; and all the diverse crustacean minutiae—copepods, ostracods, and cladocerans like the abundant daphnias. All these drifting animals multiply in sundry bizarre fashions, eat tiny plants or each other, die, and drop to the pond's bottom. Many of them have quite refined means of locomotion—they whirl, paddle, swim, slog, whip, and sinuate—but since they are so small, they are no match against even the least current in the water. Even such a sober limnologist as Robert E. Coker characterizes the movement of plankton as "milling around."

A cup of duck-pond water looks like a seething broth. If I carry the cup ₇ home and let the sludge settle, the animalcules sort themselves out, and I can concentrate them further by dividing them into two clear glass bowls. One bowl I paint all black except for a single circle where the light shines through; I leave the other bowl clear except for a single black circle against the light. Given a few hours, the light-loving creatures make their feeble way to the clear circle, and the shade-loving creatures to the black. Then, if I want to, I can harvest them with a pipette and examine them under a microscope.

There they loom and disappear as I fiddle with the focus. I run the ₈ eyepiece around until I am seeing the drop magnified three hundred times, and I squint at the little rotifer called monostyla. It zooms around excitedly, crashing into strands of spirogyra alga or zipping around the frayed edge of a clump of debris. The creature is a flattened oval; at its "head" is a circular fringe of whirling cilia, and at its "tail" a single long spike, so that it is shaped roughly like a horseshoe crab. But it is so incredibly small, as multicelled animals go, that it is translucent, even transparent, and I have a hard time telling if it is above or beneath a similarly transparent alga. Two monostyla drive into view from opposite directions; they meet, bump, reverse, part. I keep thinking that if I listen closely I will hear the high whine of tiny engines. As their drop heats from the light on the mirror, the rotifers skitter more and more frantically; as it dries, they pale and begin to stagger, and at last can muster only a halting twitch. Then I either wash the whole batch down the sink's drain, or in a rush of sentiment walk out to the road by starlight and dump them in a puddle. Tinker Creek where I live is too fast and rough for most of them.

I don't really look forward to these microscopic forays: I have been ₉ almost knocked off my kitchen chair on several occasions when, as I was following with strained eyes the tiny career of a monostyla rotifer, an enormous red roundworm whipped into the scene, blocking everything, and writhing in huge, flapping convulsions that seemed to sweep my face and fill the kitchen. I do it as a moral exercise; the microscope at my forehead is a kind of phylactery, a constant reminder of the facts of creation that I would just as soon forget. You can buy your child a microscope and say grandly, "Look, child, at the Jungle in a Little Drop." The boy looks, plays around with pond water and bread mold and onion sprouts for a month or two, and then starts shooting baskets or racing cars, leaving the microscope on the basement table staring fixedly at its own mirror forever—and you say he's growing up. But in the puddle or pond, in the city reservoir, ditch, or Atlantic Ocean, the rotifers still spin and munch, the daphnia still filter and are filtered, and the copepods still swarm hanging with clusters of eggs. These are real creatures with real organs leading real lives, one by one. I can't pretend they're not there. If I have life, sense, energy, will, so does a rotifer. The monostyla goes to the dark spot on the bowl: To which circle am I heading? I can move around right smartly in a calm; but in a real wind, in a change of weather, in a riptide, am I really moving, or am I "milling around"?

I was created from a clot and set in proud, free motion: so were they. So was this rotifer created, this monostyla with its body like a light bulb in which pale organs hang in loops; so was this paramecium created, with a thousand propulsive hairs jerking in unison, whipping it from here to there across a drop and back. *Ad majorem Dei gloriam?*[1]

Somewhere, and I can't find where, I read about an Eskimo hunter who asked the local missionary priest, "If I did not know about God and sin, would I go to hell?" "No," said the priest, "not if you did not know." "Then why," asked the Eskimo earnestly, "did you tell me?" If I did not know about the rotifers and paramecia, and all the bloom of plankton clogging the dying pond, fine; but since I've seen it I must somehow deal with it, take it into account. "Never lose a holy curiosity," Einstein said; and so I lift my microscope down from the shelf, spread a drop of duck pond on a glass slide, and try to look spring in the eye.

Using the Dictionary

How much of a barrier are the *technical terms* in this essay for you as the reader?

A. Check the following: 1. *algal* (1)   2. *filamentous* (1)   3. *diatom* (4) 4. *aquatic* (5)   5. *plankton* (6)   6. *flagellate* (6)   7. *animalcule* (6)   8. *crustacean* (6)   9. *minutiae* (6)   10. *sinuate* (6)   11. *limnologist* (6)   12. *pipette* (7)   13. *cilia* (8)   14. *translucent* (8)   15. *phylactery* (9)

B. Do a rough sorting out of the many names of plants and tiny organisms in this essay: Which are close to common language? Which are very technical? Which have a poetic touch?

The Writer's Agenda

Dillard is an alert observer who knows how to put into words what she sees and hears. Answer the following questions:

1. What familiar images or associations does the word *spring* bring to mind? In the opening paragraphs of the essay, what are striking details that go counter to

---

[1][Latin for "for the greater glory of God," said of works of art meant to honor or praise the Creator]

what we might expect? (In the first four paragraphs, take a partial inventory of the specific, concrete words used—what does each make you see?)

2. What sentence in the first half of this selection would you choose as the thesis sentence, striking the keynote for the whole selection?

3. Can you work out a rough plan for the author's selection and *ordering* of the details she includes?

4. In the passage about the "plankton bloom" and later, point out as many examples as you can of the specific, concrete words Dillard uses to describe the movements and activities of the tiny organisms.

5. Find and discuss examples of imaginative comparisons. (Many of these are **similes**, introduced by the words *like* or *as though*.) What do they make us see? What do they make us feel?

6. What, for you, is the point of the final anecdote?

For Discussion or Writing

7. For Dillard, what definition of life would include both human beings and the microscopic life that she describes?

8. Do you think Dillard is too preoccupied with what is strange or bizarre in nature?

9. Take an honest look at wild (or semiwild) animal life that you have a chance to observe at first hand. (For instance, provide an unretouched description of city pigeons, squirrels in a park, ants.) Try to break through the cliché barrier—avoid all cute or stereotyped description.

10. Help your readers visualize and recognize a kind of plant life that may be unfamiliar to them (or at which they may never really have looked closely). Include graphic details about texture, shape, color, and the like. You may want to show a tree or shrub, for instance, at different stages of its growth or its seasonal cycle. (Make use of graphic imaginative comparisons.)

11. Describe a place that would not be likely to appear on a picture postcard but that for you has a special interest or strange fascination. The place might be a railroad yard, a car dump, a building site, the site of an excavation. Use language that will help your readers share in the sights, sounds, and smells.

Branching Out

12. Describe the life and activity at a busy corner of your campus the way it might appear to a superhuman or extraterrestrial botanist who studies it the way Dillard studied the life of the pond.

BACKGROUND: N. Scott Momaday (born 1934) is a member of the Kiowa tribe and first became widely known when he published a collection of Kiowa tales, *The Journey of Tai-me* (1968), later republished as *The Way to Rainy Mountain*. Momaday was born in Lawton, Oklahoma, and studied at the University of New Mexico and Stanford University. He became a professor of English at the University of California, first at Santa Barbara and then at Berkeley. His novel *The House Made of Dawn* won the Pulitzer Prize in 1969. Many of his poems recreate with haunting beauty the songs and legends of his people; they have appeared in collections such as *The Gourd Dancer* (1976). The following essay, after which the book *The Way to Rainy Mountain* was named, was first published in *The Reporter*.

N. Scott Momaday

The Way to Rainy Mountain

GUIDE TO READING: Momaday is a writer who vividly recalls scenes and people from the past. In reading the essay, pay special attention to vividly remembered characteristic details that make places and people real for the reader. At the same time, ask yourself: "Why does the writer remember these details? What is their meaning for him?"

A single knoll rises out of the plain in Oklahoma, north and west of the Wichita range. For my people, the Kiowas, it is an old landmark, and they gave it the name Rainy Mountain. The hardest weather in the world is there. Winter brings blizzards, hot tornadic winds arise in the spring, and in the summer the prairie is an anvil's edge. The grass turns brittle and brown, and it cracks beneath your feet. There are green belts along the rivers and creeks, linear groves of hickory and pecan, willow and witch hazel. At a distance in July or August the steaming foliage seems almost to writhe in fire. Great green and yellow grasshoppers are everywhere in the tall grass, popping up like corn to sting the flesh, and tortoises crawl about on the red earth, going nowhere in the plenty of time. Loneliness is an aspect of the land. All things in the plain are isolate; there is no confusion of objects in the eye, but *one* hill or *one* tree or *one* man. To look upon that landscape in the early morning, with the sun at your back, is to lose the sense of proportion. Your imagination comes to life, and this, you think, is where Creation was begun.

I returned to Rainy Mountain in July. My grandmother had died in the spring, and I wanted to be at her grave. She had lived to be very old and at last infirm. Her only living daughter was with her when she died, and I was told that in death her face was that of a child.

I like to think of her as a child. When she was born, the Kiowas were $_3$
living the last great moment of their history. For more than a hundred years
they had controlled the open range from the Smoky Hill River to the Red,
from the headwaters of the Canadian to the fork of the Arkansas and
Cimarron. In alliance with the Comanches, they had ruled the whole of the
Southern Plains. War was their sacred business, and they were the finest
horsemen the world has ever known. But warfare for the Kiowas was
pre-eminently a matter of disposition rather than of survival, and they never
understood the grim, unrelenting advance of the U.S. Cavalry. When at last,
divided and ill provisioned, they were driven onto the Staked Plains in the
cold of autumn, they fell into panic.[1] In Palo Duro Canyon they abandoned
their crucial stores to pillage and had nothing then but their lives. In order to
save themselves, they surrendered to the soldiers at Fort Sill and were
imprisoned in the old stone corral that now stands as a military museum. My
grandmother was spared the humiliation of those high gray walls by eight or
ten years, but she must have known from birth the affliction of defeat, the
dark brooding of old warriors.

Her name was Aho, and she belonged to the last culture to evolve in $_4$
North America. Her forebears came down from the high country in western
Montana nearly three centuries ago. They were a mountain people, a mysterious tribe of hunters whose language has never been classified in any major
group. In the late seventeenth century they began a long migration to the
south and east. It was a journey toward the dawn, and it led to a golden age.
Along the way the Kiowas were befriended by the Crows, who gave them
the culture and religion of the Plains. They acquired horses, and their
ancient nomadic spirit was suddenly free of the ground. They acquired
Tai-me, the sacred sun-dance doll, from that moment the object and symbol
of their worship, and so shared in the divinity of the sun. Not least, they
acquired the sense of destiny, therefore courage and pride. When they
entered upon the Southern Plains they had been transformed. No longer
were they slaves to the simple necessity of survival; they were a lordly and
dangerous society of fighters and thieves, hunters and priests of the sun.
According to their origin myth, they entered the world through a hollow log.
From one point of view, their migration was the fruit of an old prophecy, for
indeed they emerged from a sunless world.

Though my grandmother lived out her long life in the shadow of Rainy $_5$
Mountain, the immense landscape of the continental interior lay like memory in her blood. She could tell of the Crows, whom she had never seen, and
of the Black Hills, where she had never been. I wanted to see in reality what
she had seen more perfectly in the mind's eye, and drove fifteen hundred
miles to begin my pilgrimage.

---

[1][The Staked Plains, English for the Spanish *Llano Estacado*, is the name of the great arid plateau of
southeast New Mexico, northwest Oklahoma, and west Texas.]

Yellowstone, it seemed to me, was the top of the world, a region of ₆
deep lakes and dark timber, canyons and waterfalls. But, beautiful as it is,
one might have the sense of confinement there. The skyline in all directions
is close at hand, the high wall of the woods and deep cleavages of shade.
There is a perfect freedom in the mountains, but it belongs to the eagle and
the elk, the badger and the bear. The Kiowas reckoned their stature by
distances they see, and they were bent and blind in the wilderness.

Descending eastward, the highland meadows are a stairway to the ₇
plain. In July the inland slope of the Rockies is luxuriant with flax and
buckwheat, stonecrop and larkspur. The earth unfolds and the limit of the
land recedes. Clusters of trees, and animals grazing far in the distance,
cause the vision to reach away and wonder to build upon the mind. The sun
follows a longer course in the day, and the sky is immense beyond all
comparison. The great billowing clouds that sail upon it are shadows that
move upon the grain like water, dividing light. Farther down, in the land of
the Crows and Blackfeet, the plain is yellow. Sweet clover takes hold of the
hills and bends upon itself to cover and seal the soil. There the Kiowas
paused on their way; they had come to the place where they must change
their lives. The sun is at home on the plains. Precisely there does it have the
certain character of a god. When the Kiowas came to the land of the Crows,
they could see the dark lees of the hills at dawn across the Bighorn River,
the profusion of light on the grain shelves, the oldest deity ranging after the
solstices. Not yet would they veer southward to the caldron of the land that
lay below; they must wean their blood from the northern winter and hold
the mountains a while longer in their view. They bore Tai-me in procession
to the east.

A dark mist lay over the Black Hills, and the land was like iron. At the ₈
top of a ridge I caught sight of Devil's Tower upthrust against the gray sky as
if in the birth of time the core of the earth had broken through its crust and
the motion of the world was begun. There are things in nature that engender
an awful quiet in the heart of man; Devil's Tower is one of them. Two
centuries ago, because they could not do otherwise, the Kiowas made a
legend at the base of the rock. My grandmother said:

"Eight children were there at play, seven sisters and their brother. ₉
Suddenly the boy was struck dumb; he trembled and began to run upon his
hands and feet. His fingers became claws, and his body was covered with
fur. There was a bear where the boy had been. The sisters were terrified;
they ran, and the bear after them. They came to the stump of a great tree, and
the tree spoke to them. It bade them climb upon it, and as they did so, it
began to rise into the air. The bear came to kill them, but they were just
beyond its reach. It reared against the tree and scored the bark all around
with its claws. The seven sisters were borne into the sky, and they became
the stars of the Big Dipper." From that moment, and so long as the legend
lives, the Kiowas have kinsmen in the night sky. Whatever they were in the

mountains, they could be no more. However tenuous their well-being, however much they had suffered and would suffer again, they had found a way out of the wilderness.

My grandmother had a reverence for the sun, a holy regard that now is 10 all but gone out of mankind. There was a wariness in her, and an ancient awe. She was a Christian in her later years, but she had come a long way about, and she never forgot her birthright. As a child she had been to the sun dances; she had taken part in that annual rite, and by it she had learned the restoration of her people in the presence of Tai-me. She was about seven when the last Kiowa sun dance was held in 1887 on the Washita River above Rainy Mountain Creek. The buffalo were gone. In order to consummate the ancient sacrifice—to impale the head of a buffalo bull upon the Tai-me tree—a delegation of old men journeyed into Texas, there to beg and barter for an animal from the Goodnight herd. She was ten when the Kiowas came together for the last time as a living sun-dance culture. They could find no buffalo; they had to hang an old hide from the sacred tree. Before the dance could begin, a company of soldiers rode out from Fort Sill under orders to disperse the tribe. Forbidden without cause the essential act of their faith, having seen the wild herds slaughtered and left to rot upon the ground, the Kiowas backed away forever from the tree. That was July 20, 1890, at the great bend of the Washita. My grandmother was there. Without bitterness, and for as long as she lived, she bore a vision of deicide.

Now that I can have her only in memory, I see my grandmother in the 11 several postures that were peculiar to her: standing at the wood stove on a winter morning and turning meat in a great iron skillet; sitting at the south window, bent above her beadwork, and afterwards, when her vision failed, looking down for a long time into the fold of her hands; going out upon a cane, very slowly as she did when the weight of age came upon her; praying. I remember her most often at prayer. She made long, rambling prayers out of suffering and hope, having seen many things. I was never sure that I had the right to hear, so exclusive were they of all mere custom and company. The last time I saw her she prayed standing by the side of her bed at night, naked to the waist, the light of a kerosene lamp moving upon her dark skin. Her long black hair, always drawn and braided in the day, lay upon her shoulders and against her breasts like a shawl. I do not speak Kiowa, and I never understood her prayers, but there was something inherently sad in the sound, some merest hesitation upon the syllables of sorrow. She began in a high and descending pitch, exhausting her breath to silence; then again and again—and always the same intensity of effort, of something that is, and is not, like urgency in the human voice. Transported so in the dancing light among the shadows of her room, she seemed beyond the reach of time. But that was illusion; I think I knew then that I should not see her again.

Houses are like sentinels in the plain, old keepers of the weather 12 watch. There, in a very little while, wood takes on the appearance of great age. All colors wear soon away in the wind and rain, and then the wood is burned gray and the grain appears and the nails turn red with rust. The window panes are black and opaque; you imagine there is nothing within, and indeed there are many ghosts, bones given up to the land. They stand here and there against the sky, and you approach them for a longer time than you expect. They belong in the distance; it is their domain.

Once there was a lot of sound in my grandmother's house, a lot of [13] coming and going, feasting and talk. The summers there were full of excitement and reunion. The Kiowas are a summer people; they abide the cold and keep to themselves, but when the season turns and the land becomes warm and vital they cannot hold still; an old love of going returns upon them. The aged visitors who came to my grandmother's house when I was a child were made of lean and leather, and they bore themselves upright. They wore great black hats and bright ample shirts that shook in the wind. They rubbed fat upon their hair and wound their braids with strips of colored cloth. Some of them painted their faces and carried the scars of old and cherished enmities. They were an old council of warlords, come to remind and be reminded of who they were. Their wives and daughters served them well. The women might indulge themselves; gossip was at once the mark and compensation of their servitude. They made loud and elaborate talk among themselves, full of jest and gesture, fright and false alarm. They went abroad in fringed and flowered shawls, bright beadwork and German silver. They were at home in the kitchen, and they prepared meals that were banquets.

There were frequent prayer meetings, and nocturnal feasts. When I [14] was a child I played with my cousins outside, where the lamplight fell upon the ground and the singing of the old people rose up around us and carried away into the darkness. There were a lot of good things to eat, a lot of laughter and surprise. And afterwards, when the quiet returned, I lay down with my grandmother and could hear the frogs away by the river and feel the motion of the air.

Now there is a funeral silence in the rooms, the endless wake of some [15] final word. The walls have closed in upon my grandmother's house. When I returned to it in mourning, I saw for the first time in my life how small it was. It was late at night, and there was a white moon, nearly full. I sat for a long time on the stone steps by the kitchen door. From there I could see out across the land; I could see the long row of trees by the creek, the low light upon the rolling plains, and the stars of the Big Dipper. Once I looked at the moon and caught sight of a strange thing. A cricket had perched upon the handrail, only a few inches away. My line of vision was such that the creature filled the moon like a fossil. It had gone there, I thought, to live and die, for there, of all places, was its small definition made whole and eternal. A warm wind rose up and purled like the longing within me.

The next morning, I awoke at dawn and went out on the dirt road to [16] Rainy Mountain. It was already hot, and the grasshoppers began to fill the air. Still, it was early in the morning, and birds sang out of the shadows. The long yellow grass on the mountain shone in the bright light, and a scissortail hied above the land. There, where it ought to be, at the end of a long and legendary way, was my grandmother's grave. She had at last succeeded to that holy ground. Here and there on the dark stones were ancestral names. Looking back once, I saw the mountain and came away.

Using the Dictionary

Momaday writes about the past in a solemn, reverential style. For each of the following, what would be a simpler word or expression that would serve for a more casual occasion? 1. *isolate*—adj. (1)   2. *pillage* (3)   3. *forebears* (4)   4. *kinsmen* (9)   5. *tenuous* (9)   6. *consummate* (10)   7. *impale* (10)   8. *deicide* (10)   9. *sentinels* (12)   10. *opaque* (12)   11. *domain* (12)   12. *abide* (13)   13. *enmities* (13)   14. *servitude* (13)   15. *nocturnal* (14)

The Writer's Agenda

This essay combines vivid imaginative description with far-ranging reflection on the meaning of the scenes and people described. Answer the following questions about how the essay takes shape:

1. How does the author in the opening paragraph create the *setting* for his childhood memories? Point out striking specific details; graphic, concrete words; striking imaginative comparisons or figurative language. What for you is the unifying central idea or dominant impression in this paragraph?

2. On the occasion of his grandmother's death, Momaday briefly tells the story of his people. What to you is most instructive or most memorable about their history, their legends, and their religion?

3. In the *portrait* of his grandmother that begins the last third of the essay, what details does the author use to make her real and distinctive to us as a person?

4. In his description of life at the grandmother's house, how does Momaday recreate the vanished past? What are some striking or vivid details? What for you is the unifying central idea or dominant impression? (How does the author use the **contrast** between then and now to heighten the overall impression at which he aims?)

5. How do the two concluding paragraphs take up again *earlier strands* of the essay? What is the symbolic significance of the cricket?

6. The author's style is rich in details and comments that may at times seem **paradoxical**—they may seem contradictory at first but begin to make sense on further thought. What is paradoxical about statements such as the following?

   a. Warfare for the Kiowas was pre-eminently a matter of disposition rather than of survival.
   b. Some of them . . . carried the scars of old and cherished enmities.
   c. Gossip was at once the mark and compensation of their servitude.

For Discussion or Writing

7. In writing about the Native American past, Momaday deals with a subject that has often been obscured by prejudice, stereotypes, or neglect. What in this essay confirmed or reinforced familiar ideas? What for you was new or instructive?

8. How much in this essay is nostalgia for a vanished past? How much is meaningful or relevant as guidance for the future?

9. Use the author's description of life at his grandmother's house as a model for a childhood reminiscence or nostalgic re-creation of a scene from your own past.

10. Write a tribute to a person who, like the author's grandmother, represents a distinctive way of life. Write about someone you know well from close observation.

For Branching Out

11. Describe a natural scene, including ample detail from patient first-hand observation. For instance, take a close look at a cliff, forest clearing, deserted beach, undeveloped lakefront, stretch of desert. Or describe a typical city scene, taking a close look at a parking lot, public square, major avenue, major intersection in a shopping area, main street, or the like. Aim at a unifying overall impression.

12. Use Momaday's account of the migration of the Kiowas as a model for an account of a journey or of moving from one part of the country to another. Use vivid concrete detail to make settings or stages real for your readers. Try to establish a clear pattern or to convey a sense of meaningful progression.

BACKGROUND: Gretel Ehrlich was born in Santa Barbara, California, in 1946. She was a student at Bennington College and at UCLA. She became a producer and director of award-winning documentary films and was for a time an adviser to the Navajo Film Commission. In the following essay, she takes up a topic that was for a long time a major theme in American history and literature: the wide open spaces of the West, which gave people a chance to get close to the land, to work with their hands, and to meet other people as individuals. She wrote the essay four years after she had gone to Wyoming in search of "new and unpopulated territory." Instead of leaving after a while, as she had planned, she went to work helping a sheep rancher shear, brand, and delouse his thousands of sheep. She threw away her city clothes and bought new. The following, in a slightly shortened form, is her account of what it was like for her to live and work in open country. Her book *The Solace of Wide Open Spaces* was published in 1985.

Gretel Ehrlich

Wide Open Spaces

GUIDE TO READING: Take note of the many authentic details from the author's first-hand observation. At the same time, pay special attention to how she *uses* these details to support the general impressions she has formed of the place and its people. What is special about the setting? What is the relation between the place and the people that the author describes—how does the setting in which these people live help shape their outlook and behavior?

It's May, and I've just awakened from a nap, curled against sagebrush 1 the way my dog taught me to sleep—sheltered from wind. A weather front is pulling the huge sky over me, and from the dark a hailstone has hit me on the head.

I'm trailing a band of 2000 sheep across a stretch of Wyoming badland, 2 a 50-mile trip that takes five days because sheep shade up in the hot sun and won't budge until it cools. Bunched together now, and excited into a run by the storm, they drift across dry land, tumbling into draws like water and surging out again onto the rugged, choppy plateaus that are the building blocks of this state.

The name "Wyoming" comes from an Indian word meaning "at the 3 great plains," but the plains are really valleys, great arid valleys, 1600 square miles' worth of them, with the horizon bending up on all sides into mountain ranges. This gives the vastness a sheltering look.

Winter lasts six months here. Prevailing winds spill snowdrifts to the 4 east, and new storms from the northwest replenish them. This white bulk is sometimes dizzying, even nauseating, to look at. At 20, 30, 40 degrees below zero, it is not only your car that doesn't work but also your mind and body.

The landscape hardens into a dungeon of space. During the winter, while I was riding to find a new calf, my legs half froze to the saddle, and in the silence that such cold creates, I felt like the first person on earth, or the last.

Today the sun is out—only a few clouds billowing. In the east, where the sheep have started off without me, the benchland tilts up in a series of red-earthed, eroded mesas, planed flat on top by a million years of water. Behind them, a bold line of muscular scarps rears up 10,000 feet to become the Big Horn Mountains. A tidal pattern is engraved into the ground, as if left by the sea that once covered this state. Canyons curve down like galaxies to meet the oncoming rush of flat land.

To live and work in this kind of open country, with its 100-mile views, is to lose the distinction between background and foreground. When I asked an older ranch hand to describe Wyoming's openness, he said, "It's all a bunch of nothing—wind and rattlesnakes—and so much of it you can't tell where you're going or where you've been and it don't make much difference."

John, a sheepman I know, is tall and handsome and has an explosive temperament. He has a perfect intuition about people and sheep. They call him "Highpockets" because he's so long-legged; his graceful stride matches the distances he has to cover.

"Open space hasn't affected me at all. It's all the people moving in on it," he said. The huge ranch he was born on takes up much of one county and spreads into another state. For him to put 100,000 miles on his pickup in three years and never leave home is not unusual.

Most of Wyoming has a "lean-to" look. Instead of big, roomy barns and Victorian houses, there are dugouts, low sheds, log cabins, sheep camps and fence lines that look like driftwood blown haphazardly into place. People in Wyoming still feel pride because they live in such a harsh place, part of the glamorous cowboy past, and they are determined not to be the victims of a mining-dominated future.

Most characteristic of the state's landscape is what a developer euphe-mistically describes as "indigenous growth right up to your front door"—a reference to waterless stands of salt sage, snakes, jackrabbits, deerflies, red dust, a brief respite of wildflowers, dry washes and no trees.

Sagebrush covers 58,000 square miles of Wyoming. The biggest city has a population of 50,000, and there are only five settlements that could be called cities in the whole state. The rest are towns, scattered across the expanse with as much as 60 miles between them, their populations 2000, 50 or 10. They are fugitive-looking, perched on a barren, windblown bench, or tagged onto a river or a railroad, or laid out straight in a farming valley with implement stores and a block-long Mormon church.

In the eastern part of the state, which slides down into the Great 13
Plains, the new mining settlements are boomtowns, trailer cities, metal
knots on flat land.

Despite the desolate look, there's a coziness to living in this state. 14
There are so few people (only 470,000) that ranchers who buy and sell cattle
know each other statewide. The kids who choose to go to college usually go
to the state's one university, in Laramie. Hired hands work their way around
Wyoming in a lifetime of hirings and firings. And, despite the physical
separation, people stay in touch, often driving two or three hours to another
ranch for dinner.

Seventy-five years ago, when travel was by buckboard or horseback, 15
cowboys who were temporarily out of work rode the grub line—drifting
from ranch to ranch, mending fences or milking cows, and receiving in
exchange a bed and meals. Gossip and messages traveled this slow circuit
with them, creating an intimacy among ranchers who were three and four
weeks' ride apart.

One old-time couple I know, whose turn-of-the-century homestead 16
was used by an outlaw gang as a relay station for stolen horses, recall that if
you were traveling, desperado or not, any lighted ranch house was a
welcome sign.

Even now, for someone who lives in a remote spot, arriving at a ranch 17
or coming to town for supplies is cause for celebration. To emerge from
isolation can be disorienting. Everything looks bright, new, vivid. After I had
been herding sheep for only three days, the sound of the camp-tender's
pickup flustered me. Longing for human company, I felt a foolish grin take
over my face, yet I had to resist an urgent temptation to run and hide.

Things happen suddenly in Wyoming: the change of seasons and 18
weather; for people, the violent swings into and out of isolation. But good-
naturedness goes hand in hand with severity. Friendliness is a tradition.
Strangers passing on the road wave hello.

A common sight is two pickups stopped side by side far out on a range, 19
on a dirt track winding through the sage. The drivers will share a cigarette,
uncap their Thermos bottles, and pass a battered cup, steaming with coffee,
between windows. These meetings summon up the details of several
generations, because in Wyoming private histories are largely public
knowledge.

In most parts of Wyoming, the human population is visibly outnum- 20
bered by the animal. Not far from my town of 50, I rode into a narrow valley
and startled a herd of 200 elk. Eagles look like small people as they eat
car-killed deer by the road. Antelope, moving in small, graceful bands, travel
at 60 m.p.h., their mouths open as if drinking in the space.

The solitude in which Westerners live makes them quiet. They tele- 21
graph thoughts and feelings by the way they tilt their heads and listen;
pulling their Stetsons into a steep dive over their eyes or pigeon-toeing one
boot over the other, they lean against a fence and take the whole scene in.

These detached looks of quiet amusement are sometimes cynical, but they can also come from a dry-eyed humility as lucid as the air is clear.

Conversation goes on in what sounds like a private code. A few 22 phrases imply a complex of meanings. Asking directions you get a curious list of details. While trailing sheep, I was told to "ride up to that kinda upturned rock, follow the pin wash, turn left at the dump, and then you'll see the waterhole."

I've spent hours riding to sheep camp at dawn in a pickup when 23 nothing was said and eaten meals in the cookhouse when the only words spoken were a mumbled "Thank you, ma'am" at the end of dinner. The silence is profound. Instead of talking, we seem to share one eye. The landscape is engorged with detail, every movement on it chillingly sharp. The air between people is charged.

Spring weather is capricious and mean. It snows, then blisters with 24 heat. There have been tornadoes. They lay their elephant trunks out in the sage until they find houses, then slurp everything up and leave. I've noticed that melting snowbanks hiss and rot, viperous, then drip into calm pools where ducklings hatch and livestock, being trailed to summer range, drink.

With the ice cover gone, rivers churn a milkshake brown, taking 25 culverts and small bridges with them. Water in such an arid place (the average annual rainfall where I live is less than eight inches) is like blood. It festoons drab land with green veins: a line of cottonwoods following a stream; a strip of alfalfa, and on ditchbanks, wild asparagus growing.

I try to imagine a world of uncharted land, in which one could look 26 over an uncompleted map and ride a horse past where all the lines have stopped. There is no real wilderness left; wildnerness, yes, but true wilderness has been gone on this continent since the time of Lewis and Clark's overland journey.

Two hundred years ago, the Crow, Shoshone, Arapaho, Cheyenne, and 27 Sioux roamed the intermountain West, orchestrating their movements according to hunger, season, and warfare. Once they acquired horses, they traversed the spines of all the big Wyoming ranges—the Absarokas, the Wind Rivers, the Tetons, the Big Horns—and wintered on the unprotected plains that fan out from them. Space was life. The world was their home.

What was life-giving to native Americans was often nightmarish to 28 sod-busters who arrived encumbered with families and ethnic pasts to be transplanted in nearly uninhabitable land. The great distances, the shortage of water and trees, and the loneliness created unexpected hardships for them.

In her book *O Pioneers!* Willa Cather gives a settler's version of the 29 black landscape:[1] "The little town behind them had vanished as if it had

---

[1][Willa Cather (1873–1947) grew up in the grasslands of Nebraska. In books like *O Pioneers!* (1913) and *My Antonia* (1918) she told the story of European immigrants who farmed the uncharted plains of the Midwest.]

never been, had fallen behind the swell of the prairie, and the stern frozen country received them into its bosom. The homesteads were few and far apart; here and there a windmill gaunt against the sky, a sod house crouching in a hollow."

The emptiness of the West was for others a geography of possibility. 30 Men and women who amassed great chunks of land and struggled to preserve unfenced empires were, despite their self-serving motives, unwitting geographers. They understood the lay of the land.

But by the 1850s, the Oregon and Mormon trails sported bumper-to- 31 bumper traffic. Wealthy landowners, many of them aristocratic absentee landlords, known as remittance men because they were paid to come West and get out of their families' hair, overstocked the range with more than a million head of cattle. By 1885, the feed and water were desperately short, and the winter of 1886 laid out the gaunt bodies of dead animals so closely together that when the thaw came, one rancher from Kaycee claimed to have walked on cowhide all the way to Crazy Woman Creek, 20 miles away.

Territorial Wyoming was a boy's world. The land was generous with 32 everything but water. At first there was room enough and food enough for everyone. And, as with all beginnings, an expansive mood set in. The young cowboys, drifters, shopkeepers, and schoolteachers were heroic, lawless, generous, rowdy, and tenacious. The individualism and optimism generated during those times have endured.

Cattle barons tried to control all the public grazing land by restricting 33 membership in the Wyoming Stock Growers Association, as if it were a country club. They ostracized from roundups and brandings cowboys and ranchers who were not members, then denounced them as rustlers.

One cold-blooded murder of a small-time stockman kicked off the 34 Johnson County cattle war, which was no simple good guy−bad guy shoot-out but a complicated class struggle between landed gentry and less affluent settlers—a shocking reminder that the West was not an egalitarian sanctuary after all.

Fencing ultimately enforced boundaries, but barbed wire abolished 35 space. It was stretched across the beautiful valleys, into mountains, over desert badlands, through buffalo grass.

The "anything is possible" fever—the lure of any place—was con- 36 stricted. The integrity of the land as a geographical body, and the freedom to ride anywhere on it, were lost.

I punched cows with a young man named Martin, who is the great- 37 grandson of John Tisdale. His inheritance is not the open land that Tisdale knew and prematurely lost but a rage against restraint.

In all this open space, values crystallize quickly. People are strong on 38 scruples but tenderhearted about quirky behavior. A friend and I found one ranch hand, who's "not right in the head," sitting in front of the badly decayed carcass of a cow, shaking his finger and saying, "Now, I don't want you to do this ever again!"

When I asked what was wrong with him, I was told, "He's goofier than ₃₉ hell, just like the rest of us."

Perhaps because the West is historically new, conventional morality is ₄₀ still felt to be less important than rock-bottom truths. Though there's always a lot of teasing and sparring around, people are blunt with each other, sometimes even cruel, believing honesty is stronger medicine than sympathy, which may console but often conceals.

The formality that goes hand in hand with the rowdiness is known as ₄₁ "the Western Code." It's a list of practical do's and don'ts, faithfully observed. A friend, Cliff, who runs a trapline in the winter, cut off half his foot while axing a hole in the ice. Alone, he dragged himself to his pickup and headed for town, stopping to open the ranch gate as he left, and getting out to close it again, thus losing, in his observance of rules, precious time and blood.

Later, he commented, "How would it look, them having to come to the ₄₂ hospital to tell me their cows had gotten out?"

The roominess of the state has affected political attitudes. Ranchers ₄₃ keep up with world politics and the convulsions of the economy but are basically isolationists. Used to running their own small empires of land and livestock, they're suspicious of big government.

It's a "don't fence me in" holdover from a century ago. They still want ₄₄ the elbow room their grandfathers had, so they're strongly conservative, but with a populist twist.

Summer is the season when we get our "cowboy tans"—on the lower ₄₅ parts of our faces and on three fourths of our arms. Excessive heat, in the 90s and higher, sends us outside with the mosquitoes.

After the brief lushness of summer, the sun moves south. The range ₄₆ grass is brown. Livestock has been trailed back down from the mountains. Waterholes begin to frost over at night. Last fall Martin asked me to accompany him on a pack trip. With five horses, we followed a river into the mountains behind the tiny Wyoming town of Meeteetse. Groves of aspen, red and orange, gave off a light that made us look toasted.

One of our evening entertainments was to watch the night sky. My dog, ₄₇ who also came on the trip, a dingo bred to herd sheep, is so used to the silence and empty skies that when an airplane flies over he always looks up and eyes the distant intruder quizzically.

The sky, lately, seems to be much more crowded than it used to be. ₄₈ Satellites make their silent passes in the dark with great regularity. We counted 18 in one hour's viewing. How odd to think that while they circumnavigated the planet, Martin and I had moved only six miles into our local wilderness, and had seen no other human for the two weeks we stayed there.

At night, by moonlight, the land is whittled to slivers—a ridge, a river, ₄₉ a strip of grassland stretching to the mountains, then the huge sky. One morning a full moon was setting in the west just as the sun was rising. I felt precariously balanced between the two as I loped across a meadow. For a moment, I could believe that the stars, which were still visible, work like cooper's bands, holding everything above Wyoming together.

Space has a spiritual equivalent, and can heal what is divided and 50 burdensome in us. My grandchildren will probably use space shuttles for a honeymoon trip or to recover from heart attacks, but closer to home we might also learn how to carry space inside ourselves in the effortless way we carry our skins. Space represents sanity, not a life purified, dull, or "spaced out" but one that might accommodate intelligently any idea or situation.

Using the Dictionary

A. Look up the following examples of regional vocabulary—words likely to be familiar to people in the part of the country the author writes about: 1. *plateau* (2)   2. *mesa* (6)   3. *canyon* (6)   4. *range* (3)   5. *dry wash* (11)   6. *log cabin* (10)   7. *buckboard* (15)   8. *relay station* (16)   9. *sodbuster* (28)   10. *sod house* (29)

B. Look up the following examples of **historical** terms. Check especially for information about their origins or associations: 11. *indigenous* (11)   12. *desperado* (16)   13. *ostracize* (33)   14. *drifter* (32)   15. *landed gentry* (34)   16. *egalitarian* (34)   17. *absentee landlord* (31)   18. *sanctuary* (34)   19. *isolationist* (43)   20. *populist* (44)

C. Look up examples of words more likely to appear in **formal** writing than in informal speech: 21. *replenish* (4)   22. *euphemistic* (11)   23. *respite* (11)   24. *expanse* (12)   25. *desolate* (14)   26. *traverse* (27)   27. *encumbered* (28)   28. *circumnavigate* (48)   29. *precarious* (49)   30. *lope* (49)

The Writer's Agenda

In this essay, an effective writer uses authentic details *for a purpose.* Answer the following questions about how she uses details from first-hand observation to support her general conclusions about the land and its people:

1. In the first nine paragraphs, Ehrlich presents the **dominant impression** that gives unity to her essay. Point out terms and expressions that echo her key idea of "wide open" country, where everything is on a large scale. Point out specific details that support and reinforce this key idea in these introductory paragraphs.

2. In a second section of the essay (paragraphs 10–13), the author focuses on features of the *physical setting* that make it a harsh place to live. What details about architecture, vegetation, wildlife, and geography support this point?

3. In the section starting "Despite the desolate look . . ." the author goes on to talk about a first major trait of the *people.* What is that trait, and how does she explain it? (In the next five or six paragraphs, trace the network of **related terms** that all echo or reinforce this first major point.) At the end of this section, the author goes on to a second psychological trait that she explains as the result of solitude. What is it,

and why may it seem contradictory when compared with the first?

4. In the central section of the essay, the author sketches a *brief history* of the state. Identify several major historical stages. Explain some of the attitudes or competing forces that played a major role in each.

5. In her *conclusion*, how does Ehrlich make sure that the concluding four or five paragraphs are not merely weak repetition of what she has already said? At the very end, she spells out a central idea that was implied in much of what she said earlier. What is it?

6. Study examples of figurative language in the following sample passages. What does each example make us see and hear and feel? What does it draw on for comparison?

    a. Today the sun is out—only a few clouds billowing. In the east, where the sheep have started off without me, the benchland tilts up in a series of red-earthed, eroded mesas, planed flat on top by a million years of water. Behind them, a bold line of muscular scarps rears up 10,000 feet to become the Big Horn Mountains. A tidal pattern is engraved into the ground, as if left by the sea that once covered this state. Canyons curve down like galaxies to meet the oncoming rush of flat land.

    b. Spring weather is capricious and mean. It snows, then blisters with heat. There have been tornadoes. They lay their elephant trunks out in the sage until they find houses, then slurp everything up and leave. I've noticed that melting snowbanks hiss and rot, viperous, then drip into calm pools where ducklings hatch and livestock, being trailed to summer range, drink.

For Discussion or Writing

7. Who do you think would make a better audience for this selection—people living in the country or people living in the city?

8. People are often wary of the outsider who forms superficial impressions. If you were an oldtimer in the area that the author describes, how do you think you would react to her account?

9. Gretel Ehrlich touches on several traditional traits of the American national character that observers have traced to the frontier experience: neighborliness; tolerance for eccentricity; quietness, or dislike of too much talk. Concentrate on one of these. To judge from your own observation, is it still strong, or has it changed or disappeared? Discuss detailed examples from first-hand observation.

10. Describe a part of the country that for you has a definite regional flavor— that is different in appearance or mood from other parts of the country. Concentrate on the physical setting—the landscape, the weather, and the like. Select details that allow you to build up a strong overall impression.

11. Do you know fairly well some occupation that brings people close to sights and sounds not familiar to outsiders? For instance, have you ever worked in a service station, hospital, family grocery? Describe the setting, concentrating on what the people working there see and hear and feel. Aim at a unifying overall impression.

For Branching Out

12. We are often told that Americans today are very mobile; they move on from place to place. To judge from your own observation and experience, do Americans care much or little about the area or the region where they live? Are the places where they live or grew up very special to them? Discuss some detailed evidence from your own observation.

WRITERS ON WRITING
Gretel Ehrlich on Writing and Revising

QUESTION: Your examples and descriptions are very vivid. Do you keep a journal or notebook?

ANSWER: I do—although not in a rigorous way. I note down anything and everything I find interesting—on a completely personal level: dreams, bits of conversations, thoughts . . . . Or, when I'm going to observe, I keep a notebook, if it won't be too intrusive. I know there are some people who feel that they have to write in a journal every day, but I don't. Yet, as it turns out, it's almost daily—and I write about everything from the changing seasons to my changing moods.

QUESTION: To write so vividly, you must know the art of observation well. Was it something you learned?

ANSWER: I was a documentary filmmaker for some time, so I'm sure that helped to keep me somewhat detached from a situation. It's easy to be seduced into a situation and lose track of what's going on. But I really think that part of the innate talent of being a writer is a natural curiosity or instinct. I do work on remembering. I don't have a particularly steel-trap mind, so I do have to discipline myself to remember details that help to tell a story: someone's clothes, the way people express themselves. I have to remember for those times when taking notes would be intrusive.

QUESTION: How do you discipline yourself to remember?

ANSWER: It's a conscious discipline. I don't have any choice—I have to do it—like remembering the doctor's phone number.

QUESTION: You spoke about "detachment" earlier on. Yet, you seem intensely involved in what you're writing about.

ANSWER: By "detachment," I mean continual awareness: You're completely open to the situation you're in—but your eyes are open all the time. That kind of involvement makes you more appreciative of all the nuances. It doesn't mean that you shut yourself off

QUESTION: Do you have writing rituals?

ANSWER: Not really, since my life is pretty diverse. I write whenever I get the chance. Whether that means I get to write all day or a few hours or 15 minutes a day, I try to take advantage of what I have. If it were in my nature to set up rituals for the act of writing, nothing would ever be quite right: I'd never get anything written because it's so hard to write anyway. I just try to deal with disruptions without making a big deal.

QUESTION: Do you do much revising?

ANSWER: Yes, I do. Sometimes I revise as I go along. Sometimes I put something away and let it marinate for a week—or sometimes both. Sometimes I can't stand to be around it, and other times I can't stand not to be around it. The most time-consuming part, though, is at the very beginning. Everything comes out in fragments and then it either starts to string together or it doesn't—and I have to start again.

QUESTION: Do you have someone you particularly rely on as your critic?

ANSWER: No, not really. Recently, I've had friends to help me, but that's mostly in terms of moral support. When *Solace* was put together, I had an editor who read the whole manuscript and went through making suggestions, especially about structure. She was good—and very careful about not destroying me. But, mainly, you have to do it yourself. Being a writer means knowing when your writing is good and when it isn't. That knowledge comes from experience. You learn what your own voice is and what its range is.

QUESTION: Do you like to write?

ANSWER: It's gone beyond that. I just can't not do it anymore. If I don't write for two or three days, I get cranky and on edge. I guess I do like it, but it's not a simple liking—like liking a beer in the afternoon. Maybe that sounds melodramatic, but it's true.

—From an interview with the editors of *Essay 2*

STUDENT MODEL 2

FOR READING: Study the following short selection as a possible model for writing of your own. How do you react to it overall? What makes it interesting or effective? Answer the following more specific questions:

1. (PURPOSE) What was the writer trying to do?
2. (AUDIENCE) What kind of reader would make a good reader for this selection?

3. (SOURCES) Where did the writer turn for material?
4. (THESIS) Does the selection have a central idea or unifying thesis?
5. (STRUCTURE) What is the author's overall plan or strategy?
6. (STYLE) What makes the piece effective or memorable (for instance, striking details, memorable phrases)?
7. (REVISION) What do you think the writer could or should have done differently?

Joe Pollifrone

A Day in the Life

Quickly walking through the unending maze of unblemished ivory-white hallways, I see the familiar rectangular black sign on the wall, "This elevator for employee use only." I press the lower translucent plastic button; suddenly the bell sounds, and the down arrow above the elevator door turns a bright red against the subdued fluorescent lighting. Slowly the elevator door disappears into the wall. Making sure I do not overturn my shoulder-high polished-aluminum foodtray cart (as is often done by trainees), I watch that the small black plastic wheels of the cart do not get caught in the crack between the elevator and the spotless tiled floor. Already in the capacious elevator is an orderly dressed in blue from cap to booties, standing next to a gurney with an unwrinkled snow-white sheet over a patient. As the door opens to the sullen first floor, I pull my cart into the hallway. As I turn to hold the door open, I notice a green tag dangling from the big toe of the patient, and I hear the orderly's voice: "Thanks, but I'm getting off in the basement."

The depression I always felt as a dietary technician (actually a dishwasher and gatherer of dirty dishes) at the Valley Hospital was a result of the dejecting atmosphere. Every day's sights and sounds reinforced my feeling of helplessness when confronted with pain and misery.

At six-thirty on a Sunday morning, the gentle hum of the giant black floor polishers seems to be the only sound audible in the hospital. As I pass the open doors, I catch bits of routine complaints from elderly patients. I hear the sound of coughing from behind the door of the children's ward, with the shiny round handle so high that the small hands of children cannot reach. As I enter the Intensive Care Unit, I see the nurse on duty engrossed in a book with a deserted beach on the cover—she is escaping for a short time from the suffering and dying around her. The patients have light-green name bands around their wrists. One has a cropped head of hair (impossible to tell the sex) and is chained to the bed by the drips, drains, and leads connected to a kidney machine and respirators.

I pass a cheerful young volunteer pushing a wheelchair-bound old woman past the bold red sign that reads, "Keep clear at all times—Emer-

gency Access Area." I pick up some dirty food trays from the emergency
room and move on.

"Code ninety-nine CCU east"—a calm voice breaks into the piped-in ₅
dentist's-office music that fills every hall and waiting room. As I move
through the Coronary Care Unit, I see a defenseless grey-haired old man
with tiny white stubs on his chin, lying in a fully automatic, do-everything,
criblike bed. A doctor, a stethoscope around her neck, takes a pancake-
shaped instrument with small plastic handles and black coiled wires to
place on the old man's lean chest.

"For the protection of the patients, no matches, lighters, belts, ties, or ₆
drugs of any kind beyond this point." This sign appears at eye level on the
locked door to a closed ward, my last place to pick up food trays for the day.
I pick up the nearby white telephone and state my name, title, and business.
A buzzer sounds, and I walk into the community "kitchen"—nothing more
than a green sink, a light green refrigerator, a green formica table, and white
plastic chairs. All of the utensils are made of plastic or styrofoam; there are
no knives. Four expressionless people sit around the table, as if they were
not on this planet. They look as if they had been awake for days without
sleep. They do not utter a word as I walk by.

After working in this environment for a time, I became used and ₇
perhaps immune to the depressing sights I saw around me. I gradually began
to see the invigorating parts of life in the hospital, such as the maternity
ward and the miracle of a dying patient's fighting and conquering a fatal
disease. But these positive impressions will never quite balance the feelings
of depression and helplessness that I felt in the beginning.

FOR WRITING: Give your readers an insider's tour of a museum, a theater, a jail, or
other institution that you know well or that you have had a chance to study. Provide
vivid, graphic details. Give your readers a clear sense of where they are and where
they are headed.

ADDITIONAL WRITING TOPICS 2

Observation

A. Make your readers take a fresh look at a painting, building, site, memorial,
or work of art that they are likely to know. Make it as real, vivid, and graphic as you
can. Bring your personal reactions or feelings into play. Some possible subjects:
- the Lincoln Memorial
- the Mona Lisa
- American Gothic

- the Vietnam Memorial in Washington, D.C.
- a Chagall painting
- the World Trade Center in New York City
- Michelangelo's Pietà
- the Superdome in New Orleans
- Times Square
- the Sunset Strip
- the Statue of Liberty
- the Parthenon

B. Take your readers behind the scenes to make them see a place you know well. Make them see how it looks from the inside. Some possible subjects:

- a restaurant
- a fast-food place
- a garage
- a hospital
- a psychiatric clinic
- a fire station
- a theater
- a resort
- a summer camp
- a police department
- a department store
- an amusement park

C. Tourists are often said to see (or be shown) only what is superficially strange, amusing, or picturesque. Write as a guide for a visitor who wants to see what tourists are likely to miss. Take your reader to a place like the following:

- a state or national park
- a historical site
- a reservation
- a winery
- a mission
- a waterfront
- a historical part of your town or city
- a foreign country where you have lived or visited
- a favorite museum

3

POINTS OF VIEW

Taking a Stand

OVERVIEW

Many typical writing assignments in a composition class will ask you to take a stand on an issue of current interest or general concern. Such writing does not take place in a vacuum: Our opinions take shape in the give-and-take of discussion that goes on around us. Much effective writing is part of a continuing dialogue. A question arises and we feel we have at least part of the answer. Something we care about is misrepresented, and we want to set the record straight. We are ready to take a stand; we are ready to present our personal point of view.

PURPOSE One of the basic motives of writing is our need to speak out, to make ourselves heard. We let others know where we stand so that they will take our opinion into account. Often what compels us to take a stand is personal loyalty, inside knowledge, or personal interest. Someone makes a case, and we want to show why we agree. Someone makes a proposal, and we want to show what is wrong with it. We feel the need to question a disturbing new idea, to head off an ill-considered scheme, or to correct a stereotype. Personal decisions as well as public opinion are shaped by those who care enough to speak out, to take a stand.

AUDIENCE When we state an opinion on a subject of general interest, we often aim at the imaginary educated, reasonable "general reader"—well-informed, a person of goodwill. However, we may learn more about the action-and-reaction of live debate when we write for a more localized audience closer to home—for instance, when we write about parking problems, rape prevention, or the underpaid part-time faculty on our own campus. On many current issues—changing sex roles, comparable worth, women's sports—we have to reckon with aroused, committed readers who will react strongly to a superficial or condescending treatment of a topic close to their hearts.

BENEFITS FOR THE WRITER (1) To present an informed, responsible opinion, we need to get involved in a subject; we need to work up the material. An effective writer is an alert listener and reader. To present a personal point of view effectively, we have to go beyond hearsay, prejudice, and superficial impressions. When we try to work out a responsible opinion, we learn something about the *sources* of effective writing in honest observation, first-hand experience, careful reading and listening, or systematic research.

(2) Trying to make ourselves heard, we learn how to *sum up* our key ideas effectively, how to make them stand out in such a way that they will be understood and remembered. We learn to satisfy the reader who wants to know: "What is the point? What are you trying to tell me? Where do you stand?"

(3) Trying to get a respectful hearing, we learn what it takes to *support* opinions effectively. Our readers will ask not only "*What* do you believe?" but also "*Why* do you believe what you do?" We need striking examples, relevant evidence, helpful facts and figures, supporting testimony from quoted authorities. It is true that we are "entitled to our own opinion"—but no reader is obligated to heed it unless we have learned to marshal the supporting material, unless we have learned to anchor our ideas to visible means of support.

POINTS OF VIEW
Additional Reading

Stanley Kauffmann, The Return of Rambo   (p. 405)
Barbara Tuchman, Humanity's Better Moments   (p. 460)

WRITER'S GUIDE 3

Supporting a Thesis

Much writing that is worth reading presents an informed opinion on a subject of common concern. The kind of statement that *sums up* the author's point of view is called a *thesis*. The thesis spells out the central idea of a paper. It provides the answer for the reader who wants to know: "What is the point? What are you trying to prove?" In a paper worth reading, the thesis is the result of your own honest thinking about the subject. To formulate an effective thesis, you have to add up what you know. You have to pull together what you have heard and read.

When you write a paper that presents and supports a central thesis, remember the following guidelines:

(1) *Focus on an issue of common concern.* A live issue is one that cannot simply be settled by appeals to what "everybody knows." People with a knowledge of the subject take different sides. They disagree not just from spite or ignorance but because they see things differently. They have come to the subject from different backgrounds and with different expectations. On many topics of current public debate, some people's minds may already be set in concrete, but many other people are not sure they have the right answer. They may be willing to listen to your arguments if they feel that they will learn something and that you will respect their right to make up their own minds.

A writer today should be able to find an audience for a serious discussion of issues like the following:

- Should the government take steps to reduce illegal immigration?
- Should private citizens be allowed to arm themselves for protection against criminals?
- Should people sign marriage contracts that spell out how domestic chores and child raising will be shared between the spouses?
- Should the government finance programs designed to create jobs?
- Does the separation of church and state rule out school prayer or programs related to religious holidays?
- Should Americans stress English as the single national language of instruction in the schools?

(2) *Sum up your central idea as the thesis of your paper.* The thesis is a brief one-sentence or two-sentence statement of the answer you give to the basic question raised by your paper. It clearly and directly states your point of view on the issue. It satisfies the reader who wants to know: "What

is the message? Where do you stand?" Do not use your thesis merely to set vague general directions for your paper: "We should look at *several factors* involved in prejudice" or "There are *many objections* to gun control." Use your thesis to take a definite stand:

> TOO OPEN: Like many other minority students, I have had a variety of experiences with white friends.
>
> POINTED: So-called liberals who befriend minority students are often fair-weather friends; on weekends and on social occasions, they are nowhere to be found.

> TOO OPEN: Many serious questions have been raised about the ever-present violence in movies and on TV.
>
> POINTED: The main objection to television and movie violence is that it makes killing seem swift and easy.

> TOO OPEN: Much has been written in recent years about the attitude Americans have toward work.
>
> POINTED: To judge from fashionable movies and books, many Americans today hate their work.

(3) *Use your introduction to lead directly into your central thesis.* At times, a writer will lead up to the main point indirectly or in stages. But an early statement of your thesis will focus your readers' attention and let them know what is at issue. The following might be the opening paragraph of an essay on careers open to women:

> Introduction   When a bright young woman graduate started looking for a job, why was the first question always: "Can you type?" A history of prejudice lies behind that question. Why are women thought of as secretaries, not administrators? Librarians and teachers, but not doctors and lawyers? *Be-*
>
> THESIS   *cause they are thought of as different and inferior. The happy homemaker and the contented darky are both stereotypes produced by prejudice.*   (Shirley Chisholm, "A Visiting Feminine Eye," *McCall's*)

(4) *Support your thesis with relevant evidence or detailed examples.* A thesis serves as a promise to the reader. The implied promise is, "This is what I believe, and I will show *why*." Look at the array of material that the author of the following student paper worked up in support of her thesis:

The Year of the Lout

> THESIS   *Crude and violent behavior in our society has gone beyond mere bad manners to a breakdown of respect for others.*

Dramatic representative incident	As a young pedestrian raced across the busy street to catch a bus, an oncoming car sped up, forcing the young man to dive into the rocks and shrubbery. The car then pulled into a parking space in front of a grocery store, and the driver and his wife got out. As they went into the store, the young man got up, brushing the rocks and debris off his clothes, and went after them to confront the driver. "You almost killed me, man!" the bruised and shaken jaywalker yelled at the driver. In response the driver of the car pulled out a gun and cracked the young man over the head with it.

This pedestrian was not seriously harmed, but he did miss his bus. The gun-toting motorist was later picked up and taken to jail. . . . |
Additional examples	Noisy patrons in theaters ruin the movie for the rest of the audience; graffiti deface bridges, overpasses, and subways; vandals trash restrooms or make a mess with fire extinguishers. . . .
Supporting source	Mike Royko, Chicago columnist, reports an incident in which his car was almost made the middle layer of a sandwich by two large trucks when he inadvertently caused one of the trucks to slow down. The trucker and his buddy spent twenty minutes playing highway games with Royko by pinning him in and trying to run him off the road to punish him for his "crime."
Authoritative opinion	Psychologists ask us to think about the underlying psychological mechanisms that precipitate (or prevent) violent and destructive behavior. One landscape architect in Seattle wraps newly planted trees in gauze. The gauze bandage, suggesting something wounded or vulnerable, is designed to produce a caring rather than a destructive response.

(5) *Consider including in your thesis a clue to the organization of your paper.* A thesis can serve as a preview; it can sketch out a program for the rest of a paper. Suppose you have been asked to write about a term that echoes in much current political discussion. A thesis like the following can set the direction for the development of your paper:

> THESIS   *Exploitation is using others for personal advantage: Individuals exploit other human beings; stronger nations have always exploited weaker nations.*

This thesis statment makes us expect a paper that has two major parts. First, we are likely to find examples of *individual* exploitation:

| First category | Today it is not unusual for adults to exploit children. Children are pushed into acting or modeling at a very young age by their parents.... |

In the second part of the paper, we are likely to find examples of *nations* exploiting other nations.

| Second category | In the history of modern imperialism, we see many examples of small, weak nations being invaded for their gold and diamonds, or exploited for their oil and other raw materials.... |

To sum up: A thesis is a statement in need of support. In the rough-and-tumble of public debate, it is not enough to *have* an opinion. The key question we ask of a writer is: "What makes you think so?" The point of view you present in a paper must be founded in something. It must derive from an honest look at the issue. You are entitled to your opinion, but your readers will expect you to back it up with examples, statistics, case histories, expert testimony, and other kinds of support.

Prewriting Activities 3

1. For an *opinion inventory*, write down your views on several subjects. Write freely and quickly, recording views, ideas, or reactions as they come to mind. Write on several of the following: law and order, the draft, corruption, pornography, affirmative action, nuclear power, political parties, drugs, race, war.

2. Conduct an *interview* to get the insider's view on an issue of current concern. For instance, interview an elderly person on what retirement is like, a school official on vandalism, a police officer on violence in a crime-ridden neighborhood. Prepare a set of questions (and adjust or modify them as necessary during the interview). One student obtained good results by asking a retired person questions like the following:

   a. What do you like best about retirement?
   b. What do you like least?
   c. Is there anything you are particularly angry about?
   d. If you could be fifty again, would you plan anything differently?
   e. What advice would you give young people about planning for retirement?

3. Use *discovery frames* like the following to work up a subject in a systematic, organized way. Ask yourself questions that will help you discover what you already know about a topic. Suppose a topic asks you to express your views, or take a stand, on environmental pollution. For a preliminary collection of material, write detailed responses under all or most of the following headings:

   I. *Common knowledge:* What is it that "everybody says" or "everybody knows" about this subject? What are some typical headlines? How frequently is pollution in the news? What would a reader find in recent newspaper or magazine articles on this subject?

II. *Personal experience:* Where have you yourself seen striking evidence of pollution? Is it an issue where you live? Where has it played a role in the lives or the work of people you know? What do you know about this topic from first-hand observation and experience?

III. *Long-range causes:* What are the basic causes of our current problems with pollution? What are the major long-range historical developments that explain our current dilemmas? Which in your opinion are the chief culprits (and which perhaps are merely scapegoats)?

IV. *Current efforts:* What has been done, or is being done, to clean up the environment? What are some recent successes or failures? What are major obstacles or hopeful signs?

V. *Future prospects:* What lies ahead? How optimistic or how pessimistic would your own personal forecast be, and why?

4. How good a listener are you? How often do you make the effort to understand fully the point of view of someone with whom you strongly *disagree*? Play the devil's advocate. Explain as fully and as fairly as you can an attitude, position, or point of view with which you strongly disagree.

Paragraph Practice 3

Have you ever felt the need to correct a misconception or to set the record straight? Write a paragraph in which you present the corrected view or more accurate statement as the central idea, or *topic sentence*. Then provide examples or evidence. Study and discuss the following paragraph as a possible model.

The Banning of Books

Censorship attacks good books, not poor books. The current tensions between the schools and some parents generally involve very good materials. Although the term *obscene* is used quite frequently in complaints by parents, it is very doubtful that any of the books are in fact legally obscene. The books that are most frequently the objects of complaints include John Steinbeck's *The Grapes of Wrath*, George Orwell's *1984*, Aldous Huxley's *Brave New World*, Gordon Parks' *The Learning Tree*, James Dickey's *Deliverance*, and Pearl S. Buck's *The Good Earth*. This list would be regarded by most teachers or librarians as a reasonable sample of some of the best or most relevant writers of the recent past. It should be noted that most of the writers are American writers of the twentieth century. The conflicts between some parents and schools involve the best learning materials, not the poorest.   (Adapted from Lee Burress and Edward B. Jenkinson, "Censorship Attacks Good Books")

BACKGROUND: Arthur Ashe was one of the first black athletes to gain an international reputation in tennis, until then often considered a sport reserved for the leisured white upper middle class. He won the first United States Open championship as an amateur in 1968. He won the Wimbledon tournament in England in 1975. The article reprinted here was first published in the *New York Times*. In this article, Ashe asks young readers to look beyond the seductive surface glamour of the athletic star system at the realities facing the rank and file.

Arthur Ashe

A Black Athlete

Looks at Education

GUIDE TO READING: Where does the author state his central thesis? Where does he echo or reinforce it? How does he support it?

Since my sophomore year at UCLA, I have become convinced that we 1 blacks spend too much time on the playing fields and too little time in the libraries. Consider these facts: for the major professional sports of hockey, football, basketball, baseball, golf, tennis and boxing, there are roughly only 3170 major league positions available (attributing 200 positions to golf, 200 to tennis and 100 to boxing). And the annual turnover is small.

There must be some way to assure that those who try but don't make it 2 to pro sports don't wind up on street corners or in unemployment lines. Unfortunately, our most widely recognized role models are athletes and entertainers—"runnin'" and "jumpin'" and "singin'" and "dancin'."

Our greatest heroes of the century have been athletes—Jack Johnson, 3 Joe Louis, and Muhammad Ali. Racial and economic discrimination forced us to channel our energies into athletics and entertainment. These were the ways out of the ghetto, the ways to get that Cadillac, those regular shoes, that cashmere sport coat.

Somehow, parents must instill a desire for learning alongside the 4 desire to be Walt Frazier. Why not start by sending black professional athletes into high schools to explain the facts of life?

I have often addressed high school audiences and my message is 5 always the same: "For every hour you spend on the athletic field, spend two in the library. Even if you make it as a pro athlete, your career will be over by the time you are 35. You will need that diploma."

Have these pro athletes explain what happens if you break a leg, get a 6 sore arm, have one bad year or don't make the cut for five or six tournaments. Explain to them the star system, wherein for every star earning millions there are six or seven others making $15,000 or $20,000 or $30,000. Invite a bench-warmer or a guy who didn't make it. Ask him if he sleeps every night. Ask him whether he was graduated. Ask him what he would do if he became disabled tomorrow. Ask him where his old high school athletic buddies are.

We have been on the same roads—sports and entertainment—too long. We need to pull over, fill up at the library and speed away to Congress and the Supreme Court, the unions and the business world. 7

I'll never forget how proud my grandmother was when I graduated from UCLA. Never mind the Davis Cup. Never mind the Wimbledon title. To this day, she still doesn't know what those names mean. What mattered to her was that of her more than thirty children and grandchildren, I was the first to be graduated from college, and a famous college at that. Somehow, that made up for all those floors she scrubbed all those years. 8

Using the Dictionary

For which of the following references does your dictionary provide help? What kind? 1. Jack Johnson (3)   2. Joe Louis (3)   3. Muhammad Ali (3)   4. Walt Frazier (4)   5. Davis Cup (8)   6. Wimbledon (8)

The Writer's Agenda

This short article is exceptionally well focused on a single issue. It reiterates—that is, it reinforces and drives home—a central thesis.

1. How would you sum up the author's *purpose*? What is he trying to accomplish? Who is his intended *audience*?

2. Where does he state his central *thesis*? Where is the thesis echoed or reinforced?

3. How does the author *support* the central thesis? What use does he make of examples, explanation, statistics?

4. What does the *conclusion* add to the article?

5. Where does the author touch on the deeper causes of what he describes? How is it part of a larger pattern?

For Discussion or Writing

6. Do you think this article will persuade its intended audience? Why or why not?

7. In your opinion, does recognition for outstanding black athletes and entertainers help overcome prejudice? Or does it help reinforce prejudice by keeping alive stereotypes? Take a stand and support your position.

8. How much truth is there in familiar stereotypes of the "jock"?

9. Is there too much emphasis on athletics in the American high school or college? Support your answer with detailed examples from your own observation and experience.

10. Do the mass media glorify the athlete? What image of the athlete do they create or perpetuate? In your opinion, is it a good or a bad influence on young people?

Branching Out

11. Find an editorial that takes a stand on a current issue related to sports or athletics. Report and discuss the author's point of view. How is it supported? How do you react and why?

12. Many observers have criticized the passive role of the audience in our most popular spectator sports. One such critic summed up her opinion by saying, "In time, I expect we will advance sufficiently so that no one is on the sidelines and everyone plays." Do you agree or disagree? Support your point of view.

WRITERS ON WRITING
Arthur Ashe on Professional Writers and Amateurs

QUESTION: You're a professional athlete and a successful business-man, among other titles. Why do you write?

ANSWER: I've always enjoyed writing. I enjoyed it in high school—and always got A's in English. But, then, when I went to UCLA, I had to take the freshman English exam, and I flunked it. I couldn't believe it because I always thought I wrote well. I took that "Subject A" class and whizzed right through it.

QUESTION: Did you take other English courses that were useful?

ANSWER: Oh, yes. In fact, wherever I go, I tell people that. I recently gave an address at a church I attended when I lived in Richmond to high school graduates about to enter college. I told them the same thing I tell any high school group: The most important subject you can take is English. Take as many English courses as you can. They're very necessary courses, especially if you're black and especially if you're going into the corporate world.

As a board member of one of the major Fortune 500 companies, I know that a lack of communication—writing—skills is the number one drawback to blacks getting ahead in the corporate world.

QUESTION: How does your status as a world-class athlete affect you as a writer—or does it?

ANSWER: Sure it does. I don't feel confident enough to call myself "a writer." I don't do it for a living; I just enjoy it. But readers listen to me because of who I am. If I can put what I want to say in readable form, they'll listen.

The Washington Post asks me to write for them several times a year. If something involving a black athlete becomes front page news, I'll probably be asked to do a thought piece on it. Also, I have access to the world of athletics in a way that a professional sports writer who is not an athlete doesn't. I can go into the locker room at Wimbledon; I can call star athletes.

But sometimes I just submit blind articles. For instance, I recently wrote one for the "About Men" section of *The New York Times.*

QUESTION: Did you get much response to your "Open Letter to Parents of Black Athletes" in 1977?

ANSWER: Response to that piece was greater than to anything else I've ever written. It came out at a time when people were trying to convince not only black athletes but young blacks in general to put athletics in its proper place. But one of the problems is that the very people you're trying to reach don't read these articles. When that one came out in *The New York Times*, some teacher probably read it and put it on the bulletin board. But the people who are out there having these kind of problems aren't reading *The Times.*

QUESTION: So why bother?

ANSWER: The people who have the problems may not read it, but the ones who are in a position to influence them will. Things published in authoritative papers like the *Washington Post* and *The New York Times* automatically go on the agenda of the nation. That's the way the process works.

QUESTION: I can't resist asking: is writing harder than playing tennis?

ANSWER: No, not for me, because I'm not trying to win prizes for writing. I'm not trying to win the Pulitzer. I'm not trying to sound like anybody else—not George Will or William Raspberry, even Jim Murray. I'm not a great wordsmith, but I enjoy writing. I have something to say.

—from an interview with the editors of *Essay 2*

BACKGROUND: Susan Jacoby is a journalist and essayist who has frequently written on issues related to women's rights. She has worked as education reporter for the *Washington Post* and as a columnist for the *New York Times*; a collection of her columns and magazine essays (*The Possible She*) was published in 1979. In 1969, she went to the Soviet Union for two years; she published several books about her observations and experiences there. In the essay that follows, Jacoby disagrees with the position taken on pornography by many advocates of women's rights. She champions the protection writers, artists, and entertainers have historically enjoyed under the First Amendment. Adopted as part of the Bill of Rights in 1791, the First Amendment to the U.S. Constitution, in addition to guaranteeing freedom of religion and the rights of assembly and petition, provides that "Congress shall make no law . . . abridging the freedom of speech, or of the press." (For a strong dissenting view, see Gloria Steinem's essay "Erotica and Pornography" in Unit 5 of this book.)

Susan Jacoby

Pornography and the First Amendment

GUIDE TO READING: How does the author raise the issue? Where does she take her stand? How does she attack the opposing view? What alternatives does she offer to the position she opposes?

It is no news that many women are defecting from the ranks of civil 1 libertarians on the issue of obscenity. The conviction of Larry Flynt, publisher of *Hustler* magazine—before his metamorphosis into a born-again Christian—was greeted with unabashed feminist approval. Harry Reems, the unknown actor who was convicted by a Memphis jury for conspiring to distribute the movie *Deep Throat*, has carried on his legal battles with almost no support from women who ordinarily regard themselves as supporters of the First Amendment. Feminist writers and scholars have even discussed the possibility of making common cause against pornography with adversaries of the women's movement—including opponents of the equal rights amendment and "right to life" forces.

All of this is deeply disturbing to a woman writer who believes, as I 2 always have and still do, in an absolute interpretation of the First Amendment. Nothing in Larry Flynt's garbage convinces me that the late Justice Hugo L. Black was wrong in his opinion that "the Federal Government is without any power whatsoever under the Constitution to put any type of burden on free speech and expression of ideas of any kind (as distinguished from conduct)." Many women I like and respect tell me I am wrong; I cannot remember having become involved in so many heated discussions of a public issue since the end of the Vietnam War. A feminist writer described my views as those of a "First Amendment junkie."

Many feminist arguments for controls on pornography carry the impli- 3 cit conviction that porn books, magazines and movies pose a greater threat to women than similarly repulsive exercises of free speech pose to other offended groups. This conviction has, of course, been shared by everyone— regardless of race, creed or sex—who has ever argued in favor of abridging the First Amendment. It is the argument used by some Jews who have withdrawn their support from the American Civil Liberties Union because it has defended the right of American Nazis to march through a community inhabited by survivors of Hitler's concentration camps.

If feminists want to argue that the protection of the Constitution 4 should not be extended to *any* particularly odious or threatening form of speech, they have a reasonable argument (although I don't agree with it). But it is ridiculous to suggest that the porn shops on 42nd Street are more disgusting to women than a march of neo-Nazis is to survivors of the extermination camps.

The arguments over pornography also blur the vital distinction be- 5 tween expression of ideas and conduct. When I say I believe unreservedly in the First Amendment, someone always comes back at me with the issue of "kiddie porn." But kiddie porn is not a First Amendment issue. It is an issue of the abuse of power—the power adults have over children—and not of obscenity. Parents and promoters have no more right to use their children to make porn movies than they do to send them to work in coal mines. The responsible adults should be prosecuted, just as adults who use children for back-breaking farm labor should be prosecuted.

Susan Brownmiller, in *Against Our Will: Men, Women and Rape,* has 6 described pornography as "the undiluted essence of anti-female propa- ganda." I think this is a fair description of some types of pornography, especially of the brutish subspecies that equates sex with death and por- trays women primarily as objects of violence.

The equation of sex and violence, personified by some glossy rock 7 record album covers as well as by *Hustler,* has fed the illusion that cen- sorship of pornography can be conducted on a more rational basis than other types of censorship. Are all pictures of naked women obscene? Clearly not, says a friend. A Renoir nude is art, she says, and *Hustler* is trash.[1] "Any reasonable person" knows that.

But what about something between art and trash—something, say, 8 along the lines of *Playboy* or *Penthouse* magazines? I asked five women for

---

[1][Auguste Renoir (1841–1919) was a French impressionist painter who painted female nudes in such masterpieces as the *Baigneuses,* or "Women Bathing."]

their reactions to one picture in *Penthouse* and got responses that ranged from "lovely" and "sensuous" to "revolting" and "demeaning." Feminists, like everyone else, seldom have rational reasons for their preferences in erotica. Like members of juries, they tend to disagree when confronted with something that falls short of 100 percent vulgarity.

In any case, feminists will not be the arbiters of good taste if it 9 becomes easier to harass, prosecute and convict people on obscenity charges. Most of the people who want to censor girlie magazines are equally opposed to open discussion of issues that are of vital concern to women: rape, abortion, menstruation, contraception, lesbianism—in fact, the entire range of sexual experience from a woman's viewpoint.

Feminist writers and editors and film makers have limited financial 10 resources: Confronted by a determined prosecutor, Hugh Hefner will fare better than Susan Brownmiller. Would the Memphis jurors who convicted Harry Reems for his role in *Deep Throat* be inclined to take a more positive view of paintings of the female genitalia done by sensitive feminist artists? *Ms.* magazine has printed color reproductions of some of those art works; *Ms.* is already banned from a number of high school libraries because someone considers it threatening and/or obscene.

Feminists who want to censor what they regard as harmful pornogra- 11 phy have essentially the same motivation as other would-be censors: They want to use the power of the state to accomplish what they have been unable to achieve in the marketplace of ideas and images. The impulse to censor places no faith in the possibilities of democratic persuasion.

It isn't easy to persuade certain men that they have better uses for 12 $1.95 each month than to spend it on a copy of *Hustler*? Well, then, give the men no choice in the matter.

I believe there is also a connection between the impulse toward 13 censorship on the part of people who used to consider themselves civil libertarians and a more general desire to shift responsibility from individuals to institutions. When I saw the movie *Looking for Mr. Goodbar*, I was stunned by its series of visual images equating sex and violence, coupled with what seems to me the mindless message (a distortion of the fine Judith Rossner novel) that casual sex equals death. When I came out of the movie, I was even more shocked to see parents standing in line with children between the ages of 10 and 14.

I simply don't know why a parent would take a child to see such a 14 movie, any more than I understand why people feel they can't turn off a television set their child is watching. Whenever I say that, my friends tell me I don't know how it is because I don't have children. True, but I do have parents. When I was a child, they did turn off the TV. They didn't expect the Federal Communications Commission to do their job for them.

I am a First Amendment junkie. You can't OD on the First Amendment, 15 because free speech is its own best antidote.

Using the Dictionary

Check the following as necessary: 1. *metamorphosis* (1)   2. *unabashed* (1)   3. *implicit* (3)   4. *repulsive* (3)   5. *odious* (4)   6. *sensuous* (8)   7. *demeaning* (8)   8. *erotica* (8)   9. *arbiter* (9)   10. *antidote* (15)

The Writer's Agenda

The author sets out to register and defend her disagreement with a point of view that currently has strong and articulate advocates. Answer the following questions:

1. How does Jacoby raise the issue? What is the central disagreement that she outlines in her introduction?

2. Where does she take her stand? Where and how does she state her thesis?

3. In the early paragraphs, how does she attack the opposing view and bolster her own?

4. How does the author handle such test cases as kiddie porn, sex and violence, and nudity in the arts?

5. What is the key to Jacoby's definition of censorship in the last third of her essay? What is her alternative?

6. How does Jacoby's conclusion circle back to the beginning?

For Discussion or Writing

7. To you, is the control over pornography advocated by women's groups "censorship"? Why or why not?

8. How convincing is Jacoby's alternative to censorship? Do you think many women would agree with her? (What kind of readers would make an ideal audience for her?)

9. When, if ever, is censorship justified? Where does freedom of speech end—where do you draw the line? You may want to focus on a test case or several related ones.

10. Take a stand on an issue that you consider of "vital concern to women." Choose one of those Jacoby lists or another that she does not include. Spell out and support your position on the issue as fully as you can.

Branching Out

11. A partial list of books most frequently attacked when used in the schools would include John Steinbeck's *Grapes of Wrath*, George Orwell's *1984*, William Golding's *Lord of the Flies*, Aldous Huxley's *Brave New World*, J. D. Salinger's *The Catcher in the Rye*, Mark Twain's *The Adventures of Huckleberry Finn*, Pearl Buck's

The Good Earth. Take a stand for or against censorship of reading materials for high school students. Use one or more books frequently attacked, discussing them as test cases.

WRITERS ON WRITING
Susan Jacoby on Point of View

QUESTION: You were presenting an opinion that you knew would be unpopular with a group—feminists—with whom you yourself identify. How did this situation affect your writing?

ANSWER: The piece was written for a column in *The New York Times*, so it was for a general audience. But I was particularly interested in writing about the question of censorship from the standpoint of a feminist. I think it's important to see the difference between opinion and point of view. The absolute substance of this essay is to reconcile feminism and civil libertarianism when pornography is degrading to women—that is the point of view of this article. I might write an opinion on censorship in a million ways—but that was my point of view for this article.

In any piece on a controversial subject, you have to identify your point of view—who you are. How it will be read depends very much on who you are. I would go so far as to say that any piece on a controversial subject that doesn't identify the politics of the author is doomed to failure. What axe you have to grind is very important—and it has to be taken into account as you structure your argument. Think of the Sojourner Truth statement, "I laid the bricks and ain't I a woman?" If she had been a man—so what, it wouldn't be unusual!

QUESTION: Did you set out to change people's minds with this piece?

ANSWER: No, I doubt that an argument on a controversial subject changes anyone's mind. It might change one person's mind . . . but you do a piece like this to put an intelligent viewpoint out there. . . . Writing on a controversial subject comes out of an internal need to say something—to say it intelligently—and not out of any expectation that you are going to make people agree with you by what you are writing.

QUESTION: You seem to anticipate counterarguments as you write (e.g., kiddie porn, subjectivity of "art"). Did you structure your argument by these counterpoints?

ANSWER: Yes. I think any time you're writing about a controversial subject, counterarguments structure your argument. If they don't, you leave a hole big enough for a truck to drive through. In this piece I wanted to write about the topic from the standpoint of a feminist; therefore, I was particularly interested in the objections a feminist audience might raise.

When you're doing an expository piece of writing like this one, you can't just ignore the objections that feminists raise to pornography. That is not to say that you can overcome these points of view—but you don't want to ignore them. You don't have to answer every objection you can imagine, but you have to be aware of them. When you write about anything that is politically or socially controversial, you have to account for the contradictory viewpoints.

Part of the process of writing is learning how to think about your argument in other people's terms. Making a logical argument means understanding logic and building a case, block by block. That process includes understanding other points of view besides the one you're taking in your argument.

—From an interview with the editors of *Essay 2*

BACKGROUND; Charles McCabe (1915–1983) was for many years a columnist for the *San Francisco Chronicle*. Like other newspaper columnists, he was a writer with strong opinons; and like such columnists as Jimmy Breslin in New York and Mike Royko in Chicago, he had a large, loyal local following. McCabe worked as a journalist in New York and for United Press in Washington, D.C., before going West. He often wrote about his Irish heritage and watched the passing scene with wry humor. Wrongheaded or crotchety at times, he was suspicious of politicians and intolerant of humbug. Many of his columns illustrate well what sets much writing in motion: We observe or read something that triggers a response. We feel the need to go on record with our own opinion. We feel the need to protest against a misguided attitude, to correct a misunderstanding, or to set the record straight. Often our purpose, as it was McCabe's in the following column, is to *talk back*.

Charles McCabe

Muggers and Morals

GUIDE TO READING: How does McCabe raise the issue? Where does he let us know his own opinion? How does he support it? Pay special attention to how the author uses *quoted material* to bring the issue into focus and to support his own point of view.

It was, Suzanne Geller wrote to the *New York Times* on July 1, 1981, 1 "one of those clear, comfortable days when it feels like the most exciting city street in the world on which to walk. I was stunned by what is frequently called 'an incident'—a very sad incident."

She was crossing south on 51st Street and heard a lot of shouting. She 2 turned and saw two men fighting in the middle of the crosswalk. She was watching a mugging in progress. Several pedestrians "came to the rescue of the victim of a robbery attempt and forced the perpetrator to the ground.

"My respect for the responsible citizens was short-lived, as the would- 3 be robber was held down, he was kicked, punched, stomped, and beaten. I watched in horror and heard myself scream, 'Stop beating him, stop!' Against the noise of the traffic and the ever-increasing mob, this was no more than a whisper. The attack was brief, and when the wounded man was pulled to his feet, the observers clapped and cheered.

"The hatred and anger and violence of the well-groomed 'responsible' 4 citizens was more frightening than the attempted robbery. To observe the display of uncontrolled animal-like behavior of the attaché-case carriers and the support of the crowd left me feeling sick and ashamed."

Why the *Times* ran this letter is beyond me. Its effect, if not its 5 intention, was inflammatory. To express more sympathy for a mugger than

the people who prevented what Geller admitted was an "attempted robbery" is surely something new, even in New York on the corner of 51st and
Fifth. Hysterical protests frequently reach New York city desks, but their
publication is rather more the business of the afternoon *Post*, which special-
izes in sensationalism.

A week later the *Times* published three letters protesting Geller's ₆
peculiar views. One was from an eyewitness to the incident, Edgar Tafel. "A
man in sneakers was darting between cars from the north side of the street
to the south side.

"Yes, two men dropped their attaché cases and grabbed the 'perpetra- ₇
tor' who was holding a gold chain. He tried to free himself, called his captors
filthy names, tried to strike them. They responded with their fists.

"Two traffic officers went over to help, soon joined by a police officer. ₈
All the time the captured man tried to break loose. It was then that I heard ...
a female voice: 'Don't hurt him! Don't hit him!' The other onlookers applauded the two men, who had by then returned the gold chain to the
woman who had been attacked."

Tafel concluded: "I think Suzanne Geller should have withheld her ₉
tongue and pen."

Another correspondent, David M. Kaplan, wrote: "... The overzealous- ₁₀
ness of the passersby in this incident, which Miss Geller found alarming, is
far preferable to the old stereotype of New Yorkers' unwillingness to
become involved in such incidents."

A third writer, Fred Jacobs, said, "... what is 'sad' about this incident? ₁₁
Far sadder it would have been if nobody had done anything.

"And what is wrong with giving a little roughing up (she herself says ₁₂
the attack was 'brief') to a crook when he is caught red-handed? It's the only
semblance of justice he will ever face. For the bad know that in New York, if
they are punished with any severity—if they are punished at all—they are
the exception, not the rule.

"... In fact, I kind of hope to find myself soon in a 'well-groomed mob' ₁₃
like the one Miss Geller saw. Should I witness the original incident, why, I'd
like to get in a few kicks myself."

Using the Dictionary

Which of the following would you expect the average newspaper reader to know?
Which do you have to look up?   1. *perpetrator* (2)   2. *attaché case* (4)   3.
inflammatory (5)   4. *sensationalism* (5)   5. *captor* (7)   6. *overzealousness*
(10)   7. *stereotype* (10)   8. *severity* (12)

The Writer's Agenda

The purpose of many a newspaper column is to raise an issue, to present the author's
opinion, and to offer a minimum of support. Answer the following questions about
the column you have just read:

1. How does McCabe raise the issue? What key details are we given about the original incident? How fully do we come to understand the reaction of the letter writer that triggered McCabe's response?

2. Where does McCabe state his own opinion? (Is there a sentence that could serve as his thesis?)

3. How do the other letter writers McCabe quotes support his own point of view? What reasons do the authors offer for the stand they take? What justifications do they present for people who take "justice into their own hands"?

For Discussion or Writing

4. How do you react to this column? Would you have been a receptive reader or a good audience for this column when it first appeared? Why or why not?

5. Of the points of view expressed by the letter writers, which is closest to your own? Defend the position you support.

6. Are we witnessing a return to vigilantism? To judge from your own experience and observation, how ready are frustrated citizens to take the law into their own hands? Do you think their attitude is justified?

7. Has our society become too permissive? Has there been a breakdown of law and order? (Concentrate on one major area, one major cause, or one major remedy. Make your own view the central thesis of your paper, and support it with detailed arguments and examples.)

Branching Out

8. How do newspapers deal with street crime? What picture of street crime emerges from a study of several issues of a local newspaper? What label would fit the prevailing point of view adopted in the newspaper reports—sensationalism? objectivity? moral indignation?

9. Many people have lost faith in the ability of the police to control crime. Attitudes toward the police range from extremely hostile to very supportive. What is yours? (Support the stand you take with detailed examples or other supporting material.)

BACKGROUND: George Leonard has written widely, questioning traditional patterns of thought and promoting changes of attitude designed to help us develop our intellectual and spiritual resources. He was born in 1923 in Macon, Georgia, and graduated from the University of North Carolina in 1948. He went to New York and later to San Francisco to work as a senior editor for *Look* magazine, winning several awards from educational groups for his articles on American education. In 1968, in his book *Education and Ecstasy*, he joined other radical reformers in projecting alternatives to what they considered joyless and rigid patterns of traditional education. He published *The Ultimate Athlete* in 1975. The following essay is part of a longer article he wrote for the "Ultimate Fitness" section of the May 1985 issue of *Esquire* magazine.

George Leonard

Born to Run

GUIDE TO READING: In this essay, the author sets out to present and support an ambitious central thesis. What is it? Where and how does he present it? What kind of background does he provide? Where does he turn for support?

Running is one of the primal human acts, and the particular human form it takes, using a bipedal stride in a fully upright stance, has played an essential part in shaping our destiny. It was once believed that our hominid ancestors were rather pitiable creatures compared with the other animals of the jungles and savannas; lacking the fangs, claws, and specialized physical abilities of the predators, the hominids supposedly prevailed only because of their large brains and their ability to use tools. But there is now compelling evidence that our direct ancestors of some four million years ago had relatively small brains, only about a third the size of ours. What these hominids *did* have was a fully upright stance with the modern, doubly curved spine that enters the skull at the bottom rather than the back (as is the case with the apes). The upright stance increased the field of vision and freed the forelimbs for use in inspecting and manipulating objects, thus challenging the brain to increase its capacity through the process of natural selection. We can't specify the athletic ability of our four-million-year-old ancestors, but it was sufficient for the survival of the line, even without tools and high intelligence.

Much has been made of the blazing sprint speed of the cheetah, the prodigious high jumps of the kangaroo, the underwater skills of the dolphin, and the gymnastic prowess of the chimpanzee. But no animal can match the human animal in all-around athletic ability. If we were to hold a mammal decathlon with events in sprinting, endurance running, long jumping, high jumping, swimming, deep diving, gymnastics, striking, kicking, and burrowing, other animals would win most of the individual events. But a well-trained human would come up with the best overall score. And in one event—endurance running—the human would outperform all other animals of comparable size, as well as some quite a bit larger.

It is the extraordinary human capacity to run long and hard, even in ₃ the heat of day, that might well have made early man a formidable predator. In an article in a recent *Current Anthropology*, zoologist David Carrier of the University of Michigan points out that surviving primitive people, in pursuits lasting up to two days, have outrun many kinds of animals known for their great speed. "Bushmen are reported to run down duiker, steenbok, and gemsbok during the rainy season, and wildebeest and zebra during the hot dry season. Tarahumara Indians chase deer through the mountains of northern Mexico until the animals collapse from exhaustion, and then throttle them by hand. Paiutes and Navajo of the American Southwest are reported to have hunted pronghorn antelope (one of the fastest of all mammals) with this same technique. Furthermore, aborigines of northwestern Australia are known to hunt kangaroo successfully in this way." (In the April 3, 1978, issue of *Sports Illustrated*, an Ashland, Oregon, runner named Michael Baughman described running down a deer. It turned out to be a surprisingly easy task. Even when the young buck stood trembling with its head hung low, so exhausted that its human pursuer could walk up and touch its flank, Baughman still felt "refreshed enough to be able to run for another half hour.")

This human dominance over animals known for their specialized ₄ running skills is even stranger than it might seem, for human running is not only relatively slow but also inefficient. Carrier notes that the energy cost of running (oxygen consumption per unit of body weight per unit of distance traveled) is about twice as high for humans as for most other mammals. This being the case, it would seem that a man wouldn't have a chance against a deer, but there are other factors that outweigh our energy inefficiency. Perhaps the most important is the human ability to dissipate the body heat built up during strenuous exertion. We possess the most efficient sweat glands in the animal kingdom; no other species sweats so copiously. Our evaporative cooling system works even better because of our unique nakedness, which may have evolved to make it possible for us to run long distances on hot days. Even the copious hair that remains on our heads serves this purpose, providing a shield for the head and shoulders when the sun is highest and its rays most destructive.

One thing is sure: when any animal reaches a certain core tempera- ₅ ture, it can no longer run. At a blazing sixty-two miles an hour, the cheetah generates heat at a rate sixty times greater than while at rest. Overheating is what brings this swift animal to a halt; when its body temperature reaches 105, generally in less than three quarters of a mile, it simply stops. In a long chase, the first animal to overheat loses.

Our breathing system is also superior. In four-legged animals, brea- 6
thing is tied into the motion and impact of the front feet and the bending
motion of the body. Whether the animal is walking, trotting, or galloping,
only one breath is possible for each locomotive cycle, which limits it to
certain optimum speeds for each gait. Our upright stance, however, allows
us to run with the same efficiency no matter what the speed: we spontaneously choose the breathing pattern (two strides per breath, three
strides per breath, and so on) that is the most efficient for the speed. A
marathoner, for instance, expends the same amount of energy whether he
or she runs the distance in four hours or two and a half hours.

Even our large adrenal and thyroid glands predispose us toward 7
running; they tend to increase the levels of those hormones that help the
muscles use fatty acids and glucose efficiently. And our omnivorous diet
itself, especially our capacity to load up on carbohydrates, gives us an edge
over carnivores and most other animals in long-distance running.

All of this adds up to one simple fact: we are born to run, especially to 8
run great distances. Some observers, bemused by the runners who have
overflowed from tracks and trails to city sidewalks and streets, argue that
running is only a fad or even an addiction, a form of narcissim. But to
call running a fad makes as much sense as to call thinking a fad. Endurance running is an essential human activity that preceded abstract thought
and indeed helped make it possible.

The recent debates on the value of running generally involve immedi- 9
ate, practical matters: Does it help you lose weight? Is it good for your heart?
Will it help you live longer? These are important questions, but they obscure
the underlying motivation. People might start running for any number of
practical or self-serving reasons, but those who persist experience something that entirely transcends the debate, something deeply satisfying in and
of itself: a reconnection with the roots of our race, a reaffirmation of an
ancient and noble pursuit.

Though we no longer run for food and survival, the importance of this 10
activity is still evident in the sports we most enjoy watching. Football,
basketball, baseball, and soccer, it might be said, are complicated excuses
for running. Tennis and other racket, net, and wall games involve a series of
short, dancing sprints. Pole vaulting, javelin throwing, high jumping, long
jumping, and triple jumping begin with and depend upon running. Rugby,
cricket, field hockey, team handball, hurdles, steeplechase, various forms of
tag, hide-and-seek, and capture-the-flag—all are runners' games.

At the very least, running can give you all the aerobic conditioning you 11
need, with a minimum of specialized training or expenditure of time and
equipment. For those with busy schedules, in fact, running's time demands
are so modest as to make it almost irresistible. Walking might well be the
safest and surest way to aerobic health, but it takes about three hours of
brisk walking to give you the benefits of a one-hour run. In his book
Running Without Fear, Dr. Kenneth Cooper, creator of the aerobics con-

cept and one of the pioneers of the fitness movement, recommends a minimum running distance of two miles three times a week at an eight-to-ten-minute-a-mile pace, and a maximum of three miles five times a week at the same pace. That adds up to forty-eight minutes to an hour a week at the least, and two hours to two and a half hours at the most. Anything more than that, according to Cooper, adds little or nothing in the way of health benefits.

Cooper is among those who warn against the myth that running gives 12 certain protection against heart disease (though every large-scale study has shown that vigorous exercise gives considerable protection). He also argues strongly for coronary stress-testing prior to starting any strenuous exercise program. Other experts, notably runner George Sheehan, himself a cardiologist, question the accuracy of and need for stress-testing. "If you listen to your body," Sheehan says, "running is perfectly safe. No horse ever ran itself to death without a jockey on its back. If there's any disagreement between a machine and your body, listen to your body."

By and large, however, running experts have made a turn toward 13 caution and moderation since the death of running guru Jim Fixx last summer. Joe Henderson, one of the most authoritative writers on the subject, sums it up in the December 1984 *Runner's World*: "Runners are more realistic in their thinking about what running can do for them. They take fewer risks in their approach to training and racing. They plan less for short-term success and more for long-term health and happiness."

All of this is to the good. Runners and would-be runners should be 14 offered safe and sensible programs and warned against the dangers and pitfalls of their practice. And those who wish to run for specific, practical benefits—weight control, stress reduction, a healthier heart—must be given their due. But to limit the dialogue to these practical considerations is to demean the human spirit. Many people run not to lose weight but to loosen the chains of a mechanized culture, not to postpone death but to savor life. For these runners, the admonitions of the exercise critics are moot; they run quite consciously, as informed, consenting adults, to exceed their previous limits and to press the edges of the possible, whether this means completing their first circuit of a four-hundred-meter track without walking, or fighting for victory in a triathlon, as in this episode recounted in a recent issue of *American Medical News*:

> Few moments in sports history have so poignantly captured the agony of 15 defeat as when twenty-three-year-old Julie Moss was leading the women's division of the twenty-six-mile marathon of Hawaii's Ironman Triathlon World Championship.
>
> With only one hundred yards left between her and the finish, Moss fell to 16 her knees. She then rose, ran a few more yards, and collapsed again. As TV cameras rolled, she lost control of her bodily functions. She got up again, ran, fell, and then started crawling. Passed by the second-place runner, she crawled across the finish line, stretched out her arm, and passed out.

Jim McKay of ABC Sports called it "heroic . . . one of the greatest moments [17] in the history of televised sport." Gilbert Lang, M.D., an orthopedic surgeon at Roseville (California) Community Hospital and a longtime endurance runner, calls it "stupid—very nearly fatal."

Both Lang and McKay are right: it was stupid and it was heroic. Surely [18] no runner should be encouraged to go so near the edge of death. But what kind of world would it be, how meager and pale, without such heroics? Perhaps there would be no human world at all, for there must have been countless times before the dawn of history when primitive hunters in pursuit of prey gave all of themselves in this way so that members of their bands, our distant ancestors, could live. Athletes such as Julie Moss run for all of us, reaffirming our humanity, our very existence.

Using the Dictionary

A. How does your dictionary help you with the meaning of the following words by "going to the roots" (mostly Latin, in a few cases Greek)?   1. *primal* (1)   2. *bipedal* (1)   3. *hominid* (1)   4. *predator* (1)   5. *prodigious* (2)   6. *decathlon* (2)   7. *aborigines* (3)   8. *dominance* (4)   9. *copious* (4)   10. *locomotive* (6)   11. *carnivore* (7)   12. *narcissism* (8)   13. *transcend* (9)   14. *cardiologist* (12)   15. *triathlon* (14)
B. What technical terms (*adrenal, thyroid, glucose*) need explanation for the general reader?

The Writer's Agenda

Leonard is known as a writer who forcefully and articulately presents strong personal views. Answer the following questions about how he presents his views on running in this essay.

1. What is Leonard's central *thesis*? Where does he state it? Where and how does he restate or reinforce it?

2. What point of view does the author adopt in his introductory discussion of the role of humans in the animal kingdom? What is his main point, or what are his main points?

3. What point of view does the author adopt in his discussion of the practical or physical benefits of running?

4. Throughout the essay, Leonard brings in numerous related *examples* to support his points; he makes ample use of specifics to illustrate his general points. What passages or parts of the essay make especially striking use of examples?

5. What use does Leonard make of *quoted authorities* to support his points? Which quoted or paraphrased materials are for you most striking or informative?

6. What does the final incident prove? (Do you agree that "it was stupid and it was heroic"?)

For Writing or Discussion

7. Does the reader of this essay have to be a convert or fanatic? Does Leonard go overboard as an advocate of the sport he promotes?

8. Leonard says, "To call running a fad makes as much sense as to call thinking a fad." Do you agree or disagree?

9. According to Leonard, many people run "to loosen the chains of a mechanized culture." What does he mean? Is something similar true of the sport or sports you know best?

10. Is there for you some kind (or kinds) of sport or exercise that is (or are) clearly superior to others? Present and support your choice.

11. Discuss or defend a current trend that to you is more than a fad. (Or show that a current trend taken seriously by many people is indeed a passing fad.)

Branching Out

12. Describe and discuss a trend—in fashion, entertainment, architecture, or sports—that shows something important about American society.

BACKGROUND: Margaret Mead (1901–78) became famous as a young anthropologist who went to Samoa in 1925 to live with the islanders and study their way of life. The book she wrote about her experiences, *Coming of Age in Samoa*, became one of the most widely read books in the history of anthropology. It was still the subject of scholarly debate fifty-five years after its publication in 1928. Mead grew up in New Jersey and Pennsylvania, moving frequently as required by the studies or teaching assignments of her parents. After studying at Columbia University, she ignored the advice of a famous fellow anthropologist and linguist to stay home and have children. Instead, she went on to years of field work studying the patterns of growing up of adolescent girls in cultures relatively untouched by Western civilization; she published a succession of widely read books ranging from *Growing Up in New Guinea* (1930) to *Male and Female* (1949). In the final years of her career, Mead wrote to provide young people with guidance through the challenges and confusions of our time.

Margaret Mead

We Need Taboos on
Sex at Work

GUIDE TO READING: In the essay that follows, the author identifies the central problem and discusses a familiar suggested solution. She then presents her own solution, stating a strong personal point of view. What is the problem, and how and where does she identify it? What are the possible solutions, and how are they different? What historical background does the author present to help us understand the issue? What does she do to help convince us?

What should we—what can we—do about sexual harassment on the job?

During the century since the first "type writer"—that is, the first young woman clerk who had mastered the operation of the mechanical writing machine—entered a business office and initiated a whole new female-male work relationship, women have had to struggle with the problem of sexual harassment at work. And we still are at a loss as to how to cope with it successfully.

Certainly no one of us—young or old, single or married, attractive or homely, naive or socially skilled—has escaped entirely unscathed. True, actual sexual assaults—rape and seduction—have been less common in almost any work situation than fathers and brothers once feared and predicted. But who among us hasn't met the male kiss-and-tell office flirt, the pinching prankster, the man in search of party girls, or the man who makes sex a condition for job promotion? Who has not known the man who thinks no task is too tedious, unpleasant, or demeaning for his "girl" to do in or out of office hours, the gossipmonger and—perhaps most dangerous— the apparently friendly man who subtly undercuts every direction given by a woman, depreciates every plan she offers, and devalues her every accomplishment? Some women get discouraged and give up; most women learn to be wary. But as long as so many men use sex in so many ways as a weapon to keep down the women with whom they work, how can we develop mature, give-and-take working relationships?

As I see it, it isn't more laws that we need now, but new taboos.   4

Not every woman—and certainly not every man—realizes and ac- 5 knowledges that the mid-1960s marked a watershed in the *legal* treatment of women in the working world. Beginning with the Equal Pay Act of 1963 and the Civil Rights Acts of 1964 (especially Title VII), legislation has been passed, executive orders have been issued, official guidelines have been established and decisions in a great many court cases have set forth a woman's right to be a first-class working citizen. Slowly but surely, using the new laws, women are making progress in their fight to gain what the law now so clearly defines as the right of every working person. And today almost half of all adult women are working persons.

But there are serious discrepancies. At home and at school we still 6 bring up boys to respond to the presence of women in outmoded ways—to become men who cannot be trusted alone with a woman, who are angry and frustrated by having to treat a woman as an equal—either as a female with power who must be cajoled or as a female without power who can be coerced. But at the same time we are teaching our daughters to expect a very different working world, one in which both women and men are full participants.

In keeping with this goal, we are insistent that the rights women have 7 gained must be spelled out and that women use every legal device to ensure that new rules are formulated and translated into practice. Why, then, do I think that the new laws will not be sufficient to protect women—and men too, for that matter—from the problems of sexual harassment on the job? Why do I think we need new taboos?

I realize that this must sound strange to a generation of young women 8 who have felt the need to break and abandon taboos of many kinds—from taboo against the inappropriate use of four-letter words to taboos against petty pilfering; from taboos against the use of addictive drugs to taboos against the public display of the naked human body; from the taboo against the frank enjoyment of sex to the taboos against full sexual honesty.

In some circles it has even become fashionable to call incest taboos— 9 the taboos against sex with close family members other than husband and wife—out of date and unimportant. Yet incest taboos remain a vital part of any society. They insure that most children can grow up safe in the household, learn to trust, to be loved and to be sexually safe, unexploited and unmolested within the family.

When we examine how any society works, it becomes clear that it is 10 precisely the basic taboos—the deeply and intensely felt prohibitions against "unthinkable" behavior—that keep the social system in balance. Laws are an expression of principles concerning things we can and do think about, and they can be changed as our perception of the world changes. But a taboo, even against taking a human life, may or may not be formulated in legal terms in some societies; the taboo lies much deeper in our consciousness, and by prohibiting certain forms of behavior also affirms what we hold most precious in our human relationships. Taboos break down in periods of profound change and are re-created in new forms during periods of transition.

We are in such a period now. And like the family, the modern business 11 and the modern profession must develop incest taboos. If women are to work on an equal basis with men, with men supervising women in some cases and women supervising men in others, we have to develop decent sex mores in the whole working world.

In the past, when women entered the working world as factory work- 12 ers or clerks in shops, as typists or chorus girls, they entered at the bottom; their poverty and their need for the job were part of their helplessness. Like women in domestic service, they were very vulnerable to sexual advances and seduction by men in positions of power over them. But sex also presented a precarious ladder by which a girl just might climb to become the pampered mistress or even the wife of the boss, the producer, the important politician.

For a long time after women began to work away from home, people 13 made a sharp distinction between women who virtuously lived at home and limited "work" to voluntary efforts and other women who, lacking the support and protection of a father, brother, husband, or son, were constrained to work for money. Wage-earning women were sexually vulnerable, and it was generally believed that the woman who was raped probably deserved it and that the woman who was seduced probably had tempted the man. By leaving home, a woman did not merely move beyond the range of the laws that protected her there, but beyond the areas of living made safe by the force of taboos.

In the primitive societies in which I worked and lived as a young 14 woman and as an older one, women who obeyed the accepted rules of behavior were not molested. But a woman who broke the rules—went out in the bush at night, worked alone in a distant garden or followed a lonely path without even a child companion—was asking for trouble. In general, women and men knew what was expected of them—until their lives were shaken up by change through the coming of strangers and the introduction of new kinds of work and new expectations. Then, along with other sorts of confusion, there was confusion about the sex relations of men and women. Cases of sex molestation, attack, and rape reflected the breakdown of traditional security.

Everywhere and at all times, societies have developed ways of styliz- 15 ing relations between women and men. Though the rules might be cruel and exploitative, they defined with clarity the posture and gait, the costume and the conversation, that signaled a woman's compliance with the rules as well as the circumstances in which a woman defined herself as a whore. In our own society, when women first became nurses their costume, reminiscent of the dress of nuns, at once announced the virtue of their calling. When a young American woman went away from home to teach children in one of the thousands of one-room schoolhouses that abounded in the countryside, the local community took charge of her virtue. Sometimes the rules were broken—on purpose. But the rules that protected men as well as women were known and agreed upon.

Today, with our huge and restless mobility from country to city, from 16 one city to another, from class to class and from one country to another, most of the subtle ways in which women and men related to each other in a more limited setting have broken down. And now a new element has entered into their working relations with the demands that women must be employed in unfamiliar occupations and at higher executive and profes- sional levels. Almost without warning, and certainly without considering the necessity for working out new forms of acceptable behavior, men and women are confronting each other as colleagues with equal rights.

And suddenly there is an outburst of complaints from women who find 17 themselves mistreated in ways to which they are quite unaccustomed, as well as complaints from women who have suddenly discovered that sexual harassment on the job no longer is part of the expected life of a working woman. By banding together, organizing themselves and counseling one another, women are beginning to feel their strength and are making them- selves heard, loud and clear, on the job, in the media and in the courts. Harassment on the job and wife beating at home have become part of our public consciousness.

Now, how to deal with the problems, the social discord and disso- 18 nance, in the relations between women and men? The complaints, the legal remedies and the support institutions developed by women all are part of the response to the new conception of women's rights. But I believe we need something much more pervasive, a climate of opinion that includes men as well as women, and that will affect not only adult relations and behavior on the job but also the expectations about the adult world that guide our children's progress into that world.

What we need, in fact, are new taboos that are appropriate to the new 19 society we are struggling to create—taboos that will operate within the work setting as once they operated within the household. Neither men nor women should expect that sex can be used either to victimize women who need to keep their jobs or to keep women from advancement or to help men advance their own careers. A taboo enjoins. We need one that says clearly and unequivocally, "You don't make passes at or sleep with the people you work with."

This means that girls and boys will have to grow up together expecting 20 and respecting a continuous relationship, in season and out, alone together or in a mixed group, that can withstand tension and relaxation, stimulation and frustration, frankness and reserve, without breaking down. It will have something of the relationship of brothers and sisters who have grown up together safely within a household, but it also will be different. For where brother and sister have a lifelong relationship, women and men who work together may share many years or only a few weeks or days or even hours.

In the way in which societies do develop new ways of meeting new 21 problems, I believe we are beginning to develop new ways of working together that carry with them appropriate taboos—new ways that allow women and men to work together effortlessly and to respect each other as persons.

The beginning was made not at work but in our insistence on coeduca- 22 tion in the earliest grades of school, and gradually at all levels. This has made it possible for women to have much greater freedom wherever they go—so much so that we take it almost wholly for granted. We know it is not always wholehearted, but it is a beginning we know well.

And now, in line with new attitudes toward sex and equality, many 23 students have demanded, and obtained, coeducational dormitories. Their elders mistook this as a demand for freer sexual access; but student advocates said firmly that, as young men and women, they wanted to meet under more natural circumstances and get to know one another as friends.

Today, wherever there is coeducation with a fairly even ratio between 24 the sexes and several years' experience of living in coeducational dormitories, a quiet taboo is developing without the support of formal rules and regulations, fines or public exposure, praise or censure—a taboo against serious dating within the dormitory. Young women and young men who later will have to work side by side, in superordinate and subordinate relations as well as equals and members of a team, are finding their way toward a kind of harmony in which exploitative sex is set aside in favor of mutual concern, shared interests and, it seems to me, a new sense of friendship.

This is just a beginning, and one that is far from perfect. But one of the 25 very good things is that women are discovering they can be frank and outspoken without being shrill, just as men are discovering there are pleasures in friendships without domination.

It is just a beginning, but students can set a style that will carry over 26 into working relations in which skill, ability, and experience are the criteria by which persons are judged, and appreciation of a woman or a man as a whole person will deeply modify the exploitation and the anguish of sexual inequality. Laws and formal regulations and the protection given by the courts are necessary to establish and maintain institutional arrangements. But the commitment and acceptance that are implied by taboos are critical in the formation and protection of the most meaningful human relations.

Using the Dictionary

Look up the following words, paying attention to special uses and connotations.   1. How are the words *unscathed* (3) and *scathing* related?   2. Where does the word *taboo* (4) come from, and what are its usual connotations?   3. What are the negative connotations or unfavorable associations of *demeaning* (3), *cajole* (6), and *coerce* (6)?   4. How is the word *mores* (11) related to *moral* and *morality*?   5. Where or how is the word *stylize* (15) usually employed?   6. What does *virtue* (15) mean in Mead's references to teachers and nurses? (What are other meanings of the word?)   7. What are the literal or original meanings of *discord* (18) and *dissonance* (18)?   8. Does your dictionary cover the figurative meanings of the italicized words in "legal *remedies*" (18) and "*climate* of opinion" (18)?   9. What does your dictionary tell you about *equivocal* (19)?   10. What is the difference between *pain* and *anguish* (26)?

The Writer's Agenda

In this selection, the writer first identifies the problem. She then looks at one possible solution that is not the whole answer. She then presents the other solution that is the heart of her message. Trace the way she presents and supports her strong personal point of view.

1. The author starts with a key question. The answer is summed up in a central *thesis* that becomes a program or preview for the rest of the essay. Restate the key question in your own words. Where is it echoed and expanded in the introductory paragraphs? Point out the thesis sentence and the introductory phrase that signals its appearance.

2. In her *introduction*, the author briefly but pointedly tells us what she means by her key term. Discuss her examples. (Which are most telling or convincing?) Sum up her definition and use of the term *sexual harassment*.

3. The author starts with the more familiar or predictable of the two possible solutions to the central problem. What is that solution? What, according to Mead, are the obstacles in its path?

4. Where does Mead start discussing her own alternative to reliance on legal answers? Why does she think that for many young women the notion of new "taboos" may be difficult to accept? (How does her mentioning of the "incest taboo" become relevant to the main trend of the argument?)

5. What were important results of women's entry into the "working world"? How does the author's observation of rules or taboos in primitive societies help her

explain our own past? How does she use women who worked as nurses and teachers as examples?

6. In several paragraphs that start the final third of the essay, the author *restates and expands* her central point about the need for new taboos in our modern world. (Point out several **transitional expressions** that signal the author's return from the past to the present.) What does she add here to our understanding of what taboos are and how they work?

7. The final two or three paragraphs spell out the author's basic goals in strongly idealistic or inspirational terms. Point out phrases that seem especially important or eloquent to you.

For Discussion or Writing

8. What parts of Mead's essay can you relate to your own observation or experience? Where have you observed the older patterns or traditional sex roles that she describes? Where have you seen evidence of the changes or transitional patterns she traces?

9. What in this essay is the **tone** and implied attitude toward men? Is it hostile or conciliatory, harsh or understanding? Provide evidence from the essay.

10. Do you think women and men would react differently to this essay? How or why?

11. Many people feel that private personal relations are people's own business and should not be the concern of employers or institutions. Do you agree?

12. In working toward a better future, some people put their faith in better laws. Other people put their faith in changes in people's attitudes. To you, which of the two choices seems more promising or more important? Explain and support your choice.

Branching Out

13. How much progress has there been toward equality of the sexes? Choose one major area: school, work, or home. Sum up your answer as the thesis early in your paper. Provide detailed examples to support your thesis.

STUDENT MODEL 3

First Draft and Revision

FOR READING: Compare the rough *first draft* of this paper with the *final revised draft* that is reprinted after it. What changes did the author make during her revision? Did she change her strategy or overall plan? What material did she add? What material did she omit? What changes did she make in wording or style—are they improvements? Consider the following questions as you study the final draft as a possible model for writing of your own:

1. (PURPOSE) What was the writer trying to do?
2. (AUDIENCE) What kind of reader would make a good reader for this selection?
3. (SOURCES) Where did the writer turn for material?
4. (THESIS) Does the selection have a central idea or unifying thesis?
5. (STRUCTURE) What is the author's overall plan or strategy?
6. (STYLE) What makes the piece effective or memorable (for instance, striking details, memorable phrases)?

Maureen Barney

Finding "Home Sweet Home"
(First Draft)

Mobility: The word has come to mean something that a hundred years ago was unimaginable. The basic move from one house to another because of family growth has become archaic. City-to-city, state-to-state, and even coast-to-coast moves are common occurrences. Are we losing something by this modern ability to relocate? I don't think so.

I grew up in a small town in Michigan; the population was 1000 people. The only Americans I knew were white middle-class farmers. Because I had friends out West and jobs were scarce in Michigan, I decided to move to Los Angeles. My parents and I jumped into the pickup and headed toward the airport. As I hugged my parents goodbye, I smelled the sweet hay scent of my father's clothes and I had to force myself to believe that I had made the right decision.

No amount of college or years of experience could have taught me how diversified and intricate America is as my move across the country. I had never met Filipinos, Mexicans, or Japanese. In my hometown, there was one black family. The move gave me a chance to learn and to grow. I might never have eaten grits, bagels, or burritos!

We are no longer restricted to particular towns or states because we couldn't possibly fit our belongings, children, and pets into the covered wagon and forge our way to a more prosperous region. Our options are numerous. If being in a different area would allow us to have more desirable jobs, go to better schools, or enable us to live in an environment more suitable to us, we can do it.

When I was still in high school, an older friend's parents announced that they were moving to the East Coast. My friend was reluctant; she had planned to stay, raise a family, and farm like everybody else. But she finally sold her horse, threw away her overalls, and headed east. She is now one of the few from our town with a college degree and a successful job.

Another friend of mine had grown up in Los Angeles. He had always 6
dreamed of fishing, hiking, and raising children in a quiet, country atmosphere. He stayed in the city until he obtained his college degree and then
moved to a tiny town in Iowa where, as he puts it, "even the mayor is
unemployed." He is doing odd carpentry jobs to support his family and says
his life is happier than he could ever imagine it being.

The wonderful thing about America's mobility is that we can really 7
search out and find that location in which we are happiest. Of course, the
amount of moves, distances of those moves, and the decision of whether to
move or not has to be decided according to each family's individual traits.
Constant changes of school systems and short term friendships can be
distressing. I believe, though, in moderation, that changing homes is a very
healthy and revitalizing experience.

Maureen Barney

A Good Move
(Revised Final Draft)

Mobility: The word has come to mean something that a hundred years 1
ago was unimaginable. We no longer simply move from one house to
another as the family needs more room. Today, moves from city to city, from
state to state, or from coast to coast are common. Are we losing something
as a result of this ability to pack our possessions into a truck, wave goodbye
to our neighbors, and leave our "sweet home"? I don't think so. The wonderful thing about our modern ability to move is that we can search out and find
that location where we fit in or where we can be content.

I grew up in a small town in Michigan; the population was 1000 people. 2
The only Americans I knew were white middle-class farmers. Because I had
friends out West and jobs were scarce in Michigan, I decided to move to Los
Angeles at age eighteen. I carried a jar of pickled watermelon rind and some
homemade strawberry preserves in my suitcase. At the airport, as I hugged
my parents goodbye, I smelled the sweet hay scent of my father's flannel
shirt, and I had to force myself to believe that I had made the right decision.
However, no amount of college or years of experience could have taught me
as well how diversified America is as my move across the country. In my
hometown there was only one black family. I had never met Filipinos,
Mexicans, or Japanese. Today I work and go to school with people from
many different backgrounds.

No one today is any longer restricted to any particular town or state. 3
We no longer load our belongings, children, and pets into covered wagons to
forge ahead to a new territory. But our options are numerous. We can strike
out in search of better jobs, better schools, or a more suitable environment.
In the process, we learn to cope with change, meet new people, and
establish new friendships.

Several of my friends have gone through the experience of making the   4
right move. When I was still in high school, an older friend's parents
announced that they were moving to the East Coast. My friend was reluctant. She had planned to stay in her hometown, raise a family, and farm like
everyone else. But she finally sold her horse, threw away her overalls, and
headed east. She is now one of the few from our town with a college degree
and a different career.

Finding contentment does not always mean moving away from the   5
farm. Another friend of mine had grown up in Los Angeles but had always
dreamed of fishing, hiking, and raising children in a quiet country atmosphere. He drove to the city college every day, listening to country music in
his old truck, until he earned his degree. He then moved to a tiny town in
Iowa where, as he puts it, "even the mayor is unemployed." He is doing
carpentry jobs to help support his family and is happier than ever before.

A recent survey in *Better Homes and Gardens* found that four out of   6
five people, of all genders and ages, who had moved from one state to
another were originally reluctant when the decision was first made. Three
months after those moves, though, nearly all of them had positive feelings
about the move and thought it a change for the better. People from farming
towns in Michigan, steel towns in Pennsylvania, and fishing towns in Maine
are discovering that moving can be a healthy and revitalizing experience.

FOR WRITING: On ceremonial occasions like the bicentennial of the Declaration of
Independence or the centennial of the Statue of Liberty, articles and books proliferate that take stock of distinctive features of American life or the American experience. Write a *guest editorial* for a student newspaper on one such feature currently
of concern to students on your campus or to members of your generation of
students. Try to bring the issue clearly into focus. Take a stand. Provide striking or
convincing supporting material. (Your instructor may ask you to hand in a *first draft*
for peer editing or editorial comment before you prepare your revised final draft.)

Additional Writing Topics 3

Points of View

A. Some of the following statements may cause you to say "I don't really care."
Some of them, however, may cause you to say "I agree" or "I disagree" or "I agree up
to a point." Support, or take issue with, one such statement. (If you can, explore
some of the pros and cons in preliminary class discussion.)

1. Athletics interferes with education.

2. Boy Scouts are obsolete.

3. Divorce has been made too easy.

4. A good teacher is the best curriculum.

5. Teachers reward students who agree with them.

6. Pornography is a victimless crime.

7. Single people should be taxed more heavily to encourage them to get married.

8. Local governments should fund day-care centers to help working mothers.

9. Our culture condones violence against women.

10. English should be declared the national language of the country.

11. It's useless to try to save historic buildings that stand in the way of progress.

12. Subsidized opera, theater, ballet, and music serve the interests of a small elite.

13. Schools and government agencies should have hiring quotas for minorities.

14. What consenting adults do is their own business.

15. Colleges have no business officially recognizing fraternities and sororities.

16. School prayer or any other religious observance violates the separation of church and state.

17. Toy stores should not carry war toys or war games.

18. Women should support women candidates.

19. The best managers or supervisors are those who have worked their way up from the rank and file.

20. Communities should provide shelters for the homeless.

B. If you could ask a single test question of candidates for public office before you voted for them, what would it be? What is the issue or commitment closest to your heart? Explain and defend your choice.

PART

TWO

PATTERNS

FOR

WRITING

The central part of this book focuses on the central part of the writing process. As we move beyond the preliminary stage, the crucial question becomes: How does good writing take shape? The first task of a writer is to work up the material for a substantial piece of writing. The second task is to *organize* it. To explore the subject, to collect a rich fund of promising material, is only the necessary first step. How does the material add up? What general conclusions does it justify? In what order should they be presented to the reader? A crucial second stage in the process of writing a paper is to develop a workable overall plan. Every writer has to learn to do the kind of thinking that gives shape to miscellaneous materials. As you work on your papers, learn to sort out materials that may at first seem contradictory or confusing. Set up priorities. Decide what points to take up in what order.

A well-written paper has a plan that the reader can follow. The writer has sorted things out and laid them out in a pattern. One thing follows another in an order that makes sense. Develop your own ability to organize your writing by practicing some of the basic patterns that writers use over and over as they structure their material and lay it out for the reader: *process, comparison and contrast, classification, cause and effect.*

Effective writers know how to choose (or adapt) from among such familiar patterns of organization the one that will do justice to the topic at hand. They know how to choose the pattern that will serve their purpose. The selections in this part of the book will give you a chance to learn how experienced writers work out the right pattern for the task at hand.

The patterns you are going to study and practice will at first be fairly simple or predictable. They will become more complicated, and will call for more thinking about strategy, as you go along. When you trace a process, when you compare and contrast, when you classify (or sort things out into major kinds), you can often use or adapt fairly straightforward patterns that are relatively easy to outline. But the more complicated the subject, the more challenging the working out of an overall pattern will become. When you argue about causes and effects, or define an important term, or try to persuade a reluctant reader, you may be employing a combination of strategies. You may increasingly have to rely on your ability to work out the pattern that will do the job.

4

PROCESS

How It Works

One of the most basic and widely useful patterns of organization is the pattern we use when we trace a process. Every writer has to learn to follow a process or a sequence of events in time. A good writer knows how to mark off major stages in a chain of events and how to do justice to one major step at a time. A good writer knows how to do justice to the essential details needed to make a procedure work.

PURPOSE We use the process pattern to explain how something works or how it came to be. We can use it to give directions or instructions; a "how-to" paper might show readers how to bake their own bread, or how to grow their own vegetables, or how to build an award-winning kite. Or we can use the process pattern to reconstruct a chain of events that brought about a result we want to explain. A process paper might explain how beavers build their dams and thereby change the ecology of an area until they finally move on and start a similar cycle elsewhere.

AUDIENCE Much process writing aims at a "presold" audience that has a practical need for instructions or advice. The reader might need to know how to assemble an exercise bike or how to avoid muscle fatigue. Much other process writing arouses and satisfies the reader's curiosity about processes at work in the natural world or in the world of history. In either case, writers have to judge how much inside knowledge they have to fill in for the newcomer or outsider.

BENEFITS FOR THE WRITER (1) Process writing teaches the writer to do an honest job. It is hard to fake: Recipes, instructions, and directions won't work unless the writer has mastered the essential details, knows the essential ingredients or tools, and goes through the necessary steps in the right order.

(2) Process writing teaches the writer to lay out a pattern a reader can follow. A successful process paper has to keep the reader from getting lost in miscellaneous detail; it has to divide a complicated sequence into major stages that the reader can take in one at a time.

(3) Process writing makes the writer aware of the needs of the audience. It tests the writer's ability to explain and demonstrate.

PROCESS
Additional Reading

Ed Edelson, Smart Computers—Now They Speak Our Language   (p. 382)

WRITER'S GUIDE 4

Tracing a Process

Much practical, scientific, and historical writing helps the reader understand a subject by showing how one thing leads to another in a series of steps. Remember the following guidelines when writing a paper that traces a process:

(1) *Explain the purpose or the benefits of the process.* Keep your reader aware of the *why* as well as the *how*. The following might be the introduction to a paper about how to bake bread:

A Perfect Loaf of Bread

One step toward becoming a more self-sufficient person in our consumer society is learning how to bake old-fashioned homemade bread. Bread provides carbohydrates, a basic necessity in our diet. However, much of the bread sold in stores is filled with preservatives so that it can stay on the shelves longer without spoiling. Much of it has an unnatural bleached appearance. It often has the consistency and the taste of a sponge. If we want to reduce the amount of dubious chemicals and additives in our diet, we can start by baking our own bread from natural ingredients.

(2) *Provide all necessary details.* Provide the necessary information about supplies, ingredients, and tools. The following instructions for building a concrete walkway pay careful attention to the *why*, the *what*, and the *how*:

(Why)   Before actually mixing the cement, we need to block off the area where the concrete is to be placed. This is the first step because a framework is needed to hold the concrete in place right after the ingredients are mixed. The wood used
(What)   for this frame should be rot-resistant, like redwood or cedar. We will need two 2 × 4s four feet long and two 2 × 4s two feet long. . . .

(How)   We check the area for the walkway to see that the ground is hard and free of debris. Then we position the wood in a rectangle with the pieces of equal length running parallel to each other. We nail the sides together, making sure their top surfaces are flush with the grade planned for the concrete. . . .

(3) *Explain the technical workings of things.* Whenever you are dealing with something difficult or unusual, make clear what needs to be done to make the process work. Study the amount of detailed technical

explanation that the following passage provides to make us understand how a snake can swallow its prey:

FIRST STAGE: (stalking)	Imagine you are watching a hungry rattlesnake stalk its prey in the Georgia woods on a moonless fall night. Using its sense of smell and its infrared equipment for night sight, the snake has picked up a young gopher on the way home to its gopher hole.... The rattler inches along the ground until its night sight and heat perception tell it that it is within striking range....
SECOND STAGE: (attacking)	The snake slowly, quietly coils. In a fraction of a second, it strikes with its fangs unsheathed, injects the poison, and withdraws....
THIRD STAGE: (devouring)	To get the gopher, four times the circumference of the rattler's head, into its mouth and down its gullet is a challenging feat, since the reptile has no claws for leverage or dismemberment. When it has caught a frog or large mammal, the snake will swallow its meal headfirst. *Its jaws open in back as well as in front* (human beings can open only the front part), giving it tremendous stretch. It is actually able to *unhinge its jaws and extend them around the victim's head*. Then the snake shifts from side to side, *pulling itself over the dead rodent the way a stocking slides over a leg as we pull on it....*

(4) *Divide the process into major stages.* People who are good at explaining things divide a procedure or a sequence of events into major stages. This clear division into steps or parts helps us see the broad outlines of the process as a whole. At each point during the process, it makes us feel that we know where we are. What might have seemed a confusing sequence of "one thing after another" falls into a pattern that makes sense.

When we give instructions or directions, dividing a process clearly into major steps helps us build our readers' confidence: They can feel that they will be able to master one thing at a time. The following might be the major stages for the paper on baking bread:

> I. Mixing the dough
> II. Letting the dough rise
> III. Baking the bread

Help your readers find their bearings by providing an *overview* or preview of the major stages at the beginning of your paper. If necessary, summarize, or recapitulate, the major stages again at the end. The writer describing the natural process summarized in the following passages made sure the reader would have the basic one-two-three sequence firmly in mind:

OVERVIEW: A small beetle, the mimosa girdler, undertakes *three pieces of linked, sequential behavior:* finding a mimosa tree and climbing up the trunk and out to the end of a branch; cutting a longitudinal slit and laying within it five or six eggs; and crawling back on the limb and girdling it neatly down into the cambium [the layer between the wood and the bark]. . . .

SAMPLE STEP: *The third step* is an eight-to-ten-hour task of hard labor, from which the beetle gains no food for itself—only the certainty that the branch will promptly die and fall to the ground in the next brisk wind, thus enabling the larvae to hatch and grow in an abundance of dead wood. . . .

RECAPITULATION: The beetle's brain is only a few strings of neurons connected in a modest network, capable therefore of only *three tiny thoughts, coming into consciousness one after the other:* find the right tree; get up there and lay eggs in a slit; back up and spend the day killing the branch so the eggs can hatch (Lewis Thomas, "Debating the Unknowable," *Atlantic*)

(5) *Use clear transitions to mark major stages or phases.* A transition provides the link or bridge that helps the reader move from one point to the next. The transitional phrases in the following excerpt help the reader move forward *in time* as the author identifies major phases in a historical process:

THESIS: *Asians have long encountered discrimination and exploitation in this country.* Indeed, many who have arrived in America in the last 150 years probably wished that they had stayed home.

FIRST STAGE: *During the 19th century,* thousands of poor Chinese workers were imported to this country to provide cheap labor for construction of the Western railroads. Serfs in all but name, they left a synonym in our language for exploited, underpaid workers: coolie labor. . . .

SECOND STAGE: *In later years,* sizable numbers of Japanese and Koreans went to the West Coast, mostly to work as farm laborers, although some eventually prospered in business and other fields. In 1924, amid emotional outcries about a "yellow peril," Congress passed the Alien Quota Act, which all but excluded Asians by setting numerical quotas restricting immigration almost exclusively to Europeans. . . .

THIRD STAGE: *After Pearl Harbor pushed the United States into World War II,* sentiment against Orientals intensified once again, and thousands of Japanese who lived on the West Coast were interned in prison camps. . . .

FOURTH STAGE: *In 1965, as a kind of an ancillary effect of the civil-rights movement,* Congress repealed the 1924 law, and racial quotas were abolished. . . .   (Robert Lindsay, "The New Asian Immigrants," *New York Times Magazine*)

(6) *Explain technical terms that are likely to be unfamiliar to the outsider.* Any writer providing instructions or explanations has to ask: "How much does my reader already know?" Most people will have a general idea of what a laser is, but a writer discussing its use in eye surgery will feel the need to provide an exact technical description: A laser is a device that focuses, narrows, and amplifies a beam of light to turn it into an extremely concentrated and intense ray that can be used as a powerful tool and with microscopic precision.

Remember that the writer explaining a process generally writes as the expert or insider explaining things to the newcomer or outsider. A writer explaining how early photographers worked will have to make sure that the uninitiated reader understands terms like *emulsion, autochrome, negative,* and *transparency*—terms that the reader who merely pushes the button on an instant camera is not likely to have encountered.

(7) *Use comparisons or analogies to help explain what is difficult or unfamiliar.* We can often explain something by showing how it is similar to something the reader already knows. We can clarify a difficult process by showing how it resembles a simpler, easier-to-follow procedure. When an extended comparison fits well enough to apply to several related features, we call it an **analogy**. Here is the analogy that a well-known science writer used to explain his point that we are selective in taking in the world around us—that our minds take in only what we are geared to observe:

Like other animals, we go around creating whatever the reality is that we perceive, with our own instruments, all the time. A frog, for example, has one kind of reality, which is a dark speck against a lighted background. Of course, the real "thought" that the frog has is of a fly, and if that speck doesn't move, or if it doesn't move in a flylike fashion, it doesn't get recorded in the frog's brain. He sees only the thing that he is designed to see. We might be in somewhat the same situation: we may have some things that we're designed with receptors to see and other things for which we just don't have receptors—yet, anyway. (Lewis Thomas, "Turning Points," *Quest*)

To sum up: Writing that traces a process answers the question "What does it take to make this work?" Writing tracing a process trains a writer to explain something step by step, following it through the necessary stages in the right order. Process writing has to be methodical, and it may at times seem unexciting. However, it is often educational and useful. It is hard to fake. When it is well done, it leaves readers with the feeling that they have learned something good to know.

Prewriting Activities 4

1. For *sentence practice*, write half a dozen sentences, each tracing an activity or a process in considerable detail. Start with simple physical actions or events, but go on to larger patterns. Use the following as possible models:

   a. A dirty, long-haired young man in a faded army fatigue jacket, weary from walking, reached through the barbed-wire fence to pet a mud-covered jersey milk cow grazing in a field alongside the country road.

   b. On an early January day in 1968, a volcanic eruption pushed some steaming rocks above the surface waters of the South Pacific, adding a new island to the remote Tonga archipelago.

   c. We begin as children; we mature; we leave the parental nest; we give birth to children who, in turn, grow up, leave and begin the process all over again. (Alvin Toffler)

2. Many of the things we do are so familiar to us that we do them almost unthinkingly or automatically. We become consciously aware of what is involved when we have to demonstrate to a complete newcomer how to do things right in every detail, step by step. Write foolproof *how-to instructions* for someone totally unfamiliar with an everyday activity like the following: changing an automobile tire; doing a large pile of dinner dishes; cooking a hamburger; painting one's own room.

3. Much of what we do in our bureaucratic modern society requires that we go through a series of necessary steps in the right order. As helpfully as you can, explain the *procedure* for one of the following: admission to college, registering for courses, getting married, getting divorced, buying or selling a house.

Paragraph Practice 4

Write a paragraph to give your readers basic instructions for a procedure that they might at some time find useful or necessary. Study and discuss the following student-written paragraph as a possible model.

Life or Death

Imagine yourself with a friend when suddenly heart and breathing stop as the result of a heart attack. Could you save your friend's life? If a bystander were to administer CPR—cardiopulmonary resuscitation—the victim would have a 40 percent chance to live. To start, put the victim carefully flat on the back. Place one hand under the base of the neck and lift gently; with the other hand pinch nostrils closed with thumb and index finger. Take a deep breath, open your mouth wide, and place it around the victim's mouth, making a tight seal. Blow air into the victim's mouth for several quick breaths, lifting your mouth slightly to get fresh air. Next, put the middle finger and the index finger of your right hand on the sternum—the notch at the top of the V formed by the lower part of the rib cage. Place the heel of your left hand on the breastbone next to your index finger and then move your right hand to place it on top of the left. Straighten your arms, locking your elbows. Push straight down for about fifteen compressions. Keep alternating forced breathing and chest compressions until the victim starts breathing or until trained help arrives.

BACKGROUND: Marie De Santis is one of many writers who in recent years have written urgently about the threats to our vanishing wildlife. When she was a doctoral student in the late 1960s, she decided to follow the lure of the sea. She served a brief apprenticeship on California fishing boats and became captain of her own boat. In her book *Neptune's Apprentice* (1984), she describes her eight years as a commercial fisherwoman, telling of the hard work, the dangers, and the spirit of the people shaped by the sea. In the following excerpt from her book *California Currents*, she addresses herself to readers who "wish to continue living in a world with real animals" and who want future generations to "see more than the broken spirits of the animals of the zoo." She traces the life cycle of the wild salmon threatened by the destruction (or obstruction) of its traditional spawning grounds and being replaced by fish artificially bred in hatcheries and "no more suited to the stream than the poodle is to the woods."

Marie De Santis

Last of the

Wild Salmon

GUIDE TO READING: In this selection, the author traces the life cycle of a threatened species. Does the essay have a keynote or a symbolic high point? Does the author give an overview of the process? What are the major phases of the cycle? How does the author make her account dramatic—how does she make it come to life?

In a stream so shallow that its full body is no longer submerged in the water, the salmon twists on its side to get a better grip with its tail. Its gillplate is torn, big hunks of skin hang off its sides from collisions with rocks, there are deep gouges in its body, and all around for miles to go there is only the cruelty of more jagged rocks and less and less water to sustain the swim. Surely the animal is dying! 1

And then the salmon leaps like an arrow shot from a bow; some urge and will and passion ignores the animal body and focuses on the stream. 2

Of all the extremes of adaptation to the ocean's awful toll on the young, none is more mythic in proportion than the salmon's mighty journey to the mountain streams: a journey that brings life to meet death at a point on a perfect circle, a return through miles of narrowing waters to the exact gravel-bedded streamlet of its birth. A journey to spawning and death, so clear in its resemblance to the migrations of the sperm to the egg as to entwine their meanings in a single reflection. 3

On every continent of the northern hemisphere, from the temperate zone to the arctic, there is hardly a river that hasn't teemed with the 4 salmon's spawn: the Thames, the Rhine, the rivers of France and Spain, Kamchatka and Siberia, Japan (which alone has more than 200 salmon rivers) and the arctic streams of Greenland. From the Aleutians to Monterey Bay, through the broadest byways to the most rugged and narrow gorge, the salmon have made their way home. There are many journeys for which the salmon endure more than 1000 miles.

As soon as the ice melts on the Yukon, the king salmon enter the river's 5 mouth, and for a month, the fish swim against the current, 50 miles a day for a total of 1500. And like every other salmon on its run, the king salmon fasts completely along the way. In other rivers, salmon scale vertical rocks up to 60 feet high, against hurtling waterfalls.

The salmon gets to spawn once in life, and maybe that's reason 6 enough. The salmon's instinct to return to the place of its birth is so unmodifiable and of such purity as to have inspired hundreds of spiritual rites in as many societies of human beings.

The salmon arrives battered and starved, with a mate chosen along the 7 way, and never has passion seemed less likely from two more wretched-looking beings. But, there in the gravel of the streamlet, the female fans out a nest with the sweep of her powerful tail and the male fends off intruders. The nest done, the two fish lie next to each other suspended in the water over the nest; their bodies quiver with intense vibrations, and simultaneously they throw the eggs and the sperm. Compared with the millions of eggs thrown by a cod in a stream, the salmon need throw only 2000 to 5000. Despite the predators and other hazards of the stream, these cold mountain waters are a sanctuary compared with the sea. For the next two or three days, the pair continue nesting and spawning until all the eggs are laid. Then the salmon, whose journey has spanned the ocean and the stream, lies by the nest and dies.

Soon the banks of the streams are stacked with ragged carcasses, and 8 the animals of the woods come down for a feast. The stream lies quiet in the winter's deepening cold. But within a month two black eyes appear through the skin of each egg. And two weeks later, the water is again alive with the pulsing of millions of small fish feeling the first clumsy kicks of their tails. The fingerlings stay for a while, growing on the insects and larvae that have been nurtured by the forest. Then, one day, they realize what that tail is for and begin their descent to the sea, a journey mapped in their genes by the parents they left behind.

The young salmon arrive in the estuary facing the sea, where they 9 linger again and learn to feed on shrimp, small crustaceans and other creatures of the brine. Here, also, their bodies complete an upheaval of internal and external changes that allow them to move on to the saltier sea. These adaptations require such extraordinary body transformations that when the same events occur on the stage of evolution they take millions and millions of years. In the life of the salmon, the changes take place in only a matter of months. One of life's most prohibitive barriers—that between fresh and salt water—is crossed, and the salmon swim back and forth, in and out of the sea, trying it on for size.

Then one day, the youngsters do not return. The stream is only a 10 distant memory drifting further and further back in the wake of time, only different—a memory that will resurrect and demand that its path be retraced.

So accessible is the salmon's life in the stream that more is known 11 about the reproduction of this fish than any other ocean animal. With the ease of placing cameras underwater, there isn't any aspect of this dramatic cycle that hasn't been captured in full color in some of the most spectacular film footage ever made.

But once the salmon enters the sea, the story of its life is a secret as 12 deep and dark as the farthest reaches of the ocean it roams. The human eye with its most sophisticated aids, from satellite to sonar, has never caught more than a glance of the salmon at sea. Extensive tagging programs have been carried out, but they tell us little more than that the salmon is likely to be found anywhere within thousands of miles of its origins, and even this is only a sliver of the picture because the tags are recovered only when the salmon is caught by fishermen, who work solely within the narrow coastal zone. Along with a few other pelagic fishes, like the tuna, that claim vast stretches of sea for their pasture, the salmon's life remains one of the most mysterious on earth.

Using the Dictionary

What help does your dictionary give with *technical terms* like the following? (Which of these would you expect the general reader to know?)   1. *migration* (3)   2. *predator* (7)   3. *fingerling* (8)   4. *larvae* (8)   5. *estuary* (9)   6. *crustacean* (9)   7. *sonar* (12)   8. *pelagic* (12)

The Writer's Agenda

In this essay, the author sets out to give her audience a vivid account of a process that for her has a larger symbolic meaning. Answer the following questions about how she achieves her purpose:

1. De Santis starts with what is for her the symbolic *high point* of the cycle. How does her introduction strike the keynote for the rest of the essay? What details make it especially dramatic?

2. Where does the author give her *overview* of the process? What for her is its larger symbolic meaning?

3. What are the four or five *major stages* of the process? For each stage, what are the key developments or events? What are the most striking details?

4. Find and discuss striking examples of *exact, concrete language* that make the author's account come to life.

5. What does the author's *conclusion* add to the rest of the selection? How does the point she emphasizes there relate to the earlier sections? How does she tie it in with what has gone before?

For Discussion or Writing

6. How much in this selection is *objective*, factual material; how much is *subjective*, personal feeling or attitude? How would you sum up the author's attitude toward her subject?

7. How large do you think is the audience for this kind of writing? How many people share the author's concerns? How many people care?

8. Trace the life cycle of an animal or plant that you have had a chance to study or read about (a butterfly, a frog; a fruit tree, a rosebush; any other). Identify major phases; use graphic, authentic detail. (If you write about a domestic animal or pet, be sure to avoid cute or stereotyped description.)

9. Trace the life cycle of a car, a neighborhood, a school, a waterfront, or something else that might go through major stages of development, growth, or deterioration.

10. Trace major stages in the history of a fad, fashion, or trend as it runs its course.

11. What to you are major stages or phases of growing up? (What major stages would you chart in a person's progress toward "maturity"?)

Branching Out

12. Write about an occupation or business that goes through major seasonal cycles. Mark off major stages or phases; develop them in graphic detail.

BACKGROUND: John McPhee has been called the "best nonfiction writer practicing today." He was born in Princeton, New Jersey, in 1931; and he has lived, gone to college, taught, or worked there most of his life. After some years as a staff reporter for *Time*, he became a regular contributor to the *New Yorker* magazine. In recent years, he has taught a seminar at Princeton University, "The Literature of Fact," designed to teach the application of creative writing techniques to journalism and other forms of nonfiction. Many of McPhee's *New Yorker* pieces became part of the more than a dozen books he has published. Some of his best-loved work, like *The Pine Barrens* (1968), is about places and people not yet spoiled by progress; often his pieces are based on his observations while traveling and on long, detailed interviews with local characters. He usually writes about the East, although some of his pieces take his readers to the West or to the Scotland of his ancestors. The following selection is from *Oranges* (1967), which traced the history and the life cycle of the Florida orange. A lover of freshly squeezed orange juice, McPhee here traces the process by which the "frozen people" turn oranges into the frozen concentrate from which we make what passes for orange juice today.

John McPhee

Oranges

GUIDE TO READING: What are the major stages in the process? What are striking details that make the process real? What is the overall impression or the major theme that unifies the selection?

The enormous factories that the frozen people have built more closely   1
resemble oil refineries than auto plants. The evaporators are tall assemblages of looping pipes, quite similar to the cat-cracking towers that turn crude oil into gasoline. When oranges arrive, in semitrailers, they are poured into giant bins, so that a plant can have a kind of reservoir to draw upon. At Minute Maid's plant in Auburndale, for example, forty bins hold four million oranges, or enough to keep the plant going for half a day. From samples analyzed by technicians who are employed by the State of Florida, the plant manager knows what the juice, sugar, and acid content is of the fruit in each bin, and blends the oranges into the assembly line accordingly, always attempting to achieve as uniform a product as possible. An individual orange obviously means nothing in this process, and the rise of concentrate has brought about a basic change in the system by which oranges are sold.

Growers used to sell oranges as oranges. They now sell "pounds-   2
solids," and modern citrus men seem to use the term in every other sentence they utter. The rise of concentrate has not only changed the landscape and the language; it has, in a sense, turned the orange inside out. Because the

concentrate plants are making a product of which the preponderant ingredient is sugar, it is sugar that they buy as raw material. They pay for the number of pounds of solids that come dissolved in the juice in each truckload of oranges, and these solids are almost wholly sugars. Growers now worry more about the number of pounds of sugar they are producing per acre than the quality of the individual oranges on their trees. If the concentrate plants bought oranges by weight alone, growers could plant, say, Hamlins on Rough Lemon in light sand—a scion, rootstock, and soil combination that will produce extremely heavy yields of insipid and watery oranges.

As the fruit starts to move along a concentrate plant's assembly line, it ₃ is first culled. In what some citrus people remember as "the old fresh-fruit days," before the Second World War, about forty per cent of all oranges grown in Florida were eliminated at packinghouses and dumped in fields. Florida milk tasted like orangeade. Now, with the exception of the split and rotten fruit, all of Florida's orange crop is used. Moving up a conveyor belt, oranges are scrubbed with detergent before they roll on into juicing machines. There are several kinds of juicing machines, and they are something to see. One is called the Brown Seven Hundred. Seven hundred oranges a minute go into it and are split and reamed on the same kind of rosettes that are in the centers of ordinary kitchen reamers. The rinds that come pelting out the bottom are integral halves, just like the rinds of oranges squeezed in a kitchen. Another machine is the Food Machinery Corporation's FMC In-line Extractor. It has a shining row of aluminum jaws, upper and lower, with shining aluminum teeth. When an orange tumbles in, the upper jaw comes crunching down on it while at the same time the orange is penetrated from below by a perforated steel tube. As the jaws crush the outside, the juice goes through the perforations in the tube and down into the plumbing of the concentrate plant. All in a second, the juice has been removed and the rind has been crushed and shredded beyond recognition.

From either machine, the juice flows on into a thing called the finisher, ₄ where seeds, rag, and pulp are removed. The finisher has a big stainless steel screw that steadily drives the juice through a fine-mesh screen. From the finisher, it flows on into holding tanks. Orange juice squeezed at home should be consumed fairly soon after it is expressed, because air reacts with it and before long produces a bitter taste, and the juice has fatty constituents that can become rancid. In the extractors, the finishers, and the troughs of concentrate plants, a good bit of air gets into the juice. Bacilli and other organisms may have started growing in it. So the juice has to be pasteurized. In some plants, this occurs before it is concentrated. In others, pasteurization is part of the vacuum-evaporating process—for example, in the Minute Maid plant in Auburndale, which uses the Thermal Accelerated Short Time Evaporator (T.A.S.T.E.). A great, airy network of bright-red, looping tubes, the Short Time stands about fifty feet high. Old-style evaporators keep one load of juice within them for about an hour, gradually boiling the water out. In the Short Time, juice flows in at one end in a continuous stream and comes out the other end eight minutes later.

Specific gravity, figured according to a special scale for sugar solutions, is the measurement of concentrate. The special scale, worked out by a nineteenth-century German scientist named Adolf F. W. Brix, is read in "degrees Brix." Orange juice as it comes out of oranges is usually about twelve degrees Brix—that is, for every hundred pounds of water there are twelve pounds of sugar. In the Short Time, orange juice passes through seven stages. At each stage, there are sampling valves. The juice at the start is plain, straightforward orange juice but with a notable absence of pulp or juice vesicles. By the third stage, the juice is up to nineteen degrees Brix and has the viscosity and heat of fairly thick hot chocolate. The flavor is rich and the aftertaste is clean. At the fifth stage, the juice is up to forty-six degrees Brix—already thicker than the ultimate product that goes into the six-ounce can—and it has the consistency of cough syrup, with a biting aftertaste. After the seventh stage, the orange juice can be as high as seventy degrees Brix. It is a deep apricot-orange in color. It is thick enough to chew, and its taste actually suggests apricot-flavored gum. Stirred into enough water to take it back to twelve degrees Brix, it tastes like nothing much but sweetened water.

As a season progresses, the sugar-acid ratio of oranges improves. Pineapple oranges, at their peak, are better in this respect than Hamlins at theirs; and Valencias are the best of all. So the concentrators keep big drums of out-of-season concentrate in cold-storage rooms and blend them with in-season concentrates in order to achieve even more uniformity. Advertisements can be misleading, however, when they show four or five kinds of oranges and imply that each can of the advertiser's concentrate contains an exact blend of all of them. It would be all but impossible to achieve that. The blending phase of the process is at best only an educated stab at long-term uniformity, using whatever happens to be on hand in the cold rooms and the fresh-fruit bins. The blending is, moreover, merely a mixing of old and new concentrates, still at sixty degrees Brix and still all but tasteless if reconstituted with water.

The most important moment comes when the cutback is poured in, taking the super-concentrated juice down to forty-five degrees Brix, which MacDowell and his colleagues worked out as a suitable level, because three cans of tap water seemed to be enough to thaw the juice fairly quickly but not so much that the cooling effect of the cold concentrate would be lost in the reconstituted juice. Cutback is mainly fresh orange juice, but it contains additional flavor essences, peel oil, and pulp. Among the components that get boiled away in the evaporator are at least eight hydrocarbons, four esters, fifteen carbonyls, and sixteen kinds of alcohol. The chemistry of orange juice is so subtle and complicated that most identifications are tentative, and no one can guess which components form its taste, let alone in what proportion. Some of these essences are recovered in condensation chambers in the evaporators, and they are put back into the juice. The chief flavoring element in cutback is d-limonene, which is the main ingredient of peel oil. The oil cells in the skins of all citrus fruit are ninety per cent d-limonene. It is d-limonene that burns the lips of children sucking oranges. D-limonene reddened the lips of the ladies of the seventeenth-century French court, who bit into limes for the purpose. D-limonene is what makes the leaves of all orange and grapefruit trees smell like lemons when crushed in the hand. D-limonene is what the Martini drinker rubs on the rim of his glass and then drops into his drink in a twist of lemon. The modern Martini drinker has stouter taste buds than his predecessors of the seventeenth century, when people in Europe used to spray a little peel oil on the outside of their wineglasses, in the belief that it was so strong that it would penetrate the glass and impart a restrained flavor to the wine. In the same century, peel oil was widely used in Germany in the manufacture of "preservative plague-lozenges." In the fourteenth century in Ceylon, men who dived into lakes to search the bottom for precious stones first rubbed their bodies with orange-peel oil in order to repel crocodiles and poisonous snakes. Peel oil is flammable. Peel oil is the principal flavoring essence that frozen people put into concentrated orange juice in order to attempt to recover the flavor of fresh orange juice. "We have always had the flavor of fresh oranges to come up against," MacDowell told me. "People who make things like tomato juice and pineapple juice have not had this problem." . . .

Plants that make "chilled juice" are set up as concentrate plants are, [8] but without the evaporators. Instead, the juice goes into bottles and cartons and is shipped to places as distant as Nome. Tropicana, by far the biggest company in the chilled-juice business, ships twelve thousand quarts of orange juice to Nome each month. People in Los Angeles, surprisingly enough, drink two hundred and forty thousand quarts of Tropicana orange juice a month, and the company's Los Angeles sales are second only to sales in New York.

Tropicana used to ship orange juice by sea from Florida to New York [9] in a glistening white tanker with seven hundred and thirty thousand gallons of juice slurping around in the hold. For guests of the company, the ship had four double staterooms and a gourmet chef. Among freeloaders, it was considered one of the seven wonders of commerce. To sailors of the merchant marine, it was the most attractive billet on the high seas. A typical week consisted of three nights in New York, two nights at sea, and two nights in Florida. There was almost no work to do. There were forty-two men in the crew, some with homes at each end. White as a yacht, the ship would glide impressively past Wall Street and under the bridges of the East River, put forth a stainless-steel tube, and quickly drain its cargo into tanks in Queens.

Tropicana unfortunately found that although this was a stylish way to [10] transport orange juice, it was also uneconomical. The juice now goes by rail, already packed in bottles or cartons. The cartons are being phased out because they admit too much oxygen. Tropicana people are frank in appraisal of their product. "It's the closest thing to freshly squeezed orange juice you can get and not have to do the work yourself," one of the company's executives told me. To maintain the cloud in the juice and keep it from settling, enzymes have to be killed by raising the temperature of the juice to nearly two hundred degrees. Even so, there is some loss of Vitamin C if the juice remains unconsumed too long, just as there is a loss of Vitamin C if concentrate is mixed in advance and allowed to stand for some time.

During the winter, Tropicana freezes surplus orange juice in huge 11 floes and stores it until summer, when it is cracked up, fed into an ice crusher, melted down, and shipped. In this way, the company avoids the more usual practice of chilled-juice shippers, who sell reconstituted concentrate in the summertime, adding dry juice-sacs in order to create the illusion of freshness. The juice-sacs come from California as "barreled washed pulp."

Leftover rinds, rag, pulp, and seeds at chilled-juice and concentrate 12 plants have considerable value of their own. In most years, about fourteen million dollars are returned to the citrus industry through its by-products. Orange wine tastes like a one-for-one mixture of dry vermouth and sauterne. It varies from estate-bottled types like Pool's and Vino del Sol to Florida Fruit Bowl Orange Wine, the *vin ordinaire* of Florida shopping centers, made by National Grape Products of Jacksonville, and sold for ninety-nine cents. Florida winos are said to like the price. Florida Life cordials are made from citrus fruit, as are Consul gin, Surf Side gin, Five Flag gin, Fleet Street gin, and Consul vodka.

Peel oil has been used to make not only paint but varnish as well. It 13 hardens rubber, too, but is more commonly used in perfumes and as a flavor essence for anything that is supposed to taste of orange, from candy to cake-mixes and soft drinks. Carvone, a synthetic spearmint oil which is used to flavor spearmint gum, is made from citrus peel oil. The Coca-Cola Company is one of the world's largest users of peel oil, as anyone knows who happens to have noticed the lemony smell of the d-limonene that clings to the inside of an empty Coke bottle.

A million and a half pounds of polyunsaturated citrus-seed oil is 14 processed and sold each year, for cooking. Hydrogenated orange-seed oil is more like butter, by-products researchers told me, than oleomargarine. Noticing a refrigerator in their laboratory, I asked if they had some on hand. They said they were sorry, but all they had was real butter. Would I care for an English muffin?

Looking out a window over an orange grove, one researcher re- 15 marked, "We are growing chemicals now, not oranges." Dried juice vesicles, powdered and mixed with water, produce a thick and foamy solution which is used to fight forest fires. Albedecone, a pharmaceutical which stops leaks in blood vessels, is made from hesperidin, a substance in the peels of oranges. But the main use of the leftover rinds is cattle feed, either as molasses made from the peel sugars or as dried shredded meal. Citrus pulp and chopped rinds are dried for dairy feed much in the same way that clothes are dried in a home dryer—in a drum within a drum, whirling. The exhaust vapors perfume the countryside for miles around concentrate plants with a heavy aroma of oranges. The evaporators themselves are odorless. People often assume that they are smelling the making of orange juice when they are actually smelling cattle feed. If the aroma is not as delicate as the odor of blossoms, it is nonetheless superior to the aroma of a tire and rubber plant, a Limburger cheese factory, a pea cannery, a paper mill, or an oil refinery. Actually, the orange atmospheres of the Florida concentrate towns are quite agreeable, and, in my own subjective view, the only town in the United States which outdoes them in this respect is Hershey, Pennsylvania.

Using the Dictionary

Which of the following do you have to check? Choose several of the *technical terms* to explain to an outsider.   1. *evaporator* (1)   2. *cat-cracking* (1)   3. *concentrate*, n. (1)   4. *preponderant* (2)   5. *scion* (2)   6. *insipid* (2)   7. *rosette* (3)   8. *integral* (3)   9. *perforate* (3)   10. *pasteurize* (4)   11. *specific gravity* (5)   12. *vesicle* (5)   13. *viscosity* (5)   14. *cutback* (7)   15. *ester* (7)   16. *billet* (9)   17. *enzyme* (10)   18. *floe* (11)   19. *polyunsaturated* (14)   20. *hydrogenated* (14)

The Writer's Agenda

McPhee sets out to trace the process that produces concentrate, from the arrival of the fresh orange at the plant to the orange smell given off by the cattle feed that is one of the by-products of the process. Answer the following questions:

1. What statement late in the essay best sums up its keynote or dominant impression?

2. McPhee writes about the process not as a naive outside critic but as an investigator who has thoroughly mastered the necessary *inside* information. What details in his account are for you most striking, informative, or unexpected?

3. What are the major stages in the process that produces the concentrate? (Sum up each stage, including key details.) Where do key **transitions** provide a bridge from one phase to the next?

4. In paragraph 3, McPhee uses graphic, concrete words like *culled, dumped,* and *scrubbed* to make the procedures or activities real for the reader. Find half a dozen similar words later in the paragraph. What do they make us see? What extended imaginative comparison, or **metaphor** helps us visualize the machinery?

5. In the paragraphs on "chilled juice" (8–11), we might expect to hear about *real* orange juice as contrasted with the artificial, reconstituted stuff. How do these paragraphs dispel this illusion?

For Discussion or Writing

6. How would you sum up the differences between real orange juice and juice made from concentrate? What is the "price of progress" paid by the consumer? What are the advantages of concentrate? Are they worth the price?

7. Do you think the author of this selection is biased against business? Why or why not?

8. Writers have often complained about modern "processed" foods that are a far cry from the real thing. Investigate and describe the making of a modern processed product like processed cheese, potato chips, or imitation ice cream.

9. Describe a fast-food or quick-service operation that you know from personal observation or experience.

10. Analyze a traditional manufacturing process that involves several major stages or operations (papermaking, the making of sugar, the printing of a daily newspaper). Or bring your reader up to date on modern methods or techniques that have transformed an occupation or a manufacturing process. (For instance, write about a modern chicken farm, an assembly line using robots, or another automated manufacturing system.)

Branching Out

11. Both friendly and hostile critics have at times written about schools as if they were factories turning out a product. Write a paper in which you apply or challenge the analogy.

WRITERS ON WRITING
An Editor on McPhee's Working Methods

When McPhee conducts an interview he tries to be as blank as his notebook pages, totally devoid of preconceptions, equipped with only the most elementary knowledge. He has found that imagining he knows a subject is a disadvantage, for that prejudice will limit his freedom to ask, to learn, to be surprised by unfolding evidence. Since most stories are full of unsuspected complexity, an interviewer hardly needs to *feign* ignorance; the stronger temptation is to bluff with a show of knowledge or to trick the informant into providing simple, easily digestible answers. Neither course is to McPhee's liking; he would rather risk seeming ignorant to get a solid, knotty answer....

His working methods vary according to a project, but some steps are fairly constant. He first transcribes the notebooks, typing entries in order, occasionally adding other details or current thoughts as he goes. He likens this process to a magnet's attraction of iron filings; as the notes take shape, they draw from him new ideas about placement, phrasing, or possible analogies. When finished, he may have a hundred typed sheets of notes, enough to fill a large spring binder. He makes a photocopy of the original set and shelves it for later use. He then reads and rereads the binder set, looking for areas he needs to flesh out with research and reading at Firestone Library. The reading produces more notes, the notes more typed pages for his binder. Finally, he reads the binder and makes notes on possible structures, describing patterns the story might assume.

While its structure is forming, or when he senses how the story may end, McPhee often writes out a first draft of "the lead," a term journalists use to describe openings. In newspaper writing the lead is usually a single-sentence paragraph, designed to impart the classic who-what-where particulars of a story. In McPhee's work the lead is longer (fifteen hundred to two thousand words), more dramatic, yet rather more oblique. It establishes a mood, a setting, and perhaps some main characters or events, but not in order to put the story in a nutshell or even to hint at its full dimensions. . . .

Having read the lead via telephone to an editor at *The New Yorker*, he goes back to the binder and begins to code it with structural notes, using titles like "Voyageurs," "Loons," or acronyms—"GLAT," "LASLE." These are his topics, the formal segments of narrative, which he next writes on a series of index cards. After assembling a stack, he fans them out and begins to play a sort of writer's solitaire, studying the possibilities of order. Decisions don't come easily; a story has many potential sequences, and each chain produces a calculus of desired and undesired effects, depending on factors like character and theme.

—From William L. Howarth, Introduction to *The John McPhee Reader*

BACKGROUND: Peter Meyer (born 1950) is a political writer who published a book about President Carter. He wrote the following article for *Harper's*, one of the country's oldest magazines of opinion. Magazines like *Harper's* or the *Atlantic* often publish articles that take the longer view. Many such articles are "investigative journalism" in the best sense: They are based, like this article, on the patient sifting of "hundreds of pages of reports, documents, studies, and statistics" as well as on first-hand personal observation, interviews, and private talks. Unlike fashionable exposé journalists, Peter Meyer in this article does not try to expose to public view the shady dealings or private shortcomings of individuals. Instead, he tries to make us understand some of the often impersonal forces that are at work to change or condition our lives. In this article, he takes a critical look at a process of which the bulldozer has become the symbol: the transformation of traditional rural neighborhoods into suburban developments in the name of progress.

Peter Meyer

Land Rush

GUIDE TO READING: The author of this article uses a **case history** to dramatize an important issue. He gives a faithful, detailed account of one representative case that can teach us much about other similar situations. What is the central issue? What is the process that, according to the author, is typical of what has happened in many communities across the country? What is the general significance or larger meaning of what he has described?

About two years ago I witnessed for the first time an American event 1 that in the past decade has become so saturated with meaning as to assume the significance of ritual. It was an early weekday evening in Salem, Oregon, a small but growing city like many others around the country. Downtown, in a local government building emptied of employees except for a janitor waxing and polishing the marble floor, ten or fifteen people were standing outside a small conference room, talking casually about their families, their work, their animals, and the weather. Among the group were a carpenter, a lawyer, a housewife or two, a farmer, an interior designer, a reporter, a jeweler, an electrician and his wife, and a student—as varied a group as could be found milling about the front doors of church on a Sunday morning. Some were devout believers, others only Sunday practitioners. But their devotion was to the same idol: property. The event was a land planning commission meeting convened by the three elders of the board, which was to decide whether to approve a proposed housing development on ten acres of wooded land just south of the city.

It was a raucous two-hour meeting, and it seemed that most of the 2 participant-landowners, whose title claims ranged from as little as a quarter-acre residential lot to as much as thirty acres of farmland, opposed the development planned in their backyards. Toward the end of the session a gentleman farmer, prominent in the town as a jeweler, stood to state his objections. After a few minutes of kindly debate—the commissioners arguing that the proposed subdivision land was located within the established "urban growth boundary" and would be subdivided eventually anyway, and that, in any case, the owner had a right to use his property the way he saw fit; the longtime resident saying that that was all right as long as he would be left alone—the official behind the table decided to end the discussion. "Mr. Jackson," he said in an effort to summarize, "I don't think your property is really at issue here. It's a case of apples and oranges, and our board has to concern itself with the proposal at hand. But thank you very much for your comments."

The group waited for Jackson to take his seat. The gray-haired man, 3 who had lived most of his seventy years on his eight acres of land, remained standing, rocking to and fro, his hands on the folding chair in front of him. Finally, with most of the eyes in the room now turned in his direction, Jackson blurted, "Hell! I'm not talking about apples *or* oranges! I'm talking about *bananas!*"

Stone-faced, Jackson slowly sat. His unexpected reply had prompted a 4 burst of supportive applause and laughter from his neighbors, but it was only a symbolic victory. Several minutes later the three commissioners voted to approve the development.

A few months after that, the city council, on the recommendation of 5 the planning commission, agreed to annex the property to the city, thus guaranteeing that the subdivision would be provided with sewer, water, and electrical lines and police and fire protection. Then, because of a state law that forbade "islands" of non-city land within city limits, most of the property of owners who had fought against the development was automatically annexed to the city. Next came a flock of other developers, now assured of city services, knocking on the doors of once-irate residents, offering as much as $8,000 for an acre of land that—only months before—was worth $1,000 at best. The tax assessors came, too: not only would tax rates be higher—to pay for the added services the city was obliged to provide all of its residents—but the assessed value of the property would have to be adjusted to reflect the change in market value. Almost overnight, property taxes jumped wildly. One by one the residents, many of whom had owned their ten or twenty or thirty acres of green and wooded hillsides for a generation or more, sold. Those who didn't soon began receiving notices from the city asking for permission to cross their land with sewer or water lines to the new developments. If permission was refused, the city began "condemnation" proceedings to acquire an easement on, or title to, the land it needed. Legal fees soon became another major cost of owning the land. Meanwhile, earthmoving machines were leveling hillsides, bulldozers were uprooting trees, huge dump trucks were unloading their tons of gravel, steamrollers were packing the new asphalt streets and four-lane thorough-fares were being laid over old country roads in anticipation of the traffic.

I happened recently to meet one of the landowners who had early on decided to subdivide his sixteen acres of orchard land. The man, a retired carpenter and part-time farmer, was riding his ancient caterpillar tractor, scratching away at the land owned by one of his neighbors—a man who for years had resolutely refused to sell his property to developers or make concessions to the city. When the farmer stepped down from his machine to say hello, I asked him why he was bulldozing land that wasn't his.

He bristled a bit. "The city owns this land," he said, "and this is where the street into my subdivision is going to be."

Coincidentally, I had just seen the deed to the land, and it showed that his neighbor owned it. I asked what he meant.

"Well, hell," he muttered, "the city gets what it wants anyway; and they've already given permission for the street—yesterday. If they don't own it now, they will later. So what's the difference?" With that, he turned around, climbed back on his tractor, and continued his leveling.

In almost every section of the country these days at least half the citizens in any given town or agency seem to be embroiled in a passionate land dispute. Over the past year, while sorting through hundreds of pages of reports, documents, studies, and statistics purporting to describe these arguments, I came to understand that they had as much to do with vivid myths and dreams as with the so-called facts of the matter. The metaphor of the land (whether as Eden, homestead, utopia, farm, refuge, or fortress) still exerts a commanding force on the American imagination.

This is true even though nobody knows very much about what is happening to the land or who owns it or how much of it remains open to what kind of use and settlement. Some observations, however, can be made with a certain degree of confidence. In the decade between 1965 and 1975 the value of land of all kinds and descriptions increased at an average rate of 150 percent. During the same period the population increased by 11 percent, the consumer price index by 80 percent, and the divorce rate by 100 percent. It is possible that people were paying such high prices for land only for speculative reasons, because it provided them with a defense against inflation.

But I suspect that the prices also reflected a collective and uncon-scious fear that American land might be slipping away from beneath peo-ple's feet and that its loss entailed the defeat of the great national dream. Everywhere the courts were besieged with suits from people trying to retain their holdings against what they perceived as heavy odds. Last year as much as one-fifth of the American estate was being contested in courtrooms, in legislatures, before town councils and government commissions. Huge corporations were buying more land (not that they didn't already own a great deal), and many individuals were finding themselves helpless to correct what they saw as the wanton destruction of the environment—mountainsides clearcut of timber, water courses polluted with industrial wastes, hillsides scraped bare of soil. People aligning themselves with both the commercial and the environmental interests beseeched the government at every level (municipal, state, federal) to intercede on their behalf and to help them bring about the proper management of the public lands that they regarded as part of their private inheritance.

The clamoring of people with different visions of the landscape has 13 resulted in what one federal official described as a decade of "quiet revolution." Responding to the many and contradictory appeals for justice, the federal government gradually has assumed the role of gardener and caretaker, not only for the 761 million acres that it already owned but for almost all of the 2.2 billion acres of America's vast estate. To the extent that this revolution has become known to people, it has encouraged yet another fear—that government itself will usurp the individual's right to own property. There is an irony in this worthy of a literature not yet written. Seeking to assert the inalienable right to hold property, it is possible that people have given their rights away. The unhappiness of the small landowners in Oregon testifies to the not only lingering but still powerful belief in the American dream; it also testifies to the bleak and melancholy possibility that the circumstances of modern America may no longer warrant holding to such a belief.

Using the Dictionary

A. Look up the following words and explain how each might be used: 1. *raucous* (2)   2. *embroiled* (10)   3. *purport* (10)   4. *myth* (10)   5. *metaphor* (10)   6. *entail* (12)   7. *beseech* (12)   8. *intercede* (12)   9. *usurp* (13)

B. Look up the following *technical terms* of special interest to people who own land: 10. *annex* (5)   11. *assess* (5)   12. *condemnation* (5)   13. *easement* (5)   14. *title* (5)   15. *deed* (8)   16. *speculative* (11)   17. *holdings* (12)   18. *estate* (12)   19. *contested* (12)

The Writer's Agenda

The author of this article knows how to *dramatize an issue*. He translates lifeless statistics into things that people do or that happen to people. Answer the following questions:

1. In the introductory paragraph, what does the author do to make the *setting and the people real* for the reader? (The author compares the people at the planning commission meeting to "churchgoers." How many words can you find that follow up this *analogy*?)

2. In the paragraphs that describe the meeting of the commission, the *central issue* comes into focus. What is the central issue or central dispute? (How is Jackson a symbolic figure in this section?)

3. What are the *major stages* in the process that turns the countryside into a suburb? Outline this process as it is described by the author. (What are some striking details that help make the process real for the reader?)

4. The author follows his description of the process with a brief account of how he met the man riding the tractor. What is the point of this anecdote?

5. In the final four paragraphs, the author moves from the specific case history to its more general meaning. What is "the great national dream" that he claims is threatened or defeated by current developments? What are the "myths and dreams" about land that he claims are as important as the "so-called facts of the matter"?

6. What, according to the author, are the large-scale current developments that threaten to defeat "the great national dream"?

For Discussion or Writing

7. Looking back over the essay, sum up the standards, preferences, expectations, or loyalties of the author. What labels, if any, would you attach to the outlook he represents?

8. In reading this essay, do you feel that there is another side to this story that the author leaves untold? If you had to defend the decision of the planning commission, for instance, what would you say? Explain and defend your arguments.

9. Have you been able to observe the change of a city, a neighborhood, or an area—for better or for worse? Describe the process. Identify several major stages.

10. Many people today try to learn skills that would make them more self-sufficient than the typical member of the consumer society. Give detailed instructions on how to do something like the following:
  • how to bake your own bread
  • how to grow vegetables in your own garden
  • how to make clothes from raw materials

Choose a task that would require your readers to do justice to several important stages.

11. Many industries today are implementing processes needed (or mandated by law) for environmental protection. Study one of these and explain it to readers with little technical background.

BACKGROUND: Joan Didion was born in Sacramento, California, in 1934 and was a student at the University of California at Berkeley. She went East to work for magazines like *Vogue, Saturday Evening Post*, and *Esquire*; many of her best magazine articles were collected in *Slouching Towards Bethlehem* (1968) and *The White Album* (1979). Her essays and several novels (*Play It As It Lays, A Book of Common Prayer, Run River*) made her widely known as a witty, sharp-eyed chronicler of what is freakish, plastic, eccentric, or absurd in American life. (She once said that her first writing experiments as a five-year-old revealed "a certain predilection for the extreme" that has dogged her into adult life.) Her essays on subjects like the hippie scene of the sixties helped create the popular stereotype of California as a garish lotusland where uprooted people practice bizarre rituals. However, she has also written nostalgically of the semirural California of her youth, with its summer droughts and winter floods, where she early learned that "the apparent ease of California life is an illusion."

Joan Didion

Bureaucrats

GUIDE TO READING: The author of the following essay is a sharp-eyed observer who is good at explaining how things work—and why they often don't. As she takes us behind the scenes of a traffic control center, what do we learn about its inner workings? At the same time, what, according to the author, is wrong with how the center operates? What warnings about the electronic future are implied in her account?

    The closed door upstairs at 120 South Spring Street in downtown Los Angeles is marked OPERATIONS CENTER. In the windowless room beyond the closed door a reverential hush prevails. From six A.M. until seven P.M. in this windowless room men sit at consoles watching a huge board flash colored lights. "There's the heart attack," someone will murmur, or "We're getting the gawk effect." 120 South Spring is the Los Angeles office of Caltrans, or the California Department of Transportation, and the Operations Center is where Caltrans engineers monitor what they call "the 42-Mile Loop." The 42-Mile Loop is simply the rough triangle formed by the intersections of the Santa Monica, the San Diego and the Harbor freeways, and 42 miles represents less than ten percent of freeway mileage in Los Angeles County alone, but these particular 42 miles are regarded around 120 South Spring with a special veneration. The Loop is a "demonstration system," a phrase much favored by everyone at Caltrans, and is part of a "pilot project," another two words carrying totemic weight on South Spring.

    The Loop has electronic sensors embedded every half-mile out there   2 in the pavement itself, each sensor counting the crossing cars every twenty seconds. The Loop has its own mind, a Xerox Sigma V computer which prints out, all day and night, twenty-second readings on what is and is not moving in each of the Loop's eight lanes. It is the Xerox Sigma V that makes the big board flash red when traffic out there drops below fifteen miles an hour. It is the Xerox Sigma V that tells the Operations crew when they have an "incident" out there. An "incident" is the heart attack on the San Diego, the jackknifed truck on the Harbor, the Camaro just now tearing out the Cyclone fence on the Santa Monica. "Out there" is where incidents happen. The windowless room at 120 South Spring is where incidents get "verified." "Incident verification" is turning on the closed-circuit TV on the console and watching the traffic slow down to see (this is "the gawk effect") where the Camaro tore out the fence.

As a matter of fact there is a certain closed-circuit aspect to the entire ₃ mood of the Operations Center. "Verifying" the incident does not after all "prevent" the incident, which lends the enterprise a kind of tranced distance, and on the day recently when I visited 120 South Spring it took considerable effort to remember what I had come to talk about, which was that particular part of the Loop called the Santa Monica Freeway. The Santa Monica Freeway is 16.2 miles long, runs from the Pacific Ocean to downtown Los Angeles through what is referred to at Caltrans as "the East-West Corridor," carries more traffic every day than any other freeway in California, has what connoisseurs of freeways concede to be the most beautiful access ramps in the world, and appeared to have been transformed by Caltrans, during the several weeks before I went downtown to talk about it, into a 16.2-mile parking lot.

The problem seemed to be another Caltrans "demonstration," or ₄ "pilot," a foray into bureaucratic terrorism they were calling "The Diamond Lane" in their promotional literature and "The Project" among themselves. That the promotional literature consisted largely of schedules for buses (or "Diamond Lane Expresses") and invitations to join a car pool via computer ("Commuter Computer") made clear not only the putative point of The Project, which was to encourage travel by car pool and bus, but also the actual point, which was to eradicate a central Southern California illusion, that of individual mobility, without anyone really noticing. This had not exactly worked out. "FREEWAY FIASCO," the *Los Angeles Times* was headlining page-one stories. "THE DIAMOND LANE: ANOTHER BUST BY CALTRANS." "CALTRANS PILOT EFFORT ANOTHER IN LONG LIST OF FAILURES." "OFFICIAL DIAMOND LANE STANCE: LET THEM HOWL."

All "The Diamond Lane" theoretically involved was reserving the fast ₅ inside lanes on the Santa Monica for vehicles carrying three or more people, but in practice this meant that 25 percent of the freeway was reserved for 3 percent of the cars, and there were other odd wrinkles here and there suggesting that Caltrans had dedicated itself to making all movement around Los Angeles as arduous as possible. There was for example the matter of surface streets. A "surface street" is anything around Los Angeles that is not a freeway ("going surface" from one part of town to another is generally regarded as idiosyncratic), and surface streets do not fall directly within the Caltrans domain, but now the engineer in charge of surface streets was accusing Caltrans of threatening and intimidating him. It appeared that Caltrans wanted him to create a "confused and congested situation" on his surface streets, so as to force drivers back to the freeway, where they would meet a still more confused and congested situation and decide to stay home, or take a bus. "We are beginning a process of deliberately making it harder for drivers to use freeways," a Caltrans director had in fact said at a transit conference some months before. "We are prepared to endure considerable public outcry in order to pry John Q. Public out of his car.... I would emphasize that this is a political decision, and one that can be reversed if the public gets sufficiently enraged to throw us rascals out."

Of course this political decision was in the name of the greater good, was in the interests of "environmental improvement" and "conservation of resources," but even there the figures had about them a certain Caltrans opacity. The Santa Monica normally carried 240,000 cars and trucks every day. These 240,000 cars and trucks normally carried 260,000 people. What Caltrans described as its ultimate goal on the Santa Monica was to carry the same 260,000 people, "but in 7,800 fewer, or 232,200 vehicles." The figure "232,200" had a visionary precision to it that did not automatically create confidence, especially since the only effect so far had been to disrupt traffic throughout the Los Angeles basin, triple the number of daily accidents on the Santa Monica, prompt the initiation of two lawsuits against Caltrans, and cause large numbers of Los Angeles County residents to behave, most uncharacteristically, as an ignited and conscious proletariat. Citizen guerrillas splashed paint and scattered nails in the Diamond Lanes. Diamond Lane maintenance crews expressed fear of hurled objects. Down at 120 South Spring the architects of the Diamond Lane had taken to regarding "the media" as the architects of their embarrassment, and Caltrans statements in the press had been cryptic and contradictory, reminiscent only of old communiqués out of Vietnam.

To understand what was going on it is perhaps necessary to have participated in the freeway experience, which is the only secular communion Los Angeles has. Mere driving on the freeway is in no way the same as participating in it. Anyone can "drive" on the freeway, and many people with no vocation for it do, hesitating here and resisting there, losing the rhythm of the lane change, thinking about where they came from and where they are going. Actual participants think only about where they are. Actual participation requires a total surrender, a concentration so intense as to seem a kind of narcosis, a rapture-of-the-freeway. The mind goes clean. The rhythm takes over. A distortion of time occurs, the same distortion that characterizes the instant before an accident. It takes only a few seconds to get off the Santa Monica Freeway at National-Overland, which is a difficult exit requiring the driver to cross two new lanes of traffic streamed in from the San Diego Freeway, but those few seconds always seem to me the longest part of the trip. The moment is dangerous. The exhilaration is in doing it. "As you acquire the special skills involved," Reyner Banham observed in an extraordinary chapter about the freeways in his 1971 *Los Angeles: The Architecture of Four Ecologies*, "the freeways become a special way of being alive . . . the extreme concentration required in Los Angeles seems to bring on a state of heightened awareness that some locals find mystical."

Indeed some locals do, and some nonlocals too. Reducing the number 8 of lone souls careering around the East-West Corridor in a state of mechanized rapture may or may not have seemed socially desirable, but what it was definitely not going to seem was easy. "We're only seeing an initial period of unfamiliarity," I was assured the day I visited Caltrans. I was talking to a woman named Eleanor Wood and she was thoroughly and professionally grounded in the diction of "planning" and it did not seem likely that I could interest her in considering the freeway as regional mystery. "Any time you try to rearrange people's daily habits, they're apt to react impetuously. All this project requires is a certain rearrangement of people's daily planning. That's really all we want."

It occurred to me that a certain rearrangement of people's daily 9 planning might seem, in less rarefied air than is breathed at 120 South Spring, rather a great deal to want, but so impenetrable was the sense of higher social purpose there in the Operations Center that I did not express this reservation. Instead I changed the subject, mentioned an earlier "pilot project" on the Santa Monica: the big electronic message boards that Caltrans had installed a year or two before. The idea was that traffic information transmitted from the Santa Monica to the Xerox Sigma V could be translated, here in the Operations Center, into suggestions to the driver, and flashed right back out to the Santa Monica. This operation, in that it involved telling drivers electronically what they already knew empirically, had the rather spectral circularity that seemed to mark a great many Caltrans schemes, and I was interested in how Caltrans thought it worked.

"Actually the message boards were part of a larger pilot project," Mrs. 10 Wood said. "An ongoing project in incident management. With the message boards we hoped to learn if motorists would modify their behavior according to what we told them on the boards."

I asked if the motorists had. 11

"Actually no," Mrs. Wood said finally. "They didn't react to the signs 12 exactly as we'd hypothesized they would, no. *But.* If we'd *known* what the motorist would do . . . then we wouldn't have needed a pilot project in the first place, would we."

The circle seemed intact. Mrs. Wood and I smiled, and shook hands. I [13] watched the big board until all lights turned green on the Santa Monica and then I left and drove home on it, all 16.2 miles of it. All the way I remembered that I was watched by the Xerox Sigma V. All the way the message boards gave me the number to call for CAR POOL INFO. As I left the freeway it occurred to me that they might have their own rapture down at 120 South Spring, and it could be called Perpetuating the Department. Today the California Highway Patrol reported that, during the first six weeks of the Diamond Lane, accidents on the Santa Monica, which normally range between 49 and 72 during a six-week period, totaled 204. Yesterday plans were announced to extend the Diamond Lane to other freeways at a cost of $42,500,000.

Using the Dictionary

To set the humorous **tone** of her essay, the author often uses solemn, impressive words for prosaic, everyday matters. What is the meaning of each of the following examples, and what is its usual frame of reference?   1. *reverential* (1)   2. *veneration* (1)   3. *totemic* (1)   4. *connoisseur* (3)   5. *foray* (4)   6. *putative* (4)   7. *fiasco* (4)   8. *idiosyncratic* (5)   9. *opacity* (6)   10. *proletariat* (6)   11. *secular* (7)   12. *narcosis* (7)   13. *empirically* (9)   14. *spectral* (9)   15. *hypothesize* (12)

The Writer's Agenda

In this essay, the author reports on the operations of an agency in order to make us think about the electronic, bureaucratically controlled future that may lie ahead. How does she inform us? How does she make us think?

1. In the first three paragraphs, what do we learn about the Caltrans Center? What do we learn about its task and operations? (Summarize the *factual information* the author gives us in her introductory paragraphs.)

2. In these same introductory paragraphs, the author creates the characteristic *atmosphere* or mood of the center, and she strongly suggests her personal attitude toward it. What is that atmosphere, and what is her attitude? (What are key phrases or especially revealing details?)

3. The centerpiece of this essay is the author's account of the Diamond Lane *pilot project*. What was the aim? What was the procedure? What was the result?

4. From the beginning, the author shows her strongly *negative* attitude toward the experiment. Where and how? What is the basis of her objections?

5. Throughout the essay but especially toward the end, Didion seems to use the statements or characteristic phrases of people as evidence against them. Where and how?

6. Toward the end, the author mentions an earlier pilot project. How does she use it as a *parallel* or *precedent*?

7. How does Didion's conclusion *reinforce* the basic attitudes prevailing in her essay? How does it leave the reader with a fitting sense of satisfactory completion?

For Discussion or Writing

8. Joan Didion is quick to notice the ironic contrast between good intentions and unfortunate unintended results, or between what we expect of people and what they actually do. Where and how does this kind of **irony** show in her essay?

9. Do you think Didion is playing up to familiar stereotypes about Californians? (What kind of reader would make a good audience for her?)

10. What are familiar popular notions or stereotypes of bureaucrats and bureaucracy? How do they compare with the view of bureaucracy implied in this essay? Is there something to be said *in defense* of the bureaucrats Didion attacks?

11. Do you think that what the author describes in this essay is symbolic or prophetic of what awaits us in the future?

12. Critics of innovation for its own sake often complain that much overelaborate or unnecessary technology is used without regard for what it does to people's lives. To judge from your own observation and experience, how true is this charge?

Branching Out

13. Write a paper in which you first show that a current procedure is *not* working. Then present a better way of doing the same thing. Possible subjects are traffic control, teaching a foreign language, electing a President, rehabilitating convicted criminals, providing low-income housing, curing addiction, garbage disposal, or disposing of toxic waste.

STUDENT MODEL 4

FOR READING: Study the following short selection as a possible model for writing of your own. How do you react to it overall? What makes it interesting or effective? Answer the following more specific questions:

1. (PURPOSE) What was the writer trying to do?
2. (AUDIENCE) What kind of reader would make a good reader for this selection?
3. (SOURCES) Where did the writer turn for material?
4. (THESIS) Does the selection have a central idea or unifying thesis?
5. (STRUCTURE) What is the author's overall plan or strategy?

6. (STYLE) What makes the piece effective or memorable (for instance, striking details, memorable phrases)?

7. (REVISION) What do you think the writer could or should have done differently?

Catherine A. Russell
Tree-Cutting, Country Style

This paper is dedicated to Jessie Strong, a man (then) in his seventies, who taught me everything I know about cutting down a tree. 1

In the rural Midwest, a good store of firewood is a necessity; many 2 people burn wood as the sole or at least major source of heat for winters with temperatures that may get down well below zero. Some people buy their wood from backwoods folk who cut and sell wood for a living; others, like me, prefer to cut their own wood. This paper describes the usual tree-cutting process under some rather unusual circumstances.

It was a few months after I moved to south central Missouri that 3 during a vicious storm one of two huge oaks in our front yard was struck by lightning. Although it was spring, the leaves gradually turned brown and fell off. The next spring, we hoped to see some sign of life, but there was none. One day Jessie, my neighbor, hollered from where he was sitting on the front porch, "That tree needs to come down!" This I knew only too well.

"When?" I hollered back to Jessie. 4

"Tomorrow!" 5

"O.K. About nine? Bring Old Gappy." 6

Old Gappy was Jessie's six-foot, two-man (or two-woman) cross-cut 7 saw. That saw, with jagged-tooth edge (some teeth three to four inches deep) had cut down many a tree since Jessie had gotten it thirty or so years previously. Unless one has access to a heavy-duty, long-bladed chain saw, a cross-cut saw such as Old Gappy is the main tool needed for a large tree-cutting operation. One also needs a splitting maul (a thicker and blunter version of the traditional ax with a "maul" head—about six to nine pounds of iron at the end of a sturdy hickory handle), a large iron wedge, and a traditional ax as well as a Carborundum sharpening file. For this job, Jessie also brought a thick rope to guide the fall.

Before cutting down a tree, it is always a good idea to notch it in the 8 direction where it is intended to fall. True to form, before we started, Jessie took the Carborundum file, placed it flat against one side of the ax, and gave the blade a few smooth strong outward thrusts to sharpen it—first one side, then the other. Then he took the sharpened ax and cut a wedge-shaped chip out of the trunk on the side where we wanted the tree to fall. First he cut downward at about a 45 degree angle to begin a notch approximately six inches deep into the three foot (diameter) trunk; he then cut straight at a 90 degree angle into the tree to meet the diagonal cut.

After the tree had been notched, Jessie and I each took an end of Old ₉
Gappy, grabbed ahold of the sturdy, peg-shaped handles, and set the saw
teeth against the trunk, opposite where the chip had been removed. It took a
moment of rocking side to side before we stopped forcing and started
guiding the blade. Slowly we established the familiar give-and-take movement necessary to a successful tree cutting operation. The two cutters must
synchronize their work, surrendering to the steady, common, almost metro-
nomic back-and-forth rhythm of the task. The whole body needs to be taken
over by the rhythm, rather than just one's arms. (Using only one's arms, one
tires soon.)

It is crucial to learn to let the *saw* do the work of cutting—guide rather ₁₀
than force the saw blade into the wood. If one forces the teeth, even the
slightest bit, into the wood, the blade will snag and stop, immovable, in
the trunk.

About two-thirds of the way cutting through the trunk, we stopped to ₁₁
tie the rope around the trunk a foot or so higher than we were sawing. I laid
the wedge and maul closer to the trunk so they could be handy to grab and
use when necessary. Once the rope was securely tied, we resumed sawing.

Soon the tree gave the first slight warning crack. Sometimes, when one ₁₂
gets this close to cutting through the tree, the trunk twists slightly, pinching
the saw. In this event, one must pick up the iron wedge, place it, point first, at
a 90 degree angle directly behind the blade, and pound it in with the splitting
maul until the weight of the tree is eased off the blade and one can proceed
to saw. It usually doesn't take much more sawing before, with a final, large
c-r-r-r-a-a-a-c-c-k-k-k! the tree leans and then falls.

Many people are terrified to be near a falling tree. The tendency is to ₁₃
panic and run from the tree fall. It's important, therefore, to realize that the
safest place to stand is right next to the trunk; one can then step a couple of
feet around the trunk in whatever direction is necessary to get out of the
way of the tree.

As our tree slowly began to fall, Jessie took ahold of the rope and ₁₄
gently guided the tree to one side, and it fell right on target in the middle of
the driveway. What satisfaction to have the job done!

Now that the tree was down, it only remained to cut it into firewood. ₁₅
Another neighbor helped, and in less than three hours, the three of us had
the tree cut up and toted to the woodpile near the house. Throughout the
next winter, thanks, in part, to that lightning-struck oak, I had plenty of
wood to burn for heat.

FOR WRITING: Do you remember an experience that taught you how to do something
or how something works? Or do you remember an experience where *you* taught
someone else something important? Write a paper about such a learning or teaching
experience. Trace the process for your reader.

ADDITIONAL WRITING TOPICS 4

Process

A. Write a "how-to" essay offering practical instructions, directions, or advice. Choose a topic like the following:

1. how to bake your own bread
2. how to prepare a (gourmet or vegetarian or Mexican) meal
3. how to lose weight
4. how to plant and care for a lawn or a vegetable garden
5. how to use a word processor
6. how to teach a youngster to drive
7. how to make a house a home
8. how to raise prize-winning dogs
9. how to do a computer search
10. how to take apart and reassemble an engine
11. how to make a marriage last
12. how to arrange your own divorce
13. how to organize an old-style wedding
14. how to become a successful competitor
15. how to make your own clothes
16. how to handle people who tend to lose their tempers
17. how to meet people and make new friends
18. how to lose friends
19. how to make a backpacking trip a success
20. how to aid a drowning victim

B. Trace a process to explain "how it works" or how something came to be. Divide the process into major stages; fill in accurate, graphic detail; explain technical terms. Choose a topic like the following:

1. producing a campus newspaper
2. the Americanization of a new immigrant
3. a new treatment or medical procedure
4. a promotional campaign for a new product
5. a body-building contest or similar contest
6. how a computer stores and retrieves information
7. the staging of a theatrical production
8. the life cycle of a fad
9. the workings of a lawsuit
10. the making of a pearl
11. finding oil
12. being arrested
13. becoming a model
14. starting a business
15. making pottery

COMPARISON AND CONTRAST

Guiding Our Choices

OVERVIEW

We compare and contrast two things to get a clear picture of similarities and differences. How are the two things alike? How are they different? Many occasions that require some organized thinking call for comparison and contrast. Car buyers, for example, compare prices, engines, interiors, gas mileage, and optional equipment. If they start asking themselves, "Why trade it in?" they may compare payments, maintenance costs, and fuel costs for a new model with estimated repair and fuel costs of their old car.

PURPOSE Well-used comparison or contrast helps readers notice, it helps them understand, and it helps them choose. We become more vividly aware of the bare, boxy, glass-and-steel style of many downtown office buildings when a writer contrasts it with the ornamented stone facades of earlier high rises. We begin to understand the workings of nuclear fusion when a writer systematically compares and contrasts it with the more familiar process of nuclear fission, releasing energy through the splitting of the atom. We are persuaded to retire our clattering old typewriter when an article graphically demonstrates, on the one hand, the messy erasures, cutting and pasting, and tedious recopying of traditional typing and, on the other hand, the ease of revision and recopying of current word-processing equipment. Comparison or contrast is a widely useful tool, serving a writer in many different situations.

AUDIENCE A writer using comparison and contrast often writes as an expert guide for readers who have an immediate practical need for explanations or instructions. In other cases, the writer is an insider or expert writing for a general audience curious about or interested in the subject. In still other cases, however, the audience for writing that compares and contrasts is a relatively knowledgeable, specialized audience reading to see how new developments compare with more familiar ideas and practices in a special field.

BENEFITS FOR THE WRITER (1) Systematic use of comparison or contrast teaches you to organize. It requires you to organize a body of material that has no obvious built-in sequence or ground plan. You will have to *work out* the pattern that best helps your reader see important connections. You will have to line things up so that important similarities and differences stand out.

(2) By the same token, the planning for a comparison-and-contrast paper will usually require more than an informal scratch outline. As you line up major points for comparison, you learn how to use a *formal outline* to organize a substantial body of material. You learn to check the built-in road map your paper provides for your reader for detours, backtrackings, and dead ends.

COMPARISON AND CONTRAST
Additional Reading

Lewis Thomas, Ant City and Human Society   (p. 364)
Isaac Asimov, Nuclear Fusion   (p. 374)
D. Cossina (student theme), A Good Neighbor   (p. 513)

WRITER'S GUIDE 5

Comparison and Contrast

Effective comparison and contrast line things up in such a way that we can see important connections and become aware of important distinctions. Remember the following points about the *why* and *how* of papers devoted to comparison and contrast:

(1) *Use comparison and contrast to call attention, to make things stand out.* The basic function of comparison and contrast is to help open our eyes, to make us notice things that we might otherwise overlook. The following are two key passages from a column about the author's return from a weekend trip to the country. By going from the friendly, warm small-town atmosphere of the holiday weekend to the suspicious, cold workaday world of city streets, we become more vividly aware of both:

(The rural community)   The weekend is over, and we drive down the country road from the cottage to the pier, passing out our last supply of waves. We wave at people walking and wave at people riding. We wave at people we know and wave at people who are strangers.... When we arrive at the pier, the boat is already crowded with the end-of-summer exodus. Island emigrants help each other stack cat carriers and lift bags onto the back of the boat....

(The city)   To easy my reentry into workaday life, I decide to walk the last mile home. I am left at a familiar, safe city corner and, yes, almost immediately, my accent changes. I begin to "speak" in the city's body language: neutral and wary. Suddenly conscious of my own adjustments, I notice how few eyes meet on this mile. Women do not look at men. Old people do not look at teenagers. Men do not smile at each other.... (Ellen Goodman, "Wave of the Past," *Washington Post*)

(2) *Use comparison and contrast to help explain.* We can use important similarities to help the reader go from the familiar to the unfamiliar. Then we can point to important differences to help explain what made the unfamiliar strange and new. In the following sample passage, the writer helps us visualize the musk-ox, at one time nearly extinct, by comparing it with its more familiar cousin, the bison, or buffalo:

A robust and shaggy animal, the musk-ox at first glance resembles a bison because of its humped shoulders and stocky build. Like the bison, it feeds on plants, but it is smaller, growing to about six feet in length and the height of a man's chest. Designed to thrive in the cold, the musk-ox has a coat so thick that it needs no barn to shelter it from Arctic blizzards. It retains body heat with two thicknesses of hair: an outer coat of long black hair that completely covers the animal except for the lips and nostrils, shedding the rain, and an inner coat of soft, gray-brown hair, called qiviut, that is so dense that neither cold nor moisture can penetrate it.   (Noel Vietmeyer, "The Return of the Musk-Ox," *Quest*)

(3) *Use comparison and contrast to help the reader make choices.* Writers often compare things in order to guide our evaluation—to show us which is preferable and why. A magazine article may provide a detailed comparison to make us choose mass transit over private cars, private health insurance over "socialized medicine," or coal-burning plants over nuclear reactors. The following excerpts focus on the advantages that an old familiar method of hauling loads has over more modern ones. Note the thesis that states the point of the comparison:

Time to Get a Horse

THESIS:	Draft horses are back in fashion. *Work horses do some jobs better than tractors or trucks.* During a recent blizzard, the animal keepers at Chicago's Brookfield Zoo found that the only way to haul feed through the snow was using their team of Clydesdales. . . .
AREAS OF APPLICATION (1) Forestry	In Oregon, Washington, and Montana, more and more horses are being used in forestry, especially in selective logging. The animals are gentle to the forest floor: within weeks there is no record that they were there . . . .
(2) Farming	All over the country, small farmers are finding it harder and harder to meet the cost of buying and operating machinery designed for big acreage. Recent analysis of horse-powered Amish farms in Pennsylvania shows that consumption of fossil fuel is minuscule, and profitability is higher than on neighboring mechanized farms. . . .
(3) Special hauling	Horses also seem to have a future in special haulage: utility companies in Washington and some Southern states, for instance, use horses to pull electric and telephone cables through broken terrain . . . . (Noel Vietmeyer, *Quest*)

(4) *Line things up clearly for a point-by-point comparison.* To organize your comparison, you first have to line up possible similarities and differences clearly in your own mind. To make sure the reader sees the important connections, you may decide to try a **point-by-point** comparison. You first identify perhaps three or four major areas or features where

comparison would prove instructive. Then you take up each of these in turn. Jade Snow Wong, author of "Fifth Chinese Daughter," was raised in the strict Chinese tradition of her immigrant parents, but she slowly adopted contrasting American ways. On some points, the two traditions are similar: The parents' dedication to hard work has its parallel in the traditional American work ethic. However, on other points, such as the methods of education, the two traditions are strikingly different. An outline for a point-by-point comparison might look like this:

Chinese Tradition and the American Way

THESIS: Jade Snow Wong was raised in the strict Chinese tradition but gradually adopted more modern American ways.

I. The work ethic
   A. The traditional Chinese way
   B. The American way
II. The authority of parents
   A. The traditional Chinese way
   B. The American way
III. The methods of education
   A. The traditional Chinese way
   B. The American way
IV. The different roles of men and women
   A. The traditional Chinese way
   B. The American way

(5) *Line things up clearly for a parallel-order comparison.* When comparing two people or two institutions, we may decide that we should do a separate portrait of each in order to do them justice. However, in order to help the reader make the necessary connections, we try to take up the same or similar points in the same order. For example, a writer intrigued by the resemblances between a school and a jail might describe each institution separately but discuss major points in the same order: first, the role of the *authorities*; then, the duties of the *inmates*; finally, the system of *punishments and rewards.*

In such a **parallel-order** comparison, we must help the reader see the pattern and make the right connections at each point. (A conclusion that summarizes the similarities or differences can help make sure that such a paper does not break into two separate halves.) The following is a sample outline of a paper comparing two characters from imaginative literature: the shrewd Odysseus (or Ulysses) of Homer's *Odyssey* and the glorious Achilles of Homer's *Iliad*. Each half of the paper takes up key qualities of the traditional heroes *in the same order*: their fame as warriors, their eloquence as leaders, and their personal temperament.

The Fox and the Lion

THESIS: Odysseus and Achilles are both great traditional heroes, but Odysseus is closer to an ideal blending of brain and brawn.

I. Odysseus as a traditional hero
   A. Great warrior (unsurpassed in archery)
   B. Eloquent speaker
   C. Shrewd counselor (carefully weighing the facts)
   D. Very human character (lover of good food and wine)
II. Achilles as a traditional hero
   A. Great warrior
   B. Not a great speaker
   C. Impulsive person (insolent and resentful)
   D. Half divine (indifferent to food)

Notice the strategy the writer has chosen for ordering the four parallel points: The paper takes us from the most familiar or predictable, to which we will readily assent (their being great warriors) to the less obvious (their qualities as speakers and planners, for instance—the qualities that relate more to the brain than to brawn).

(6) *Group similarities and differences together in separate parts of your paper if this division seems the best strategy.* You may first want to show why two things seem superficially different but then go on to show underlying similarities. Or you may want to show that two things are superficially alike but then go on to show underlying differences.

Many writers have compared human beings to ants or have commented on the amazing, almost-human working together of numberless ants or bees as part of one huge insect society. A writer following up such a comparison in detail might first make us aware of the surface resemblances between such insect societies and our own: In a big city, the masses of pedestrians hurrying to and fro may seem like the restlessly scurrying columns of ants; the teams of workers on a big construction job may seem like the restless worker bees busy in the hive. But in the second part of the essay, the writer may start to stress the qualities that make us human: our ability to move on and strike out on our own, or our capacity for taking on many different tasks and trying new and different ways.

(7) *Provide the signals that will guide your reader.* Whatever overall plan you adopt, use the necessary links or **transitional expressions** that serve as signposts for the reader. We steer the reader toward similarities by words and phrases such as *like, similarly, in similar fashion.* We signal a contrast by such words and phrases as *however, whereas, by contrast, on the other hand.*

To sum up: Systematic comparison or contrast forces a writer to work out a clear overall strategy for a paper. It requires a writer to organize the material in such a way that important similarities or differences become clear to the reader. When well done, comparison and contrast can make us see important connections, alert us to important differences, and help us make important choices.

Prewriting Activities 5

1. The following passages are adapted from a description of New York City elementary schools of many years ago. For a *"then-and-now" contrast*, provide contrasting material from your own grade-school experience. Write a paragraph or two for each of the four headings.

   I. *The students*: Many students were the children of poor immigrants. Their parents spoke Italian or German or Yiddish at home. Often their parents and their "greenhorn" relatives knew little or no English. Though they worked in the sweatshops, many of these immigrants believed in America as a haven from persecution and as the land of opportunity. . . .

   II. *The teachers*: The teachers were almost all women. They wore long dresses with high lace collars and black, shiny, "pointy" shoes. They were all extraordinarily clean-looking. Most of them seemed to be called Miss McDonald. . . .

   III. *Goals*: Teachers often did not seem to like, let alone love, us students. But they taught us—firmly, thoroughly, and relentlessly. They did not ask or seem to care who their students were or where they came from. But the teachers knew what students were in school for—to become civilized, to be Americanized, to learn to read and write English. . . .

   IV. *Tools:* The main teaching tool was the "reader," a collection of readings somewhat stuffy, stodgy, "noble," and, at times, mind-stretching. The readers were filled with "memory gems"—lines, phrases, and thoughts that echoed in the students' minds. . . .

2. For a *preliminary collection of material,* jot down ideas for a possible comparison and contrast of one of the following:
   - a dormitory and a hotel
   - a school and a jail
   - a college lecture and a television news broadcast
   - learning to swim and learning to write
   - having a roommate and being married
   - being a passenger and being a driver

Write quickly. First, jot down any possible similarities. Then jot down possible differences. Include striking details, examples, explanations.

3. A familiar figure in much modern literature is the alienated, frustrated, or lonely individual. Prepare a preliminary outline for a *parallel-order comparison* of

two such figures. Choose characters from books you have read or from plays or movies you have seen. After each subheading in your outline, jot down some details that show what kind of detail you would use to develop each point.

4. For *sentence practice*, write half a dozen sentences that sum up an important contrast in a pointed, memorable form. Use the following sentences as possible models:

a. Scientists have to be interested in things, not persons. (Marie Curie)

b. To err is human; to forgive, divine. (Alexander Pope)

c. To do good is noble; to teach others to do good is nobler, and no trouble. (Mark Twain)

d. The summer soldier and the sunshine patriot will, in this crisis, shrink from the service of his country, but he that stands it now deserves the love and thanks of man and woman. (Thomas Paine)

e. The practical person comes out of the house, sees the rain clouds, and goes back for an umbrella; the poetic person comes out of the house, says, "Look at those clouds!" and walks off into the rain.

Paragraph Practice 5

Write a paragraph about a changing trend. Work out a then-and-now contrast or a contrast between now and what is to come. Study and discuss the following paragraph as a possible model.

The Russians Are Coming

Not since the Nixon-era cop-and-vigilante cycle has the action film become so blatant an arena for political wish fulfillment. In the early seventies, however, the demons were American. These days they strike from the outside. Given the current climate, it now seems remarkable that as recently as 1983, *Octopussy* employed James Bond's first Russian antagonist in two decades. With the informal detente of the mid-sixties, Russians were supplanted by Chinese or East Germans as screen villains—and, in films and television series like *The Russians are Coming! The Russians are Coming!* and "The Man From U.N.C.L.E.," they even appeared in a sympathetic light. These days, the only good Russian is a dead Russian—or a defector. Either way, Main Street is the enemy's goal, infusing movies as otherwise disparate as *White Nights* and *Red Dawn, Moscow on the Hudson* and *Invasion U.S.A.* with a backbeat of paranoia and an undercurrent of narcissism. (J. Hoberman, "The Fascist Guns," *American Film*)

BACKGROUND: The following article was written by an associate dean of the Columbia University Graduate School of Journalism (and former Washington reporter) for the "My Turn" column of *Newsweek* magazine. Carolyn Lewis has had a successful career in print, radio, and television journalism and taught broadcast journalism first at Boston University and then at Columbia. She is the author of *Reporting for Television*, published in 1983. In the article that follows, she develops a contemporary version of a contrast that has been a favorite topic of writers through the ages: life in the city and life in the country.

Carolyn Lewis

A Different Drummer

GUIDE TO READING: This article is a very informal exploration of two contrasting lifestyles. Look for striking or revealing details that provide a clue to a basic difference. Try to sort them out—try to line them up under major headings.

My two sons live lives starkly different from my own. They make their   1
homes in small rural places, and theirs are lives of voluntary simplicity.

They have chosen work that gives service to others, requires no great   2
competitiveness, and does no harm in the name of greater good. They share
a singular lack of interest in accruing possessions. Their clothes would
make Brooks Brothers shudder, and they drive automobiles that are both
ancient and uncomely.

They till the earth around their modest houses to grow vegetables,   3
trees, and flowers. They are entertained by shared festivities with neighbors, wives, and children. They have records for music, books for learning,
and each lives close enough to the sea to enjoy the esthetic pleasures of blue
vistas and open sky.

This curious phenomenon—of ambitious, competitive, urban parents   4
spawning gentle, unambitious, country offspring—is not unique to my own
experience. I observe it all around me and listen with amusement to the
puzzled comments of middle-aged parents faced with this unexpected
generational shift.

"We gave him everything, and he chooses to weave blankets in Maine,"   5
they say accusingly. Or, "We invested in Andover and Harvard, and he cuts
trees in Oregon." The refrain is sorrowful, even embarrassed, as though our
children have somehow turned against us by choosing to live in ways
different from our own.

But I confess that every time I return to the big city after visiting my   6
children, I am haunted by a psychic malaise. I go through my days comparing this with that, and more and more the *that* is looking better.

What my sons have is a world that is small enough to be readily understood, where those responsible wear a human face. When I talk about the big city where I live, in the only terms that can grasp its enormity—about groups and studies, trends and polls—my sons smile sweetly and speak of people who live around the corner, have specific names and definitive problems. Theirs are flesh-and-blood realities instead of my pale, theoretical formulations. They remind me that the collective humanity I measure and label is far less interesting and vital than the individual who, mercifully, in the end will defy categorization.

When I ask him how he likes living in a town of 500 people three hours away from the nearest large city, my son Peter says: "Just fine. You see, I know who I am here."

That statement resonates in my brain. It's true; he has a definable space to call his own. He has warming relationships with family and neighbors. He has what E. F. Schumacher would call "good work." [1]

On the other hand, he certainly cannot be labeled rich. His income is hardly the kind that makes the GNP go into a tailspin. When the sophisticated instruments of measurement are applied to his life—husband, wife, two children (family of four earning so much)—they mark him low income.

I, by comparison, living in my overpriced city apartment, walking to work past putrid sacks of street garbage, paying usurious taxes to local and state governments I generally abhor, I am rated middle class. This causes me to wonder, do the measurements make sense? Are we measuring only that which is easily measured—the numbers on the money chart—and ignoring values more central to the good life?

For my sons there is of course the rural bounty of fresh-grown vegetables, line-caught fish, and the shared riches of neighbors' orchards and gardens. There is the unpaid baby-sitter for whose children my daughter-in-law baby-sits in return, and neighbors who barter their skills and labor. But more than that, how do you measure serenity? Sense of self? The feeling that, in order to get ahead, you don't have to trample on somebody else's skull?

I don't want to idealize life in small places. There are times when the outside world intrudes brutally, as when the cost of gasoline goes up or developers cast their eyes on untouched farmland. There are cruelties, there is bigotry, there are all the many vices and meannesses in small places that exist in large cities. Furthermore, it is harder to ignore them when they cannot be banished psychologically to another part of town or excused as the vagaries of alien groups—when they have to be acknowledged as "part of us."

---

[1][E. F. Schumacher, German-born British economist, in *Small Is Beautiful* (1973), developed proposals for technology on a smaller, more human scale and for a society not depending on continuous economic growth.]

Nor do I want to belittle the opportunities for small decencies in ₁₄ cities—the eruptions of one-stranger-to-another caring that always surprise and delight. But these are, sadly, more exceptions than rules and are often overwhelmed by the awful corruptions and dangers that surround us.

In this society, where material riches and a certain notoriety are ₁₅ considered admirable achievements, it takes some courage to say, no thanks, not for me. The urban pleasures and delights—restaurants, museums, theater, crowds in the streets—continue to have an urgent seductiveness for many young people. For parents like myself, who strove to offer our children these opportunities and riches, it is hard to be reconciled to those same children spurning the offer and choosing otherwise.

Plainly, what my sons want and need is something different—some- ₁₆ thing smaller, simpler, and more manageable. They march to a different drummer, searching for an ethic that recognizes limits, that scorns overbearing competition and what it does to human relations, and that says simply and gently, enough is enough.

Is my sons' solution to the complexity and seeming intractability of ₁₇ modern problems the answer for everyone? Of course not. Some of us have to stay in the cities, do what we can, fight when it is necessary, compete in order to survive. Maybe if we are diligent, we can make things a little better where we are.

But to choose small places, modest ambitions, and values that are ₁₈ tolerant and loving is surely an admirable alternative. It may in the end be the only alternative we have to an urban culture in which we have created so much ugliness, and where we seem to inflict so much pain on each other through neglect, selfishness, and failure of will.

Using the Dictionary

Which of the following words do you need to check?   1. *accrue* (2)   2. *refrain* (5)   3.   *malaise* (6)   4. *categorization* (7)   5. *resonate* (9)   6. *putrid* (11)   7. *usurious*   (11)   8. *bounty*   (12)   9. *serenity*   (12)   10. *bigotry* (13)   11. *vagary* (13)   12. *notoriety* (15)   13. *ethic* (16)   14. *intractability* (17)   15. *diligent* (17)

The Writer's Agenda

Lewis sets out to explore a contrast that confronts people with basic choices. Answer the following questions about how this contrast comes into focus for her readers.

1. As you follow the author's informal exploration of the two contrasting lifestyles, what for you are some of the most striking or revealing *details*? What for you are key terms or revealing phrases that provide important clues to the basic contrast?

2. What are major points of contrast between the two *settings*? For instance, how do people relate to their environment and to other people?

3. What are some of the basic underlying contrasts in *attitude*—toward success, toward competition, toward "limits"?

4. Contrast easily leads to exaggeration, with a heightening or oversimplifying of differences. In paragraph 11 and elsewhere, how does the author protect herself against charges of *oversimplification*?

5. After she weighs the choices, what is the author's *summing up*? What is her verdict on the small-town lifestyle and the "urban culture"?

For Discussion or Writing

6. Editors of publications like *Newsweek* often describe the intended reader of the publication for potential advertisers or subscribers. When the editors published this article, what kind of audience did they have in mind? What features would you include in a *capsule portrait* of the intended *Newsweek* reader?

7. Which of the two lifestyles contrasted in this essay do *you* prefer? Defend your choice.

8. Many observers feel that a new generation of students has turned in the opposite direction from that sketched in this essay—turning excessively ambitious, becoming totally preoccupied with careers. How much evidence have you personally seen of this trend?

9. Develop a detailed contrast between
   - a personal setting (where those involved or responsible wear a "human face") and a very impersonal setting;
   - a world "small enough to be readily understood" and one whose workings or larger purposes we cannot grasp; or
   - a setting where the "small decencies" are observed and one where they are neglected.

10. Choose two styles of living that you have had a chance to compare. For instance, choose city and suburban living, Snowbelt and Sunbelt living, or army life and civilian life. Focus on three or four key features. Prepare a clear *parallel-order* or *point-by-point* comparison.

BACKGROUND: William George Ouchi (born 1943) was one of the first students of management to study systematically the factors that in the sixties and seventies began to give Japanese industry the competitive edge in world markets. A professor of management at UCLA, Ouchi started his research at a time when Japanese products were replacing Swiss watches, German cameras, British motorcycles, and American cars. He published his conclusions in *Theory Z: How American Business Can Meet the Japanese Challenge* in 1981. His findings have since been widely quoted and reprinted; his book became one of the best-known in a flood of books and articles with titles like *Japan as No. 1: Lessons for America.* In the following excerpt, Ouchi compares and contrasts traditional cultural patterns that for him provide a central part of the answer to the familiar question: "What has Japan got that other countries haven't got?"

William Ouchi

The Competitive Edge: Japanese and Americans

GUIDE TO READING: What is Ouchi's central thesis? How does he explain, elaborate, and support it? What use does he make of key examples? What use does he make of contrasting historical information about the two countries?

Perhaps the most difficult aspect of the Japanese for Westerners to comprehend is the strong orientation to collective values, particularly a collective sense of responsibility. Let me illustrate with an anecdote about a visit to a new factory in Japan owned and operated by an American electronics company. The American company, a particularly creative firm, frequently attracts attention within the business community for its novel approaches to planning, organizational design, and management systems. As a consequence of this corporate style, the parent company determined to make a thorough study of Japanese workers and to design a plant that would combine the best of East and West. In their study they discovered that Japanese firms almost never make use of individual work incentives, such as piecework or even individual performance appraisal tied to salary increases. They concluded that rewarding individual achievement and individual ability is always a good thing.

In the final assembly area of their new plant, long lines of young Japanese women wired together electronic products on a piece-rate system: the more you wired, the more you got paid. About two months after opening, the head foreladies approached the plant manager. "Honorable plant manager," they said humbly as they bowed, "we are embarrassed to be so forward, but we must speak to you because all of the girls have threatened to quit work this Friday." (To have this happen, of course, would be a great disaster for all concerned.) "Why," they wanted to know, "can't our plant have the same compensation system as other Japanese companies? When you hire a new girl, her starting wage should be fixed by her age. An eighteen-year-old should be paid more than a sixteen-year-old. Every year on her birthday, she should receive an automatic increase in pay. The idea that any of us can be more productive than another must be wrong, because none of us in final assembly could make a thing unless all of the other people in the plant had done their jobs right first. To single one person out as being more productive is wrong and is also personally humiliating to us." The company changed its compensation system to the Japanese model.

Another American company in Japan had installed a suggestion system much as we have in the United States. Individual workers were encouraged to place suggestions to improve productivity into special boxes. For an accepted idea the individual received a bonus amounting to some fraction of the productivity savings realized from his or her suggestion. After a period of six months, not a single suggestion had been submitted. The American managers were puzzled. They had heard many stories of the inventiveness, the commitment, and the loyalty of Japanese workers, yet not one suggestion to improve productivity had appeared.

The managers approached some of the workers and asked why the suggestion system had not been used. The answer: "No one can come up with a work improvement idea alone. We work together, and any ideas that one of us may have are actually developed by watching others and talking to others. If one of us was singled out for being responsible for such an idea, it would embarrass all of us." The company changed to a group suggestion system, in which workers collectively submitted suggestions. Bonuses were paid to groups which would save bonus money until the end of the year for a party at a restaurant or, if there was enough money, for family vacations together. The suggestions and productivity improvements rained down on the plant.

One can interpret these examples in two quite different ways. Perhaps the Japanese commitment to collective values is an anachronism that does not fit with modern industrialism but brings economic success despite that collectivism. Collectivism seems to be inimical to the kind of maverick creativity exemplified in Benjamin Franklin, Thomas Edison, and John D. Rockefeller. Collectivism does not seem to provide the individual incentive to excel which has made a great success of American enterprise. Entirely apart from its economic effects, collectivism implies a loss of individuality, a loss of the freedom to be different, to hold fundamentally different values from others.

The second interpretation of the examples is that the Japanese collectivism is economically efficient. It causes people to work well together and to encourage one another to better efforts. Industrial life requires interdependence of one person on another. But a less obvious but far-reaching implication of the Japanese collectivism for economic performance has to do with accountability.

In the Japanese mind, collectivism is neither a corporate or individual 7 goal to strive for nor a slogan to pursue. Rather, the nature of things operates so that nothing of consequence occurs as a result of individual effort. Everything important in life happens as a result of teamwork or collective effort. Therefore, to attempt to assign individual credit or blame to results is unfounded. A Japanese professor of accounting, a brilliant scholar trained at Carnegie-Mellon University who teaches now in Tokyo, remarked that the status of accounting systems in Japanese industry is primitive compared to those in the United States. Profit centers, transfer prices, and computerized information systems are barely known even in the largest Japanese companies, whereas they are a commonplace in even small United States organizations. Though not at all surprised at the difference in accounting systems, I was not at all sure that the Japanese were primitive. In fact, I thought their system a good deal more efficient than ours.

Most American companies have basically two accounting systems. 8 One system summarizes the overall financial state to inform stockholders, bankers, and other outsiders. That system is not of interest here. The other system, called the managerial or cost accounting system, exists for an entirely different reason. It measures in detail all of the particulars of transactions between departments, divisions, and key individuals in the organization, for the purpose of untangling the interdependencies between people. When, for example, two departments share one truck for deliveries, the cost accounting system charges each department for part of the cost of maintaining the truck and driver, so that at the end of the year, the performance of each department can be individually assessed, and the better department's manager can receive a larger raise. Of course, all of this information processing costs money, and furthermore may lead to arguments between the departments over whether the costs charged to each are fair.

In a Japanese company a short-run assessment of individual performance is not wanted, so the company can save the considerable expense of 9 collecting and processing all of that information. Companies still keep track of which department uses a truck how often and for what purposes, but like-minded people can interpret some simple numbers for themselves and adjust their behavior accordingly. Those insisting upon clear and precise measurement for the purpose of advancing individual interests must have an elaborate information system. Industrial life, however, is essentially integrated and interdependent. No one builds an automobile alone, no one carries through a banking transaction alone. In a sense the Japanese value of collectivism fits naturally into an industrial setting, whereas the Western individualism provides constant conflicts. The image that comes to mind is of Chaplin's silent film "Modern Times" in which the apparently insignificant hero played by Chaplin successfully fights against the unfeeling machinery of industry. Modern industrial life can be aggravating, even hostile, or natural: all depends on the fit between our culture and our technology.

. . .

The *shinkansen* or "bullet train" speeds across the rural areas of 10 Japan giving a quick view of cluster after cluster of farmhouses surrounded by rice paddies. This particular pattern did not develop purely by chance, but as a consequence of the technology peculiar to the growing of rice, the staple of the Japanese diet. The growing of rice requires the construction and maintenance of an irrigation system, something that takes many hands to build. More importantly, the planting and the harvesting of rice can only be done efficiently with the cooperation of twenty or more people. The "bottom line" is that a single family working alone cannot produce enough rice to survive, but a dozen families working together can produce a surplus. Thus the Japanese have had to develop the capacity to work together in harmony, no matter what the forces of disagreement or social disintegration, in order to survive.

Japan is a nation built entirely on the tips of giant, suboceanic volca- 11 noes. Little of the land is flat and suitable for agriculture. Terraced hillsides make use of every available square foot of arable land. Small homes built very close together further conserve the land. Japan also suffers from natural disasters such as earthquakes and hurricanes. Traditionally homes are made of light construction materials, so a house falling down during a disaster will not crush its occupants and also can be quickly and inexpensively rebuilt. During the feudal period until the Meiji restoration of 1868, each feudal lord sought to restrain his subjects from moving from one village to the next for fear that a neighboring lord might amass enough peasants with which to produce a large agricultural surplus, hire an army and pose a threat. Apparently bridges were not commonly built across rivers and streams until the late nineteenth century, since bridges increased mobility between villages.

Taken all together, this characteristic style of living paints the picture 12 of a nation of people who are homogeneous with respect to race, history, language, religion, and culture. For centuries and generations these people have lived in the same village next door to the same neighbors. Living in close proximity and in dwellings which gave very little privacy, the Japanese survived through their capacity to work together in harmony. In this situation, it was inevitable that the one most central social value which emerged, the one value without which the society could not continue, was that an individual does not matter.

To the Western soul this is a chilling picture of society. Subordinating 13 individual tastes to the harmony of the group and knowing that individual needs can never take precedence over the interests of all is repellent to the Western citizen. But a frequent theme of Western philosophers and sociologists is that individual freedom exists only when people willingly subordinate their self-interests to the social interest. A society composed entirely of self-interested individuals is a society in which each person is at war with the other, a society which has no freedom. This issue, constantly at the heart of understanding society, comes up in every century, and in every society, whether the writer be Plato, Hobbes, or B. F. Skinner.[1]

In order to complete the comparison of Japanese and American living situations, consider flight over the United States. Looking out of the window high over the state of Kansas, we see a pattern of a single farmhouse surrounded by fields, followed by another single homestead surrounded by fields. In the early 1800s in the state of Kansas there were no automobiles. Your nearest neighbor was perhaps two miles distant; the winters were long, and the snow was deep. Inevitably, the central social values were self-reliance and independence. Those were the realities of that place and age that children had to learn to value.

The key to the industrial revolution was discovering that non-human forms of energy substituted for human forms could increase the wealth of a nation beyond anyone's wildest dreams. But there was a catch. To realize this great wealth, non-human energy needed huge complexes called factories with hundreds, even thousands of workers collected into one factory. Moreover, several factories in one central place made the generation of energy more efficient. Almost overnight, the Western world was transformed from a rural and agricultural country to an urban and industrial state. Our technological advance seems to no longer fit our social structure: in a sense, the Japanese can better cope with modern industrialism. While Americans still busily protect our rather extreme form of individualism, the Japanese hold their individualism in check and emphasize cooperation.

Using the Dictionary

A. Check the following: 1. *anachronism* (5) 2. *inimical* (5) 3. *maverick* (5) 4. *interdependence* (6) 5. *assess* (8) 6. *feudal* (11) 7. *homogeneous* (12) 8. *proximity* (12) 9. *precedence* (13) 10. *repellent* (13)

B. Ouchi uses the term *collectivism* (5) without its usual negative connotations. What are the more positive associations it acquires in this essay?

The Writer's Agenda

The author sets out to show basic underlying differences between two societies that have become superficially very much alike. Answer the following questions about how he develops the basic contrast:

1. Ouchi states his *key idea* very early in this selection. Where and how does

---

[1][The ancient Greek philosopher Plato (*The Republic*), the seventeenth-century British philosopher Thomas Hobbes (*Leviathan*), and the twentieth-century American psychologist B. F. Skinner (*Walden Two*) all constructed imaginary or hypothetical future societies.]

he elaborate or explain it later in the essay? What key terms or phrases for you best sum up the two contrasting attitudes?

2. Ouchi starts this selection with two extended *examples*. What makes them effective test cases or strategic choices?

3. How is the author's description of the two different accounting systems relevant to his argument?

4. How does the author use his account of different historical traditions to help explain the basic contrast?

5. To Westerners, the collective spirit of the Japanese may seem an anachronism, something our society has outgrown. Where and how does the author turn the tables? What, according to him, is anachronistic or obsolete about cherished American values?

For Discussion or Writing

6. What is Ouchi's attitude toward his American audience? Does he show an understanding of American attitudes?

7. What questions would you like to ask the author? (How do you think he would answer them?)

8. On the basis of what Ouchi says, what recommendations would you prepare for American management? What changes or improvements are feasible? What obstacles do you anticipate, and how might they be overcome?

9. Compare and contrast two areas of American life—one in which independence or individualism is very strong, and one in which interdependence or teamwork plays a central role.

10. Compare and contrast two areas (institutions, activities) that are in some ways alike but that also are separated by underlying differences. Possible examples:
- advertising and political campaigns
- a business and a school
- living together and marriage
- exercise and sports
- love and friendship

BACKGROUND: Gloria Steinem (born 1935), the granddaughter of a prominent American suffragette, early became a widely heard and widely respected advocate of women's rights. She grew up in poverty in east Toledo, Ohio. After graduating from Smith College with a degree in government, she went to New York to work as a free-lance writer. In 1968, while a columnist for *New York* magazine, she attended a meeting of a women's liberation group; during the next few years, she became an effective and influential leader of the women's movement. An editor of *Ms.*, which was founded in 1971 and became one of the most widely known feminist journals in the country, Steinem has worked as a campaigner, lecturer, and fund raiser on behalf of liberal political causes. In 1983, she published *Outrageous Acts and Everyday Rebellions*, a collection of her essays.

Gloria Steinem

Erotica and

Pornography

GUIDE TO READING: In this essay, Steinem sets up a contrast between two key terms that are likely to be confused in the minds of her readers. How does she lead up to the central issue? Why and how do the two terms overlap? What is the key to the distinction that she is trying to make? What does she do to make the distinction clear and convincing to her readers?

Human beings are the only animals that experience the same sex drive at times when we can—and cannot—conceive.

Just as we developed uniquely human capacities for language, planning, memory, and invention along our evolutionary path, we also developed sexuality as a form of expression; a way of communicating that is separable from our need for sex as a way of perpetuating ourselves. For humans alone, sexuality can be and often is primarily a way of bonding, of giving and receiving pleasure, bridging differentness, discovering sameness, and communicating emotion.

We developed this and other human gifts through our ability to change our environment, adapt physically, and in the long run, to affect our own evolution. But as an emotional result of this spiraling path away from other animals, we seem to alternate between periods of exploring our unique abilities to change new boundaries, and feelings of loneliness in the unknown that we ourselves have created; a fear that sometimes sends us back to the comfort of the animal world by encouraging us to exaggerate our sameness.

The separation of "play" from "work," for instance, is a problem only in the human world. So is the difference between art and nature, or an intellectual accomplishment and a physical one. As a result, we celebrate play, art, and invention as leaps into the unknown; but any imbalance can send us back to nostalgia for our primate past and the conviction that the basics of work, nature, and physical labor are somehow more worthwhile or even moral.

In the same way, we have explored our sexuality as separable from conception: a pleasurable, empathetic bridge to strangers of the same species. We have even invented contraception—a skill that has probably existed in some form since our ancestors figured out the process of birth— in order to extend this uniquely human difference. Yet we also have times of atavistic suspicion that sex is not complete—or even legal or intended-by-god—if it cannot end in conception.

No wonder the concepts of "erotica" and "pornography" can be so crucially different, and yet so confused. Both assume that sexuality can be separated from conception, and therefore can be used to carry a personal message. That's a major reason why, even in our current culture, both may be called equally "shocking" or legally "obscene," a word whose Latin derivative means "dirty, containing filth." This gross condemnation of all sexuality that isn't harnessed to childbirth and marriage has been increased by the current backlash against women's progress. Out of fear that the whole patriarchal structure might be upset if women really had the autonomous power to decide our reproductive futures (that is, if we controlled the most basic means of production), right-wing groups are not only denouncing prochoice abortion literature as "pornographic," but are trying to stop the sending of all contraceptive information through the mails by invoking obscenity laws. In fact, Phyllis Schlafly recently denounced the entire Women's Movement as "obscene."[1]

Not surprisingly, this religious, visceral backlash has a secular, intellectual counterpart that relies heavily on applying the "natural" behavior of the animal world to humans. That is questionable in itself, but these Lionel Tiger-ish studies make their political purpose even more clear in the particular animals they select and the habits they choose to emphasize.[2] The message is that females should accept their "destiny" of being sexually dependent and devote themselves to bearing and rearing their young.

Defending against such reaction in turn leads to another temptation: to merely reverse the terms, and declare that all nonprocreative sex is good. In fact, however, this human activity can be as constructive as destructive, moral or immoral, as any other. Sex as communication can send messages

---

[1][Phyllis Schlafly became known for her strong antifeminist views and her campaign against the Equal Rights Amendment.]

[2][Lionel Tiger is a Canadian-born anthropologist who has written about the relation between biology and culture and who looks with a critical eye at current patterns of marriage and divorce.]

as different as life and death; even the origins of "erotica" and "pornography" reflect that fact. After all, "erotica" is rooted in *eros* or passionate love, and thus in the idea of positive choice, free will, the yearning for a particular person. (Interestingly, the definition of erotica leaves open the question of gender.) "Pornography" begins with a root meaning "prostitution" or "female captives," thus letting us know that the subject is not mutual love, or love at all, but domination and violence against women. (Though, of course, homosexual pornography may imitate this violence by putting a man in the "feminine" role of victim.) It ends with a root meaning "writing about" or "description of" which puts still more distance between subject and object, and replaces a spontaneous yearning for closeness with objectification and a voyeur.

The difference is clear in the words. It becomes even more so by example. 9

Look at any photo or film of people making love; really making love. 10 The images may be diverse, but there is usually a sensuality and touch and warmth, an acceptance of bodies and nerve endings. There is always a spontaneous sense of people who are there because they *want* to be, out of shared pleasure.

Now look at any depiction of sex in which there is clear force, or an 11 unequal power that spells coercion. It may be very blatant, with weapons or torture or bondage, wounds and bruises, some clear humiliation, or an adult's sexual power being used over a child. It may be much more subtle: a physical attitude of conqueror and victim, the use of race or class difference to imply the same thing, perhaps a very unequal nudity, with one person exposed and vulnerable while the other is clothed. In either case, there is no sense of equal choice or equal power.

The first is erotic: a mutually pleasurable, sexual expression between 12 people who have enough power to be there by positive choice. It may or may not strike a sense-memory in the viewer, or be creative enough to make the unknown seem real; but it doesn't require us to identify with a conqueror or a victim. It is truly sensuous, and may give us a contagion of pleasure.

The second is pornographic: its message is violence, dominance, and 13 conquest. It is sex being used to reinforce some inequality, or to create one, or to tell us the lie that pain and humiliation (ours or someone else's) are really the same as pleasure. If we are to feel anything, we must identify with conqueror or victim. That means we can only experience pleasure through the adoption of some degree of sadism or masochism. It also means that we may feel diminished by the role of conqueror, or enraged, humiliated, and vengeful by sharing identity with the victim.

Perhaps one could simply say that erotica is about sexuality, but 14 pornography is about power and sex-as-weapon—in the same way we have come to understand that rape is about violence, and not really about sexuality at all.

Yes, it's true that there are women who have been forced by violent ₁₅ families and dominating men to confuse love with pain; so much so that they have become masochists. (A fact that in no way excuses those who administer such pain.) But the truth is that, for most women—and for men with enough humanity to imagine themselves into the predicament of women— true pornography could serve as aversion therapy for sex.

Of course, there will always be personal differences about what is and ₁₆ is not erotic, and there may be cultural differences for a long time to come. Many women feel that sex makes them vulnerable and therefore may continue to need more sense of personal connection and safety before allowing any erotic feelings. We now find competence and expertise erotic in men, but that may pass as we develop those qualities in ourselves. Men, on the other hand, may continue to feel less vulnerable, and therefore more open to such potential danger as sex with strangers. As some men replace the need for submission from childlike women with the pleasure of cooperation from equals, they may find a partner's competence to be erotic, too.

Such group changes plus individual differences will continue to be ₁₇ reflected in sexual love between people of the same gender, as well as between women and men. The point is not to dictate sameness, but to discover ourselves and each other through sexuality that is an exploring, pleasurable, empathetic part of our lives; a human sexuality that is unchained both from unwanted pregnancies and from violence.

But that is a hope, not a reality. At the moment, fear of change is ₁₈ increasing both the indiscriminate repression of all nonprocreative sex in the religious and "conservative" male world, and the pornographic vengeance against women's sexuality in the secular world of "liberal" and "radical" men. It's almost futuristic to debate what is and is not truly erotic, when many women are again being forced into compulsory motherhood, and the number of pornographic murders, tortures, and woman-hating images are on the increase in both popular culture and real life.

It's a familiar division: wife or whore, "good" woman who is constantly ₁₉ vulnerable to pregnancy or "bad" woman who is unprotected from violence. *Both* roles would be upset if we were to control our own sexuality. And that's exactly what we must do.

In spite of all our atavistic suspicions and training for the "natural" ₂₀ role of motherhood, we took up the complicated battle for reproductive freedom. Our bodies had borne the health burden of endless births and poor abortions, and we had a greater motive for separating sexuality and conception.

Now we have to take up the equally complex burden of explaining that ₂₁ all nonprocreative sex is *not* alike. We have a motive: our right to a uniquely human sexuality, and sometimes even to survival. As it is, our bodies have too rarely been enough our own to develop erotica in our own lives, much less in art and literature. And our bodies have too often been the objects of pornography and the woman-hating, violent practice that it preaches. Consider also our spirits that break a little each time we see ourselves in chains or full labial display for the conquering male viewer, bruised or on our knees, screaming a real or pretended pain to delight the sadist, pretending to enjoy what we don't enjoy, to be blind to the images of our sisters that really haunt us—humiliated often enough ourselves by the truly obscene idea that sex and the domination of women must be combined.

Sexuality *is* human, free, separate—and so are we.   22

But until we untangle the lethal confusion of sex with violence, there   23
will be more pornography and less erotica. There will be little murders in our beds—and very little love.

Using the Dictionary

A. Which of the following terms do you need to check?   1. *evolutionary* (2)   2. *primate* (4)   3. *empathetic* (5)   4. *atavistic* (5)   5. *patriarchal* (6)   6. *autonomous* (6)   7. *visceral* (7)   8. *secular* (7)   9. *objectification* (8)   10. *coercion* (11)   11. *blatant* (11)   12. *predicament* (15)   13. *expertise* (16)   14. *futuristic* (18)   15. *lethal* (23)

B. Check the origin of the following key terms: *obscene, erotic, pornography, voyeur, sadism, masochism.*

The Writer's Agenda

The purpose of this essay is to show a vital distinction between two forms of expression that are often confused—lumped together in the minds of people who condemn both. How does the author develop the central contrast?

1. In her opening paragraphs, how does Steinem explain the reasons for the common confusion between erotica and pornography? (What current backlash is reinforcing that confusion? How is someone who is trying to distinguish the two terms caught between two extremes?)

2. How would you sum up Steinem's basic *distinction* between the two concepts? (Where do you think it is stated most clearly or forcefully?)

3. What *examples* or supporting materials serve best to make the distinction real for you?

4. What *synonyms* and other related words or phrases cluster around the two opposing terms—words with positive connotations for the one, with negative connotations or associations for the other?

5. What *concessions* does Steinem make, or what objections does she try to meet, toward the end of her essay?

6. How, at the end, does Steinem relate her topic to major familiar feminist themes or concerns?

For Discussion or Writing

7. Does Steinem's basic distinction between erotica and pornography seem valid to you? Why or why not?

8. Who would be Steinem's ideal audience? Does a reader have to be a feminist to sympathize with her point of view? Does the reader have to be a woman?

9. Can you develop a contrast between objectionable and acceptable treatment of love and sex in the media? (Can you develop a contrast between objectionable and acceptable treatment of violence?)

10. Do you agree that "woman-hating images are on the increase in both popular culture and real life"?

Branching Out

11. Develop a detailed comparison and contrast between two areas that may in some ways overlap but that are set apart by basic differences. Choose one:
- work and play
- art and nature
- management and labor
- country and rock
- abstract and representational art

BACKGROUND: Amy Gross (born 1942) is a feature editor for *Vogue* who has written on women's issues and women's lives for publications including *Redbook* and the *New York Times*. She wrote the following essay for *Mademoiselle* in 1976. At the time, the term *androgny* was first being widely used by feminist psychologists trying to overcome traditional stereotyped assumptions about masculine and feminine roles. Combining the Greek root words for *man* and *woman*, the term reflects the assumption that members of both sexes combine in different degrees "male" and "female" psychological traits. In her article, Gross followed the lead of researchers exploring the implications of a "liberated sexual identity." She applauded the androgynous man as she reevaluated, from a woman's perspective, the meaning of masculine appeal.

Amy Gross

The Appeal of the
Androgynous Man

GUIDE TO READING: The author discusses the "androgynous" man informally, using personal anecdote and humorous asides. What are the major features of the androgynous man that emerge from her discussion? What are the major points of contrast with the traditional "macho" image of the male? How does she buttress her personal impressions with references to psychological studies?

James Dean was my first androgynous man.[1] I figured I could talk to him. He was anguished and I was 12, so we had a lot in common. With only a few exceptions, all the men I have liked or loved have been a certain kind of man: a kind who doesn't play football or watch the games on Sunday, who doesn't tell dirty jokes featuring broads or chicks, who is not contemptuous of conversations that are philosophically speculative, introspective, or otherwise foolish according to the other kind of man. He is more self-amused, less inflated, more quirky, vulnerable and responsive than the other sort (the other sort, I'm visualizing as the guys on TV who advertise deodorant in the locker room). He is more like me than the other sort. He is what social scientists and feminists would call androgynous: having the characteristics of both male and female.

Now the first thing I want you to know about the androgynous man is that he is neither effeminate nor hermaphroditic. All his primary and

---

[1] [James Dean, who died young in an automobile accident, was the moody, gloomy hero of movies about rebellious, alienated youth.]

secondary sexual characteristics are in order and I would say he's all-man, but that is just what he is not. He is more than all-man.

The merely all-man man, for one thing, never walks to the grocery ₃ store unless the little woman is away visiting her mother with the kids, or is in the hospital having a kid, or there is no little woman. All-men men don't know how to shop in a grocery store unless it is to buy a 6-pack and some pretzels. Their ideas of nutrition expand beyond a 6-pack and pretzels only to take in steak, potatoes, scotch or rye whiskey, and maybe a wad of cake or apple pie. All-men men have absolutely no taste in food, art, books, movies, theatre, dance, how to live, what are good questions, what is funny, or anything else I care about. It's not exactly that the all-man's man is an uncouth illiterate. He may be educated, well-mannered, and on a first-name basis with fine wines. One all-man man I knew was a handsome individual who gave the impression of being gentle, affectionate, and sensitive. He sat and ate dinner one night while I was doing something endearingly feminine at the sink. At one point, he mutely held up his glass to indicate in a primitive, even ape-like way, his need for a refill. This was in 1967, before Women's Liberation. Even so, I was disturbed. Not enough to break the glass over his handsome head, not even enough to mutely indicate the where-abouts of the refrigerator, but enough to remember that moment in all its revelatory clarity. No androgynous man would ever brutishly expect to be waited on without even a "please." (With a "please," maybe.)

The brute happened to be a doctor—not a hard hat—and, to all ₄ appearances, couth. But he had bought the whole superman package, complete with that fragile beast, the male ego. The androgynous man arrives with a male ego too, but his is not as imperialistic. It doesn't invade every area of his life and person. Most activities and thoughts have nothing to do with masculinity or femininity. The androgynous man knows this. The all-man man doesn't. He must keep a constant guard against anything even vaguely feminine (*i.e.*, "sissy") rising up in him. It must be a terrible strain.

Male chauvinism is an irritation, but the real problem I have with the ₅ all-man man is that it's hard for me to talk to him. He's alien to me, and for this I'm at least half to blame. As his interests have not carried him into the sissy, mine have never taken me very far into the typically masculine terrains of sports, business and finance, politics, cars, boats and machines. But blame or no blame, the reality is that it is almost as difficult for me to connect with him as it would be to link up with an Arab shepherd or Bolivian sandalmaker. There's a similar culture gap.

It seems to me that the most masculine men usually end up with the ₆ most feminine women. Maybe they like extreme polarity. I like polarity myself, but the poles have to be within earshot. As I've implied, I'm very big on talking. I fall in love for at least three hours with anyone who engages me in a real conversation. I'd rather a man point out a paragraph in a book—wanting to share it with me—than bring me flowers. I'd rather a man ask what I think than tell me I look pretty. (Women who are very pretty and accustomed to hearing that they are pretty may feel differently.) My experience is that all-men men read books I don't want to see paragraphs of, and don't really give a damn what I or any woman would think about most issues so long as she looks pretty. They have a very limited use for women. I suspect they don't really like us. The androgynous man likes women as much or as little as he likes anyone.

Another difference between the all-man man and the androgynous man is that the first is not a star in the creativity department. If your image of the creative male accessorizes him with a beret, smock and artist's palette, you will not believe the all-man man has been seriously short-changed. But if you allow as how creativity is a talent for freedom, associated with imagination, wit, empathy, unpredictability, and receptivity to new impressions and connections, then you will certainly pity the dull, thick-skinned, rigid fellow in whom creativity sets no fires.

Nor is the all-man man so hot when it comes to sensitivity. He may be true-blue in the trenches, but if you are troubled, you'd be wasting your time trying to milk comfort from the all-man man.

This is not blind prejudice. It is enlightened prejudice. My biases were confirmed recently by a psychologist named Sandra Lipsetz Bem, a professor at Stanford University. She brought to attention the fact that high masculinity in males (and high femininity in females) has been "consistently correlated with lower overall intelligence and lower creativity." Another psychologist, Donald W. MacKinnon, director of the Institute of Personality Assessment and Research at the University of California in Berkeley, found that "creative males give more expression to the feminine side of their nature than do less creative men . . . [They] score relatively high on femininity, and this despite the fact that, as a group, they do not present an effeminate appearance or give evidence of increased homosexual interests or experiences. Their elevated scores on femininity indicate rather an openness to their feelings and emotions, a sensitive intellect and understanding self-awareness and wide-ranging interests including many which in the American culture are thought of as more feminine . . ."

Dr. Bem ran a series of experiments on college students who had been categorized as masculine, feminine, or androgynous. In three tests of the degree of nurturance—warmth and caring—the masculine men scored painfully low (painfully for anyone stuck with a masculine man, that is). In one of those experiments, all the students were asked to listen to a "troubled talker"—a person who was not neurotic but simply lonely, supposedly new in town and feeling like an outsider. The masculine men were the least supportive, responsive or humane. "They lacked the ability to express warmth, playfulness and concern," Bem concluded. (She's giving them the benefit of the doubt. It's possible the masculine men didn't express those qualities because they didn't possess them.)

The androgynous man, on the other hand, having been run through the same carnival of tests, "performs spectacularly. He shuns no behavior just because our culture happens to label it as female and his competence crosses both the instrumental [getting the job done, the problem solved] and the expressive [showing a concern for the welfare of others, the harmony of the group] domains. Thus, he stands firm in his opinion, he cuddles kittens and bounces babies and he has a sympathetic ear for someone in distress."

Well, a great mind, a sensitive and warm personality are fine in their ₁₂ place, but you are perhaps skeptical of the gut appeal of the androgynous man. As a friend, maybe, you'd like an androgynous man. For a sexual partner, though, you'd prefer a jock. There's no arguing chemistry, but consider the jock for a moment. He competes on the field, whatever his field is, and bed is just one more field to him: another opportunity to perform, another fray. Sensuality is for him candy to be doled out as lure. It is a ration whose flow is cut off at the exact point when it has served its purpose— namely, to elicit your willingness to work out on the field with him.

Highly masculine men need to believe their sexual appetite is far ₁₃ greater than a woman's (than a nice woman's). To them, females must be seduced. Seduction is a euphemism for a power play, a con job. It pits man against woman (or woman against man). The jock believes he must win you over, incite your body to rebel against your better judgment: in other words—conquer you.

The androgynous man is not your opponent but your teammate. He ₁₄ does not seduce: he invites. Sensuality is a pleasure for him. He's not quite so goal-oriented. And to conclude, I think I need only remind you here of his greater imagination, his wit and empathy, his unpredictability, and his receptivity to new impressions and connections.

Using the Dictionary

What does each of the following terms mean in the context in which it is used in the essay?   1. *anguished* (1)   2. *speculative* (1)   3. *vulnerable* (1) 4. *effeminate* (2)   5. *uncouth* (3)   6. *revelatory* (3)   7. *imperialistic* (4)   8. *terrains* (5)   9. *empathy* (7)   10. *correlated* (9)   11. *supportive* (10)   12. *humane* (10)   13. *sensuality* (12)   14. *elicit* (12)   15. *incite* (13)

The Writer's Agenda

The author uses comparison and contrast to explain and defend a strong personal preference. Answer the following questions about how she proceeds.

1. In the first five or six paragraphs, what are the major *points of contrast* between the androgynous man and the stereotypical "all-man" man? Can you fit them into some overall pattern?

2. In these early paragraphs, Gross frequently forestalls *misunderstandings* or misconceptions. What are some examples?

3. How do the *research findings* cited by the author confirm her "biases"? What are the most striking or most important points that emerge from this part of the essay?

4. In her discussion of men as sexual partners, the author uses the athlete as an example of the highly masculine man. How and with what results does she use the imagery of sports?

5. Throughout the essay, the author cites as examples *concrete situations* or activities that put men to the test. As you look back over the essay, which of these do you remember best, or which do most to make the basic contrast clear?

For Discussion or Writing

6. Who is Gross's intended audience? Is she writing mainly for other women?

7. Is there a single clue or a central trait that for you helps explain the basic contrast between the two types examined by the author? What for you is the most essential difference?

8. In Gross's essay, how much is merely personal preference? How much to you seems valid observation of general patterns of behavior? What in her essay reminds you of personal experience or observation?

9. Is there something to be said in defense of the "all-man" man?

10. Prepare an essay that would be the logical companion piece to the author's article: "The Appeal of the Androgynous Woman." Develop the contrast between her and a traditional "female" image.

11. Prepare a "then-and-now" paper in which you contrast the changing images of one of the following: a good mother (father); a successful marriage; the ideal male (or female) movie star; the ideal minister.

12. Has the androgynous ideal influenced the portrayal of men in movies or on television?

WRITERS ON WRITING
Amy Gross on Writing and Revising

QUESTION: "The Androgynous Man" has many delightful examples from your own experience. How do you keep track of them—a journal?

ANSWER: I don't keep a journal. I used to keep a notebook of quotes—things I've read, epigrams, something bright someone said in the course of a book review, or a passage from a novel—but I've never kept a kind of poet's notebook of phrases. I think the way I work is to focus on subjects so that the images just come. I type an article over and over again, and often my fingers will surprise me by throwing something new on the page.

QUESTION: When you revise, do you add or subtract?

ANSWER: The longer I've been writing, the more it's a matter of subtracting. Maybe that's because I'm doing so much editing now. I like cleaner copy.

QUESTION: You were in "The Androgynous Man." Did you detach yourself so that you were writing about a character rather than yourself?

ANSWER: No. I think when I wrote the article I felt exactly the way I wrote about myself—that's who I was. I write much less now from a personal viewpoint. I'm not comfortable with it now.

QUESTION: Why not?

ANSWER: When I was at *Mademoiselle*, I wrote as though I were picking up the phone. I trusted and believed that the readers were my friends and very much like me. *Vogue*'s audience is not just much larger than *Mademoiselle*'s was, but it's a much less homogeneous group. *Vogue*'s readers are anywhere from 18 to 70. They're more sophisticated. The *Mademoiselle* reader was a very smart young woman, but the *Vogue* reader, at least as I think of her, is a cooler, more worldly, more formal person. You don't sidle up to her, assuming intimacy.

QUESTION: Where do you spend most of your writing time?

ANSWER: In revision.

QUESTION: Once you've done a draft, do you put the piece away?

ANSWER: No, I just sit there suffering, imagining what would happen if this were a lead, if that were a lead. I stare and stare, and now that I have a word processor, instead of retyping and retyping, I read and reread. I always wish that I had the time to put something away. I assume that time is the best editor.

QUESTION: Do you ever get stuck?

ANSWER: Always. And then I eat a lot; I used to gain five pounds an article. I'd go to the refrigerator, walk around; I'd feel it was hopeless, there was no point, why was I writing? I'd think I was stupid: I hated the sound of my own voice. And then I'd write some more.

But when I wrote my last piece, the first one I had done in a year, I felt tremendously excited. The writing—three-quarters of it, any-way—is throwing stuff out. I would look at what I'd written and get ill at the boring, banal stuff my brain had done. I would sit there hating myself and what I had written. Then I would start to see the thread and how it linked the different beads of sections. It was thrilling to me, and I felt alive, engaged. Then I felt once again that I was temperamentally a writer. Writing is often sitting there waiting for my brain to make connections that I don't know.

—from an interview with the editors of *Essay 2*

STUDENT MODEL 5

FOR READING: Study the following short selection as a possible model for writing of your own. How do you react to it overall? What makes it interesting or effective? Answer the following more specific questions:

1. (PURPOSE) What was the writer trying to do?
2. (AUDIENCE) What kind of reader would make a good reader for this selection?
3. (SOURCES) Where did the writer turn for material?
4. (THESIS) Does the selection have a central idea or unifying thesis?
5. (STRUCTURE) What is the author's overall plan or strategy?
6. (STYLE) What makes the piece effective or memorable (for instance, striking details, memorable phrases)?
7. (REVISION) What do you think the writer could or should have done differently?

Mina Lunt

L-Mode, R-Mode

When I picture my artist friends, I see them clustered on grass like a bevy of quail, looking at each other's paintings. Their clothes, as they say, "make a statement": Some wear sandals (and a few are barefoot); most wear paint-spattered jeans and old shirts or sweaters. They are lost in a world of cadmium yellow and veridian green as they talk shop about lines and textures and paints.

When I picture my business friends, I see them sitting around a conference table. They wear the sales manager's uniform: dark suits (in shades of gray and blue and black), with ties or scarves of subdued patterns. In their regulation attaché cases, they carry the graphs, flowcharts, printouts and statistical tables that link them to the outside world.

Do artists and business people only look different—or do they think ₃ differently? To an artist, ordinary prosaic work is only a means to an end; mundane "outside" work may be necessary for survival. What matters is the expression of inner feelings; the reward is in the pleasure of working on whatever current project designed to make a comment on some aspect of life.

For the business-oriented person, work is one of a series of never- ₄ ending steps toward that ultimate, unobtainable, nebulous goal of success. Feelings and emotions are likely to get in the way. What matters is not the creative moment now but the goals, the objectives, the projections of tomorrow's campaign, of next year's "bottom line."

Neither the artistic person nor the practical person is right or wrong in ₅ his or her perception of and reaction to reality. Each is experiencing life and relating to life from a different perspective. According to one theory, much in these different approaches can be traced to different styles of thinking represented by the right and left hemispheres of the brain. In her book, *Drawing on the Right Side of the Brain*, Betty Edwards quotes Roger Sperry (who pioneered this theory in the late sixties) as saying, "There appear to be two modes of thinking, verbal and nonverbal, represented rather separately in the left and right hemispheres. . . ." Edwards says, "Both hemispheres are involved in higher cognitive functioning, with each half of the brain specialized in complementary fashion for different modes of thinking, both highly complex."

The left hemisphere of the brain is responsible for cognitive mental ₆ processes such as math, language, and consecutive reasoning. This L-mode is linear; it analyzes step by step; it keeps track of time by sequencing one thing after another; it verbalizes to describe or define; it draws conclusions based on systematic logical reasoning.

The right hemisphere is responsible for perceptual and visual activity ₇ (such as art) and for the emotions. This R-mode is synthetic (it puts things together to form patterns or wholes) rather than analytic. It is without a sense of time. It seizes analogies and similarities (it creates metaphors). It has a nonverbal awareness of things. It is intuitive rather than logical and sees things holistically (as wholes) rather than dissecting them in linear fashion.

We are told that the left hemisphere is usually dominant. It is therefore ₈ no surprise that business and science are dominant in our society. By righting the balance, we can broaden our perceptions and come closer to a well-rounded life.

FOR WRITING: Write a paper in which you explore the clash between two strong opposites. Set up a pattern that makes the key differences vivid for your reader.

ADDITIONAL WRITING TOPICS 5

Comparison and Contrast

A.   Choose a pair like the following, and do a detailed comparison and contrast to justify your preference:

1. bus travel and plane travel
2. public school and private school
3. home cooking and cafeteria food
4. marriage and the single life
5. friends from your own or from a different background
6. classical music vs. jazz or rock
7. traditional or modern painting
8. living in a house or in an apartment
9. living in a hot or in a cold climate
10. working for a male or female boss
11. living in America or abroad
12. working or going to school
13. writing a paper or giving a speech
14. a large school and a small school
15. living in a big city or in a small town
16. growing up in a small or in a large family
17. an office job or a job outdoors
18. traditional cooking or a different kind
19. partying or working out
20. football and baseball

B.   Write a "then-and-now" paper that compares and contrasts the past and the present. Choose a topic like the following:

1. the old downtown shopping street and the modern shopping mall
2. an old hotel and a modern motel
3. the old-style family farm and the modern farm
4. an old car and the latest model
5. a neighborhood before and after urban renewal
6. an area before and after yuppification
7. earlier and current election campaigns
8. old-style TV comedy and current fare
9. a childhood setting revisited
10. work before and after a promotion

C.   Write a "before-and-after" essay that compares and contrasts prejudice and reality, or idealized expectation and the real thing. Choose a topic like the following:

1. going to Mexico
2. the person of my dreams

3. first week on campus
4. my first black, white, or Asian friends
5. I move to a mixed neighborhood
6. you're in the army now
7. discovering wedded bliss
8. the Greek life
9. welfare myths and realities
10. leaving home

6

CLASSIFICATION

Sorting Things Out

OVERVIEW

One of the most basic organizing skills required of a writer is the ability to sort out a mass of material into major categories. When we start sorting our miscellaneous material, what goes together and why? Sometimes ready-made categories are built into the subject or come with the territory: lower class, middle class, upper class; single, married, divorced. More often, we have to set up our own categories or modify existing ones so that they will serve our present purpose.

PURPOSE Basically, we sort things and people out into categories in order to help our readers find their way. In much of the writing we do, we do the kind of sorting and labeling that helps readers find their bearings. For instance, we put labels on people, classifying them with others of the same kind: introvert and extrovert; gifted, average, and retarded; workaholics, time servers, and dropouts. When such categories are carefully set up, they help us understand people, and they guide us in our dealings with them. Often, appropriate classification provides a guide to appropriate action. A book on mental illness has to go beyond large catchall categories like "nervous breakdown" to identify specific nervous conditions, often requiring very different treatment.

AUDIENCE Classification is a very basic organizing skill, and the needs it serves range from the practical needs of a very specialized audience to the needs of the general reader who likes to stay well informed. Much writing in both the natural and the social sciences aims at an audience especially interested in problems of classification. An article in a journal devoted to educational psychology, for instance, may propose a new classification of essential learning skills, with implications for the work of teachers, textbook authors, and curriculum specialists.

BENEFITS FOR THE WRITER (1) Setting up a workable system of classification requires organizing skills that will serve a writer well in a great variety of writing tasks. A writer doing an honest job often accumulates material that at first seems confusing or even contradictory, and the basic question often is "What goes with what?"

(2) Sorting things out into workable categories requires a writer to think a subject through. Do our categories truly represent major recurrent kinds, or do they give undue weight to exceptions or types that are really rare though perhaps flashy and noticeable? When does something that we present as a representative type become a narrow stereotype? Individuals often complain that the labels we put on them do not do them justice; they feel misrepresented, nailed into a box.

(3) Writing that sets up a scheme of classification tests our ability to *follow through*. To make a category seem viable and representative, we present a rich array of convincing, representative examples. (Or we may substantiate each category with an exceptionally detailed, convincing case history that our readers will recognize as typical of many other similar cases.)

CLASSIFICATION
Additional Reading

George Orwell, Politics and the English Language   (p. 503)

WRITER'S GUIDE 6

Division and Classification

The two most widely useful methods of organizing a paper are division and classification. We use these methods again and again to bring order into a mass of material. We use them to set up a strategy allowing us to take up one major part of our subject at a time. Some subjects divide along already established lines. A brief guide describing American colleges to foreign students might take up in turn two-year colleges, four-year colleges, and graduate schools. But more often you as the writer will have to set up the categories that suit your purpose. You will have to sort out and classify— pigeonholing examples and details according to a system that you yourself have worked out.

A clearly worked out scheme of division or classification will often organize a paper or an article as a whole. When organizing such a paper, remember the following guidelines:

(1) *Use ready-made lines of division when they suit your purpose.* Often major lines of division are already built into the subject matter, ready for use. A writer charting changing patterns of immigration might classify people who have come from abroad according to their legal status. In this case, major boundary lines are already established by law. The writer's scheme of classification might look like this:

A Nation of Immigrants

THESIS: As in earlier days, Americans today everywhere encounter representatives of a new wave of immigrants, legal and illegal.

    I. Temporary visitors (who are in the country legally for a limited time for study, visits, or travel)
    II. Illegal aliens (who have entered the country, or stayed on, without valid legal papers)
    III. Resident aliens (who have entered legally to work and live here but who are not, or not yet, U.S. citizens)
    IV. Naturalized U.S. citizens

However, for a different purpose a writer might sort out people coming to this country along different lines. A writer who is opposed to an increased flow of immigration might focus on what *entitles* people to immigrate:

    I. Traditional national quotas
    II. Marriage to U.S. citizens or close kinship

III. Preferred occupational categories

IV. Legalized illegal immigrants (through amnesties or in hardship cases, for instance)

(2) *Set up your own categories as needed or appropriate.* Often you will have to draw your own boundary lines, setting up major kinds. As you set up your scheme of classification, ask yourself: "How well do my categories accommodate the evidence? How effectively will they help my readers find their way?" A scheme like the following will be convincing if it seems to fit many (or all) of the examples that come to mind. The system of classification will work if it enables readers to pigeonhole many of the books about schools that they have read:

GENERAL
SCHEME:
School novels may be divided and subdivided, but the essential distinction—perhaps it is also the essential distinction among students—separates those that are proschool from those that are antischool.

FIRST
CATEGORY:
In proschool novels, school is the seat of order and civilization, the clean well-lighted place where conventions are learned and values accepted ... prizes and demerits are justly given, the class has a top and a bottom, and the Head, in his (or her) wisdom, separates the sheep from the goats....

SECOND
CATEGORY:
Antischool novels assume that school is the place where we learn the conventions of oppression and hypocrisy.... Antischool novels are written from the point of view of the anarchic student, ever hopeful that something deliciously awful will happen, that all the teachers, the bores, and the pillars of the community will by some happy accident be unveiled .... (Frances Taliaferro, "Blackboard Art," *Harper's*)

(3) *Set up your major categories according to a consistent principle of classification.* Suppose you wanted to sort out the students at your college into major kinds. You could classify them according to their occupational goals, or according to how serious they are about their studies, or according to their political outlook. If your principle of classification is political outlook, for instance, your groupings might range from radical through moderate to ultraconservative. Confusion starts when your basic principle of selection is not clear, or when you unexpectedly shift from one to the other.

The writer's purpose will determine the basic principle of selection. In his autobiography, Theodore H. White, known for his chronicles of presidential campaigns, writes about the pecking order among students at Harvard University. He accordingly organizes this section of the book according to the students' *social class*:

A Touch of Class

THESIS:
The general
scheme

Students divide themselves by their own discriminations in every generation, and the group I ran with had a neat system of classification. Harvard was divided into three groups—white men, gray men, and meatballs. I belonged to the meatballs, by self-classification.

FIRST GROUP:
The
"aristocracy"

White men were youngsters of great name; my own class held a Boston Saltonstall, a New York Straus, a Chicago Marshall Field, two Roosevelts (John and Kermit), a Joseph P. Kennedy, Jr. . . . Students of such names had automobiles; they went to Boston deb parties, football games, the June crew race against Yale; they belonged to clubs. . . .

SECOND GROUP:
The "solid
middle class"

Between white men above and meatballs at the bottom came the gray men. The gray men were mostly public high school boys, sturdy sons of America's middle class. They went out for football and baseball, manned the *Crimson* and the *Lampoon*, ran for class committees and, later in life, for school committees and political office. They came neither of the aristocracy nor of the deserving poor, as did most meatballs and scholarship boys. . . .

THIRD GROUP:
The "mobile
lower middle
classes"

Meatballs were usually day students or scholarship students. We were at Harvard not to enjoy the games, the girls, the burlesque shows of the Old Howard, the companionship, the elms, the turning leaves of fall, the grassy banks of the Charles. We had come to get the Harvard badge, which says "Veritas," but really means a job somewhere in the future, in some bureaucracy, in some institution, in some school, laboratory, university, or law firm.   ("Growing Up in the Land of Promise," *Atlantic*)

(4) *Base your classification on a combination of related criteria when they clearly serve your purpose.* Often several related factors work together to help us sort out people or things into categories. A marketing study, for instance, might set up the following four major groups of consumers:

I. Late teens
II. College students
III. Working singles
IV. Young marrieds

This scheme roughly follows chronological order, but age is only one of the factors that shape the buying habits of each group. (In strictly chronological terms the categories overlap.) Other factors, such as occupational and marital status, combine with age level to determine the buying patterns of each category. College students, for instance, are as a group relatively young (and often active and in good health). They are often single (but with strong remaining ties to home and parents). A consumer's profile of the typical college student would show the combined effect of these factors:

- (Living habits) They spend much money on snacks, milk, and orange juice; they are seldom seen in expensive or pretentious restaurants.
- (Activities) They are buyers of sports equipment; they own, on the average, three pairs of shoes used in active sports.
- (Family status) They are away from home and, as a result, are travelers; in the last twelve months, 34 percent of them bought traveler's checks. On the average, they make six long-distance calls a month during the school year.

(5) *Develop each category with relevant examples and convincing details.* In a paper about stereotypes perpetuated by the media, a black student wrote about stereotypical images of blacks found in movies and on television. He set up three major categories, proceeding in roughly chronological order from the loyal Negro servants of *Gone with the Wind* to today's athletic superstars:

I. Stereotypes concerning social class
   (tendency to appear in menial occupations, as gardeners, servants, and the like)
II. Stereotypes concerning lifestyle
   (natural inclination toward music and dancing)
III. Stereotypes concerning athletic ability
   (tendency to excel in physical rather than intellectual or creative pursuits)

The following paragraph contains the kind of detailed example needed for each of these categories:

> Many of the stereotypes we see in the area of athletics are not openly offensive but nevertheless damaging. Many sports announcers consciously or unconsciously reinforce subtle stereotypes. *For example*, a black running back may fake out the defense and run for a touchdown. The announcer will compliment the black player on his superb "instinct." This term implies that the running back did not have to think—he just had to take the ball and run and let his "natural rhythm" take him into the end zone.

To convince your readers that your categories are valid, you will have to make sure that your examples are not isolated instances but are representative. Often a mix of several examples briefly surveyed or summarized and then one or two followed up in detail will best do the job.

(6) *Use transitions to show the logical relationships between your categories*. Provide the logical links that show how your categories fit into the larger picture you are sketching out. Avoid lame transitions that merely add without showing *why*: "*Another* common stereotype is . . . ." or "We should *also* mention that . . . ." In a paper about stereotypes, use transitions that show how each category fits into your overall plan. Are you going from the crude and obvious to the more subtle? Are you looking at contradictory or opposed images—perhaps in order to look later for a common thread? Provide the necessary signals for your reader:

> *At one extreme*, we see the handsome, macho young single who wears designer jeans, drives a fast car, and is pursued by beautiful women . . . .

> *At the opposite extreme*, we see the clumsy young husband who is displayed hopelessly attempting to make the waffles while his son, after patiently waiting, says, "Why don't you make them like Mom does?"

To sum up: Organizing a paper often means breaking up a subject into its major parts or sorting material out into major kinds. A crucial part of your planning for a paper will often be to construct an outline that sets up major divisions or major categories. Ask yourself: Do the dividing lines do justice to the subject matter? Do your categories serve your purpose? Have you made the overall plan clear enough for the reader?

Prewriting Activities 6

1. Many *widely used schemes* of classification channel our thinking almost without our being consciously aware of them. Choose one of the following schemes. For each of the three or four subheadings, write down associations, details, or images as they come to mind. Write quickly. Try to work up a rich fund of material for use in class discussion of the usefulness and limitations of the system of classification you have chosen. Write on one of the following:

- upper class, middle class, lower class
- urban, suburban, rural
- child, adolescent, adult, the elderly
- right wing, moderate, left wing
- single, married, divorced

2. Working alone or as a member of a team, conduct an informal *opinion survey* on your campus. Use a questionnaire or informal interviews to sample students' opinions on a subject like the following:

- attitudes toward marriage
- attitudes toward apartheid (or other political issue)
- attitudes toward beauty contests

- attitudes toward pornography
- attitudes toward politicians
- attitudes toward the military
- attitudes toward the police
- attitudes toward Arabs (Asians) (Hispanics)
- attitudes toward college football

Sort out your findings and set up a system of classification. For instance, can you range students' opinions on a scale going from old-fashioned to moderate to modern? Can you set up several representative types?

3. Set up a scheme of classification that would help you classify *friends and acquaintances*. For instance, you may want to set up three or four categories on a scale from introvert to extrovert, or from serious student to casual student. Describe and illustrate each category.

Paragraph Practice 6

Write a paragraph in which you identify and illustrate three or four major *current trends* in popular music, male or female fashions, interior decorating, available student housing, or the like. Make your reader see what your underlying criteria or principles of selection are. Study and discuss the following student-written paragraph as a possible model.

Birds of a Feather

My favorite pastime is sitting in a small city park to watch the young men who walk, strut, and saunter across my field of vision. Most of these males can be assigned to three categories according to their style of dress and the way they act toward the other sex. Each style is modeled on the appearance of a movie star or rock star. The first type appears in the rough, tough image of a blue-collar worker. This Bruce Springsteen look is as commonly sighted as the spring robin, the reason for the large population being the easy acquisition of the wardrobe: lace-up construction boots, well-soaked and bleached blue jeans, short-sleeve T-shirts, with keys jangling from hip belt loops. These men, while apparently not conscious of their physique, acknowledge all women in their age range. The next type, with its spring-pastel layered look, is the Miami Vice peacock. This flamboyant number is less frequently sighted because of the expense and frequent dry cleaning required: baggy pants with a matching oversized blazer with shoulder pads—never buttoned to reveal the form-fitting, ribbed knit shirt worn underneath. A rich dark tan is required to set off the light-colored clothes. These men seldom look at women because they know women are always looking at them. The rarest of all sightings is the wacky Woody Allen look-alike, seldom seen because normally hidden in the back row of foreign film theaters. Layers of dark winterish clothing cover the frail white forms: tweed jacket, oversized khaki-colored pants, blue shirts with button-down collar. Heavy black eyeglasses, too large for the face, are frequently pushed back into position to provide a measure of exercise. These Woody Allen clones are flattered silly by the attention of any female and respond by chattering nonstop, emitting multisyllable words nobody understands.

BACKGROUND: Jane Brody (born 1941) has for years been writing a legendary "Personal Health" column for the section titled "Living" in the *New York Times*. Her writing illustrates the kind of practical nonfiction prose for which there seems to be a virtually unlimited market in our society: books on health, cookbooks, diet guides, exercise manuals. Author or coauthor of several books on health and nutrition, Brody is the kind of earnest counselor who often seems more concerned about our health than we are. One faithful reader commented on her "excess of caution": Her advice on cocktail parties, for instance, is to shorten them, to place the bar "in a relatively inaccessible place," and to be prepared for guests who want to start with plain water. The following selection, designed to help her readers understand and overcome fatigue, is from *Jane Brody's New York Times Guide to Personal Health*, published in 1982.

Jane Brody

Three Kinds

# of Fatigue

GUIDE TO READING: How does the author arouse our concern or get us involved in her subject? How does she sort out the causes of fatigue? How practical or useful is her advice?

Fatigue is one of the most common complaints brought to doctors, 1 friends, and relatives. You'd think in this era of labor-saving devices and convenient transportation that few people would have reason to be so tired. But probably more people complain of fatigue today than in the days when hay was baled by hand and laundry scrubbed on a washboard. Witness these typical complaints:

"It doesn't seem to matter how long I sleep—I'm more tired when I 2 wake up than when I went to bed."

"Some of my friends come home from work and jog for several miles 3 or swim laps. I don't know how they do it. I'm completely exhausted at the end of a day at the office."

"I thought I was weary because of the holidays, but now that they're 4 over, I'm even worse. I can barely get through the week, and on the weekend I don't even have the strength to get dressed. I wonder if I'm anemic or something."

"I don't know what's wrong with me lately, but I've been so collapsed 5 that I haven't made a proper meal for the family in weeks. We've been living on TV dinners and packaged mixes. I was finally forced to do a laundry because the kids ran out of underwear."

The causes of modern-day fatigue are diverse and only rarely related [6] to excessive physical exertion. The relatively few people who do heavy labor all day long almost never complain about being tired, perhaps because they expect to be. Today, physicians report, tiredness is more likely a consequence of underexertion than of wearing yourself down with over-activity. In fact, increased physical activity is often prescribed as a *cure* for sagging energy.

There are three main categories of fatigue: [7]

Physical. This is the well-known result of overworking your muscles [8] to the point where metabolic waste products—carbon dioxide and lactic acid—accumulate in your blood and sap your strength. Your muscles can't continue to work efficiently in a bath of these chemicals. Physical fatigue is usually a pleasant tiredness, such as that which you might experience after playing a hard set of tennis, chopping wood, or climbing a mountain. The cure is simple and fast: You rest, giving your body a chance to get rid of accumulated wastes and restore muscle fuel.

Pathological. Here fatigue is a warning sign or consequence of some [9] underlying physical disorder, perhaps the common cold or flu or something more serious like diabetes or cancer. Usually other symptoms besides fatigue are present that suggest the true cause.

Even after an illness has passed, you're likely to feel dragged out for a [10] week or more. Take your fatigue as a signal to go slow while your body has a chance to recover fully even if all you had was a cold. Pushing yourself to resume full activity too soon could precipitate a relapse and almost certainly will prolong your period of fatigue.

Even though illness is not a frequent cause of prolonged fatigue, it's [11] very important that it not be overlooked. Therefore, anyone who feels drained of energy for weeks on end should have a thorough physical checkup. But even if nothing shows up as a result of the various medical tests, that doesn't mean there's nothing wrong with you.

Unfortunately too often a medical work-up ends with a battery of [12] negative test results, the patient is dismissed, and the true cause of serious fatigue goes undetected. As Dr. John Bulette, a psychiatrist at the Medical College of Pennsylvania Hospital in Philadelphia, tells it, this is what happened to a Pennsylvania woman who had lost nearly fifty pounds and was "almost dead—so tired she could hardly lift her head up." The doctors who first examined the woman were sure she had cancer. But no matter how hard they looked, they could find no sign of malignancy or of any other disease that could account for her wasting away. Finally, she was brought to the college hospital, where doctors noted that she was severely depressed.

They questioned her about her life and discovered that her troubles [13] had begun two years earlier, after her husband died. Once treated for depression, the woman quickly perked up, gained ten pounds in just a few weeks, then returned home to continue her recovery with the aid of psychotherapy.

Psychological. Emotional problems and conflicts, especially de- 14 pression and anxiety, are by far the most common causes of prolonged fatigue. Fatigue may represent a defense mechanism that prevents you from having to face the true cause of your depression, such as the fact that you hate your job. It is also your body's safety valve for expressing repressed emotional conflicts, such as feeling trapped in an ungratifying role or an unhappy marriage. When such feelings are not expressed openly, they often come out as physical symptoms, with fatigue as one of the most common manifestations. "Many people who are extremely fatigued don't even know they're depressed," Dr. Bulette says. "They're so busy distracting themselves or just worrying about being tired that they don't recognize their depression."

One of these situations is so common it's been given a name—tired 15 housewife syndrome. The victims are commonly young mothers who day in and day out face the predictable tedium of caring for a home and small children, fixing meals, dealing with repairmen, and generally having no one interesting to talk to and nothing enjoyable to look forward to at the end of their boring and unrewarding day. The tired housewife may be inwardly resentful, envious of her husband's job, and guilty about her feelings. But rather than face them head-on, she becomes extremely fatigued.

Today, with nearly half the mothers of young children working outside 16 the home, the tired housewife syndrome has taken on a new twist: that of conflicting roles and responsibilities and guilt over leaving the children, often with an overlay of genuine physical exhaustion from trying to be all things to all people.

Emotionally induced fatigue may be compounded by sleep distur- 17 bance that results from the underlying psychological conflict. A person may develop insomnia or may sleep the requisite number of hours but fitfully, tossing and turning all night, having disturbing dreams, and awakening, as one woman put it, feeling as if she "had been run over by a truck."

Understanding the underlying emotional problem is the crucial first 18 step toward curing psychological fatigue and by itself often results in considerable lessening of the tiredness. Professional psychological help or career or marriage counseling may be needed.

There is a great deal you can do on your own to deal with both severe 19 prolonged fatigue and those periodic washed-out feelings. Vitamins and tranquilizers are almost never the right answer, sleeping pills and alcohol are counterproductive, and caffeine is at best a temporary solution that can backfire with abuse and cause life-disrupting symptoms of anxiety. Instead, you might try:

Diet. If you eat a skimpy breakfast or none at all, you're likely to 20 experience midmorning fatigue, the result of a drop in blood sugar, which your body and brain depend on for energy. For peak energy in the morning, be sure to eat a proper breakfast, low in sugar and fairly high in protein, which will provide a steady supply of blood sugar throughout the morning. Coffee and a doughnut are almost worse than nothing, providing a brief boost and then letting you down with a thud.

The same goes for the rest of the day: Frequent snacking on sweets is a   21 false pick-me-up that soon leaves you lower than you were to begin with. Stick to regular, satisfying, well-balanced meals that help you maintain a trim figure. Extra weight is tiring both physically and psychologically. Getting your weight down to normal can go a long way toward revitalizing you.

Exercise. Contrary to what you may think, exercise enhances, rather   22 than saps, energy. Regular conditioning exercises, such as jogging, cycling, or swimming, help you to resist fatigue by increasing your body's ability to handle more of a work load. You get tired less quickly because your capability is greater.

Exercise also has a well-recognized tranquilizing effect, which helps   23 you work in a more relaxed fashion and be less dragged down by the tensions of your day. At the end of a day exercise can relieve accumulated tensions, give you more energy in the evening, and help you sleep more restfully.

Sleep. If you know you're tired because you haven't been getting   24 enough sleep, the solution is simple: Get to bed earlier. There's no right amount of sleep for everyone, and generally sleep requirements decline with age. Find the amount that suits you best, and aim for it. Insomnia and other sleep disorders should not be treated with sleeping pills, alcohol, or tranquilizers, which can actually make the problem worse.

Know yourself. Try to schedule your most taxing jobs for the time of   25 day when you're at your peak. Some are "morning people" who tire by midafternoon; others do their best work in the evening. Don't overextend yourself, trying to climb the ladder of success at a record pace or to meet everyone's demands or expectations. Decide what you want to do and what you can handle comfortably, and learn to say no to additional requests. Recognize your energy cycles and plan accordingly. Many women have a low point premenstrually, during which time extra sleep may be needed and demanding activities are particularly exhausting.

Take breaks. No matter how interesting or demanding your work,   26 you'll be able to do it with more vigor if now and again you stop, stretch, and change the scenery. Instead of coffee and a sweet roll on your break, try meditation, yoga, calisthenics, or a brisk walk. Even running up and down the staircase can provide refreshment from a sedentary job. If your job is physically demanding, relax in a quiet place for a while. The do-something-different rule also applies to vacation; "getting away from it all" for a week or two or longer can be highly revitalizing, helping you to put things in perspective and enabling you to take your job more in stride upon your return.

Using The Dictionary

The following are words that Brody expects her newspaper audience to know. Which of them do you have to look up?   1. *diverse* (6)   2. *metabolic* (8)   3. *precipitate* (10)   4. *malignancy* (12)   5. *psychotherapy* (13)   6. *manifestation* (14)   7. *syndrome* (15)   8. *tedium* (15)   9. *yoga* (26)   10. *sedentary* (26)

The Writer's Agenda

Brody's writing serves an immediate practical purpose. How does she accomplish it? Answer the following questions:

1. Do you make a good audience for this kind of writing? Why or why not?

2. How does Brody bring her subject into *focus*? What is the common misunderstanding she sets out to correct?

3. What would you include in a capsule summary of each of her three *categories*?

4. In what *order* does she present her categories, and why?

5. Brody knows how to translate her subject into *nontechnical* terms; she knows how to bring it "close to home." What examples or passages do most to help make the subject real for you? How or why?

6. Would you call the author's suggested solutions "common-sense" advice? Is it mostly familiar and predictable? Does any part of it seem new or doubtful to you?

For Discussion or Writing

7. How concerned are young Americans about their health? Are they generally in good health? Are they generally in poor health?

8. College students are often said to suffer from stress, anxiety, or frustration. Do you agree with this observation? Do some sorting out: Sort out some major kinds or causes of stress. Or classify major personality types according to how they respond to stress.

9. We can classify people according to their degree of involvement with alcohol, from teetotaler through the social drinker to the alcoholic. Prepare a paper in which you classify different types of people according to their degree of involvement with alcohol, smoking, or drugs.

10. Some people seem to have the secret of contentment; others seem to be chronic complainers. Set up several major categories of people according to their tendency to be content or dissatisfied.

11. Assume you are a columnist for a major newspaper. Write a column in which you discuss and give advice on a major health problem you see in young Americans.

Branching Out

12. Study some of the personal-advice literature in local bookstores or on the book racks in supermarkets. Set up a system of classification based on subject matter, degree of usefulness, or some other principle of selection that helps you sort them out.

BACKGROUND: Some of our most popular columnists look at the conflicts and uncertainties of our times and serve as interpreters and guides for others. One of the best-known of such columnists is Ellen Goodman, the author of the first two portraits of contemporary American types in the following set of three. She wrote the two columns reprinted here for the *Boston Globe*, whose office she has called one of the more "congenial newspaper offices in the country" and also "a good place to think." In many of her widely read and often-reprinted columns, she draws on her own experiences and those of her friends and family. Sam Keen, a contributing editor of *Psychology Today*, is the author of the third portrait of a representative type included here. He wrote it as part of a magazine article exploring our shifting self-images and "visions of the good life." Like Ellen Goodman an alert and sensitive watcher of trends, he wrote the article to help his readers chart "a weather map of our times."

Ellen Goodman and

Sam Keen

Americans at Work:

Three Portraits

GUIDE TO READING: Each of the three short selections in this group discusses a type of person we encounter in the world of work. What makes each a representative type? Pay special attention to how the authors define the three types: What are their attitudes toward work? What is the role work plays in their lives? How does work affect their attitudes toward life and their relations with other people?

(1) Ellen Goodman

The Company Man

He worked himself to death, finally and precisely, at 3:00 A.M. Sunday morning.

The obituary didn't say that, of course. It said he died of a coronary thrombosis—I think that was it—but everyone among his friends and acquaintances knew it instantly. He was a perfect Type A, a workaholic, a classic, they said to each other and shook their heads—and thought for five or ten minutes about the way they lived.

This man who worked himself to death finally and precisely at 3:00 A.M. Sunday morning—on his day off—was fifty-one years old and a vice-president. He was, however, one of six vice-presidents, and one of three who might conceivably—if the president died or retired soon enough—have moved to the top spot. Phil knew that.

He worked six days a week, five of them until eight or nine at night, during a time when his own company had begun the four-day week for everyone but the executives. He worked like the Important People. He had no outside "extracurricular activities," unless, of course, you think about a monthly golf game that way. To Phil, it was work. He always ate egg salad sandwiches at his desk. He was, of course, overweight, by 20 or 25 pounds. He thought it was okay, though, because he didn't smoke.

On Saturdays, Phil wore a sports jacket to the office instead of a suit, because it was the weekend.

He had a lot of people working for him, maybe sixty, and most of them liked him most of the time. Three of them will be seriously considered for his job. The obituary didn't mention that.

But it did list his "survivors" quite accurately. He is survived by his wife, Helen, forty-eight years old, good woman of no particular marketable skills, who worked in an office before marrying and mothering. She had, according to her daughter, given up trying to compete with his work years ago, when the children were small. A company friend said, "I know how much you will miss him." And she answered, "I already have."

"Missing him all these years," she must have given up part of herself which had cared too much for the man. She would be "well taken care of."

His "dearly beloved" eldest of the "dearly loved" children is a hard-working executive in a manufacturing firm down South. In the day and a half before the funeral, he went around the neighborhood researching his father, asking the neighbors what he was like. They were embarrassed.

His second child is a girl, who is twenty-four and newly married. She lived near her mother and they are close, but whenever she was alone with her father, in a car driving somewhere, they had nothing to say to each other.

The youngest is twenty, a boy, a high-school graduate who has spent the last couple of years, like a lot of his friends, doing enough odd jobs to stay in grass and food. He was the one who tried to grab at his father, and tried to mean enough to him to keep the man at home. He was his father's favorite. Over the last two years, Phil stayed up nights worrying about the boy.

The boy once said, "My father and I only board here."

At the funeral, the sixty-year-old company president told the forty-eight-year-old widow that the fifty-one-year-old deceased had meant much to the company and would be missed and would be hard to replace. The widow didn't look him in the eye. She was afraid he would read her bitterness and, after all, she would need him to straighten out the finances—the stock options and all that.

Phil was overweight and nervous and worked too hard. If he wasn't at the office, he was worried about it. Phil was a Type A, a heart-attack natural. You could have picked him out in a minute from a lineup.

So when he finally worked himself to death, at precisely 3:00 A.M. 15
Sunday morning, no one was really surprised.

By 5:00 P.M. the afternoon of the funeral, the company president had 16
begun, discreetly of course, with care and taste, to make inquiries about his
replacement. One of the three men. He asked around: "Who's been working
the hardest?"

(2) Ellen Goodman

Superworkingmom or Superdrudge?

There weren't any stunning revelations in the news last week. The 17
Bureau of Labor reported that the wage gap between men and women was
on the increase, while a *Newsweek* cover story analyzed the fact that the
numbers gap between working men and women was on the decrease.

No, there were no stunning bulletins. The monkey-in-the-middle of all 18
this change was again described as the average employed mother who is not
only working more and earning less, but bearing the full load of family care.
In short, the only equality she's won after a decade of personal and social
upheaval is with the working mothers of Russia.

Many of the back-to-work women are still apologizing for changing 19
the rules of the mating game as they were writ back in 1955. They are doing
penance by "doing it all," or "juggling" as the magazines put it so cutely. They
read cheerleading articles that say, "You, too, Dora Daring, can manage a
home and job, can keep your roots blond, your children squeaky clean and
have their permission slips signed on time if only you learn a few organizing
tricks!"

But one thing that is apparent is that the younger women of America 20
aren't buying it. Superworkingmom looks more like Superdrudge to them.

A generation ago, young women felt that they had to choose between 21
being a housewife and a career woman. Today's young women often feel
their choice is between Superdrudge or not mothering at all. Most of the
college women I have talked with look upon motherhood as The End. When
you talk about having babies, they stare at you.

The "best and the brightest" women in their twenties not only have a 22
horror of being housewives but a dread of getting on that working-mother
treadmill.

Still, they may not be seeing the whole story. Both of the main pieces in 23
the *Newsweek* article ended on the note, "Men may well have to spend more
time running the house and raising the children." But that isn't future-think.
It's happening right now in the bumper crop of two-parent working families
bearing their first child in their thirties.

Many of those men already found out that they would have to share 24
the kids if they wanted them. These days, there is a new version of the old

play, *Lysistrata.*[1] In this one, child-bearing-age women—especially those
with high aspirations—are simply rejecting pregnancy until they get some
assurances of partnership parenting.

For a while, it looked as if this generation would simply choose to be   25
"child-free." But now it appears that they have charted a new trend.

Many of these couples discuss everything short of college tuition for   26
the kids before they conceive them. Because of the hesitations of women,
the burden of proof has often been shifted onto the men.

It is often the men in their thirties who are pushed to really "decide" if   27
they want to raise, not just "have" children. One friend quizzed her husband
as if she were an Internal Revenue agent: "Will you get up in the middle of
the night? Will you stay home half the time when the kids are sick? Who will
call for the sitter?"

As her husband recalls, "She was sure that the minute we had a child,   28
she would have two jobs and I would be sitting in the living room waiting for
din-din."

But, in fact, these couples have gone into parenting differently and   29
seem to offer the most appealing shared life pattern to emerge slowly out of
the morass of guilt and conflict in changing expectations.

They may well be the cutting edge of a massive change in the life cycle.   30
By the thirties, after all, many of us have settled some of the issues of
personal confidence and professional competence. Many are ready to make
compromises, or simply ready to raise children.

In any case the first-time thirties parents seem better prepared for the   31
pressures and ready to share them. The thing that seems to surprise them is
the pleasure. They are enjoying kids, not just crisply coping. No one seems
to have warned them about that.

(3) Sam Keen

A New Breed

Jay, a carpenter who has worked for me on several occasions, is a   32
barrel of a man, stout as an oak log. Though not yet thirty years old, his
convictions are well seasoned; he is true to the grain of his own wood. On
good days he shows up for work between 9 and 10 a.m. If it is raining, or his
dog needs to go to the veterinarian, or he has promised to help a friend, or
there is an exhibit of Zen art at the museum, he may not get here at all. As yet
he hasn't called to say the day is too beautiful to spend working. But I
wouldn't be surprised if he did. When he arrives, he unwraps his bundles of

---

[1][Aristophanes' comedy *Lysistrata* was first performed in Athens in 411 B.C. In the play, the women of
Athens refuse to sleep with their husbands in order to force them to make peace with Sparta.]

Japanese woodworking tools, removes the fine saws and chisels from their mahogany cases, puts some shakuhachi flute music on his tape deck, and begins methodically to sculpt the elaborate joints in the beams that will form the structure of the studio we are building. He works slowly, pausing to watch a hawk circle overhead, to tell a joke, to savor the smell of the wood. Occasionally I try to hurry him. "That looks close enough, Jay," I say. "May as well take the time to do it right the first time," he replies and goes on working at his own pace. After several days he announces that the beams are ready to be hoisted into place. We lift and tug and push. Notch joins notch. Tongue slips into groove. The puzzle fits together. We sigh with relief. A satisfying day.

Some would say Jay is an underachiever, a dropout, that he lacks ambition. A college graduate with honors in football, he works sporadically, for carpenter's wages. He has no pension, no health insurance, no fringe benefits. He drives an old truck and lives in a funky neighborhood near the industrial district of Oakland. When he doesn't need money, he tends his garden, writes poetry, paints, and studies Japanese and wood joinery. "I get by," he says. "It doesn't make any sense to sell your soul for security and have no time left to do the things you love."

I say Jay is one of a new breed of Americans who are refusing to make work the central value in their lives. These light-hearted rebels have paused to consider the lilies of the field (executive coronaries and the pollution of the Love Canal) and have decided neither to toil nor to spin. They are turning everything upside down and calling into question the traditional, orthodox virtues of the Protestant work ethic and American dream. They are inventing new "life-styles," forging new myths and visions of the good life, new definitions of happiness.

The rebellion is directed *against* the long-reigning secular theology of work that is best summed up in the words of Ayn Rand, whose popular philosophy romanticized capitalism and sanctified selfishness: ". . . your work is the process of achieving your values . . . your body is a machine, but your mind is its driver . . . your work is the purpose of your life, and you must speed past any killer who assumes the right to stop you . . . any value you might find outside your work, any other loyalty or love, can be only travelers you choose to share your journey with and must be travelers going on their own power in the same direction."[2] The rebels reject the sacred symbol $ and refuse to judge the worth of their lives by the economic equivalent of the Last Judgment—The Bottom Line. Disillusioned with the ideal of Progress, they are no longer willing to sacrifice present happiness for the promise of future economic security. In short, they have declared: the great God Work is dead.

[2][Ayn Rand (1905-82), Russian-born advocate of a philosophy of competitiveness and self-reliance, wrote *The Fountainhead* (1943) and *Atlas Shrugged* (1957).]

Using the Dictionary

Columnists like Ellen Goodman are trend-watchers who look out not only for new ideas but also for the new expressions and "buzzwords" that we use to talk about them. Check your dictionary for the following expressions. Then choose three of them that are not treated in your dictionary or treated very briefly. For each, write a short paragraph explaining its meaning, implications, and typical uses.   1. *workaholic* (2)   2. *stock option* (13)   3. *parenting* (24)   4. *cutting edge* (30)   5. *coping* (31)   6. *underachiever* (33)   7. *dropout* (33)   8. *life-style* (34)   9. *work ethic* (34)   10. *bottom line* (35)

The Writer's Agenda

Study the way these two authors sketch out types that many of their readers will recognize as representative of general trends.

1. Goodman gives us a vivid dramatized account of what she considers a typical "company man." What are the features that for her make the person representative of a widespread type? What are some of the most telling details?

2. What are the key features in Goodman's portrait of the "average employed mother"? What guidance does she provide for the future in her discussion of choices facing young women?

3. Sam Keen assembles characteristic details that help define a person representing "a new breed of Americans." What are the most important or striking of these details? What are the major points he makes when tracing the *contrast* with "orthodox" or traditional values?

4. Our sense of *irony* makes us react with bitter amusement or with a wry smile when people fail to live up to expectations—whether our own or those of society. Find and discuss several examples of this kind of irony in this group of selections.

For Discussion or Writing

5. What in these three selections do you recognize as typical or representative? Turning to your own experience, discuss examples or observations that would bear out the general descriptions given by the two authors.

6. Whenever we describe something as typical, we run the risk of giving a one-sided or oversimplified picture. Where in these three selections do you feel there is a danger of oversimplification or exaggeration?

7. How do the types of workers described in these selections fit into a more general picture of Americans at work? Prepare your own portrait of one major type that is not included in these brief portraits.

8. Do a close-up of a representative person. Choose a type that you know well from personal observation or experience. Possible types are the unemployed teen-

ager, the person running a small store or other business, the career woman, the high school principal. Model your portrait of the type on one of the portraits you have read.

9. Set up your own classification of several representative types of workers. Identify and describe several major categories or types. Use one or a combination of the following as the basis of your classification: the kind of work they do, the attitude toward work, and the role work plays in their lives. For instance, on the basis of different attitudes toward work, major types might range from people considering their work a calling or vocation (ministers, missionaries) to people disliking their work and working strictly to make a living. Give detailed examples.

BACKGROUND: Judith Viorst (born 1931) is a poet, journalist, and author of children's books who knows how to treat serious subjects in a lighter vein. She was born in Newark, New Jersey, and graduated from Rutgers University. She has said of her humorous poems that they are "more or less based on the family life of the Viorsts. I also steal from all my friends' lives." She has worked as a contributing editor and columnist for *Redbook* magazine, and she has contributed poems and articles to publications including *New York*, the *New York Times*, and *Holiday*. She has written fiction and science books for children. Her best-known books include *It's Hard to Be Hip over Thirty, and Other Tragedies of Married Life* (1968); *Yes, Married: A Saga of Love and Complaint* (1972); and *Love and Guilt and the Meaning of Life, Etc.* (1979). The following essay first appeared in *Redbook* in October 1977.

Judith Viorst

Friends, Good Friends—and Such Good Friends

GUIDE TO READING: What does friendship mean to the author? In her informal stock-taking of kinds of friends, what sets one type apart from the other? How does she make each kind real for her readers?

Women are friends, I once would have said, when they totally love and support and trust each other, and bare to each other the secrets of their souls, and run—no questions asked—to help each other, and tell harsh truths to each other (no, you can't wear that dress unless you lose ten pounds first) when harsh truths must be told.

Women are friends, I once would have said, when they share the same affection for Ingmar Bergman, plus train rides, cats, warm rain, charades, Camus, and hate with equal ardor Newark and Brussels sprouts and Lawrence Welk and camping.[1]

In other words, I once would have said that a friend is a friend all the way, but now I believe that's a narrow point of view. For the friendships I

---

[1][Ingmar Bergman is the Swedish filmmaker admired by lovers of the cinema for art films including *The Seventh Seal* (1956) and *Wild Strawberries* (1957). Albert Camus is the existentialist French novelist and essayist whose *The Stranger* (1942) became a classic of the modern literature of alienation. At the opposite end of the spectrum of sophistication, Lawrence Welk for many years produced a musical variety show devoted to old popular favorites, which he called "champagne music."]

have and the friendships I see are conducted at many levels of intensity, serve many different functions, meet different needs and range from those as all-the-way as the friendship of the soul sisters mentioned above to that of the most nonchalant and casual playmates.

Consider these varieties of friendship: 4

1. Convenience friends. These are the women with whom, if our   5 paths weren't crossing all the time, we'd have no particular reason to be friends: a next-door neighbor, a woman in our car pool, the mother of one of our children's closest friends or maybe some mommy with whom we serve juice and cookies each week at the Glenwood Co-op Nursery.

Convenience friends are convenient indeed. They'll lend us their cups   6 and silverware for a party. They'll drive our kids to soccer when we're sick. They'll take us to pick up our car when we need a lift to the garage. They'll even take our cats when we go on vacation. As we will for them.

But we don't, with convenience friends, ever come too close or tell too   7 much; we maintain our public face and emotional distance. "Which means," says Elaine, "that I'll talk about being overweight but not about being depressed. Which means I'll admit being mad but not blind with rage. Which means I might say that we're pinched this month but never that I'm worried sick over money."

But which doesn't mean that there isn't sufficient value to be found in   8 these friendships of mutual aid, in convenience friends.

2. Special-interest friends. These friendships aren't intimate, and   9 they needn't involve kids or silverware or cats. Their value lies in some interest jointly shared. And so we may have an office friend or a yoga friend or a tennis friend or a friend from the Women's Democratic Club.

"I've got one woman friend," says Joyce, "who likes, as I do, to take   10 psychology courses. Which makes it nice for me—and nice for her. It's fun to go with someone you know and it's fun to discuss what you've learned, driving back from the classes." And for the most part, she says, that's all they discuss.

"I'd say that what we're doing is *doing* together, not being together,"   11 Suzanne says of her Tuesday-doubles friends. "It's mainly a tennis relationship, but we play together well. And I guess we all need to have a couple of playmates."

I agree.   12

My playmate is a shopping friend, a woman of marvelous taste, a   13 woman who knows exactly *where* to buy *what*, and furthermore is a woman who always knows beyond a doubt what one ought to be buying. I don't have the time to keep up with what's new in eyeshadow, hemlines and shoes and whether the smock look is in or finished already. But since (oh, shame!) I care a lot about eyeshadow, hemlines and shoes, and since I don't *want* to wear smocks if the smock look is finished, I'm very glad to have a shopping friend.

3. Historical friends. We all have a friend who knew us when ... 14
maybe way back in Miss Meltzer's second grade, when our family lived in
that three-room flat in Brooklyn, when our dad was out of work for seven
months, when our brother Allie got in that fight where they had to call the
police, when our sister married the endodontist from Yonkers and when, the
morning after we lost our virginity, she was the first, the only friend we told.

The years have gone by and we've gone separate ways and we've little 15
in common now, but we're still an intimate part of each other's past. And so
whenever we go to Detroit we always go to visit the friend of our girlhood.
Who knows how we talked before our voice got un-Brooklyned. Who knows
what we ate before we learned about artichokes. And who, by her presence,
puts us in touch with an earlier part of ourself, a part of ourself it's important
never to lose.

"What this friend means to me and what I mean to her," says Grace, "is 16
having a sister without sibling rivalry. We know the texture of each other's
lives. She remembers my grandmother's cabbage soup. I remember the way
her uncle played the piano. There's simply no other friend who remembers
those things."

4. Crossroads friends. Like historical friends, our crossroads 17
friends are important for *what was*—for the friendship we shared at a
crucial, now past, time of life. A time, perhaps, when we roomed in college
together; or worked as eager young singles in the Big City together, or went
together, as my friend Elizabeth and I did, through pregnancy, birth and that
scary first year of new motherhood.

Crossroads friends forge powerful links, links strong enough to en- 18
dure with not much more contact than once-a-year letters at Christmas. And
out of respect for those crossroads years, for those dramas and dreams we
once shared, we will always be friends.

5. Cross-generational friends. Historical friends and crossroads 19
friends seem to maintain a special kind of intimacy—dormant but always
ready to be revived and though we may rarely meet, whenever we do
connect, it's personal and intense. Another kind of intimacy exists in the
friendships that form across generations in what one woman calls her
daughter-mother and her mother-daughter relationships.

Evelyn's friend is her mother's age—"but I share so much more than I 20
ever could with my mother"—a woman she talks to of music, of books and
of life. "What I get from her is the benefit of her experience. What she
gets—and enjoys—from me is a youthful perspective. It's a pleasure for
both of us."

I have in my own life a precious friend, a woman of 65 who has lived 21
very hard, who is wise, who listens well; who has been where I am and can
help me understand it; and who represents not only an ultimate ideal
mother to me but also the person I'd like to be when I grow up.

In our daughter role we tend to do more than our share of self- 22
revelation; in our mother role we tend to receive what's revealed. It's

another kind of pleasure—playing wise mother to a questing younger person. It's another very lovely kind of friendship.

6. Part-of-a-couple friends. Some of the women we call our friends ²³ we never see alone—we see them as part of a couple at couples' parties. And though we share interests in many things and respect each other's views, we aren't moved to deepen the relationship. Whatever the reason, a lack of time or—and this is more likely—a lack of chemistry, our friendship remains in the context of a group. But the fact that our feeling on seeing each other is always, "I'm *so* glad she's here" and the fact that we spend half the evening talking together says that this too, in its own way, counts as a friendship.

(Other part-of-a-couple friends are the friends that came with the ²⁴ marriage, and some of these are friends we could live without. But sometimes, alas, she married our husband's best friend, and sometimes, alas, she is our husband's best friend. And so we find ourself dealing with her, somewhat against our will, in a spirit of what I'll call *reluctant* friendship.)

7. Men who are friends. I wanted to write just of women friends, but ²⁵ the women I've talked to won't let me—they say I must mention man-woman friendships too. For these friendships can be just as close and as dear as those that we form with women. Listen to Lucy's description of one such friendship:

"We've found we have things to talk about that are different from what ²⁶ he talks about with my husband and different from what I talk about with his wife. So sometimes we call on the phone or meet for lunch. There are similar intellectual interests—we always pass on to each other the books that we love—but there's also something tender and caring too."

In a couple of crises, Lucy says, "he offered himself, for talking and for ²⁷ helping. And when someone died in his family he wanted me there. The sexual, flirty part of our friendship is very small, but *some*—just enough to make it fun and different." She thinks—and I agree—that the sexual part, though small is always *some*, is always there when a man and a woman are friends.

It's only in the past few years that I've made friends with men, in the ²⁸ sense of a friendship that's *mine*, not just part of two couples. And achieving with them the ease and the trust I've found with women friends has value indeed. Under the dryer at home last week, putting on mascara and rouge, I comfortably sat and talked with a fellow named Peter. Peter, I finally decided, could handle the shock of me minus mascara under the dryer. Because we care for each other. Because we're friends.

There are medium friends, and pretty good friends, and very good ²⁹ friends indeed, and these friendships are defined by their level of intimacy. And what we'll reveal at each of these levels of intimacy is calibrated with care. We might tell a medium friend, for example, that yesterday we had a fight with our husband. And we might tell a pretty good friend that this fight with our husband made us so mad that we slept on the couch. And we might tell a very good friend that the reason we got so mad in that fight that we slept on the couch had something to do with that girl who works in his office. But it's only to our very best friends that we're willing to tell all, to tell what's going on with that girl in his office.

The best of friends, I still believe, totally love and support and trust ₃₀ each other, and bare to each other the secrets of their souls, and run—no questions asked—to help each other, and tell harsh truths to each other when they must be told.

But we needn't agree about everything (only 12-year-old girl friends ₃₁ agree about *everything*) to tolerate each other's point of view. To accept, without judgment. To give and to take without ever keeping score. And to *be* there, as I am for them and as they are for me, to comfort our sorrows, to celebrate our joys.

Using the Dictionary

Which of the following do you need to check?　1. *nonchalant* (3)　2. *yoga* (9)　3. *endodontist* (14)　4. *sibling* (16)　5. *dormant* (19)　6. *context* (23)　7. *calibrate* (29)

The Writer's Agenda

Viorst's purpose is to show the whole range of friendship by describing the many kinds of friends that play a role in her life. Answer the following questions:

1. What for you are the key features in the author's original definition of friendship? (Which elements seem to you most essential?) How, according to her introduction, has she changed or broadened her definition?

2. In your own words (one sentence each), how would you sum up *each kind* of friend that she includes in her informal listing? How does she make each kind or type real for her readers?

3. Can you further sort out the types of friends she includes in her inventory-taking? Do some of them share key features?

4. Toward the end of her essay, Viorst classifies friendships according to the degree of intimacy. Looking back over the types she has discussed earlier, how would you assign them to her categories of "medium friends," "pretty good friends," and "very good friends indeed"?

For Discussion or Writing

5. What do you think made the author write this article? What kind of reader would make a receptive audience?

6. For you, are some of the kinds of friendships Viorst discusses too casual or limited to be included when we consider "true friends"? Where would you draw the line?

7. Can friendship without sex or romance exist between men and women?

8. What types of friends would you include in your own survey of kinds of friendships? Set up your own system of classification. Start with a preview or overview. Then identify and illustrate each major type.

9. People used to claim that it is easier for men than for women to become true friends. Do you agree? (Use detailed evidence from your observation, experience, or reading.)

10. Write a paper in which you classify people in a large group like one of the following. Set up several major categories. Identify them clearly and illustrate them well. Possible topics:

- high school teachers
- politicians
- football players
- successful women
- preachers
- television stars
- sales representatives
- immigrants
- people on welfare
- babysitters

Branching Out

11. Movie critics have pointed out that many successful American movies over the years have dealt not with love between the sexes but with male friendship—the adventures or tribulations of two "buddies." Discuss several examples. Present and support your conclusions about what they have in common or what accounts for their appeal.

12. Write a classification paper about kinds of people you dislike, hate, disapprove of, or detest. Label major categories and illustrate them well.

WRITERS ON WRITING
Judith Viorst on the Influence of Reading

In books I've read since I was young I've searched for heroines who could serve as ideals, as models, as possibilities—some reflecting the secret self that dwelled inside me, others pointing to whole new ways that a woman (if only she dared!) might try to be. The person that I am today was shaped by Nancy Drew; by Jo March, Jane Eyre and Heathcliff's soul mate Cathy; and by other fictional females whose attractiveness or character or audacity for a time were the standards by which I measured myself.

I return to some of these books to see if I still understand the powerful hold that these heroines once had on me. I still understand.

Consider teen-aged Nancy Drew—beautiful, blond-haired, blue-eyed girl detective—who had the most terrific life that I as a ten-year-old could ever imagine. Motherless (in other words, quite free of maternal controls), she lived with her handsome indulgent lawyer father in a large brick house set back from the street with a winding tree-lined driveway on the outside and a faithful, nonintrusive house-keeper Hannah cooking yummy meals on the inside. She also had a boy friend, a convertible, nice clothes and two close girl friends—not as perfect as she, but then it seemed to me that no one could possibly be as perfect as Nancy Drew, who in dozens and dozens of books (*The Hidden Staircase, The Whispering Statue, The Clue in the Diary, The Clue of the Tapping Heels*) was resourceful and brave and intelligent as she went around solving mysteries left and right, while remaining kind to the elderly and invariably polite and absolutely completely delightfully feminine.

I mean, what else *was* there?

I soon found out what else when I encountered the four March sisters of *Little Women*, a sentimental, old-fashioned book about girls growing up in Civil War time in New England. About spoiled, vain, pretty Amy. And sickly, saintly Beth. And womanly, decent Meg. And about—most important of all—gawky, bookworm Jo. Dear Jo, who wasn't as flawless as the golden Nancy Drew but who showed me that girls like her—like *us*—could be heroines. Even if we weren't much to look at. Even if we were clumsy and socially gauche. And even if the transition into young womanhood often appeared to our dubious eye to be difficult and scary and even unwelcome.

—from Judith Viorst, "How Books Helped Shape My Life," *Redbook*

BACKGROUND: Marya Mannes was born in 1904 in New York City. She worked as writer and editor for publications including *Vogue, The Reporter, McCall's*, and the *New York Times*. She became widely known as a television critic who vigorously condemned the failure of the medium to live up to its educational and cultural potential. In addition to her role as a television critic with high standards, she wrote as a playwright, feature editor, radio scriptwriter, drama critic, and author of satirical verse. In 1961, she published *The New York I Know*, a "fierce, loving, and critical" portrait of her native city. Her autobiographical *Out of My Time* appeared in 1971. Her work is that of a true professional, combining sharp-eyed observation, outspoken advocacy of her convictions, and satirical bite. She was an early critic of the "gigantic dosage of violence" in television entertainment. In the following article, first published in 1970, she took aim at another target that has since attracted the attention of many writers: the stereotyping of women in television commercials.

Marya Mannes

Television: The Splitting Image

GUIDE TO READING: Pay special attention to how this author *sorted out* the constant stream of images in television commercials. What recurrent types did she identify— types of people that appeared in commercials again and again? What examples did she give to make each type real? What were her objections to each of the major types she described? How have things changed?

A bride who looks scarcely fourteen whispers, "Oh, Mom, I'm so ₁ *happy!*" while a doting family adjusts her gown and veil and a male voice croons softly, "A woman is a harder thing to be than a man. She has more feelings to feel." The mitigation of these excesses, it appears, is a feminine deodorant called Secret, which allows our bride to approach the altar with security as well as emotion.

A successful actor turned pitchman bestows his attention on a lady ₂ with two suitcases, which prompt him to ask her whether she has been on a journey. "No," she says, or words to that effect, as she opens the suitcases. "My two boys bring back their soiled clothes every weekend from college for me to wash." And she goes into the familiar litany of grease, chocolate, mud, coffee, and fruit-juice stains, which presumably record the life of the average American male from two to fifty. The actor compliments her on this happy device to bring her boys home every week and hands her a box of Biz, because "Biz *is* better."

Two women with stony faces meet cart to cart in a supermarket as one ₃ takes a jar of peanut butter off a shelf. When the other asks her in a voice of nitric acid why she takes that brand, the first snaps, "Because I'm choosy for my family!" The two then break into delightful smiles as Number Two makes Number One taste Jif for "mothers who are choosy."

If you have not come across these dramatic interludes, it is because 4 you are not at home during the day and do not watch daytime television. It also means that your intestinal tract is spared from severe assaults, your credibility unstrained. Or, for that matter, you may look at commercials like these every day and manage either to ignore them or find nothing—given the fact of advertising—wrong with them. In that case, you are either so brainwashed or so innocent that you remain unaware of what this daily infusion may have done and is doing to an entire people as the long-accepted adjunct of free enterprise and support of "free" television.

"Given the fact" and "long-accepted" are the key words here. Only 5 socialists, communists, idealists (or the BBC) fail to realize that a mass television system cannot exist without the support of sponsors, that the massive cost of maintaining it as a free service cannot be met without the massive income from selling products. You have only to read of the unending struggle to provide financial support for public, noncommercial television for further evidence.

Besides, aren't commercials in the public interest? Don't they help you 6 choose what to buy? Don't they provide needed breaks from programming? Aren't many of them brilliantly done, and some of them funny?

Tick off the yeses and what have you left? You have, I venture to 7 submit, these intangible but possibly high costs: the diminution of human worth, the infusion and hardening of social attitudes no longer valid or desirable, pervasive discontent, and psychic fragmentation.

Should anyone wonder why deception is not an included detriment, I 8 suggest that our public is so conditioned to promotion as a way of life, whether in art or politics or products, that elements of exaggeration or distortion are taken for granted. Nobody really believes that a certain shampoo will get a certain swain, or that an unclogged sinus can make a man a swinger. People are merely prepared to hope it will.

But the diminution of human worth is much more subtle and just as 9 pervasive. In the guise of what they consider comedy, the producers of television commercials have created a loathsome gallery of men and women patterned, presumably, on a Mr. and Mrs. America. Women liberationists have a major target in the commercial image of woman flashed hourly and daily to the vast majority. There are, indeed, only four kinds of females in this relentless sales procession: the gorgeous teen-age swinger with bouncing locks; the young mother teaching her baby girl the right soap for skin care; the middle-aged housewife with a voice like a power saw; and the old lady with dentures and irregularity. All these women, to be sure, exist. But between the swinging sex object and the constipated granny there are millions of females rarely shown in commercials. These are—married or single—intelligent, sensitive women who bring charm to their homes, who work at jobs as well as lend grace to their marriage, who support themselves, who have talents or hobbies or commitments, or who are skilled at their professions.

We are left with the full-time housewife in all her whining glory: obsessed with whiter wash, moister cakes, shinier floors, cleaner children, softer diapers, and greaseless fried chicken. In the rare instances when these ladies are not in the kitchen, at the washing machine, or waiting on hubby, they are buying beauty shops (fantasy, see?) to take home so that their hair will have more body. Or out at the supermarket being choosy.

If they were attractive in their obsessions, they might be bearable. But they are not. They are pushy, loud-mouthed, stupid, and—of all things now—bereft of sexuality. Presumably, the argument in the tenets of advertising is that once a woman marries she changes overnight from plaything to floor-waxer.

To be fair, men make an equivalent transition in commercials. The swinging male with the mod hair and the beautiful chick turns inevitably into the paunchy slob who chokes on his wife's cake. You will notice, however, that the voice urging the viewer to buy the product is nearly always male: gentle, wise, helpful, seductive. And the visible presence telling the housewife how to get shinier floors and whiter wash and lovelier hair is almost invariably a man: the Svengali in modern dress, the Trilby (if only she were!), his willing object.[1]

Woman, in short, is consumer first and human being fourth. A wife and mother who stays at home all day buys a lot more than a woman who lives alone or who—married or single—has a job. The young girl bent on marriage is the next most susceptible consumer. It is entirely understandable, then, that the potential buyers of detergents, foods, polishes, toothpastes, pills, and housewares are the housewives, and that the sex object spends most of *her* money on cosmetics, hair lotions, soaps, mouthwashes, and soft drinks.

Here we come, of course, to the youngest class of consumers, the swinging teen-agers so beloved by advertisers keen on telling them (and us) that they've "got a lot to live, and Pepsi's got a lot to give." This affords a chance to show a squirming, leaping, jiggling group of beautiful kids having a very loud high on rock and—of all things—soda pop. One of commercial TV's most dubious achievements, in fact, is the reinforcement of the self-adulation characteristic of the young as a group.

As for the aging female citizen, the less shown of her the better. She is useful for ailments, but since she buys very little of anything, not having a husband or any children to feed or house to keep, nor—of course—sex appeal to burnish, society and commercials have little place for her. The same is true, to be sure, of older men, who are handy for Bosses with Bad

---

[1][Svengali is the evil hypnotist in the novel *Trilby* (1894) by George du Maurier.]

Breath or Doctors with Remedies. Yet, on the whole, men hold up better than women at any age—in life or on television. Lines of their faces are marks of distinction, while on women they are signatures of decay.

There is no question, in any case, that television commercials (and [16] many of the entertainment programs, notably the soap serials that are part of the selling package) reinforce, like an insistent drill, the assumption that a woman's function is that of wife, mother, and servant of men: the inevitable sequel to her earlier function as sex object and swinger.

At a time when more and more women are at long last learning to [17] reject these assumptions as archaic and demeaning, and to grow into individual human beings with a wide option of lives to live, the sellers of the nation are bent upon reinforcing the ancient pattern. They know only too well that by beaming their message to the Consumer Queen they can justify her existence as the housebound Mrs. America: dumber than dumb, whiter than white.

The conditioning starts very early: with the girl child who wants the [18] skin Ivory soap has reputedly given her mother, with the nine-year-old who brings back a cake of Camay instead of the male deodorant her father wanted. (When she confesses that she bought it so she could be "feminine," her father hugs her, and, with the voice of a child-molester, whispers, "My little girl is growing up on me, huh.") And then, before long, comes the teenaged bride who "has feelings to feel."

It is the little boys who dream of wings, in an airplane commercial; [19] who grow up (with fewer cavities) into the doers. Their little sisters turn into *Cosmopolitan* girls, who in turn become housewives furious that their neighbors' wash is cleaner than theirs.

There is good reason to suspect that this manic obsession with cleanli- [20] ness, fostered, quite naturally, by the giant soap and detergent interests, may bear some responsibility for the cultivated sloppiness of so many of the young in their clothing as well as in their chosen hideouts. The compulsive housewife who spends more time washing and vacuuming and polishing her possessions than communicating to, or stimulating her children creates a kind of sterility that the young would instinctively reject. The impeccably tidy home, the impeccably tidy lawn are—in a very real sense—unnatural and confining.

Yet the commercials confront us with broods of happy children, some [21] of whom—believe it or not—notice the new fresh smell their clean, white sweatshirts exhale thanks to Mom's new "softener."

Who are, one cannot help but ask, the writers who manage to combine [22] the sales of products with the selling-out of human dreams and dignity? Who people this cosmos of commercials with dolts and fools and shrews and narcissists? Who know so much about quirks and mannerisms and ailments and so little about life? So much about presumed wants and so little about crying needs?

Do they not know, these extremely clever creators of commercials, [23] what they could do for their audience even while they exploit and entertain them? How they could raise the levels of manners and attitudes while they sell their wares? Or do they really share the worm's-eye view of mass communication that sees, and addresses, only the lowest common denominator?

It can be argued that commercials are taken too seriously, that their 24 function is merely to amuse, engage, and sell, and that they do this brilliantly. If that were all to this wheedling of millions, well and good. But it is not. There are two more fallouts from this chronic sales explosion that cannot be measured but that at least can be expected. One has to do with the continual celebration of youth at the expense of maturity. In commercials only the young have access to beauty, sex, and joy in life. What do older women feel, day after day, when love is the exclusive possession of a teenage girl with a bobbing mantle of hair? What older man would not covet her in restless impotence?

The constant reminder of what is inaccessible must inevitably pro- 25 duce a subterranean but real discontent, just as the continual sight of things and places beyond reach has eaten deeply into the ghetto soul. If we are constantly presented with what we are not or cannot have, the dislocation deepens, contentment vanishes, and frustration reigns. Even for the substantially secure, there is always a better thing, a better way, to buy. That none of these things makes a better life may be consciously acknowledged, but still the desire lodges in the spirit, nagging and pulling.

This kind of fragmentation works in potent ways above and beyond 26 the mere fact of program interruption, which is much of the time more of a blessing than a curse, especially in those rare instances when the commercial is deft and funny: the soft and subtle sell. Its overall curse, due to the larger number of commercials in each hour, is that it reduces the attention span of a people already so conditioned to constant change and distraction that they cannot tolerate continuity in print or on the air.

Specifically, commercial interruption is most damaging during that 10 27 percent of programming (a charitable estimate) most important to the mind and spirit of people: news and public affairs, and drama.

To many (and among these are network news producers), commer- 28 cials have no place or business during the vital process of informing the public. There is something obscene about a newscaster pausing to introduce a deodorant or shampoo commercial between an airplane crash and a body count. It is more than an interruption; it tends to reduce news to a form of running entertainment, to smudge the edges of reality by treating death or disaster or diplomacy on the same level as household appliances or a new gasoline.

Enormous amounts of time, money, and talent go into commercials. 29 Technically they are often brilliant and innovative, the product not only of the new skills and devices but of imaginative minds. A few of them are both funny and endearing.

Among the enlightened sponsors, moreover, are some who manage to ₃₀ combine an image of their corporation and their products with accuracy and restraint.

What has to happen to mass medium advertisers as a whole, and ₃₁ especially on TV, is a totally new approach to their function not only as sellers but as social influencers. They have the same obligation as the broadcast medium itself: not only to entertain but to reflect, not only to reflect but to enlarge public consciousness and human stature.

This may be a tall order, but it is a vital one at a time when Americans ₃₂ have ceased to know who they are and where they are going, and when all the multiple forces acting upon them are daily diminishing their sense of their own value and purpose in life, when social upheaval and social fragmentation have destroyed old patterns, and when survival depends on new ones.

If we continue to see ourselves as the advertisers see us, we have no ₃₃ place to go. Nor, I might add, has commercial broadcasting itself.

Using the Dictionary

Marya Mannes uses many words with strong negative connotations. Explain what is unflattering about each italicized word in the following phrases. Check unfamiliar words in your dictionary.   1. a *doting* family (1)   2. a male voice *croons* (1)   3. an actor turned *pitchman* (2)   4. a familiar *litany* (2)   5. a *dubious* achievement (14)   6. *self-adulation* of the young (14)   7. *archaic* and *demeaning* assumptions (17)   8. a *manic* obsession (20)   9. a kind of *sterility* (20)   10. *dolts . . . shrews* and *narcissists* (22)   11. *quirks* and *mannerisms* (22)   12. this *wheedling* (24)   13. restless *impotence* (24)   14. the *dislocation* deepens (25)

The Writer's Agenda

To many jaded viewers, commercials on television mean merely one pleading or cajoling sales message after the other. The author of this article wanted to make us *pay attention*. She did so by focusing on several recurring types who people these commercials and who together add up to a revealing pattern.

1. What is the author's central thesis? Sum up and explain the major charges that she brings against television commercials in this article.

2. The author has classified the women who appear in television commercials under *four major headings*. What are the four major types? Describe each type, drawing on concrete details the author provides in different parts of the article.

3. What, according to the author, makes each of these types a damaging misrepresentation or stereotype? What are her *objections* to each? Where does she most forcefully or most directly champion the truths misrepresented by these stereotypes?

4. The author is determined to be fair in her account of how *men* are represented in commercials. On the one hand, what negative or stereotyped images of men does she find in commercials? On the other hand, what features of commercials make men appear in superior traditional roles?

5. Toward the end of her introduction and again in her concluding paragraphs, Mannes discusses some of the *larger issues* raised by the role television plays in our lives. What are the standards she applies or the goals she sets for television as a medium? (Does she have anything good to say about the medium as she observed it?)

6. Mannes has a gift for *satire*—she knows how to use cruel humor as a weapon in attacking things she deplores. She has a gift for the memorable concrete phrase or image with a strong satirical touch ("the worm's-eye view of mass communication"). Find and discuss a few striking examples.

For Discussion or Writing

7. Compare the image of women projected in current television commercials with the situation described by the author. Do the stereotypes she describes survive? Where and how? Has there been progress toward a more balanced or truthful picture of women in commercials and advertising? (Give detailed examples.)

8. What stereotypes about women, other than those observed by Mannes in commercials, exist in our society? How and where are they kept alive? Identify three or four major stereotypes and give detailed examples for each. (What are their probable causes or origins? What harm do they do? What are possible remedies?)

9. Do the media, and especially movies and television, keep alive stereotypes about men? Sort out and classify prevailing male stereotypes. Limit yourself to several major types and give detailed examples for each.

10. Like Mannes, many television critics see on television much that appeals to the "lowest common denominator." Set up a system of classification for shows that in your judgment fall under this general heading. Describe and illustrate fully three or four major types.

11. How much truth is there in a stereotype? Of the many groups in our society that are misrepresented by stereotypes, choose one that you know well from personal observation or experience. Write a paper that "talks back" to the stereotype—or that shows to what extent the stereotype may be true. In the first half of your paper, explore the prevailing stereotype as it is promoted by jokes and stories, movies and television, or other means. In the second half, draw on your own observation of or experience with the group. Try to show the reality that is obscured or misrepresented by the stereotype. Choose from groups like the following: a. (social or occupational groups) members of motorcycle clubs, politicians, "schoolmarms," police officers, athletes, "good ole boys," sales representatives; b. (ethnic or regional groups) the Irish, Texans, Italians, Germans, Asians, Mexicans, Jews, native Americans, Arabs.

STUDENT MODEL 6

FOR READING: Study the following short selection as a possible model for writing of your own. How do you react to it overall? What makes it interesting or effective? Answer the following more specific questions:

1. (PURPOSE) What was the writer trying to do?
2. (AUDIENCE) What kind of reader would make a good reader for this selection?
3. (SOURCES) Where did the writer turn for material?
4. (THESIS) Does the selection have a central idea or unifying thesis?
5. (STRUCTURE) What is the author's overall plan or strategy?
6. (STYLE) What makes the piece effective or memorable (for instance, striking details, memorable phrases)?
7. (REVISION) What do you think the writer could or should have done differently?

Sandra Bouslaugh

New Options, New Attitudes

The working woman is not new to society. However, in recent years we have seen dramatic changes in the kind of work she does. What we need today is similar changes in our attitudes toward the major kinds of women's work. Rather than classify the woman without a salaried outside career as non-working, we should refer to her as a woman who works in the home, because that is a more accurate description of a homemaker—who represents the first of three patterns of women's work. Second is the woman employed in traditional female occupations, who had few options to choose from—options that are still too often thought of and treated as second class. The third pattern allows women a freer choice of careers—but these choices are not always met by open minds. Along with changing the kinds of work women do, we need to change our attitudes toward working women and their careers.

Most common of the three patterns has long been the woman who works in the home. We should realize that she has often functioned as a cook, a tailor, a merchant (selling produce and buying supplies), an agricultural worker (tending livestock and working in the fields), and a teacher (teaching manners, social skills, and work habits) as well as a wife, mother, and housekeeper. The spinning wheel, the sewing machine, the ironing board, and the wash trough were long familiar symbols of her toil and tools of her trade.

Although working in the home has been and should continue to be an ₃
honored and legitimate choice, many women have decided against this
option out of necessity. The necessity to support herself and others, the
desire to relate to an environment other than the home, and the longing to
be known as an independent being rather than as an appendage of her
family are just a few of the reasons women began to seek outside employment. Often, however, the employment women found was limited to areas
that became stereotyped as traditional "women's work."

Nurses, teachers, social workers, waitresses, stewardesses, librarians, ₄
beauticians—these are examples of women doing traditional women's
work. Regardless of their skills, dedication, and hard work, the women in
these occupations were and still are often given low status and low pay.
Perhaps because many of these women are in service occupations (rather
than in positions involving manufacturing or supervision), people in other
lines of work have often treated them condescendingly—with employers
often calling the woman worker simply "the girl" or worse yet "my girl,"
implying ownership or a parent-child relationship.

A story told me by a former employer shows that such attitudes persist
as employment patterns change. While attending law school, Susan worked
as a legal assistant to acquaint herself with the workings of a law office as
well as help finance her education. However, when she graduated at the top
of her class, she had trouble becoming established in her profession. She
discovered later that her colleagues found it hard to accept her because
they remembered her in a "subservient" position.

Women who do what was traditionally "women's work" are entitled to ₅
the same respect as those in the third category—those who chose a career
because their aptitudes lay in that area, rather than having it chosen for
them because they were female. Women finally are given an opportunity
men have had for centuries—to choose their own careers. This free choice
has produced female engineers, pilots, authors, executives, scientists, and
more. Yet when we think of these and other professionals, many of us still
think of men. In an old episode of "All in the Family," Mike, the liberal
son-in-law, proposes a riddle to Archie, the chauvinistic head of the household who is set in his ways. As Mike tells the story, a boy and his father are
involved in a car accident. The boy is injured and the father is killed. When
the boy is wheeled into the operating room at a hospital, the doctor looks at
him and announces: "I can't operate on this patient. He is my son." "What is
the explanation?" Mike wants to know.

After thinking for a while, Archie guesses that the doctor or the man in ₆
the car was the boy's stepfather. Maybe the boy was adopted. Maybe the
doctor was some kind of religious figure who calls everyone his son. Finally,
Mike confronts Archie with the truth: The doctor is a woman. This possibility had never occurred to Archie, and he calls the riddle stupid, because it
doesn't specify a *woman* doctor. Archie, like much of our society, assumes

that a doctor is a man, even though the word includes no reference to sex, as there is in *salesman* or *stewardess*.

Now that the patterns of women's work are changing, our attitudes ⁊ must also change. History has given us three patterns of women's work. Homemaking, the first pattern, evolved into the second as women increasingly found work outside the home. This second pattern, however, put unfair limits on the careers women could choose, and society undervalued the work they performed. Finally, we see a third pattern where women can choose any employment but are still faced with outdated ideas and attitudes. Soon perhaps we can look forward to a fourth stage where all employees, male and female, are respected for the career choices they have made and are judged equally, without distinction.

FOR WRITING: Write a classification paper that requires you to *reclassify* what you observe as familiar patterns shift or change. For instance, you may want to set up new categories for new kinds of jobs for today's students, for changing levels of social status, for new kinds of popular music, or for new types of nonconventional students on campus. Set up a clear overall pattern for your paper; use striking, convincing examples or evidence.

ADDITIONAL WRITING TOPICS 6

Classification

A. Write a classification paper that will serve as a guide to a confused newcomer or outside observer. Choose a topic like the following:

1. kinds of restaurants
2. current fashions
3. kinds of parents
4. ways to dress for success
5. styles of cooking
6. most common personality types on campus
7. types of jokes, or kinds of humor
8. type of drivers
9. favorite hangouts of the younger crowd
10. kinds of vacations (or vacationers)
11. ways of dealing with trouble or bad news
12. ways of making a fool of yourself in public
13. roads to academic success
14. relationships
15. new television shows
16. different kinds of religious people
17. successful politicians

18. performers who are (current) (all-time) audience favorites
19. people who sell
20. people who wait on tables

B. Study television news or news reports in a newspaper over a period of a week or so. Write a classification paper in which you sort out and report on the major recurrent kinds of news. Label them clearly; describe them; use striking examples. (Or you may want to concentrate and sort out the subcategories of one major kind of news, such as crime news.)

7

ARGUMENT

Cause and Effect

OVERVIEW

In a structured argument, one thing follows from the other. We take the reader along step by logical step. When we are really serious about a subject, or when the conclusions to be drawn seem especially important, we may want to leave little to the reader's goodwill or personal perference. We try to lay the subject out in such a way that a rational person, looking at the matter coolly and objectively, will reach the same logical conclusions that we did.

One important kind of systematic, step-by-step reasoning is the analysis of causes and effects. Cause-and-effect thinking is built into much of the reasoning that helps us understand our world and enables us to function in it. We explain a present situation by tracing the causes that produced it. We argue the merits of a proposal by showing what its consequences would be if adopted. We project current trends into the future by showing the results that similar causes will produce if they continue to operate.

PURPOSE In many situations that require a choice among alternatives, we use cause-and-effect reasoning to guide the reader. The basic purpose of cause-and-effect reasoning is to explain *why*: We trace the causes of something to show why it came about, to show why things are as they are. At the same time, understanding the *why* provides us with clues to the *how*: Analyzing causes and their effects provides guidance for the future. When we understand the causes of something, we can change our behavior in order to produce different or more desirable effects. Much cause-and-effect writing is done by writers who view with alarm: they analyze the causes of ominous current trends—our threatened wildlife, the poisoning of the environment—and they recommend action to head off the predicted results.

AUDIENCE Cause-and-effect writing often aims at readers seriously concerned with decisions that affect either their personal lives or the public welfare. The writer expects readers to take seriously such topics as why women earn less than men, what factors precipitate divorce, what can be done about toxic waste, how public transit can be made into a viable alternative to the private automobile. Cause-and-effect thinking dominates writing on technical subjects, where to understand something typically means to know the causes that bring it about. But much writing on nontechnical subjects tries to apply cause-and-effect thinking to social or economic concerns in order to affect our decisions about the future.

BENEFITS FOR THE WRITER (1) Cause-and-effect writing helps us think clearly and objectively. It can teach us to go beyond what we would *like* to see; it makes us take into account hard facts and unwelcome evidence. Careful study of cause and effect can help us counteract our tendency to shortcut thinking: sweeping generalizations, hasty conclusions, scapegoating.

(2) Cause-and-effect writing helps teach a writer to work out a structured, step-by-step argument. Working out a chain of cause and effect, a writer has to make sure the readers see the logical connections at each point; at the same time, readers need a clear sense of where they are headed, of how each detail fits into the larger picture.

(3) Cause-and-effect writing, like other kinds of structured argument, can teach us to hold our own in the give-and-take of serious debate. We learn to reckon with opposing arguments, to anticipate objections. It is often not enough to promote our own theories or explanations—we may also have to argue *against* alternative theories that might be used to undercut or discredit our own.

CAUSE AND EFFECT
Additional Reading

Rachel Carson, Our War Against Nature   (p. 368)

WRITER'S GUIDE 7

Analyzing Causes and Effects

Much serious current writing applies cause-and-effect reasoning to issues ranging from the banning of pesticides to the future of the family. Often the writers ask similar questions: "What are the causes of current trends? What will the results be if current trends continue? What would we have to do to bring about different results?"

Systematic analysis of cause and effect may provide the basic structure for a single paragraph or for a paper as a whole. The following guidelines chart strategies for papers that focus on causes and their results:

(1) *Trace a chain of cause and effect.* Much cause-and-effect writing traces a sequence of events, showing not only how it happened but also why. The writer makes sure to include each necessary development that triggered the next stage or phase in the sequence.

Much writing about social and cultural trends traces a chain of cause-and-effect relationships to explain how people act and why. Notice that the **transitions** in the following paragraph signal major links in a chain of causes. The **topic sentence**, or statement of the key idea, sums up the basic cause-and-effect relationship:

TOPIC SENTENCE:	*The hostility toward work that has developed in this generation comes largely from sons of fathers who were workaholics.* The fathers of today's middle-class children lived
Root cause:	through and were wounded by the great Depression. Anyone who grew up in the 1940's lives with the fear that the tide of prosperity might recede again, as it did in 1931, and
Second link:	then there would be no jobs. *As a result*, most of the men who have risen to middle-management positions devoted themselves to their work and their corporations with reli-
Third link:	gious zeal: the job was the center of their lives. *And so* a generation of sons and daughters identify "work" as the villain who took Daddy away from them and returned him tired and used-up at the end of the day. A thousand times in the average middle-class home a child eager to play with Daddy was told, "Not now, Daddy's tired" or "Daddy has to go to work." (Sam Keen, "Lovers vs. Workers," *Quest*)

(2) *Trace the varied consequences of a single major cause.* Often cause-and-effect writing shows the repercussions of an important change or historical development. An article might focus on a single root cause and then show its far-reaching effects:

The Car Explosion

THESIS: *The car is probably the foremost example of a technological innovation which developed, as it spread, vast and largely unforeseen social consequences.*

First result: Immediately there was the matter of *traffic congestion*. . . .

Second result: *Pollution* of the air by car fumes, though first denied by the car companies, was later proved by scientists in California. . . .

Third result: *Court dockets* became so crowded with accident cases that about a decade ago relief was sought through no-fault insurance. . . .

Fourth result: Growing dependence on foreign sources for oil highlighted the role of the car as a consumer of an increasingly *scarce natural resource*. . . .

Fifth result: Probably the least well-perceived consequence of the car is its impact on the *center cities*. . . .

(3) *Recognize a range of possible contributing causes*: Often several causes work together to produce a combined result. A writer may still want to close in on the most important cause, or the one that could most easily be corrected to help solve a problem. However, readers become wary of *oversimplification*. They need to see evidence that the writer is aware of the different possible causes that may be contributing to the same result. The following excerpts might represent an introductory survey of possible causes, but they could also provide the outline for a paper as a whole:

As American as Apple Pie

Cause 1: Some say there is so much violence in our nation simply because there are *too many of us*—the census strangling the senses. . . .

Cause 2: Some say it's because we have become *too permissive*—failing to understand that when anything goes, everything may go. . . .

Cause 3: Some say it's because violence is an *entertainment* for jaded appetites—part of the side show of our time—perhaps not arranged but certainly exploited by television and the other media to keep their profits high. . . .

Cause 4: Some say violence is *big business*, that crime does pay—handsomely. . . .

Cause 5:   Some say that violence is merely a crude form of *redistribution of wealth. . . .* (Bess Myerson, *Redbook*)

Note: Concentrating on a single chief cause and ignoring other factors leads to familiar kinds of shortcut thinking:

- The first of these is **scapegoating**: Confronted with a problem, we identify a single cause and make it the culprit. Much scapegoat thinking sets up a single, easily reached target for our anger. When students can't read, newspapers and parents like to blame the teachers. The teachers chosen as scapegoats are likely to point to other factors: Reading ability varies statistically with the income level of the parents; students are kept from books by jazzed-up visual entertainment; their peer culture and society at large place little value on books and book learning.
- The opposite kind of shortcut thinking is the search for the **panacea**: We look for a single (and preferably cheap) remedy for complicated ills.
- A special kind of shortcut thinking confuses *after* and *because*. The **post hoc fallacy** (from the Latin "after this") makes us jump to conclusions when events follow each other closely in time. Harassing phone calls start after a hostile-looking neighbor moves in across the street. A wet, cold summer follows the eruption of a volcano. Cause and effect? Or merely a hunch that would have to be confirmed by some substantial evidence?

(4) *Go beyond surface appearances to trace underlying causes.* When we take a serious look at a subject, we go beyond surface impressions to identify those factors that do not meet the eye. The following might be the outline of a magazine article helping us understand a complex issue:

The Open Door

FAMILIAR VIEW: We usually think of our immigration policies as inspired by high-minded, idealistic motives. We hear speakers say that we are all immigrants or the children of immigrants. We quote the familiar lines about the huddled masses of the old continent seeking refuge in the New World. However, *the real reasons for continuing large-scale immigration are often less flattering and more down-to-earth. . . .*

First cause: Much support for immigration is motivated by *selfish interests*. In the words of one observer, "The primary selfish interest in unimpeded immigration is the desire of employers for cheap labor, particularly in industries and trades that offer degrading work. . . ."

Second cause: Much support for continued immigration is motivated by *practical political considerations*. In the past, rabid opponents of immigration used to warn that the country was being overrun by foreigners of supposedly inferior genetic stock. As a result, today the politician who votes to restrict immigration is likely to be accused of prejudice, bigotry, isolationism, and racism....

Third cause: Much illegal immigration is made possible by our traditional American *distaste for police-state methods*. We would need an army of immigration officers to seal off our coasts and our borders. We would need a national system of I.D. cards and fingerprinting to keep illegal aliens out of jobs....

(5) *Weigh the consequences of alternative courses of action*. Many of our everyday decisions are the result of our asking ourselves: "What will happen if I follow course A? What will happen if I follow course B?" Often a structured argument will weigh different possible courses of action in order to make us choose the most promising or least painful one. Often the writer will proceed by **eliminating alternatives** in order to lead up to the remaining logical choice.

The following might be the outline of a paper weighing alternatives. Under each major heading, the writer would present arguments pro and con, first examining favorable and then unfavorable effects:

Our Crowded Jails

THESIS: Ironically, at a time when public opinion is clamoring for stiffer sentences, courts and prison officials are looking for ways to keep or move more people out of our overcrowded jails.

I. More use of plea bargaining
   A. Favorable results
   B. Unfavorable results

II. Lowering bail requirements
   A. Statistics in support
   B. Important cautions

III. Granting earlier paroles
   A. Desirable results
   B. Undesirable results

IV. Leniency for "victimless" crimes
   A. Arguments in favor
   B. Predictable opposition

To sum up: The purpose of a structured argument is to convince the reader, to carry the reader along step by step. Often, the most important links in an argument are relationships between cause and effect. When analyzing causes and effects, we have to make sure not to take too much for granted. We have to show the actual workings of causes and their effects in convincing detail. We have to be alert to different possible causes contributing to the same result.

Prewriting Activities 7

1. The following excerpts identify possible reasons for a high dropout rate for students from one population group. Study these excerpts. Then do your own preliminary survey of four or five major *possible causes* of a similar situation that you have studied or observed. Fill in observations, details, facts, or figures for each cause you identify. Choose a situation like the following: high unemployment among one population group; success of foreign imports in a specific field; weight problems; high divorce rates; drug abuse among young people; inflation; growth of teenage gangs.

Strangers in Their Own Land

Possible cause 1:
Mexican Americans have a higher dropout rate than any other comparable group in the nation. One of the principal reasons for the high dropout rate of Mexican Americans has been simply that Mexican American youngsters *tend to be over age in grade levels*. By the time they get to the point where they are able to function in English and do the required first-grade work, they should chronologically be in the second grade. . . .

Possible cause 2:
There is no doubt that the high dropout rate of Mexican Americans is directly linked to *tests and measurements*. Of the many Mexican American children who were found to be over age in grade levels in a study at Arizona State University, their median performance on most tests was about one standard deviation below the Anglo groups. . . .

Possible cause 3:
Not only do Mexican American children enter school at a measurable disadvantage, but the disadvantage becomes more pronounced as they move up through the grades. With such factors reinforcing the "failure-syndrome" and "negative self-concept," little wonder that Mexican American youngsters leave school in such great numbers. . . .

Possible cause 4:
The *lack of emphasis on education in the home* cannot be considered a significant factor in the high dropout rate of Mexican Americans. Studies have concluded that there is

little difference between Mexican American families and other families in the emphasis on education. . . .   (Philip D. Ortego, "A Need for Bilingual Education," in *The Chicanos*)

2. Investigate the causes behind a current problem on your campus or in your neighborhood. First, examine an apparent, alleged, or official reason. Then, examine what you consider the real reason or the deeper cause. Prepare a rough *first draft* of a paper using your findings.

Paragraph Practice 7

Write a paragraph that focuses on a distinctive behavior pattern and the result it produces. Focus, for instance, on what being a cheerleader, or holding two jobs, or getting behind in one's studies does to a person's life. Study and discuss the following sample paragraph as a possible model.

Mind Over Water

I have been working on swimming since I was ten, four hours a day or more, every day, skipping the greater part of my social life. What I do is analogous to other long-distance competitions: running, cycling, rowing, those sports where training time far exceeds actual competition time. But swimming burns more calories per minute than anything else. The lungs, heart and muscles must all be working at peak efficiency for this sport, which doesn't require brute strength but rather the strength of endurance. I can do a thousand sit-ups in the wink of an eye—and I never do sit-ups on a regular basis. I've run the mile in 5:15, not exactly Olympic caliber, but better than most women can do. My lung capacity is six-point-one liters, greater than that of a lot of football players. My heartbeat is forty-seven or forty-eight when I am at rest, compared to the normal seventy-two for other people. A conditioned athlete usually has a heartbeat of sixty plus. These characteristics are not due to genetics—I attained them by swimming hour after hour, year after year.   (Diana Nyad)

BACKGROUND: Sheila Tobias (born 1935) helped make the terms "math avoider" and "math anxiety" the familiar buzzwords they are today. She went to college at Radcliffe and Columbia University. She became a college teacher and administrator and was a founding member of the National Organization of Women. In 1978, she published *Overcoming Math Anxiety*. In this book, she drew on a mass of statistics, published research, and expert opinion to answer questions like the following: Why is math a major hurdle for many students? Is it true that young women, especially, avoid math? If so, are the causes biological? Are they psychological? Are they cultural—determined by patterns built into our culture? After the publication of her book, Tobias helped found a training and consulting service running math clinics for adults. The following article, first published in the *Atlantic*, uses key excerpts from her book.

Sheila Tobias

Who's Afraid of Math, and Why?

GUIDE TO READING: In this essay, the author carefully and systematically examines possible causes of failure, and fear of failure, at math. What are the major possible causes? What is the most important evidence the author presents or reviews for each? What seems to be her final verdict on each of the major possibilities?

The first thing people remember about failing at math is that it felt like sudden death. Whether the incident occurred while learning "word problems" in sixth grade, coping with equations in high school, or first confronting calculus and statistics in college, failure came suddenly and in a very frightening way. An idea or a new operation was not just difficult, it was impossible! And, instead of asking questions or taking the lesson slowly, most people remember having had the feeling that they would never go any further in mathematics. If we assume that the curriculum was reasonable, and that the new idea was but the next in a series of learnable concepts, the feeling of utter defeat was simply not rational; yet "math anxious" college students and adults have revealed that no matter how much the teacher reassured them, they could not overcome that feeling.

A common myth about the nature of mathematical ability holds that one either has or does not have a mathematical mind. Mathematical imagination and an intuitive grasp of mathematical principles may well be needed to do advanced research, but why should people who can do college-level work in other subjects not be able to do college-level math as well? Rates of learning may vary. Competency under time pressure may differ. Certainly low self-esteem will get in the way. But where is the evidence that a student needs a "mathematical mind" in order to succeed at learning math?

Consider the effects of this mythology. Since only a few people are supposed to have this mathematical mind, part of what makes us so passive in the face of our difficulties in learning mathematics is that we suspect all the while we may not be one of "them," and we spend our time waiting to find out when our nonmathematical minds will be exposed. Since our limit will eventually be reached, we see no point in being methodical or in attending to detail. We are grateful when we survive fractions, word problems, or geometry. If that certain moment of failure hasn't struck yet, it is only temporarily postponed.

Parents, especially parents of girls, often expect their children to be nonmathematical. Parents are either poor at math and had their own sudden-death experiences, or, if math came easily for them, they do not know how it feels to be slow. In either case, they unwittingly foster the idea that a mathematical mind is something one either has or does not have.

Mathematics and Sex

Although fear of math is not a purely female phenomenon, girls tend to drop out of math sooner than boys, and adult women experience an aversion to math and math-related activities that is akin to anxiety. A 1972 survey of the amount of high school mathematics taken by incoming freshmen at Berkeley revealed that while 57 percent of the boys had taken four years of high school math, only 8 percent of the girls had had the same amount of preparation. Without four years of high school math, students at Berkeley, and at most other colleges and universities, are ineligible for the calculus sequence, unlikely to attempt chemistry or physics, and inadequately prepared for statistics and economics.

Unable to elect these entry-level courses, the remaining 92 percent of the girls will be limited, presumably, to the career choices that are considered feminine: the humanities, guidance and counseling, elementary school teaching, foreign languages, and the fine arts.

Boys and girls may be born alike with respect to math, but certain sex differences in performance emerge early according to several respected studies, and these differences remain through adulthood. They are:

1. Girls compute better than boys (elementary school and on).
2. Boys solve word problems better than girls (from age thirteen on).
3. Boys take more math than girls (from age sixteen on).
4. Girls learn to hate math sooner and possibly for different reasons.

Why the differences in performance? One reason is the amount of math learned and used at play. Another may be the difference in male-female maturation. If girls do better than boys at all elementary school tasks, then they may compute better for no other reason than that arithmetic is part of the elementary school curriculum. As boys and girls grow older, girls become, under pressure, academically less competitive. Thus, the falling off of girls' math performance between ages ten and fifteen may be because:

1. Math gets harder in each successive year and requires more work and commitment.
2. Both boys and girls are pressured, beginning at age ten, not to excel in areas designated by society to be outside their sex-role domains.
3. Thus girls have a good excuse to avoid the painful struggle with math; boys don't.

Such a model may explain girls' lower achievement in math overall, 9 but why should girls even younger than ten have difficulty in problem-solving? In her review of the research on sex differences, psychologist Eleanor Maccoby noted that girls are generally more conforming, more suggestible, and more dependent upon the opinion of others than boys (all learned, not innate, behaviors). Being so, they may not be as willing to take risks or to think for themselves, two behaviors that are necessary in solving problems. Indeed, in one test of third-graders, girls were found to be not nearly as willing to estimate, to make judgments about "possible right answers," or to work with systems they had never seen before. Their very success at doing what is expected of them up to that time seems to get in the way of their doing something new.

If readiness to do word problems, to take one example, is as much a 10 function of readiness to take risks as it is of "reasoning ability," then mathematics performance certainly requires more than memory, computation, and reasoning. The differences in math performance between boys and girls—no matter how consistently those differences show up—cannot be attributed simply to differences in innate ability.

Still, if one were to ask the victims themselves, they would probably 11 disagree: they would say their problems with math have to do with the way they are "wired." They feel they are somehow missing something—one ability or several—that other people have. Although women want to believe they are not mentally inferior to men, many fear that, where math is concerned, they really are. Thus, we have to consider seriously whether mathematical ability has a biological basis, not only because a number of researchers believe this to be so, but because a number of victims agree with them.

The Arguments from Biology

The search for some biological basis for math ability or disability is 12 fraught with logical and experimental difficulties. Since not all math underachievers are women, and not all women are mathematics-avoidant, poor performance in math is unlikely to be due to some genetic or hormonal difference between the sexes. Moreover, no amount of research so far has unearthed a "mathematical competency" in some tangible, measurable substance in the body. Since "masculinity" cannot be injected into women to test whether or not it improves their mathematics, the theories that attribute such ability to genes or hormones must depend for their proof on circumstantial evidence. So long as about 7 percent of the Ph.D.'s in mathematics are earned by women, we have to conclude either that these women have genes, hormones, and brain organization different from those of the rest of us, or that certain positive experiences in their lives have largely undone the negative fact that they are female, or both.

Genetically, the only difference between males and females (albeit a 13 significant and pervasive one) is the presence of two chromosomes designated X in every female cell. Normal males exhibit an X-Y combination. Because some kinds of mental retardation are associated with sex-chromosomal anomalies, a number of researchers have sought a converse linkage between specific abilities and the presence or absence of the second X. But the linkage between genetics and mathematics is not supported by conclusive evidence.

Since intensified hormonal activity commences at adolescence, a time 14 during which girls seem to lose interest in mathematics, much more has been made of the unequal amounts in females and males of the sex-linked hormones androgen and estrogen. Biological researchers have linked estrogen—the female hormone—with "simple repetitive tasks," and androgen—the male hormone—with "complex restructuring tasks." The assumption here is not only that such specific talents are biologically based (probably undemonstrable) but also that one cannot be good at *both* repetitive and restructuring kinds of assignments.

Sex Roles and Mathematics Competence

The fact that many girls tend to lose interest in math at the age they 15 reach puberty (junior high school) suggests that puberty might in some sense cause girls to fall behind in math. Several explanations come to mind: the influence of hormones, more intensified sex-role socialization, or some extracurricular learning experience exclusive to boys of that age.

One group of seventh-graders in a private school in New England gave 16 a clue as to what children themselves think about all of this. When asked why girls do as well as boys in math until the sixth grade, while sixth-grade boys do better from that point on, the girls responded: "Oh, that's easy. After sixth grade, we have to do real math." The answer to why "real math" should be considered to be "for boys" and not "for girls" can be found not in the realm of biology but only in the realm of ideology of sex differences.

Parents, peers, and teachers forgive a girl when she does badly in math [17] at school, encouraging her to do well in other subjects instead. "'There, there,' my mother used to say when I failed at math," one woman says. "But I got a talking-to when I did badly in French." Lynn Fox, who directs a program for mathematically gifted junior high boys and girls on the campus of Johns Hopkins University, has trouble recruiting girls and keeping them in her program. Some parents prevent their daughters from participating altogether for fear that excellence in math will make them too different. The girls themselves are often reluctant to continue with mathematics, Fox reports, because they fear social ostracism.

Where do these associations come from? [18]

The association of masculinity with mathematics sometimes extends [19] from the discipline to those who practice it. Students, asked on a questionnaire what characteristics they associate with a mathematician (as contrasted with a "writer"), selected terms such as rational, cautious, wise, and responsible. The writer, on the other hand, in addition to being seen as individualistic and independent, was also described as warm, interested in people, and altogether more compatible with a feminine ideal.

As a result of this psychological conditioning, a young woman may [20] consider math and math-related fields to be inimical to femininity. In an interesting study of West German teenagers, Erika Schildkamp-Kuendiger found that girls who identified themselves with the feminine ideal underachieved in mathematics, that is, did less well than would have been expected of them based on general intelligence and performance in other subjects.

Street Mathematics: Things, Motion, Scores

Not all the skills that are necessary for learning mathematics are [21] learned in school. Measuring, computing, and manipulating objects that have dimensions and dynamic properties of their own are part of the everyday life of children. Children who miss out on these experiences may not be well primed for math in school.

Feminists have complained for a long time that playing with dolls is [22] one way of convincing impressionable little girls that they may only be mothers or housewives—or, as in the case of the Barbie doll, "pinup girls"—when they grow up. But doll-playing may have even more serious consequences for little girls than that. Do girls find out about gravity and distance and shapes and sizes playing with dolls? Probably not.

A curious boy, if his parents are tolerant, will have taken apart a [23] number of household and play objects by the time he is ten, and, if his parents are lucky, he may even have put them back together again. In all of this he is learning things that will be useful in physics and math. Taking parts out that have to go back in requires some examination of form. Building something that stays up or at least stays put for some time involves working with structure.

Sports is another source of math-related concepts for children which tends to favor boys. Getting to first base on a not very well hit grounder is a lesson in time, speed, and distance. Intercepting a football thrown through the air requires some rapid intuitive eye calculations based on the ball's direction, speed, and trajectory. Since physics is partly concerned with velocities, trajectories, and collisions of objects, much of the math taught to prepare a student for physics deals with relationships and formulas that can be used to express motion and acceleration.

What, then, can we conclude about mathematics and sex? If math anxiety is in part the result of math avoidance, why not require girls to take as much math as they can possibly master? If being the only girl in "trig" is the reason so many women drop math at the end of high school, why not provide psychological counseling and support for those young women who wish to go on? Since ability in mathematics is considered by many to be unfeminine, perhaps fear of success, more than any bodily or mental dysfunction, may interfere with girls' ability to learn math.

Using the Dictionary

How technical is the author's vocabulary? Check the following as necessary:
1. *intuitive* (2) 2. *methodical* (3) 3. *aversion* (5) 4. *maturation* (8) 5. *computation* (10) 6. *fraught* (12) 7. *genetic* (12) 8. *tangible* (12) 9. *albeit* (13) 10. *anomaly* (13) 11. *converse* (13) 12. *socialization* (15) 13. *realm* (16) 14. *ostracism* (17) 15. *trajectory* (24) 16. *velocity* (24) 17. *dysfunction* (25)

The Writer's Agenda

In this essay, the author sets out to analyze causes and effects in order to find possible solutions to a widespread problem. Answer the following questions:

1. From the beginning, what basic assumptions does the author make about her *audience*?

2. Tobias sets her essay in motion by attacking a common *misconception*. What is it, and what harm does it do?

3. Where and how does the author most effectively dramatize the *issue* for you—make you see its bearings or its importance?

4. A key argument in many discussions of sex roles concerns the influence of biology, or genetic factors. What are key facts or arguments that Tobias reviews? What seems to be her last word on the subject?

5. How much weight does Tobias attach to the influence of traditional social or cultural roles—of a traditional "feminine ideal"?

6. According to Tobias, how do different traditional patterns of play and of sports affect mathematical aptitude or mathematical performance?

7. What positive advice or guidance does Tobias leave us with? How valid does it seem to you?

For Discussion or Writing

8. Are you a "math avoider"? Do you suffer from "math anxiety"? What do you think caused *you* to be poor or good at math?

9. Do you think this essay would have been more effective or less effective if the author had concentrated exclusively on math anxiety experienced by women?

10. In your experience, how does our culture guide the way boys and girls relate to math, science, or technology? (Are familiar patterns of cultural conditioning changing? Why and how?)

11. Voluminous reports and proposals preaching a return to excellence in the nation's schools have recently probed the causes of academic achievement. What for you are the major causes of academic success (or academic failure)? How do you know?

12. Why are some people good at taking tests? Why do others do poorly? (Or, for you what makes the difference between a good and a bad test?)

13. Do students have feelings similar to "mathophobia" about other academic subjects? Examine the causes of students' aversion or hostility toward what you think is a least favorite subject.

Branching Out

14. In her book *Games Your Mother Never Taught You,* Betty Lehan Harragan claims that young males have a competitive edge in American business because they tend to be more familiar than young women with two areas from which business draws analogies, key terms, and inspiration. These two areas are military life and team sports. Can you show the influence or role of one of these in what you have seen of American business?

WRITERS ON WRITING

Sheila Tobias on Math Anxiety and Writing Anxiety

QUESTION: Are there parallels between math anxiety and writing anxiety?

ANSWER: Yes, I think so. The essence of the parallel is that people feel—wrongly—that they are incapable of doing well in these subjects. More specifically, the getting-started issues are the same. A student looking at a math problem with trepidation may think he must know exactly where he is going—it's comparable to writing. A writing student thinks he's supposed to have a completed plan—to know just what the finished product will look like—yet both good math students and good writers dive in or start to work knowing that they will figure out where to go from the inside.

In solving a math problem, think about it as if you were doing a jigsaw puzzle, and do the same for writing. You don't start by knowing the whole picture: You start by finding the edges, by finding a little of the blue here, the yellow there—and you're on your way.

Real mathematicians looking at a problem they've never seen before don't wait for a plan. They go right in. Your instincts get massaged by getting going, and most people, I think, have pretty good instincts in math and in writing. But, if you stand back chewing on your pencil, you have no way to draw on your instincts, the resources of your intuitions.

Secondly, I firmly believe that good writers vary from bad writers *not* in the quality of the first draft—most of those probably look pretty much the same—but in the revising process. I say of my own work, "Only my wastebasket knows for sure!"

It's a cycle: The more confident you are, the more willing you are to take risks, and the more willing you are to take risks, the more experience you get—and the better you get.

QUESTION: How do you get math-anxious students to dive in? Would the same techniques work for anxious writers?

ANSWER: In the first draft, the important thing is not to be inhibited. In math, we suggest even the simplest things that may seem silly—having students rewrite the question in their own words, substitute simpler numbers, anything to get intuition going.

All anybody can do, really, is to help people learn about their own idiosyncrasies. It's a very personal thing to figure out strategies, to understand our own processes.

In our workshops, we teach "interventions"; one of them is closely related to writing. We get people to keep a journal to make them aware of their own processes. We use double entry journals—on the one side, they work on the problem; on the other, they describe the process (what they are thinking, how they are feeling). Then we use these journals as the subject for discussion—to show there's not just one right way to do things.

The good student, I believe, varies from a bad student in the degree to which she understands how she learns and can, therefore, transfer whatever the task is into what she does best.

QUESTION: Do both math and writing as problem-solving processes suffer from our need to find clear (and absolute) answers?

ANSWER: Math is sold to students as being "right-answer producing," and in my book I point out that arithmetic involves going from a question to an answer, but mathematics means going from an answer to a question. In teaching writing or math, we need to teach people to formulate questions.

A student who does well in the kind of psychological environment where there are "right" answers has difficulty adjusting to the atmosphere of the writing class where there is no "right answer."

When I taught humanities to engineers, I found that they were uncomfortable with my not being able to tell them—*exactly*—what they could do to get an "A." Students find two very incompatible sets of expectations in the same school. I'm not saying that people who are good in math are not good writers or vice versa—that's not true at all. Many people are very good at both.

QUESTION: Do sex roles affect attitudes or ability in writing as you claim they do in math?

ANSWER: Women are less inhibited, though not necessarily more talented, in writing. But that's important because they are encouraged to verbalize when men are not. So women may find it easier to write.

—From an interview with the editors of *Essay 2*

BACKGROUND: Garrett Hardin (born in 1915 in Dallas, Texas) is the author of books and articles on "human ecology"—the study of how human life is sustained on this planet. He completed his doctoral work in biology at Stanford University in 1941. He was on the faculty of the University of California at Santa Barbara for many years, and he has lectured at many other universities. His writings, including the widely reprinted article "The Tragedy of the Commons," attack the conventional American self-image of good intentions and philanthropy around the world. Hardin represents a new kind of conservative intellectual trying to counter the views of the "guilt-ridden," "conscience-stricken" humanitarian liberal with a more "hard-nosed" view of America's interests as a nation. The essay reprinted here was published as part of a longer article in *Psychology Today*.

Garrett Hardin

Lifeboat Ethics

GUIDE TO READING: This essay makes us ask, "If we choose one course over another, what will be the consequences of our actions?" What are the well-intentioned proposals that the author argues against in this essay? How does he repeatedly trace a chain of cause and effect to the predicted consequences in order to make us reject the proposals?

Environmentalists use the metaphor of the earth as a "spaceship" in trying to persuade countries, industries and people to stop wasting and polluting our natural resources. Since we all share life on this planet, they argue, no single person or institution has the right to destroy, waste, or use more than a fair share of its resources. 1

But does everyone on earth have an equal right to an equal share of its resources? The spaceship metaphor can be dangerous when used by misguided idealists to justify suicidal policies for sharing our resources through uncontrolled immigration and foreign aid. In their enthusiastic but unrealistic generosity, they confuse the ethics of a spaceship with those of a lifeboat. 2

A true spaceship would have to be under the control of a captain, since no ship could possibly survive if its course were determined by committee. Spaceship Earth certainly has no captain; the United Nations is merely a toothless tiger, with little power to enforce any policy upon its bickering members. 3

If we divide the world crudely into rich nations and poor nations, two thirds of them are desperately poor, and only one third comparatively rich, with the United States the wealthiest of all. Metaphorically each rich na- 4 tion can be seen as a lifeboat full of comparatively rich people. In the ocean outside each lifeboat swim the poor of the world, who would like to get in, or at least to share some of the wealth. What should the lifeboat passengers do?

First, we must recognize the limited capacity of any lifeboat. For example, a nation's land has a limited capacity to support a population and as the current energy crisis has shown us, in some ways we have already exceeded the carrying capacity of our land. So here we sit, say 50 people in our lifeboat. To be generous, let us assume it has room for 10 more, making a total capacity of 60. Suppose the 50 of us in the lifeboat see 100 others swimming in the water outside, begging for admission to our boat or for handouts. We have several options: we may be tempted to try to live by the Christian ideal of being "our brother's keeper," or by the Marxist ideal of "to each according to his needs." Since the needs of all in the water are the same, and since they can all be seen as our "brothers," we could take them all into our boat, making a total of 150 in a boat designed for 60. The boat swamps; everyone drowns. Complete justice, complete catastrophe.

Since the boat has an unused excess capacity of 10 more passengers, we could admit just 10 more to it. But which 10 do we let in? How do we choose? Do we pick the best 10, the neediest 10, "first come, first served"? And what do we say to the 90 we exclude? If we do let an extra 10 into our lifeboat, we will have lost our "safety factor," an engineering principle of critical importance. For example, if we don't leave room for excess capacity as a safety factor in our country's agriculture, a new plant disease or a bad change in the weather could have disastrous consequences.

Suppose we decide to preserve our small safety factor and admit no more to the lifeboat. Our survival is then possible, although we shall have to be constantly on guard against boarding parties.

While this last solution clearly offers the only means of our survival, it is morally abhorrent to many people. Some say they feel guilty about their good luck. My reply is simple: "Get out and yield your place to others." This may solve the problem of the guilt-ridden person's conscience, but it does not change the ethics of the lifeboat. The needy person to whom the guilt-ridden person yields his place will not himself feel guilty about his good luck. If he did, he would not climb aboard. The net result of conscience-stricken people giving up their unjustly held seats is the elimination of that sort of conscience from the lifeboat.

This is the basic metaphor within which we must work out our solutions. Let us now enrich the image, step by step, with substantive additions from the real world, a world that must solve real and pressing problems of overpopulation and hunger.

The harsh ethics of the lifeboat become even harsher when we consider the reproductive differences between the rich nations and the poor nations. The people inside the lifeboats are doubling in numbers every 87 years; those swimming around outside are doubling, on the average, every

35 years, more than twice as fast as the rich. And since the world's resources are dwindling, the difference in prosperity between the rich and the poor can only increase.

As of 1973, the U. S. had a population of 210 million people, who were 11 increasing by 0.8 percent per year. Outside our lifeboat, let us imagine another 210 million people (say the combined populations of Colombia, Ecuador, Venezuela, Morocco, Pakistan, Thailand, and the Philippines), increasing at a rate of 3.3 percent per year. Put differently, the doubling time for this aggregate population was 21 years, compared to 87 years for the U.S.

Now suppose the U.S. agreed to pool its resources with those seven 12 countries, with everyone receiving an equal share. Initially the ratio of Americans to non-Americans in this model would be one-to-one. But consider what the ratio would be after 87 years, by which time the Americans would have doubled to a population of 420 million. By then, doubling every 21 years, the other group would have swollen to 354 billion. Each American would have to share the available resources with more than eight people.

But, one could argue, this discussion assumes that current population 13 trends will continue, and they may not. Quite so. Most likely the rate of population increase will decline much faster in the U.S. than it will in the other countries, and there does not seem to be much we can do about it. In sharing with "each according to his needs," we must recognize that needs are determined by population size, which is determined by the rate of reproduction, which at present is regarded as a sovereign right of every nation, poor or not. This being so, the philanthropic load created by the sharing ethic of the spaceship can only increase.

The fundamental error of spaceship ethics, and the sharing it requires, 14 is that it leads to what I call "the tragedy of the commons." Under a system of private property, people who own property recognize their responsibility to care for it, for if they don't they will eventually suffer. A farmer, for instance, will allow no more cattle in a pasture than its carrying capacity justifies. If he overloads it, erosion sets in, weeds take over, and he loses the use of the pasture.

If a pasture becomes a commons open to all, the right of each to use it 15 may not be matched by a corresponding responsibility to protect it. Asking everyone to use it with discretion will hardly do, for the considerate herdsman who refrains from overloading the commons suffers more than a selfish one who says his needs are greater. If everyone would restrain himself, all would be well; but it takes only one less than everyone to ruin a system of voluntary restraint. In a crowded world of less than perfect human beings, mutual ruin is inevitable if there are no controls. This is the tragedy of the commons.

One of the major tasks of education today should be the creation of 16 such an acute awareness of the dangers of the commons that people will recognize its many varieties. For example, the air and water have become polluted because they are treated as commons. Further growth in the population or per-capita conversion of natural resources into pollutants will only make the problem worse. The same holds true for the fish of the oceans. Fishing fleets have nearly disappeared in many parts of the world; technological improvements in the art of fishing are hastening the day of complete ruin. Only the replacement of the system of the commons with a responsible system of control will save the land, air, water and oceanic fisheries.

In recent years there has been a push to create a new commons called 17 a World Food Bank, an international depository of food reserves to which nations would contribute according to their abilities and from which they would draw according to their needs. This humanitarian proposal received support from many liberal international groups, and from such prominent citizens as Margaret Mead, the U.N. Secretary General, and Senator Edward Kennedy.

A world food bank appeals powerfully to our humanitarian impulses. 18 But before we rush ahead with such a plan, let us ask if such a program would actually do more good than harm, not only momentarily but also in the long run. Those who propose a food bank usually refer to a current "emergency" or "crisis" in terms of world food supply. But what is an emergency? Although they may be infrequent and sudden, everyone knows that emergencies will occur from time to time. A well-run family, company, organization or country prepares for the likelihood of accidents and emergencies. It expects them, it budgets for them, it saves for them.

What happens if some organizations or countries budget for accidents 19 and others do not? If each country is solely responsible for its own well-being, poorly managed ones will suffer. But they can learn from experience. They may mend their ways, and learn to budget for infrequent but certain emergencies. For example, the weather varies from year to year, and periodic crop failures are certain. A wise and competent government saves out of the production of the good years in anticipation of bad years to come. Joseph taught this policy to Pharaoh in Egypt more than 2,000 years ago. Yet the great majority of the governments in the world today do not follow such a policy. They lack either the wisdom or the competence, or both. Should those nations that do manage to put something aside be forced to come to the rescue each time an emergency occurs among the poor nations?

"But it isn't their fault!" some kind-hearted liberals argue. "How can 20 we blame the poor people who are caught in an emergency? Why must they suffer for the sins of their governments?" The concept of blame is simply not relevant here. The real question is, what are the operational consequences of establishing a world food bank? If it is open to every country every time a need develops, slovenly rulers will not be motivated to take Joseph's advice. Someone will always come to their aid. Some countries will deposit food in the world food bank, and others will withdraw it. There will be almost no overlap. As a result of such solutions to food shortage emergencies, the poor countries will not learn to mend their ways, and will suffer progressively greater emergencies as their populations grow.

On the average, poor countries undergo a 2.5 percent increase in 21 population each year; rich countries, about 0.6 percent. Only rich countries have anything in the way of food reserves set aside, and even they do not have as much as they should. Poor countries have none. If poor countries received no food from the outside, the rate of their population growth would be periodically checked by crop failures and famines. But if they can always draw on a world food bank in time of need, their population can continue to grow unchecked, and so will their "need" for aid. In the short run, a world food bank may diminish that need, but in the long run it actually increases the need without limit.

Without some system of worldwide food sharing, the proportion 22 of people in the rich and poor nations might eventually stabilize. The overpopulated poor countries would decrease in numbers while the rich countries that had room for more people would increase. But with a well-meaning system of sharing, such as a world food bank, the growth differential between the rich and the poor countries will not only persist, it will increase. Because of the higher rate of population growth in the poor countries of the world, 88 percent of today's children are born poor, and only 12 percent rich. Year by year the ratio becomes worse as the fast-reproducing poor outnumber the slow-reproducing rich.

A world food bank is thus a commons in disguise. People will have 23 more motivation to draw from it than to add to any common store. The less provident and less able will multiply at the expense of the abler and more provident, bringing eventual ruin upon all who share in the commons. Besides, any system of "sharing" that amounts to foreign aid from the rich nations to the poor nations will carry the taint of charity, which will contribute little to the world peace so devoutly desired by those who support the idea of a world food bank.

As past U.S. foreign-aid programs have amply and depressingly dem- 24 onstrated, international charity frequently inspires mistrust and antagonism rather than gratitude on the part of the recipient nation.

The modern approach to foreign aid stresses the export of technology 25 and advice, rather than money and food. As an ancient Chinese proverb goes: "Give a man a fish and he will eat for a day; teach him how to fish and he will eat for the rest of his days." Acting on this advice, the Rockefeller and Ford Foundations have financed a number of programs for improving agriculture in the hungry nations. Known as the "Green Revolution," these programs have led to the development of "miracle rice" and "miracle wheat," new strains that offer bigger harvests and greater resistance to crop damage.

Whether or not the Green Revolution can increase food production as 26 much as its champions claim is a debatable but possibly irrelevant point. Those who support this well-intended humanitarian effort should first consider some of the fundamentals of human ecology. Ironically, one man who did was the late Alan Gregg, a vice president of the Rockefeller Foundation. Two decades ago he expressed strong doubts about the wisdom of such attempts to increase food production. He likened the growth and spread of humanity over the surface of the earth to the spread of cancer in the human body, remarking that "cancerous growths demand food, but, as far as I know, they have never been cured by getting it."

Every human born constitutes a draft on all aspects of the environment: food, air, water, forests, beaches, wildlife, scenery and solitude. Food can, perhaps, be significantly increased to meet a growing demand. But what about clean beaches, unspoiled forests, and solitude? If we satisfy a growing population's need for food, we necessarily decrease its per capita supply of the other resources needed by people.

India, for example, now has a population of 600 million, which increases by 15 million each year. This population already puts a huge load on a relatively impoverished environment. The country's forests are now only a small fraction of what they were three centuries ago, and floods and erosion continually destroy the insufficient farmland that remains. Every one of the 15 million new lives added to India's population puts an additional burden on the environment, and increases the economic and social costs of crowding. However humanitarian our intent, every Indian life saved through medical or nutritional assistance from abroad diminishes the quality of life for those who remain, and for subsequent generations. If rich countries make it possible, through foreign aid, for 600 million Indians to swell to 1.2 billion in a mere 28 years, as their current growth rate threatens, will future generations of Indians thank us for hastening the destruction of their environment? Will our good intentions be sufficient excuse for the consequences of our actions?

Without a true world government to control reproduction and the use of available resources, the sharing ethic of the spaceship is impossible. For the foreseeable future, our survival demands that we govern our actions by the ethics of a lifeboat, harsh though they may be. Posterity will be satisfied with nothing less.

Using the Dictionary

Check examples of a formal, impersonal vocabulary: 1. *ethics* (2)   2. *abhorrent* (8)   3. *substantive* (9)   4. *reproductive* (10)   5. *aggregate* (11)   6. *ratio* (12)   7. *sovereign* (13)   8. *philanthropic* (13)   9. *discretion* (15)   10. *antagonism* (24)

The Writer's Agenda

Hardin traces in detail several imaginative comparisons, or metaphors, that can guide our thinking about the ethics of survival on our crowded planet. Each metaphor makes us think in a different way about important causes and their effects.

1. "Spaceship Earth" became a widely echoed slogan of the environmental movement. What are its implications? Why does Hardin reject it?

2. In much of the early part of the essay, the author uses the lifeboat analogy as the basic metaphor "within which we must work out our solutions." If we follow the logic of the lifeboat analogy, what are our basic options and their consequences?

3. How does Hardin interpret the statistics concerning population growth that he presents when applying the lifeboat image to conditions in the "real world"? Summarize and explain his projections.

4. In the latter half of the essay, Hardin introduces his second key analogy— the "commons." What is its original context? What psychological mechanisms is it meant to dramatize for the reader? What modern examples of its workings does Hardin examine?

5. Hardin's discussion of the "Green Revolution" takes his argument an important step further. How?

6. "Protecting the environment" and safeguarding "the quality of life" are familiar aims of the "well-intentioned" liberals whose proposals Hardin generally rejects. How does he appropriate these aims for his own purposes?

7. Hardin relies mainly on the logic of his arguments to sway the reader. However, he also freely uses strong *connotative language* to express disapproval or ridicule. Explain how expressions like the following are meant to steer the reactions of the reader: "misguided idealists," "toothless tiger," "boarding parties," "guilt-ridden person," "conscience-stricken people," "kind-hearted idealists," "spread of cancer."

For Discussion or Writing

8. Which of the three basic survival metaphors do you prefer—the spaceship, the lifeboat, the commons? (Argue for the most convincing or against the least convincing of these metaphors.)

9. What kind of audience is likely to have a hostile reaction to Hardin's arguments? Put yourself in the position of a hostile reader and take on one of Hardin's arguments.

10. People who agree with Hardin tend to pride themselves on their "realism" or "pragmatism." Their opponents often accuse them of "cynicism" or callousness. To you, is Hardin a realist or a cynic?

11. Do you agree with Hardin's arguments in part? Prepare a "Yes, but" paper in which you show to what extent you agree and disagree.

12. Choose an issue that presents officials or the voters with a choice among different courses of action. Prepare a paper in which you examine different options and their consequences. Choose an issue that you have had a chance to study or investigate. Possible choices:
- welfare policy
- rent control
- liberalized immigration laws

- the draft and its alternatives
- the legal drinking age
- publicly financed abortions
- objectionable books in high school libraries

Branching Out

13. Examine the implications and possible limitations of a key metaphor that has played a role in much political discussion. Possible examples include the "arms race," the "cold war," the "iron curtain," the "family of nations," "brotherhood," "sisterhood," the "melting pot," the "sexual revolution," the "silent majority," the "taxpayers' revolt."

BACKGROUND: Carl Sagan is an American astrophysicist who became famous for his television series, "Cosmos." He was born in New York in 1934 and did his undergraduate and graduate work at the University of Chicago. He has taught or done research at Berkeley, Harvard, and Cornell and has lectured widely at other institutions. He has written widely on our solar system and planetary exploration; and he participated in the preparation of the Mariner and Viking space missions to Venus, Mars, and Jupiter and Saturn. Sagan was part of the panel of scientists who developed the data used to predict a "nuclear winter," a catastrophic blotting out of the sun's light and warmth as the result of nuclear war. He often writes as a concerned scientist sounding a warning about current uses (or abuses) of science and technology. His best-known books are *The Dragons of Eden: Speculations on the Evolution of Human Intelligence* (1977) and *Broca's Brain* (1979).

Carl Sagan

The Warming

---

of the World

GUIDE TO READING: What causes the basic warming process? What effects will it produce? What are the possible solutions or remedies? What is the author's final advice to his readers?

When humans first evolved—in the savannahs of East Africa a few million years ago—our numbers were few and our powers feeble. We knew almost nothing about controlling our environment—even clothing had yet to be invented. We were creatures of the climate, utterly dependent upon it.

A few degrees hotter or colder on average, and our ancestors were in trouble. The toll taken much later by the ice ages, in which average land temperatures dropped some 8°C (centigrade, or Celsius), must have been horrific. And yet, it is exactly such climatic change that pushed our ancestors to develop tools and technology, science and civilization. Certainly, skills in hunting, skinning, tanning, building shelters and refurbishing caves must owe much to the terrors of the deep ice age.

Today, we live in a balmy epoch, 10,000 years after the last major glaciation. In this climatic spring, our species has flourished; we now cover the entire planet and are altering the very appearance of our world. Lately—within the last century or so—humans have acquired, in more ways than one, the ability to make major changes in that climate upon which we are so dependent. The Nuclear Winter findings are one dramatic indication that we can change the climate—in this case, in the spasm of nuclear war. But I wish here to describe a different kind of climatic danger, this one slower, more subtle and arising from intentions that are wholly benign.

It is warm down here on Earth because the Sun shines. If the Sun were 4 somehow turned off, the Earth would rapidly cool. The oceans would freeze, eventually the atmosphere itself would condense out and our planet would be covered everywhere by snowbanks of solid oxygen and nitrogen 10 meters (about 30 feet) high. Only the tiny trickle of heat from the Earth's interior and the faint starlight would save our world from a temperature of absolute zero.

We know how bright the Sun is; we know how far from it we are; and 5 we know what fraction of the sunlight reaching the Earth is reflected back to space (about 30 percent). So we can calculate—with a simple mathematical equation—what the average temperature of the Earth should be. But when we do the calculation, we find that the Earth's temperature should be about 20°C below the freezing point of water, in stark contradiction to our everyday experience. What have we done wrong?

As in many such cases in science, what we've done wrong is to forget 6 something—in this case, the atmosphere. Every object in the universe radiates some kind of light to space; the colder the object, the longer the wavelength of radiation it emits. The Earth—much colder than the Sun— radiates to space mainly in the infrared part of the spectrum, not the visible. Were the Sun turned off, the Earth would soon be indetectable in ordinary visible light, though it would be brilliantly illuminated in infrared light.

When sunlight strikes the Earth, part is reflected back into the sky; 7 much of the rest is absorbed by the ground and heats it—the darker the ground, the greater the heating. The ground radiates back upward in the infrared. Thus, for an airless Earth, the temperature would be set solely by a balance between the incoming sunlight absorbed by the surface and the infrared radiation that the surface emits back to space.

When you put air on a planet, the situation changes. The Earth's 8 atmosphere is, generally, still transparent to visible light. That's why we can see each other when we talk, glimpse distant mountains and view the stars.

But in the infrared, all that is different. While the oxygen and nitrogen 9 in the air are transparent in both the infrared and the visible, minor constituents such as water vapor (H_2O) and carbon dioxide (CO_2) tend to be much more opaque in the infrared. It would be useless for us to have eyes that could see at a wavelength, say, of 15 microns in the infrared, because the air is murky black there.

Accordingly, if you add air to a world, you heat it: The surface now has 10 difficulty when it tries to radiate back to space in the infrared. The atmosphere tends to absorb the infrared radiation, keeping heat near the surface and providing an infrared blanket for the world. There is very little CO_2 in the Earth's atmosphere—only 0.03 percent. But that small amount is enough to make the Earth's atmosphere opaque in important regions of the infrared spectrum. CO_2 and H_2O are the reason the global temperature is not well below freezing. We owe our comfort—indeed, our very existence—to the fact that these gases are present and are much more transparent in the visible than in the infrared. Our lives depend on a delicate balance of invisible gases. Too much blanket, or too little, and we're in trouble.

This property of many gases to absorb strongly in the infrared but not 11 in the visible, and thereby to heat their surroundings, is called the "greenhouse effect." A florist's greenhouse keeps its planty inhabitants warm. The phrase "greenhouse effect" is widely used and has an instructive ring to it, reminding us that we live in a planetary-scale greenhouse and recalling the admonition about living in glass houses and throwing stones. But, in fact, florists' greenhouses do not keep warm by the greenhouse effect; they work mainly by inhibiting the movement of air inside, another matter altogether.

We need look only as far as the nearest planet to see an example of an 12 atmospheric greenhouse effect gone wild. Venus has in its atmosphere an enormous quantity of carbon dioxide (roughly as much as is buried as carbonates in all the rocks of the Earth's crust). There is an atmosphere of CO_2 on Venus 90 times thicker than the atmosphere of the Earth and containing some 200,000 times more CO_2 than in our air. With water vapor and other minor atmospheric constituents, this is enough to make a greenhouse effect that keeps the surface of Venus around 470°C (900°F)—enough to melt tin or lead.

When humans burn wood or "fossil fuels" (coal, oil, natural gas, etc.), 13 they put carbon dioxide into the air. One carbon atom (C) combines with a molecule of oxygen (O_2) to produce CO_2. The development of agriculture, the conversion of dense forest to comparatively sparsely vegetated farms, has moved carbon atoms from plants on the ground to carbon dioxide in the air. About half of this new CO_2 is removed by plants or by the layering down of carbonates in the oceans. On human time-scales, these changes are irreversible: Once the CO_2 is in the atmosphere, human technology is helpless to remove it. So the overall amount of CO_2 in the air has been growing—at least since the industrial revolution. If no other factors operate, and if enough CO_2 is put into the atmosphere, eventually the average surface temperature will increase perceptibly.

There are other greenhouse gases that are increasingly abundant in 14 the Earth's atmosphere—halocarbons, such as the freon used in refrigerator cooling systems; or nitrous oxide (N_2O), produced by automobile exhausts and nitrogenous fertilizers; or methane (CH_4), produced partly in the intestines of cows and other ruminants.

But let's for the moment concentrate on carbon dioxide: How long, at 15 the present rates of burning wood and fossil fuels, before the global climate becomes significantly warmer? And what would the consequences be?

It is relatively simple to calculate the immediate warming from a given 16 increase in the CO_2 abundance, and all competent calculations seem to be in good agreement. More difficult to estimate are (1) the rate at which carbon dioxide will continue to be put into the atmosphere (it depends on population growth rates, economic styles, alternative energy sources and the like) and (2) feedbacks—ways in which a slight warming might produce other, more drastic, effects.

The recent increase in atmospheric CO_2 is well documented. Over the last century, this CO_2 buildup should have resulted in a few tenths of a degree of global warming, and there is some evidence that such a warming has occurred. [17]

The National Academy of Sciences estimates that the present atmospheric abundance of CO_2 is likely to double by the year 2065, although experts at the academy predict a one-in-20 chance that it will double before 2035—when an infant born today becomes 50 years old. Such a doubling would warm the air near the surface of the Earth by 2°C or 3°C—maybe by as much as 4°C. These are average temperature values; there would naturally be considerable local variation. High latitudes would be warmed much more, although a baked Alaska will be some time coming. [18]

There would be precipitation changes. The annual discharge of rivers would be altered. Some scientists believe that central North America—including much of the area that is now the breadbasket of the world—would be parched in summer if the global temperature increases by a few degrees. There would be some mitigating effects; for example, where plant growth is not otherwise limited, more CO_2 should aid photosynthesis and make more luxuriant growth (of weeds as well as crops). If the present CO_2 injection into the atmosphere continued over a few centuries, the warming would be greater than from all other causes over the last 100,000 years. [19]

As the climate warms, glacial ice melts. Over the last 100 years, the level of the world's oceans has risen by 15 centimeters (6 inches). A global warming of 3°C or 4°C over the next century is likely to bring a further rise in the average sea level of about 70 centimeters (28 inches). An increase of this magnitude could produce major damage to ports all over the world and induce fundamental changes in the patterns of land development. A serious speculation is that greenhouse temperature increases of 3°C or 4°C could, in addition, trigger the disintegration of the West Antarctic Ice Sheet, with huge quantities of polar ice falling into the ocean. This would raise sea level by some 6 meters (20 feet) over a period of centuries, with the eventual inundation of all coastal cities on the planet. [20]

There are many other possibilities that are poorly understood, including the release of other greenhouse gases (for example, methane from peat bogs) accelerated by the warming climate. The circulation of the oceans might be an important aspect of the problem. The scientific community is attempting to make an environmental-impact statement for the entire planet on the consequences of continued burning of fossil fuels. Despite the [21] uncertainties, a kind of consensus is in: Over the next century or more, with projected rates of burning of coal, oil and gas, there is trouble ahead.

The problem is difficult for at least three different reasons: 22

(1) We do not yet fully understand how severe the greenhouse con- 23 sequences will be.

(2) Although the effects are not yet strikingly noticeable in everyday 24 life, to deal with the problem, the present generation might have to make sacrifices for the next.

(3) The problem cannot be solved except on an international scale: 25 The atmosphere is ignorant of national boundaries. South African carbon dioxide warms Taiwan, and Soviet coal-burning practices affect productivity in America. The largest coal resources in the world are found in the Soviet Union, the United States and China, in that order. What incentives are there for a nation such as China, with vast coal reserves and a commitment to rapid economic development, to hold back on the burning of fossil fuels because the result might, decades later, be a parched American sunbelt or still more ghastly starvation in sub-Saharan Africa? Would countries that might benefit from a warmer climate be as vigorous in restraining the burning of fossil fuels as nations likely to suffer greatly?

Fortunately, we have a little time. A great deal can be done in decades. 26 Some argue that government subsidies lower the price of fossil fuels, inviting waste; more efficient usage, besides its economic advantage, could greatly ameliorate the CO_2 greenhouse problem. Parts of the solution might involve alternative energy sources, where appropriate: solar power, for example, or safer nuclear fission reactors, which, whatever their other dangers, produce no greenhouse gases of importance. Conceivably, the long-awaited advent of commercial nuclear fusion power might happen before the middle of the next century.

However, any technological solution to the looming greenhouse prob- 27 lem must be worldwide. It would not be sufficient for the United States or the Soviet Union, say, to develop safe and commercially feasible fusion power plants: That technology would have to be diffused worldwide, on terms of cost and reliability that would be more attractive to developing nations than a reliance on fossil fuel reserves or imports. A serious, very high-level look at patterns of U.S. and world energy development in light of the greenhouse problem seems overdue.

During the last few million years, human technology, spurred in part 28 by climatic change, has made our species a force to be reckoned with on a planetary scale. We now find, to our astonishment, that we pose a danger to ourselves. The present world order is, unfortunately, not designed to deal with global-scale dangers. Nations tend to be concerned about themselves, not about the planet; they tend to have short-term rather than long-term objectives. In problems such as the increasing greenhouse effect, one nation or region might benefit while another suffers. In other global environmental issues, such as nuclear war, all nations lose. The problems are connected: Constructive international efforts to understand and resolve one will benefit the others.

Further study and better public understanding are needed, of course. [29] But what is essential is a global consciousness—a view that transcends our exclusive identification with the generational and political groupings into which, by accident, we have been born. The solution to these problems requires a perspective that embraces the planet and the future. We are all in this greenhouse together.

Using the Dictionary

Check the following as necessary. How much help does your dictionary give you with technical **scientific terms**? 1. *evolve* (1) 2. *refurbish* (2) 3. *glaciation* (3) 4. *radiate* (6) 5. *emit* (6) 6. *infrared* (6) 7. *spectrum* (6) 8. *constituent* (9) 9. *opaque* (9) 10. *carbonate* (12) 11. *irreversible* (13) 12. *halocarbons* (14) 13. *nitrous oxide* (14) 14. *ruminant* (14) 15. *precipitation* (19) 16. *photosynthesis* (19) 17. *inundation* (20) 18. *ameliorate* (26) 19. *diffuse*, vb. (27) 20. *global* (28)

The Writer's Agenda

This selection is a classic example of an essay taking us from a problem to its solution. How does the author proceed?

1. How does Sagan's introduction put the problem in historical perspective? What major point does it lead up to?

2. What is the greenhouse effect? How does Sagan explain it to his readers? (Why is the term not literally accurate or appropriate?) How does Sagan use the comparison with Venus to reinforce the main point?

3. What *causes* are at work to raise the global temperature? What *effects* will they produce?

4. What are the possible *solutions* or remedies? What are the obstacles in their way? What is the major requirement that Sagan stresses in his conclusion?

5. Sagan has become widely known for his gift for translating technical concepts into nontechnical language for a general audience. What are some helpful or striking examples of plain language, everyday comparisons, touches of humor?

For Discussion or Writing

6. Does Sagan's essay succeed in arousing your concern? Why or why not?

7. To judge from your observation and reading, how much progress has our society made toward improved environmental awareness?

8. Investigate and take a stand on a controversial scientific innovation that has been the subject of much public concern, such as gene splicing, test-tube babies, the artificial heart.

9. Write about one of the unintended by-products of progress: toxic waste, water shortages, hard-to-dispose-of garbage, smog. What is the problem? What is the solution?

Branching Out

10. Investigate the causes and possible solutions to a problem that you see as a long-range trend in our society. Choose a topic like the following:

- the "merchandising" of political candidates
- the rising cost of a college education
- the scarcity of marriageable males
- the spread of cults
- vulgar or offensive rock lyrics

BACKGROUND: Michael Novak (born 1933), a native of western Pennsylvania, is a teacher and writer with strong conservative views. He has made the influence of his ideas felt as a professor of philosophy and religious studies, as a government consultant, and as a syndicated columnist. He has written numerous articles and books about the changing Catholic church and about Catholic life in America. His book *The Rise of the Unmeltable Ethnics* (1972) played a major role in the ethnic revival of the seventies that led many Americans to revise their conventional "melting-pot" theories about American culture. Novak and others claimed that the "white ethnics"—such as the descendants of Irish, Italian, Polish, or Czech immigrants—had often found their own background or experience ignored in the schools, in the media, or in traditional American literature. In the name of assimilation, official mainstream culture—White Anglo-Saxon Protestant—had tried to force a superficial uniformity on millions of Americans with cultural roots and group loyalties of their own. In the essay reprinted here, Novak champions a cause close to the heart of many representatives of the "white ethnics"—often predominantly Catholic, and often strong defenders of the traditional family.

Michael Novak

The Family

Out of Favor

GUIDE TO READING: In coming to the defense of an embattled institution, Novak traces major causes that combine to produce powerful social trends. Sort out and outline the causes and effects he surveys under two major headings: What are the major causes that have been at work to weaken the traditional family unit? As a result, what benefits and traditional values are in danger of being lost?

Recently a friend of mine told me the following anecdote. At lunch in a restaurant, he had mentioned that he and his wife intended to have a second child soon. His listener registered the words, stood, and reached out his hand with unmistakable fervor: "You are making a political statement. Congratulations!"

We live in lucky times. So many, so varied, and so aggressive are the antifamily sentiments in our society that brave souls may now have (for the first time in centuries) the pleasure of discovering for themselves the importance of the family. Choosing to have a family used to be uninteresting. It is, today, an act of intelligence and courage. To love family life, to see in family life the most potent moral, intellectual, and political cell in the body politic is to be marked today as a heretic.

Orthodoxy is usually enforced by an economic system. Our own system, postindustrial capitalism, plays an ambivalent role with respect to the family. On the one hand, capitalism demands hard work, competition, sacrifice, saving, and rational decision-making. On the other, it stresses liberty and encourages hedonism.

Now the great corporations (as well as the universities, the political professions, the foundations, the great newspapers and publishing empires, and the film industry) diminish the moral and economic importance of the family. They demand travel and frequent change of residence. Teasing the heart with glittering entertainment and gratifying the demands of ambition, they dissolve attachments and loyalties. Husbands and wives live in isolation from each other. Children of the upwardly mobile are almost as abandoned, emotionally, as the children of the ghetto. The lives of husbands, wives, and children do not mesh, are not engaged, seem merely thrown together. There is enough money. There is too much emotional space. It is easier to leave town than to pretend that one's lives truly matter to each other. (I remember the tenth anniversary party of a foreign office of a major newsmagazine; none of its members was married to his spouse of ten years before.) At an advanced stage capitalism imparts enormous centrifugal forces to the souls of those who have most internalized its values; and these forces shear marriages and families apart.

To insist, in the face of such forces, that marriage and family still express our highest moral ideals is to awaken hostility and opposition. For many, marriage has been a bitter disappointment. They long to be free of it and also of the guilt they feel, a residual guilt which they have put to sleep and do not want awakened. They loathe marriage. They celebrate its demise. Each sign of weakness in the institution exonerates them of personal failure.

Urban industrial life is not designed to assist families. Expressways divide neighborhoods and parishes. Small family bakeries, cheese shops, and candy stores are boarded up. Social engineers plan for sewers, power lines, access roads, but not for the cultural ecology which allows families of different histories and structures to flower and prosper. The workplace is not designed with family needs in mind; neither are working hours.

Yet, clearly, the family is the seedbed of economic skills, money habits, attitudes toward work, and the arts of financial independence. The family is a stronger agency of educational success than the school. The family is a stronger teacher of the religious imagination than the church. Political and social planning in a wise social order begin with the axiom *What strengthens the family strengthens society.* Highly paid, mobile, and restless professionals may disdain the family (having been nurtured by its strengths), but those whom other agencies desert have only one institution in which to find essential nourishment.

The role of a father, a mother, and of children with respect to them, is the absolutely critical center of social force. Even when poverty and disorientation strike, as over the generations they so often do, it is family strength that most defends individuals against alienation, lassitude, or despair. The world around the family is fundamentally unjust. The state and its agents, and the economic system and its agencies, are never fully to be trusted. One could not trust them in Eastern Europe, in Sicily, or in Ireland—and one cannot trust them here. One unforgettable law has been learned painfully through all the oppressions, disasters, and injustices of the last thousand years: *If things go well with the family, life is worth living; when the family falters, life falls apart.*

These words, I know, go against the conventional grain. In America, 9 we seem to look to the state for every form of social assistance. Immigrant Jews and Catholics have for fifty years supported progressive legislation in favor of federal social programs: for minimum wage, Social Security, Medicare, civil rights. Yet dignity, for most immigrant peoples, resides first of all in family strength. Along with Southern blacks, Appalachians, Latins, and Indians, most immigrants to America are family people. Indeed, virtually all Americans, outside our professional classes, are family people.

As for the media, outrageous myths blow breezily about. Everyone 10 says that divorces are multiplying. They are. But the figures hide as much as they reveal. Some 66 percent of all husbands and wives stick together until death do them part. In addition, the death that "parts" a marriage comes far later now than it did in any previous era. Faithful spouses stay together for a longer span of years than ever. For centuries, the average age of death was, for a female, say, thirty-two, and, for a male, thirty-eight. That so many modern marriages carry a far longer span of years with a certain grace is an unprecedented tribute to the institution.

Finally, aggressive sentiments against marriage are usually expressed 11 today in the name of "freedom," "openness," "play," or "serious commitment to a career." Marriage is pictured as a form of imprisonment, oppression, boredom, and chafing hindrance. Not all these accusations are wrong; but the superstition surrounding them is.

Before one can speak intelligently of marriage, one must discuss the 12 superstition that blocks our vision. We lack the courage nowadays to live by creeds, or to state our doctrines clearly (even to ourselves). Our highest moral principle is flexibility. Guided by sentiments we are embarrassed to put into words, we support them not by argument but by their trendiness.

The central idea of our foggy way of life, however, seems unambig- 13 uous enough. It is that life is solitary and brief, and that its aim is self-fulfillment. Total mastery over one's surroundings, control over the disposition of one's time—these are necessary conditions for self-fulfillment. ("Stand not in my way.") Autonomy we understand to mean protection of our inner kingdom—protection around the self from intrusions of chance, irrationality, necessity, and other persons. ("My self, my castle.") In such a vision of the self, marriage is merely an alliance. It entails as minimal an abridgment of inner privacy as one partner or the other may allow. Children are not a welcome responsibility, for to have children is, plainly, to cease being a child oneself.

For the modern temper, great dreads here arise. Sanity, we think, 14 consists in centering upon the only self one has. Surrender self-control, surrender happiness. And so we keep the other out. We then maintain our belief in our unselfishness by laboring for "humanity"—for women, the oppressed, the Third World, or some other needy group. The solitary self needs distant collectivities to witness to its altruism. It has a passionate need to love humankind. It cannot give itself to a spouse or children. "Individual people" seek happiness through concentration upon them-selves, although perhaps for the sake of service to others. Most television cops, detectives, cowboys, and doctors are of this tribe. The "family people" define themselves through belonging to others: spouse, children, parents, siblings, nieces, cousins, and the rest. For the family people, to be human is to be, so to speak, molecular. I am not solely I. I am husband, father, son, brother, uncle, cousin; I am a family network.

There is, beyond the simplicities of half-hour television, a gritty real- 15 ism in family life. Outside the family, we choose our own friends, like-minded folk whose intellectual and cultural passions resemble ours. Inside the family, however, divergent passions, intellections, and frustrations slam and batter us. Families today bring together professions, occupations, social classes, and sometimes regional, ethnic, or religious differences. Family life may remain in the United States the last stronghold of genuine cosmopolitanism and harsh, truthful differences.

For a thousand years, the family was the one institution the peoples of 16 Eastern and Southern Europe, the Irish, and others could trust. The family constitutes their political, economic, and educational strength. The public schools of the United States failing them, they reached into their families and created an astonishingly successful system of parochial schools. Hardly literate, poor, and diffident peoples, they achieved something of an educa-tional miracle. Economically, the Jews, the Greeks, the Lebanese estab-lished one another in as many small businesses as they could open. The Italians, the Poles, the Slovaks, the Croatians gave each other economic help amounting to two or three thousands of dollars a year per family. Cousin Joe did the electrical work; Pete fixed cars; Emil helped paint the house; aunts and uncles and grandparents canned foods, minded the chil-dren; fathers in their spare time built playrooms, boats, and other luxuries in the basements of row houses.

The family network was also a political force in precinct, ward, or 17 district. People of the upper classes could pass on to their children advan-tages of inheritance, admission to exclusive schools, and high-level con-tacts. Children of the immigrants also made their families the primary networks of economic and political strength. Kinship is a primary reality in many unions and in all urban political "machines." Mothers and fathers instructed their children simultaneously, "Don't trust anybody," and "The family will never let you down."

In contemporary conditions, of course, these old family methods and 18 styles have atrophied. There is no way of going back to the past. (Not everything about the past, in any case, was attractive.) Education media help children to become sophisticated about everything but the essentials: love, fidelity, childbearing, mutual help, care for parents and the elderly. Almost everything about mobile, impersonal, distancing life in the United States—tax policies, real-estate policies, the demands of the corporations, and even the demands of modern political forms—makes it difficult for families that feel ancient moral obligations to care for their aged, their mentally disturbed, their retarded, their needy.

It is difficult to believe that the state is a better instrument for satis- 19 fying such human needs than the family. If parents do not keep after the children to do their schoolwork, can the large, consolidated school educate? Some have great faith in state services: in orphanages, child-care centers, schools, job-training programs, and nursing homes. Some want the state to become one large centralized family. Such faith taxes credulity. Much of the popular resistance to federal child care arises from distrust of social workers and childhood engineers who would be agents of state power. Families need help in child care, but many distrust the state and the social-work establishment.

An economic order that would make the family the basic unit of social 20 policy would touch every citizen at the nerve center of daily life. The family is the primary teacher of moral development. In the struggles and conflicts of marital life, husbands and wives learn the realism and adult practicalities of love. Through the love, stability, discipline, and laughter of parents and siblings, children learn that reality accepts them, welcomes them, invites their willingness to take risks. The family nourishes "basic trust." From this spring creativity, psychic energy, social dynamism. If infants are injured here, not all the institutions of society can put them back together.

Economic and educational disciplines are learned only in the home 21 and, if not there, hardly at all. Discipline in black families has been traditionally severe, very like that in white working-class families. Survival has depended on family discipline. Working-class people, white and black, cannot count on having their way; most of the time they have to be docile, agreeable, and efficient. Otherwise, they are fired. They cannot quit their jobs too often; otherwise their employment record shows instability. Blacks as well as whites survive by such rules, as long as authority in the home is strong. From here, some find the base for their mobility, up and out. Without a guiding hand, however, the temptations to work a little, quit, enjoy oneself, then work a little, are too much encouraged by one's peers on the street. *Either* the home, *or* the street: This is the moral choice. Liberals too seldom think about the economic values of strong family life; they neglect their own source of strength, and legislate for others what would never have worked for themselves.

Using the Dictionary

Check ten of the following in your dictionary: 1. *fervor* (1)   2. *heretic* (2)   3. *orthodoxy* (3)   4. *ambivalent* (3)   5. *hedonism* (3)   6. *residual* (5)   7. *exonerate* (5)   8. *alienation* (8)   9. *lassitude* (8)   10. *myth* (10)   11. *autonomy* (13)   12. *altruism* (14)   13. *cosmopolitanism* (15)   14. *fidelity* (18)   15. *dynamism* (20)

The Writer's Agenda

Novak's aim in this essay is twofold: to trace the causes that work against the traditional family, and to speak up in defense of the benefits and traditional values that are being lost as a result. Answer the following questions:

1. How does the *introduction* lead up to and spell out the central thesis hinted at in the title?

2. Early in the essay, Novak discusses *two basic causes* that work against the traditional family—an "upwardly mobile" lifestyle and the conditions of "urban industrial life." What are the cause-and-effect relationships that he traces here?

3. In the central portion of the essay, the author discusses *myths and superstitions* that reinforce our modern tendency to be "individual people" rather than "family people." What are the ideas and attitudes he attacks here? What are their sources?

4. Much of the author's idealized description of family life centers on the *ethnic family.* How does he define it? What does he say about its history? What does he say about its psychological, educational, economic, and political role?

5. In his concluding paragraphs, Novak rejects two kinds of *substitute family*—the "state" and the "street." How does he contrast their roles with that of the family?

For Discussion or Writing

6. Is the traditional family doomed? In your judgment, what causes are working for it or against it? What factors shape the thinking of people in your own generation about marriage and family?

7. Novak says that the "family nourishes basic trust. . . . If infants are injured here, not all the institutions of society can put them back together." Test his generalization against what you know from your own observation or experience.

8. Novak agrees with people who distrust and resist the expansion of government services in such areas as child care, job training, or nursing homes. What is your own stand on this issue? Why do you agree or disagree?

9. Prepare a paper in which you discuss major causes for a current trend that you have studied or read about. Choose a topic like the following:
   • a low birthrate
   • the decline of American industry

- unemployment in a special field
- the plight of the inner city
- high divorce rates
- teacher strikes
- the new poor
- the decline of manners

STUDENT MODEL 7

FOR READING: Study the following short selection as a possible model for writing of your own. How do you react to it overall? What makes it interesting or effective? Answer the following more specific questions:

1. (PURPOSE) What was the writer trying to do?

2. (AUDIENCE) What kind of reader would make a good reader for this selection?

3. (SOURCES) Where did the writer turn for material?

4. (THESIS) Does the selection have a central idea or unifying thesis?

5. (STRUCTURE) What is the author's overall plan or strategy?

6. (STYLE) What makes the piece effective or memorable (for instance, striking details, memorable phrases)?

7. (REVISION) What do you think the writer could or should have done differently?

Karen McLaughlin
Stress: The Combat Zone

When one of my fellow students at the house where I live double-parks her Mustang, blocking my Ford, I get upset. To make sure she does not repeat the offense, I leave nasty notes on her windshield and in her mailbox. Also, I am offended when people think I am still in high school. When I was shopping for Christmas cards, the cashier at the Hallmark store made the mistake of misjudging my age, mumbling, "I just don't understand why banks these days are giving checking accounts to such young people." Face flushed, I gave her the whole story: I was nineteen, a student at the university, and so on. I concluded by muttering under my breath that I could not understand why Hallmark allowed such old people to work there. In retrospect, I realize that this incident was not life-threatening and that I made too much of it. Unfortunately, incidents like this one occur all the time and everywhere, making our public behavior an embarrassment. If standards of public behavior are going to improve, people, including myself, must learn to control their outbursts of anger and frustration.

We live in a stressful society. To be successful, we are supposed to "do it all." We rush from work to the gym or fitness center, then home for a quick bite of dinner, then off to a meeting or open house, then home to rush through some homework before going to bed. We are caught in crawling commuter traffic, already late for work or class, and our adrenaline starts pumping, with no way to put it to work by running to make up lost time or by punching someone in the nose. We compete for grades or for promotion, and we are hypersensitive to slights or insults that make us feel that we don't count. Rush, rush, rush! Compete, compete, compete! With so many pressures building up, it is only natural for us to feel tense and frustrated; thus we seek an outlet for our pent-up frustrations. Unfortunately, we often release our built-up aggression in public, using as our target an innocent old lady in a Hallmark store.

In the campus bookstore where I work, every customer seems to be in a hurry. Each customer thinks it is my fault, and mine alone, that the math book is not on the shelf where it is supposed to be. I try to explain: more books are on order; we have received only a partial shipment; the books are still in a box stacked in the receiving area. The response is always the same: a bright red face, clenched teeth and fists, a vocabulary reduced to a few choice words. What can be done to calm people down? Judging by the number of books available at the store that deal with ways to combat stress (about thirty by a rough count), and by the variety of classes offered that deal with stress management, a conscious effort is being made to help people.

Drivers represent new lows of deteriorating standards of public behavior. Isn't it annoying when we are in a hurry to get to work to see someone dare drive slow in the fast lane? Don't people realize that if they want to drive slowly (that is, observe the speed limit) they should keep to the right lanes? Frustrated drivers flash their lights, blast their horns, and use a variety of hand motions, all while staying within six inches of the car ahead. At a gas station, a driver may be waiting an eternity behind a car parked at the premium pump. She finally pulls around in front of the other car to use the unleaded pump ahead. When ready to leave, the other driver, although there is plenty of room to back up, starts blasting his horn and shouting obscenities at the person he had kept waiting.

What is the answer? To help people prevent frustration from building up during the daily commute, the local newspaper published a series of articles this summer, featuring interviews with commuters. One woman said she spent the time flirting with other drivers. Another said she munched on candy or other snacks. One driver played relaxation tapes on his car stereo. There are various ways to make the drive more enjoyable, and people need to find something they enjoy doing (other than rude gestures): listening to language tapes, reciting poetry.

When frustrated people act out their frustrations in public, they start a 6
chain reaction of anger and latent violence. We live in a society where
irrational violence may erupt anytime anywhere. Therefore, today, when
that Mercedes cuts us off on the way home, or if the cashier in the cafeteria
is a little slow, let us take a deep breath and reaffirm that we are above going
ape in public.

FOR WRITING: Write about a problem that affects your own life or that of people
close to you. Explore its causes, effects, and possible solutions. Make the problem
vivid or real to your readers; show them the connection between causes and effects.

Additional Writing Topics 7

Cause and Effect

A. Which of the following topics makes you want to say "Let me explain why"?
Choose one and trace causes and effect. Use detailed examples, case histories, or
other supporting evidence.

1. why diets don't work
2. why discipline is a problem in high schools
3. why women earn less than men
4. why vandalism is on the rise
5. why motorists fail to support safety regulations
6. why women object to beauty contests
7. why people tell ethnic jokes
8. why students cheat
9. why young Americans join religious cults
10. why people are having few children, or none
11. why couples split up
12. why people like horror movies
13. why people read horoscopes
14. why people join the Marines
15. why parents prefer private schools
16. why minority citizens distrust the police
17. why minority students drop out
18. why men are on the defensive
19. why young Americans distrust their government
20. why people like their jobs

B. Conduct a survey—query your fellow students to find the answers to one
of the following questions:

1. What makes people choose cars?
2. What makes voters vote for a candidate?

3. What makes moviegoers hate a movie?
4. What makes people listen to talk shows?
5. What do its fans like about science fiction?

C. Look at a current trend and project it into the future. What will be the effects if it continues? Make use of detailed evidence or support. Choose one:

1. What if college costs continue to rise?
2. What if immigration continues unchecked?
3. What if Americans continue to insist on using their private cars?
4. What if unemployment continues in the ghetto?
5. What if the current backlash against permissiveness continues?
6. What if we allow religious groups to censor books and movies?
7. What if competition for good grades gets more intense?
8. What if we cut back on welfare costs?
9. What if women increase their political strength?
10. What if academic standards are strictly enforced for athletes?

8

DEFINITION

Drawing the Line

OVERVIEW

A good writer knows how to keep an argument from bogging down in a dispute over words. When we define an important term, we map out the territory it covers; we set it off from other related or opposite terms. We may have to clarify a confusing term by tracing its history. We may have to look at several case histories to find a common denominator. An extended definition of a key term can clarify the reader's thinking on an important issue; it can provide a rallying point or imply a program for action.

PURPOSE Effective definition helps us clear up confusion and clarify important choices. Arguments over issues easily turn into disputes over words. Sooner or later, when we argue an important issue, someone is likely to say: "What do you mean by equal opportunity?" or "What do you mean by reverse discrimination?" Reading an editorial or article, we often want to ask: "Where do we draw the line?" Where do we draw the "poverty line"? Is creationism a "science"? Is nudity "obscene"? Often an important decision hinges on how we interpret a key term. What is censorship—and what is merely the legitimate exercise of the parents' rights or the school board's duty? When should a juvenile offender be tried as an adult? One important task of writers who write to define is to *update* a term whose meaning may have shifted over the years: *liberal, patriotism, marriage.*

AUDIENCE Writing that sets out to define usually aims at serious readers who expect to see distinctions carefully worked out. The intended audience is often the general reader interested in current issues and recent trends. For example, the reader may care to know what is behind a current buzzword—*mainstreaming, macho, sexual harassment, upscale,* or *gentrification.* Often an extended definition assumes a reader willing to see current issues in historical perspective. (What are the historical roots of our commitment to free speech? What is the history of civil disobedience?) More specifically targeted writing may work out definitions for a specialized audience with special needs. For instance, legislators, lawyers and their clients, judges, and jurors need to concern themselves with what constitutes *negligence, discrimination,* or *insanity.*

BENEFITS FOR THE WRITER (1) Writing papers that define will help teach you to weigh your words. It will make you take words more seriously, it will make you aware of their full range of meaning (and sometimes their double meanings).

(2) Practice in working out instructive definitions will make you think of a key term as a *promise* to the reader. To make a term like *equal opportunity* meaningful, you have to show some striking examples of what it takes to make opportunity equal in typical situations. The American Dream may mean one thing to you and another to your reader—you will need to give some striking examples of the images that recur in the dream.

(3) Awareness of the need for definition makes a writer lower the abstraction count. Writing becomes unconvincing when it uses too many loosely defined abstractions—large, sweeping terms like *commitment, social justice, exploitation,* and *reverse discrimination.* We use such abstractions less freely once we realize that each of them needs follow-up, explanation, and demonstration.

DEFINITION
Additional Reading

Tom Wolfe, The Right Stuff   (p. 413)

WRITER'S GUIDE 8

Writing to Define

Often a writer will clarify an important word in passing, as needed in the course of an explanation or argument. We can often define a limited technical term in a sentence or in a phrase:

Air bags—*cushions that inflate on impact to protect passengers in a crash*—have been the subject of hotly debated experiments.

Unfortunately, few of the terms that become the bone of contention in an argument are limited in this fashion. Terms like *censorship* or *discrimination* are "umbrella terms"; in the words of one observer, they provide a tent to cover "a large and active circus." To clarify such a term, the writer will often have to provide an **extended definition** that answers questions like the following: Why is this term important? What is its basic or most commonly agreed-upon meaning? What are typical examples of its use? What are borderline situations? Where do we draw the line?

Remember the following guidelines when writing a paper whose major purpose is to define an important term:

(1) *To sum up your definition, place the term in a general category and then specify what sets it apart.* A summary following this traditional format is called a **formal definition**. It works like a road atlas that directs us first to a general area and then narrows it down by more specific coordinates. The format of a formal definition can be adapted to a wide range of words, from narrow technical terms to large abstractions:

TERM	GENERAL CLASS	SPECIFICS
A zebra is	a swift, horselike animal	with dark stripes on a white or tawny body.
Entitlements are	federal benefits	for which people qualify automatically, by virtue of their age, income, or occupation.
Prejudice is	thinking ill of individuals	merely because of their membership in a group.
Democracy is	a form of government	that allows people to elect their representatives and encourages the free expression of political views.

An extended definition often starts with such a summary and then develops its implications in detail. In the following example, the writer spells out the full meaning of a definition of *entitlements* that focuses on a single key criterion: The benefits are *automatic*; the government is legally obligated to provide them to all who are eligible.

Entitlements

FORMAL DEFINITION:

Key examples:

Entitlements, sometimes called "payments to individuals," are technically defined as benefits for which people qualify automatically, by virtue of their age or income or occupation. Social Security is such an entitlement, by far the largest. So are medical programs such as Medicare and Medicaid, civil-service and military pensions, unemployment insurance and price-supported payments for farmers. . . .

Contrast:

If the Congress appropriates $2 billion to build a dam or a highway, it can be confident that no more than $2 billion may legally be spent. But when it authorizes extended unemployment benefits, or a different reimbursement formula under Medicare, it can set no limit on the money that will ultimately flow from the Treasury . . . .

Common misunderstanding:

The "entitlement problem" is often thought of as a "welfare problem." To a trivial extent, it is: most federal programs for the needy, including the classic welfare program, AFDC (Aid to Families with Dependent Children), do fall within the entitlement budget. But they make up a small part of the whole. . . . (James Fallows, "Entitlements," *Atlantic*)

In arguments dealing with human behavior or with political trends, important terms can seldom be reduced to a single test criterion. Often, an informative definition has to specify several major requirements that *combine* to mark off what a term covers. The following might be the outline of an extended definition of *colonialism*:

The End of Empire

FORMAL DEFINITION:

Colonialism is the systematic domination and exploitation—military, economic, and cultural—of one country by another. Classic colonialism followed military conquest and was marked by several distinguishing features. . . .

KEY CRITERIA:

First, the imperial mother country controlled the colonial economy. It used the colony as a source of raw materials and as a market for finished goods. . . .

Second, the mother country controlled the currency of the colony and imposed taxes or tariffs. . . .

Third, the mother country maintained military control of the colony, raising colonial troops to be used in the service of the mother country. . . .

Fourth, the mother country imposed its language upon the subject people, as in the case of Portuguese in Brazil, Spanish in most of the rest of South America, or English and French in many parts of Africa.

Note: Careful wording of a definition makes sure that it accurately reflects what a term takes in and what it leaves out. For instance, sociologists have begun to use the term *underclass* to describe a new social class of the chronically unemployed urban poor, including large numbers of high school dropouts and single mothers on welfare. The definition of the term would have to be worded in such a way that it *excludes* people who work regularly but are poor because they are poorly paid, or an older class of rural poor less reliant on welfare support.

(2) *Show what the word means in practice.* Verbal definitions remain lifeless and abstract unless they are followed up with vivid, convincing examples. The term *welfare mentality* will remain a mere catchword unless we look at actual people on welfare—the way they live and make ends meet. One basic ground plan for a definition paper is to start with a general definition and then apply it to a range of detailed examples.

Here is an outline for an extended definition that presents a general definition as the initial thesis and then shows how it applies in several important examples:

Censors and the Schools

DEFINITION: Censorship is interference by officials, organizations, or individuals that employs threats, reprisals, legal means, or force to hamper the free expression of ideas.

I. "Obscene" books in high school libraries
II. The battle of the dictionaries
III. The controversy over evolution

Many words that sound good—*rehabilitation, equal opportunity*—easily remain empty promises. To give concrete meaning to such a term, we usually have to ask: "Where can we see it in action? How can we bring it about?"

(3) *With difficult or debatable terms, study test cases in order to arrive at a common denominator.* To find solid common ground, we may

want to ask our readers to look first of all at several situations where the word clearly applies. We can then ask: "What do these situations have in common?"

In much recent controversy, for instance, the word *insanity* seems to have been stretched beyond its commonsense meaning. Editorial writers deplore an "insanity defense" that is used to clear people charged with what seem deliberate acts. Radical psychiatrists charge that modern society itself is insane, forcing truly sane people to withdraw into a private world of their own. What is a basic definition of insanity that would provide some common basis for discussion? The following is a simplified outline of a magazine article that sets out *in search of* a common meaning:

Going Crazy

(Informal introductory example)	There are "crazy people on the street" in all our cities, I suppose—angry black war veterans sniping from a hotel rooftop in New Orleans, shaven-headed girls with knives prowling the hills above Los Angeles—but New York, being the biggest and most anarchic and most enraged of all cities, seems at times to have a lunatic on every block. In some the lunacy is quite harmless. I once knew a man in a threadbare tweed coat, ornamented by an American flag at the lapel, whose only occupation was to board the Forty-second Street crosstown bus and preach the Gospel in a thick Swedish accent....
EXTENDED CASE HISTORY 1:	Emanuel Plaitakis was talking about a young man named Steve Cloud, of 92-41 190th Street, Jamaica, Queens, who went crazy at 10:30 on the morning of October 18, 1973. Plaitakis had just finished a cup of coffee in Deli City, right next to the Empire State Building, and he was wheeling himself out onto Thirty-fourth Street when he saw "one of those crazy people," later identified as Cloud, "walking up and down without any reason...."
EXTENDED CASE HISTORY 2:	To Bellevue the city's ambulances bring its tired, its poor, its huddled masses and wretched refuse. One morning I noticed behind the admissions desk a young Puerto Rican who tugged and strained against the white cloth tapes that held his wrists and ankles to a wheeled stretcher....
EXTENDED CASE HISTORY 3:	Michael Mooney, Jr., was there early in 1973, and he had a vision. He is a husky youth of twenty-one with large blue eyes and moderately long reddish-brown hair. He had dropped out of Harvard to become a musician—he plays the piano, guitar, saxophone, and bass—but he grew increasingly subject to fits of paranoia....

(Brief personal experience leading up to) GENERAL DEFINITION	...During that moment, however, I think that I was standing on the border of what we call insanity. *The main symptoms were all there: a breakdown in the machinery of perception, or a breakdown in the rational mind's ability to receive and combine perceptions and to make judgments from them....* (Otto Friedrich, "Going Crazy," *Harper's*)

An article following this pattern reverses the familiar pattern that starts with a general claim as its thesis and then provides support. Instead, it *leads up to* a thesis that is the result of a common search shared by writer and reader. We call a pattern of thought or writing that funnels material into a final conclusion an **inductive pattern**. The inductive pattern presents examples first, generalizations last. It makes special claims on the attention of the reader, but it can produce lasting conviction when well done.

(4) *Explore the different uses of a term.* Often the meaning of a term shifts with the area where it is used, or with the purposes of the people using it. We can clear up apparent contradictions by showing why and how the same term means different things to different people. For instance, we could organize a paper exploring the uses of the term *insanity* by looking at the meanings of the term in different contexts:

I. *Commonsense definition*—guiding many people's personal reactions:
Insanity means mental illness that causes wildly erratic behavior and renders people incapable of caring for themselves as well as dangerous to others.

II. *Medical definition*—serving as a framework for treatment or therapy:
Insanity is a derangement or disease of the mind occurring usually as a specific disorder (like schizophrenia), not to be confused with mental retardation or different forms of neurosis.

III. *Legal definition*—serving as a guide in fixing legal responsibility:
Insanity is an impairment of the mental faculties rendering a person unable to enter into legal contracts or relationships or to assume responsibility for illegal acts.

IV. *Statistician's definition*—making possible the gathering of figures that can help guide legislators and others:
The narrowest definition of mental illness might limit the concept to people who actually enter a mental hospital for treatment—somewhat over half a million Americans every year.

(5) *Use comparison and contrast with closely related terms to mark off the boundaries of a term.* To help define something new, we often show how it differs from something familiar. A writer trying to define the "superhero" of much current fantasy literature and popular entertainment may emphasize the contrast with the traditional heroes of folklore and history:

TRADITIONAL: A hero is a human being who through discipline, bravery, determination, and perhaps divine assistance accomplishes seemingly incredible feats. Heroes generally must be good and serve a good cause, though sometimes brave and generous men in the service of an evil cause are deemed to be heroes—usually tragic but noble figures. . . .

NEW: A superhero, *by contrast*, is not a real human being, but a fantasy creature—Superman, Batman, Captain Marvel, Wonder Woman, *et al.* Superheroes, unlike the heroes of Greek mythology, have no Achilles' heel. Superman himself is vulnerable to the mineral kryptonite, but of course he will never be killed by it—unlike the great Achilles. Unlike the more traditional heroes of folklore and of reality, modern superheroes have no moral context. They are generally in the service of "good" and against "evil," of course. But the good that they serve is undefined. . . . (Harold O.J. Brown, "Superman on the Screen," *Christianity Today*)

A writer often establishes the boundaries of a term by marking it off from several of its closest cousins or look-alikes. For instance, *affection, passion*, and *infatuation* appear as near-synonyms of *love*; they stand for something closely related but not exactly the same. By showing how each is different, a writer could mark off the boundaries of "true love."

(6) *Trace the history of a term to clarify its changing meanings.* Terms like *anarchist, pacifism, liberal*, or *democracy* are likely to remain confusing unless we clarify their historical roots and discuss some of the major historical developments in which they played a role. A writer may trace the history of such a term in order to *redefine* it for our times:

REVOLUTIONARY FIRST STAGE: The development of a sense of patriotism was a strong unifying force during our Revolution and its insecure aftermath. Defined then and now as "love of country," patriotism was an extremely important motivating force with which to confront foreign threats to the young nation. It was no happenstance that *The Star Spangled Banner* was composed during the War of 1812 . . . .

EXPANSIONIST SECOND STAGE: As the United States moved into the 20th century and became a world power, far-flung alliances and wars fought thousands of miles away stretched the boundaries of patriotism. "Making the world safe for democracy" was the grandiose way Woodrow Wilson put it. . . .

MODERN THIRD STAGE: World War II was the last war that all Americans fought with conviction. Thereafter, when "bombs bursting in air" would be atomic bombs, world war became a suicidal risk. . . . Wars that could be so final and so swift lost their

glamour even for the most militaristically minded. When
we became the most powerful nation on earth, the old
insecurity that made patriotism into a conditioned reflex of
"my country right or wrong" should have given way to a
thinking process; as expressed by Carl Schurz: "Our country ... when right, to be kept right. When wrong, to be put
right." ... (Ralph Nader, "We Need a New Kind of Patriotism,"
Life)

To sum up: Careful definition of important words helps us say what we
mean. Much misunderstanding is brought on by words that have different
meanings for different people. Much controversy is caused by words whose
meanings have begun to shift and whose exact bearings have to be spe-
cified. Without definition, many impressive or inspirational words that roll
smoothly off the tongue remain just words.

Prewriting Activities 8

1. The media constantly supply us with new *buzzwords* for developments and
trends. Choose one of these. For a preliminary collection of material, jot down any
ideas, examples, catchwords, quotations, or relevant incidents that come to mind:
- no-fault divorce
- single-parent family
- ethnic revival
- freedom of information
- white flight
- reverse discrimination
- the Moral Majority
- gentrification
- the underclass
- mainstreaming
- invasion of privacy

2. Do a preliminary inventory of material for an extended definition of a term
that has played or is playing an important role in American political life. Choose a
term like *segregation, feminism, dissent, patronage, due process, corruption, the
Jewish vote, welfare state*. Fill in material under all or most of the following
headings:

I. *Surface meaning* (What common associations or misconceptions cluster
around the term?)

II. *Historical roots* (For instance, what are the roots of segregation in the
history of slavery and abolition? What are famous names in the history of
dissent?)

III. *Media coverage* (For instance, when is the last time you have seen segregation play a major role in news coverage?)

IV. *Personal experience* (Where in your own life or in the lives of relatives and friends has segregation or dissent or the welfare state become more than a distant abstraction?)

V. *Related or contrasting terms* (In defining *feminism*, what use would you make of related terms like *suffragist, women's rights, emancipation, women's liberation?*)

VI. *Common denominator* (What to you are key elements or dimensions of the term to which a definition would have to do justice?)

3. Each of the following model sentences clarifies or brings into focus an important term. Study the model sentences and the student-written imitations. For each model, write an imitation of your own that clarifies or brings into focus an important term. Follow the pattern or structure of the original sentence as closely as you can.

MODEL 1: Economy is the art of making the most of life. (George Bernard Shaw)

IMITATION: Procrastination is the art of avoiding today's mistakes by putting them off until tomorrow.

MODEL 2: Courage is not the absence of fear; it is the control over fear. (Dickie Chapelle)

IMITATION: Positive thinking is not the absence of negative thoughts; it is the control over negative thoughts.

MODEL 3: Love is as necessary to human beings as food and shelter. (Aldous Huxley)

IMITATION: Attention is as essential to children as are clothes and shoes.

MODEL 4: Marriage, like many other institutions, brings restrictions as well as benefits.

IMITATION: Idealism, like other philosophies, produces hope as well as despair.

MODEL 5: What makes democratic politics different from most other professions is that, occasionally, the politician has a duty to risk his job by performing it conscientiously. (George F. Will)

IMITATION: What makes women different from men is that often a woman is able to reach a better decision by adding the human factor to cold facts.

Paragraph Practice 8

Write a paragraph to define and illustrate a term important in discussions of American history or American culture. Choose a term like *macho, the work ethic, Jim Crow, the melting pot, pluralism, assimilation, the pioneer, the Southern belle, middle-class values.* Study and discuss the following sample paragraph as a possible model.

Loving Your Work

Some would ascribe our interest in jobs to that vague web of convictions called the Protestant work ethic. Of course you do not have to work or be Protestant to subscribe to this ethic; more to the point, if you are not Protestant, or do not want to work, you may feel compelled to support its validity with a great deal of verbal zeal. This work ethic is expressed in phrases like "an honest day's pay for an honest day's work," "I'd rather be called a son-of-a-bitch than be called lazy," "God helps those that help themselves," and many other gems of folk wisdom. John Cotton, the first great leader of the Boston Church, preached to the Puritans on their Christian calling, their duty to work for the Lord. Ben Franklin opens his autobiography by acknowledging his rise from poverty to success through work. He goes on to admonish his readers that in following his example they should not only avoid bad habits but also should take care to appear to be hard-working and thrifty citizens. No wonder that, for many Americans, the appearance of work has often seemed more important than the reality.   (Joseph F. Trimmer and Robert R. Kettler, *American Oblique*)

BACKGROUND: Susannah Lessard worked as an editor for the *Washington Monthly* and became a staff writer for the *New Yorker*. She writes reflective pieces about the current American scene and American values, on subjects ranging from Oyster Bay, Long Island, to the architecture of skyscrapers, which she examined in an article called "The Towers of Light." She wrote the following definition of *conservatism* as part of a longer article called "Civility, Community, Humor: The Conservatism We Need," which was published in the *Washington Monthly* in 1973. Like many other commentators at the time, she was writing to explain a general swing "to the right" in America. Her definition helps us understand a general conservative trend in American politics and morals, shown in examples ranging from "back to basics" in the schools to a backlash against "permissive" personal morality.

Susannah Lessard

The Real
Conservatism

GUIDE TO READING: This definition maps out essential elements that combine to make up a conservative outlook. What are the key elements in the definition? What are the major areas to which the author applies the term? What related terms or near-synonyms help us understand the term? What opposite or contrasting terms set the conservative outlook off from competing attitudes?

One autumn Saturday afternoon I was listening to the radio when the 1 station switched to the Dartmouth-Harvard game. The game had not begun, and the announcer was rambling on about the nip in the air, the autumn colors, past games, this year's players, their names and hometowns—a seminostalgic discourse that, despite an aversion for football talk, I found unexpectedly moving. Autumn, a new crop of players, New England: The world was on a steady keel after all. I could not remember having felt that quiet sense of cycle, of ongoing life and the past floating so serenely to the surface, in a long time.

That morning, anyway, I felt like a conservative. 2

I am not a conservative. I think the government not only should try to, 3 but can, improve life for its citizens; yet for the first time I've begun to understand the value of tradition, both for the counterpoint it can provide to the Left and for the different perspective it offers on the drift rightward of the electorate.

Two elementary attitudes underlie the conservative tradition. The first 4 is a passionate sense of the need to conserve—the land, the culture, the institutions, codes of behavior—and to revere and protect those elements that constitute "civilization." The conservative looks to the enduring values of the past—to holding on to what we've got—in forming his political positions, rather than to alluring, idealistic visions of what the future could be.

The second attitude is a cautious view of raw democracy, or direct representational government. The conservative believes firmly in the rights of minorities and those institutions that protect minorities from the whims of the majority, such as the Supreme Court—an elite, appointed body—and the Constitution, particularly the First Amendment. The concern behind this attitude is less for racial, ethnic or religious groups than for intellectual minorities—the educated elite—to which conservatives have always belonged.

These institutions that restrain the mass will are precious in the conservative view, not just because they protect the few from being trampled by the many, but also because they protect the majority from its own mistakes. This awareness that the majority can often be wrong (so easily forgotten by social crusaders) produces a mental habit. Conservatives tend to be automatically uncomfortable with any idea or trend that smacks of mob psychology—anything that gains a swift and wide popularity—to the point of appearing to enjoy embracing unpopular positions and dropping wet blankets on the emotional political moods to which this country is prone.

An outgrowth of these attitudes—and one with particular value—is the humor that the skeptical turn of the conservative mind can bring to bear on the confused, disaster-prone but unreservedly grand schemes for the betterment of mankind, which the quixotic and too often humorless liberal is forever earnestly pressing to perpetrate.

Using the Dictionary

How much do you learn from your dictionary about the history of each word, its range of meaning or major uses, and possible overtones or associations? 1. *counterpoint* (3) 2. *code* (4) 3. *elite* (5) 4. *crusader* (6) 5. *mob* (6) 6. *skeptical* (7) 7. *quixotic* (7)

The Writer's Agenda

The author of this definition in a very short space maps out an important term. Answer the following questions about how she proceeds:

1. This selection starts with a *personal anecdote* that effectively links a mere word to concrete experience. What major elements help create the **mood** of this introduction? What to you is the central clue to the conservative temperament that the author provides here?

2. Of the two basic conservative attitudes that Lessard enumerates, the first is the more conventional or familiar. What is the key element here? What are the major areas to which it applies?

3. In going on to a second fundamental conservative attitude, the author clears up a misunderstanding that might arise from her reference to the "rights of minorities." Why would this misunderstanding arise? How does she clear it up?

4. Much of the second half of this definition deals with practical political implications of conservative attitudes. What, according to the author, is the conservative attitude toward "raw democracy" and "mob psychology"? What are its practical political results?

5. Where and how does Lessard *contrast* conservatism with its liberal counterpoint? How does the concluding paragraph round out the contrast between the two opposed terms?

For Discussion or Writing

6. Would a conservative or a liberal make a better audience for this selection?

7. Prepare your own one-sentence definitions of several of the key terms used in this essay: *conservative, liberal, elite, raw democracy, mob psychology.* Compare your definitions with those prepared by your classmates.

8. Discuss major synonyms and related terms that cluster around the word *conservative* in this selection: *tradition, values, culture, civilization.* How are they related? Where do we encounter them? How are they typically used?

9. Where have you seen evidence of a general conservative trend in our society? Provide your own working definition of *conservative*, and discuss striking examples. Or identify an important countertrend. Provide a definition and detailed examples.

10. Many arguments hinge on distinctions between related words. Choose one: When does a conservative become a reactionary? When does a liberal become a radical? When does an authoritarian government become totalitarian?

11. Prepare your own extended definition of a term often used by critical observers of American culture. Choose one: *sentimentality, sensationalism, materialism, permissiveness,* or *optimism.* Provide a definition and detailed examples. Mark the term off from other related or opposite terms as needed.

WRITERS ON WRITING
Susannah Lessard on Choosing and Developing a Topic

QUESTION: How do you come up with topics?

ANSWER: It's not good to choose a topic by asking if people will like it or if it will be popular. You have to be looking for your own response to the subject. That's my experience anyway. But other people might have a different experience and can write really well about something they know is popular.

A journal helps. It's an indispensable device because you're not writing for the public. You're writing just for yourself. In that way, you get to see what you're interested in. Keeping a journal for me is a really important exercise.

I think it's also important to have a "free zone" for writing—time set aside where writing isn't required. I can sit down and do whatever I want—it can be as bad as anything. I can really have fun writing, and it's a growth area. That kind of writing allows me to be surprised by myself. It's different from journal writing, which still has some craft to it. In the "free zone," I might write a lot of garbage—but that's okay because it might lead somewhere.

QUESTION: The popular wisdom is that journalists write fast—deadlines are a comfortable fact of life. True?

ANSWER: That's not true for me. I think some people may work fast, especially newspaper journalists. But *The New Yorker* doesn't have deadlines—they know that different pieces require different amounts of time and only the writer can really know that. I work slowly through several drafts.

QUESTION: Where do you spend most of your time: planning, drafting, revising?

ANSWER: Pretty much in equal parts.

QUESTION: How do you plan?

ANSWER: I use outlines. Sometimes I look at other pieces that are similar to the form I want, and sometimes I even outline them. I outline my own pieces—there's really no more efficient way. In many ways, the most intense work is the thinking before writing. I have a tremendous impulse to put pencil to paper, to get to the typewriter. But the most important part of writing is thinking and clarifying before putting pen to paper.

The outline is part of that thinking process. I might in the end depart from it, but I need a way to put my thoughts together, and the outline is the best way I know.

QUESTION: Your piece appears in the section of our text on "definition." Do you think about forms like definition and comparison when you write?

ANSWER: It's helpful at a certain point to recognize that this piece you're writing is a particular form—definition. Settling on a definite form or writing strategy is similar to setting up an outline: You don't want to do that prematurely. Pieces have an independent life, and they gravitate toward what they want to be.

—From an interview with the editors of *Essay 2*

BACKGROUND: Jane Howard (born 1935) is a journalist who became known for her books about the changing American scene. She was born in Springfield, Illinois, and attended the University of Michigan. She went to work and live in New York City, working for *Life* magazine first as a reporter and later as editor and staff writer. Her books include *A Different Woman* (1973) and her widely reviewed *Families* (1978), from which the following article was adopted for publication in the *Atlantic* magazine. Unlike trend watchers who merely chart changing patterns of American life, Howard points new directions for readers who are looking for guidance in a time of shifting values. She helps us adapt old concepts or ways of thinking to changing circumstances in changing times. Her most recent book is *Margaret Mead: A Life* (1984).

Jane Howard

In Search of the Good Family

GUIDE TO READING: In this essay, the author sets out to give new meaning to an old familiar term. Why does she feel the need to redefine the word? What synonyms, near-synonyms, and other related terms does she bring in, and how are they related to her central term? As she maps out the area covered by her central term, what part of the territory is familiar? What part is new or strange?

Call it a clan, call it a network, call it a tribe, call it a family. Whatever you call it, whoever you are, you need one. You need one because you are human. You didn't come from nowhere. Before you, around you, and presumably after you, too, there are others. Some of these others must matter a lot—to you, and if you are very lucky, to one another. Their welfare must be nearly as important to you as your own. Even if you live alone, even if your solitude is elected and ebullient, you still cannot do without a clan or tribe.

The trouble with the clans and tribes many of us were born into is not that they consist of meddlesome ogres but that they are too far away. In emergencies we rush across continents and if need be oceans to their sides, as they do to ours. Maybe we even make a habit of seeing them, once or twice a year, for the sheer pleasure of it. But blood ties seldom dictate our addresses. Our blood kin are often too remote to ease us from our Tuesdays to our Wednesdays. For this we must rely on our families of friends. If our relatives are not, do not wish to be, or for whatever reasons cannot be our friends, then by some complex alchemy we must try to transform our friends into our relatives. If blood and roots don't do the job, then we must look to water and branches, and sort ourselves into new constellations, new families.

These new families, to borrow the terminology of an African tribe (the 3 Bangwa of the Cameroons), may consist either of friends of the road, ascribed by chance, or friends of the heart, achieved by choice. Ascribed friends are those we happen to go to school with, work with, or live near. They know where we went last weekend and whether we still have a cold. Just being around gives them a provisional importance in our lives, and us in theirs. Maybe they will still matter to us when we or they move away; quite likely they won't. Six months or two years will probably erase us from each other's thoughts, unless by some chance they and we have become friends of the heart.

Wishing to be friends, as Aristotle[1] wrote, is quick work, but friendship 4 is a slowly ripening fruit. An ancient proverb he quotes in his *Ethics* had it that you cannot know a man until you and he together have eaten a peck of salt. Now a peck, a quarter of a bushel, is quite a lot of salt—more, perhaps, than most pairs of people ever have occasion to share. We must try though. We must sit together at as many tables as we can. We must steer each other through enough seasons and weathers so that sooner or later it crosses our minds that one of us, God knows which or with what sorrow, must one day mourn the other.

We must devise new ways, or revive old ones, to equip ourselves with 5 kinfolk. Maybe such an impulse prompted whoever ordered the cake I saw in my neighborhood bakery to have it frosted to say "HAPPY BIRTHDAY SURROGATE." I like to think that this cake was decorated not for a judge but for someone's surrogate mother or surrogate brother: loathsome jargon, but admirable sentiment. If you didn't conceive me or if we didn't grow up in the same house, we can still be related, if we decide we ought to be. It is never too late, I like to hope, to augment our families in ways nature neglected to do. It is never too late to choose new clans.

The best-chosen clans, like the best friendships and the best blood 6 families, endure by accumulating a history solid enough to suggest a future. But clans that don't last have merit too. We can lament them but we shouldn't deride them. Better an ephemeral clan or tribe than none at all. A few of my life's most tribally joyous times, in fact, have been spent with people whom I have yet to see again. This saddens me, as it may them too, but dwelling overlong on such sadness does no good. A more fertile exercise is to think back on those times and try to figure out what made them, for all their brevity, so stirring. What can such times teach us about forming new and more lasting tribes in the future?

New tribes and clans can no more be willed into existence, of course, 7

[1][ancient Greek philosopher (382–322 B.C.), whose *Nicomachean Ethics* includes friendship among the key virtues that contribute to the good life]

than any other good thing can. We keep trying, though. To try, with gritted teeth and girded loins, is after all American. That is what the two Helens and I were talking about the day we had lunch in a room way up in a high-rise motel near the Kansas City airport. We had lunch there at the end of a two-day conference on families. The two Helens were social scientists, but I liked them even so, among other reasons because they both objected to that motel's coffee shop even more than I did. One of the Helens, from Virginia, disliked it so much that she had brought along homemade whole wheat bread, sesame butter, and honey from her parents' farm in South Dakota, where she had visited before the conference. Her picnic was the best thing that happened, to me at least, those whole two days.

"If you're voluntarily childless and alone," said the other Helen, who 8 was from Pennsylvania by way of Puerto Rico, "it gets harder and harder with the passage of time. It's stressful. That's why you need support systems." I had been hearing quite a bit of talk about "support systems." The term is not among my favorites, but I can understand its currency. Whatever "support systems" may be, the need for them is clearly urgent, and not just in this country. Are there not thriving "mega-families" of as many as three hundred people in Scandinavia? Have not the Japanese for years had an honored, enduring—if perhaps by our standards rather rigid—custom of adopting nonrelatives to fill gaps in their families? Should we not applaud and maybe imitate such ingenuity?

And consider our own Unitarians. From Santa Barbara to Boston they 9 have been earnestly dividing their congregations into arbitrary "extended families" whose members are bound to act like each other's relatives. Kurt Vonnegut, Jr.[2] plays with a similiar train of thought in his fictional *Slapstick*. In that book every newborn baby is assigned a randomly chosen middle name, like Uranium or Daffodil or Raspberry. These middle names are connected with hyphens to numbers between one and twenty, and any two people who have the same middle name are automatically related. This is all to the good, the author thinks, because "human beings need all the relatives they can get—as possible donors or receivers not of love but of common decency." He envisions these extended families as "one of the four greatest inventions by Americans," the others being *Robert's Rules of Order*, the Bill of Rights, and the principles of Alcoholics Anonymous.

This charming notion might even work, if it weren't so arbitrary. 10 Already each of us is born into one family not of our choosing. If we're going to devise new ones, we might as well have the luxury of picking the members ourselves. Clever picking might result in new families whose benefits would surpass or at least equal those of the old. As a member in reasonable standing of six or seven tribes in addition to the one I was born

[2][American novelist, master of satire and fantasy, who wrote *Slaughterhouse Five* (1969) and many other books]

to, I have been trying to figure which characteristics are common to both kinds of families.

1) Good families have a chief, or a heroine, or a founder—someone [11] around whom others cluster, whose achievements, as the Yiddish word has it, let them *kvell*[3], and whose example spurs them on to like feats. Some blood dynasties produce such figures regularly; others languish for as many as five generations between demigods, wondering with each new pregnancy whether this, at last, might be the messianic baby who will redeem them. Look, is there not something gubernatorial about her footstep, or musical about the way he bangs with his spoon on his cup? All clans, of all kinds, need such a figure now and then. Sometimes clans based on water rather than blood harbor several such personages at one time.

2) Good families have a switchboard operator—someone who can- [12] not help but keep track of what all the others are up to, who plays Houston Mission Control to everyone else's Apollo. This role is assumed rather than assigned. The person who volunteers for it often has the instincts of an archivist, and feels driven to keep scrapbooks and photograph albums up to date, so that the clan can see proof of its own continuity.

3) Good families are much to all their members, but everything to [13] none. Good families are fortresses with many windows and doors to the outer world. The blood clans I feel most drawn to were founded by parents who are nearly as devoted to what they do outside as they are to each other and their children. Their curiosity and passion are contagious. Everybody, where they live, is busy. Paint is spattered on eyeglasses. Mud lurks under fingernails. Person-to-person calls come in the middle of the night from Tokyo and Brussels. Catcher's mitts, ballet slippers, overdue library books, and other signs of extrafamilial concerns are everywhere.

4) Good families are hospitable. Knowing that hosts need guests as [14] much as guests need hosts, they are generous with honorary memberships for friends, whom they urge to come early and often and to stay late. Such clans exude a vivid sense of surrounding rings of relatives, neighbors, teachers, students, and godparents, any of whom at any time might break or slide into the inner circle. Inside that circle a wholesome, tacit emotional feudalism develops: you give me protection, I'll give you fealty. Such pacts begin with, but soon go far beyond, the jolly exchange of pie at Thanksgiving or cake on a birthday. They mean that you can ask me to supervise your children for the fortnight you will be in the hospital, and that however inconvenient this might be for me, I shall manage to do so. It means I can phone you on what for me is a dreary, wretched Sunday afternoon and for you is the eve of a deadline, knowing you will tell me to come right over, if

[3][Leo Rosten, in *The Joys of Yiddish*, defines *kvell* as "beam with immense pride and pleasure . . . doting with conspicuous pride."]

only to watch you type. It means we need not dissemble. ("To yield to seeming," as Martin Buber wrote, "is man's essential cowardice, to resist it is his essential courage . . . one must at times pay dearly for life lived from the being, but it is never too dear.")[4]

5) Good families deal squarely with direness. Pity the tribe that 15 doesn't have, and cherish, at least one flamboyant eccentric. Pity too the one that supposes it can avoid for long the woes to which all flesh is heir. Lunacy, bankruptcy, suicide, and other unthinkable fates sooner or later afflict the noblest of clans with an undertow of gloom. Family life is a set of givens, someone once told me, and it takes courage to see certain givens as blessings rather than as curses. It surely does. Contradictions and inconsistencies are givens, too. So is the battle against what the Oregon patriarch Kenneth Babbs calls malarkey. "There's always malarkey lurking, bubbles in the cesspool, fetid bubbles that pop and smell. But I don't put up with malarkey, between my stepkids and my natural ones or anywhere else in the family."

6) Good families prize their rituals. Nothing welds a family more than 16 these. Rituals are vital especially for clans without histories, because they evoke a past, imply a future, and hint at continuity. No line in the seder service at Passover reassures more than the last: "Next year in Jerusalem!" A clan becomes more of a clan each time it gathers to observe a fixed ritual (Christmas, birthdays, Thanksgiving, and so on), grieves at a funeral (anyone may come to most funerals; those who do declare their tribalness), and devises a new rite of its own. Equinox breakfasts can be at least as welding as Memorial Day parades. Several of my colleagues and I used to meet for lunch every Pearl Harbor Day, preferably to eat some politically neutral fare like smorgasbord, to "forgive" our only ancestrally Japanese friend, Irene Kubota Neves. For that and other things we became, and remain, a sort of family . . . .

7) Good families are affectionate. This of course is a matter of style. I 17 know clans whose members greet each other with gingerly handshakes or, in what pass for kisses, with hurried brushes of jawbones, as if the object were to touch not the lips but the ears. I don't see how such people manage. "The tribe that does not hug," as someone who has been part of many *ad hoc* families recently wrote to me, "is no tribe at all. More and more I realize that everybody, regardless of age, needs to be hugged and comforted in a brotherly or sisterly way now and then. Preferably now."

8) Good families have a sense of place, which these days is not 18 achieved easily. As Susanne Langer wrote in 1957, "Most people have no home that is a symbol of their childhood, not even a definite memory of one place to serve that purpose . . . all the old symbols are gone." Once I asked a

[4][Martin Buber (1878–1965) was an Austrian-born Israeli philosopher and theologian.]

roomful of supper guests if anyone felt a strong pull to any certain spot on the face of the earth. Everyone was silent, except for a visitor from Bavaria. The rest of us seemed to know all too well what Walker Percy means in *The Moviegoer* when he tells of the "genie-soul of a place, which every place has or else is not a place [and which] wherever you go, you must meet and master or else be met and mastered." All that meeting and mastering saps plenty of strength. It also underscores our need for tribal bases of the sort which soaring real estate taxes and splintering families have made all but obsolete.

So what are we to do, those of us whose habit and pleasure and doom 19 is our tendency, as a Georgia lady put it, to "fly off at every other whipstitch"? Think in terms of movable feasts, that's what. Live here, wherever here may be, as if we were going to belong here for the rest of our lives. Learn to hallow whatever ground we happen to stand on or land on. Like medieval knights who took their tapestries along on Crusades, like modern Afghanis with their yurts, we must pack such totems and icons as we can to make short-term quarters feel like home. Pillows, small rugs, watercolors can dispel much of the chilling anonymity of a motel room or sublet apartment. When we can, we should live in rooms with stoves or fireplaces or at least candlelight. The ancient saying is still true: Extinguished hearth, extinguished family.

Round tables help too, and as a friend of mine once put it, so do "too 20 many comfortable chairs, with surfaces to put feet on, arranged so as to encourage a maximum of eye contact." Such rooms inspire good talk, of which good clans can never have enough.

9) Good families, not just the blood kind, find some way to connect 21 with posterity. "To forge a link in the humble chain of being, encircling heirs to ancestors," as Michael Novak has written, "is to walk within a circle of magic as primitive as humans knew in caves." He is talking of course about babies, feeling them leap in wombs, giving them suck. Parenthood, however, is a state which some miss by chance and others by design, and a vocation to which not all are called. Some of us, like the novelist Richard P. Brickner, look on as others "name their children and their children in turn name their own lives, devising their own flags from their parents' cloth." What are we who lack children to do? Build houses? Plant trees? Write books or symphonies or laws? Perhaps, but even if we do these things, there should be children on the sidelines if not at the center of our lives.

It is a sadly impoverished tribe that does not allow access to, and make 22 much of, some children. Not too much, of course; it has truly been said that never in history have so many educated people devoted so much attention to so few children. Attention, in excess, can turn to fawning, which isn't much better than neglect. Still, if we don't regularly see and talk to and laugh with people who can expect to outlive us by twenty years or so, we had better get busy and find some.

10) Good families also honor their elders. The wider the age range, 23 the stronger the tribe. Jean-Paul Sartre[5] and Margaret Mead, to name two spectacularly confident former children, have both remarked on the central importance of grandparents in their own early lives. Grandparents are now in much more abundant supply than they were a generation or two ago, when old age was more rare. If actual grandparents are not at hand, no family should have too hard a time finding substitute ones to whom to pay unfeigned homage. The Soviet Union's enchantment with day-care centers, I have heard, stems at least in part from the state's eagerness to keep children away from their presumably subversive grandparents. Let that be a lesson to clans based on interest as well as to those based on genes.

Using the Dictionary

In her **allusions** to other cultures and other periods in history, Howard uses many terms that have come into English from other languages. Check ten of the following. What language or part of the world does the word come from?   1. *alchemy* (2)   2. *constellation* (2)   3. *dynasty* (11)   4. *demigod* (11)   5. *messianic* (11)   6. *feudalism* (14)   7. *fealty* (14)   8. *flamboyant* (15)   9. *patriarch* (15)   10. *seder* (16)   11. *smorgasbord* (16)   12. *genie* (18)   13. *yurt* (19)   14. *totem* (19)   15. *icon* (19)

The Writer's Agenda

Howard sets out to give a contemporary meaning to a traditional concept. Answer the following questions about how she redefines her key term:

1. Where does the author first sum up her *redefinition* of the central term as the **thesis** of her essay? What does she say about the need for redefining the term? Find several sentences that reiterate—restate, explain, reinforce—her central thesis.

2. Howard brings in many *related terms* that cluster around the central concept. Discuss some of the traditional terms she uses: *clan, tribe, kin, dynasty, blood, roots, patriarch.* What are their meanings, associations, uses? What are the origins and implications of more modern terms like *network, surrogate mother, support system, extended family*?

3. Among the characteristics of good families listed by the author, select the three or four that to you seem most basic or most essential. What does the author say about them? Where or how have you observed them in action?

4. Among the characteristics of good families listed by the author, select those that seem to you most surprising—least conventional or least predictable. What does the author say about them? Does she make their inclusion plausible?

---

[5][leading French philosopher, novelist, playwright, and political activist of the post–World War II period, who helped popularize the philosophy of existentialism]

5. How successful is the author in showing what her ideas mean *in practice*? Discuss some of the examples, anecdotes, precedents, or parallels that for you are most helpful or most convincing.

For Discussion or Writing

6. Make your own list of the essential characteristics of "good families." Rearrange the order of those listed by Howard to reflect your own priorities. What characteristics would you add and why? Which would you delete?

7. Where would you place the ideal reader for Howard's article on a scale ranging from very traditional to very modern? (Is there a point where very traditional people would draw the line?)

8. Terms like *family* and *marriage* change their meanings as legal boundaries and attitudes shift. What would you include in an extended definition of marriage as an institution? (Does it require legal or official certification? Does it have to be sanctified by a religious rite? Does it have to be with someone of the other sex? What are its key responsibilities or obligations?)

9. Write an extended definition of the ideal family, or of true friendship, or of true love. If needed, set your key term off from other related or opposed terms.

Branching Out

10. Howard makes us reconsider some familiar human needs or key elements in people's lives. Prepare a paper in which you explore one of the following. Pay special attention to changing attitudes or conventions.
- the importance of ritual or ceremony in our lives
- the differences in how people show affection
- traditions of hospitality
- the way we treat or think of elders
- attitudes toward engagements

BACKGROUND: Ralph Nader became famous as a crusading consumer advocate who forced large corporations and government agencies to face up to their responsibility for the public welfare. He was born in Winsted, Connecticut, in 1934 and studied at Princeton University and Harvard Law School. As a young lawyer working for the U.S. Department of Labor, he did the research that led to his *Unsafe at Any Speed* (1965), an exposé of the automobile industry's disregard for passenger safety. In 1969, he helped found the Center for Study of Responsive Law. The center employed idealistic young students (informally known as "Nader's Raiders") to serve as watchdogs for the rights of individuals threatened by the callousness of large bureaucratic institutions and big business. In "A New Kind of Patriotism," first published in *Life* magazine in 1971, Nader speaks as the voice of a generation that rejected the unquestioning patriotism of their elders.

Ralph Nader
A New Kind
of Patriotism

GUIDE TO READING: In this essay, the author sets out to redefine a traditional term to reflect the changing values of a new generation. What historical background does he provide? What synonyms or related terms does he introduce? What are the key requirements for the new kind of patriotism?

At a recent meeting of the national PTA, the idealism and commitment 1
of many young people to environmental and civil rights causes were being discussed. A middle-aged woman, who was listening closely, stood up and asked: "But what can we do to make young people today patriotic?"

In a very direct way, she illuminated the tensions contained in the idea 2
of patriotism. These tensions, which peak at moments of public contempt or respect for patriotic symbols such as the flag, have in the past few years divided the generations and pitted children against parents. Highly charged exchanges take place between those who believe that patriotism is automatically possessed by those in authority and those who assert that patriotism is not a pattern imposed but a condition earned by the quality of an individual's, or a people's, behavior. The struggle over symbols, epithets and generalities impedes a clearer understanding of the meaning and value of patriotism. It is time to talk of patriotism, not as an abstraction steeped in nostalgia, but as behavior that can be judged by the standard of "liberty and justice for all."

Patriotism can be a great asset for any organized society, but it can 3
also be a tool manipulated by unscrupulous or cowardly leaders and elites.

The development of a sense of patriotism was a strong unifying force during our Revolution and its insecure aftermath. Defined then and now as "love of country," patriotism was an extremely important motivating force with which to confront foreign threats to the young nation. It was no happenstance that *The Star Spangled Banner* was composed during the War of 1812 when the Redcoats were not only coming but already here. For a weak frontier country beset by the competitions and aggressions of European powers in the New World, the martial virtues were those of sheer survival. America produced patriots who never moved beyond the borders of their country. They were literally defenders of their home.

As the United States moved into the 20th century and became a world power, far flung alliances and wars fought thousands of miles away stretched the boundaries of patriotism. "Making the world safe for democracy" was the grandiose way Woodrow Wilson put it. At other times and places (such as Latin America) it became distorted into "jingoism." World War II was the last war that all Americans fought with conviction. Thereafter, when "bombs bursting in air" would be atomic bombs, world war became a suicidal risk. Wars that could be so final and swift lost their glamour even for the most militaristically minded. When we became the most powerful nation on earth, the old insecurity that made patriotism into a conditioned reflex of "my country right or wrong" should have given way to a thinking process; as expressed by Carl Schurz: "Our country . . . when right, to be kept right. When wrong, to be put right." It was not until the Indochina war that we began the search for a new kind of patriotism.

If we are to find true and concrete meaning in patriotism, I suggest these starting points. First, in order that a free and just consensus be formed, patriotism must once again be rooted in the individual's own conscience and beliefs. Love is conceived by the giver (citizens) when merited by the receiver (the governmental authorities). If "consent of the governed" is to have any meaning, the abstract ideal of country has to be separated from those who direct it; otherwise the government cannot be evaluated by its citizens. The authorities in the State Department, the Pentagon, or the White House are not infallible; they have been and often are wrong, vain, misleading, shortsighted or authoritarian. When they are, leaders like these are shortchanging, not representing, America. To identify America with them is to abandon hope and settle for tragedy. Americans who consider themselves patriotic in the traditional sense do not usually hesitate to heap criticism in domestic matters over what they believe is oppressive or wasteful or unresponsive government handling of their rights and dignity. They should be just as vigilant in weighing similar government action which harnesses domestic resources for foreign involvements. Citizenship has an obligation to cleanse patriotism of the misdeeds done in its name abroad.

The flag, as the Pledge of Allegiance makes clear, takes its meaning from that "for which it stands"; it should not and cannot stand for shame, injustice and tyranny. It must not be used as a bandanna or a fig leaf by those unworthy of this country's leadership.

Second, patriotism begins at home. Love of country in fact is insepar-   7 able from citizen action to make the country more lovable. This means working to end poverty, discrimination, corruption, greed and other conditions that weaken the promise and potential of America.

Third, if it is unpatriotic to tear down the flag (which is a symbol of the   8 country), why isn't it more unpatriotic to desecrate the country itself—to pollute, despoil and ravage the air, land and water? Such environmental degradation makes the "pursuit of happiness" ragged indeed. Why isn't it unpatriotic to engage in the colossal waste that characterizes so many defense contracts? Why isn't it unpatriotic to draw our country into a mistaken war and then keep extending the involvement, with untold casualties to soldiers and innocents, while not telling Americans the truth? Why isn't the deplorable treatment of returning veterans by government and industry evaluated by the same standards as is their dispatch to war? Why isn't the systematic contravention of the U.S. Constitution and the Declaration of Independence in our treatment of minority groups, the poor, the young, the old and other disadvantaged or helpless people crassly unpatriotic? Isn't all such behavior contradicting the innate worth and the dignity of the individual in America? Is it not time to end the tragic twisting of patriotism whereby those who work to expose and correct deep injustices, and who take intolerable risks while doing it, are accused of running down America by the very forces doing just that? Our country and its ideals are something for us to uphold as individuals and together, not something to drape, as a deceptive cloak, around activities that mar or destroy these ideals.

Fourth, there is no reason why patriotism has to be so heavily associ-   9 ated, in the minds of the young as well as adults, with military exploits, jets and missiles. Citizenship must include the duty to advance our ideals actively into practice for a better community, country and world, if peace is to prevail over war. And this obligation stems not just from a secular concern for humanity but from a belief in the brotherhood of man—"I am my brother's keeper"—that is common to all major religions. It is the classic confrontation—barbarism *vs.* the holy ones. If patriotism has no room for deliberation, for acknowledging an individual's sense of justice and his religious principles, it will continue to close minds, stifle the dissent that has made us strong, and deter the participation of Americans who challenge in order to correct, and who question in order to answer. We need only to recall recent history in other countries where patriotism was converted into an epidemic of collective madness and destruction. A patriotism manipulated by the government asks only for a servile nod from its subjects. A new patriotism requires a thinking assent from its citizens. If patriotism is to have any "manifest destiny," it is in building a world where all mankind is our bond in peace.

Using the Dictionary

A. Check the following as necessary: 1. *illuminate* (2) 2. *epithet* (2) 3. *impede* (2) 4. *abstraction* (2) 5. *unscrupulous* (3) 6. *elite* (3) 7. *aftermath* (3) 8. *martial* (3) 9. *grandiose* (4) 10. *concrete*, adj. (5) 11. *infallible* (5) 12. *vigilant* (5) 13. *desecrate* (8) 14. *ravage* (8) 15. *degradation* (8) 16. *contravention* (8) 17. *innate* (8) 18. *barbarism* (9) 19. *servile* (9) B. Prepare a *one-sentence* definition of the following key terms: 20. *jingoism* (4) 21. *militaristic* (4) 22. *consensus* (5) 23. *authoritarian* (5) 24. *manifest destiny* (9)

The Writer's Agenda

In this essay, Nader sets out in search of "a new kind of patriotism" to take the place of the "my-country-right-or-wrong" patriotism of past generations. Answer the following questions:

1. How does Nader set his essay in motion? What sentence early in the essay strikes the *keynote* or raises the key issue of the essay?

2. How does Nader's treatment of the *history* of his central term provide common ground for a potentially divided audience?

3. Where in his short history of patriotism does Nader reach the important turning point? (What is the difference between "love of country" and "jingoism"?)

4. What are Nader's requirements or criteria for "true patriotism"? Which of them come through most forcefully or seem most important?

5. Why and how does Nader use familiar *slogans* like "consent of the governed" or "making the world safe for democracy" or "manifest destiny"? (What are other examples?)

6. How does Nader's conclusion sum up his thesis? What does he do in his conclusion to give added force to his central argument?

For Discussion or Writing

7. For you, what is the most important change, or the central element, in Nader's redefinition of patriotism for a new generation? (How would you define Nader's generation? What kind of reader would make an ideal audience for him?)

8. Do you agree with Nader? What is your own definition of *true patriotism*?

9. Nader makes sweeping charges against the political and economic establishment. Choose one that you can either substantiate or refute and examine it in detail.

10. Is it true that we have recently seen a return to old-fashioned patriotism? What signs of it (or what contrary evidence) have you observed?

11. What do we mean when we accuse people of sexism, chauvinism, manipulation, bigotry, or fanaticism? Choose one of these. Where do you draw the line?

12. How important are symbols to people's convictions or beliefs? For instance, what role does the flag play, or what role do uniforms play, in promoting patriotism?

13. Write about a term that many people have had to reexamine or that has changed its meaning. For instance, what does (or should) *fidelity* mean for the current generation? Is there such a thing as "reverse racism"? Is romantic love obsolete?

Branching Out

14. Terms like the following are often used in the heat of argument: *militarism, fascism, communism, imperialism, colonialism.* Work out a truly instructive or informative definition for one of these—use historical material as appropriate.

BACKGROUND: Richard Rodriguez (born 1944) grew up in Sacramento, California, as the son of Mexican immigrants. On his first day of school, he found himself in a class of white middle-class children in which he was the only Mexican American, able to understand "some fifty stray English words." His widely praised autobiography, *Hunger of Memory* (1981), is the history of his education as a "disadvantaged" child who went on to become a scholarship student and a successful writer and lecturer. An English major in college, he studied English literature at prestigious places including Stanford, Berkeley, and the British Museum in London. A major theme of his book is the price of assimilation: his growing separation from the world of his parents and relatives; his gradual estrangement from the familiar, intimate Spanish of his childhood home as English, the "public" language of school and office, slowly became his primary language. Like other bilingual, bicultural Americans, he remained an alert observer of the American scene, looking beyond its surface contradictions for clues to our common identity. The essay that follows first appeared in *Harper's* magazine in March 1984.

Richard Rodriguez

Does America
Still Exist?

GUIDE TO READING: Like many writers before him, this author sets out in search of a definition of America and the American way. What contradictions make the search difficult for him? What for him are important clues to our common culture? Does he arrive at a common denominator?

For the children of immigrant parents the knowledge comes easier. 1
America exists everywhere in the city—on billboards, frankly in the smell of French fries and popcorn. It exists in the pace: traffic lights, the assertions of neon, the mysterious bong-bong-bong through atriums of department stores. America exists as the voice of the crowd, a menacing sound— the high nasal accent of American English.

When I was a boy in Sacramento (California, the fifties), people would 2
ask me, "Where you from?" I was born in this country, but I knew the question meant to decipher my darkness, my looks.

My mother once instructed me to say, "I am an American of Mexican 3
descent." By the time I was nine or ten, I wanted to say, but dared not reply, "I am an American."

Immigrants come to America and, against hostility or mere loneliness, 4
they recreate a homeland in the parlor, tacking up postcards or calendars of some impossible blue—lake or sea or sky. Children of immigrant parents

are supposed to perch on a hyphen between two countries. Relatives assume the achievement as much as anyone. Relatives are, in any case, surprised when the child begins losing old ways. One day at the family picnic the boy wanders away from their spiced food and faceless stories to watch other boys play baseball in the distance.

There is sorrow in the American memory, guilty sorrow for having left 5 something behind—Portugal, China, Norway. The American story is the story of immigrant children and of their children—children no longer able to speak to grandparents. The memory of exile becomes inarticulate as it passes from generation to generation, along with wedding rings and pocket watches—like some mute stone in a wad of old lace. Europe. Asia. Eden.

But, it needs to be said, if this is a country where one stops being 6 Vietnamese or Italian, this is a country where one begins to be an American. America exists as a culture and a grin, a faith and a shrug. It is clasped in a handshake, called by a first name.

As much as the country is joined in a common culture, however, 7 Americans are reluctant to celebrate the process of assimilation. We pledge allegiance to diversity. America was born Protestant and bred Puritan, and the notion of community we share is derived from a seventeenth-century faith. Presidents and the pages of ninth-grade civics readers yet proclaim the orthodoxy: We are gathered together—but as individuals, with separate pasts, distinct destinies. Our society is as paradoxical as a Puritan congregation: We stand together, alone.

Americans have traditionally defined themselves by what they refused 8 to include. As often, however, Americans have struggled, turned in good conscience at last to assert the great Protestant virtue of tolerance. Despite outbreaks of nativist frenzy, America has remained an immigrant country, open and true to itself.

Against pious emblems of rural America—soda fountain, Elks hall, 9 Protestant church, and now shopping mall—stands the coldhearted city, crowded with races and ambitions, curious laughter, much that is odd. Nevertheless, it is the city that has most truly represented America. In the city, however, the millions of singular lives have had no richer notion of wholeness to describe them than the idea of pluralism.

"Where you from?" the American asks the immigrant child. "Mex- 10 *ico," the boy learns to say.*

Mexico, the country of my blood ancestors, offers formal contrast to 11 the American achievement. If the United States was formed by Protestant individualism, Mexico was shaped by a medieval Catholic dream of one world. The Spanish journeyed to Mexico to plunder, and they may have gone, in God's name, with an arrogance peculiar to those who intend to convert. But through the conversion, the Indian converted the Spaniard. A new race was born, the *mestizo*, wedding European to Indian. José Vasconcelos, the Mexican philosopher, has celebrated this New World creation, proclaiming it the "cosmic race."

Centuries later, in a San Francisco restaurant, a Mexican-American [12] lawyer of my acquaintance says, in English, over *salade niçoise*, that he does not intend to assimilate into gringo society.[1] His claim is echoed by a chorus of others (Italian-Americans, Greeks, Asians) in this era of ethnic pride. The melting pot has been retired, clanking, into the museum of quaint disgrace, alongside Aunt Jemima and the Katzenjammer Kids.[2] But resistance to assimilation is characteristically American. It only makes clear how inevitable the process of assimilation actually is.

For generations, this has been the pattern. Immigrant parents have [13] sent their children to school (simply, they thought) to acquire the "skills" to survive in the city. The child returned home with a voice his parents barely recognized or understood, couldn't trust, and didn't like.

In Eastern cities—Philadelphia, New York, Boston, Baltimore—class [14] after class gathered immigrant children to women (usually women) who stood in front of rooms full of children, changing children. So also for me in the 1950s. Irish-Catholic nuns. California. The old story. The hyphen tipped to the right, away from Mexico and toward a confusing but true American identity.

I speak now in the chromium American accent of my grammar [15] school classmates—Billy Reckers, Mike Bradley, Carol Schmidt, Kathy O'Grady.... I believe I became like my classmates, became German, Polish, and (like my teachers) Irish. And because assimilation is always reciprocal, my classmates got something of me. (I mean sad eyes; belief in the Indian Virgin; a taste for sugar skulls on the Feast of the Dead.) In the blending, we became what our parents could never have been, and we carried America one revolution further.

"Does America still exist?" Americans have been asking the question [16] for so long that to ask it again only proves our continuous link. But perhaps the question deserves to be asked with urgency—now. Since the black civil rights movement of the 1960s, our tenuous notion of a shared public life has deteriorated notably.

The struggle of black men and women did not eradicate racism, but it [17] became the great moment in the life of America's conscience. Water hoses, bulldogs, blood—the images, rendered black, white, rectangular, passed into living rooms.

It is hard to look at a photograph of a crowd taken, say, in 1890 or in [18] 1930 and not notice the absence of blacks. (It becomes an impertinence to wonder if America *still* exists.)

In the sixties, other groups of Americans learned to champion their [19] rights by analogy to the black civil rights movement. But the heroic vision

[1][*Salade niçoise* is a French salad featuring tuna and anchovies, likely to be found in expensive American restaurants.]
[2][The beaming face of Aunt Jemima (the black cook working in white folks' kitchens) is no longer used to advertise pancake mix. The ethnic humor of the Katzenjammer Kids, forever playing crude pranks on klutzy elders who speak English with a heavy German accent, is also a thing of the past.]

faded. Dr. Martin Luther King Jr. had spoken with Pauline eloquence of a nation that would unite Christian and Jew, old and young, rich and poor.[3] Within a decade, the struggles of the 1960s were reduced to a bureaucratic competition for little more than pieces of a representational pie. The quest for a portion of power became an end in itself. The metaphor for the American city of the 1970s was a committee: one black, one woman, one person under thirty . . . .

If the small town had sinned against America by too neatly defining 20 who could be an American, the city's sin was a romantic secession. One noticed the romanticism in the antiwar movement—certain demonstrators who demonstrated a lack of tact or desire to persuade and seemed content to play secular protestants. One noticed the romanticism in the competition among members of "minority groups" to claim the status of Primary Victim. To Americans unconfident of their common identity, minority standing became a way of asserting individuality. Middle-class Americans—men and women clearly not the primary victims of social oppression—brandished their suffering with exuberance.

The dream of a single society probably died with *The Ed Sullivan* 21 *Show*. The reality of America persists. Teenagers pass through big-city high schools banded in racial groups, their collars turned up to a uniform shrug. But then they graduate to jobs at the phone company or in banks, where they end up working alongside people unlike themselves. Typists and tellers walk out together at lunchtime.

It is easier for us as Americans to believe the obvious fact of our 22 separateness—easier to imagine the black and white Americas prophesied by the Kerner report (broken glass, street fires)—than to recognize the reality of a city street at lunchtime.[4] Americans are wedded by proximity to a common culture. The panhandler at one corner is related to the pamphleteer at the next who is related to the banker who is kin to the Chinese old man wearing an MIT sweatshirt. In any true national history, Thomas Jefferson begets Martin Luther King Jr. who begets the Gray Panthers. It is because we lack a vision of ourselves entire—the city street is crowded and we are each preoccupied with finding our own way home—that we lack an appropriate hymn.

Under my window now passes a little white girl softly rehearsing to 23 herself a Motown obbligato.

Using the Dictionary

How does your dictionary define the following terms? How clear and helpful are the definitions? 1. *orthodoxy* (7)   2. *paradoxical* (7)   3. *nativist* (8)   4. *emblem* (9)   5. *pluralism* (9)   6. *melting pot* (12)   7. *reciprocal* (15)   8. *tenuous*

---

[3][Much of the teaching of the early Christian church is contained in the writings of St. Paul, an apostle who wrote several New Testament epistles.]
[4][The Kerner report presented the results of an investigation into the causes of racial violence.]

(16)   9. *impertinence* (18)   10. *secession* (20)   11. *secular* (20)   12. *proximity* (22)   13. *obbligato* (23)

The Writer's Agenda

Rodriguez writes from an urgent sense that our "notion of a shared public life has deteriorated." Answer the following questions about how he tries to counteract this trend.

1. Look at some of the many details that for Rodriguez are typical or symbolic of America. What is their meaning or importance? Are they related? Is there any *common thread* or common denominator?

2. What, according to the author, is the pattern that many children of immigrant parents have lived through as they react to the old-country ways of their parents?

3. Rodriguez discusses the small rural town and the big city as two opposed symbols of what America stands for. What definition of America does each represent? Which for him is more truly American? Why?

4. What does the contrast between the history of Mexico and the "American achievement" contribute to the essay?

5. A **paradox** is an apparent contradiction that may begin to make sense as we give it further thought. The central paradox in this essay is that according to Rodriguez "resistance to assimilation is characteristically American." What does he mean? How does he explain or justify this paradox?

6. Toward the end of his essay, Rodriguez is critical of middle-class Americans who are "unconfident of their common identity." What is the nature or the basis of his criticism?

For Discussion or Writing

7. How would you sum up the "confusing but true American identity" that the author sketches out for himself in this essay?

8. Pluralism became popular in the sixties and seventies as an alternative to traditional ideals of Americanism. What definition of *pluralism* emerges from this essay?

9. Choose a collection of things or ideas that for you are typically American. Try to find a common denominator.

10. Is the "melting pot" a thing of the past? To judge from your observation and experience, is assimilation still working in America?

11. Is it true that "America has remained an immigrant country, open and true to itself?"

12. Write your own extended definition of one of the following as it works (or fails to work) in American society today: individualism, tolerance, orthodoxy, pluralism.

Branching Out

13. Where would you draw the line between chauvinism (or rah-rah patriotism) and true love of one's country?

14. At what point does an immigrant (or descendant of immigrants) become truly American?

STUDENT MODEL 8

FOR READING: Study the following short selection as a possible model for writing of your own. How do you react to it overall? What makes it interesting or effective? Answer the following more specific questions:

1. (PURPOSE) What was the writer trying to do?
2. (AUDIENCE) What kind of reader would make a good reader for this selection?
3. (SOURCES) Where did the writer turn for material?
4. (THESIS) Does the selection have a central idea or unifying thesis?
5. (STRUCTURE) What is the author's overall plan or strategy?
6. (STYLE) What makes the piece effective or memorable (for instance, striking details, memorable phrases)?
7. (REVISION) What do you think the writer could or should have done differently?

Veda Anderson (student editorial)
Reversing Discrimination

Affirmative action is not reverse discrimination. Affirmative action is necessary. Job discrimination on the basis of sex or race, although not blatant, is very real. In 1980, 45,382 complaints of race and sex biases were filed with the Equal Employment Opportunity Commission. In 1984, 52,130 complaints were filed. There is a grave need for a plan that helps women and minorities advance and achieve racial balance in the work force. There is a need to correct the problems that have resulted from past discrimination.

The passage of the Civil Rights Act in 1964 provided the legal opportunity for equality, but it did not guarantee equal opportunity. Unfortunately, in this society, equality in the work force realistically can be achieved only by federal policy that pushes affirmative action and many times enforces quotas. In Chicago, quotas were critically important in overcoming the racial and sexual imbalance in the police and fire departments. Under a

1974 court order, the minority and female share of the police payroll jumped from 18 to 28 percent.

Ninety-five percent of 128 big companies said that they would use ₃ hiring and promotion goals even if the government stopped requiring them. And in May, the National Association of Manufacturers voted to continue a new program involving affirmative action. These companies and departments have realized and accepted the fact that discrimination is detrimental to a woman's or a minority's chance of finding and keeping a job.

One argument against affirmative action is that it is reverse discri- ₄ mination. But there is a problem with that argument. Discrimination is based on contempt or even loathing for the excluded group. Affirmative action is not, and it does not stigmatize others. Rather, it increases the social and economic strength of formerly victimized groups.

Another argument against affirmative action is that it creates a situa- ₅ tion in which jobs are no longer filled on the basis of quality. However, this is not necessarily so. Many times minority job candidates are just as skilled as their white counterparts but are denied jobs or overlooked because they are stereotyped as undesirable. There are serious problems with the education of minorities in this country, but the excuse from employers that there are no qualified minority candidates out there is just what it is—an excuse.

And it can still be argued that under the circumstances it is acceptable ₆ and understandable to give a female or a member of a minority a chance even if he or she is less qualified. After all, a look into the past reveals that blacks were deprived of a chance for equal education and opportunities for a long time. It can also be argued that the environment in which many minorities are raised is enough to set them back. So, how fair is the competition anyway?

It would be ideal if everyone were given the same type and amount of ₇ education, but unfortunately that is not the case. What needs to be realized is that many times, all an individual needs is a chance to compete. Affirmative action gives minorities and women that chance.

Indeed, a burden is imposed on the person who is denied a position so ₈ that a member of a minority or a woman can be given a chance. But is that such a high price to pay to help a group that has been held down? Helping people who have been oppressed and are still being restrained by continued stereotyping is for the public good.

—From *Spartan Daily*

FOR WRITING: Write a *guest editorial* for a student newspaper. Define one of the buzzwords frequently heard in current discussion of political or social issues: *mainstreaming, comparable worth, freedom of information, doublespeak, welfare mentality, right to privacy, workfare,* or the like.

ADDITIONAL WRITING TOPICS 8

Definition

A. Terms like the following sometimes come too easily to our lips. We may use them too quickly or thoughtlessly for praise or blame (or as an excuse). For which of these can you say, "I can show the true meaning of that term"? Define the term, using detailed examples.

1. sincerity
2. a truly friendly person
3. just a kid
4. an unreliable person
5. a fanatic
6. "using" other people
7. good looks
8. irresponsibility
9. a waffler
10. a drag
11. true generosity
12. a superficial person
13. callousness
14. a grind
15. selfishness

B. The need for definition often arises when someone asks us, "Where do you draw the line?" Work out a well-illustrated definition to answer a question like the following. (Your instructor may ask you to include a brief description of your intended *audience*. What kind of person is likely to ask the question you chose, and why?)

1. Where is the line between ordinary and natural foods?
2. When does a rough manner become abusive behavior?
3. When does an active child become a troublemaker?
4. When should a building be preserved as a historic monument?
5. Where does ordinary carelessness become culpable negligence?
6. When is humor in bad taste?
7. Where is the line between a vivacious person and a flirt?
8. When does loyalty to family become nepotism?
9. When does a foreigner begin to become an American?
10. When does an offender become a "hardened criminal"?
11. Where is the line between the social drinker and the alcoholic?
12. Where is the line between a habit and addiction?
13. Where is the line between emotional problems and mental illness?
14. Where is the line between realism and cynicism?
15. Where is the line between opposition and treason?

C.   The following are terms frequently heard in current discussion. Which of them make you say, "I can show what is truly involved"? Write an extended definition of one of these, explaining its significance and tracing its ramifications. Use detailed examples.

1. the macho mystique
2. the moral majority
3. born again
4. single-issue politics
5. the underclass
6. the welfare mentality
7. the new poor
8. sexual harassment
9. comparable worth
10. the feminization of poverty

9

PERSUASION

The Power of Words

OVERVIEW

Persuasion is the art of changing the reader's mind. Our power of persuasion is put to the test when we need to convince someone who disagrees with us, when we need to gain the support of a reluctant listener or reader, when we need to make people confront issues they would rather evade. An experienced writer knows how to work out the right strategy, how to put the reader in a receptive mood, how to overcome obstacles, and how to lead up to what is difficult and controversial. Persuasive writers know how to arouse the reader's concern. They know how to appeal to shared values, how to mobilize latent goodwill.

PURPOSE More so than other kinds of writing, persuasion aims at results. We write to change the reader's mind or the reader's ways. The result we aim at may be something tangible and practical: a vote, a contribution, a sale, a job, a raise, early parole, a waived requirement. Often the aim of persuasive writing is to make readers agree to a course of action, to influence policy, to enlist support for a good cause, or to head off an ill-considered scheme. Often the aim is to change attitudes: to counteract prejudice, to discredit corrupt or oppressive authority, to calm undue fears.

AUDIENCE Audiences for persuasive writing range all the way from the like-minded, receptive audience that cheers us on to the hostile audience whose resistance we have to overcome. When we aim mainly at people who are basically on our side, we can invoke common goals, we can make strong statements about the opposition, and we can channel the enthusiasm of the audience in productive directions. When we aim at people who are lukewarm or hostile toward our cause, we need to *find* common ground. We have to defuse objections; we have to be careful not to alienate readers by negative or sarcastic remarks at the expense of people they admire. Often the real test of our gift for persuasion comes when we take a stand *unpopular* with our intended audience—when we defend rock records (and their lyrics) to long-suffering parents; when we defend general education courses to students impatient to finish college and find a job.

BENEFITS FOR THE WRITER (1) Effective persuasion requires attention to a basic rule for all effective writing: *Know your reader.* An effective writer has learned to anticipate the smiles and frowns (and sometimes the catcalls) of the audience.

(2) Practice in persuasive writing will help you discover the power of words. You will learn something about what *moves* the reader—what it takes to arouse anger, indignation, sympathy, or compassion.

(3) Practice in persuasive writing will give you practice in making your writing serve your purpose. No one becomes a really good writer merely by doing dutiful writing exercises and assignments. We write with drive and conviction when our writing becomes a means of making our own ideas, interests, and commitments prevail.

PERSUASION
Additional Reading

Richard Harsham, A Beeper for Violence   (p. 409)
Jonathan Schell, What Happened at Hiroshima   (p. 440)
Jonathan Swift, A Modest Proposal   (p. 494)

WRITER'S GUIDE 9

The Strategies of Persuasion

What strategies of persuasion will work with a critical reader? What are pitfalls that the writer has to avoid? Remember the following guidelines when trying to make your writing more persuasive:

(1) *Make yourself heard.* In order to change people's minds, we must get their attention. To overcome indifference or break through the crust of apathy, we must first get a hearing. It is true that at times we will need to be diplomatic. We may have to prepare the ground. We may want to approach a booby-trapped subject like abortion or the draft cautiously. But finally a persuasive writer must be able to make a strong plea. Important points must receive proper **emphasis;** the writer must know how to give full weight to what truly matters.

The authors of the following excerpts know how to state key points emphatically. They know how to make essential points stand out. They know how to sum up important ideas in memorable form—we will remember these ideas and ponder them as they sink in:

> The time to look upon the Mexican American as the poor, uneducated, tortilla-eating peon who is the victim of some fate stemming from Quetzal-coatl's disapproval is over. Mexican Americans are descendants of a proud race. As Americans they deserve their rightful place in the American sun. (Philip D. Ortego)

> Women predominate in the lower-paying, menial, unrewarding, dead-end jobs, and when they do reach better positions, they are invariably paid less than a man gets for the same job. (Shirley Chisholm)

As you write or revise a persuasive paper, ask yourself: Can I point to a passage of the paper that sums up my central message or major plea in a quotable, memorable form? What can I do to highlight it or give it additional force?

(2) *Use language that brings the readers' emotions into play and appeals to their basic values.* It is true that a persuasive writer must know how to present facts that objective readers can verify. But a writer who wants to influence opinions and actions cannot afford to remain neutral and detached, pondering the pros and cons with folded arms. Effective persuasive writing makes strategic use of emotive or connotative language—language that triggers the right attitudes and steers the readers' emotions. A writer attacking the traditional big-car policy of American automakers will not simply refer to "big, powerful cars" but more likely to "road locomo-

tives," "gas guzzlers," "American behemoths," "postwar dinosaurs," or "the world's biggest compacts."

Note: Language charged with strong emotions is a double-edged weapon. It can arouse powerful feelings of solidarity and common purpose in an audience that is already half-convinced. Strong charges and passionate appeals may work well with an "in-group" audience that is more than half-ready to follow the author's lead. However, strong language can easily seem inflammatory and prejudiced to the uncommitted. It may alienate fair-minded readers, and it may inflame the opposition. Avoid personal abuse: *peacenik, do-gooder, redneck,* or *fem-libber.* Avoid sexist condescension (*lady politician*) and racist slurs.

(3) *Dramatize dry facts.* To be persuasive, writers must know how to bring issues to life. They must know how to highlight facts and select striking evidence. They must know how to present examples that will stir sympathy or indignation. Know how to support your main points with a variety of vivid, dramatic material:

- A striking *example* can effectively bring an issue into focus:

    Recently a woman filed a lawsuit because she had slipped into a grave while attending a funeral; after being stuck for half an hour looking up at a coffin suspended overhead, she suffered nightmares, for which the court awarded her $400,000 in damages. In no other country would she have been given the time of day for anything so ridiculous. Nowhere else have personal irresponsibility and the refusal to accept the unavoidable risks of life become so institutionalized that lawyers get their 30 percent regardless, and insurance pays for everything. (Patrick Bogan, "The $310 Million Paranoia Subsidy," *Harper's*)

- Striking *statistics*, strategically used, may help impress a previously indifferent reader.

    The smiling brown face sandwiched between mortarboard and high-necked dark gown is becoming the educational exception, more and more. At rates even worse than in the days of overt discrimination, the American school system is rejecting the Hispanic student. Now, only 55 percent of our Latino youth are graduating from high school. Only 21 percent are entering college. Only 8 percent are completing a four-year curriculum. (Cecilia Preciado Burciaga, "Voices," *Nuestro*)

- Telling *comparisons* can impress the true meaning of facts and figures on readers who have become jaded or blasé. Writing about the amount spent on the trial of a would-be assassin of a President, this writer uses comparison to make the figure meaningful:

Three million dollars would pay the cost to the federal government of 2,380,952 free school lunches for poor children, at $1.26 per lunch. If a similar amount were spent to decide the guilt or innocence of each of the more than 20,000 persons charged with murder or manslaughter and the more than 150,000 charged with using firearms in aggravated assaults in the United States every year, it would add up to more than $500 billion.   (Stuart Taylor, Jr., "Too Much Justice," *Harper's*)

- Revealing *contrasts* can steer the reader's attention in the desired direction:

Over 10,000 people are killed with handguns every year in the United States. Other civilized countries with proper gun control laws, such as Britain and Japan, consider forty deaths a year by handguns excessive. The exact figures on those killed by handguns in a recent year were Great Britain, 8; Japan, 48; Canada, 52; West Germany, 42; and the United States, 10,728.

(4) *Work out an effective overall plan.* Often the basic strategy of a persuasive writer is to go from the simple to the difficult—from what is easy to accept to what is hard to believe. In order to be persuasive, we will often first try to find *common ground* with our readers. We will try to strengthen their trust in our good sense and good faith. Having put our readers in an assenting, receptive mood, we can then hope to take them with us as we go on to the difficult or the new.

In a lecture reprinted later in this book, the American historian Barbara Tuchman set out to counteract the widespread modern pessimism about humanity's potential for good or evil. She assumed that a modern audience would be skeptical about our capacity for dedication and achievement. It would see in much of history a record of violence and corruption. To restore our faith in human nature, Tuchman started her lecture by reminding us of achievements that we are least likely to question. Only then did she go on to the area that many modern readers find disillusioning or demoralizing—political history:

Humanity's Better Moments

- the *exploits of seafarers and explorers* from the Vikings to the explorers of the North American continent
- the *glories of painters and architects*
- the *benefits of modern medicine*
- the *politics of reform,* with the abolitionist movement in England and the United States as an outstanding example
- the *struggle for liberty,* from the Jews fighting the Romans under the leadership of the Maccabees to the American colonists risking their property and their lives

(5) *Use an extended case history when it is the best means of proving your point.* A writer may decide that the best way to prove charges of discrimination or to alert us to the dangers of pollution is to examine one famous case in point in detail. The more earnestly or painstakingly the story is told, the harder it will be for reluctant readers to brush off the author's charges.

The outline of a magazine article on a famous case of environmental pollution may look somewhat like this:

Love Canal and the Poisoning of America

I. Innocent beginnings
(An unfinished canal, left from a period of growth and boosterism, is used as a chemical dump and then filled in; homes and a school are built on or near the site.)

II. First hints of trouble
(Foul-smelling substances are found in backyards and basements; skin rashes and suspicious ailments plague children and adults.)

III. The refusal to believe
(Public officials and corporate officers belittle charges and evade responsibility.)

IV. The emerging truth
(Determined sleuthing reveals the truth as isolated incidents become part of a pattern and the extent of the disaster becomes clear.)

V. Belated remedies
(Half-hearted or belated remedies are applied as victims organize and lawsuits proliferate.)

(6) *Challenge your opposition.* Writers aiming at effective persuasion often find that it is not enough to advance their own cause. They have to counteract opposing arguments. They have to head off rival claims to the reader's allegiance or support. To be persuasive, you will often have to make it your business to know competing proposals or rival claims—and to refute or discredit them if you can.

To help your own position prevail, you may have to do the following:

• Show *weaknesses* or contradictions in your opponents' proposals:

> Any prayer used in a school would have to be composed by a committee and made innocuous enough to satisfy all the different religious groups that make up the population of this republic. Catholics, Protestants, Jews, Buddhists, Moslems, and all the others would have to agree that the language is not propaganda for the opposition. Thus, no mention of Yahweh, Jesus, Buddha, or Mahomet would be possible; we would have some lamebrained little homily with a muttered reference to God.   (Pete Hamill, "Prayers for the Past," *San Francisco Chronicle*)

- Counteract *myths* or wishful thinking by citing contrary facts:

> We never had a country in which every schoolchild said his prayers in a classroom every day. A study made in 1960 by Richard B. Dierenfield of Macalaster College in St. Paul, Minn., showed that 91 percent of Western school systems and 74 percent in the Midwest never had school prayers. There were prayers in Southern schools and schools in the Northeast, but 50 percent of all American public schools had no prayers at all.   (Pete Hamill, "Prayers")

- Point out *conflicts of interest* or ulterior motives:

> In our system of jurisprudence anyone can sue anyone else for practically anything. The real question is, "Can I sue and win?" Increasingly, the answer to that question is—no. Too often litigation *works only to the economic advantage of the attorneys.* The more protracted the litigation, *the more hours are spent and the more fees are generated.* By tacit agreement in the profession, litigation is usually conducted with the old bury-them-in-paperwork sleight of hand. . . . Abraham Lincoln said, "A lawyer's time is *his stock in trade.*" Lawyers today work hard at ensuring a bullish market for that stock.   (Stanley J. Lieberman, "A No-Lose Proposition," *Newsweek*)

Remember, however, that personal attacks often backfire. When you are tempted to belittle and ridicule the opposition, remember the standards of the fair-minded reader. Avoid the appearance of a mere **ad hominem** attack—an attack aimed "at the person" and sidestepping or evading the issues.

To sum up: Persuasion is effective when the reader decides to support a cause, or to agree to a course of action, or to change an attitude. To write persuasively, you have to develop a sense of how your audience is likely to respond to what you say. You have to be able to make a strong plea, using strong language where appropriate to dramatize needs or to express strong feelings. But you also have to be able to approach a subject cautiously, leading up gradually to something difficult or controversial. The more emphatic your writing becomes, the closer you will move to the line where statement becomes overstatement, or where strong assertion turns into exaggeration. An independent and experienced reader resents being pushed or manipulated. The art of writing persuasively is the art of making a strong plea without alienating the intelligent, fair-minded reader.

Prewriting Activities 9

1. Choose a recent commercial, political advertisement, fund-raising letter, or the like that you found exceptionally persuasive—or exceptionally ineffective. Prepare a *critique*—explain and illustrate what makes it good or bad persuasion. (If you can, provide a copy of the original piece for your readers.)

2. Assume you have a last-minute chance to speak up in support of (or in opposition to) a person or proposal that you care about. For instance, imagine a favorite teacher (real person) being denied tenure or in danger of being laid off. Or imagine you have a chance to talk to undecided voters about a favorite candidate in a current or recent election. Or imagine you have a chance to head off an ill-considered scheme affecting your campus or community. Write a *quick* letter—work up a strategy and be as persuasive as you can.

3. In preparation for a persuasive paper, prepare a *profile* of what you would consider a typical or representative reader in a group like the following:
  • a group of local business people
  • art majors
  • a women's caucus on campus
  • local police officers
  • tenants in low-income housing
  • people operating family farms
Do not take too much for granted: Avoid stereotypes or oversimplification. Sketch out major shared attitudes, values, and expectations that you would take into account in addressing the group.

4. Study the following brief report on a familiar controversy. Then write a strong plea designed to persuade ordinary motorists either to support or oppose a compulsory safety device, such as air bags or self-buckling seat belts.

Should the government require that new cars be equipped with air bags—cushions that inflate on impact to protect passengers in a crash? Like nuclear power, this is an issue where reasonable minds may differ, but reasonable minds are hard to find. To Ralph Nader, airbags have provided a litmus test of political virtue ever since the last Corvair rolled off the assembly line in the mid-sixties. Nader bitterly denounced his protégée Joan Claybrook for not immediately requiring the devices when she was director of highway safety for Jimmy Carter. Opponents of airbags see them as the prime example of statist meddling. *Car and Driver*, a magazine for auto enthusiasts, refers to Nader and Claybrook as "Safety Nazis."   ("Harper's Journal," *Harper's*)

5. Record your candid reactions to the following passage. Explain or defend your reactions in some detail. How persuasive is the writer? Then compare your reactions with those of your classmates and discuss differences in the reactions of different readers.

In view of our society's callous unconcern for existing children who are, in fact, unwanted, it is hard to listen tolerantly to the hypocritical cant which defends the "rights" of minute cells of human tissue which have had the mischance to be fertilized. Despite the dramatic gains of genetics in recent years, there will probably always be human beings misshapen in mind or body because of heredity, accident, disease, war, famine, or the lack of loving nurture. To them, a humane people owes the kind of support and rehabilitative effort which is now no more than a utopian dream. Surely it is a form of madness to insist on adding to this still-unaccepted burden responsibility for thousands of children, rejected even before they are born. (Marion K. Sanders, "The Right Not to Be Born," *Harper's*)

Paragraph Practice 9

Write a paragraph in which you commend or attack a current trend or recent innovation. Try to influence the attitudes of undecided or hostile readers. Study and discuss the following paragraph as a possible model.

Snarling Cars

For decades, one of Detroit's major advertising ploys was to market its products as instruments of violence. During the entire postwar period, in fact, Detroit's marketing strategy was not to sell automobiles as sensible family transportation, as one might expect in a reasonably civilized society, but as vehicles of mayhem and destruction. What's in a name? In Detroit's case, plenty. Because over the years, as an auto writer once observed, the very names Detroit managers gave to their cars reveal quite plainly the industry's appeal to motives of violence and aggression. Consider the Oldsmobile *Cutlass*, the Buick *Le Sabre*, the Plymouth *Fury*, the Plymouth *Barracuda*, the Chevrolet Corvette *Stingray*, the Ford Mustang *Cobra*, the American Motors *Matador*, the Mercury *Lynx*, Mercury *Bobcat*, and Mercury *Cougar*—killers all. . . . The theme of violence in these names has a cunning economic logic behind it. As we now know, Detroit management's guiding theology during the postwar era was: big car, big profit; small car, small profit. And what better way to sell big, powerful cars than to link them in the public's mind with the libidinal release of destructive impulses? (Howell Raines, *New Republic*)

BACKGROUND: George F. Will (born 1941) is a widely read conservative columnist who probes the moral issues underlying the passing events of the day. He was born in Champaign, Illinois; he was educated at Trinity College in Connecticut, at Oxford, and at Princeton. He taught politics at several universities before he went to Washington as a congressional aide. He became the Washington editor of the *National Review* in 1973. Will became widely known for his column in the *Washington Post;* within a short time it was syndicated to 275 daily newspapers. At the age of thirty-five, he was awarded the Pulitzer Prize for Distinguished Commentary. A collection of his newspaper and *Newsweek* columns was published in 1978 under the title, *The Pursuit of Happiness, and Other Sobering Thoughts.* He has said that the purpose behind his writing is to look "for the kernel of principle and other significance that exists, recognized or not, inside events, actions, policies, and manners." Will knows how to present strong opinions in a calm, rational manner, drawing on formidable resources of learning and wit.

George F. Will
The Barbarity
of Boxing

GUIDE TO READING: What is Will's strategy for persuading his readers? How does he proceed? What appeals or techniques does he use? What are the basic values or standards that he expects his readers to share?

For 150 years people have been savoring Macaulay's judgment that the Puritans hated bearbaiting not because it gave pain to the bear but because it gave pleasure to the spectators.[1] However, there are moments, and this is one, for blurting out the truth: The Puritans were right. The pain to the bear was not a matter of moral indifference, but the pleasure of the spectators was sufficient reason for abolishing that entertainment.

Now another boxer has been beaten to death. The brain injury he suffered was worse than the injury the loser in a boxing match is supposed to suffer. It is hard to calibrate such things—how hard an opponent's brain should be banged against the inside of his cranium—in the heat of battle.

From time immemorial, in immemorial ways, men have been fighting for the entertainment of other men. Perhaps in a serene, temperate society boxing would be banned along with other blood sports—if, in such a society, the question would even arise. But a step toward the extinction of

[1] [Thomas Babington Macaulay (1800-1859) was a British essayist and historian whose opinions were widely respected by his Victorian audience.]

boxing is understanding why that is desirable. One reason is the physical injury done to young men. But a sufficient reason is the quality of the pleasure boxing often gives to spectators.

There is no denying that boxing like other, better sports, can exemplify excellence. Boxing demands bravery and, when done well, is beautiful in the way that any exercise of finely honed physical talents is. Furthermore, many sports are dangerous. But boxing is the sport that has as its object the infliction of pain and injury. Its crowning achievement is the infliction of serious trauma on the brain. The euphemism for boxing is "the art of self-defense." No. A rose is a rose is a rose, and a user fee is a revenue enhancer is a tax increase, and boxing is aggression.

It is probable that there will be a rising rate of spinal cord injuries and deaths in football. The force of defense players (a function of weight and speed) is increasing even faster than the force of ball carriers and receivers. As a coach once said, football is not a contact sport—dancing is a contact sport—football is a collision sport. The human body, especially the knee and spine, is not suited to that. But football can be made safer by equipment improvements and rules changes such as those proscribing certain kinds of blocks. Boxing is fundamentally impervious to reform.

It will be said that if two consenting adults want to batter each other for the amusement of paying adults, the essential niceties have been satisfied, "consent" being almost the only nicety of a liberal society. But from Plato on, political philosophers have taken entertainments seriously and have believed the law should, too.[2] They have because a society is judged by the kind of citizens it produces, and some entertainments are coarsening. Good government and the good life depend on good values and passions, and some entertainments are inimical to these.

Such an argument cuts no ice in a society where the decayed public philosophy teaches that the pursuit of happiness is a right sovereign over all other considerations; that "happiness" and "pleasure" are synonyms, and that there is no hierarchy of values against which to measure particular appetites. Besides, some persons will say, with reason, that a society in which the entertainment menu includes topless lady mud wrestlers is a society past worrying about.

Sports besides boxing attract persons who want their unworthy passions stirred, including a lust for blood. I remember Memorial Day in the Middle West in the 1950s, when all roads led to the Indianapolis Speedway, where too many fans went to drink Falstaff beer and hope for a crash. But boxing is in a class by itself.

Richard Hoffer of the *Los Angeles Times* remembers the death of Johnny Owen, a young 118-pound bantamweight who died before he had

---

[2][In *The Republic*, the Greek philosopher Plato (428–348 B.C.) describes an imaginary ideal society founded in justice. In *The Republic*, Socrates, Plato's teacher, proposes to outlaw frivolous entertainments and unworthy stories about the gods and traditional heroes.]

fulfilled his modest ambition of buying a hardware store back home in Wales. Hoffer remembers that "Owen was put in a coma by a single punch, carried out of the Olympic (arena) under a hail of beer cups, some of which were filled with urine."

The law cannot prudently move far in advance of mass taste, so boxing 10 cannot be outlawed. But in a world in which many barbarities are unavoidable, perhaps it is not too much to hope that some of the optional sorts will be outgrown.

Using the Dictionary

Will writes in a fairly formal style, with an occasional informal touch. Which of the following do you have to look up?   1. *calibrate* (2)   2. *cranium* (2)   3. *serene* (3)   4. *trauma* (4)   5. *euphemism* (4)   6. *impervious* (5)   7. *nicety* (6)   8. *inimical* (6)   9. *sovereign* (7)   10. *synonym* (7)   11. *hierarchy* (7)   12. *prudently* (10)   13. *barbarity* (10)

The Writer's Agenda

In this piece from his column, Will maintains his image of a writer who knows how to be reasonable while championing strong opinions. How does he make his writing persuasive?

1. Who is the real target of Will's attack—the boxers? the promoters? the audience? Where does he deliver his most telling blow at his chief target?

2. In the early paragraphs, Will uses some very *strong language* to arouse the reader's emotions. Where?

3. What does Will do in this column to maintain the stance of the *reasonable observer* who gives credit where credit is due?

4. For what purpose does Will use his strategic comparison with football?

5. Where and how does the author most directly spell out the principles or *values* underlying his criticism of boxing?

6. What is the position that Will expects his readers to accept? (Is it different from what you had expected? Why or how?)

For Discussion or Writing

7. Do you make a good audience for this column? Do you find Will's argument persuasive? Why or why not?

8. Is it true that football promotes violence by glorifying force rather than skill? Support the charge, or defend the sport against the charge.

9. Argue for or against a ban on boxing—or on hunting as a "blood sport." Try to persuade an audience that is likely to disagree.

10. Is it true that popular sports mirror the moral values of the society in which they flourish? Concentrate on one major sport—or on several that seem to you symbolic or revealing: wrestling, boxing, baseball, bullfighting, or other.

11. Write a paper on "The Barbarity of ...." Fill in a barbaric practice or condition that you strongly feel should be corrected.

Branching Out

12. In recent years, critics have attacked war toys as promoting a war mentality, and Barbie dolls as promoting sexism. Argue against or in defense of one of these, or of another kind of toy that has possible political significance.

BACKGROUND: Fern Kupfer was born in the Bronx, New York, in 1946 and graduated from a college of the State University of New York. After moving to Iowa, she did graduate work at Iowa State University and taught in a community college. In 1982, she published *Before and After Zachariah,* in her words, "a personal narrative about what happens to a family, and to a marriage, when a damaged child is born." She has written for *Redbook* and *Newsweek* and has been praised for her outspokenness and honesty in dealing with a subject often shrouded in euphemisms and taboos. Zachariah was the Kupfer's second child, severely brain-damaged from birth and deteriorating in spite of the best available help.

Fern Kupfer

Institution Is Not a

Dirty Word

GUIDE TO READING: The author of this article champions an unpopular point of view. She tries to change her readers' minds on an emotion-laden subject. What is her strategy? What does she do to counteract the widely accepted opposing view? What does she do to defend and advance her own?

I watched Phil Donahue recently. He had on mothers of handicapped children who talked about the pain and blessing of having a "special" child. As the mother of a severely handicapped six-year-old boy who cannot sit, who cannot walk, who will be in diapers all of his days, I understand the pain. The blessing part continues to elude me—notwithstanding the kind and caring people we've met through this tragedy.

What really makes my jaws clench, though, is the use of the word "special." The idea that our damaged children are "special," and that we as parents were somehow picked for the role, is one of the myths that come with the territory. It's reinforced by the popular media, which present us with heartwarming images of retarded people who marry, of quadriplegics who fly airplanes, of those fortunate few who struggle out of comas to teach us about the meaning of courage and love. I like these stories myself. But, of course, inspirational tales are only one side of the story. The other side deals with the daily care of a family member who might need more than many normal families can give. Parents who endure with silent stoicism or chin-up good humor are greeted with kudos and applause. "I don't know how you do it," the well-wishers say, not realizing, of course, that no one has a choice in this matter. No one would consciously choose to have a child anything less than healthy and normal. The other truth is not spoken aloud: "Thank God, it's not me."

One mother on the Donahue show talked about how difficult it was to ₃
care for her severely brain-damaged daughter, but in the end, she said
serenely, "She gives much more than she takes from our family." And no, she
would never institutionalize her child. She would never "put her away." For
"she is my child," the woman firmly concluded as the audience clapped in
approval. "I would never give her up."

Everyone always says how awful the institutions are. Don't they have ₄
bars on the windows and children lying neglected in crowded wards? Aren't
all the workers sadists, taking direction from the legendary Big Nurse?
Indeed, isn't institutionalizing a child tantamount to locking him away?
Signing him out of your life forever? Isn't it proof of your failure
as a parent—one who couldn't quite measure up and love your child, no
matter what?

No, to all of the above. And love is beside the point. ₅

Our child Zachariah has not lived at home for almost four years. I ₆
knew when we placed him, sorry as I was, that this was the right decision,
for his care precluded any semblance of normal family life for the rest of us.
I do not think that we "gave him up," although he is cared for daily by nurses,
caseworkers, teachers and therapists, rather than by his mother and father.
When we come to visit him at his "residential facility," a place housing 50
severely physically and mentally handicapped youngsters, we usually see
him being held and rocked by a foster grandma who has spent the better
part of the afternoon singing him nursery rhymes. I do not feel that we have
"put him away." Perhaps it is just a question of language. I told another
mother who was going through the difficult decision regarding placement
for her retarded child, "Think of it as going to boarding school rather than
institutionalization." Maybe euphemisms help ease the pain a little bit. But
I've also seen enough to know that institution need not be a dirty word.

The media still relish those institution horror stories: a page-one photo ₇
of a retarded girl who was repeatedly molested by the janitor on night duty.
Oh, the newspapers have a field day with something like that. And that is
how it should be, I suppose. To protect against institutional abuse we need
critical reporters with sharpened pencils and a keen investigative eye. But
there are other scenes from the institution as well. I've seen a young
caseworker talk lovingly as she changed the diapers of a teen-age boy. I've
watched as an aide put red ribbons into the ponytail of a cerebral-palsied
woman, wipe away the drool and kiss her on the cheek. When we bring Zach
back to his facility after a visit home, the workers welcome him with hugs
and notice if we gave him a haircut or a new shirt.

The reporters don't make news out of that simple stuff. It doesn't mesh ₈
with the anti-institutional bias prevalent in the last few years, or the tendency to canonize the handicapped and their accomplishments. This anti-
institutional trend has some very frightening ramifications. We force mental
patients out into the real world of cheap welfare hotels and call it "community placement." We parole youthful offenders because "jails are such danger-

ous places to be," making our city streets dangerous places for the law-abiding. We heap enormous guilt on the families that need, for their own survival, to put their no-longer-competent elderly in that dreaded last stop: the nursing home.

Another danger is that in a time of economic distress for all of us, ₉ funds could be cut for human-service programs under the guise of anti-institutionalization. We must make sure, before we close the doors of those "awful" institutions, that we have alternative facilities to care for the clientele. The humanitarians who tell us how terrible institutions are should be wary lest they become unwilling bedfellows to conservative politicians who want to walk a tight fiscal line. It takes a lot of money to run institutions. No politician is going to say he's against the handicapped, but he can talk in sanctimonious terms about efforts to preserve the family unit, about families remaining independent and self-sufficient. Translated, this means, "You got your troubles, I got mine."

Most retarded people do not belong in institutions any more than most ₁₀ people over 65 belong in nursing homes. What we need are options and alternatives for a heterogeneous population. We need group homes and halfway houses and government subsidies to families who choose to care for dependent members at home. We need accessible housing for independent handicapped people; we need to pay enough to foster-care families to show that a good home is worth paying for. We need institutions. And it shouldn't have to be a dirty word.

Using The Dictionary

Explain ten of the following terms. Which of them have emotional associations or overtones?   1. *myth* (2)   2. *quadriplegic* (2)   3. *stoicism* (2)   4. *kudos* (2)   5. *Big Nurse* (4)   6. *tantamount* (4)   7. *semblance* (6)   8. *euphemism* (6)   9. *canonize* (8)   10. *law-abiding* (8)   11. *clientele* (9)   12. *humanitarian* (9)   13. *sanctimonious* (9)   14. *heterogeneous* (10)   15. *halfway house* (10)

The Writer's Agenda

The author of this article takes on the difficult task of changing the reader's attitudes on an emotion-laden subject. Study her strategy as a persuasive writer:

1. The author first attacks *currently fashionable* attitudes. According to her, how do the media treat the subject of the handicapped, and what are her objections?

2. The author's overall strategy is to *lead up* to an unpopular point of view. Where does she first raise the issue of institutionalization, and how? Where and how does she first state her own point of view?

3. Where and how does Kupfer match her own *personal experience* against the "myths" and images projected by the media?

4. Toward the end of her essay, the author makes charges that serve to *discredit* those who represent the current "anti-institutional" trend. What examples does she cite of ironic contradictions and ulterior motives?

5. How does the author's conclusion appeal to readers who like to find not just grievances or complaints but *positive suggestions* and workable solutions?

6. In the last paragraph, the author's language becomes assertive and insistent. What features of *sentence style* help produce this effect?

For Discussion or Writing

7. Has this article in any way changed your mind? Why or why not? Where is the author most persuasive? Where least? (What kind of reader is most likely or least likely to be persuaded by her article?)

8. What has been your own experience with the central issue raised by this article? What is it like to be handicapped, or to help people cope with their handicaps?

9. Have you yourself encountered evidence of a current "anti-institutional" bias in our society? What causes it? How does it show? To what degree is it justified?

10. Is it true that the media tend to treat the subject of the handicapped in an upbeat or inspirational fashion? What other subjects do the media tend to treat inspirationally?

11. Write a persuasive paper championing an unpopular view or one that many people do not share. Choose a debatable question or controversial issue: school prayer, divorce, homosexuality, police brutality, "debriefing" of converts to religious cults. Try to persuade an audience whose views differ from your own.

WRITERS ON WRITING
Fern Kupfer on Writer and Audience

QUESTION: Did negative responses to your article affect you?

ANSWER: Not really ... except I wrote back to one woman who also had a child who had Down's syndrome and who disagreed strongly with my position. We began corresponding—and eventually became good friends. We each softened our positions through listening to the other.

QUESTION: Did you expect many responses? Did you anticipate negative ones?

ANSWER: I didn't think about responses or worry about the negative ones. It all comes down to having something important to say. I knew many people would disagree with me and my friends warned me— but I didn't want to protect myself because I felt that what I was saying was really terribly important and that other people might be helped by it.

I think a sense of audience comes from having something really important to say. I have received thousands of letters from women, mothers who have handicapped children—these are not writers and many are not even educated. But the letters are eloquent—a strong voice that comes from having something they want to say—a truthfulness. I used the letters in my book [as chapter openings] because they are so beautiful, heartbreaking.

QUESTION: Who was your audience? People with an opposing view?

ANSWER: No, I wasn't trying to change those who chose another route. I was concerned about the stereotypes about institutions—the television and media portrayal of institutions as terrible places. So, I looked at these clichés and was just telling people that this is not the way it is—to challenge the stereotypes and myths about the handicapped.

You know, when someone says out loud what other people have been thinking, it has power. That's what I think happened to me. It was like Betty Friedan in *The Feminine Mystique* when she wrote that she was a housewife with a comfortable income, lovely children, and a nice husband—but she was unhappy and felt guilty for being unhappy. She said what many people were thinking.

QUESTION: Did the responses clarify your thinking or make you change anything or explain it differently?

ANSWER: Not really. The positive ones made me feel good. Often, I heard from professionals who work with handicapped children and who wrote that they had been judgmental about parents who put their children in institutions—and now they understood better.

But sometime the letters really did make me think. I received one from a mother of a handicapped child; she wrote that she "longed to be the girl I used to be," that she would never be the same again. I thought about that—about how any tragedy makes us think about ourselves in before and after terms—before this happened, I was one way, now I am another—so it was really this concept that made me come up with the title for my book: *Before and After Zachariah.*

—From an interview with the editors of *Essay 2*

BACKGROUND: For a generation of readers, Kurt Vonnegut's novels and short stories embodied the psychedelic fantasy, far-out humor, and turned-off antiestablishment satire of the sixties and early seventies. Kurt Vonnegut, Jr., was born in 1922 in Indianapolis; he was drafted while in college during World War II. In the spring of 1945, he was a prisoner of war in Germany and witnessed the fire bombing of Dresden, which killed an estimated 135,000 people. Years later, this experience became the center of his classic antiwar novel, *Slaughterhouse Five* (1969). Its hero, Billy Pilgrim, like other Vonnegut characters, tries to maintain his sanity in a world gone mad. The following excerpt is from a speech Vonnegut gave at the 92nd Street YM-YWHA in New York City, printed in *The Nation* in January 1984. The speech shows a master satirist in action, employing his far-ranging imagination and gift for zany humor to persuade his audience.

Kurt Vonnegut, Jr.
War Preparers
Anonymous

GUIDE TO READING: **Satire** uses humor as a means of persuasion, holding abuses up to ridicule and scorn. In this excerpt, how does a master satirist use his imagination to dramatize the issue—to bring it to life? How does he use humor to sway the audience?

What has been America's most nurturing contribution to the culture of this planet so far? Many would say jazz. I, who love jazz, will say this instead: Alcoholics Anonymous.

I am not an alcoholic. If I were, I would go before the nearest AA meeting and say, "My name is Kurt Vonnegut. I am an alcoholic." God willing, that might be my first step down the long, hard road back to sobriety.

The AA scheme, which requires a confession like that, is the first to have any measurable success in dealing with the tendency of some human beings, perhaps 10 percent of any population, to become addicted to substances that give them brief spasms of pleasure but in the long term transmute their lives and the lives of those around them into ultimate ghastliness.

The AA scheme, which, again, can work only if the addicts regularly admit that this or that chemical is poisonous to them, is now proving its effectiveness with compulsive gamblers, who are not dependent on chemicals from a distillery or a pharmaceutical laboratory. This is no paradox. Gamblers, in effect, manufacture their own dangerous substances. God help them, they produce chemicals that elate them whenever they place a bet on simply anything.

If I were a compulsive gambler, which I am not, I would be well advised to stand up before the nearest meeting of Gamblers Anonymous and declare, "My name is Kurt Vonnegut. I am a compulsive gambler."

Whether I was standing before a meeting of Gamblers Anonymous or Alcoholics Anonymous, I would be encouraged to testify as to how the chemicals I had generated within myself or swallowed had alienated my friends and relatives, cost me jobs and houses, and deprived me of my last shred of self-respect.

I now wish to call attention to another form of addiction, which has not been previously identified. It is more like gambling than drinking, since the people afflicted are ravenous for situations that will cause their bodies to release exciting chemicals into their bloodstreams. I am persuaded that there are among us people who are tragically hooked on preparations for war.

Tell people with that disease that war is coming and we have to get ready for it, and for a few minutes there they will be as happy as a drunk with his martini breakfast or a compulsive gambler with his paycheck bet on the Super Bowl.

Let us recognize how sick such people are. From now on, when a national leader, or even just a neighbor, starts talking about some new weapons system that is going to cost us a mere $29 billion, we should speak up. We should say something on the order of, "Honest to God, I couldn't be sorrier for you if I'd seen you wash down a fistful of black beauties with a pint of Southern Comfort."

I mean it. I am not joking. Compulsive preparers for World War III, in this country or any other, are as tragically and as repulsively addicted as any stockbroker passed out with his head in a toilet in the Port Authority bus terminal.

For an alcoholic to experience a little joy, he needs maybe three ounces of grain alcohol. Alcoholics, when they are close to hitting bottom, customarily can't hold much alcohol.

If we know a compulsive gambler who is dead broke, we can probably make him happy with a dollar to bet on who can spit farther than someone else.

For us to give a compulsive war-preparer a fleeting moment of happiness, we may have to buy him three Trident submarines and a hundred intercontinental ballistic missiles mounted on choo-choo trains.

If Western Civilization were a person—

If Western Civilization, which blankets the world now, as far as I can tell, were a person—

If Western Civilization, which surely now includes the Soviet Union and China and India and Pakistan and on and on, were a person—

If Western Civilization were a person, we would be directing it to the nearest meeting of War Preparers Anonymous. We would be telling it to stand up before the meeting and say, "My name is Western Civilization. I am a compulsive war-preparer. I have lost everything I ever cared about. I should have come here long ago. I first hit bottom in World War I."

Western Civilization cannot be represented by a single person, of course, but a single explanation for the catastrophic course it has followed during this bloody century is possible. We the people, because of our ignorance of the disease, have again and again entrusted power to people we did not know were sickies. [18]

And let us not mock them now, any more than we would mock someone with syphilis or smallpox or leprosy or yaws or typhoid fever or any of the other diseases to which the flesh is heir. All we have to do is separate them from the levers of power, I think. [19]

And then what? [20]

Western Civilization's long, hard trip back to sobriety might begin. [21]

Using the Dictionary

Check the following as needed: 1. *sobriety* (2) 2. *transmute* (3) 3. *compulsive* (4) 4. *pharmaceutical* (4) 5. *paradox* (4) 6. *ravenous* (7) 7. *repulsive* (10)

The Writer's Agenda

Vonnegut's task is to break through the crust of apathy—to make his audience pay renewed attention to a problem that they are likely to consider beyond their control. Answer the following questions:

1. How well does Vonnegut's basic **analogy** fit? Do you find it persuasive? Why or why not?

2. A writer may set out to shock and provoke his readers—or to put them first in an assenting mood. Which is Vonnegut's strategy? What makes his opening paragraphs eloquent or effective?

3. What makes the gambling analogy an effective **transition** or bridge to his real topic?

4. Where and how does Vonnegut use the vocabulary of disease? With what effect?

5. In this piece, what are some extremely *informal* touches? (Why do you think the author includes them?) Where and how does his style nevertheless get solemn and insistent?

For Discussion or Writing

6. What kind of readers would make a good audience for Vonnegut? (What kind of readers would be the *wrong* audience?)

7. Many people are fatalistic about the possibility of nuclear war, feeling that there is nothing anyone can do. Do you share this view? Attack or defend this attitude.

8. For you, is humor (like Vonnegut's) appropriate or inappropriate in serious political discussion?

9. Much political discussion in recent years has focused on the choice between "guns or butter," between national defense and domestic social programs. Take a stand on this issue. Try to persuade a hostile or uncommitted audience.

10. Write a satirical or imaginative attack on a current danger to personal health or the welfare of society, such as alcoholism, drug abuse, smoking, gambling, or a faulty diet. Try a fresh, imaginative approach to reach an audience that is likely to be tired of the subject.

Branching Out

11. What do *you* think has been an outstanding American contribution to the culture of this planet?

BACKGROUND: Martin Luther King, Jr. (1929–68) was born in Atlanta, Georgia, and became a Baptist minister like his father. He was the pastor of the Dexter Avenue Baptist Church in Montgomery, Alabama, when a black woman challenged the back-of-the-bus rule of the city's bus system. King organized the successful 381-day boycott of the segregated transit system that marked the birth of the modern civil rights movement, of which he became the acknowledged leader. He founded the Southern Christian Leadership Conference in 1957. Millions were stirred by broadcasts of his sermons and embraced the philosophy of nonviolent revolution that he preached in books like *Letter from Birmingham Jail* (1963) and *Why We Can't Wait* (1964). The movement he led helped bring about the 1964 Civil Rights Act and the 1965 Voting Rights Act. His eloquence and his example inspired a new generation of black leaders, from Andrew Young, who became U.S. ambassador to the United Nations and later mayor of Atlanta, to Julian Bond, Shirley Chisholm, and Jesse Jackson. King was jailed many times, spied on by government agents, stabbed and reviled; he was finally struck down by the bullet of an assassin in Memphis on April 4, 1968. "I Have a Dream" is the speech he gave in Washington, D.C., in August 1963 after he led a march of 200,000 people to commemorate the one hundredth anniversary of Lincoln's proclamation freeing the slaves.

Martin Luther King, Jr.

I Have a Dream

GUIDE TO READING: King's eloquence gave hope and a new sense of dignity to millions of black people while at the same time it stirred the conscience of the white majority. Where in this speech is he speaking most directly to his black followers? Where is he speaking most directly to the white majority? Where does he appeal most strongly to shared common values?

Five score years ago, a great American, in whose symbolic shadow we stand, signed the Emancipation Proclamation. This momentous decree came as a great beacon light of hope to millions of Negro slaves who had been seared in the flames of withering injustice. It came as a joyous daybreak to end the long night of captivity. 1

But one hundred years later, we must face the tragic fact that the Negro is still not free. One hundred years later, the life of the Negro is still sadly crippled by the manacles of segregation and the chains of discrimination. One hundred years later, the Negro lives on a lonely island of poverty in the midst of a vast ocean of material prosperity. One hundred years later, the Negro is still languishing in the corners of American society and finds himself an exile in his own land. So we have come here today to dramatize an appalling condition. 2

In a sense we have come to our nation's capital to cash a check. When 3 the architects of our republic wrote the magnificent words of the Constitution and the Declaration of Independence, they were signing a promissory note to which every American was to fall heir. This note was a promise that all men would be guaranteed the unalienable rights of life, liberty, and the pursuit of happiness.

It is obvious today that America has defaulted on this promissory note 4 insofar as her citizens of color are concerned. Instead of honoring this sacred obligation, America has given the Negro people a bad check; a check which has come back marked "insufficient funds." But we refuse to believe that the bank of justice is bankrupt. We refuse to believe that there are insufficient funds in the great vaults of opportunity of this nation. So we have come to cash this check—a check that will give us upon demand the riches of freedom and the security of justice. We have also come to this hallowed spot to remind America of the fierce urgency of *now.* This is no time to engage in the luxury of cooling off or take the tranquilizing drugs of gradualism. *Now* is the time to make real the promises of Democracy. *Now* is the time to rise from the dark and desolate valley of segregation to the sunlit path of racial justice. *Now* is the time to open the doors of opportunity to all of God's children. *Now* is the time to lift our nation from the quicksands of racial injustice to the solid rock of brotherhood.

It would be fatal for the nation to overlook the urgency of the moment 5 and to underestimate the determination of the Negro. This sweltering summer of the Negro's legitimate discontent will not pass until there is an invigorating autumn of freedom and equality. 1963 is not an end, but a beginning. Those who hope that the Negro needed to blow off steam and will now be content will have a rude awakening if the nation returns to business as usual. There will be neither rest nor tranquility in America until the Negro is granted his citizenship rights. The whirlwinds of revolt will continue to shake the foundations of our nation until the bright day of justice emerges.

But there is something I must say to my people who stand on the warm 6 threshold which leads into the palace of justice. In the process of gaining our rightful place we must not be guilty of wrongful deeds. Let us not seek to satisfy our thirst for freedom by drinking from the cup of bitterness and hatred. We must forever conduct our struggle on the high plane of dignity and discipline. We must not allow our creative protest to degenerate into physical violence. Again and again we must rise to the majestic heights of meeting physical force with soul force. The marvelous new militancy which has engulfed the Negro community must not lead us to a distrust of all white people, for many of our white brothers, as evidenced by their presence here today, have come to realize that their destiny is tied up with our destiny and their freedom is inextricably bound to our freedom. We cannot walk alone.

And as we walk, we must make the pledge that we shall march ahead. 7

We cannot turn back. There are those who are asking the devotees of civil rights, "When will you be satisfied?" We can never be satisfied as long as the Negro is the victim of the unspeakable horrors of police brutality. We can never be satisfied as long as our bodies, heavy with the fatigue of travel, cannot gain lodging in the motels of the highways and the hotels of the cities. We cannot be satisfied as long as the Negro's basic mobility is from a smaller ghetto to a larger one. We can never be satisfied as long as a Negro in Mississippi cannot vote and a Negro in New York believes he has nothing for which to vote. No, no, we are not satisfied, and will not be satisfied until justice rolls down like waters and righteousness like a mighty stream.

I am not unmindful that some of you have come here out of great trials 8
and tribulations. Some of you have come fresh from narrow jail cells. Some of you have come from areas where your quest for freedom left you battered by the storms of persecution and staggered by the winds of police brutality. You have been the veterans of creative suffering. Continue to work with the faith that unearned suffering is redemptive.

Go back to Mississippi, go back to Alabama, go back to South Caro- 9
lina, go back to Georgia, go back to Louisiana, go back to the slums and ghettos of our northern cities, knowing that somehow this situation can and will be changed. Let us not wallow in the valley of despair.

I say to you today, my friends, that in spite of the difficulties and 10
frustrations of the moment I still have a dream. It is a dream deeply rooted in the American dream.

I have a dream that one day this nation will rise up and live out the true 11
meaning of its creed: "We hold these truths to be self-evident; that all men are created equal."

I have a dream that one day on the red hills of Georgia the sons of 12
former slaves and the sons of former slaveowners will be able to sit down together at the table of brotherhood.

I have a dream that one day even the state of Mississippi, a desert state 13
sweltering with the heat of injustice and oppression, will be transformed into an oasis of freedom and justice.

I have a dream that my four little children will one day live in a nation 14
where they will not be judged by the color of their skin but by the content of their character.

I have a dream today. 15

I have a dream that one day the state of Alabama, whose governor's 16
lips are presently dripping with the words of interposition and nullification, will be transformed into a situation where little black boys and black girls will be able to join hands with little white boys and white girls and walk together as sisters and brothers.

I have a dream today. 17

I have a dream that one day every valley shall be exalted, every hill and 18
mountain shall be made low, the rough places will be made plain, and the

crooked places will be made straight, and the glory of the Lord shall be revealed, and all flesh shall see it together.

This is our hope. This is the faith with which I return to the South. With 19 this faith we will be able to hew out of the mountain of despair a stone of hope. With this faith we will be able to transform the jangling discords of our nation into a beautiful symphony of brotherhood. With this faith we will be able to work together, to pray together, to struggle together, to go to jail together, to stand up for freedom together, knowing that we will be free one day.

This will be the day when all of God's children will be able to sing with 20 new meaning

> My country, 'tis of thee,
> Sweet land of liberty,
>   Of thee I sing:
> Land where my fathers died,
> Land of the pilgrims' pride,
> From every mountain-side
>   Let freedom ring.

And if America is to be a great nation this must become true. So let 21 freedom ring from the prodigious hilltops of New Hampshire. Let freedom ring from the mighty mountains of New York. Let freedom ring from the heightening Alleghenies of Pennsylvania!

Let freedom ring from the snowcapped Rockies of Colorado! 22

Let freedom ring from the curvaceous peaks of California! 23

But not only that; let freedom ring from Stone Mountain of Georgia! 24

Let freedom ring from Lookout Mountain of Tennessee! 25

Let freedom ring from every hill and molehill of Mississippi. From 26 every mountainside, let freedom ring.

When we let freedom ring, when we let it ring from every village and 27 every hamlet, from every state and every city, we will be able to speed up that day when all of God's children, black men and white men, Jews and Gentiles, Protestants and Catholics, will be able to join hands and sing in the words of the old Negro spiritual, "Free at last! free at last! thank God almighty, we are free at last!"

Using the Dictionary

King uses a number of terms that have played a major role in American history or politics. How does your dictionary define each of the following? (For two or three of these, write a one-paragraph definition that sums up what the term has meant in American life.)   1. *emancipation* (1)   2. *segregation* (2)   3. *gradualism* (4)   4. *brotherhood* (4)   5. *militancy* (6)   6. *civil rights* (7)   7. *police brutality* (7)   8. *the American dream* (10)   9. *interposition* (16)   10. *nullification* (16)

The Writer's Agenda

In writing this famous speech, Martin Luther King had a double aim: to mobilize the aspirations of the black community, and to appeal to the conscience of white Americans. Answer the following questions:

1. Examine King's use of vivid **figurative language** to dramatize the evil of racism and to give emotional force to his appeals:

   a. Point out and discuss several striking imaginative comparisons (for instance, the "tranquilizing drugs of gradualism"). What is their emotional or inspirational appeal?
   b. Point out and discuss examples of imaginative comparisons that are **antithetical**—lined up as balanced opposites (daybreak/night, island/ocean). What is their appeal or effect?
   c. As an example of a **sustained or extended metaphor,** examine the bad-check analogy in the fourth paragraph. How is it carried through into related details? What is its persuasive effect?

2. King appeals to *shared values* by quoting from or alluding to famous American historical documents, the Bible, and Negro spirituals (as well as Shakespeare, adapting his "the winter of our discontent"). What are some striking examples? What do you think is their effect on the audience?

3. Where does King speak most directly to "my people"? What warnings or cautions does he address to them? Where does he most forcefully give voice to their grievances?

4. In what parts of the speech does King address himself most directly to the *white majority?* What warnings does he address to them? In your judgment, how or where does he appeal most effectively to their consciences?

5. In the second half of his speech, King makes extensive use of **emphatic repetition** as a traditional oratorical device. Examine his repetition of words and phrases as well as his use of parallel sentence structure. What makes his use of repetition varied, emphatic, and eloquent rather than monotonous?

For Discussion or Writing

6. King said in this speech that his dream of the future was "a dream deeply rooted in the American dream." What did he mean?

7. King preached nonviolent revolution, adapting the philosophy of nonviolence taught by Gandhi in India during the struggle for independence from British rule. Argue for or against nonviolence as a means of social reform or political revolution. Make your arguments persuasive for a skeptical or reluctant audience.

8. In his speech, King addressed himself to members of America's minorities who were able to vote but who believed they had "nothing for which to vote." In our society today, what is the power of the right to vote? Make your argument persuasive for a skeptical audience.

9. Since King's death, various initiatives or efforts designed to combat segregation have been much debated: affirmative action, racial quotas, busing, and the like. Argue for or against one such major initiative, trying to persuade a skeptical or hostile audience.

10. What has done most to shape your own views of racial tension, racial prejudice, or discrimination? What has been the role of books, television, movies? Give a vivid account of experiences that had a major impact on you.

11. Many observers feel that apathy has to a large extent replaced the moral fervor of the early days of the civil rights movement. Examine some current editorials or short articles that deal with social issues or social injustice. How persuasive are they? Do they seem too bland, conciliatory, or uninvolved?

STUDENT MODEL 9

FOR READING: Study the following short selection as a possible model for writing of your own. How do you react to it overall? What makes it interesting or effective? Answer the following more specific questions:

1. (PURPOSE) What was the writer trying to do?
2. (AUDIENCE) What kind of reader would make a good reader for this selection?
3. (SOURCES) Where did the writer turn for material?
4. (THESIS) Does the selection have a central idea or unifying thesis?
5. (STRUCTURE) What is the author's overall plan or strategy?
6. (STYLE) What makes the piece effective or memorable (for instance, striking details, memorable phrases)?
7. (REVISION) What do you think the writer could or should have done differently?

Sally Finnegan (student editorial)
Getting MADD

Three years ago a 23-year-old man with a blood alcohol nearly three 1 times the 0.10 legal limit, crashed head-on into a car carrying Jackie Masso, her husband Patrick, her daughter Patty, and a friend at 4:30 in the afternoon. Today Jackie Masso faces two to three more operations on her legs. Her husband must get his lungs pumped about three times a year because of congestive heart failure and her 21-year-old daughter, after having her crushed nose broken and reset two times, faces yet more plastic surgery.

Masso got MADD. She and her husband are co-presidents of the local 2 chapter of Mothers Against Drunk Driving, which has 400—500 paying members and 1,000 on a mailing list.

Masso said she has noticed something in the many courtrooms where ₃ she has sat with families who have had a son or daughter killed or badly injured. She has noticed that the drunken drivers with multiple offenses tend to always blame their car, the weather, or the other driver but never themselves.

"I've never heard a drunken driver say he's sorry," she said. ₄

If drunken drivers are not sorry, at least MADD has helped to make ₅ drunken driving penalties stiffer and raised public awareness. *Time* magazine reported May 20 that deaths of drunken drivers had decreased by 32 percent since 1980. But still too many teen-age and college-age people persist in drinking and driving.

Time reported in the same article that one out of five freshmen at the ₆ University of Minnesota admitted to being a heavy drinker, which was two times the 1975 rate. There are an estimated 10 million alcoholics in the United States, with a growing number belonging to the younger age brackets.

Many high schools now have Students Against Drunk Driving orga- ₇ nizations. SADD requires the teenager to sign a contract with an adult, a parent, a teacher, or an older friend pledging to call the adult if ever the teenager finds himself too drunk to drive. In return, the adult pledges to pick up the drunken teenager, reserving any questions for a later time.

The closest formalized approach to alcohol awareness we have on ₈ campus is within the Greek system. Kevin Rice, president of the Intra-fraternity Council, and Kathy Rivers, president of the Panhellenic, said that individual houses coordinate alcohol awareness programs through their national offices. Rivers, who estimates that there are more than 300 women within the Panhellenic, said each house presents at least one alcohol awareness program per semester.

Rice said emphasis on alcohol within fraternities has decreased the ₉ past few years. Fraternities now keep rush dry until the weekend parties. "Alcohol is not necessarily a motivating factor anymore," he said. Russ Lunsford, public information officer for the UPD, does not yet have last year's statistics for alcohol-related arrests, but, as he said, "One drunken driver is one too many."

Masso said she had never been involved in anything like MADD before ₁₀ that drunken driver hit her car head-on at 70—75 mph. "I'm not sitting back," she said. "I'm doing something." We can do something before a drunken driver hits another one of us head-on.

(From *Spartan Daily*)

FOR WRITING: Write a letter to the editor of your local newspaper. Try to counteract or overcome public apathy on a topic that is of special concern to you or to people close to you.

ADDITIONAL WRITING TOPICS 9

Persuasion

A. Assume that your audience is a group of young voters about to vote for the first time. Choose an issue that you care about. Persuade the group to vote your way. Choose an issue like the following:

1. a higher or lower driving age
2. a higher or lower drinking age
3. using state lotteries to help finance public education
4. banning smoking in public places
5. ending registration for the draft
6. legalizing marijuana
7. allowing religious groups to use campus facilities
8. abolishing the death penalty
9. mandatory retirement age for teachers
10. keeping ROTC off the campus

B. Write a persuasive letter designed to overcome the resistance of a reluctant or hostile reader. Advocate a cause or proposal close to your heart. Work out a strategy for bringing the reader over to your side. For instance, do one of the following:

1. Persuade a friend who likes the indoors to go hiking, backpacking, mountain climbing, or the like.
2. Persuade a friend who is a tightwad to contribute money to help protect wildlife.
3. Persuade a conservative owner of a business to employ more women as managers.
4. Persuade a rock and roll fan to become interested in classical music.
5. Persuade a hard-nosed business type to come to an art museum with you.
6. Persuade a relative opposed to your friendship (or intended marriage) with someone of a different ethnic or religious background to join the two of you for a meal.
7. Persuade a nonathletic friend to support the idea of a new sports arena or stadium.
8. Persuade the city council to bar zoning changes that would permit rapid growth.
9. Persuade a developer to help save low-income housing.
10. Persuade the college administration to ban or permit alcohol in campus eateries.

C. Write a guest editorial aimed at a group of which you are a member or whose aims and policies you normally support. Try to dissuade the group from a policy or course of action that you consider ill-advised. For instance, do one of the following:

1. Dissuade your church group from supporting censorship.

2. Dissuade a women's group from supporting a current policy.

3. Dissuade fellow environmentalists from opposing a new freeway or ski resort.

4. Dissuade fellow blacks from supporting a position that might alienate whites.

5. Dissuade fellow students from campaigning for more flexible graduation requirements.

PART
THREE
AREAS
FOR
WRITING

In the final part of this book, you will find essays that represent major areas of interest, major areas for writing. Writers do not write in a vacuum. They have a grounding in a special area; they develop their expertise in a special field; they cater to an audience that shares a common background or a common commitment. Writers of nonfiction prose may write as nature writers, as science writers, or as historians. They may write as journalists— reporters, feature writers, copy writers, columnists. They may write as reviewers—music critics, drama critics, film critics, restaurant critics.

Your own writing in college will not be limited to English classes. You may encounter writing situations and writing tasks across the curriculum. You may become familiar with the special requirements, varying styles, and characteristic expectations that help shape writing in different fields. The units that follow will ask you to read and write in several major areas:

- SCIENCE. A society hooked on science and technology urgently needs writers who can mediate between the experts and a lay audience.

- MEDIA. Some of the most colorful writing we encounter looks into the mirror that the media hold up to American life and American popular culture.

- HISTORY. Some of the most sobering writing we read explores the lessons we should learn from the past and the directions they point for the future.

The final unit in this part presents CLASSIC ESSAYS by writers whose alert intelligence and creative imagination enable them to provide the link between expository prose and imaginative literature.

10

SCIENCE WRITING

Writing to Inform

OVERVIEW

The first duty of a writer is to shed light on the subject. The more technical the subject, the more the task of enlightening the reader may become the writer's chief concern. Much writing on topics in science, technology, or medicine aims to make expert knowledge understandable to the general reader. To make us understand the subject, the writer presents essential facts, explains what is new or difficult, and shows important connections. We judge such writing by how successfully it makes technical information accessible to the newcomer or the outsider.

PURPOSE The technology that science has created and the theories it has constructed shape how we live and what we think. But although science reaches everywhere into our lives, the advance of specialized scientific knowledge has far outstripped the science education of the ordinary citizen. Much of what goes on in science is a mystery to anyone outside a small group of highly trained specialists, united by a special kind of dedication to and absorption in their work. In our science-conscious and technology-dominated society, there is a constant need for writing that can bridge the gap between the specialist and the general public.

AUDIENCE Science writers and "popularizers" write for a lay audience as experts making what is new or difficult accessible to the outsider. Typically they assume an audience that is curious and interested—not entirely uninitiated but having, say, the science background of the typical college graduate. Their writing supposes readers who are interested in science and technology as voters, consumers, or simply as intelligent and concerned citizens. Writers aiming at this kind of audience need to show their respect for the reader's intelligence. They must show that their central aim is to enlighten rather than to manipulate, cajole, or bamboozle the reader.

BENEFITS FOR THE WRITER (1) Writing about technical subjects provides us with training in *objectivity*. It can help teach us a respect for facts, careful attention to detail, and a preference for theories that can be tested or verified. It can help make us wary of superficial impressions, wild guesses, and prejudice.

(2) Writing about technical subjects for the general reader, we learn to respect the needs and limitations of the audience. We learn to serve the *reader's needs*—to explain what is different, to lay out information in an intelligible pattern, to use parallels and analogies that will tie difficult concepts to the world of familiar experience.

WRITER'S GUIDE 10

Writing to Inform

In much informative writing, the writer serves as a guide whose task it is to do justice to the subject at hand. Such writing has to be **objective**. It concentrates on showing and explaining what is "out there." It plays down personal, subjective thoughts, feelings, and preferences (although it often reflects the author's fascination with or commitment to the subject). Observe the following guidelines when writing papers whose major purpose is to inform and explain:

(1) *Show your respect for observable facts.* Reassure readers who want to know: On what kind of observation are these data based? How could this statement be verified? Whenever possible, show your capacity for patient first-hand observation, as did the author of the following passage:

> Once, years ago, I saw red blood cells whip, one by one, through the capillaries in a goldfish's transparent tail. The goldfish was etherized. Its head lay in a wad of wet cotton wool; its tail lay on a tray under a dissecting microscope.... The red blood cells in the goldfish's tail streamed and coursed through narrow channels invisible save for glistening threads of thickness in the general translucency. They never wavered or slowed or ceased flowing.... They streamed redly around, up, and on, one by one, more, and more, without end.   (Annie Dillard, *Pilgrim at Tinker Creek*)

(2) *Include essential information.* Ask yourself: "What does the reader need to know? What parts does the reader need to know in order to understand the whole? What basic steps does the reader have to trace in order to see how a process works?" Give your reader the answers to the basic fact-finding questions: What? Where? When? How? Why? The following description of comets provides essential information about what they are, when and where they are observed, and how they behave and why:

(Where is it found?)   Edmund Halley (1656–1742) was the first to state that comets are members of the solar system, traveling in elliptical orbits. Billions of comets continually circle the sun like a halo at distances of over 10 billion miles. Occasionally one is "kicked" out of its track by the gravitational attraction of a star or planet. It may then be wrenched into a new smaller orbit which makes it travel into the interior of the solar system, looping around the sun....

(What is it made
up of?)   A comet is merely an accumulation of frozen gases and grit, no more than a few miles in diameter, with a density much less than that of water....

(How does it work?)

Off by itself in space, a comet has no tail. But when it approaches the sun, solar energy vaporizes its outer layers to form a swollen head and then drives some of this material away to form a tail of incandescence pointing out toward space. . . .

(What is striking evidence or a striking example?)

The Great Comet of 1843 had a tail that streamed out more than 500 million miles. . . .

(3) *Build on what is familiar.* Go from the simple to the difficult. Authors who write about technical subjects and yet reach large audiences know how to start from reassuringly familiar everyday knowledge. They constantly return to it for comparison and illustration.

Here is a famous science writer talking about the protein molecules that are the basic building blocks of our bodies. Although the information becomes technical, everyday comparisons help us see what it means in terms that we can understand:

> To begin with, proteins consist of large molecules. Even a protein molecule of only average size is made up of a conglomeration of perhaps four hundred thousand atoms. *In comparison, a water molecule is made up of three atoms and a molecule of table sugar of forty-five atoms.*
>
> Atoms within the protein molecule are arranged in combinations called amino acids, each of which is made up of anywhere from ten to thirty atoms. The amino acids are strung together, *like beads in a necklace*, to form a protein molecule. . . .
>
> The interesting thing is that if two protein molecules are made up of the same number of the same types of amino acids, they will *still* be different if the order in which those amino acids occur in the chain differs. It is *as if you were to make a necklace out of twenty beads—five red, five yellow, five blue, and five green. Depending on the order in which you arranged them you could make twelve billion different patterns.*   (Isaac Asimov, *Is Anyone There?*)

(4) *Proceed in a systematic fashion.* The less familiar the subject is to the reader, the more the writer has to be sure to cover essential parts of the subject in a clear, step-by-step order. Writing whose main aim is to inform is usually more rigorously organized than other kinds. The businesslike, systematic, step-by-step development is a signal to readers that they need to pay *attention*: If they blink, they might miss an important step. Often, the writer will be tracing a chain of events that will not make sense if important links are left out.

Even when the writer is not tracing a step-by-step process or a chain of cause and effect, informative writing usually has the kind of systematic forward movement in which the different stages are not really optional. Instead, one step leads to and helps us understand another. For instance, a writer may trace the same principle through several related applications. In the following excerpt, the writer shows the same basic reaction at work in three different examples. But he does so in order to *lead up* from familiar ones to one that is less familiar and especially important:

GENERAL PRINCIPLE: First example (vaccination)	*The body builds up special defensive proteins (antibodies) that react with foreign molecules and neutralize them.* This is one of its best defenses against invading bacteria and viruses. Once someone has formed an antibody against the measles virus, he is immune to further attacks....
Second example (allergies)	A negative instance of the same use of proteins is the fact that the body may also accidentally become sensitive to foreign substances that are fairly harmless in themselves; to the proteins of certain types of pollen, for instance, or to certain types of food. A person will in such a case suffer from hay fever or food allergy....
Third example (rejection of grafts)	A particular antibody can always distinguish between a foreign substance and the molecules present in the body it belongs to. If an antibody can distinguish between two proteins, those two proteins must in some way be different. That being so, no two human beings, except for identical twins, can have proteins that are completely alike. The proof of this is that a skin graft will fail unless it is taken from another part of the patient's own body, or, at furthest remove, from the body of his identical twin, if he is lucky enough to have one. (Isaac Asimov, *Is Anyone There?*)

(5) *Explain necessary technical terms.* We cannot say much about a complex subject like body chemistry without using technical terms, any more than an auto mechanic can function efficiently without using terms like *carburetor, differential, valve,* and *gasket.* A writer must select technical terms that are clearly useful or necessary and must make sure to explain them and illustrate their use. When introducing several important technical terms at a time, the writer must make a special effort to provide enough commonsense description to keep the terms clear:

> The heart has four chambers—two atria and two ventricles—and four valves, two of which control the flow of blood from atrium to ventricle, and two of which control the pumping of the blood from the ventricles out into the arteries. The atria—the two chambers at the top of the heart—are *little more than reservoirs* for blood returning via the veins to the heart. They collect blood returned to the heart from the body and lungs, and deliver it to the heart's larger active chamber below. The first set of valves simply insures that the blood *flows only one way*, from the atria to the ventricles. The ventricles are *the blood pumps* that do the true work of the heart. These two larger

chambers contract forcefully to pump the blood to the lungs and throughout the body.

To sum up: Practice in informative writing is good training for writers who otherwise might tend to take too much for granted. Trying to explain a technical subject to the nonspecialist, we learn to pay attention to the legitimate needs and expectations of the reader. We learn something about the difficulties of trying to say what we mean, but also about the satisfaction that comes from reaching an audience.

Prewriting Activities 10

1. Find and photocopy a textbook passage that explains a basic scientific principle or concept exceptionally well. Choose a passage on a topic like gravity, magnetism, combustion, inertia, friction, catalysts. Explain what use the writer makes of explanation, examples, comparison, contrast, or other helps for the reader.

2. Write as a guide for the interested consumer: Explain the advantages of an advanced camera over a simple one, of a diesel engine, of four-wheel traction, or of some recent technical innovation. Make sure you explain technical points to a lay audience.

3. Prepare a *preliminary collection* of material on the future of robots and robotics. Draw on a variety of possible sources: personal observation, science fiction, current newspaper and magazine articles about robots in factories, books by authorities on the subject.

Paragraph Practice 10

Write a paragraph to bring clearly into focus what we mean by a familiar term from the world of science or technology. For instance, you may choose a term like *genetics, biochemistry, electricity, chemotherapy, automation.* Make use of explanation, example, comparison, contrast, analogy, or whatever will help you to clarify the key principle for the reader. Study and discuss the following paragraph as a possible model.

In Defense of Technology

Before there were human beings there was technology. Fossil remains of our predecessors dating from more than a million years ago show that our remote ancestors made tools out of pebbles and animal bones. And that's what technology is: toolmaking. The human animal doesn't have the speed of a horse, the fighting teeth of a chimpanzee, the wings of an eagle, the claws of a tiger, or the protective fleece of a sheep. But we have discovered (or invented) technology. We make tools, where other species make physiological adaptations. We have fire and all the energy-producing engines stemming from it. We travel faster than the horse, fly higher than the eagle, fight much more devastatingly than any predator, and protect our bodies with not only sheep's wool, but artificial fabrics as well. One man alone can't kill a mammoth. But a handful of men, armed with nothing more sophisticated than stone-tipped spears and fire, apparently drove the mammoths into extinction. By the time the last glaciation dwindled, humankind was the supreme ruler of every land mass on Earth, except isolated Antarctica. And we ruled with fire, spear, awl, scraper: technology.   (Ben Bova, "Where Do We Go *From?*" *Analog*)

BACKGROUND: Lewis Thomas (born 1913) has had a distinguished career as a research professor and administrator at university medical centers and medical schools. He became dean at Yale University Medical School and president of the Memorial Sloan-Kettering Cancer Center in New York. Through widely read articles and books, Thomas has become known as a writer serving as interpreter and guide to readers bewildered by modern science. He has made his special interest— biology, the study of the origins and workings of life—fascinating to a large public. He does not merely share scientific information; he makes us think about the motives of the scientist, the nature of science, and its role in our culture. He once described the urge to know that underlies true scientific work as a deeply placed human instinct. He said, "I don't know of any other human occupation in which the people engaged in it are so caught up, so totally preoccupied, so driven beyond their strength and resources." In many of his essays, Thomas appears as the opposite of the narrow specialist; he explores the border area between reason and imagination, between fact and myth. Many of his essays first appeared in the *New England Journal of Medicine.* They were collected in *The Lives of a Cell: Notes of a Biology Watcher* (1974) and *The Medusa and the Snail* (1979).

Lewis Thomas
Ant City and
Human Society

GUIDE TO READING: In reading this essay, pay special attention to the perspective the author sets up in the opening paragraph: What does the introduction make you expect—on what does it focus your attention as a reader? Then, as you read on, take stock of the similarities between insects and human beings, both considered as "social animals." At the same time, take stock of the differences that set them apart. What is the central difference that concerns the author?

Not all social animals are social with the same degree of commitment. ₁ In some species, the members are so tied to each other and interdependent as to seem the loosely conjoined cells of a tissue. The social insects are like this. They move, and live all their lives, in a mass; a beehive is a spherical animal. In other species, less compulsively social, the members make their homes together, pool resources, travel in packs or schools, and share the food, but any single one can survive solitary, detached from the rest. Others are social only in the sense of being more or less congenial, meeting from time to time in committees, using social gatherings as *ad hoc* occasions for feeding and breeding. Some animals simply nod at each other in passing, never reaching even a first-name relationship.

It is not a simple thing to decide where we fit, for at one time or 2 another in our lives we manage to organize in every imaginable social arrangement. We are as interdependent, especially in our cities, as bees or ants, yet we can detach if we wish and go live alone in the woods, in theory anyway. We feed and look after each other, constructing elaborate systems for this, even including vending machines to dispense ice cream in gas stations, but we also have numerous books to tell us how to live off the land. We cluster in family groups, but we tend, unpredictably, to turn on each other and fight as if we were different species. Collectively, we hanker to accumulate all the information in the universe and distribute it around among ourselves as though it were a kind of essential foodstuff, ant-fashion. (The faintest trace of real news in science has the action of a pheromone, lifting the hairs of workers in laboratories at the ends of the earth.) But each of us also builds a private store of his own secret knowledge and hides it away like untouchable treasure. We have names to label each as self, and we believe without reservation that this system of taxonomy will guarantee the entity, the absolute separateness of each of us, but the mechanism has no discernible function in the center of a crowded city; we are essentially nameless, most of our time.

Nobody wants to think that the rapidly expanding mass of mankind, 3 spreading out over the surface of the earth, blackening the ground, bears any meaningful resemblance to the life of an anthill or hive. Who would consider for a moment that the more than 3 billion of us are a sort of stupendous animal when we become linked together? We are not mindless, nor is our day-to-day behavior coded out to the last detail by our genomes. Nor do we seem to be engaged together, compulsively, in any single, universal, stereotyped task analogous to the construction of a nest. If we were ever to pull all our brains together in fact, to make a common mind the way the ants do, it would be an unthinkable thought, way over our heads.

Social animals tend to keep at a particular thing, generally something 4 huge for their size; they work at it ceaselessly under genetic instructions and genetic compulsion, using it to house the species and protect it, assuring permanence.

There are, to be sure, superficial resemblances in some of the things 5 we do together, like building glass and plastic cities on all the land and farming under the sea, or assembling in armies, or landing samples of ourselves on the moon, or sending memoranda into the next galaxy. We do these together without being quite sure why, but we can stop doing one thing and move to another whenever we like. We are not committed or bound by our genes to stick to one activity forever, like the wasps. Today's behavior is no more fixed than when we tumbled out over Europe to build cathedrals in the twelfth century. At that time we were convinced that it would go on forever, that this was the way to live, but it was not; indeed, most of us have already forgotten what it was all about. Anything we do in this transient, secondary social way, compulsively and with all our energies but only for a brief period of our history, cannot be counted as social behavior in the biological sense. If we can turn it on and off, on whims, it isn't likely that our genes are providing the detailed instructions. Constructing Chartres[1] was good for our minds, but we found that our lives went on, and it is no more likely that we will find survival in Rome plows or laser bombs, or rapid mass transport or a Mars lander, or solar power, or even synthetic protein. We do tend to improvise things like this as we go along, but it is clear that we can pick and choose.

For practical purposes, it would probably be best for us not to be 6 biologically social, in the long run. Not that we have a choice, of course, or even a vote. It would not be good news to learn that we are all roped together intellectually, droning away at some featureless, genetically driven collective work, building something so immense that we can never see the outlines. It seems especially hard, even perilous, for this to be the burden of a species with the unique attribute of speech, and argument. Leave this kind of life to the insects and birds, and lesser mammals, and fish.

Using the Dictionary

How much help does your dictionary give you with *technical terms*? Compare the treatment of the following specialized terms in two college-level dictionaries. Which dictionary provides more help for the general reader? How or why? Check the following: 1. *ad hoc* (1)   2. *species* (2)   3. *pheromone* (2)   4. *taxonomy* (2)   5. *genome* (3)   6. *genetic* (4)   7. *gene* (5)   8. *galaxy* (5)   9. *laser* (5)   10. *protein* (5)

The Writer's Agenda

The author of this essay makes us aware of striking similarities in the behavior of "social animals" and human beings. But his final aim is to show a key difference that sets social animals and human beings apart. Answer the following questions:

1. In the opening paragraph, the author distinguishes *four kinds* of social animals. What are the four kinds, and what sets them apart?

2. How does the author prepare us from the beginning for the later comparison and contrast with human behavior? Point out and discuss the terms that are taken from the sphere of human life and here applied to animals.

3. In the second paragraph, the author begins to make us aware of some of the *surface similarities* between human beings and social animals. What are they?

4. In the second paragraph, the author pairs the similarities between human and animal life with facts that point the opposite way. What are the *differences* that he mentions in this paragraph?

[1][The cathedral at Chartres, built between 1130 and 1260, is one of the most famous examples of medieval Gothic architecture.]

5. In the second half of this essay, the author closes in on what to him is the most important difference between the social animals and human society. Explain the *basic difference* in your own words. What are some of the key terms that the author uses to make the distinction? What are key examples that he uses to prove his point?

6. In the final paragraph, the author most clearly goes beyond scientific description to *judgments of value*. What are the judgments he makes here? Show how his attitudes and preferences are reflected in strongly **connotative** words that he uses in this conclusion.

7. Lewis Thomas is a writer who knows how to be serious without being glum. Point out passages or expressions in this essay that show his ability to provide a lighter touch.

For Discussion or Writing

8. How much background does a reader need to bring to this essay?

9. How basically alike or how fundamentally different are we when compared with our animal kindred? What similarities between the lives of ants or bees and human life seem most striking or fundamental to you?

10. What is the key feature that sets human beings apart from animals? Discuss some of the different possible answers to this question, or defend your own.

11. Thomas says that not all social animals "are social with the same degree of commitment." Apply the same perspective to human beings. Choose two groups of people that you know well. Compare and contrast them on the basis of how social they are—and how closely they interact with others. The two groups you choose could be age groups, religious or ethnic groups, occupational groups, or the like.

Branching Out

12. There has been much recent research into the behavior patterns of animals in the wild—wolves, lions, orangutans. Choose one such species and report on recent research.

13. There has been much controversy over the necessity and abuses of animal experiments. Research the topic. Prepare a paper in which you present your findings and take a stand.

BACKGROUND: Rachel L. Carson (1907–64) was a dedicated scientist with a gift for sharing not only scientific knowledge but also her fascination with the beauty and mystery of nature. She studied biology at the Pennsylvania College for Women and continued her work as a biologist at Johns Hopkins University in Baltimore and at the Marine Biological Laboratory at Woods Hole, Massachusetts. She instructed and delighted many readers with her books about the "mystery and meaning of the sea": *The Sea Around Us* (which won the National Book Award in 1951), *Under the Sea Wind,* and *The Edge of the Sea.* Her classic *Silent Spring* (1962) predicted a future in which our remaining wildlife has been destroyed by the heedless use of pesticides; it became a call to arms in the crusade to save the environment. Her chief target was DDT, a powerful insecticide that had been spectacularly successful against such scourges as malaria, carried by mosquitoes. However, DDT was eventually banned because of the poisonous concentrations built up as the chemical traveled up the food chain through insects to birds and mammals. The following essay is part of chapter 2 of *Silent Spring.*

Rachel Carson

Our War

Against Nature

GUIDE TO READING: In recent years, much attention has focused on the unexpected or harmful results that are the *unintended* by-products of human interference in the workings of nature. In reading this essay, pay special attention to the cause-and-effect relationships traced by the author—those that are part of the workings of nature, and those that result from human intervention.

It took hundreds of millions of years to produce the life that now inhabits the earth—eons of time in which that developing and evolving and diversifying life reached a state of adjustment and balance with its surroundings. The environment, rigorously shaping and directing the life it supported, contained elements that were hostile as well as supporting. Certain rocks gave out dangerous radiation; even within the light of the sun, from which all life draws its energy, there were short-wave radiations with power to injure. Given time—time not in years but in millennia—life adjusts, and a balance has been reached. For time is the essential ingredient; but in the modern world there is no time.

The rapidity of change and the speed with which new situations are created follow the impetuous and heedless pace of man rather than the deliberate pace of nature. Radiation is no longer merely the background radiation of rocks, the bombardment of cosmic rays, the ultraviolet of the sun that have existed before there was any life on earth; radiation is now the unnatural creation of man's tampering with the atom. The chemicals to which life is asked to make its adjustment are no longer merely the calcium and silica and copper and all the rest of the minerals washed out of the rocks and carried in rivers to the sea; they are the synthetic creations of man's inventive mind, brewed in laboratories, and having no counterparts in nature.

To adjust to these chemicals would require time on the scale that is nature's; it would require not merely the years of a man's life but the life of generations. And even this, were it by some miracle possible, would be futile, for the new chemicals come from our laboratories in an endless stream; almost five hundred annually find their way into actual use in the United States alone. The figure is staggering and its implications are not easily grasped—500 new chemicals to which the bodies of men and animals are required somehow to adapt each year, chemicals totally outside the limits of biologic experience.

Among them are many that are used in our war against nature. Since the mid-1940's over 200 basic chemicals have been created for use in killing insects, weeds, rodents, and other organisms described in the modern vernacular as "pests"; and they are sold under several thousand different brand names.

These sprays, dusts, and aerosols are now applied almost universally to farms, gardens, forests, and homes—nonselective chemicals that have the power to kill every insect, the "good" and the "bad," to still the song of birds and the leaping of fish in the streams, to coat the leaves with a deadly film, and to linger on in soil—all this though the intended target may be only a few weeds or insects. Can anyone believe it is possible to lay down such a barrage of poisons on the surface of the earth without making it unfit for all life? They should not be called "insecticides," but "biocides."

The whole process of spraying seems caught up in an endless spiral. Since DDT was released for civilian use, a process of escalation has been going on in which ever more toxic materials must be found. This has happened because insects, in a triumphant vindication of Darwin's principle of the survival of the fittest, have evolved super races immune to the particular insecticide used, hence a deadlier one has always to be developed—and then a deadlier one than that. It has happened also because destructive insects often undergo a "flareback," or resurgence, after spraying, in numbers greater than before. Thus the chemical war is never won, and all life is caught in its violent crossfire.

Along with the possibility of extinction by nuclear war, the central problem of our age has therefore become the contamination of our total environment with such substances of incredible potential for harm—substances that accumulate in the tissues of plants and animals and even penetrate the germ cells to shatter or alter the very material of heredity upon which the shape of the future depends.

Some would-be architects of our future look toward a time when it will be possible to alter the human germ plasm by design. But we may easily be doing so now by inadvertence, for many chemicals, like radiation, bring about gene mutations. It is ironic to think that man might determine his own future by something so seemingly trivial as the choice of an insect spray.

All this has been risked—for what? Future historians may well be amazed by our distorted sense of proportion. How could intelligent beings seek to control a few unwanted species by a method that contaminated the entire environment and brought the threat of disease and death even to their own kind? Yet this is precisely what we have done. We have done it, moreover, for reasons that collapse the moment we examine them. We are told that the enormous and expanding use of pesticides is necessary to maintain farm production. Yet is our real problem not one of *overproduction*? Our farms, despite measures to remove acreages from production and to pay farmers *not* to produce, have yielded such a staggering excess of crops that the American taxpayer by 1962 is paying out more than one billion dollars a year as the total carrying cost of the surplus-food storage program. And is the situation helped when one branch of the Agriculture Department tries to reduce production while another states, as it did in 1958, "It is believed generally that reduction of crop acreages under provisions of the Soil Bank will stimulate interest in use of chemicals to obtain maximum production on the land retained in crops."

All this is not to say there is no insect problem and no need of control. I am saying, rather, that control must be geared to realities, not to mythical situations, and that methods employed must be such that they do not destroy us along with the insects.

The problem whose attempted solution has brought such a train of disaster in its wake is an accompaniment of our modern way of life. Long before the age of man, insects inhabited the earth—a group of extraordinarily varied and adaptable beings. Over the course of time a small percentage of the more than half a million species of insects have come into conflict with human welfare in two principal ways: as competitors for the food supply and as carriers of human disease.

Disease-carrying insects become important where human beings are crowded together, especially under conditions where sanitation is poor, as in time of natural disaster or war or in situations of extreme poverty and deprivation. Then control of some sort becomes necessary. It is a sobering fact, however, that the method of massive chemical control has had only limited success, and also threatens to worsen the very conditions it is intended to curb.

Under primitive agricultural conditions the farmer had few insect problems. These arose with the intensification of agriculture—the devotion of immense acreages to a single crop. Such a system set the stage for explosive increases in specific insect populations. Single-crop farming does not take advantage of the principles by which nature works; it is agriculture as an engineer might conceive it to be. Nature has introduced great variety into the landscape, but man has displayed a passion for simplifying it. Thus we undo the built-in checks and balances by which nature holds the species within bounds. One important natural check is a limit on the amount of suitable habitat for each species. Obviously then, an insect that lives on wheat can build up its population to much higher levels on a farm devoted to wheat than on one in which wheat is intermingled with other crops to which the insect is not adapted.

The same thing happens in other situations. A generation or more ago, 14 the towns of large areas of the United States lined their streets with the noble elm tree. Now the beauty they hopefully created is threatened with complete destruction as disease sweeps through the elms, carried by a beetle that would have only limited chance to build up large populations and to spread from tree to tree if the elms were only occasional trees in a richly diversified planting.

Another factor in the modern insect problem is one that must be 15 viewed against a background of geologic and human history: the spreading of thousands of different kinds of organisms from their native homes to invade new territories. This worldwide migration has been studied and graphically described by the British ecologist Charles Elton in his book *The Ecology of Invasions*. During the Cretaceous Period, some hundred million years ago, flooding seas cut many land bridges between continents and living things found themselves confined in what Elton calls "colossal separate nature reserves." There, isolated from others of their kind, they developed many new species. When some of the land masses were joined again, about 15 million years ago, these species began to move out into new territories—a movement that is not only still in progress but is now receiving considerable assistance from man.

The importation of plants is the primary agent in the modern spread of 16 species, for animals have almost invariably gone along with the plants, quarantine being a comparatively recent and not completely effective innovation. The United States Office of Plant Introduction alone has introduced almost 200,000 species and varieties of plants from all over the world. Nearly half of the 180 or so major insect enemies of plants in the United States are accidental imports from abroad, and most of them have come as hitchhikers on plants.

In new territory, out of reach of the restraining hand of the natural 17 enemies that kept down its numbers in its native land, an invading plant or animal is able to become enormously abundant. Thus it is no accident that our most troublesome insects are introduced species.

These invasions, both the naturally occurring and those dependent on 18 human assistance, are likely to continue indefinitely. Quarantine and massive chemical campaigns are only extremely expensive ways of buying time. We are faced, according to Dr. Elton, "with a life-and-death need not just to find new technological means of suppressing this plant or that animal";

instead we need the basic knowledge of animal populations and their relations to their surroundings that will "promote an even balance and damp down the explosive power of outbreaks and new invasions."

Much of the necessary knowledge is now available but we do not use it. We train ecologists in our universities and even employ them in our governmental agencies but we seldom take their advice. We allow the chemical death rain to fall as though there were no alternative, whereas in fact there are many, and our ingenuity could soon discover many more if given opportunity. [19]

It is not my contention that chemical insecticides must never be used. I do contend that we have put poisonous and biologically potent chemicals indiscriminately into the hands of persons largely or wholly ignorant of their potentials for harm. We have subjected enormous numbers of people to contact with these poisons, without their consent and often without their knowledge. If the Bill of Rights contains no guarantee that a citizen shall be secure against lethal poisons distributed either by private individuals or by public officials, it is surely only because our forefathers, despite their considerable wisdom and foresight, could conceive of no such problem. [20]

I contend, furthermore, that we have allowed these chemicals to be used with little or no advance investigation of their effect on soil, water, wildlife, and man himself. Future generations are unlikely to condone our lack of prudent concern for the integrity of the natural world that supports all life. [21]

Using the Dictionary

Check the following specialized or technical terms.   1. *eon* (1)   2. *millennium* (1)   3. *bombardment* (2)   4. *silica* (2)   5. *toxic* (6)   6. *resurgence* (6)   7. *plasm* (8)   8. *mutation* (8)   9. *habitat* (13)   10. *Cretaceous* (15)

The Writer's Agenda

In this essay, the author projects the "shape of the future" on the basis of what has happened in the past and of what is happening now. Answer the following questions:

1. In the introductory paragraphs, Carson sets up the basic *contrast* between the workings of nature and the effects of human intervention. What are the crucial differences? What are her key examples?

2. Where does the author first state her central thesis? At what other points in the essay do you find emphatic or eloquent restatements of her central idea?

3. According to the author, what causes the "endless spiral," or escalation, in the use of pesticides?

4. The expanding use of pesticides is often justified by urgent need. How does the author deal with this justification?

5. In a central portion of this essay, the author traces our current insect problems to our human tampering with the "built-in checks and balances" of nature. What are her key examples? Explain the causes and effects at work in each case.

6. Toward the end of her essay, Carson strongly implies that alternatives exist to the massive use of pesticides. What are they?

For Discussion or Writing

7. In the controversies that followed the publication of *Silent Spring*, environmentalists have been labeled "one-sided," "biased," "unrealistic," and "alarmist." Does this essay by Carson seem to you objective or biased, balanced or exaggerated? Where and how?

8. Plagues and blights figure prominently in the earliest written records going back to biblical times. Choose one that has recently been in the news: the gypsy moth, elm disease, pigeons, rats, cockroaches, the medfly, or the like. Investigate the cause-and-effect relationships involved in its appearance and in efforts to combat it.

9. Carson said in *Silent Spring* that "only within the moment of time represented by the present century" has one species—ours—acquired the power to alter the nature of our world. Investigate the cause-and-effect relationships involved in one prominent example of this power: acid rain, dust bowls, "dead" lakes, the growth of deserts, or the like.

10. In recent years, public opinion has become vividly aware of the unintended consequences or undesirable side effects of well-intentioned actions and projects. Focus on one major area, such as law, foreign policy, or medicine. Discuss examples (or one extended example) of good intentions followed by unintended consequences.

BACKGROUND: Isaac Asimov (born 1920) is one of this country's leading authors of factual science writing as well as of science fiction. He came to New York City from Russia with his immigrant parents when he was three years old. He went to high school in Brooklyn, and he graduated from Columbia University with a degree in chemistry when he was nineteen. He became a professor of biochemistry at the Boston University School of Medicine but soon started to devote most of his time to writing. "From an early age," he says, "I had known I was a writer." As a boy, Asimov had become fascinated with early science fiction magazines such as *Amazing Stories* when his father would not let him read gory dime-store novels. He started his own career as a writer by publishing science fiction on topics including robots, time travel, and life on other planets. Many of his over 160 books, however, are nonfiction, explaining topics "on the frontiers of science" to the general reader. He says about his work as a science writer: "I can read a dozen dull books and make one interesting book out of them. I'm on fire to explain, and happiest when it's something reasonably intricate which I can make clear step by step."

Isaac Asimov

Nuclear Fusion

GUIDE TO READING: As you read Asimov's essay, pay special attention to how he sizes up the needs of the reader. What, in the judgment of the author, does the nonspecialist need to know and to have explained? What familiar or everyday knowledge does the author build on? Which points become clear to you; which remain confusing, and why?

The world faces a crisis that may destroy civilization in our own 1 lifetime. It is usually referred to as an energy crisis, but it isn't. It is an oil crisis. The earth's oil wells may begin to run dry in 30 years, and without oil it would seem that the industrial world will clank to a grinding halt and that there will be no way in which the teeming population of the world could be supported.

Yet who says oil is the only source of energy? It is, at present, the most 2 convenient source; at present, the most versatile. Matters do not, however, have to stay in the present.

The early decades of the 21st century may see oil supplies at a useless 3 trickle and yet find energy plentiful and electricity coursing through the nerves and veins of industry. With plentiful, unending electricity, we could even manufacture our own oil to fill indispensable needs: Electricity can break down water to hydrogen and oxygen; the oxygen can be discarded, and the hydrogen can be combined with carbon dioxide from the air to form gasoline. The gasoline can then be burned and will combine with the discarded oxygen to form water and carbon dioxide again.

Nothing will be used up but electricity, and the electricity can come from the greatest and most copious source of energy on our planet—the hydrogen in seawater. That hydrogen represents the great ark in which humanity can ride out the oil shortage that now threatens to overwhelm us and come to rest finally on the quiet uplands of energy plenty.

There is a catch. The ark is not yet quite within reach. Our hands still grope for it, but we cannot yet squeeze the energy out of hydrogen.

The simplest way of getting energy out of hydrogen is to combine it with oxygen—to let it burn and deliver heat. Such a process, however, involves merely the outermost fringe of the hydrogen atom and delivers only a tiny fraction of the energy store available at its compact "nucleus."

Something other than hydrogen-burning—something much more dramatic—takes place at the center of the sun. Under enormous gravitational pressures, the substance at the sun's core is squeezed together, raising the temperature there to a colossal 15 million degrees Centigrade (24 million degrees Fahrenheit).

At such pressures and temperatures, the very atoms of matter smash to pieces. Their outer shells break away and expose the tiny nuclei at the center, which then drive into each other at thousands of miles per second and sometimes stick. When hydrogen nuclei stick together to form the slightly larger nuclei of helium atoms, the process is called "hydrogen fusion."

Every second, 650 million tons of hydrogen are fusing into 645.5 million tons of helium at the sun's center. This process produces energy. Each missing 4.5 million tons per second represents the energy that pours out of the sun in all directions. A very small fraction is intercepted by the earth, and on that energy all life is supported.

Though it takes an incredible amount of hydrogen fusion each second to support the sun, there is so much hydrogen in that giant object that, even after some 5 billion years, it is still mostly hydrogen. The sun can continue to produce energy for perhaps 7 billion more years before its fusion mechanism begins to falter.

Can we somehow take advantage of this process on earth?

The trouble is we can't duplicate the conditions at the center of the sun in the proper way. To begin with, we need enormous temperatures. One way of achieving such temperatures is to explode an "atomic bomb" that is powered by uranium fission. For just a brief period of time, temperatures in the millions of degrees are produced at the center of that explosion. If hydrogen in some appropriate form is present there, it will fuse. The result is that the atomic bomb becomes the trigger for the greater blast of a "hydrogen bomb."

Naturally, we can't run the world by exploding hydrogen bombs. We [13] want *controlled* fusion—the kind that produces energy a little bit at a time in usable, nondestructive quantities.

One way would be to start with a small quantity of hydrogen and heat [14] it until it fuses. There would only be a small amount of energy produced. This could be bled away while the new hydrogen is added to the mix to undergo fusion in its turn.

Heating hydrogen to the required temperature isn't easy, but it can be [15] done by electric currents or by pumping in energetic subatomic particles. The trouble is that hydrogen expands as it's heated, and its atoms drift irretrievably away in all directions. We must hold the hydrogen in place while it is being heated. But how? The sun holds its hydrogen in place with its enormous gravitational field, but we can't imitate the sun's gravity on earth.

Nor can we force the hydrogen to remain in place by keeping it in a [16] container. The heat might cause the container to vaporize. On the other hand, if we kept the container cool while the hydrogen heated up, the hydrogen would lose heat again upon contact with the cool container.

One possibility is to use a magnetic field. A magnetic field is not matter [17] and is neither hot nor cold. As the hydrogen is heated, its atoms break down to electrically charged fragments, and these are repelled by the magnetic field. The fragments can't break through the magnetic field and must stay in place.

The problem is designing a magnetic field of the proper shape and [18] intensity that will remain stable and not spring a leak. It's not an easy job. Scientists in the U.S., Great Britain and the Soviet Union have been working at it for nearly 30 years. The best device proposed thus far is the "tokamak," first developed in the Soviet Union.

But even a tokamak won't do the job for ordinary hydrogen. In the [19] center of the sun, a temperature of 15 million degrees Centigrade is sufficient because the hydrogen is squeezed together very densely. On earth we must work with much thinner gas, and that requires still higher temperatures. Fortunately, there is a kind of hydrogen easier to fuse called deuterium. Only one out of every 6500 hydrogen atoms is deuterium, but even so there is enough in each gallon of seawater to equal the energy supplied by burning 300 gallons of gasoline. Since there are 3.6 quintillion gallons of seawater on earth, there is enough deuterium to last billions of years at the present rate of energy use.

The temperature required can be lowered further if a still-rarer kind of [20] hydrogen called tritium is added to the deuterium. Tritium is radioactive and hardly occurs in nature, but it can be manufactured in the laboratory. If a quantity of deuterium-tritium mixture is made dense enough, heated hot enough and kept in confinement long enough, it will fuse. There are well-worked-out figures for what is needed for all three conditions, and scientists have been edging toward the critical combination. Recent work with tokamaks at Princeton University and the Massachusetts Institute of Technology has confirmed that fusion induced by magnetic confinement is a real possibility—once a better tokamak can be built. But this, experts say, is still many years away.

But magnetic confinement isn't the only route to fusion power. It's only needed when the hydrogen is heated slowly and would therefore expand and drift away while it is being heated. 21

Suppose the hydrogen were heated very rapidly. It might then reach fusion temperature so rapidly that the hydrogen has no time to expand before it starts fusing. That's what happens in a hydrogen bomb. The uranium fission develops its high temperature so rapidly that any hydrogen present fuses before it can scatter. 22

We can't use a fission bomb for controlled fusion, however. Some other way must be found to raise the temperature very rapidly. One way is to make use of a laser. Lasers, first developed in 1960, produce light in a very tight beam. The total energy may not be unusually great, but the beam can be focused on such a microscopic point that the concentrated energy raises the temperature at the point to millions of degrees in a fraction of a second. 23

Imagine a mixture of deuterium and tritium inside a tiny, thin-walled glass bubble. If the bubble is struck simultaneously by a number of laser beams from different directions, the heating takes place all around the outer skin of the bubble. What expansion there is forces the gas upward. The inner portion of the bubble goes way up in density, further up in temperature, and begins to fuse. 24

We can imagine bubble after bubble dropping into position and being fused by accurately timed bursts of laser light. Work is underway at the University of California's Lawrence Livermore Laboratory to determine the feasibility of laser fusion. 25

Of course, it takes considerable energy to keep the lasers going, and they are expensive devices. Simpler and more efficient might be beams of high-energy subatomic particles such as electrons. We still haven't reached controlled fusion in this fashion either. Larger, more reliable lasers are needed—or more powerful electron beams. 26

Still, at the rate we are going now, it seems that sometime before the mid-1980s, one or the other of the methods—magnetic fields, lasers or electron beams—will work. Perhaps all three will work. 27

And how exciting that would be. We have atomic power now in the form of uranium fission, but hydrogen fusion would be much better: 28

• Fission uses uranium and plutonium as fuel—rare metals that are hard to get and handle. Fusion uses hydrogen, easy to obtain and handle. 29

• Fission must work with large quantities of uranium or plutonium, so runaway reactions can take place by accident and cause damage. Fusion works with tiny quantities of hydrogen at one time, so even runaway fusions would produce only a small pop. 30

• Fission produces radioactive ash, which can be extremely danger- 31
ous and may not be disposed of safely. Fusion produces helium, which is
completely safe; plus neutrons and tritium, which can be used up as fast as
they are produced.

• Finally, fission only produces a 10th as much energy as fusion, 32
weight for weight.

Of course, even after we finally attain controlled fusion in the labora- 33
tory, it may take as long as 30 years to translate that into large fusion-power
stations. There may be many engineering difficulties between a small demonstration that pleases scientists and a large, reliable supply that runs the
world.

It may well be 2020, then, before we are a fusion society. It would be 34
wise to conserve oil supplies and to substitute other energy sources (coal,
shale, wind, flowing water, tides, hot springs, and so on) to keep us going
until fusion can take over. And we might also strive to develop solar energy,
making use of the nuclear fusion power that already exists and that we call
the sun.

Using the Dictionary

How much help does your dictionary give you with basic scientific terms? Select ten
such terms from this essay and check them in your dictionary. For each, prepare a
one-sentence definition for the general reader.

The Writer's Agenda

Asimov starts from a familiar problem, presents his own solution, and then systematically examines the difficulties that need to be overcome. Answer the following
questions:

1. Asimov starts by correcting a *misconception* about the problem to be
solved. What is the misconception, and how does he correct it?

2. According to Asimov, how can we make gasoline from water and how does
the sun generate energy from hydrogen? (What imaginative comparisons or figures
of speech help set the positive, optimistic tone for this section of the essay?)

3. What *difficulties* and possible solutions do we have to consider when
trying to duplicate on earth the way the sun produces energy? Outline and explain
these for the nonspecialist. (Draw on the concrete expressive language and everyday comparisons used by the author.)

4. According to Asimov, what are the *advantages* nuclear fusion would have
when compared with nuclear fission? Outline them and explain them to the nonspecialist as clearly as you can.

5. The essay concludes with some final *cautions* or warnings. What are they?

For Discussion or Writing

6. When you read this essay as a nonspecialist reader, what parts became especially clear for you, and why? What parts remained difficult or confusing, and why?

7. In most Western countries, there is now strong opposition to nuclear power. What are the sources of that opposition? What forms does it take?

8. Do you think Asimov's essay would reassure or otherwise influence readers opposed to nuclear energy? Why or why not?

9. Fears about the safety of nuclear installations come to a head on occasions like the accidents at Three Mile Island and Chernobyl or the licensing of the Diablo Canyon nuclear plant in California. Study and present some basic technical information that would help a voter understand some of the safety issues involved.

10. At times the media present alarming reports on such topics as public health hazards or the dangers of mind control or genetic manipulation. Do research on one such topic, and use the results to enlighten readers who lack the technical or scientific background to understand the complex issues involved. Investigate a topic like the following:

- splicing of genes
- biochemical causes of mental illness
- harmful side effects of a medication or therapy
- health hazards caused by asbestos or another widely used material

---

WRITERS ON WRITING

Isaac Asimov on Writing to Inform

QUESTION: You are a successful writer of science fiction, something most people consider far more exciting than nonfiction. Yet you write an enormous amount of nonfiction. What is its appeal for you?

ANSWER: I think the nonfiction is more exciting—and more important, too. When I write matters on straight science, I'm hoping that more people will understand science, will appreciate it. That's important— for the future of the world. When I write science fiction, I try to get across something about science, but I don't expect people will concentrate on it.

QUESTION: How do you decide on or develop your topics for the nonfiction articles?

ANSWER: Sometimes I'm asked to write something—"Would you write a book on Haley's comet, because it is returning next year?" If I feel like it, I do it. Sometimes they ask me to write on something that doesn't interest me very much or about which I know very little, and then I refuse to do it. Sometimes I write a book because I am driven to do it by myself. I wrote a two-volume book on Shakespeare, and I didn't know if anyone would publish it. But I wrote it because I'm interested in that subject.

QUESTION: Students envy such freedom of choice.

ANSWER: I didn't always have it; I earned the right to choose my own subjects after twenty years of writing—it took me that long to earn my living as a writer, too. This didn't come easily to me.

QUESTION: What assumptions do you make about your general reading audience—the non-science types?

ANSWER: I assume they're interested in what I'm writing about—or at least interested to hear what I have to say. I don't write down to them. I don't expect them to be stupid. I expect them to be intelligent.

QUESTION: Is part of your purpose when you do this writing (such as "Nuclear Fusion") that you'll increase your reader's interest in the subject as well as her understanding?

ANSWER: Yes. In other words, if they feel they are a little bit interested, I want them to be more interested once they've read the article than when they started. I want them to sense the excitement of science. I want them to feel the pleasure of arousing and, in part at least, satisfying their curiosity. Ideally, I would hope that when they have finished some book of mine, that they'll want to find out more.

QUESTION: I read that you became interested in writing about scientific principles when you realized how much you enjoyed explaining them to your family.

ANSWER: It wasn't exactly my family. I was at a party at a time when I was doing postdoctoral work. Some person asked me casually what my subject was. I said I was investigating antimalarials and started explaining. I got lost! I disregarded the fact that it was a social gathering—everyone seemed interested, so I gave a lecture. Then I decided, why don't I write this?

QUESTION: How do you know where to start when explaining a scientific idea?

ANSWER: I suppose everyone works out his own way. I usually take the historical approach because that's what happens in real life. What the first notions were, why it wasn't the final solution—and little by little I get into the hard part.

QUESTION: Do you use the historical approach even when you are explaining a process, such as how something works?

ANSWER: Oh yes. If you are going to describe how the brain works, even though nobody really knows, you can start with Aristotle who thought the brain was merely an air conditioning device to cool you down. Then you ask why it needs to be so large when all it's needed for is to cool blood. And why is it so protected—more than any other organ? Then you carry on like that. You raise questions and then show how different people showed possible answers.

The difficulty with starting off with "This is how the brain works" is that it somehow sounds like it was handed down from Mount Sinai. People are much more interested in how you came to know about it, what started people thinking a certain way.

—From an interview with the editors of *Essay 2*

BACKGROUND: Ed Edelson (born 1932) lives in Jamaica, New York, and is the science editor of the New York *Daily News*. A graduate of New York University and a Sloan-Rockefeller fellow in the Advanced Science Writing Program, he formerly served as president of the National Association of Science Writers. In addition to magazine articles, Edelson has written numerous books on science, including *Healers in Uniform, Visions of Tomorrow*, and, recently, *Who Goes There?*, a study of the search for extraterrestrial intelligence. In the article reprinted here, Edelson writes as the kind of popularizer whom we turn to when new developments in technology seem to outstrip our ability to understand them and adjust to them. Ready or not, we find that computers are transforming the way we learn, bank, do business, keep records, and spend our leisure time. Afraid to be left behind as a new generation grows up with "computer literacy," we turn to writers who can translate advanced technical information into reassuring everyday terms for a general audience.

Ed Edelson
Smart Computers—
Now They Speak
Our Language

GUIDE TO READING: In this essay, the author discusses two contrasting approaches to the development of computers that respond to instructions in ordinary English. What is the basic principle on which each contrasting system is based? What key terms does the author have to define for us? What examples or illustrations does he use?

In front of just *any* computer I wriggle a bit when asked to make it do 1 something meaningful. But this time, in front of a new *smart* computer, I'm confident.

"When did Fred join us?" I typed on the keyboard, asking the hulk to 2 search its electronic files for a specific piece of data. The response on the CRT display:

1. WHEN DID SOMEONE JOIN THE COMPANY?
2. WHEN DID X JOIN THE HUMAN RACE?
3. WHEN DID X JOIN THE HOMO SAPIENS?

I had to be more specific, so I typed "3"—and got Fred's birthday. 3
Who's Fred? He's really just a fictitious name stored in a demonstra- 4

tion computer program. But what makes him so important is that I could get his data without knowing any formal computer language. My question was in plain English; my answer came back in the same understandable way.

Anyone who has struggled with BASIC or any other computer lan- 5 guage knows just how revolutionary this plain-talk computing can be. Suddenly, the computer isn't something to be approached warily and only after special training; it's a helpful companion you can chat with almost conversationally.

The people who have developed these "user-friendly" natural- 6 language programs think the future belongs to them. To find out just what that future may be like, I had two hands-on demonstrations of plain-English computing—one in Albuquerque, N.M.; the other in Waltham, Mass., just outside Boston. The two systems are as far apart philosophically as they are geographically.

The Waltham company, Artificial Intelligence Corporation, has a pro- 7 gram called Intellect. It makes a rigorous analysis of every sentence you enter to understand its meaning.

The Albuquerque company, Excalibur Technologies Corporation, has Savvy. It works by transforming your statements into three-dimensional patterns and comparing them with those representing previous statements. Savvy doesn't really understand what you're saying—in a sense, it intuits the answer.

The difference between the way these programs "think" is similar to 8 the way our own brains work—the left-brain/right-brain theory. Nobel prize winner Roger Sperry found that the two halves of our brain have distinctly different ways of operating. The left brain processes information through analysis and logic; cold, mathematical reasoning prevails. The right side, however, finds an answer by using creativity, intuition, and imagination.

It was this left-brain/right-brain theory that gave James Dowe III the 9 idea for Savvy in 1979, when he was associate director of the University of New Mexico computing center.

A friend sent him a copy of a book called *The Origin of Consciousness* 10 *in the Breakdown of the Bicameral Mind*, by Julian Jaynes, a Princeton psychologist. It was Dowe's first exposure to the left-brain/right-brain difference, and that, he says, "got me to think that the conventional way of having computers understand plain language by rigorous analysis ['computational linguistics,' to use the formal term] wasn't good enough."

The result was Savvy, from Excalibur Technologies—a company 11 tucked away in a shopping center near Albuquerque's Old Town. Its sneakers-and-jeans atmosphere makes it seem more like a research lab than an office.

As the youthful-looking, 39-year-old Dowe explains, Savvy takes the 12 intuitive approach. It assigns a weighting factor—a number—to each letter as it is typed. The letter "A" may be a "1," for example, a "B" equal to "2," and so on. As the letters are entered, a sort of bar graph is produced—words in a sentence create a pattern. The pattern becomes a mathematical representation of the sentence. Being a city boy, I compared the pattern to the New York skyline. Dowe, a country boy at heart, calls it a "terrain."

"Given this terrain, how does it compare with past terrains?" said 13 Dowe. "Now it's a problem of matching terrains, not analyzing words. If Savvy has seen the terrain before, it will solve the problem exactly. If not, it will give the closest fit."

The idea of using pattern analysis to understand ordinary language 14 has been around for years. "What you do is create a conceptual mathematical space," says Gary Hendrix of the Machine Intelligence Corporation in Palo Alto, Calif. "Then you try to locate the meanings of sentences by locating features on this space. Things are related in meaning if they are close in these dimensions."

But most people in the field have dropped the idea because, they 15 claim, they simply couldn't fit enough patterns into a computer's memory to make the method useful. Dowe, however, says that Savvy has a way of packing more patterns into a relatively small amount of computer memory, and it has a fast way of matching them with the incoming patterns. How? "We prefer to keep that a trade secret," Dowe said curtly.

To show some of what Savvy can do, Dowe sat me down at a computer 16 terminal. Its memory contained simulated payroll information for a small company with nine workers. It wasn't a highly realistic demonstration, for a couple of reasons. First, the Savvy program was on a disc, which meant that it worked rather slowly. The machine would stop and "think" for 10 or 15 seconds after I typed a question. Second, I was encouraged to word my questions in a way that would fool the program—to show how it handles unusual requests.

My first try—getting Fred's birth date—was successful, but I also got 17 some idea of the chinks in Savvy's armor. When I typed in, "What will we pay out to workers next month?" the answer was GOSH, I DON'T KNOW THIS EMPLOYEE. When I typed in "How mny people are on the payroll?" I was told to leave the typo uncorrected as a test. Savvy gave four possibilities, none of which applied precisely.

"That sort of problem is potentially manageable," says Howard 18 Morgan, a professor of decisions sciences at the University of Pennsylvania, who has been keeping tabs on Savvy. But it demonstrates an essential weakness in pattern analysis.

"The major question is how much basic dictionary can they build in 19 about applications so the kind of failure you experienced can be handled," Morgan said. "If 'workers' had been entered as one of the concepts before, the system would have understood."

The problem is how far you can get with a system that works on the 20 computer equivalent of intuition, said Morgan. "They're taking a shortcut, and the shortcut is getting them a very useful level of performance. But they admit their system doesn't have any deep-level understanding. They're saying it can be useful without any understanding."

Still, knowing Savvy's limitations, Morgan was impressed enough to [21] buy a few hundred shares of Excalibur stock after seeing a demonstration. And after its experts looked over Savvy for months, the Microdata Corporation, McDonnell Douglas's computer subsidiary, agreed last December to buy one million shares of Excalibur stock, pumping as much as $6 million into the company.

One reason for the enthusiasm is another Savvy capability that Dowe [22] demonstrated. "Tell it what you want to do," he said, "and it will write the programs for you." As I watched, Dowe instructed Savvy to set up a file on customers of a mythical corporation—names, addresses, and so on. Savvy, acting on its own, then produced a series of programs for handling the customer data. It even displayed the programs so you could make detailed changes in them.

If you believe Dowe, Savvy is going to put most computer program- [23] mers out of business. In years to come, anyone will be able to sit down at a computer and have programs written to order by Savvy, with no technical expertise needed.

Harrison Miller, a farmer-entrepreneur who works out of the unlikely [24] locality of Waterproof, La., believes it. He set up American Business Computers to market Savvy. "It's not just a pipe dream. I'm totally committed to the prospect that anyone can learn programming on a mail-order basis. I've never had a lesson in computer language in my life, and I can take Savvy and do anything I can think through. It's an equalizer. It makes me the equal of anyone with a degree in computer sciences."

If you fly north and east to Massachusetts, you'll find a colder climate [25] about Savvy. "It's an interesting toy, an adult game," says Jerrold M. Diesenroth, sales director for Artificial Intelligence. "They have in no way attacked the root problem. They've taken a limited technique and come up with a partial solution."

Far from a shopping-center storefront, Artificial Intelligence is in one [26] of the newly sprouted office buildings just off Route 128. Here, three-piece suits set the all-businesslike tone. Makers of Intellect, they have taken the analytical approach to the left-brain/right-brain theory.

Larry Harris started with the thought that a program has to have full [27] understanding of what it's told in order to be useful. "Take something as simple as the word 'and,'" Harris said. "It has surprisingly ambiguous meanings.

"If you're doing a data-base query and you ask for the names of all [28] employees who are married and live in New York, you're asking for things that are members of two sets. That's a search intersection. If you ask for data on the men's department and the women's department, you're asking for a union of two sets. If you ask for the names of employees who make between $20,000 and $30,000, you're asking for a range selection. That's three different meanings for the word 'and.'" He adds, "The intelligence of a pattern-recognition system ends as soon as it says, 'I recognize the word "and."'"

Harris began developing Intellect in the 1970's, when he was still in his twenties. (He's 34 now.) He took his degree at Cornell in artificial intelligence—the science of getting machines to do thinking tasks—and went on to the computer-sciences department at Dartmouth. There he worked on natural-language understanding—getting computers to comprehend ordinary English—and data-base query, extracting information from the data stored in a computer's memory. 29

It was natural to apply one subject to the other and develop a natural-language program that would allow people to get information from a data base. It wasn't a new idea; plenty of computer companies saw there was money to be made from a program that gave executives simple, instant access to computerized information. But the way Harris went about making the idea work was unique. 30

The basic principle of his approach is simple. When a question is typed into a terminal, the program first looks up the meanings of the words. If the question is "How many workers are on the payroll?" for example, the program looks up the meaning of "workers" and "payroll" in an electronic dictionary. Then it parses the sentence, analyzing it grammatically: "Are" is a verb, "workers" and "payroll" are nouns, and so on. When it understands the question, it gets the answer from the data base. 31

Put that way, it sounds simple. But Intellect works only because it contains an enormous amount of information—information about the meaning of specific words, information about English grammar, information about the ways in which people can bend or break grammatical rules, information about colloquialisms and slang. Think back to the school days when your English teacher made you take a sentence apart, listing every word by part of speech and function, and you'll have a good idea of what Intellect does. It uses the accumulated body of knowledge about the English language to grasp exactly what it's being told. 32

Most efforts to make such a system work have failed because natural language isn't as simple as it seems. The human brain can sort out meanings that baffle a computer program. To take a simple example, "How many cars are green?" asks for a color, while "How many cars are Fords?" asks for a manufacturer. A basic problem in developing a program is to devise an electronic dictionary that would include all the meanings of all the words that the program would encounter. Such dictionaries tend to be so big and cumbersome that the program has only limited value. 33

Harris's solution was to organize the data into categories. The category in which a word is listed provides many of the definitions (replacing the need for every word to have its own specific definition). "Green" is listed in the data base under colors, for example, while "Ford" is listed under auto manufacturers. By devising a way for the program to extract such informa- 34 tion from the data base, based on its category, Harris kept the dictionary to a manageable size.

It wasn't as simple as it sounds, of course. "We spent five years and $10 million writing this program," Jerrold Diesenroth said. The details are carefully guarded proprietary secrets. 35

There's an air of sleek prosperity in the offices of Artificial Intelligence. Diesenroth happily ticked off the names of Intellect users: Chase Manhattan Bank, Ford, Boeing, Xerox, Du Pont, and more. They're paying from $40,000 to over $60,000 to have the use of Intellect. 36

When I had my demonstration, I could see why. Intellect easily answered such questions as "How many women in the Western region were over quota last year?"—and from a data base that included hundreds of names and lots of other information. It can also go on to answer casually worded follow-up questions: "Where do they live?" or "How long have they been with the company?" Ask Intellect, "Give me a bar graph showing actual sales by division and our estimates," and it will do so in seconds. 37

This sophisticated, expensive approach seems a far cry from the world of personal computers that Savvy hopes to conquer. At the moment, Intellect can be run only on mainframe computers, the giants that are used by very large enterprises, and it's expensive. But Harris and Diesenroth say it's just a matter of time before Intellect is available for smaller businesses and then for the personal-computer market. "We're negotiating right now with manufacturers who make minis," Harris said, referring to the office-sized computers that are becoming commonplace in small businesses. 38

How long before Intellect is available for microcomputers, the kind you can take home with you? "A fairly long time," Harris said. How long? A thoughtful look came over him, and I expected to hear something about the year 2000. "Maybe three to five years," he said finally. 39

About the only thing that Dowe and Harris agree upon is that voice-pattern recognition will someday provide the next major step in computer communication: Instead of typing a command, you'll just speak it and the computer will understand. Speech recognition is one of the toughest challenges for a computer program—given the variety of accents, grammatical mistakes, and general sloppiness of any "human" language. What we say and how we say it may defy logical analysis, but it can yield to pattern-recognition techniques. Harris sees a voice-recognition system as the front end of a rigorously analytical natural-language computer program such as Intellect. Dowe sees it as a logical extension of a pattern-recognition program such as Savvy. Neither of them doubts that the natural-language revolution is happening. 40

Using the Dictionary

Check the origins of the following, and explain the connection between the earliest meanings and current uses.   1. *computer* (1)   2. *electronic* (2)   3. *data* (2)   4.

intelligence (7)   5. *simulated* (16)   6. *disc* (16)   7. *micro-* (21)   8. *program* (22)   9. *intersection* (28)   10. *mini-* (38)

The Writer's Agenda

The author's task in this essay is to make clear what before was mysterious and bewildering to many of his readers. Answer the following questions:

1. In the introductory paragraphs, the author several times alludes to his previous *struggles* when dealing with computers. What effect are these allusions meant to have on his audience? How do they lead up to the main point he wants to make about the new plain-language computers?

2. The right-brain/left-brain theory assigns familiar analytical and mathematical reasoning to the left hemisphere of the brain. What *right-brain* functions do the developers of Savvy try to build on or simulate?

3. How does the author explain the contrasting *analytical approach* to plain-language computers employed by the developers at Artificial Intelligence? (What does *parsing* mean? What makes the word *and* ambiguous—what distinctions must the computer make to handle different uses of the word? What problems are illustrated by the pair of contrasting questions about cars?)

4. Where in this essay is the "anyone can . . ." kind of optimism that is often seen in promoters of new technology strongest? Where do possible *doubts* or reservations come through most strongly?

5. For many observers, the computer, like much modern technology, is forbiddingly *impersonal* or even inhuman. What does the author do to personalize and humanize his account of the new technologies?

For Discussion and Writing

6. What has been your own experience with computers? What do they do? What problems do they cause? What changes do they bring about in people's lives?

7. "Computer literacy" is becoming a buzzword in our society. Interview an expert on this subject, perhaps a professor in the computer science department of your school, about what concepts or operations he or she feels are fundamental to achieving computer literacy. Explain these to a readership generally unfamiliar with the world of computers.

8. Explain the advantages of replacing a specific manual or mechanical operation with a computerized one. Write for an audience that is familiar with the task or operation but largely unfamiliar with computers. For instance, argue the advantages of a word processor over a typewriter, or of a computerized accounting system over manual bookkeeping.

9. The left-brain/right-brain theory has been much publicized lately. Read two or three newspaper or magazine articles on this subject. Explain some of the basic principles and implications to a lay audience.

Branching Out

10. A cherished possession of the Smithsonian Institution is a letter one of the Wright brothers wrote trying to show the feasibility of human flight. Choose a similar moment or situation in the history of science and technology. Predict and explain an important future advance to a skeptical contemporary audience.

WRITERS ON WRITING

Ed Edelson on Using the Word Processor

QUESTION: How long have you written on the word processor?

ANSWER: The newspaper introduced it about five years ago, and I bought myself one; I've been working on one ever since.

QUESTION: Has it changed the way you write?

ANSWER: Yes, in a number of ways. I don't like to rewrite. I used to try to get it perfect the first time. Now I can go back, I can move paragraphs around and change sentences, so I don't take as many pains. But it's not faster; it's about the same. I still don't like to do much revision.

QUESTION: Do you think the word processor makes writing easier?

ANSWER: No. I don't think a word processor makes much difference for a professional writer. Writing is always going to be a hand craft. A newspaper room is one of the few places in the world you can still walk into and see people making products by hand: They're writing. The word processor is a tool, but it's still a question of an individual craftsman.

QUESTION: Do you think the word processor might help with writer's block?

ANSWER: No, that's for beginners. I've been writing nearly every day for more than twenty years and I still get what people call writer's block. I don't think there's any writer who doesn't. So what do I do? Well, practice may not make perfect, but you do learn. The big problem is getting started. Writing's hard work, and naturally everybody tries to put off hard work as long as possible. Over the years you learn to just sit down and have at it.

—From an interview with the editors of *Essay 2*

STUDENT MODEL 10

FOR READING: Study the following short selection as a possible model for writing of your own. How do you react to it overall? What makes it interesting or effective? Answer the following more specific questions:

    1. (PURPOSE) What was the writer trying to do?
    2. (AUDIENCE) What kind of reader would make a good reader for this selection?
    3. (SOURCES) Where did the writer turn for material?
    4. (THESIS) Does the selection have a central idea or unifying thesis?
    5. (STRUCTURE) What is the author's overall plan or strategy?
    6. (STYLE) What makes the piece effective or memorable (for instance, striking details, memorable phrases)?
    7. (REVISION) What do you think the writer could or should have done differently?

Dolores LaGuardia

Talking to Apes

Do animals have language? Birds like many mammals have mating calls; they have shrill cries of warning. Bats exchange high-pitched greetings. Scientists interpret many of the thumpings and roarings of other animals as their way of staking out or claiming a territory. But all of these signals are expressions of immediate needs and desires. Only humans, it was thought, had true language: They could label, describe, and evaluate specific objects of fear and desire.

Recent experiments with teaching sign language to chimpanzees have shaken our assumptions about if and how animals can "talk." Because of its evolutionary closeness to humans, the chimpanzee was a logical choice for experiments to determine if communication between humans and animals was possible. However, despite their similar body structure and nervous system, chimps lack the anatomical equipment—the voice box—needed to make the many varied sounds that make up human language. The limitations of the chimpanzee are similar to that of deaf humans, who, although they do have voice boxes, cannot *hear* the sounds of language and therefore have difficulty imitating and reproducing them. Scientists concluded that if deaf humans could communicate nonverbally through the use of sign language, perhaps chimpanzees could do so also.

Ameslan, the American sign or gesture language for the deaf or mute, is known to an estimated 18 million people. Psychologists such as Beatrice and Robert Gardner (who taught their chimp Washoe and others) succeeded in teaching sign language to chimpanzees, with some of these acquiring a vocabulary of 100 to 200 words. Some of the signals the chimps learned enabled them to articulate basic needs. For example, Washoe learned that by rubbing her middle three fingers from her mouth to chin (using the Ameslan sign for *W*), she could ask for water. After twisting her index and middle finger (the symbol for *H*), she would be fed.

The chimps' communication was not limited to basic needs, however.   4
They started to use labels like *drink* or *cat* to identify pictures in a magazine. As humans do in using language, they combined signals to make up new labels for new things. Washoe signaled *water bird* when seeing a duck land in a pond. As humans do in putting words together in a sentence, the chimps eventually distinguished the different meanings of signals put together in a different order: "Lucy tickle Roger" is different from "Roger tickle Lucy." When taught the word *dirty* after having soiled her clothes, Washoe later used the word for evaluation: To a rhesus monkey who bothered her, she repeatedly signed "dirty monkey, dirty monkey."

Can animals "talk"? The successful teaching of sign language to chim-   5
panzees has led scientists to reconsider the evidence showing that other species are able to communicate with each other. Dolphins, for instance, apparently communicate through a series of high-pitched squeaks similar to underwater sonar. Carl Sagan, in *The Dragons of Eden*, tells the story of Boyce Rensberger, a *New York Times* reporter whose parents could not speak or hear and whose first language was Ameslan. Rensberger was assigned to look into the Gardners' experiment in teaching sign language to chimpanzees. After spending some time with Washoe, Rensberger reported: "Suddenly I realized I was conversing with a member of another species in my native tongue."

FOR WRITING: Prepare a report on a significant experiment or discovery for the general reader. Try to make your readers see the problem or the issue involved. Try to make the procedure and the details real, striking, or dramatic for them. Interpret the significance of the findings. (You may want to write about a milestone in the history of science or technology as if you were a contemporary. For instance, you may want to report the discovery of the moons of Jupiter, first experiments with human flight, or the first splitting of the atom.)

Additional Writing Topics 10

Science

A. Write an informative paper that explains some basic scientific concept or technical process. Write for fellow students who find science a hard subject but aspire to be well-informed citizens or consumers. Choose a topic like the following:

1. dating fossils
2. DNA
3. AM and FM radio
4. an ordinary and a diesel engine
5. how a jet engine works
6. evolution: our immediate ancestors
7. the nature of comets
8. how computer chips work
9. what hormones do
10. one-cell organisms
11. how earthquakes happen
12. the ozone layer
13. medical uses of lasers
14. basic physics of space travel
15. splitting the atom

B. Assume that you are serving as a consultant for a policy decision that requires some technical expertise. Investigate one of the following subjects and share your conclusions with your readers. Support your findings.

1. a neglected source of alternative energy
2. the best form of rapid transit
3. bears, parks, and people
4. the safety of sugar substitutes
5. off-shore drilling—pro and con
6. robots and the factory of the future
7. which pain killers work and how
8. animal experiments—pro and con
9. new ways of prolonging life
10. gene splicing—pro and con
11. how to save the condors
12. damming the last wild rivers
13. replenishing the water supply
14. much ado about cholesterol
15. disposing of toxic waste

11

MEDIA AND POPULAR CULTURE
Writing to Evaluate

OVERVIEW

People who write successfully about the mass media and American popular culture do not just report and catalog. They *interpret* what they see and hear—helping us understand what is ambiguous or obscure, making us compare our own understanding of a program or performance with theirs. They *evaluate* what they observe—making us reconsider our own reactions, helping us clarify our own critical standards. Critical interpretation and evaluation of media offerings and of popular culture bring into play a large measure of personal preference, of individual taste. They confront the writer with the need to clarify and support personal judgments. They challenge the writer to convey to readers attitudes ranging from nostalgia and amusement to bitter, slashing wit.

PURPOSE Much current writing about the media shows a fascination with the media as a mirror of American life and American popular culture. At one time, critics ignored or deplored the world of "mass culture." Television was the great wasteland; movies were assumed to appeal to the lowest common denominator. But over the years, popular culture achieved a kind of critical respectability. Screen comedy of the silent-film era was resurrected in countless retrospectives; classics like *Citizen Kane* became cult movies. In the Western and in *Star Trek* critics found myths that are a basic part of the American heritage and of the collective unconscious of the nation. Many of us today look in the mirror of the media for clues to a better understanding of our society and of ourselves.

AUDIENCE Audiences for writing about the media range from film buffs to media watchers who look at television advertising with a jaundiced eye. The writer addressing an in-group of aficionados or long-time critics must obviously take special loyalties, nostalgias, and phobias into account. But much media writing is aimed at the general reader—an amused (or bemused) spectator of the passing scene, looking for critical guidance on what to watch, what to read, what to look for, and what to shun.

BENEFITS FOR THE WRITER (1) Writing about media or popular culture requires us to explain, justify, or defend personal judgments. It requires us to clarify our standards and marshal the evidence showing how they apply. It requires us to reckon with the standards and preferences of others.

(2) Writing about the media can alert us to things that might escape the literal-minded observer: the emotional overtones of words, the force of loaded words, the symbolic meanings that we attach to familiar images. Whether we write about the media appreciatively or critically, we are likely to become involved in the attitudes and emotions they bring into play.

(3) Writing and reading about the media can help us extend our range of *style*. Effective writing ranges from deadly serious to serious with a lighter touch to boisterously witty and irreverent. Some writing by media watchers is very earnest, but much of it ranges from mildly humorous to bitterly, cuttingly satirical.

WRITER'S GUIDE 11

Writing to Evaluate

Critical writing—writing that interprets and evaluates art, entertainment, reading—is more than a record of likes and dislikes. When you write effectively about what you have observed, you do not merely praise what you admire and condemn what you deplore. You present your *considered* judgment, and you back it up with explanation, evidence, and other kinds of support. Remember the following guidelines:

(1) *Establish your credentials as an alert viewer, spectator, or reader.* Anchor your interpretations and judgments to vivid details that tell your reader: "I have taken a careful firsthand look at this—my reactions are based on more than hearsay, a casual first impression, or a quick look." Sooner or later (and preferably sooner), bring in the kind of striking detail that makes a film, a program, or a book real for your reader:

> A woman stalks batlike creatures with a knife, tossing one into the food processor, frying a second in the microwave, and slaying a third. But another monster almost strangles her before she is rescued by her son. This is a scene from Steven Spielberg's movie *Gremlins*, intended mainly for young viewers....

Often a critical review will include (or start with) a brief summary of the plot, an overview that includes enough striking detail to convince the reader that the critic knows the subject—and knows it well:

> Chunky, muscle-bound Sylvester Stallone looks repulsive one moment, noble the next, and sometimes both at once. In *Rocky*, which he wrote and stars in, he's a thirty-year-old club fighter who works as a strong-arm man, collecting money for a loan shark. Rocky never got anywhere, and he has nothing; he lives in a Philadelphia tenement, and even the name he fights under—the Italian Stallion—has become a joke. But the world heavyweight champion, Apollo Creed (Carl Weathers), who's a smart black jester like Muhammad Ali, announces that for his Bicentennial New Year's fight he'll give an unknown a shot at the title, and he picks the Italian Stallion for the racial-sexual overtones of the contest. This small romantic fable is about a palooka gaining his manhood; it's Terry Malloy finally getting his chance to be somebody. *Rocky* is a threadbare patchwork of old-movie bits (*On the Waterfront, Marty, Somebody Up There Likes Me*, Capra's *Meet Joe Doe*, and maybe even a little of Preston Sturges's *Hail the Conquering Hero*), yet it's engaging, and the naive elements are emotionally effective....A more painstaking director would have been too proud to shoot the mildewed ideas and would

have tried to throw out as many as possible and to conceal the others—and would probably have wrecked the movie. (Pauline Kael, *When the Lights Go Down*)

(2) *Go beyond factual detail or plot summaries to interpretation.* Do not merely retell the story. Ask yourself: "What does it mean? Why does it matter?" Much current discussion of television and movie fare assumes that it mirrors the values of the audience or caters to its needs. Much current criticism takes seriously the effect television and movie entertainment has on its audience—the myths or fantasies it acts out:

> Sugar-sweet movies of the Disney variety fail to take seriously the world of the child—the immense problems with which children have to struggle as they grow up, to make themselves free of the bonds that tie them to their parents, and to test their own strength. Instead of helping children, who want to understand the difficulties ahead, these shows talk down to them, insult their intelligence, and lower their aspirations. While most of the popular shows for children fall far short of what children need most, others at least provide them with some of the fantasies that relieve pressing anxieties, and this is the reason for their popularity. Superman, Wonder Woman, and the Bionic Woman stimulate children's fantasies about being strong and invulnerable, and this offers some relief from being overwhelmed by the powerful adults who control their existence. (Bruno Bettelheim, "The Art of Moving Pictures," *Harper's*)

(3) *Spell out your standards of evaluation.* What criteria are you applying? How does what you describe measure up or fall short? When you use a label like *sentimental*, explain what you mean ("allowing us to bask in a warm self-approving glow of sympathy for society's outcasts or the unfortunate"); give examples (the mobster who tries to protect his adoring teenage daughter). Look at how a well-known movie critic shows and condemns the workings of "lynch law" in recent "action movies":

> Once, quite a while ago, I had lunch with Graham Greene, and during our talk he deplored most Westerns as embodiments of lynch law. I thought of Greene during *Cobra*. The Western has of course become the Urban. The lone rider who took vengeance into his own hands has evolved into the detective who disregards the rules. Lynch law, in *Cobra* and its antecedents, is now perpetrated by men with badges. Oh, once again the proprieties get ritual obeisance—the routine scene in the commissioner's office in which Cobra is warned he's going too far, the "square" detective who tells Cobra he's sicker than the criminals he's hunting. But, as usual, these scenes imply that legal procedures are dumb and pointless. In fact, at the finish, the official who had earlier berated Cobra congratulates him on the job he's done. The very last line on the screen, after the closing credit crawl, is: "Patrons are warned not to imitate any of the stunts and action in this film." Patrons are not warned

against mind-warping on the subjects of crime, police, and law. (Stanley Kauffmann, "On Film," *The New Republic*)

(4) *Try to unify your discussion around a central theme.* What is your strongest impression? What matters to you most about what you describe? Study the unifying theme that runs through the following excerpts from a *Time* article on theme parks:

As for the twin fountainheads of theme parks—Disneyland in Anaheim, Calif., and the gigantic Walt Disney World outside Orlando—they offer nothing less than *a dream of America as it once or never was: a homogenized, turn-of-the-century village propelled into the future* by space-age science and the relentless optimism of its founding dreamer....

No rickety roller coasters, no sucker-fleecing games of chance, no sideshow tawdriness for Uncle Walt. At his place *every path would be as spotless as Formica; every doorway would be scaled to just above kid-size; every "attraction" (not ride) would be sweet enough for "guests"* (not customers) of all ages to enjoy....

All the visitors behave here, even when waiting in line 45 min. for a Frontierland hot dog. *All the employees smile,* even the teenagers in French Foreign Legion uniforms sweeping up cigarette butts in front of the imitation-Aztec Mexican pavilion....

In this *sanitized* sensory bombardment, *everything is so clean, so controlled, so world-put-back-in-joint,* that the place seems ... an experimental prototype community of yesterday.... (Richard Corliss, "If Heaven Ain't a Lot Like Disney," *Time*)

(5) *Protect yourself against charges of being biased, opinionated, or one-sided.* Try to do justice to the whole; do not put excessive weight on a phrase, an image, a scene taken out of context. Try to take into account the intentions of writers, artists, actors, directors. Be willing to recognize exceptions to conclusions you draw or charges you make:

... The argument in the tenets of advertising is that once a woman marries she changes overnight from plaything to floor-waxer. *To be fair, men make an equivalent transition in commercials. The swinging male with the mod hair and the beautiful chick turns inevitably into the paunchy slob who chokes on his wife's cake.* You will notice, however, that the voice urging the viewer to buy the product is nearly always male: gentle, wise, helpful, seductive. And the visible presence telling the housewife how to get shinier floors and whiter wash and lovelier hair is almost invariably a man. (Marya Mannes, "Television: The Splitting Image," *Saturday Review*)

(6) *Turn to authoritative sources for support.* When you might be accused of being too subjective or too self-centered in your judgments, quote respected critics, authoritative studies, informed opinion. In the following

passage, an author shows that his negative view of a media stereotype does not merely represent one person's private resentment:

> A recent research study has confirmed what Americans of Italian origin already know: Negative stereotyping of Italian Americans pervades the U.S. media. A team affiliated with Columbia and George Washington Universities studied prime-time television programs. . . . Among the major findings:
> - Television portrays one out of six Italian-American characters as criminals.
> - Viewers could conclude, judging from TV presentations, that most Italian Americans hold low-status jobs and are unable to speak English correctly.
> - Italian Americans who are not portrayed as villains or criminals are generally pictured as lovable, laughable dimwits. . . . (Vincent Romano, "The Godfather Image Persists," *NEA Today*)

(7) *Set and maintain the right tone.* Writing about the media and popular culture ranges from the very formal to the very informal—from the preachy through the half-serious and half-amused to the broadly humorous or sharply satirical. Think about the attitude you are adopting toward your subject and toward your audience. Think about where your writing is going to be positioned on the spectrum from formality to informality:

FORMAL Some of the best writing providing critical guidance to the media, to the arts, or to entertainment is **formal** without being stuffy. The following passage by a well-known television critic uses the vocabulary of serious discussion. Much of her vocabulary is close to spoken English, but she also draws on words found more frequently on the printed page than in everyday talk. She brings these in because they convey the right shade of meaning or the right attitude:

> Society forgets that not all women are naturally *maternal.* . . . All of us must know by now that the large family is no more a blessing than the childless couple is a crime. In fact, the woman who is *a copious* breeder is doing infinitely more harm than good to this suffocating planet and its crowded *broods.* The rest of us really want more men in our lives, not fewer. We want their *comradeship* at work as well as their company at home. We refuse a life that forces us to live ten hours of every weekday confined to the company of children and women. (Marya Mannes, "How Men Will Benefit from the Women's Power Revolution," *Midwest*)

MODERATELY FORMAL (with an informal touch) A critic may deliberately use selected **informal** language to help set a humorous tone—to suggest a half-amused, half-serious attitude. Look at the selective, deliberate use of informal language in the following passage:

One of the saddest but most pervasive legacies of the '60s, when we *let it all hang out*, is that there is no longer a clear distinction between the adult and the juvenile in the murky realms of sex, profanity, and worldliness.... When we sit down with the *kiddies* for diversions brought to us by the wits of New York and Los Angeles, we giggle together over sitcoms that leer and peek and whistle about sexual business.... It is no exaggeration to say that the notorious Brooke Shields blue jean advertisements, at which 1980s America glances with scarcely a moment's pause, would have been centerfold material for the *stag magazines* of the 1950s—and would have been cause for a spanking had a nice boy been caught *eyeballing* them. The advertising on television, all of which is seen by children, routinely makes overt sexual *pitches* and frequently relies on sexual jokes to *get its message across*. (Jonathan Yardley, "Explicit Lyrics, Explicit Society," *The Washington Post*)

VERY INFORMAL A writer writing about the more sensational or freakish aspects of American life may deliberately draw on **slang** to help create a jazzy, disrespectful effect. Slang is *extremely* informal; it is more aggressively unconventional than ordinary informal language. In writing about the hard-drinking, fast-driving, rough-talking test pilots from among whom America's astronauts were selected, Tom Wolfe, author of *The Right Stuff*, uses a jazzy, slangy style to shock and entertain the reader:

... staggered, *bawled*, and sang ... like a *jerk* ... like a *zombie* ... get more *wasted* or else more quietly *fried* ... cheap PX *booze* ... *barreling* down the highway ... *chalked it up* to youth ... *slapping* oxygen tank cones on their faces ... *revved up* with adrenalin.

To sum up: Writing about the media and popular culture tests your ability to observe, to interpret, and to evaluate. It requires you to clarify your standards, to justify your choices, to defend your preferences. It will make you more alert to implied attitudes and emotional overtones, and it will make you more sensitive to the attitudes and expectations of your audience.

Prewriting Activities 11

1. For sentence practice, write a series of one-sentence *capsule plots* for recent or well-remembered movies and television shows. Pack each sentence with characteristic detail or telling information. Divide your capsule plots into two sets: In the first set, use **formal** language to describe serious films or programs (or those that you want the reader to take seriously). In the second set, use more **informal** language for shows with humorous intent or shows that you want to put in a humorous light. Study the following sentences as possible models:

(Formal language)

a. A stranded reptilelike alien, befriended by human children, escapes from the planet Earth by salvaging parts from a toy chest in order to make a radio transmitter.

b. Sir Thomas More, a man of high position, with the respect of his peers and the friendship of his king, is brought to disgrace, ruin, and even execution by his inability to abandon his conscience.

c. Clint Eastwood, never allowing his jaws to move while talking, portrays the man with no name, who killed for a fistful of dollars in the Old West.

d. Diana Ross, in *Lady Sings the Blues*, portrayed Billie Holiday's upbringing in Harlem, success in entertainment as a jazz singer, and tragic downfall from drinking and drugs.

(Informal language)

e. A determined if unwilling Rambolina, overcoming the human obstacles posed by a cynical space-age yuppie, duels a grotesque alien Supermom to the death.

f. A hypochondriac photographer and a sloppy sportswriter sharing an apartment get on each other's nerves as the original "odd couple."

g. Meggie, poor kinfolk living on her rich aunt's sheep ranch, falls in love with a handsome young priest and dreams that one day he will kick the habit, so to speak, and tie the knot.

2. Start a *viewer's log* on any current television viewing (or other media watching) you are doing. Include notes on plot and characters, striking scenes or details, technical features that interest you, as well as your personal reactions or comments. Develop your log as a possible resource for papers about the media.

3. Authors who write on American popular culture often aim at a snappy, jazzy, or otherwise unconventional style, reflecting a half-serious, half-amused attitude toward their subject. Study the following short sample passages. Select one of them as the model for an imitation or parody.

a. Blackmail. Abortion. Teenage runaways. Drug addiction. Rape. Lies up the wazoo. And that's not even a good day. On a good day, college dorms will echo with screams:
"Don't do it, Luke!"
"Erica, how *could* you?"
Once the domain of grandmothers, housewives, and nightshift nurses, soap operas have now become the national campus pastime. But consider their content. It's not reality. It's not comedy. It's a relentlessly oppressive world tainted by horrible audio, cheap sets, lugubrious pacing and an excess of Farrah Fawcett hair. These assets notwithstanding, and not to mention the *real* sex, drugs, and alcohol readily available on campus, you'd think college students wouldn't require massive doses of soap operas to make it through the afternoon. But they do. (Lisa Birnbach, "The Daze of Our Lives," *Rolling Stone*)

b. The center was not holding. It was a country of bankruptcy notices and public-auction announcements and commonplace reports of casual killings and misplaced children and abandoned homes and vandals who misspelled even the four-letter words they scrawled. It was a country in which families routinely disappeared, trailing bad checks and repossession papers. Adolescents drifted from city to torn city, sloughing off both the past and the future as snakes shed their skins, children who were never taught and would never now learn the games that had held the society together. People were missing. Children were missing. Parents were missing. Those left behind filed desultory missing-persons reports, then moved on themselves.   (Joan Didion, *Slouching Towards Bethlehem*)

Paragraph Practice 11

Study the following one-paragraph movie review from *The New Yorker*. Look at the way it combines information, evaluation, and entertainment. Write a similar brief review in which you can include plot essentials, key thematic or symbolic elements, and amusing or informative sidelights.

Planet of the Apes

This is one of the liveliest science-fiction fantasies ever to come out of Hollywood. The writing, by Michael Wilson and Rod Serling, who adapted Pierre Boulle's novel *Monkey Planet*, is often fancy-ironic in the old school of poetic disillusion, but the construction is first-rate. An American astronaut finds himself in the future, on a planet run by apes; the audience is rushed along with this hero, who keeps going as fast as possible to avoid being castrated or lobotomized. All this wouldn't be so forceful or so funny if it weren't for the use of Charlton Heston in the role. With his perfect, lean-hipped, powerful body, Heston is a godlike hero; built for strength, he's an archetype of what makes Americans win. He doesn't play a nice guy; he's harsh and hostile, self-centered and hot-tempered. Yet we don't hate him, because he's so magnetically strong; he represents American power—and he has the profile of an eagle. He is the perfect American Adam for this black-comedy entertainment. The director, Franklin Schaffner, has thought out the action in terms of the wide screen, and he uses space and distance dramatically. The makeup (there is said to be a million dollars' worth) and the costuming of the actors playing the apes are rather witty, and the apes have a wonderful nervous, hopping walk. The best little hopper is Kim Hunter, as an ape doctor; she somehow manages to give a distinctive, charming performance in this makeup.

BACKGROUND: Andrew A. Rooney—reporter, scriptwriter, free-lance journalist, television commentator, syndicated columnist—knows the mass media as an insider. He was born in 1919 in Albany, New York, and attended Colgate University. During World War II, he worked as a reporter for the G.I. newspaper *Stars and Stripes*. He went to Hollywood to write material for radio programs (including the legendary Arthur Godfrey show) and in due time switched to writing for—and later producing—television shows. He became widely known as a commentator on the CBS television newsmagazine *60 Minutes*, with one reviewer calling him "the most listened-to curmudgeon in recent times." He started his widely read newspaper column in 1979; collections of his television commentaries and newspaper columns have topped the best-seller list of the *New York Times*. Rooney, who bills himself as a normal, ordinary person and the "all-American consumer," is known for his gift for dealing with everyday topics in down-to-earth fashion and with homey wit.

Andy Rooney
There's One Born Every Minute

GUIDE TO READING: Rooney here responds in his own fashion to the aggressive huckstering that is one of the petty annoyances of every day. How does he deal with it? What is his real target? What standards does he apply?

Just as soon as my $2 million comes from *Reader's Digest*, I'll probably be retiring. 1

It seems almost certain that I'll be a winner, according to the postcards 2 I've been getting from Betty B. Glass at the *Reader's Digest*'s Bureau of Control in Pleasantville, N.Y. In addition to the $2 million in checks to be drawn on the Bank of New York for deposit in my account, I'll be getting an additional $15,000 a day as a bonus award if I'm the Grand Prize Winner. There may be some misunderstanding here, because I estimate that if I live another 30 years or 10,950 days, that would come to $164,250,000.

That isn't all, either. I could qualify for an extra prize of $100,000 cash if 3 I find a gold seal attached to my Sweepstakes cards. You probably got one of these cards yourself from Betty, who is "Sweepstakes Director" for the *Digest*.

Because I wanted to get a little better idea of what my chances are, I 4 called *Reader's Digest* and asked for her. A very pleasant, British-sounding woman answered the phone.

"Betty Glass," the voice said. 5

"Hi," I said. "I'm Andy Rooney." 6

"Andy Rooney!" the voice said. "Are you for real?" 7

Well, she had taken the words right out of my mouth, because I had 8 called fully expecting to find that the "Betty Glass" who signed my Sweepstakes card was not a real person.

Wrong. Betty Glass is real. She came to the United States from En- 9 gland 35 years ago, went to work for the *Digest* almost right away and has worked there ever since. I think Betty ought to be ashamed of herself, but she's proud of her job at the *Digest*.

After talking with Betty, I was less hopeful of getting the whole 10 $2 million plus the $100,000 plus the $15,000 a day. It turns out that the most anyone has ever won is not $2 million plus those extras but only about $350,000. Whoever wins the Sweepstakes this year will get an annuity of $167,000 a year, even though it says in six places on this card they sent me that the Grand Prize is $2 million.

The *Digest* doesn't actually run this so-called $2 million Sweepstakes 11 itself. It hires someone else to do that. That company must subscribe to the old maxim, "Never underestimate the stupidity of the average person."

It has done everything it can to borrow the appearance and wording 12 from legitimate documents to make the Sweepstakes card look official. If you inspect it carefully, it looks about as honest and trustworthy as a card game at a carnival.

"URGENT NOTIFICATION" (in red)

"THIS IS TO CERTIFY . . . "

"RECORD OF REGISTRATION"

"NOT FOR TRANSFER"

"DOCUMENTATION OF PRIZE ELIGIBILITY"

"RETAIN FOR YOUR RECORDS"

The only thing the card doesn't say is "HOGWASH!" 13

I don't know what's gotten into the *Reader's Digest*, anyway. I bought 14 a copy of the July issue because it has an article of mine in it. I was surprised to read on the flap covering the front of the *Digest* the title of one of the articles: "What Men Call Extraordinary Sex."

Is this the dependable, All-American, old *Reader's Digest* we all know 15 and love? Is it going in for that stuff, too? Are sweepstakes and sex what it has to do for circulation?

The *Digest* not only tried to attract readers to this issue with the 16 promise of something sexy; it then failed to produce. "What Men Call Extraordinary Sex" is about as sexy as leftover spaghetti.

It's sad that *Reader's Digest* can't survive by doing what it started out 17 doing—that is, editing an interesting, populist little magazine that opened up new avenues of interest to millions of Americans.

If I win the $2 million Sweepstakes, I'm going to buy Betty Glass a bus 18
ticket to Atlantic City and a subscription to *Playboy* so she can tell her
editors about real longshot chances and real extraordinary sex.

Using the Dictionary

What is the difference between a popular and a "populist" publication?

The Writer's Agenda

Rooney in this column writes as the critic or watchdog who endeavors to maintain
standards and to draw the line in cases of questionable judgment or poor taste.
Answer the following questions:

1. What is Rooney's basic criticism in this column? Where does it come
through most directly or effectively? What are the standards he is trying to uphold?

2. A traditional technique of the satirist is to pretend to be the perfect naive,
gullible victim. Where and how does Rooney employ this technique?

3. We expect a columnist to be a person with strong personal opinions. What
is the proportion of fact to opinion in this column?

4. How widespread or typical are the promotional techniques Rooney criti-
cizes? Does he convince you that they are a matter of serious concern?

For Discussion or Writing

5. Look at current examples of aggressive advertising techniques. What
appeals do they employ? What motives do they bring into play, or to what needs do
they cater? What estimate of the audience do they imply?

6. Looking at several recent issues, study the front page of your daily newspaper as a clue to what its publishers consider most important. To what interests or
needs does the paper cater? What priorities has it set for itself?

7. William Safire, another columnist, says that a key question we ask about a
column is "Is this the product of a committee?"—or of a flesh-and-blood individual
with a distinct personality and private crotchets? Study a series of columns by a
widely read columnist. What is the characteristic point of view? What is the columnist's distinct personality?

8. Study several issues of a publication that aims at a large popular audience,
such as *People, Sports Illustrated,* or *Reader's Digest.* Who would be the ideal
reader? What are typical topics or materials? Is there a recurrent slant or point of
view?

9. Using Rooney's column as a possible model, write a newspaper column (or
a guest editorial for a student newspaper) on a similar topic, such as state-run
lotteries, commercials for used cars, charitable appeals, promotions for educational
television, or appeals for another good cause.

BACKGROUND: Stanley Kauffmann reviews movies for the *New Republic*. He was born in 1916 in New York and turned to theater and film criticism after a career as playwright, actor, director, and editor. He published his memoirs, *Albums of Early Life*, in 1980. Like such movie critics as *The New Yorker*'s Pauline Kael, Kauffmann is an opinion maker whose reviews are widely read (and argued with) by people who care about filmmaking and the cinema. He once said that a critic needs "a commitment to the art, a passion to see it improve, a disregard for any kind of popularity." Like other critics, he deplores the increasing dependence of the movie industry on blockbuster successes that hurt the chances of good films that may not enjoy a huge commercial success. "Money," he says, "is the strangulating factor for the present film situation in this country, because of both the great losses and the great successes."

Stanley Kauffmann

The Return of Rambo

GUIDE TO READING: Kauffmann is a reviewer who takes movies seriously. How much of his review provides background for the movie? How much do we learn about the actual movie? How much is interpretation or evaluation, and how does it show? What is the central point or message of the review?

"Symbol of the American Spirit." That's the headline in the ads for Rambo, which is about its hero's foray into Vietnam today to rescue American POWs. The subject has been used before, in *Uncommon Valor* with Gene Hackman, in *Missing in Action* and *Missing in Action II*, with Chuck Norris: but *Rambo* outdistances them. Three facts: *Rambo* is the current box-office champion in the country. (*"Rambo* Ahead by a Mile," *Variety*, June 5.) Like the second Norris film, *Rambo* is a sequel. (In the earlier one, *First Blood*, also starring Sylvester Stallone, Rambo, a returned Vietnam vet, went on a rampage against civilians and National Guardsmen because of mistreatment of Vietnam vets.) *Rambo* is cinematically no piece of schlock; it was made with prime professional skills. (Cinematography by Jack Cardiff, an Oscar winner.) In credibility, the action is as ludicrous as old Saturday-afternoon serials; in execution, the skills help it to skate over the incredibilities.

Rambo's character is constructed with equal care. Stallone wrote the script with James Cameron, using materials devised by David Morrell, and the recipe is right. Rambo is of half-Indian, half-German stock. The Indian blood, I suppose, explains his wilderness skills, his prowess with a knife and with a (modernized) bow. In this simplistic genetic formula, the German half is apparently meant to explain his talents with modern weaponry and with aircraft. From this union, perhaps, Rambo also has enormous biceps and pecs that, day or night, gleam.

The "American Spirit" that Rambo symbolizes is strong, taciturn, 3 self-reliant, and *wronged.* At the start, he is breaking rock in a penitentiary, where he is doing time as a result of his adventures in *First Blood.* His release is negotiated by a colonel who knows him and wants him for a special mission in Vietnam. Rambo asks: "Do we get to win this time?" (Read: "Will we be allowed to win this time?") Rambo has already personified the slighted Vietnam veteran; now he carries forward the stab-in-the-back theory, and it leads to political complications.

The mission, on which he is sent via helicopter and parachute from a 4 U.S. base in Thailand, is to spend 36 hours taking photographs of a Vietnam camp that he knows only too grimly well—to check if there are any American POWs. As soon as Rambo has left, his friend the colonel asks the civilian chief of the base, Murdock, about the existence of such POWs. Murdock doubts it. Evidently he wants his doubt confirmed. But Rambo finds half a dozen, rescues one, and gets him back to the "extraction point," the place where a helicopter is scheduled to lift him out. When the approaching pilot radios the base that Rambo has a POW with him, Murdock orders the pilot to abort the mission—to abandon Rambo and the POW.

At the base the furious colonel storms at Murdock, who explains that 5 the appearance of a POW back home might start agitation for armed invasion: that North Vietnam had wanted $4.5 billion ransom for prisoners back in 1972, that the money was not forthcoming then, and is even less likely to be paid now.

Soon Rambo is captured by a squad of Soviet soldiers, who are not 6 only Vietnamese allies but supply them with arms. The Soviet chief has him tortured to try to make him broadcast a false message to the U.S. base. Despite torture, Rambo refuses; his only broadcast message is to tell Murdock that he is coming back to get *him.* Helped by a Vietnamese girl who had been secretly briefed to guide him, Rambo escapes. (The girl is soon killed, so Rambo is left uncluttered by affection.)

Thus he has three political enemies: the Vietnamese, who want to kill 7 him; the Soviets, who want to kill him; and the American Murdock, whom he wants to kill. Many explosions later, he gets all six of the American POWs out, is himself unhurt, and corners the frightened Murdock, whose life he contemptuously spares.

Rambo tells the friendly colonel that there are more Americans in 8 Nam camps. (How does he know?) When the colonel asks him to join up again and help, he refuses. Apparently he is now a disillusioned loner. The colonel asks him whether he loves his country, and Rambo replies fiercely that he and all other Vietnam vets love their country—what they want is for their country to love *them.* As he walks away, the colonel asks how he will live. Rambo: "Day by day."

Obviously, then, *Rambo* is not just one more guts-and-glory series of ₉ impossible exploits. It's a statement of political beliefs, genuinely held or cynically utilized. America lost the Vietnam War but could not have lost it fairly: Americans don't lose fairly fought wars. They must have been betrayed—by elements in the government and the public that are still manipulating and betraying. The Vietnam experience bred a corps of veterans who are stalwart, long-suffering, deeply resentful. (Of course *Rambo* was made before the many recent moves to restore veterans' morale.) If given the chance, they can and will prove that history is not a closed book.

Some other matters loom out of *Rambo*. I can't argue here with the ₁₀ back-stab theory or any other political aspect of the quagmire. Nor do I want to be offhand about a misery that, along with hundreds of thousands of others, took 60,000 American lives. But *Rambo* and its film kin demonstrate that Vietnam today has become a mythological place, somewhat akin to those territories on ancient maps marked "Here there bee tygers." One after another, the heroes set off into that mysterious land to try their courage, to risk their lives in exploits without the complications of war, morally sanctified because the quest is humane and the enemy monstrous. Who needs Westerns now? In fact, quite adroitly, *Rambo* ingests the Western by making its hero half-Indian.

And there's another appeal in *Rambo*. Simplicity. Successful action ₁₁ justifies all. Are you frustrated by the plagues of complex politics? Do you feel cut off from the chance of immediate physical release by the gigantic finality of nuclear war? Take comfort—find promise, even—in those gleaming pecs and the modernized bow.

Using the Dictionary

Many of the following terms carry positive or negative **connotations**, helping the critic convey value judgments and attitudes. What *are* their connotations?   1. *foray* (1)   2. *rampage* (1)   3. *schlock* (1)   4. *cinematography* (1)   5. *ludicrous* (1)   6. *prowess* (2)   7. *simplistic* (2)   8. *taciturn* (3)   9. *manipulate* (9)   10. *stalwart* (9)   11. *mythological* (10)   12. *sanctified* (10)   13. *adroit* (10)

The Writer's Agenda

Kauffmann tries to get at the central message of the movie, showing us how it caters to the values or psychological needs of its public. Answer the following questions:

1. What **tone** does Kauffmann establish in his two introductory paragraphs? Do you expect the rest of the review to be biased or balanced? serious or tongue-in-cheek?

2. What is for Kauffmann the central message or the *central theme* of the movie? Where is the keynote first sounded in this review? Where and how is the central theme most fully spelled out later?

3. How does Kauffmann's account of the plot and the characters *support* his interpretation of its central message?

4. What is the "mythology" about Vietnam that is being promoted by movies like *Rambo*? (What kind of literature or entertainment does Kauffmann have in mind when he explains their basic appeal?) What are the implied parallels with the Western of days past?

5. Kauffmann says that he "can't argue here with the back-stab theory." What *is* his overall attitude toward the movie? What is his verdict? How and where does it show?

For Discussion or Writing

6. As a judge of popular entertainment, does Kauffmann seem too critical or too negative to you? Why or why not?

7. What evidence have you seen of the "back-stab" theory as a factor in American politics or entertainment? (How do *you* react to it?)

8. One of Kauffmann's fellow critics approved of *Rambo* as entertainment for adults but said that it would have a harmful effect on children, since it totally misled them about the suffering and heartbreak of war. What do you think?

9. Write a movie review, modeled on Kauffmann's, of a current or recent movie that has a strong subliminal message or serves a psychological need of the audience.

10. What role models do current movies offer to women?

Branching Out

11. Have you recently seen a revival of one of the classics of the screen? What was the secret of its audience appeal? What does it show about the expectations or needs of the movie-going public of its time? Choose a movie like *Birth of a Nation, Gone with the Wind, Citizen Kane, Jules and Jim, The Blue Angel, Casablanca.*

BACKGROUND: Richard Harsham is a free-lance writer in Cincinnati. His writing has appeared in publications including the *San Francisco Chronicle* and others. Like other television critics, he takes on what is often a thankless task: In an attempt to break through the crust of public apathy, he tried to alert us to the danger in something that we have come to take for granted.

Richard Harsham

A Beeper

---

for Violence

GUIDE TO READING: What does the author do to dramatize the issue? How effective is his presentation of the problem? How convincing is his solution?

To say that television violence is often unjustified, wanton and gratuitous will spark about as much controversy as saying that playing with matches causes fires. 1

But when proposals are made for alleviating the daily dose of small-screen mayhem children of tender years are exposed to, television executives decry the very idea as unthinkable, calling such efforts, in the words of George Schweitzer, a CBS vice president, "blatantly repressive policy." This, however, is not to deny that some pretty deadly force is being meted out by TV toughs for the benefit of an engrossed child audience. 2

Last July, a 9-year-old Wisconsin boy was murdered by three disgruntled kids who only wanted to take a spin on the boy's bike. His assailants—two boys, ages 14 and 12, and their female accomplice, a little girl all of 11 years—inflicted multiple stab wounds to their murder victim in addition to kicks to the head. 3

In an even more recent case, a 14-year-old Kentucky boy raped a 12-year-old girl and then calmly returned home, where police arrested him following the girl's report to them. 4

Are these acts of childish behavior? Or are they the frenzied acting out by overwrought youngsters who only did what they'd so often seen done before on TV? 5

According to the National Institute of Mental Health in Bethesda, Md., by the time an American child has reached the age of 16, he or she has logged between 10,000 and 15,000 hours in front of the television, witnessing an average 18,000 murders. 6

For anyone who doubts that televised dramas can trigger imitative behavior, there is a sobering statistic: After *The Deer Hunter*, a movie about 7

Americans' lost innocence in Vietnam, was shown on TV—29 viewers from around the country shot themselves acting out the movie's powerful Russian-roulette scenes.

So it should come as no surprise that in a recent National Council of 8 Churches report on television sex and violence, the question is raised: how to protect children from violent TV fare without violating constitutional guarantees of free speech? Seeking a reduction in TV violence, at the same time it vehemently opposes censorship, the National Council of Churches' study urges the Federal Communications Commission to assume an oversight role.

Is there a way to bring about some restraint by TV producers without 9 infringing on their First Amendment rights and, at the same time, give parents some practical control over the level of TV violence their children see? I think there is.

The television industry, in cooperation with the FCC, should impanel a 10 group of acclaimed child psychologists to review the TV programs in advance of their airing and rate the level of violence. Something akin to the star-rating system could be employed, substituting a snub-nosed revolver for the five-pointed star.

A program that a majority of the child psychologists felt portrayed a 11 high level of violence could be listed in TV Guide and newspaper schedules with four guns after the title. On the other hand, if a show had some but not much violence, one gun would appear after its program listing. Thus, parents could be forewarned about the level of violence in any given program their children wanted to see.

Then, for good measure, before opening credits of a program that was 12 deemed by the psychologists to be especially violent in content, a distinct warning tone could be sounded. It should be long enough to alert parents who want to be doubly certain that their impressionable children will not be watching depictions of human violence that are in no way ennobling.

This remedy avoids censorship, but at the same time it encourages 13 television producers to seriously reconsider infusing their shows with violence.

We all tend to forget how influential and everpresent TV is in our lives. 14 In 1951, the average American watched four-and-a-half hours of TV daily. Now the average American is plunked in front of a glowing TV for more than seven-and-a-half hours a day, according to the A. C. Nielsen Co.

Couple that with the National Institute of Mental Health's five-year 15 study of television-induced violence in children which concludes: "Violence on television does lead to aggressive behavior by children and teenagers who watch the programs."

If you're skeptical about such correlations, take time to tally a week's 16 worth of murders, beatings, rapes, robberies and brutal getting-evens that go down on the small screen. Then imagine the millions of wide-eyed kids who were watching along with you. They didn't miss a thing any more than you did at their age.

Using the Dictionary

A. Check the following as necessary: 1. *gratuitous* (1)   2. *alleviate* (2)   3. *mayhem* (2)   4. *blatant* (2)   5. *mete out* (2)   6. *engrossed* (2)   7. *infringe* (9)   8. *depiction* (12)   9. *infuse* (13)   10. *correlation* (16)

B.   Point out some examples of *informal* language that the author uses to provide a lighter touch.

The Writer's Agenda

Like other critics who view the increasing violence on television with alarm, the author tries to counteract public apathy. How? How successfully?

1. How does Harsham try to arouse the audience? In particular, look at his use of
- strong, graphic language
- striking provocative examples
- telling statistics

2. How does Harsham begin his essay? How does he end it?

3. What is his overall plan or general strategy? In what order does he present his material?

4. How serious is his proposed solution? How practical is his proposal?

5. Do you think his proposal constitutes censorship? Why, or why not?

6. How do you think Harsham visualized his intended audience? What attitudes or commitments does he appeal to or count on?

For Discussion or Writing

7. Do you think television programs have become more violent? Has the violence become more brutal? Draw on some detailed comparisons from your past and present viewing.

8. Network presidents frequently receive mail objecting to obscene lyrics in rock videos, nudity, stereotypical treatment of minorities, or other offensive material. Investigate one such complaint. Does it seem well-founded to you?

9. Study a type of television program at the highbrow end (*Masterpiece Theater*) or the lowbrow end (professional wrestling) of current television fare. Try to arrive at a portrait of the ideal audience or ideal viewer for this type of program.

10. Investigate and discuss the *formula* for a type of programming—sitcoms, crime shows, primetime soaps—currently popular with viewers.

Branching Out

11. In recent years, critics have looked seriously at the images of American life and at the underlying myths or values in some of the perennial audience favorites that live on in reruns and revivals. Study one such series—*I Love Lucy, The Honeymooners, Star Trek, The Mary Tyler Moore Show*—from this point of view.

BACKGROUND: Tom Wolfe (born 1931) started his career with a doctorate in American studies from Yale. He went on to work as a journalist for *The Washington Post* and started to publish articles in *Esquire*, *New York* magazine, and other publications. He became legendary as the inventor of the "New Journalism," a freewheeling, flamboyant, disrespectful, razzle-dazzle style of reportage that abandoned the reporter's conventional stance of detachment and objectivity. Instead, Wolfe plunged his readers into a stream of images, striking details, and snatches of conversation to make them imagine themselves as participants, sharing in the immediacy and excitement of the experience described. He became a leading chronicler of American popular culture, often seeming mesmerized by its surface glitter and zaniness but also looking for the deeper symbolic significance of trends and fads like the demolition derby, rock concerts, surfers, pot, the "me" generation, and radical chic. His colorful prose was collected in a succession of books, including *The Kandy-Kolored Tangerine-Flake Streamline Baby* (1965), *The Electric Kool-Aid Acid Test* (1968), *Radical Chic and Mau-Mauing the Flak Catchers* (1970), *The Painted Word* (1975), and *From Bauhaus to Our House* (1981). In 1981, Wolfe published *The Right Stuff*, a runaway bestseller about the astronauts of Project Mercury, America's first program for manned spacecraft. In the excerpt reprinted here, Wolfe describes the flight training of future astronauts early in their career.

Tom Wolfe

The Right Stuff

GUIDE TO READING: What is "the right stuff"? How does Wolfe use example and contrast to show us the meaning of his central term? What is his attitude toward the people he describes and the mystique they represent?

A young man might go into military flight training believing that he was entering some sort of technical school in which he was simply going to acquire a certain set of skills. Instead, he found himself all at once enclosed in a fraternity. And in this fraternity, even though it was military, men were not rated by their outward rank as ensigns, lieutenants, commanders, or whatever. No, herein the world was divided into those who had it and those who did not. This quality, this *it*, was never named, however, nor was it talked about in any way.

As to just what this ineffable quality was . . . well, it obviously involved bravery. But it was not bravery in the simple sense of being willing to risk your life. The idea seemed to be that any fool could do that, if that was all that was required, just as any fool could throw away his life in the process. No, the idea here (in the all-enclosing fraternity) seemed to be that a man should have the ability to go up in a hurtling piece of machinery and put his hide on the line and then have the moxie, the reflexes, the experience, the coolness, to pull it back in the last yawning moment—and then to go up again *the next day*, and the next day, and every next day, even if the series should prove infinite—and, ultimately, in its best expression, do so in a cause that means something to thousands, to a people, a nation, to humanity, to God. Nor was there *a test* to show whether or not a pilot had this righteous quality. There was, instead, a seemingly infinite series of tests. A career in flying was like climbing one of those ancient Babylonian pyramids made up of a dizzy progression of steps and ledges, a ziggurat, a pyramid extraordinarily high and steep; and the idea was to prove at every foot of the way up that pyramid that you were one of the elected and anointed ones who had *the right stuff* and could move higher and higher and even—ultimately, God willing, one day—that you might be able to join that special few at the very top, that elite who had the capacity to bring tears to men's eyes, the very Brotherhood of the Right Stuff itself.

None of this was to be mentioned, and yet it was acted out in a way ₃ that a young man could not fail to understand. When a new flight (i.e., a class) of trainees arrived at Pensacola, they were brought into an auditorium for a little lecture. An officer would tell them: "Take a look at the man on either side of you." Quite a few actually swiveled their heads this way and that, in the interest of appearing diligent. Then the officer would say: "One of the three of you is not going to make it!"—meaning, not get his wings. That was the opening theme, the *motif* of primary training. We already know that one-third of you do not have the right stuff—it only remains to find out who.

Furthermore, that was the way it turned out. At every level in one's ₄ progress up that staggeringly high pyramid, the world was once more divided into those men who had the right stuff to continue the climb and those who had to be *left behind* in the most obvious way. Some were eliminated in the course of the opening classroom work, as either not smart enough or not hardworking enough, and were left behind. Then came the basic flight instruction, in single-engine, propeller-driven trainers, and a few more—even though the military tried to make this stage easy—were washed out and left behind. Then came more demanding levels, one after the other, formation flying, instrument flying, jet training, all-weather flying, gunnery, and at each level more were washed out and left behind. By this point easily a third of the original candidates had been, indeed, eliminated ... from the ranks of those who might prove to have the right stuff.

In the Navy, in addition to the stages that Air Force trainees went ₅ through, the neophyte always had waiting for him, out in the ocean, a certain grim gray slab; namely, the deck of an aircraft carrier; and with it perhaps the most difficult routine in military flying, carrier landings. He was shown films about it, he heard lectures about it, and he knew that carrier landings were hazardous. He first practiced touching down on the shape of a flight deck painted on an airfield. He was instructed to touch down and gun right off. This was safe enough—the shape didn't move, at least—but it could do terrible things to, let us say, the gyroscope of the soul. *That shape!—it's so damned small!* And more candidates were washed out and left behind. Then came the day, without warning, when those who remained were sent out over the ocean for the first of many days of reckoning with the slab. The first day was always a clear day with little wind and a calm sea. The carrier was so steady that it seemed, from up there in the air, to be resting on pilings, and the candidate usually made his first carrier landing successfully, with relief and even *élan*. Many young candidates looked like terrific aviators up to that very point—and it was not until they were actually standing on the carrier deck that they first began to wonder if they had the proper stuff, after all. In the training film the flight deck was a grand piece of gray geometry, perilous, to be sure, but an amazing abstract shape as one looks down upon it on the screen. And yet once the newcomer's two feet were on it . . . *Geometry*—my God, man, this is a . . . *skillet!* It *heaved*, it moved up and down underneath his feet, it pitched up, it pitched down, it rolled to port (this great beast *rolled!*) and it rolled to starboard, as the ship moved into the wind and, therefore, into the waves, and the wind kept sweeping across, sixty feet up in the air out in the open sea, and there were no railings whatsoever. This was a *skillet!*—a frying pan!—a short-order grill!—not gray but black, smeared with skid marks from one end to the other and glistening with pools of hydraulic fluid and the occasional jet-fuel slick, all of it still hot, sticky, greasy, runny, virulent from God knows what traumas—still ablaze!—consumed in detonations, explosions, flames, combustion, roars, shrieks, whines, blasts, horrible shudders, fracturing impacts, as little men in screaming red and yellow and purple and green shirts with black Mickey Mouse helmets over their ears skittered about on the surface as if for their very lives (you've said it now!), hooking fighter planes onto the catapult shuttles so that they can explode their afterburners and be slung off the deck in a red-mad fury with a *kaboom!* that pounds through the entire deck—a procedure that seems absolutely controlled, orderly, sublime, however, compared to what he is about to watch as aircraft return to the ship for what is known in the engineering stoicisms of the military as "recovery and arrest." To say that an F-4 was coming back onto this heaving barbecue from out of the sky at a speed of 135 knots . . . that might have been the truth in the training lecture, but it did not begin to get across the idea of what the newcomer saw from the deck itself, because it created the notion that perhaps the plane was gliding in. On the deck one knew differently! As the aircraft came closer and the carrier heaved on into the waves and the plane's speed did not diminish and the deck did not grow steady—indeed, it pitched up and down five or ten feet per greasy heave—one experienced a neural alarm that no lecture could have prepared him for: This is not an *airplane* coming toward me, it is a brick with some poor sonofabitch riding it (*someone much like myself!*), and it is not *gliding*, it is *falling*, a fifty-thousand-pound brick, headed not for a stripe on the deck but for *me*—and with a horrible *smash!* it hits the skillet, and with a blur of momentum as big as a freight train's it hurtles toward the far end of the deck—another blinding storm!—another roar as the pilot pushes the throttle up to full military power and another smear of rubber screams out over the skillet—and this is nominal!—quite okay!—for a wire stretched across the deck has grabbed the hook on the end of the plane as it hit the deck tail down, and the smash was the rest of the fifteen-ton brute slamming onto the deck, as it tripped up, so that it is now straining against the wire at full throttle, in case it hadn't held and the plane had "boltered" off the end of the deck and had to struggle up into the air again. And already the Mickey Mouse helmets are running toward the fiery monster . . . .

And the candidate, looking on, begins to *feel* that great heaving sun-blazing deathboard of a deck wallowing in his own vestibular system—and suddenly he finds himself backed up against his own limits. He ends up going to the flight surgeon with so-called conversion symptoms. Overnight he develops blurred vision or numbness in his hands and feet or sinusitis so severe that he cannot tolerate changes in altitude. On one level the symptom is real. He really cannot see too well or use his fingers or stand the pain. But somewhere in his subconscious he knows it is a plea and a beg-off; he shows not the slightest concern (the flight surgeon notes) that the condition might be permanent and affect him in whatever life awaits him outside the arena of the right stuff. 6

Those who remained, those who qualified for carrier duty—and even more so those who later on qualified for *night* carrier duty—began to feel a bit like Gideon's warriors. *So many have been left behind!* The young warriors were now treated to a deathly sweet and quite unmentionable sight. They could gaze at length upon the crushed and wilted pariahs who had washed out. They could inspect those who did not have that righteous stuff.

The military did not have very merciful instincts. Rather than packing up these poor souls and sending them home, the Navy, like the Air Force and the Marines, would try to make use of them in some other role, such as flight controller. So the washout has to keep taking classes with the rest of his group, even though he can no longer touch an airplane. He sits there in the classes staring at sheets of paper with cataracts of sheer human mortification over his eyes while the rest steal looks at him . . . this man reduced to an ant, this untouchable, this poor sonofabitch. And in what test had he been found wanting? Why, it seemed to be nothing less than *manhood* itself. Naturally, this was never mentioned, either. Yet there it was. *Manliness, manhood, manly courage* . . . there was something ancient, primordial, irresistible about the challenge of this stuff, no matter what a sophisticated and rational age one might think he lived in. 8

Perhaps because it could not be talked about, the subject began to 9 take on superstitious and even mystical outlines. A man either had it or he didn't! There was no such thing as having *most* of it. Moreover, it could blow at any seam. One day a man would be ascending the pyramid at a terrific clip, and the next—bingo!—he would reach his own limits in the most unexpected way. Conrad and Schirra met an Air Force pilot who had had a great pal at Tyndall Air Force Base in Florida. This man had been the budding ace of the training class; he had flown the hottest fighter-style trainer, the T-38, like a dream; and then he began the routine step of being checked out in the T-33. The T-33 was not nearly as hot an aircraft as the T-38; it was essentially the old P-80 jet fighter. It had an exceedingly small cockpit. The pilot could barely move his shoulders. It was the sort of airplane of which everybody said, "You don't get into it, you *wear* it." Once inside a T-33 cockpit this man, this budding ace, developed claustrophobia of the most paralyzing sort. He tried everything to overcome it. He even went to a psychiatrist, which was a serious mistake for a military officer if his superiors learned of it. But nothing worked. He was shifted over to flying jet transports, such as the C-135. Very demanding and necessary aircraft they were, too, and he was still spoken of as an excellent pilot. But as everyone knew—and, again, it was never explained in so many words— only those who were assigned to fighter squadrons, the "fighter jocks," as they called each other with a self-satisfied irony, remained in the true fraternity. Those assigned to transports were not humiliated like wash-outs—*somebody* had to fly those planes—nevertheless, they, too, had been *left behind* for lack of the right stuff.

Or a man could go for a routine physical one fine day, feeling like a million dollars, and be grounded for *fallen arches*. It happened!—just like that! (And try raising them.) Or for breaking his wrist and losing only *part* of his mobility. Or for a minor deterioration of eyesight, or for any of hundreds of reasons that would make no difference to a man in an ordinary occupation. As a result all fighter jocks began looking upon doctors as their natural enemies. Going to see a flight surgeon was a no-gain proposition; a pilot could only hold his own or lose in the doctor's office. To be grounded for a medical reason was no humiliation, looked at objectively. But it was a humiliation, nonetheless!—for it meant you no longer had that indefinable, unutterable, integral stuff.

Using the Dictionary

Wolfe likes to dazzle his readers with a vocabulary ranging from slang (*moxie*, *washed out*) to **allusions** to distant history. What is the meaning and the source of each of the following examples? 1. *ineffable* (2) 2. *ziggurat* (2) 3. *anointed* (2) 4. *motif* (3) 5. *neophyte* (5) 6. *gyroscope* (5) 7. *élan* (5) 8. *virulent* (5) 9. *stoicism* (5) 10. *Gideon* (7) 11. *pariah* (7) 12. *mortification* (8) 13. *primordial* (8) 14. *mystical* (9) 15. *claustrophobia* (9)

The Writer's Agenda

Wolfe writes a highly charged prose designed to dazzle, shock, impress, and entertain the reader. Answer the following questions about how he achieves these results:

1. In the introductory paragraph, the author alerts us to expect more than a literal-minded, uninitiated, unimaginative observer would see. How does he establish an *insider's* perspective; how does he create an air of mystery and importance?

2. Though the author repeatedly says that "the right stuff" is indefinable and unutterable, he does define *key qualities* that are involved. What are they? How and where does he deal with them?

3. Wolfe's dramatic account of carrier landings is a spectacular example of his colorful, emotion-charged kind of "action writing." How does he use his tools as a writer to create the desired dramatic effect? How does he use point of view, striking details, vivid language, striking comparisons?

4. How does the final third of the essay drive home the idea of the *exclusiveness*, the select quality, of the group?

5. Wolfe often writes satirically, with a quick eye for what is cheap, gaudy, pretentious, or contradictory. What is his own *attitude* toward the trainees and the program they go through? Are we as readers expected to admire or glorify the people who have "the right stuff"? (Do *you* admire them? Why or why not?)

For Discussion or Writing

6. One of the oldest myths perpetuated by American popular entertainment is that of the lone rugged individual, facing danger and adventure. How do the space cowboys of popular science fiction use or adapt this myth? Is Wolfe's mystique of "the right stuff" in the same tradition?

7. At a time when women are joining the ranks of pilots and astronauts, is Wolfe's mystique of "manliness, manhood, manly courage" becoming obsolete?

8. Prepare a paper in which you explain what would be "the right stuff" for some other profession or calling: minister, teacher, lawyer, social worker, nurse, sales representative, or the like.

9. The astronauts became celebrities, with extensive media coverage of their private lives, personalities, and beliefs. What is the role of celebrities in the world of American media? What is their influence, or what needs do they serve? Are there different kinds?

10. Do a reportage in the Tom Wolfe style of some scene that is part of American popular culture: the rodeo, the gambling casino, the small-town parade, a prizefight, a beauty contest, or the like.

Branching Out

11. To judge from American popular entertainment, what are our current folk heroes? Are there several major recurrent types?

WRITERS ON WRITING
Tom Wolfe on Fact and Fiction

QUESTION: John Hersey wrote a piece in a recent *Yale Review* criticizing the New Journalism. He said that it's hard to distinguish between fact and fiction.

ANSWER: ... To me, it's extremely important to be accurate, because a lot of the voltage of narrative nonfiction is that the reader is able to believe. I think there are very few readers who want to read fantasy. They read novels because they're getting a picture of the emotional life of human beings that they can't get in any way except in the best forms of nonfiction. But if people start to ask, "I wonder if he makes up the parts in between that he doesn't know about," that's when you're undercutting the whole enterprise if you indulge in it.

QUESTION: So you make it a point not to fictionalize?

ANSWER: No, not even in the slightest. It's a tremendous mistake to do it. And also it's as if you violated the rules of your own game. There's a great satisfaction in taking the actual facts insofar as you can get them and turning this material into something that is as engrossing as fiction, and in some cases more so, when you succeed.

QUESTION: Often you reconstruct someone's inner thoughts.

ANSWER: You have to do it by interview. You can argue that people who can't remember very well will lie. That's a risk. You have to have faith that the writer went conscientiously about doing this—believed his source was leveling with him. We do this in autobiography all the time. We tend to believe that an individual can remember his emotions and report them accurately. We hardly even blink. I feel that in a way the nonfiction writer is writing parts of other people's autobiographies. And what he comes up with should be given at least the credence that we give other autobiographies.

QUESTION: How do your subjects feel? Did you get any feedback from the astronauts?

ANSWER: I've had varied reactions. Some of them really seemed to like it, or at least to have said that it's accurate, which means more to me than whether or not they really liked it. Alan Shepard, I know, doesn't like it because every time he's asked he says, "I haven't read it and I'm not going to." John Glenn, who in the minds of reviewers came out worst of the seven, wrote me a very funny, friendly letter. I was surprised, incidentally, that he came off the way that he did. In my mind, I was presenting a rare and strangely colorful figure of our time. It's very rare to see a man in our day—outside the Church—who is a moral zealot and who doesn't hide the fact; who constantly announces what he believes in and the moral standards he expects people to follow. To me that's much rarer and more colorful than the Joe Namath-rake figure who is much more standard these days.

QUESTION: Do you feel ambivalent about "the right stuff"?

ANSWER: In the sense that to me it wasn't nearly so important to say "Here is this great quality" as to point out that this is the core of the competition for status that drives these people. It wasn't this great quality that everyone should aspire to. Since then, people have asked me: Wouldn't you say that one can also speak of the "right stuff" in journalism, in the business world, everybody's up against difficult moments; and I always said no, there is no analogy. It involves risking your life in an essentially sporting way. But there's no halo around it.

(From Joshua Gilder, "Tom Wolfe," *Saturday Review*)

STUDENT MODEL 11

FOR READING: Study the following short selection as a possible model for writing of your own. How do you react to it overall? What makes it interesting or effective? Answer the following more specific questions:

1. (PURPOSE) What was the writer trying to do?
2. (AUDIENCE) What kind of reader would make a good reader for this selection?
3. (SOURCES) Where did the writer turn for material?
4. (THESIS) Does the selection have a central idea or unifying thesis?
5. (STRUCTURE) What is the author's overall plan or strategy?
6. (STYLE) What makes the piece effective or memorable (for instance, striking details, memorable phrases)?
7. (REVISION) What do you think the writer could or should have done differently?

Anne Gelhaus
Portraying Rape: Realism and Ratings

A recent television movie, *Silent Witness*, depicted the fictional trial of three men suspected of gang rape. During the course of the trial the defense lawyer continually harassed the victim about her alcoholism and mental illness. The lawyer persuaded the jury that the woman was drunk at the time of the rape and therefore left herself open to sexual advances.

California state law makes this line of defense illegal. A rape victim's past cannot be used as evidence against her unless she has a history of extreme sexual promiscuity. But a rape victim who is unaware of her rights might be deterred from reporting the crime after viewing such harsh treatment. This type of media portrayal perpetuates society's attitude that a victim sexually provokes the rapist into committing the crime.

When dealing with an issue as sensitive as rape, television programmers should strive for realism rather than ratings. The media reflect and shape this country's values. Many stereotypes have become intrinsic to our culture with the help of repeated false characterization in television and movies.

Research indicates that almost half of the rapes in the United States go unreported. Victims are often too humiliated to seek legal action, said Delinda Rounsville, a counselor at the San Jose Women's Alliance.

Television programs should be more sensitive to a rape victim's fragile psychological state. *Silent Witness* and shows of its kind might confirm a victim's fears that she is the criminal. A woman may continue to suffer in silence rather than face society's ridicule.

This silence is not only detrimental to a victim's mental health, it hinders the judiciary's attempts to protect her rights and increase the number of rape convictions. Many people who deal with rapists and their victims believe that increased convictions will lower the general incidence of rape, Rounsville said.

"The only way the legal system is going to change is by victims speaking out," she said.

In one landmark case, a rape victim sued her landlord on the grounds that her apartment was unsafe, Rounsville said. After her rape, the woman discovered that the previous tenant had also been assaulted. Both times, the rapist entered the apartment through a window with a broken lock. The woman won her case.

The media need to take cases such as this into consideration before airing shows that deal with rape. Most television programs are now designed to increase public awareness that rape is a violent crime and not a sexual act, Rounsville said. Talk shows feature interviews with victims and psychologists, and David Soul recently starred in another television movie as a convicted rapist who was rehabilitated through a prison support group, she said. However, the media should not assume that one responsible show cancels out one dramatization. Emotions sometimes speak louder than facts.

(From *Spartan Daily*)

FOR WRITING: Single out a current offering or trend in the world of media for praise or blame. Clarify the standards you apply; try to convince a fair-minded reader. Use striking examples or telling evidence.

Additional Writing Topics 11

Media

A. Write a paper on a topic of interest to media watchers. Focus your paper on some major point(s) or issue(s); present a conclusion or thesis and provide detailed support. Aim at an audience that is interested in the media as a mirror of American life but that may not have more than a vague recollection of the details and episodes you use as examples. Choose a topic like the following:

1. the children's hour: Saturday morning cartoons
2. the people of soap opera
3. people who call in to talk shows
4. a favorite movie or television critic
5. the gospel according to Jerry Falwell
6. reruns: nostalgia time
7. the word from William F. Buckley
8. Westerns and the Native American
9. a movie classic
10. Dear Abby: where to turn for good advice
11. Miss Manners: a lost cause?
12. white television and the black comic
13. the women's page: obsolete?
14. *The Wizard of Oz* and *The Wiz*
15. Bob Hope forever

B. With your classmates, prepare a class publication, such as a class newspaper, magazine, or collection of student writing. Set up an editorial committee; farm out different features or functions to different members of the class.

UNIT

12

WRITING ABOUT HISTORY

In Search of the Past

OVERVIEW

Historians study the past in order to provide guidance or warnings for the future. They try to make sense of the contradictory marchings and countermarchings of historical events; they try to find the larger pattern in the zigzags of historical developments. They try to find the kernel of fact in the charges and countercharges, grievances, special pleadings, and biased testimony of contemporaries. They try to make us see not only *what* happened but also *how* and *why*.

PURPOSE Historians try to get close to the actual events, looking at eyewitness reports, contemporary documents. They try to get at primary sources—rather than relying on secondhand accounts that may already be selective, biased, distorted. We expect historians to rise above the passions of the moment to get at some more objective, lasting truth.

Nevertheless, much writing on historical subjects aims at an audience that is expected to share the writer's commitments or basic goals. The people we turn to for eyewitness reports of historic events are often not detached observers but people who were involved. They are often setting down for the record something that had for them an intense personal meaning. Other writers look back at past events to reaffirm a sense of common purpose, to relive moments when they experienced the sense of solidarity that comes from a shared commitment to a common cause. Still others write to raise voices of warning, trying to teach us the lessons of past experience.

AUDIENCE Even more than other readers, an audience seriously interested in historical subjects is likely to be wary of mere superficial opinion. When we look for the lessons of recent history, we turn to the testimony of the committed participant or to the writer who has seriously studied the record and weighed the evidence. Serious writing on historical subjects shows the writer's respect for the possible doubts of the audience and for its sense of fairness.

BENEFITS FOR THE WRITER (1) Writers on historical subjects have to marshal a mass of initially confusing or contradictory material. We can learn from them how to sort out conflicting evidence, how to weigh the pro and con. We can learn from them how to take into account a range of relevant sources. Writing on historical subjects tests our ability to *organize*—to bring a subject under control.

(2) Writers on historical subjects have to separate fact from hearsay, legend, and biased testimony. We can learn from them how to judge the reliability of our sources. We learn to test secondhand information against *primary* sources: eyewitness reports, contemporary documents, the testimony of survivors.

(3) Writers on historical subjects must know how to choose, how to use and adapt material for their own purposes. We can learn from them how to summarize or excerpt; how to use a telling, revealing quotation; when to paraphrase and when to quote.

WRITER'S GUIDE 12

Using and Documenting Sources

How does a writer become an authority on a subject? We consider an authority someone who has made a careful study of a subject, is familiar with different approaches, and can give balanced answers to difficult questions. We feel confident that such a writer has turned for information to people who should know or who have made the effort to find out. We feel that the writer has taken seriously views different from his or her own and has explored the pros and cons of open issues.

When we want to stake out a claim as an authority on a subject, we will often follow the conventions of a **documented paper**—a paper that draws on a variety of sources and clearly identifies them for the reader. Whether in a short research report or in a full-length research paper, we follow the conventions of the documented paper when the origin of our facts and the validity of our judgments are major issues. In a documented paper, we clearly mark all quoted material. We clearly show the sources of facts or opinions borrowed or adapted from other writers. We give exact information about the who, what, where, and when of published material.

Remember the following guidelines when writing a documented paper:

(1) *Clearly identify your sources.* When you draw on a variety of sources, make clear to your readers who said what. Provide clear answers to questions like the following: "How do we know this? Where does this material come from? Who said this—when and where?" The following examples show how Langston Hughes identifies sources in his biography of Harriet Tubman:

Early biography	A number of books have been written about her. The first one, *Scenes in the Life of Harriet Tubman*, by Sarah H. Bradford, appeared in 1869....
Contemporary historian	And at the great public meetings of the North, as the Negro historian William Wells Brown wrote in 1854, "all who frequented anti-slavery conventions, lectures, picnics, and fairs, could not fail to have seen a black woman of medium size...."
Contemporary newspaper report	As reported by the Boston *Commonwealth*, for July 10, 1863, they "under the guidance of a black woman, dashed into the enemy's country, struck a bold and effective blow, destroying millions of dollars' worth of commissary stores...." (Langston Hughes, "Harriet Tubman, the Moses of Her People")

(2) *Use a variety of techniques for reproducing material from your sources.* Remember the most basic rule: Identify as a quotation anything that you copy verbatim, word for word, from a printed source. Use different ways of adapting material—ranging from extended direct quotation to a brief summary of an author's argument in your own words:

DIRECT QUOTATION Quote word for word to show that you have gone to the actual source and studied it at firsthand. Do not merely copy long, undigested, unevaluated passages: Quote a whole sentence or short passage when it sums up well an important idea, or when it shows well the author's stand on a controversial point. Similarly, quote verbatim when a statement shows well the spirit or tone of something you have read. *Excerpt* longer passages when it seems especially important to reproduce ideas or arguments in the actual words used by the original author.

Study different uses of **direct quotation** in the following examples:

- The following passage quotes an authority on a *debatable point.* It shows the standard way of quoting a complete, self-controlled short statement. (A colon could replace the comma that precedes the quotation.)

    William Labov, a noted linguist, once said about the use of black English, "It is the goal of most black Americans to acquire full control of the standard language without giving up their own culture."

- The quotation in the following passage spells out a *central idea* in exceptionally graphic, vivid terms. (The person quoting has shortened the quotation and used three dots—an **ellipsis** to show the omission.)

    In his 1973 attack on judicial sentencing, *Criminal Sentences: Law Without Order*, the distinguished federal judge Marvin E. Frankel claimed that in "the great majority of federal criminal cases . . . a defendant who comes up for sentencing has no way of knowing or reliably predicting whether he will walk out of the courtroom on probation, be locked up for a term of years that may consume the rest of his life, or something in between."

- The following passage reproduces as a **block quotation**—set off from the text, *no* quotation marks—a passage that shows the characteristic language of advocates of censorship:

    Several organizations hailed the removal of the dictionaries from the Texas list as a major victory. Educational Research Analysts, which bills itself as the "nation's largest textbook review clearing house," noted:

God gave parents a number of victories. In Texas alone, the State Textbook Committee did a good job of selecting the best of the available books. Then, the State Commissioner of Education removed ten books, including the dictionaries with vulgar language and unreasonable definitions.

- The following passage illustrates the way *short, apt quotations* are used to lend an authentic touch to much biographical and historical writing:

> Encouraged by her sister-in-law to "write something that would make the whole nation feel what an accursed thing slavery is," Stowe began drawing from long-stored memories of her experience living in Cincinnati's "Little Africa" to write *Uncle Tom's Cabin*. While caring for her seven children, doing laundry, baking bread, mending clothes, and teaching a group of young women, she seized every odd moment to scribble her story on whatever was at hand, often brown wrapping paper. Eighteen months later, in 1852, Stowe's labors resulted in the publication of the book Lincoln said "made the big war." (Judy Mednick, "The Right to Write," *California English*)

SUMMARY AND PARAPHRASE

Try not to quote big chunks of undigested material. Excerpt, summarize, explain. Anticipate the questions of the reader who asks, "What part of this is important? What am I supposed to make of this? Why is this in here?" Often you will **paraphrase** material—put it in your own words. This way you show that you have made the material your own. You can emphasize what is most important; you can condense and explain the material at the same time.

Here are some examples of how authors summarize or paraphrase material from their sources. Remember that in a documented paper summarized or paraphrased material will also have to be credited to its source.

- A writer will often summarize *facts and figures* without direct quotation:

> Most writers have not led easy or comfortable lives. A recent survey of P.E.N., the international writers' organization, found that the annual median income from writing was $4,700, with 68 percent making under $10,000.

- In the following passage, a writer summarizes a *researcher's findings*. Note that key terms taken directly from the original study appear in quotation marks:

> There is what Harvard psychologist Robert Rosenthal once called the "Pygmalion effect." In his now-classic study, he told teachers that certain randomly selected elementary school children were "intellectual bloomers" and would show great intellectual gains in the coming year. Sure enough,

those children did indeed show gains compared with children not labeled "bloomers."

(3) *Aim at a fair and balanced treatment of your sources.* Even when you refer to a source only briefly, you are responsible for not misrepresenting the author's intentions or point of view. Quote from others as you would have them quote from you: Do not take a quotation out of context. Show that you have identified an author's point of view, that you have traced the major steps in an argument, and that you have noted key examples. When you disagree, do not just dismiss or brush off unwelcome data or an opposing view. Do not seem to be pouncing on a single weak link in an extended argument.

The following example shows how a writer tries to do justice to a major source. Notice the mix of summary, paraphrase, and direct quotation:

Source identified	It is instructive to go back to the late 1950s and read *Seventeen* magazine, or *Mademoiselle*, or such an etiquette book as *On Becoming a Woman*, by Mary McGee Williams and Irene Kane, which went through 17 printings and sold hundreds of thousands of copies.
MAIN IDEA	Throughout the book, the assumption reigned that marriage and motherhood were every woman's sole destiny and reason for existence. The book contained lists of things girls were supposed to do to please their adolescent dates. There was no suggestion that the boy had to please the girl.
Key example	She was supposed to steer the conversation toward automobile engines, baseball, and such subjects, and defer to
Quoted title	his interests and knowledge. A typical chapter is called "It's Not Too Soon to Dream of Marriage."
Key example with quote	The image of the desirable girl was almost entirely a passive one. Under no circumstances was a girl to phone a boy and ask him out. "In dating, like dancing," we read, "a boy likes to take the lead: a girl's role, traditionally, is to follow." On a dinner date, the girl was supposed to tell the boy her choices and he would tell the waiter.
Key quote	Chastity was also a constant theme. "Boys," we read, "will only respect you if you say no." (Jeffrey Hart, "The 1950's," *National Review*)

(4) *Establish connections between your different sources.* When we seriously explore a range of sources, we encounter different points of view, authorities drawing on different sources of information, confident assertions clashing with strong doubts. Our task is to find areas of agreement and disagreement. Our challenge is to weigh differing testimony and to reconcile conflicting views.

In the following paragraph a writer brings together evidence and testimony from several different sources to support a *general conclusion*:

<table>
<tr><td>General point</td><td>American women who were successful writers often had to overcome incredible opposition and discouragement. When Phillis Wheatley, a freed Negro slave, published her *Poems on Various Subjects, Religious and Moral*, there was widespread skepticism about her being the true au-</td></tr>
<tr><td>First source</td><td>thor. She was subjected to a public examination to test her knowledge of the Bible and of Latin and Greek. Her examiners signed a document, included in the 1773 edition of her poems, which concluded that "Phillis, a young Negro girl, who but a few years since was brought an uncultivated barbarian from Africa" was qualified to have written the</td></tr>
<tr><td>Second source</td><td>poems. Louisa May Alcott, the author of *Little Women*, became a published playwright at 16, but only because, in her own words, "a certain editor labored under the delusion that the writer was a man." In her autobiography, *The*</td></tr>
<tr><td>Third source</td><td>*Living of Charlotte Perkins Gilman*, the author describes a consultation with a nerve specialist who told her to end all intellectual activity, never to "touch pen, brush, or pencil," as long as she lived.</td></tr>
</table>

(5) *Document your sources fully to demonstrate your good faith as a writer.* Documented writing, whether on historical, political, or scientific subjects, has a glass-house effect: Readers are free to inspect the evidence. They are welcome to *verify* information—to go to the original sources and see for themselves. Documentation provides all necessary information about the *who, what, where,* and *when* of the sources consulted by the author.

Follow the style of documentation described in a handbook or style manual recommended by your instructor. You are likely to be asked to include page references (and *brief* identification of the source as necessary) in parentheses in the text of your paper. A final bibliography, or alphabetical list of "Works Cited," will provide full information for each source. Study the sample pages on pp. 430–31.

To sum up: An authoritative study of a subject often draws on a variety of relevant sources. It brings in facts and figures from reliable studies. It weighs the conflicting opinions of experts. When you draw on the work of other writers, you have to learn to choose material and put it to good use. You have to convince your audience that you have been a fair-minded, responsive reader. You have to show clearly your indebtedness to others, and you have to identify your sources in such a way that your readers can check them and see for themselves.

Frank Graham, Jr., writing in <u>Audubon</u> magazine, reported a current estimate of 5,000 bald eagles left in the lower forty-eight states. According to his figures, only 627 nests remained active, and they produced approximately 500 young (99). In 1981, Steven C. Wilson and Karen C. Hayden, writing in the <u>National Geographic</u>, reported a count of 76 for wild whooping cranes left in the United States, up from a dismal count of 21 thirty years earlier (37-38). Another estimate puts the current population at 95 (Freedman 89). Angered by the notorious "massacre of Jackson's Canyon" (Christopherson 39), the author of several authoritative articles on our endangered bird populations said, "The notion that eagles are simply feathered vermin dies hard, especially in the Far West" (Lamotte, "Bald Eagles" 168). As D. H. Lawrence said about another "lord of life,"

> The voice of my education said to me
> He must be killed.   (218)

page references only

authors identified

one of several articles identified

block quotation (poetry)

Works Cited

"Aging." Encyclopaedia Britannica: Macro-
     paedia. 1983.

Alexander, Shana. "Getting Old in Kids'
     Country." Newsweek 11 Nov. 1974: 124.

Blalock, Rebecca. "Gray Power: Work of Maggie
     Kuhn." Saturday Evening Post Mar. 1979:
     32-34, 127.

Browning, Robert. Poetical Works. London:
     Oxford UP, 1967.

Comfort, Alex. A Good Age. New York: Simon,
     1976.

---. "Old Age: Facts and Fancies." Saturday
     Evening Post Mar. 1977: 45.

de Beauvoir, Simone. The Coming of Age. Trans.
     Patrick O'Brian. New York: Putnam's, 1972.

"Early Retirement Rejected by Many." Christian
     Science Monitor 24 Apr. 1979: 19.

Fischer, David Hackett. "Aging: The Issue of
     the 1980's." New Republic 2 Dec. 1979:
     31-36.

Neugarten, Bernice. "Grow Old Along with Me!
     The Best Is Yet to Be." Growing Old. Ed.
     Gordon Moss and Walter Moss. New York:
     Simon, 1975. 112-116.

Peterson, David A., Chuck Powell, and Lawne
     Robertson. "Aging in America: Toward the
     Year 2000." Gerontologist 16 (1976): 264-
     75.

encyclopedia article

standard entry: magazine

subtitle

standard entry: book

same author

translated work

anonymous article

inclusive page numbers

article in collection

several authors

Prewriting Activities 12

1. Consulting the card catalog, the *Readers' Guide*, the *Book Review Digest*, or other sources, locate three articles and books that take stock of the American involvement in Vietnam. Study each article (or selected chapter from a book). Prepare a brief report on the perspective adopted by each author, the nature of the writer's involvement, the scope and purpose of the work, and the use of sources or personal experience. Include several representative and instructive quotations from each of the three works.

2. In recent years, publishers have printed much biographical material on outstanding representatives of minority groups. Assume that you are preparing a biographical paper devoted to one such figure. Using the card catalog and periodical indexes, prepare a short list of promising sources. Follow conventional format. Include six or more items. (If possible, include one or more book-length biographical or autobiographical sources.) Choose a figure from the following list, or choose your own outstanding representative of a minority group:

César Chavez	Piri Thomas	Frederick Douglass
Maya Angelou	Leontyne Price	Mahalia Jackson
N. Scott Momaday	Martin Luther King, Jr.	James Baldwin
Lorraine Hansberry	Langston Hughes	Alex Haley
Richard Wright	Maxine Hong Kingston	Thurgood Marshall
Paul Robeson	Simon J. Ortiz	Shirley Chisholm
José Antonio Villareal	Alice Walker	Cicely Tyson
	Harriet Tubman	

Paragraph Practice 12

The following paragraph is from a review of a book about Eugene Debs, an early hero of the American labor movement. Study and discuss it as a possible model for a similar passage of your own. Do research for, and write, a similar paragraph about a historical figure you admire or dislike.

Hero of American Labor

On Christmas Day 1921, a tall, thin 66-year-old man began to walk through the empty yard of the federal penitentiary in Atlanta—free after serving two years and nine months for denouncing World War I and the government's prosecution of its opponents. ("While there is a lower class, I am in it," he said at his sentencing; "While there is a criminal element, I am of it; while there is a soul in prison, I am not free.") As his emaciated figure became visible from behind the bars of the main building, 2,300 inmates broke into a thunderous cheer. Slowly the old man turned, his gaunt face streaming with tears, and raised his arms in a symbolic embrace. Three days later, in Terre Haute, Indiana, 25,000 people welcomed him home, as men who had vied for the honor pulled him from the depot to his house in the same wagon that had carried him over the same route on his return from prison after the Pullman Strike of 1894.   (William H. Harbaugh, "Radical Democrat," *New Republic*)

BACKGROUND: Larry C. Heinemann writes about the Vietnam war as an eyewitness who shares the "blunt and heartfelt bitterness" of the veterans who "had been lied to and used by arrogant and selfish men." He was born in 1944 in Chicago; he graduated from Columbia College there and later returned to the college to teach writing. During his service in the U.S. Army from 1966 to 1968, he became a sergeant in the infantry, serving in Vietnam. Much of his writing focuses on what the war did to those who served in it. He published *Close Quarters*, a novel based on his experience in Vietnam, in 1977. In an article in the April 1985 *Harper's*, he reports on his interviews with Vietnam war veterans—some of them living in self-imposed isolation, subject to depression, paranoid suspicion, and nightmare flashbacks; others having successfully "skinned back the layers of their delayed stress to resume their lives." The following selection is an excerpt from the article, in which Heinemann says: "Tens of thousands of GIs got chewed up in the Vietnam War, and there are tens of thousands upon whom the war still chews."

Larry Heinemann

Tour of Duty

GUIDE TO READING: What are the sources of the material in this essay? What does Heinemann do to put the experience of the Vietnam veteran in perspective? How does he make the traumatic experience of the veteran real for the reader?

During World War I, the Allied military, and the British especially, 1
weren't interested in attributing the soldiers' responses to battle and butchery to any unmanly newfangled psychological or emotional causes. Rather, it was believed that the very shock, the concussion, from an artillery round had an irresistible effect upon the body itself. "Shell shock" seemed a perfectly reasonable explanation for what happened to the men in the trenches.

During World War II, the troops suffered "combat fatigue"—the boys 2
were just tired. World War II veterans did not escape the effects associated with delayed stress. The psychiatric casualties were 300 percent higher in the early years of World War II than in World War I. But the way soldiers fought in World War II, and the way they stopped fighting after it, were different from what happened in Vietnam—and this difference would prove crucial. During World War II, a unit trained together and shipped overseas together. You humped North Africa, Italy and Sicily, then France and Germany, or you island-hopped from Tarawa and Guadalcanal and Peleliu to Iwo Jima and Okinawa. You were in for the duration, as the saying went. After the war, waiting to be shipped home, you had time to share the sympathetic support of men with whom you had a particular intimacy not often permitted in this culture. (It wasn't "buddies," the dead-flat, shopworn

newspaper cliché that trivialized a complex and powerful relationship. "Buddy-up" was something you did at Boy Scout camp, when everyone would mosey down to the lake for a swim. Boy Scout camp may be many things, but it ain't the straight-leg, ground-pounding infantry.)

Waiting, you got to work some of the war out of your system; to release 3 the grief for men long dead; to feel keenly, perhaps for the first time, your survivor's guilt; to feel as well the sharp personal guilt for murdering prisoners, say, or for shelling villages good and hard that you later discovered were filled with women and children, or for firebombing Dresden; to recognize the delight you took in destruction (what the Bible calls "lust of the eye") and the warm, grim satisfaction of your firm and bitter anger. Waiting, you had time for crying jags, public and private; you had time for fistfights to settle old scores once and for all. By the time your ship docked, you had worked much of the stress out of your system, though the annual depressions (usually coinciding with anniversaries), the periodic screaming, thrashing nightmares (vivid and colorful recollections of the worst times of your life), and the rest would linger for years—delayed stress (though no one yet called it by that name) a permanent fixture in your life.

In the Vietnam War, everyone served a one-year tour—the assumption 4 being that any dipstick could keep his buttons buttoned *that* long—though you could volunteer to stay as long as you liked. (United States Marine Corps esprit dictated that every Marine would serve one year and one month. *Semper Fi*, Mac.) But the one-year tour created a reverberating and lingering turmoil of emotional problems unlike anything known after World War II.

Vietnam was a war of individuals. You went through Basic Training 5 with one group, Advanced Individual Training with another. You shipped overseas with a planeload of total strangers, and when you reached your outfit—a rifle company out in the middle of nowhere, say—the astonishment on your face and the bright sheen of your uniform pegged you as a 'cruit, the newbee, the fucking new guy.

You have never seen those people before in your life. Everyone avoids 6 you (dumb guys never last, we used to say). At the very least, you have replaced a highly experienced and valuable man whose tour was up. He was as smooth as silk when he took the point, and no John Wayne. You, on the other hand, have hardly seen an M-16 and do not know your ass from a hole in the ground. The heat and humidity are withering, and you're so exhausted by ten in the morning, pouring sweat, that when they call a break in place you can't even stand up to piss.

As you begin your tour, the short-timers finish theirs, mount their 7 choppers and leave, and are never heard from again; other FNGs arrive. Your first firefight is a bloody, nasty mess, and it is a pure wonder you are not killed. Slowly you become accustomed to the weather and the work—the *grinding*, backbreaking humps, the going over the same ground day in and day out, aboard choppers and on foot. More short-timers leave; more FNGs arrive. This is the ugliest, most grueling, and most spiritless work you have ever done. But you soon discover you're a pretty good tunnel rat or booby-trap man, or especially canny and efficient on night ambush. You come to know the ground around your base camp and firebases like the back of your hand. In camp, on standdown, you smoke dope in earnest; you drink like a fish; you party with a serious frenzy.

More short-timers leave; more FNGs arrive. With every firefight the men around you drop like flies. You endure jungle rot, heat exhaustion, crabs and head lice, and an endless diarrhea from the one-a-day malaria pills. You take your five-day R&R in Bangkok, a culinary and sexual rampage. When you get back to the field more short-timers have disappeared; more FNGs have replaced them. You are sprayed with Agent Orange; the dust is in your hair, in your water, on your food. They send you to sharpshooter school; you return with an M-14 with scope and carrying case and a $500 pair of field glasses—the company sniper. You can draw a bead and drop a VC—man, woman, or child—in his tracks at 500 meters, and he never knows what hit him. You have many kills. More short-timers leave; more FNGs arrive. You are promoted to sergeant and made a squad leader. Your platoon leader, an ROTC first lieutenant, admires and trusts you: you will go anywhere and do anything. Humping is a snap, and you live in the midst of an alien ease. 8

The firefights and ambushes are bloody and nasty, businesslike massacres with meat all over everything. The one-year tour is the topic of endless conversation; you know exactly when your tour will end, and *that* is what keeps you going. You don't care about anything but finishing your tour—you just don't care. 9

Then one morning you wake up and it is finally your turn—not a day too soon, you understand. You say your goodbyes, hop in your chopper, and leave. You will never see or hear of these men again. The next morning you hitch a ride to the airfield in time to catch the plane to Saigon. You have hacked it, but you are exhausted. Your body is as tight as a drum. The plane finally comes: a Boeing 707. The replacements file off and you and your fellow passengers walk across the tarmac, and load up—a ritual unbelievably ordinary and benign. 10

On the plane you sit in a space both anonymous and claustrophobic, more glad and more guilty than tongue can tell. Sick, lame or lazy, blind, crippled or crazy—you just want out. The plane ride is nineteen hours of canned music and beach-blanket movies. At Oakland Army Terminal you're mustered out—given a bum's rush of a physical and a new baggy, smelly uniform, and issued your outstanding pay in greenback cash. You are free to go. 11

Your entire family meets you at the airport and takes you home to the house where you grew up. Yesterday or the day before you were surrounded by men who humped guns and grenades, up to their eyeballs in bloody murder (mean and evil sons-of-bitches, you bet). Now you're dumped into a 12 maelstrom—walk/don't-walk lights, Levi's and daytime TV; mom and dad and the dog on the couch—that bears no relationship to anything you're accustomed to. You're with people who love you, but they don't have the faintest inkling how to help you. You want to sit and tell them what happened—what you saw, what you did, what you became—but more often than not they don't want to hear about it. Your father, a World War II Marine, perhaps, shrugs his shoulders and, struggling with his own residual delayed stress, says, Everybody did those things, grow up, forget it (it's all right). But you sit in that clean kitchen, smelling the eggs and bacon, and warming your hands on a cup of coffee, and it is not all right.

And no "validating" ritual—no parade or Vietnam War memorial— 13 will make it so.

And make no mistake: if you have any healthy impulses left at all, you 14 want to find a woman and take her to bed. Skip the date; skip the dinner; skip the movie. You want to feel good in your body and re-establish those powerful human feelings. Maybe you manage it, but just as likely you don't: some women refuse to date veterans, and then brag to them about it.

You get your old job back (it's the law) stocking shelves at the A&P. 15 The work is easy and dull, and the money's decent, but the petty harassment is galling. The boss doesn't want you around, the way you *stare* when the customers ask their endlessly stupid questions. You drift from job to job. Sometimes, as soon as you mention you're a veteran, the clerk behind the counter tells you to beat it; they don't need junkies and they don't need freaks.

You cannot concentrate. You begin having nightmares; you jerk out of 16 sleep, pouring sweat. You drink to anesthetize yourself against the dreams and the daydream flashbacks (drunks don't dream very well). You try to stay up as long as you can. You know you will dream about the night you shivved that wounded VC who kept waving his hands in your face, shaking his head and whispering man to man, "No, no," while he squirmed against your knife with all his might.

You cannot stand crowds or people walking too close behind you. You 17 discover an abrupt and furious temper; you startle into a crouch at the damnedest things. You become self-destructive, picking fights and driving your car crazily. There is the nagging thought that you didn't do enough, that you never should have left Vietnam. Everyone you came to trust has disappeared from your life, dead by now, for all you know. How does that make you feel? You withdraw into isolation. Why put up with the grief?

Using the Dictionary

A. Check the following as necessary: 1. *sympathetic* (2)   2. *trivialize* (2)   3. *esprit* (4)   4. *reverberate* (4)   5. *culinary* (8)   6. *benign* (10)   7. *claustrophobic* (11)   8. *maelstrom* (12)   9. *residual* (12)   10. *validate* (13)   11. *anesthetize* (16)

B. How much use does Heinemann make of extremely informal language, slang, and obscenities? (Choose examples and check how they are treated in your dictionary.) What is the effect on the reader? Do you find his use of language objectionable?

The Writer's Agenda

Heinemann writes about a traumatic chapter in recent American history as an eyewitness who wants to make us see and understand "how it was." Answer the following questions:

1. Heinemann's purpose is to make us understand men who upon their return home felt misunderstood, stereotyped, and rejected. How successful is he?

2. What is the purpose of his *introductory* discussion of earlier wars? What are the major contrasts it sets up?

3. Where does he state his central *thesis*?

4. What are major *stages* or mileposts in the progress of the "tour of duty"? Is there an overall pattern?

5. What details are for you most striking? What statements or passages do most to make the subject real for you?

6. What is the **tone** of this piece? Is it accusing, solemn, bitter, self-pitying, defiant—or what? How would you sum up the author's overall attitude?

7. How much of Heinemann's essay seems derived from direct personal experience? What other material does he use, and what do you think are its sources?

For Discussion or Writing

8. What if anything do you learn from this essay? How much of it confirms what you thought or knew before? Does the essay change your ideas about the war or your attitude toward the veterans?

9. Many people want to forget the American experience in Vietnam; others, like Heinemann, feel that we need to confront and come to terms with what happened there. Where do you stand?

10. Have you had a chance to study the relation between stereotype and reality in some area of recent history or current events? For instance, what is behind the stereotype of the Vietnam vet, the ex-Marine, the antiwar protester, the CIA, the terrorist?

11. Write about a traumatic period in your life or the life of someone close to you. Write about the events and their emotional aftermath.

Branching Out

12. The modern mass media have brought live history "into our living rooms." How have movies and television shaped your views on a subject like World War II,

Vietnam, civil wars in Latin America, strife in the Near East, apartheid in South Africa?

WRITERS ON WRITING
Larry Heinemann on the Process of Writing

QUESTION: How do you manage to maintain perspective when you are writing about something with which you are intensely involved?

ANSWER: I've been thinking and talking and reading about the war since I got back in 1968—which now is 18 years. Getting the distance on the event to be able to write about it has always been a problem. To write about the war is to relive the experience; you really don't get a distance. A lot of the same emotions I went through when I was overseas are still accessible, and that's both good and bad. They're there to write about, and your memory is highly developed. But it seems like the part of you that's not a writer is always embroiled in what went on.

The short answer is that you're really trading off. You take a distance to see the subject overall. At the same time, you have a human connection with your story.

QUESTION: We teachers tend to tell our students to write about what they know; then we caution them about the need for distance. Is this contradictory advice?

ANSWER: No, it isn't. I used to tell my students (I taught freshman writing and creative writing) to write what they knew about, the things they can do well, and begin with that. You're always doing two things at once anyway. You're asking them to write about something they know so that they can be sure they know what they are talking about. But if you ask them to write about something that might be a traumatic experience, you're asking them to deal with something as writers, not as people—a kind of special responsibility.

When you sit down at a typewriter, you have to put a lot of personal feelings aside. That's not to say ignore them, but you have to work through them. If you define any kind of writing as storytelling, what the writer has to do is tell the story and tell it as vividly as possible.

QUESTION: You have interviewed many Vietnam veterans for your work. How do you balance their words, their testimony, at the same time you are interpreting?

ANSWER: When I first started, I didn't know the questions to ask. I basically set up a rapport. I got them to talk about what happened when they were overseas, and I talked about what happened to me. Out of those conversations would come questions. Everybody had stories—everybody remembered vividly—a heightened experience. So you ask these kinds of leading questions, but when you get to the vivid imagery—when you sense that this is something the guy has remembered for a long time—you may ask more and more. You may ask them to repeat.

Then to take all that raw material and boil it down into an article—I can't remember how I did that! I knew there would be imagery that would illustrate my argument. You never exclude strong imagery because it doesn't exactly fit—any strong imagery you have to include in some way—so there has to be a way to use it, even if it's just one line. There's one quote in the article from a guy I talked to at a picnic all afternoon. He said he felt like "a qualified animal, successful species that had made it out of the lab." So I had to find a place in the piece to use it. It was such a strong, really remarkable image.

QUESTION: Teachers tell students that writing is a way to clarify experience. Did writing about Vietnam do that for you?

ANSWER: Yes—and we're not the first ones to say that. We write to find out what we think. Even doing something as simple as writing in a journal—intellectual doodling—you're figuring out things. Writing is a way of laying things out. You write to find out what you think, what you know, and what you don't know.

—From an interview with the editors of *Essay 2*

BACKGROUND: Jonathan Schell (born in New York in 1943) has been for many years a writer for *The New Yorker*. In 1976, he published *The Time of Illusion*, a study of the Nixon presidency that has been described as likely to become "one of the classic accounts of the Vietnam-Watergate era." In 1982, Schell published a series of three long, painstakingly researched articles on the threat of nuclear war. He attacked the widespread refusal to think about the threat of a nuclear holocaust that could mean not only the end of modern civilization but the biological destruction of humanity. Schell said that the bare statistics about bomb yields and probable secondary effects tell us nothing about the human reality of nuclear destruction: "We seek a human truth and come up with a handful of figures." To give his readers a glimpse of that human truth, Schell in the following excerpt turns to the testimony of the survivors of the bombing of Hiroshima on August 6, 1945. Originally published in *The New Yorker*, Schell's articles were reprinted as a book (*The Fate of the Earth*, 1982) that stirred heated debate and succeeded in forcing us "to confront head on the nuclear peril in which we all find ourselves" (*The New York Times*).

Jonathan Schell

What Happened

---

at Hiroshima

GUIDE TO READING: The following account brings together eyewitness accounts from different published sources. Why has the author chosen the quotations he presents? What does each contribute to the selection as a whole? What is the overall pattern in which the author has arranged these quoted materials? How well do they serve his overall purpose?

On August 6, 1945, at 8:16 A.M., a fission bomb with a yield of twelve and a half kilotons was detonated about nineteen hundred feet above the central section of Hiroshima. By present-day standards, the bomb was a small one, and in today's arsenals it would be classed among the merely tactical weapons. Nevertheless, it was large enough to transform a city of some three hundred and forty thousand people into hell in the space of a few seconds. "It is no exaggeration," the authors of *Hiroshima and Nagasaki* tell us, "to say that the whole city was ruined instantaneously." In that instant, tens of thousands of people were burned, blasted, and crushed to death. Other tens of thousands suffered injuries of every description or were doomed to die of radiation sickness. The center of the city was flattened, and every part of the city was damaged. The trunks of bamboo trees as far away as five miles from ground zero—the point on the ground directly under the center of the explosion—were charred. Almost half the trees within a mile and a quarter were knocked down. Windows nearly seventeen miles away were broken. Half an hour after the blast, fires set by the thermal pulse and by the collapse of the buildings began to coalesce into a firestorm, which lasted for six hours. Starting about 9 A.M. and lasting until late afternoon, a "black rain" generated by the bomb (otherwise, the day was fair) fell on the western portions of the city, carrying radioactive fallout from the blast to the ground. For four hours at midday, a violent whirlwind, born of the strange meteorological conditions produced by the explosion, further devastated the city. The number of people who were killed outright or who died of their injuries over the next three months is estimated to be a hundred and thirty thousand. Sixty-eight percent of the buildings in the city were either completely destroyed or damaged beyond repair, and the center of the city was turned into a flat, rubble-strewn plain dotted with the ruins of a few of the sturdier buildings.

In the minutes after the detonation, the day grew dark, as heavy clouds ₂ of dust and smoke filled the air. A whole city had fallen in a moment, and in and under its ruins were its people. Among those still living, most were injured, and of these most were burned or had in some way been battered or had suffered both kinds of injury. Those within a mile and a quarter of ground zero had also been subjected to intense nuclear radiation, often in lethal doses. When people revived enough from their unconsciousness or shock to see what was happening around them, they found that where a second before there had been a city getting ready to go about its daily business on a peaceful, warm August morning, now there was a heap of debris and corpses and a stunned mass of injured humanity. But at first, as they awakened and tried to find their bearings in the gathering darkness, many felt cut off and alone. In a recent volume of recollections by survivors called *Unforgettable Fire*, in which the effects of the bombing are rendered in drawings as well as in words, Mrs. Haruko Ogasawara, a young girl on that August morning, recalls that she was at first knocked unconscious. She goes on to write:

> How many seconds or minutes had passed I could not tell, but, regaining ₃ consciousness, I found myself lying on the ground covered with pieces of wood. When I stood up in a frantic effort to look around, there was darkness. Terribly frightened, I thought I was alone in a world of death, and groped for any light. My fear was so great I did not think anyone would truly understand. When I came to my senses, I found my clothes in shreds, and I was without my wooden sandals.

Soon cries of pain and cries for help from the wounded filled the air. ₄ Survivors heard the voices of their families and their friends calling out in the gloom. Mrs. Ogasawara writes:

> Suddenly, I wondered what had happened to my mother and sister. My ₅ mother was then forty-five, and my sister five years old. When the darkness

began to fade, I found that there was nothing around me. My house, the next door neighbor's house, and the next had all vanished. I was standing amid the ruins of my house. No one was around. It was quiet, very quiet—an eerie moment. I discovered my mother in a water tank. She had fainted. Crying out, "Mama, Mama," I shook her to bring her back to her senses. After coming to, my mother began to shout madly for my sister: "Eiko! Eiko!"

I wonder how much time had passed when there were cries of searches. 6 Children were calling their parents' names, and parents were calling the names of their children. We were calling desperately for my sister and listening for her voice and looking to see her. Suddenly, Mother cried "Oh Eiko!" Four or five meters away, my sister's head was sticking out and was calling my mother. . . . Mother and I worked desperately to remove the plaster and pillars and pulled her out with great effort. Her body had turned purple from the bruises, and her arm was so badly wounded that we could have placed two fingers in the wound.

Others were less fortunate in their searches and rescue attempts. In 7 *Unforgettable Fire,* a housewife describes a scene she saw:

A mother, driven half-mad while looking for her child, was calling his name. 8 At last she found him. His head looked like a boiled octopus. His eyes were half-closed, and his mouth was white, pursed, and swollen.

Throughout the city, parents were discovering their wounded or dead 9 children, and children were discovering their wounded or dead parents. Kikuno Segawa recalls seeing a little girl with her dead mother:

A woman who looked like an expectant mother was dead. At her side, a girl 10 of about three years of age brought some water in an empty can she had found. She was trying to let her mother drink from it.

The sight of people in extremities of suffering was ubiquitous. Kinzo 11 Nishida recalls:

While taking my severely wounded wife out to the riverbank by the side of 12 the hill of Nakahiro-machi, I was horrified, indeed, at the sight of a stark naked man standing in the rain with his eyeball in his palm. He looked to be in great pain, but there was nothing that I could do for him.

Many people were astonished by the sheer sudden absence of the 13 known world. The writer Yoko Ota later wrote:

I just could not understand why our surroundings had changed so greatly in 14 one instant. . . . I thought it might have been something which had nothing to do with the war—the collapse of the earth, which it was said would take place at the end of the world, and which I had read about as a child.

And a history professor who looked back at the city after the explo- 15
sion remarked later, "I saw that Hiroshima had disappeared."

As the fires sprang up in the ruins, many people, having found injured 16
family members and friends, were now forced to abandon them to the
flames or to lose their own lives in the firestorm. Those who left children,
husbands, wives, friends, and strangers to burn often found these experiences the most awful of the entire ordeal. Mikio Inoue describes how one
man, a professor, came to abandon his wife:

> It was when I crossed Miyuki Bridge that I saw Professor Takenaka, 17
> standing at the foot of the bridge. He was almost naked, wearing nothing but
> shorts, and he had a ball of rice in his right hand. Beyond the streetcar line, the
> northern area was covered by red fire burning against the sky. Far away from
> the line, Ote-machi was also a sea of fire.
>
> That day, Professor Takenaka had not gone to Hiroshima University, and 18
> the A-bomb exploded when he was at home. He tried to rescue his wife, who
> was trapped under a roofbeam, but all his efforts were in vain. The fire was
> threatening him also. His wife pleaded, "Run away, dear!" He was forced to
> desert his wife and escape from the fire. He was now at the foot of Miyuki
> Bridge.
>
> But I wonder how he came to hold that ball of rice in his hand. His naked 19
> figure, standing there before the flames with that ball of rice, looked to me as a
> symbol of the modest hopes of human beings.

In *Hiroshima*, John Hersey describes the flight of a group of German 20
priests and their Japanese colleagues through a burning section of the city:

> The street was cluttered with parts of houses that had slid into it, and with 21
> fallen telephone poles and wires. From every second or third house came the
> voices of people buried and abandoned, who invariably screamed, with formal
> politeness, *"Tasukete kure!* Help, if you please!" The priests recognized sever-
> al ruins from which these cries came as the homes of friends, but because of
> the fire it was too late to help.

And thus it happened that throughout Hiroshima all the ties of affec- 22
tion and respect that join human beings to one another were being pulled
and rent by the spreading firestorm. Soon processions of the injured—
processions of a kind that had never been seen before in history—began to
file away from the center of the city toward its outskirts. Most of the people
suffered from burns, which had often blackened their skin or caused it to
sag off them. A grocer who joined one of these processions has described
them in an interview with Robert Jay Lifton which appears in his book
Death in Life:

> They held their arms bent [forward] . . . and their skin—not only on their 23
> hands but on their faces and bodies, too—hung down . . . . If there had been

only one or two such people . . . perhaps I would not have had such a strong impression. But wherever I walked, I met these people . . . . Many of them died along the road. I can still picture them in my mind—like walking ghosts. They didn't look like people of this world.

The grocer also recalls that because of people's injuries "you couldn't 24 tell whether you were looking at them from in front or in back." People found it impossible to recognize one another. A woman who at the time was a girl of thirteen, and suffered disfiguring burns on her face, has recalled, "My face was so distorted and changed that people couldn't tell who I was. After a while I could call others' names but they couldn't recognize me." In addition to being injured, many people were vomiting—an early symptom of radiation sickness. For many, horrifying and unreal events occurred in a chaotic jumble. In *Unforgettable Fire*, Torako Hironaka enumerates some of the things that she remembers:

1. Some burned work-clothes.
2. People crying for help with their heads, shoulders, or the soles of their feet injured by fragments of broken window glass. Glass fragments were scattered everywhere.
3. [A woman] crying, saying "Aigo! Aigo!" (a Korean expression of sorrow).
4. A burning pine tree.
5. A naked woman.
6. Naked girls crying, "Stupid America!"
7. I was crouching in a puddle, for fear of being shot by a machine gun. My breasts were torn.
8. Burned down electric power lines.
9. A telephone pole had burned and fallen down.
10. A field of watermelons.
11. A dead horse.
12. What with dead cats, pigs, and people, it was just a hell on earth.

Physical collapse brought emotional and spiritual collapse with it. The 25 survivors were, on the whole, listless and stupefied. After the escapes, and the failures to escape, from the firestorm, a silence fell over the city and its remaining population. People suffered and died without speaking or otherwise making a sound. The processions of the injured, too, were soundless. Dr. Michihiko Hachiya has written in his book *Hiroshima Diary*:

Those who were able walked silently toward the suburbs in the distant 26 hills, their spirits broken, their initiative gone. When asked whence they had come, they pointed to the city and said, "That way," and when asked where they were going, pointed away from the city and said, "This way." They were so broken and confused that they moved and behaved like automatons.

Their reactions had astonished outsiders, who reported with amazement 27 the spectacle of long files of people holding stolidly to a narrow, rough path when close by was a smooth, easy road going in the same direction. The outsiders could not grasp the fact that they were witnessing the exodus of a people who walked in the realm of dreams.

Those who were still capable of action often acted in an absurd or an [28] insane way. Some of them energetically pursued tasks that had made sense in the intact Hiroshima of a few minutes before but were now utterly inappropriate. Hersey relates that the German priests were bent on bringing to safety a suitcase, containing diocesan accounts and a sum of money, that they had rescued from the fire and were carrying around with them through the burning city. And Dr. Lifton describes a young soldier's punctilious efforts to find and preserve the ashes of a burned military code book while people around him were screaming for help. Other people simply lost their minds. For example, when the German priests were escaping from the firestorm, one of them, Father Wilhelm Kleinsorge, carried on his back a Mr. Fukai, who kept saying that he wanted to remain where he was. When Father Kleinsorge finally put Mr. Fukai down, he started running. Hersey writes:

> Father Kleinsorge shouted to a dozen soldiers, who were standing by the [29] bridge, to stop him. As Father Kleinsorge started back to get Mr. Fukai, Father LaSalle called out, "Hurry! Don't waste time!" So Father Kleinsorge just requested the soldiers to take care of Mr. Fukai. They said they would, but the little, broken man got away from them, and the last the priests could see of him, he was running back toward the fire.

In the weeks after the bombing, many survivors began to notice the [30] appearance of petechiae—small spots caused by hemorrhages—on their skin. These usually signaled the onset of the critical stage of radiation sickness. In the first stage, the victims characteristically vomited repeatedly, ran a fever, and developed an abnormal thirst. (The cry "Water! Water!" was one of the few sounds often heard in Hiroshima on the day of the bombing.) Then, after a few hours or days, there was a deceptively hopeful period of remission of symptoms, called the latency period, which lasted from about a week to about four weeks. Radiation attacks the reproductive function of cells, and those that reproduce most frequently are therefore the most vulnerable. Among these are the bone-marrow cells, which are responsible for the production of blood cells. During the latency period, the count of white blood cells, which are instrumental in fighting infections, and the count of platelets, which are instrumental in clotting, drop precipitously, so the body is poorly defended against infection and is liable to hemorrhaging. In the third, and final, stage, which may last for several weeks, the victim's hair may fall out and he may suffer from diarrhea and may bleed from the intestines, the mouth, or other parts of the body, and in the end he will either recover or die. Because the fireball of the Hiroshima bomb did not touch the ground, very little ground material was mixed with the fission products of the bomb, and therefore very little local fallout was generated.

(What fallout there was descended in the black rain.) Therefore, the fatalities from radiation sickness were probably all caused by the initial nuclear radiation, and since this affected only people within a radius of a mile and a quarter of ground zero, most of the people who received lethal doses were killed more quickly by the thermal pulse and the blast wave. Thus, Hiroshima did not experience the mass radiation sickness that can be expected if a weapon is ground-burst. Since the Nagasaki bomb was also burst in the air, the effect of widespread lethal fallout on large areas, causing the death by radiation sickness of whole populations in the hours, days, and weeks after the blast, is a form of nuclear horror that the world has not experienced.

In the months and years following the bombing of Hiroshima, after radiation sickness had run its course and most of the injured had either died of their wounds or recovered from them, the inhabitants of the city began to learn that the exposure to radiation they had experienced would bring about a wide variety of illnesses, many of them lethal, throughout the lifetimes of those who had been exposed. An early sign that the harm from radiation was not restricted to radiation sickness came in the months immediately following the bombing, when people found that their reproductive organs had been temporarily harmed, with men experiencing sterility and women experiencing abnormalities in their menstrual cycles. Then, over the years, other illnesses, including cataracts of the eye and leukemia and other forms of cancer, began to appear in larger than normally expected numbers among the exposed population. In all these illnesses, correlations have been found between nearness to the explosion and incidence of the disease. Also, fetuses exposed to the bomb's radiation in utero exhibited abnormalities and developmental retardation. Those exposed within the mile-and-a-quarter radius were seven times as likely as unexposed fetuses to die in utero, and were also seven times as likely to die at birth or in infancy. Surviving children who were exposed in utero tended to be shorter and lighter than other children, and were more often mentally retarded. One of the most serious abnormalities caused by exposure to the bomb's radiation was microcephaly—abnormal smallness of the head, which is often accompanied by mental retardation. In one study, thirty-three cases of microcephaly were found among a hundred and sixty-nine children exposed in utero.

What happened at Hiroshima was less than a millionth part of a holocaust at present levels of world nuclear armament. The more than millionfold difference amounts to more than a difference in magnitude; it is also a difference in kind. The authors of *Hiroshima and Nagasaki* observe that "an atomic bomb's massive destruction and indiscriminate slaughter involves the sweeping breakdown of all order and existence—in a word, the collapse of society itself," and that therefore "the essence of atomic destruction lies in the totality of its impact on man and society." This is true also of a holocaust, of course, except that the totalities in question are now not single cities but nations, ecosystems, and the earth's ecosphere. Yet with the exception of fallout, which was relatively light at Hiroshima and Nagasaki (because both the bombs were air-burst), the immediate devastation caused by today's bombs would be of a sort similar to the devastation in those cities. The immediate effects of a twenty-megaton bomb are not different in kind from those of a twelve-and-a-half-kiloton bomb; they are only more extensive. (The proportions of the effects do change greatly with yield, however. In small bombs, the effects of the initial nuclear radiation are important, because it strikes areas in which people might otherwise have remained alive, but in larger bombs—ones in the megaton range—the consequences of the initial nuclear radiation, whose range does not increase very much with yield, are negligible, because it strikes areas in which everyone will have already been burned or blasted to death.) In bursts of both weapons, for instance, there is a radius within which the thermal pulse can ignite newspapers: for the twelve-and-a-half-kiloton weapon, it is a little over two miles; for the twenty-megaton weapon, it is twenty-five miles. (Since there is no inherent limit on the size of a nuclear weapon, these figures can be increased indefinitely, subject only to the limitations imposed by the technical capacities of the bomb builder—and of the earth's capacity to absorb the blast. The Soviet Union, which has shown a liking for sheer size in so many of its undertakings, once detonated a sixty-megaton bomb.) Therefore, while the total effect of a holocaust is qualitatively different from the total effect of a single bomb, the experience of individual people in a holocaust would be, in the short term (and again excepting the presence of lethal fallout wherever the bombs were ground-burst), very much like the experience of individual people in Hiroshima. The Hiroshima people's experience, accordingly, is of much more than historical interest. It is a picture of what our whole world is always poised to become—a backdrop of scarcely imaginable horror lying just behind the surface of our normal life, and capable of breaking through into that normal life at any second. Whether we choose to think about it or not, it is an omnipresent, inescapable truth about our lives today that at every single moment each one of us may suddenly become the deranged mother looking for her burned child; the professor with the ball of rice in his hand whose wife has just told him "Run away, dear!" and died in the fires; Mr. Fukai running back into the firestorm; the naked man standing on the blasted plain that was his city, holding his eyeball in his hand; or, more likely, one of millions of corpses. For whatever our "modest hopes" as human beings may be, every one of them can be nullified by a nuclear holocaust.

Using the Dictionary

How up to date is your dictionary? What help, if any, does it give you with terms like the following?   1. *kiloton* (1)   2. *tactical weapons* (1)   3. *ground zero* (1)   4.

thermal pulse (1)   5. *fallout* (1)   6. *radiation* (2)   7. *holocaust* (32)   8. *megaton* (32)   9. *ecosphere* (32)   10. *ecosystem* (32)

The Writer's Agenda

In this account, the author tries to put the unspeakable into words. Study the pattern that takes shape as he uses the survivors' testimony to recreate the physical and psychological impact of the events for his readers.

1. In the first paragraph, the author provides *facts and figures* about the explosion and its immediate results. Which of these would you include in a short "bare-facts" summary? Which of the facts and details included here do most to make the catastrophe real in the reader's mind? Which sentence best sums up the author's central point?

2. The first seven or eight extensive quotations describe the *aftermath* of the explosion as experienced by the survivors. Why did the author choose these quotations from the many available ones? Are there any common threads in these survivors' testimonies?

3. In several paragraphs in the middle of the essay, the author tries to sum up the *emotional or psychological* impact that the nightmare events had on the survivors. What are some of his generalizations, and how are they supported?

4. Schell begins the last third of this excerpt by discussing the *aftereffects* of the bombing. What are some details that make this section read more like matter-of-fact reporting than other parts of the essay? Why do you think the author chose to make this section more "factual" than earlier sections?

5. In the final paragraph, the author tries to sum up the human meaning of what happened in Hiroshima. What sentence for you best sums up his **thesis**?

6. An effective **conclusion** often comes full circle by taking up or pointing back to something the author introduced earlier in the essay. How does Schell's conclusion fit this pattern?

For Discussion or Writing

7. What was your reaction as a reader as you read this selection? Did it change your thinking about Hiroshima or about the threat of nuclear war? What was your attitude toward the author and what he was trying to do?

8. To judge from your observation and reading, what are major attitudes, expectations, or rationalizations current in our society regarding the threat of nuclear war?

9. Have you had a chance to listen to, or do you have a chance to interview, eyewitnesses of some upheaval in recent history? Report and interpret the testimony of participants—veterans, refugees, survivors.

10. In their treatment of recent history, the mass media—movies, television, popular nonfiction books—reflect changing attitudes and intellectual fashions.

Discuss the treatment in the media of a topic like the following: the Holocaust, Pearl Harbor, Vietnam, Hitler, World War II, World War I. Discuss detailed examples.

11. Find full bibliographical information for as many of Schell's sources as you can. Prepare a Hiroshima bibliography, using these and other relevant sources that you encounter. (Include Schell's own work.) Be sure to check for author cards and title cards in the card catalog of your library. Use conventional format.

12. Prepare a bibliography for another topic from the annals of inhumanity: Auschwitz, My Lai, Cambodia, Andersonville, or other.

BACKGROUND: Alice Walker (born 1944) is a black writer and feminist from Georgia who became widely known after the publication of her Pulitzer Prize-winning novel, *The Color Purple* (1982). (She said that she wrote the book in a place in northern California that looked a lot like the town in Georgia that most of her characters were from, "only it was more beautiful and the local swimming hole was not segregated.") While a student at Spelman College in Atlanta, Walker participated in the rallies, sit-ins, and freedom marches of the civil rights movement, which, she said later, "broke the pattern of black servitude in this country." She worked as an editor for *Ms.* magazine, and she has written and lectured widely on the relationship between black men and women, between black and white women, and between her own work and that of the black women writers who were her inspiration. Many of her essays, articles, and reviews were collected in *In Search of Our Mothers' Gardens* (1983). In the following essay, after which the collection was named, she sets out in search of the women who were her spiritual forebears.

Alice Walker

In Search of Our
Mothers' Gardens

GUIDE TO READING: As you read this essay, ask yourself how Walker uses her personal memories and her knowledge of black writers and artists to answer her two central questions: "What did it mean for a black woman to be an artist in our grandmothers' time?" What does it mean to be "an artist and a black woman" today?

I described her own nature and temperament. Told how they needed a   1
larger life for their expression. . . . I pointed out that in lieu of proper channels, her emotions had overflowed into paths that dissipated them. I talked, beautifully I thought, about an art that would be born, an art that would open the way for women the likes of her. I asked her to hope, and build up an inner life against the coming of that day. . . . I sang, with a strange quiver in my voice, a promise song.   (Jean Toomer, "Avey," *Cane*)

(The poet speaking to a prostitute who falls asleep while he's talking)[1]

When the poet Jean Toomer walked through the South in the early   2
twenties, he discovered a curious thing: black women whose spirituality

[1][Jean Toomer (1894–1967) was born in Washington, D.C., and published *Cane*, a collection of poems and stories, in 1923.]

was so intense, so deep, so *unconscious* that they were themselves unaware of the richness they held. They stumbled blindly through their lives: creatures so abused and mutilated in body, so dimmed and confused by pain, that they considered themselves unworthy even of hope. In the selfless abstractions their bodies became to the men who used them, they became more than "sexual objects," more even than mere women: they became "Saints." Instead of being perceived as whole persons, their bodies became shrines: what was thought to be their minds became temples suitable for worship. These crazy Saints stared out at the world, wildly, like lunatics— or quietly, like suicides; and the "God" that was in their gaze was as mute as a great stone.

Who were these Saints? These crazy, loony, pitiful women? 3

Some of them, without a doubt, were our mothers and grandmothers. 4

In the still heat of the post-Reconstruction South, this is how they 5 seemed to Jean Toomer: exquisite butterflies trapped in an evil honey, toiling away their lives in an era, a century, that did not acknowledge them, except as "the *mule* of the world." They dreamed dreams that no one knew—not even themselves, in any coherent fashion—and saw visions no one could understand. They wandered or sat about the countryside crooning lullabies to ghosts, and drawing the mother of Christ in charcoal on courthouse walls.

They forced their minds to desert their bodies and their striving spirits 6 sought to rise, like frail whirlwinds from the hard red clay. And when those frail whirlwinds fell, in scattered particles, upon the ground, no one mourned. Instead, men lit candles to celebrate the emptiness that remained, as people do who enter a beautiful but vacant space to resurrect a God.

Our mothers and grandmothers, some of them: moving to music not 7 yet written. And they waited.

They waited for a day when the unknown thing that was in them would 8 be made known; but guessed, somehow in their darkness, that on the day of their revelation they would be long dead. Therefore to Toomer they walked, and even ran, in slow motion. For they were going nowhere immediate, and the future was not yet within their grasp. And men took our mothers and grandmothers, "but got no pleasure from it." So complex was their passion and their calm.

To Toomer, they lay vacant and fallow as autumn fields, with harvest 9 time never in sight: and he saw them enter loveless marriages, without joy; and become prostitutes, without resistance; and become mothers of children, without fulfillment.

For these grandmothers and mothers of ours were not Saints, but 10 Artists; driven to a numb and bleeding madness by the springs of creativity in them for which there was no release. They were Creators, who lived lives of spiritual waste, because they were so rich in spirituality—which is the basis of Art—that the strain of enduring their unused and unwanted talent drove them insane. Throwing away this spirituality was their pathetic attempt to lighten the soul to a weight their work-worn, sexually abused bodies could bear.

What did it mean for a black woman to be an artist in our grand- 11 mothers' time? In our great-grandmothers' day? It is a question with an answer cruel enough to stop the blood.

Did you have a genius of a great-great-grandmother who died under 12 some ignorant and depraved white overseer's lash? Or was she required to bake biscuits for a lazy backwater tramp, when she cried out in her soul to paint watercolors of sunsets, or the rain falling on the green and peaceful pasturelands? Or was her body broken and forced to bear children (who were more often than not sold away from her)—eight, ten, fifteen, twenty children—when her one joy was the thought of modeling heroic figures of rebellion, in stone or clay?

How was the creativity of the black woman kept alive, year after year 13 and century after century, when for most of the years black people have been in America, it was a punishable crime for a black person to read or write? And the freedom to paint, to sculpt, to expand the mind with action did not exist. Consider, if you can bear to imagine it, what might have been the result if singing, too, had been forbidden by law. Listen to the voices of Bessie Smith, Billie Holiday, Nina Simone, Robert Flack, and Aretha Franklin, among others, and imagine those voices muzzled for life. Then you may begin to comprehend the lives of our "crazy," "Sainted" mothers and grandmothers. The agony of the lives of women who might have been Poets, Novelists, Essayists, and Short-Story Writers (over a period of centuries), who died with their real gifts stifled within them.

And, if this were the end of the story, we would have cause to cry out in 14 my paraphrase of Okot p'Bitek's great poem:

O, my clanswomen
Let us all cry together!
Come,
Let us mourn the death of our mother,
The death of a Queen
The ash that was produced
By a great fire!
O, this homestead is utterly dead
Close the gates
With *lacari* thorns,
For our mother
The creator of the Stool is lost!
And all the young women
Have perished in the wilderness!

But this is not the end of the story, for all the young women—our 15 mothers and grandmothers, *ourselves*—have not perished in the wilderness. And if we ask ourselves why, and search for and find the answer, we will know beyond all efforts to erase it from our minds, just exactly who, and of what, we black American women are.

One example, perhaps the most pathetic, most misunderstood one, [16] can provide a backdrop for our mothers' work: Phillis Wheatley, a slave in the 1700s.[2]

Virginia Woolf, in her book *A Room of One's Own*, wrote that in order [17] for a woman to write fiction she must have two things, certainly: a room of her own (with key and lock) and enough money to support herself.[3]

What then are we to make of Phillis Wheatley, a slave, who owned not [18] even herself? This sickly, frail black girl who required a servant of her own at times—her health was so precarious—and who, had she been white, would have been easily considered the intellectual superior of all the women and most of the men in the society of her day.

Virginia Woolf wrote further, speaking of course not of our Phillis, that [19] "any woman born with a great gift in the sixteenth century [insert "eighteenth century," insert "black woman," insert "born or made a slave"] would certainly have gone crazed, shot herself, or ended her days in some lonely cottage outside the village, half witch, half wizard [insert "Saint"], feared and mocked at. For it needs little skill and psychology to be sure that a highly gifted girl who had tried to use her gift for poetry would have been so thwarted and hindered by contrary instincts [add "chains, guns, the lash, the ownership of one's body by someone else, submission to an alien religion"], that she must have lost her health and sanity to a certainty."

The key words, as they relate to Phillis, are "contrary instincts." For [20] when we read the poetry of Phillis Wheatley—as when we read the novels of Nella Larsen or the oddly false-sounding autobiography of that freest of all black women writers, Zora Hurston—evidence of "contrary instincts" is everywhere.[4] Her loyalties were completely divided, as was, without question, her mind.

But how could this be otherwise? Captured at seven, a slave of [21] wealthy, doting whites who instilled in her the "savagery" of the Africa they "rescued" her from . . . one wonders if she was even able to remember her homeland as she had known it, or as it really was.

Yet, because she did try to use her gift for poetry in a world that made [22] her a slave, she was "so thwarted and hindered by . . . contrary instincts, that she . . . lost her health. . . ." In the last years of her brief life, burdened not only with the need to express her gift but also with a penniless, friendless

---

[2][Phillis Wheatley (c. 1753–94), an African slave, wrote *Poems on Various Subjects, Religious and Moral*, published in 1773.]

[3][Virginia Woolf (1882–1941) was a leading British novelist and critic whose best-known novels are *Mrs. Dalloway* (1925) and *To the Lighthouse* (1927).]

[4][Zora Neale Hurston (1901–1960) wrote *Mules and Men*, a collection of black legend and folklore. Her novels include *Their Eyes Were Watching God*, which Alice Walker has praised for its "sense of black people as complete, complex, *undiminished* human beings."]

"freedom" and several small children for whom she was forced to do strenuous work to feed, she lost her health, certainly. Suffering from malnutrition and neglect and who knows what mental agonies, Phillis Wheatley died.

So torn by "contrary instincts" was black, kidnapped, enslaved Phillis [23] that her description of the "Goddess"—as she poetically called the Liberty she did not have—is ironically, cruelly humorous. And, in fact, has held Phillis up to ridicule for more than a century. It is usually read prior to hanging Phillis's memory as that of a fool. She wrote:

> The Goddess comes, she moves divinely fair,
> Olive and laurel binds her *golden* hair.
> Wherever shines this native of the skies,
> Unnumber'd charms and recent graces rise. [My italics]

It is obvious that Phillis, the slave, combed the "Goddess's" hair every [24] morning; prior, perhaps, to bringing in the milk, or fixing her mistress's lunch. She took her imagery from the one thing she saw elevated above all others.

With the benefit of hindsight we ask, "How could she?" [25]

But at last, Phillis, we understand. No more snickering when your stiff, [26] struggling, ambivalent lines are forced on us. We know now that you were not an idiot or a traitor; only a sickly little black girl, snatched from your home and country and made a slave; a woman who still struggled to sing the song that was your gift, although in a land of barbarians who praised you for your bewildered tongue. It is not so much what you sang, as that you kept alive, in so many of our ancestors, *the notion of song.*

Black women are called, in the folklore that so aptly identifies one's [27] status in society, "the *mule* of the world," because we have been handed the burdens that everyone else—*everyone* else— refused to carry. We have also been called "Matriarchs," "Superwomen," and "Mean and Evil Bitches." Not to mention "Castraters" and "Sapphire's Mama." When we have pleaded for understanding, our character has been distorted; when we have asked for simple caring, we have been handed empty inspirational appellations, then stuck in the farthest corner. When we have asked for love, we have been given children. In short, even our plainer gifts, our labors of fidelity and love, have been knocked down our throats. To be an artist and a black woman, even today, lowers our status in many respects, rather than raises it: and yet, artists we will be.

Therefore we must fearlessly pull out of ourselves and look at and [28] identify with our lives the living creativity some of our great-grandmothers were not allowed to know. I stress *some* of them because it is well known that the majority of our great-grandmothers knew, even without "knowing" it, the reality of their spirituality, even if they didn't recognize it beyond what happened in the singing at church—and they never had any intention of giving it up.

How they did it—those millions of black women who were not Phillis 29
Wheatley, or Lucy Terry or Frances Harper or Zora Hurston or Nella Larsen or Bessie Smith; or Elizabeth Catlett, or Katherine Dunham, either—brings me to the title of this essay, "In Search of Our Mothers' Gardens," which is a personal account that is yet shared, in its theme and its meaning, by all of us. I found, while thinking about the far-reaching world of the creative black woman, that often the truest answer to a question that really matters can be found very close.

In the late 1920s my mother ran away from home to marry my father. 30
Marriage, if not running away, was expected of seventeen-year-old girls. By the time she was twenty, she had two children and was pregnant with a third. Five children later, I was born. And this is how I came to know my mother: she seemed a large, soft, loving-eyed woman who was rarely impatient in our home. Her quick, violent temper was on view only a few times a year, when she battled with the white landlord who had the misfortune to suggest to her that her children did not need to go to school.

She made all the clothes we wore, even my brothers' overalls. She 31
made all the towels and sheets we used. She spent the summers canning vegetables and fruits. She spent the winter evenings making quilts enough to cover all our beds.

During the "working" day, she labored beside—not behind—my 32
father in the fields. Her day began before sunup, and did not end until late at night. There was never a moment for her to sit down, undisturbed, to unravel her own private thoughts; never a time free from interruption—by work or the noisy inquiries of her many children. And yet, it is to my mother—and all our mothers who were not famous—that I went in search of the secret of what has fed that muzzled and often mutilated, but vibrant, creative spirit that the black woman has inherited, and that pops out in wild and unlikely places to this day.

But when, you will ask, did my overworked mother have time to know 33
or care about feeding the creative spirit?

The answer is so simple that many of us have spent years discovering 34
it. We have constantly looked high, when we should have looked high— and low.

For example: in the Smithsonian Institution in Washington, D.C., there 35
hangs a quilt unlike any other in the world. In fanciful, inspired, and yet simple and identifiable figures, it portrays the story of the Crucifixion. It is considered rare, beyond price. Though it follows no known pattern of quilt-making, and though it is made of bits and pieces of worthless rags, it is obviously the work of a person of powerful imagination and deep spiritual feeling. Below this quilt I saw a note that says it was made by "an anonymous Black woman in Alabama, a hundred years ago."

If we could locate this "anonymous" black woman from Alabama, she [36] would turn out to be one of our grandmothers—an artist who left her mark in the only materials she could afford, and in the only medium her position in society allowed her to use.

As Virginia Woolf wrote further, in *A Room of One's Own:* [37]

> Yet genius of a sort must have existed among women as it must have existed among the working class. [Change this to "slaves" and "the wives and daughters of sharecroppers."] Now and again an Emily Brontë or a Robert Burns [change this to "a Zora Hurston or a Richard Wright"] blazes out and proves its presence. But certainly it never got itself on to paper. When, however, one reads of a witch being ducked, of a woman possessed by devils [or "Sainthood"], of a wise woman selling herbs [our root workers], or even a very remarkable man who had a mother, then I think we are on the track of a lost novelist, a suppressed poet, of some mute and inglorious Jane Austen. . . . Indeed, I would venture to guess that Anon, who wrote so many poems without signing them, was often a woman. . . .

And so our mothers and grandmothers have, more often than not [38] anonymously, handed on the creative spark, the seed of the flower they themselves never hoped to see: or like a sealed letter they could not plainly read.

And so it is, certainly, with my own mother. Unlike "Ma" Rainey's [39] songs, which retained their creator's name even while blasting forth from Bessie Smith's mouth, no song or poem will bear my mother's name. Yet so many of the stories that I write, that we all write, are my mother's stories. Only recently did I fully realize this: that through years of listening to my mother's stories of her life, I have absorbed not only the stories themselves, but something of the manner in which she spoke, something of the urgency that involves the knowledge that her stories—like her life—must be recorded. It is probably for this reason that so much of what I have written is about characters whose counterparts in real life are so much older than I am.

But the telling of these stories, which came from my mother's lips as [40] naturally as breathing, was not the only way my mother showed herself as an artist. For stories, too, were subject to being distracted, to dying without conclusion. Dinners must be started, and cotton must be gathered before the big rains. The artist that was and is my mother showed itself to me only after many years. This is what I finally noticed:

Like Mem, a character in *The Third Life of Grange Copeland*, my [41] mother adorned with flowers whatever shabby house we were forced to live in. And not just your typical straggly country stand of zinnias, either. She planted ambitious gardens—and still does—with over fifty different varieties of plants that bloom profusely from early March until late November. Before she left home for the fields, she watered her flowers, chopped up the grass, and laid out new beds. When she returned from the fields she might divide clumps of bulbs, dig a cold pit, uproot and replant roses, or prune branches from her taller bushes or trees—until night came and it was too dark to see.

Whatever she planted grew as if by magic, and her fame as a grower of flowers spread over three counties. Because of her creativity with her flowers, even my memories of poverty are seen through a screen of blooms—sunflowers, petunias, roses, dahlias, forsythia, spirea, delphiniums, verbena . . . and on and on. [42]

And I remember people coming to my mother's yard to be given cuttings from her flowers; I hear again the praise showered on her because whatever rocky soil she landed on, she turned into a garden. A garden so brilliant with colors, so original in its design, so magnificent with life and creativity, that to this day people drive by our house in Georgia—perfect strangers and imperfect strangers—and ask to stand or walk among my mother's art. [43]

I notice that it is only when my mother is working in her flowers that she is radiant, almost to the point of being invisible—except as Creator: hand and eye. She is involved in work her soul must have. Ordering the universe in the image of her personal conception of Beauty. [44]

Her face, as she prepares the Art that is her gift, is a legacy of respect she leaves to me, for all that illuminates and cherishes life. She has handed down respect for the possibilities—and the will to grasp them. [45]

For her, so hindered and intruded upon in so many ways, being an artist has still been a daily part of her life. This ability to hold on, even in very simple ways, is work black women have done for a very long time. [46]

This poem is not enough, but it is something, for the woman who literally covered the holes in our walls with sunflowers: [47]

They were women then
My mama's generation
Husky of voice—Stout of
Step
With fists as well as
Hands
How they battered down
Doors
And ironed
Starched white
Shirts
How they led
Armies
Headragged Generals
Across mined
Fields
Booby-trapped
Kitchens

To discover books
Desks
A place for us
How they knew what we
Must know
Without knowing a page
Of it
Themselves.

Guided by my heritage of a love of beauty and a respect for strength— 48
in search of my mother's garden, I found my own.

And perhaps in Africa over two hundred years ago, there was just such 49
a mother; perhaps she painted vivid and daring decorations in oranges and
yellows and greens on the walls of her hut; perhaps she sang—in a voice
like Roberta Flack's—*sweetly* over the compounds of her village; perhaps
she wove the most stunning mats or told the most ingenious stories of all the
village story-tellers. Perhaps she was herself a poet—though only her
daughter's name is signed to the poems that we know.

Perhaps Phillis Wheatley's mother was also an artist. 50

Perhaps in more than Phillis Wheatley's biological life is her mother's 51
signature made clear.

Using the Dictionary

Check the following as necessary: 1. *dissipate* (1)   2. *fallow* (9)   3. *precarious*
(18)   4. *doting* (21)   5. *strenuous* (22)   6. *ambivalent* (26)   7. *matriarch*
(27)   8. *appellation* (27)   9. *fidelity* (27)   10. *vibrant* (32)   11. *radiant*
(44)   12. *legacy* (45)   13. *ingenious* (49)

The Writer's Agenda

In this essay, Walker rediscovers and reevaluates a part of her spiritual history.
Answer the following questions:

1. What is the meaning of the title? How does it point forward to the major
theme or central message of the essay?

2. What is the common strand in Walker's quotations from the black poet Jean
Toomer and the British novelist Virginia Woolf?

3. Which of the black singers whom Walker mentions do you recognize? How
is her discussion of them related to her main trend of thought in this essay?

4. What, according to Walker, is the story of Phillis Wheatley? What is the
meaning of that story for Walker? (How does she want us to revise more conventional judgments of Wheatley's role?)

5. What, for you, is most striking or memorable about Walker's tribute to her
mother?

6. Walker writes with a poet's gift for metaphor, for vivid figurative language. For instance, what is striking or unusual about expressions like "exquisite butterflies trapped in an evil honey" or "frail whirlwinds from the hard red clay"? Find and discuss several other examples of vivid imaginative language.

7. How much does Walker draw on her family history or personal experience? How much on printed sources? What other sources does she draw on?

For Discussion or Writing

8. How would you sum up the author's answer to her central questions? What is the central lesson or inspiration that Walker draws from her look at the past?

9. Should the ideal reader for this essay be black? female? an artist? Do you think the author excludes men or whites from her audience?

10. What definition of art, or what view of the role of the artist, underlies Walker's essay?

11. What role have art or artists played in your own life? Does contemporary art as you know it have a spiritual or vital significance?

12. Write a tribute to someone who has had a major influence on your life or view of the world.

Branching Out

13. Alice Walker's novel *The Color Purple* and the movie based on it produced a range of different critical reactions. Find two or more differing critical perspectives on the book or the movie and discuss the differences in point of view.

14. Prepare a brief *biography* of one of the women mentioned in Walker's essay: Zora Hurston, Lucy Terry, Frances Harper, Nella Larsen, Bessie Smith, Billie Holiday, Ma Rainey, Nina Simone, Roberta Flack, Aretha Franklin, Elizabeth Catlett, Katherine Dunham. (You may have to turn to histories or anthologies of black literature, historical studies of black music, and similar sources for material.)

BACKGROUND: Barbara W. Tuchman was born in 1912 in New York City. She graduated from Radcliffe College and worked as a foreign correspondent, reporting on the
Spanish Civil War from Madrid in 1937. In 1962, she published *The Guns of August*, a
book about the beginning of World War I. The book won a Pulitzer Prize and made
her one of the nation's best-known historians. In 1978, she published *A Distant
Mirror*, about the calamities of Europe in the fourteenth century, the age of the
plague or Black Death, an age of "depopulation and disaster, extravagance and
splendor." She said about her motives in writing this book: "After the experiences of
the terrible twentieth century, we have greater fellow-feeling for a distraught age
whose rules were breaking down under the pressure of adverse and violent events."
In her historical writings, Tuchman employs her mastery of carefully researched
detail to create narratives full of life and suspense. The article that follows is
abridged from a lecture she gave in 1980. Although much of her own work as a
historian deals with catastrophe, with war and disease, she here tries to counteract
what she calls the "negative overload" of recorded history—the disproportionate
survival in historical records "of the bad side—of evil, misery, contention, and
harm."

Barbara Tuchman

Humanity's Better

Moments

GUIDE TO READING: In this essay, the author tries to counteract our prevailing
modern pessimism about human nature and about the future of humanity. How does
she proceed? What examples of human achievement or what evidence of positive
qualities does she present, and in what order?

For a change from prevailing pessimism, I should like to recall some of   1
the positive and even admirable capacities of the human race. We hear very
little of them lately. Ours is not a time of self-esteem or self-confidence—as
was, for instance, the nineteenth century, when self-esteem may be seen
oozing from its portraits. Victorians, especially the men, pictured themselves as erect, noble, and splendidly handsome. Our self-image looks more
like Woody Allen or a character from Samuel Beckett.[1] Amid a mass of
worldwide troubles and a poor record for the twentieth century, we see our
species—with cause—as functioning very badly, as blunderers when not

---

[1][Samuel Beckett's best-known play is *Waiting for Godot* (1954), in which two tramps spend much of
their time in aimless conversation, vacillating between self-pity and self-disgust.]

knaves, as violent, ignoble, corrupt, inept, incapable of mastering the forces that threaten us, weakly subject to our worst instincts; in short, decadent.

The catalogue is familiar and valid, but it is growing tiresome. A study 2 of history reminds one that humanity has its ups and downs and during the ups has accomplished many brave and beautiful things, exerted stupendous endeavors, explored and conquered oceans and wilderness, achieved marvels of beauty in the creative arts and marvels of science and social progress; has loved liberty with a passion that throughout history has led men to fight and die for it over and over again; has pursued knowledge, exercised reason, enjoyed laughter and pleasures, played games with zest, shown courage, heroism, altruism, honor, and decency; experienced love; known comfort, contentment, and occasionally happiness. All these qualities have been part of human experience, and if they have not had as important notice as the negatives nor exerted as wide and persistent an influence as the evils we do, they nevertheless deserve attention, for they are currently all but forgotten.

Among the great endeavors, we have in our own time carried men to 3 the moon and brought them back safely—surely one of the most remarkable achievements in history. Some may disapprove of the effort as unproductive, too costly, and a wrong choice of priorities in relation to greater needs, all of which may be true but does not, as I see it, diminish the achievement. If you look carefully, all positives have a negative underside— sometimes more, sometimes less—and not all admirable endeavors have admirable motives. Some have sad consequences. Although most signs presently point from bad to worse, human capacities are probably what they have always been. If primitive man could discover how to transform grain into bread, and reeds growing by the riverbank into baskets; if his successors could invent the wheel, harness the insubstantial air to turn a millstone, transform sheep's wool, flax, and worms' cocoons into fabric— we, I imagine, will find a way to manage the energy problem.

Consider how the Dutch accomplished the miracle of making land out 4 of sea. By progressive enclosure of the Zuider Zee over the last sixty years, they have added half a million acres to their country, enlarging its area by eight percent and providing homes, farms, and towns for close to a quarter of a million people. The will to do the impossible, the spirit of can-do that overtakes our species now and then, was never more manifest than in this earth-altering act by the smallest of the major European nations. Today the *Afsluitdijk*, or Zuider Zee road, is a normal thoroughfare. To drive across it between the sullen ocean on one side and new land on the other is for that moment to feel optimism for the human race.

Even when the historical tide is low, a particular group of doers may 5 emerge in exploits that inspire awe. Shrouded in the mists of the eighth century, long before the cathedrals, Viking seamanship was a wonder of daring, stamina, and skill. Pushing relentlessly outward in open boats, the

Vikings sailed south, around Spain to North Africa and Arabia, north to the top of the world, west across uncharted seas to American coasts. They hauled their boats overland from the Baltic to make their way down Russian rivers to the Black Sea. Why? We do not know what engine drove them, only that it was part of the human endowment.

What of the founding of our own country, America? We take the 6
Mayflower for granted—yet think of the boldness, the enterprise, the determined independence, the sheer grit it took to leave the known and set out across the sea for the unknown where no houses or food, no stores, no cleared land, no crops or livestock, none of the equipment or settlement of organized living awaited.

Equally bold was the enterprise of the French in the northern forests 7
of the American continent, who throughout the seventeenth century explored and opened the land from the St. Lawrence to the Mississippi, from the Great Lakes to the Gulf of Mexico. They came not for liberty like the Pilgrims, but for gain and dominion, whether in spiritual empire for the Jesuits or in land, glory, and riches for the agents of the King; and rarely in history have people willingly embraced such hardship, such daunting adventure, and persisted with such tenacity and endurance. They met hunger, exhaustion, frostbite, capture and torture by Indians, wounds and disease, dangerous rapids, swarms of insects, long portages, bitter weather, and hardly ever did those who suffered the experience fail to return, re-enter the menacing but bountiful forest, and pit themselves once more against danger, pain, and death.

Above all others, the perseverance of La Salle in his search for the 8
mouth of the Mississippi was unsurpassed. While preparing in Quebec, he mastered eight Indian languages. From then on he suffered accidents, betrayals, desertions, losses of men and provisions, fever and snow blindness, the hostility and intrigues of rivals who incited the Indians against him and plotted to ambush or poison him. He was truly pursued, as Francis Parkman wrote, by "a demon of havoc."[2] Paddling through heavy waves in a storm over Lake Ontario, he waded through freezing surf to beach the canoes each night, and lost guns and baggage when a canoe was swamped and sank. To lay the foundations of a fort above Niagara, frozen ground had to be thawed by boiling water. When the fort was at last built, La Salle christened it Crèvecoeur—that is, Heartbreak. It earned the name when in his absence it was plundered and deserted by its half-starved mutinous garrison. Farther on, a friendly Indian village, intended as a destination, was found laid waste by the Iroquois with only charred stakes stuck with skulls standing among the ashes, while wolves and buzzards prowled through the remains.

---

[2][Francis Parkman (1823–93), author of *The Oregon Trail* and *Pioneers of France in the New World*, was the leading nineteenth-century historian of the American frontier.]

When at last, after four months' hazardous journey down the Great ₉
River, La Salle reached the sea, he formally took possession in the name of
Louis XIV of all the country from the river's mouth to its source and of its
tributaries—that is, of the vast basin of the Mississippi from the Rockies to
the Appalachians—and named it Louisiana. The validity of the claim, which
seems so hollow to us (though successful in its own time), is not the point.
What counts is the conquest of fearful adversity by one man's extraordinary
exertions and inflexible will.

Our greatest recourse and most enduring achievement is art. At its ₁₀
best, it reveals the nobility that coexists in human nature along with flaws
and evils, and the beauty and truth it can perceive. Whether in music or
architecture, literature, painting or sculpture, art opens our eyes, ears, and
feelings to something beyond ourselves, something we cannot experience
without the artist's vision and the genius of his craft. The placing of Greek
temples, like the Temple of Poseidon on the promontory at Sunion, outlined
against the piercing blue of the Aegean Sea, Poseidon's home; the majesty of
Michelangelo's sculptured figures in stone; Shakespeare's command of
language and knowledge of the human soul; the intricate order of Bach, the
enchantment of Mozart; the purity of Chinese monochrome pottery with its
lovely names—celadon, oxblood, peach blossom, clair de lune; the exuberance of Tiepolo's ceilings where, without picture frames to limit movement,
a whole world in exquisitely beautiful colors lives and moves in the sky; the
prose and poetry of all the writers from Homer to Cervantes to Jane Austen
and John Keats to Dostoevski and Chekhov—who made all these things?
We—our species—did.[3]

If we have (as I think) lost beauty and elegance in the modern world, ₁₁
we have gained much, through science and technology and democratic
pressures, in the material well-being of the masses. The change in the lives
of, and society's attitude toward, the working class marks the great divide
between the modern world and the old regime. From the French Revolution
through the brutal labor wars of the nineteenth and twentieth centuries, the
change was earned mainly by force against fierce and often vicious opposition. While this was a harsh process, it developed and activated a social
conscience hardly operative before. Slavery, beggary, unaided misery, and
want have, on the whole, been eliminated in the developed nations of the
West. That much is a credit in the human record, even if the world is uglier as
a result of adapting to mass values. History generally arranges these things
so that gain is balanced by loss, perhaps in order not to make the gods
jealous.

---

[3][In her list of great artists, the author includes, along with those who are universally known, the
Italian painter Tiepolo (1696–1770); the Spanish novelist Cervantes (1547–1616), author of the
mock-heroic *Don Quixote*; the British novelist Jane Austen (1775–1817), author of *Pride and
Prejudice*; and the Russian short-story writer and dramatist Anton Chekhov (1860–1904), author of
The Cherry Orchard.]

The material miracles wrought by science and technology—from the [12] harnessing of steam and electricity to anesthesia, antisepsis, antibiotics, and woman's liberator, the washing machine, and all the labor-savers that go with it—are too well recognized in our culture to need my emphasis. Pasteur is as great a figure in the human record as Michelangelo or Mozart—probably, as far as the general welfare is concerned, greater.[4] We are more aware of his kind of accomplishment than of those less tangible. Ask anyone to suggest the credits of mankind and the answer is likely to start with physical things. Yet the underside of scientific progress is prominent and dark. The weaponry of war in its ever-widening capacity to kill is the deadly example, and who is prepared to state with confidence that the over-all effect of the automobile, airplane, telephone, television, and computer has been, on balance, beneficent?

Pursuit of knowledge for its own sake has been a more certain good. [13] There was a springtime in the eighteenth century when, through knowledge and reason, everything seemed possible; when reason was expected to break through religious dogma like the sun breaking through fog, and man, armed with knowledge and reason would be able at last to control his own fate and construct a good society.

Although the Enlightenment may have overestimated the power of [14] reason to guide human conduct, it nevertheless opened to men and women a more humane view of their fellow passengers. Slowly the harshest habits gave way to reform—in treatment of the insane, reduction of death penalties, mitigation of the fierce laws against debtors and poachers, and in the passionately fought cause for abolition of the slave trade.

The humanitarian movement was not charity, which always carries an [15] overtone of being done in the donor's interest, but a more disinterested benevolence or altruism, motivated by conscience. It was personified in William Wilberforce, who in the later eighteenth century stirred the great rebellion of the English conscience against the trade in human beings. In America the immorality of slavery had long troubled the colonies. By 1789 slavery had been legally abolished by the New England states followed by New York, New Jersey, and Pennsylvania, but the southern states, as their price for joining the Union, insisted that the subject be excluded from the Constitution.

In England, where the home economy did not depend on slave labor, [16] Wilberforce had more scope. His influence could have carried him to the Prime Minister's seat if personal power had been his goal, but he channeled his life instead toward a goal for humanity. He instigated, energized, inspired a movement whose members held meetings, organized petitions, collected information on the horrors of the middle passage, showered

---

[4][Louis Pasteur (1822-95) was the French chemist who pioneered the prevention of disease through inoculation and after whom the process of pasteurization is named.]

pamphlets on the public, gathered Nonconformist middle-class sentiment into a swelling tide that, in Trevelyan's phrase, "melted the hard prudence of statesmen."[5] Abolition of the slave trade under the British flag was won in 1807. The British Navy was used to enforce the ban by searches on the high seas and regular patrols of the African coast. When Portugal and Spain were persuaded to join in the prohibition, they were paid a compensation of £300,000 and £400,000 respectively by the British taxpayer. Violations and smuggling continued, convincing the abolitionists that, in order to stop the trade, slavery itself had to be abolished. Agitation resumed. By degrees over the next quarter-century, compensation reduced the opposition of the West Indian slave-owners and their allies in England until emancipation of all slaves in the British Empire was enacted in 1833. The total cost to the British taxpayer was reckoned at £20 million.

Through recent unpleasant experiences we have learned to expect ambition, greed, or corruption to reveal itself behind every public act, but, as we have just seen, it is not invariably so. Human beings do possess better impulses, and occasionally act upon them, even in the twentieth century. Occupied Denmark, during World War II, outraged by Nazi orders for deportation of its Jewish fellow citizens, summoned the courage of defiance and transformed itself into a united underground railway to smuggle virtually all eight thousand Danish Jews out to Sweden, and Sweden gave them shelter. Far away and unconnected, a village in southern France, Le Chambon-sur-Lignon, devoted itself to rescuing Jews and other victims of the Nazis at the risk of the inhabitants' own lives and freedom. "Saving lives became a hobby of the people of Le Chambon," said one of them. The larger record of the time was admittedly collaboration, passive or active. We cannot reckon on the better impulses predominating in the world, only that they will always appear. 17

The strongest of these in history, summoner of the best in us, has been zeal for liberty. Time after time, in some spot somewhere on the globe, people have risen in what Swinburne called the "divine right of insurrection"—to overthrow despots, repel alien conquerors, achieve independence—and so it will be until the day power ceases to corrupt, which, I think, is not a near expectation. 18

The ancient Jews rose three times against alien rulers, beginning with the revolt of the Maccabees against the effort of Antiochus to outlaw observance of the Jewish faith.[6] Mattathias the priest and his five sons, assembling loyal believers in the mountains, opened a guerrilla war which, 19

---

[5][The Nonconformists were English protestants who refused to conform to the official Anglican state church and who commanded a strong following among the middle class. G. M. Trevelyan, long a professor of history at Cambridge University, first published his widely read *History of England* in 1926.]

[6][The revolt of the Maccabees against the Syrians under King Antiochus took place in the second century B.C. Hadrian was the Roman emperor at the time of the final Jewish rebellion against Roman rule in the second century A.D.]

after the father's death, was to find a leader of military genius in his son Judah, called Maccabee or the Hammer. Later honored in the Middle Ages as one of the Nine Worthies of the world, he defeated his enemies, rededicated the temple, and re-established the independence of Judea. In the next century the uprising of the Zealots against Roman rule was fanatically and hopelessly pursued through famines, sieges, the fall of Jerusalem and destruction of the temple until a last stand of fewer than a thousand on the rock of Masada ended in group suicide in preference to surrender. After sixty years as an occupied province, Judea rose yet again under Simon Bar Kochba, who regained Jerusalem for a brief moment of Jewish control but could not withstand the arms of Hadrian. The rebellion was crushed, but the zeal for selfhood, smoldering in exile through eighteen centuries, was to revive and regain its home in our time.

The phenomenon continues in our own day, in Algeria, in Vietnam, 20 although, seen at close quarters and more often than not manipulated by outsiders, contemporary movements seem less pure and heroic than those polished by history's gloss—as, for instance, the Scots under William Wallace, the Swiss against the Hapsburgs, the American colonies against the mother country.[7]

I have always cherished the spirited rejoinder of one of the great 21 colonial landowners of New York who, on being advised not to risk his property by signing the Declaration of Independence, replied, "Damn the property; give me the pen!" On seeking confirmation for purposes of this essay, I am deeply chagrined to report that the saying appears to be apocryphal. Yet not its spirit, for the signers well knew they were risking their property, not to mention their heads, by putting their names to the Declaration.

Is anything to be learned from my survey? I raise the question only 22 because most people want history to teach them lessons, which I believe it can do, although I am less sure we can use them when needed. I gathered these examples not to teach but merely to remind people in a despondent era that the good in humanity operates even if the bad secures more attention. I am aware that selecting out the better moments does not result in a realistic picture. Turn them over and there is likely to be a darker side, as when Project Apollo, our journey to the moon, was authorized because its glamour could obtain subsidies for rocket and missile development that otherwise might not have been forthcoming. That is the way things are.

Whole philosophies have evolved over the question whether the hu- 23 man species is predominantly good or evil. I only know that it is mixed, that you cannot separate good from bad, that wisdom, courage, and benevolence

[7][William Wallace (1272–1305) led the Scots in their fight for independence from English rule. Switzerland has through the centuries been the symbol of a small country that successfully defended its independence against powerful neighbors, such as the Austrian-Hungarian empire ruled by the House of Hasberg.]

exist alongside knavery, greed, and stupidity; heroism and fortitude alongside vainglory, cruelty, and corruption.

It is a paradox of our time in the West that never have so many people 24 been so relatively well off and never has society been more troubled. Yet I suspect that humanity's virtues have not vanished, although the experiences of our century seem to suggest that they are in abeyance. A century that took shape in the disillusion which followed the enormous effort and hopes of World War I, that saw revolution in Russia congeal into the same tyranny it overthrew, saw a supposedly civilized nation revert under the Nazis into organized and unparalleled savagery, saw the craven appeasement by the democracies, is understandably marked by suspicion of human nature. A literary historian, Van Wyck Brooks, discussing the 1920s and '30s, wrote that whereas Whitman and Emerson "had been impressed by the worth and good sense of the people, writers of the new time" were struck by their lusts, cupidity, violence, and had come to dislike their fellow men. The same theme reappeared in a recent play in which a mother struggled against her two "pitilessly contemptuous" children. Her problem was that she wanted them to be happy and they did not want to be. They preferred to watch horrors on television. In essence this is our epoch. It insists upon the flaws and corruptions, without belief in valor or virtue or the possibility of happiness. It keeps turning to look back on Sodom and Gomorrah; it has no view of the Delectable Mountains.[8]

We must keep a balance, and I know of no better prescription than a 25 phrase from Condorcet's eulogy on the death of Benjamin Franklin: "He pardoned the present for the sake of the future."

Using the Dictionary

In each of the following pairs, a word from this essay appears with a similar or related word. How are the words in each pair related? How are they different or alike? 1. *decadent—decay* (1)   2. *altruism—charity* (2)   3. *manifest—manifesto* (4)   4. *dominion—domain* (7)   5. *adversity—adversary* (9)   6. *promontory—peninsula* (10)   7. *regime—government* (11)   8. *dogma—doctrine* (13)   9. *humane—human* (14)   10. *mitigation—leniency* (14)   11. *disinterested—uninterested* (15)   12. *collaboration—cooperation* (17)   13. *chagrined—annoyed* (21)   14. *apocryphal—apocalyptic* (21)   15. *era—epoch* (22)

The Writer's Agenda

Tuchman sets out to overcome the modern reader's pessimism about human history and human nature. To overcome the skepticism of her audience, her general strategy is to go from the relatively safe and undisputed to the debatable or questionable.

[8][a symbol for salvation or the promise of eternal life]

1. What is the modern "self-image" that Tuchman sets out to counteract? What are major areas or major points in her *preview* of the kinds of human accomplishment that she will discuss?

2. Describe the author's *early examples* of the "spirit of can-do," from the Zuider Zee to La Salle's journey. What in this section is familiar or predictable? What is striking or unexpected? What do these achievements have in common?

3. The author labels *art* humanity's "greatest recourse" and "most enduring achievement." How does she define its functions or its purpose?

4. For the author, a profound change in the attitude toward the *working class* marks the "great divide" between the modern world and earlier periods. What forces, according to her, brought this change about, and how?

5. Tuchman pays tribute to *humanitarian reform* as the major legacy of the eighteenth century—the Age of Reason, or the Enlightenment. What data and details does she use to justify this judgment?

6. In the remaining portion of her essay, Tuchman tackles our pervading modern pessimism about *politics*. What key examples does she use in this section? What are striking facts or details that she uses to convince her readers?

7. Throughout her essay, the author reassures her readers that she is aiming at a *balanced* point of view. She wants them to feel that she is not painting a foolishly optimistic picture. Discuss several of her references to the "darker side."

For Discussion or Writing

8. Which of the accomplishments Tuchman describes seem most familiar or most convincing? Which to you seem most questionable or subject to interpretation, and why?

9. Tuchman attributes to modern readers a pervading pessimism about history or disillusionment with human nature. Is this pessimistic outlook shared by members of your own generation? In their view of history or human nature, do you feel most people your age tend to be pessimists, fatalists, realists, optimists, cynics?

10. People in the author's generation often looked to art, architecture, or music for inspiration. They expected art to reveal "the nobility that coexists in human nature along with flaws and evil." Has art lost this power to inspire or to ennoble for young people today?

11. Much modern history is written by "revisionist" historians—people who reexamine and revise cherished illusions or traditional views. Have you had occasion to revise your own views of American history or world history? How and why?

12. Write an essay in defense of skepticism, pessimism, optimism, or a similar term of your choice.

STUDENT MODEL 12

FOR READING: Study the following short selection as a possible model for writing of your own. How do you react to it overall? What makes it interesting or effective? Answer the following more specific questions:

1. (PURPOSE) What was the writer trying to do?
2. (AUDIENCE) What kind of reader would make a good reader for this selection?
3. (SOURCES) Where did the writer turn for material?
4. (THESIS) Does the selection have a central idea or unifying thesis?
5. (STRUCTURE) What is the author's overall plan or strategy?
6. (STYLE) What makes the piece effective or memorable (for instance, striking details, memorable phrases)?
7. (REVISION) What do you think the writer could or should have done differently?

J. Strum

Growing Up Liberal

Since the McCarthy period of the 1950s, Communists have been ostra- 1 cized in American society. Although there were many members of the Communist party in the 1930s, by the end of the 1950s most people had come to the conclusion that communism had become as corrupt as capitalism; many of these people became the liberals of the 1960s.

My father was among those party members who became disenchanted 2 with the Soviet Union after it invaded Hungary in 1956. Unlike many of his friends, however, he refused to turn over to the FBI the names of other members of the party; as a result, he was persecuted in many subtle ways. Our hometown newspaper would periodically have stories about his involvement in some liberal cause or other, headlined "Red Supports Peace March" or "Commie Organizes Coalition." To say the least, these articles limited his political effectiveness; they also had adverse effects on his earning power. Employers got nervous when they saw such headlines, however false. In reaction to these assaults on our father, we children developed an unquestioning and unwavering loyalty towards him.

Nevertheless, some painful realizations came to me as I grew up. 3 Despite my father's willingness to listen to my ideas, I could never sway his opinions. Trying to understand why I felt rebellious, I realized that I had experienced several injustices. I had been coerced by my parents into working for their causes before I was mature enough to understand them. I had participated in political demonstrations based on their indoctrination.

Many of my own needs and wishes were subordinated to their concern for the world at large. Philosophically, I felt betrayed, because they had used authoritarian means to achieve their liberal ends.

Just as other children are forced to go to church on Sunday, we were forced to help promote our parents' religion: politics. Every few weeks, the family would pitch in to put out a mailing for some organization or other. I became adept at collating, stapling, stuffing, and sealing envelopes. We were enlisted to distribute leaflets in front of a polling place, although at age three I did not understand the complexities of the issues on the ballot. I walked in my first peace march at age eight. Along with thousands of others, we walked nine miles supporting nuclear disarmament.

Sacrifice for the greater good was a prerequisite to being a good liberal. While an infant, I had to be raised by my mother alone, while my father traveled on behalf of liberal causes. When I was a child, we lived on the border of slums, as my father was living the life of a blue-collar worker, true to his belief in the working class. When I was attacked by black students in junior high school, my parents did not run screaming to the principal. Instead, they lectured me about acting hateful; they told me to understand that black students were angry at white people, not at me.

Friends whose parents were quibbling with them over the length of their hair told me that I was lucky. It seems I was supposed to be grateful that my parents were not members of the Ku Klux Klan or Nazis. "Be glad," my friends would say. "Your parents know where it's at." I wasn't so sure. *It*—the answer, truth, wisdom—comes from a process of evaluating ideas, not from "laying a trip"—even a liberal trip—on children.

FOR WRITING: What experience have you had that might be of interest to a historian of the future? For instance, could you write a firsthand eyewitness report on a subject like the ethnic family, the deterioration of the city, the vanishing family farm, the shift to a service economy, the welfare mentality, the soaring divorce rate, changing child custody laws, or the like? Try to show what a general historical trend means in the lives of those involved.

ADDITIONAL WRITING TOPICS 12

History

A. For a history class of the future, explain the meaning of one of the following and its role in contemporary life. Trace causes or origins; discuss problems and possible remedies; make projections for the future. Choose one:

1. the new South
2. the rise of the yuppie

3. la raza
4. Reaganomics
5. neo-Nazis
6. the sexual revolution
7. right to life
8. redevelopment
9. the women's movement
10. post-modernist architecture
11. punk
12. Black Muslims
13. ecumenism
14. deregulation
15. the fitness movement

B. Investigate the history of a religious, ethnic, racial, or occupational group of which you are a member or to which you have close ties. Concentrate on a major phase or a major set of issues. Write a historical paper that has a strong unifying thread or major theme. Draw on several different sources; identify them for your readers.

13

CLASSIC ESSAYS

Prose and the Imagination

OVERVIEW

The essays in this last section of the book are on the borderline between expository prose and imaginative literature. Imaginative literature draws on the full resources of language; it brings our full range of thought and feeling into play. The writers in this unit know how to translate ideas into vivid images. They speak to our feelings as well as to our intelligence. Their tone ranges from bitterness or nostalgia to warm humor or slashing wit. Their writing is far removed from averaged-out committee prose; they speak with an unmistakable personal voice. These writers remind us that the best expository prose is personal and committed, alive with vivid images and honest feeling.

PURPOSE Prose with a strong imaginative dimension makes us see, think, and feel. It brings into play capacities for observation, thought, and feeling that often go unused in hurried routine living. Such prose makes us more sensitive to our surroundings and the people around us. It broadens our sympathies by making us share in the experience of others. It makes us feel gladness and sorrow, compassion and indignation. It makes us feel more fully alive as human beings.

AUDIENCE Today's bestsellers, we are often told, are written according to formula. They give the audience "what it wants"; they are conceived or commissioned by people who study the audience and exploit its weaknesses. This unit brings together authors who write according to the opposite principle. They write for an imaginary ideal reader—a reader who, in the words of Virginia Woolf, becomes the author's "fellow-worker and accomplice." The writers in this unit share a common faith in the reader's understanding and goodwill. They trust us as readers to appreciate shades of meaning, to think seriously about things that matter, and to use our imagination to look at familiar subjects in a new light. They cater to the highest common denominator; their essays show what they expect us as readers to be capable of when we are at our best.

BENEFITS FOR THE WRITER

(1) Writing that appeals strongly to the imagination steers clear of clichés; it uses fresh vivid language; it is alive with vivid images and telling details. We can learn from it how to act out and dramatize rather than merely summarize ideas.

(2) Imaginative writing does justice to the emotional dimension of language. We can learn from it how to express attitudes and feelings candidly and without false notes.

(3) Imaginative writing goes beyond the tried and only partly true. It makes us take a new look at what is familiar; it makes us see connections that we might have overlooked. We can learn from it how to look at things from a fresh perspective. We can learn from it how to break out of familiar patterns and experiment with something new.

WRITER'S GUIDE 13

The Elements of Style

When writing has style, we read it with the pleasure that comes from seeing something difficult done well. The writer has learned to do skillfully and gracefully what people at first do laboriously, as if holding the pencil with both hands. Part of our pleasure in reading good writing comes from the *individual* style of an author. In reading someone like Mark Twain, we seem to hear the author's personal voice. We come to recognize the wit or the eloquence that is an author's trademark. But many features or elements of an effective style are found over and over in good prose. To make your own writing more effective, remember the following guidelines:

(1) *Speak your mind.* A basic test of effective style is our ability to speak up and make ourselves heard. Many successful writers reached a large audience not because they catered to popular opinion but because they knew how to take a stand. They knew how to make what matters stand out. We remember emphatic statements like the following:

> When a sixth of the population of a nation which has undertaken to be the refuge of liberty are slaves, . . . I think that it is not too soon for honest men to rebel and revolutionize. (Henry David Thoreau)

> Official war propaganda, with its disgusting hypocrisy and self-righteousness, tends to make thinking people sympathize with the enemy. (George Orwell)

> The quality of strength lined with tenderness is an unbeatable combination, as are intelligence and necessity when unblunted by formal education. (Maya Angelou)

(2) *Use accurate words.* The right word does not merely give us "the general idea"; it gives us the right shade of meaning. A large vocabulary enables the writer to choose the word that carries just the right meaning and the right attitude. Writers who care about words expect their readers to appreciate distinctions like the following:

> The way to be *safe* is never to be *secure*. (Benjamin Franklin)

> Rage cannot be *hidden*; it can only be *dissembled*. (James Baldwin)

> For the gifted young woman today, such a life . . . is not a *destiny* but a *fate*. (Mary McCarthy)

Such differences are partly in the **denotations** of words—what the words point to. But they are often also in the **connotations** of words—the attitudes or judgments they imply. A person who *toils* carries more of a burden than one who merely *works*, and makes more of a claim to our sympathy. A person who *squanders* an inheritance does so more recklessly and foolishly than one who *wastes* it. Often a single well-chosen word carries information and attitudes more effectively than a roundabout explanation.

(3) *Translate the abstract into the concrete.* Relate general ideas to the world of sights and sounds. When we state general ideas, we necessarily abstract, or "draw away" from specific people and events. But good writers never move away too far or for too long from what we can see and hear, what we can imagine and visualize. They resist "mere abstractions"— general words that have been cut loose from their roots in concrete reality.

Passages like the following reassure us that, to their authors, words are not just words. The writers easily and naturally relate their general ideas to the world of everyday experience:

The West begins *where the annual rainfall drops below twenty inches.* (Bernard DeVoto)

The only natural force over which we have any control out here is water, and that only recently. In my memory California summers were characterized by *the coughing of the pipes that meant the well was dry,* and California winters by *all-night watches on rivers about to crest,* by *sandbagging,* by *dynamite on the levees and flooding on the first floor.* (Joan Didion)

(4) *Use fresh figurative language to call up the right images and feelings.* Use imaginative comparisons that will create vivid images in the reader's mind and bring the right feelings and attitudes into play. Effective figurative language makes prose come to life. It makes readers take a fresh look; it appeals to their emotions as well as to their minds.

When the imaginative comparison, or figure of speech, is clearly presented as a comparison (introduced by words such as *like, as,* and *as if*), we call it a **simile**:

His son spent money *as if he were trying to see the bottom of the mint.* (Alice Walker)

Prose consists less and less of words chosen for their meaning, and more and more of phrases tacked together *like the sections of a prefabricated hen-house.* (George Orwell)

When a writer talks about something as if it actually were the thing to which it is being compared, we call the imaginative comparison a **metaphor**:

I kept wishing that he would talk about himself, hoping to *break through the wall of rhetoric.* (Joan Didion)

> Everyone is *a moon* and has *a dark side which he never shows to anybody.*
> (Mark Twain)

A sustained or extended metaphor follows the same basic comparison through several related details:

> In the midst of *this chopping sea of civilized life,* such are *the clouds and storms and quicksands* . . . that a man has to live, if he would not *founder and go to the bottom* and not *make his port* at all, by dead reckoning, and he must be a great calculator indeed who succeeds. (Henry David Thoreau)

Metaphors can wear out, however. When we hear them over and over, they become merely a tired, secondhand way of stating a familiar idea. We can tell that metaphors no longer call up a vivid image when we find two combined in a mixed cliché. ("Young people today will have to *roll up their sleeves* if they want to *take their places at the banquet of life.*") Avoid **mixed metaphors** that show you are no longer paying attention to the images your figurative expressions call up in the reader's mind:

> CONSISTENT: There are a thousand *hacking away at the branches* of evil to one who is *striking at the root.* (Thoreau)
>
> MIXED: The potential for disaster was there; only a *spark plug* was needed to *unleash* these tragic events.
>
> The *long arm* of federal tyranny is reaching out to *crush us under its boot.*

(5) *Make full use of the resources of the English sentence.* A short, pointed sentence sums up. It is easy to remember and to quote:

> As long as possible live free and uncommitted. (Thoreau)
>
> Economy is the art of making the most of life. (G.B. Shaw)
>
> Punctuality is the thief of time. (Oscar Wilde)

A long, elaborate sentence can follow through. It can explain; it can drive home a point; it can fill in detail:

> The mild-mannered man who turns into a bear behind the wheel of a car—i.e., who finds in the power of the automobile a vehicle for the release of his inhibitions—is part of American folklore. (Tom Wolfe)

Study the way the first-rate writers use the short, pointed sentence to sum up a key point and then follow up with a more elaborate sentence that explains or provides details:

SHORT: | *The great enemy of clear language is insincerity.*
LONG: | When there is a gap between one's real and one's declared aims, one turns as it were instinctively to long words and exhausted idioms, like a cuttlefish squirting out ink. (George Orwell)

A good writer has an ear for how a well-built sentence sounds. Many well-balanced sentences owe their rhythm to the way related ideas have been lined up in similar grammatical form. Such lining up of related sentence elements is called **parallel structure**:

It is about time we realize that many women make
  better teachers than mothers,
  better actresses than wives,
  better diplomats than cooks. (Marya Mannes)

Other sentences owe their rhythm to the balanced lining up of opposites. We call such a lining up of clear-cut opposites an **antithesis**. Here is an example of such antithetical balance:

We have exchanged *being known in small communities* for
          being anonymous in huge populations.
          (Ellen Goodman)

(6) *Use humor and irony for their leavening effect.* When you write on a serious subject, you want to assure your readers that you take your subject and your audience seriously. But when writing becomes *too* serious, it can easily become humorless and forbidding. An occasional humorous or ironic touch will assure your readers that they are listening to a human being. One way a writer can steer away from deadly seriousness is to use occasional touches of verbal humor, or **word play**:

The *settlement* of America had its origin in the *unsettlement* of Europe. (Lewis Mumford)

The trouble with the *profit system* has always been that it was highly *unprofitable* to most people. The profits went to the few; the work went to the many. (E.B. White)

A writer with a lively sense of **irony** will keep prose from getting dull by pointing up revealing contradictions:

Individualism is the belief that we should all paddle our own canoes, *especially on the high seas.*

A writer with a sharp wit will surprise us by giving an unexpected twist to a familiar phrase or a familiar pious sentiment:

To do good is noble; to teach others to do good is nobler, and no trouble. (Mark Twain)

To sum up: Writers with a sense of style have learned to look at their own writing through the reader's eyes—to listen to it with a reader's ears. They sense whether the words they choose will make things clear for the reader or befog the subject. Their ear for sentences tells them whether a sentence will read well. Putting themselves in the reader's place, they sense when their writing becomes too solemn and plodding—or too chummy and frivolous. Good writing shows the writer's faith in the reader's ability to know the difference.

Prewriting Activities 13

1. For *sentence practice*, select sentences from the following categories as model sentences. Write sentences that use your own subject matter but that imitate the style of the original as closely as possible. Choose your model sentences from the following sections of this Writer's Guide:

a. emphatic sentences—section (1)
b. figurative sentences—section (4)
c. short, pointed sentences—section (5)
d. sentences with parallel structure—section (5)
e. antithetical sentences—section (5)
f. sentences with an ironic or humorous touch—section (6)

2. A favorite *stylistic exercise* for essayists has been the traditional "informal essay." It is often whimsical in its choice of a topic and leisurely and humorous in style. However, it often has serious undertones as it reveals to the reader the writer's personality or view of life. Write one or two paragraphs on a subject that allows you to be half serious and half humorous. Make your paragraphs a half-serious defense of something that some people may criticize but that to many people is not a serious issue: dirt roads, pigeons, cheerleaders, fast-food restaurants, low riders, T-shirt messages.

Paragraph Practice 13

Study the use the following paragraph makes of familiar elements of style: emphatic repetition and parallelism, sustained figurative language, antithetical opposition. Write a similar emphatic or eloquent passage about some important decision you have made or a turn your life has taken.

Driving Life into a Corner

I went to the woods because I wished to live deliberately, to front only the essential facts of life, and see if I could not learn what it had to teach, and not, when I came to die, discover that I had not lived. I did not wish to live what was not life, living is so dear; nor did I wish to practice resignation, unless it was quite necessary. I wanted to live deep and suck out all the marrow of life, to live so sturdily and Spartan-like as to put to rout all that was not life, to cut a broad swath and shave close, to drive life into a corner, and reduce it to its lowest terms, and, if it proved to be mean, why then to get the whole and genuine meanness of it, and publish its meanness to the world; or if it were sublime, to know it by experience, and be able to give a true account of it in my next excursion. For most men, it appears to me, are in a strange uncertainty about it, whether it is of the devil or of God, and have *somewhat hastily* concluded that it is the chief end of man here to "glorify God and enjoy him forever." (Henry David Thoreau, *Walden*)

BACKGROUND: Maxine Hong Kingston stands out among writers who in recent decades have made Americans more aware of their manifold cultural and ethnic heritage. She was born in 1940, the daughter of Chinese immigrants who ran a laundry in Stockton, California. Relatives who had stayed in China were caught up in the turmoil of the Communist revolution. She has taught as a high school teacher in California and Hawaii and has been a visiting professor at the University of Hawaii in Honolulu. Kingston's writing draws on a rich fund of personal observation, family legend, and traditional tales. She has written with intense emotion and often great bitterness about growing up as a girl within the narrow boundaries of traditional Chinese culture. Her autobiographical *The Woman Warrior: Memoirs of a Childhood Among Ghosts* won the nonfiction award of the National Book Critics Circle in 1976. In her second book, *China Men* (1980), she has written about the barriers and humiliations immigrants from China encountered in America.

Maxine Hong Kingston
The Woman
Warrior

GUIDE TO READING: In this intensely personal account of her experiences, Kingston writes from a deep-seated sense of injustice. What caused it? How does she deal with it?

My American life has been such a disappointment. 1

"I got straight A's, Mama." 2

"Let me tell you a true story about a girl who saved her village." 3

I could not figure out what was my village. And it was important that I 4
do something big and fine, or else my parents would sell me when we made our way back to China. In China there were solutions for what to do with little girls who ate up food and threw tantrums. You can't eat straight A's.

When one of my parents or the emigrant villagers said, "Feeding girls 5
is feeding cowbirds," I would thrash on the floor and scream so hard I couldn't talk. I couldn't stop.

"What's the matter with her?" 6

"I don't know. Bad, I guess. You know how girls are. There's no profit in 7
raising girls. Better to raise geese than girls."

"I would hit her if she were mine. But then there's no use wasting all 8
that discipline on a girl. 'When you raise girls, you're raising children for strangers.'"

"Stop that crying!" my mother would yell. "I'm going to hit you if you 9 don't stop. Bad girl! Stop!" I'm going to remember never to hit or scold my children for crying, I thought, because then they will only cry more.

"I'm not a bad girl," I would scream. "I'm not a bad girl. I'm not a bad 10 girl." I might as well have said, "I'm not a girl."

"When you were little, all you had to say was 'I'm not a bad girl,' and 11 you could make yourself cry," my mother says, talking-story about my childhood.

I minded that the emigrant villagers shook their heads at my sister and 12 me. "One girl—and another girl," they said, and made our parents ashamed to take us out together. The good part about my brothers being born was that people stopped saying, "All girls," but I learned new grievances. "Did you roll an egg on *my* face like that when *I* was born?" "Did you have a full-month party for *me?*" "Did you turn on all the lights?" "Did you send *my* picture to Grandmother?" "Why not? Because I'm a girl? Is that why not?" "Why didn't you teach me English?" "You like having me beaten up at school, don't you?"

"She is very mean, isn't she?" the emigrant villagers would say. 13

"Come, children. Hurry. Hurry. Who wants to go out with Great- 14 Uncle?" On Saturday mornings, my great-uncle, the ex-river pirate, did the shopping. "Get your coats, whoever's coming."

"I'm coming. I'm coming. Wait for me." 15

When he heard girls' voices, he turned on us and roared, "No girls!" and 16 left my sisters and me hanging our coats back up, not looking at one another. The boys came back with candy and new toys. When they walked through Chinatown, the people must have said, "A boy—and another boy—and another boy!" At my great-uncle's funeral I secretly tested out feeling glad that he was dead—the six-foot bearish masculinity of him.

I went away to college—Berkeley in the sixties—and I studied, and I 17 marched to change the world, but I did not turn into a boy. I would have liked to bring myself back as a boy for my parents to welcome with chickens and pigs. That was for my brother, who returned alive from Vietnam.

If I went to Vietnam, I would not come back; females desert families. It 18 was said, "There is an outward tendency in females," which meant that I was getting straight A's for the good of my future husband's family, not my own. I did not plan ever to have a husband. I would show my mother and father and the nosey emigrant villagers that girls have no outward tendency. I stopped getting straight A's.

And all the time I was having to turn myself American-feminine, or 19 no dates.

There is a Chinese word for the female *I* —which is "slave." Break the 20 women with their own tongues!

I refused to cook. When I had to wash dishes, I would crack one or two. 21 "Bad girl," my mother yelled, and sometimes that made me gloat rather than cry. Isn't a bad girl almost a boy?

"What do you want to be when you grow up, little girl?" 22

"A lumberjack in Oregon." 23

Even now, unless I'm happy, I burn the food when I cook. I do not feed 24 people. I let the dirty dishes rot. I eat at other people's tables but won't invite them to mine, where the dishes are rotting.

If I could not-eat, perhaps I could make myself a warrior like the 25 swordswoman who drives me. I will—I must—rise and plow the fields as soon as the baby comes out.

Once I get outside the house, what bird might call me; on what horse 26 could I ride away? Marriage and childbirth strengthen the swordswoman, who is not a maid like Joan of Arc. Do the women's work; then do more work, which will become ours too. No husband of mine will say, "I could have been a drummer, but I had to think about the wife and kids. You know how it is." Nobody supports me at the expense of his own adventure. Then I get bitter: no one supports me; I am not loved enough to be supported. That I am not a burden has to compensate for the sad envy when I look at women loved enough to be supported. Even now China wraps double binds around my feet.

When urban renewal tore down my parents' laundry and paved over 27 our slum for a parking lot, I only made up gun and knife fantasies and did nothing useful.

From the fairy tales, I've learned exactly who the enemy are. I easily 28 recognize them—business-suited in their modern American executive guise, each boss two feet taller than I am and impossible to meet eye to eye.

I once worked at an art supply house that sold paints to artists. "Order 29 more of that nigger yellow, willya?" the boss told me. "Bright, isn't it? Nigger yellow."

"I don't like that word," I had to say in my bad, small-person's voice 30 that makes no impact. The boss never deigned to answer.

I also worked at a land developer's association. The building industry 31 was planning a banquet for contractors, real estate dealers, and real estate editors. "Did you know the restaurant you chose for the banquet is being picketed by CORE and the NAACP?" I squeaked.

"Of course I know." The boss laughed. "That's why I chose it." 32

"I refuse to type these invitations," I whispered, voice unreliable. 33

He leaned back in his leather chair, his bossy stomach opulent. He 34 picked up his calendar and slowly circled a date. "You will be paid up to here," he said. "We'll mail you the check."

If I took the sword, which my hate must surely have forged out of the 35 air, and gutted him, I would put color and wrinkles into his shirt.

It's not just the stupid racists that I have to do something about, but the 36 tyrants who for whatever reason can deny my family food and work. My job is my own only land.

To avenge my family, I'd have to storm across China to take back our 37 farm from the Communists; I'd have to rage across the United States to take back the laundry in New York and the one in California. Nobody in history has conquered and united both North America and Asia. A descendant of eighty pole fighters, I ought to be able to set out confidently, march straight down our street, get going right now. There's work to do, ground to cover. Surely, the eighty pole fighters, though unseen would follow me and lead me and protect me, as is the wont of ancestors.

Or it may well be that they're resting happily in China, their spirits 38 dispersed among the real Chinese, and not nudging me at all with their poles. I mustn't feel bad that I haven't done as well as the swordswoman did; after all, no bird called me, no wise old people tutored me. I have no magic beads, or water gourd sight, no rabbit that will jump in the fire when I'm hungry. I dislike armies.

I've looked for the bird. I've seen clouds make pointed angel wings 39 that stream past the sunset, but they shred into clouds. Once at a beach after a long hike I saw a seagull, tiny as an insect. But when I jumped up to tell what miracle I saw, before I could get the words out I understood that the bird was insect-size because it was far away. My brain had momentarily lost its depth perception. I was that eager to find an unusual bird.

The news from China has been confusing. It also had something to do 40 with birds. I was nine years old when the letters made my parents, who are rocks, cry. My father screamed in his sleep. My mother wept and crumpled up the letters. She set fire to them page by page in the ashtray, but new letters came almost every day. The only letters they opened without fear were the ones with red borders, the holiday letters that mustn't carry bad news. The other letters said that my uncles were made to kneel on broken glass during their trials and had confessed to being land-owners. They were all executed, and the aunt whose thumbs were twisted off drowned herself. Other aunts, mothers-in-law, and cousins disappeared; some suddenly began writing to us again from communes or from Hong Kong. They kept asking for money. The ones in communes got four ounces of fat and one cup of oil a week, they said, and had to work from 4 A.M. to 9 P.M. They had to learn to do dances waving red kerchiefs; they had to sing nonsense syllables. The Communists gave axes to the old ladies and said, "Go and kill yourself. You're useless." If we overseas Chinese would just send money to the Communist bank, our relatives said, they might get a percentage of it for themselves. The aunts in Hong Kong said to send money quickly; their children were begging on the sidewalks and mean people put dirt in their bowls.

When I dream that I am wire without flesh, there is a letter on blue 41 airmail paper that floats above the night ocean between here and China. It must arrive safely or else my grandmother and I will lose each other.

My parents felt bad whether or not they sent money. Sometimes they 42 got angry at their brothers and sisters for asking. And they would not simply ask but have to talk-story too. The revolutionaries had taken Fourth Aunt and Uncle's store, house, and lands. They attacked the house and killed the grandfather and oldest daughter. The grandmother escaped with the loose cash and did not return to help. Fourth Aunt picked up her sons, one under each arm, and hid in the pig house, where they slept that night in cotton clothes. The next day she found her husband, who had miraculously escaped. The two of them collected twigs and yams to sell while their children begged. Each morning they tied the faggots on each other's back. Nobody bought from them. They ate the yams and some of the children's rice. Finally Fourth Aunt saw what was wrong. "We have to shout 'Fuel for sale' and 'Yams for sale,'" she said. "We can't just walk unobtrusively up and down the street." "You're right," said my uncle, but he was shy and walked in back of her. "Shout," my aunt ordered, but he could not. "They think we're carrying these sticks home for our own fire," she said. "Shout." They walked about miserably, silently, until sundown, neither of them able to advertise themselves. Fourth Aunt, an orphan since the age of ten, mean as my mother, threw her bundle down at his feet and scolded Fourth Uncle, "Starving to death, his wife and children starving to death, and he's too damned shy to raise his voice." She left him standing by himself and afraid to return empty-handed to her. He sat under a tree to think, when he spotted a pair of nesting doves. Dumping his bag of yams, he climbed up and caught the birds. That was when the Communists trapped him, in the tree. They criticized him for selfishly taking food for his own family and killed him, leaving his body in the tree as an example. They took the birds to a commune kitchen to be shared.

It is confusing that my family was not the poor to be championed. They were executed like the barons in the stories, when they were not barons. It is confusing that birds tricked us. [43]

What fighting and killing I have seen have not been glorious but slum grubby. I fought the most during junior high school and always cried. Fights are confusing as to who has won. The corpses I've seen had been rolled and dumped, sad little dirty bodies covered with a police khaki blanket. My mother locked her children in the house so we couldn't look at dead slum people. But at news of a body, I would find a way to get out; I had to learn about dying if I wanted to become a swordswoman. Once there was an Asian man stabbed next door, word on cloth pinned to his corpse. When the police came around asking questions, my father said, "No read Japanese. Japanese words. Me Chinese." [44]

I've also looked for old people who could be my gurus. A medium with red hair told me that a girl who died in a far country follows me wherever I go. This spirit can help me if I acknowledge her, she said. Between the head line and the heart line in my right palm, she said, I have the mystic cross. I could become a medium myself. I don't want to be a medium. I don't want to be a crank taking "offerings" in a wicker plate from the frightened audience, who, one after another, asked the spirits how to raise rent money, how to cure their coughs and skin disease, how to find a job. And martial arts are for unsure little boys kicking away under fluorescent lights. [45]

I live now where there are Chinese and Japanese, but no emigrants 46
from my own village looking at me as if I had failed them. Living among
one's own emigrant villagers can give a good Chinese far from China glory
and a place. "That old busboy is really a swordsman," we whisper when he
goes by, "He is a swordsman who's killed fifty. He has a tong ax in his closet."
But I am useless, one more girl who couldn't be sold. When I visit the family
now, I wrap my American successes around me like a private shawl; I *am*
worthy of eating the food. From afar I can believe my family loves me
fundamentally. They only say, "When fishing for treasures in the flood, be
careful not to pull in girls," because that is what one says about daughters.
But I watched such words come out of my own mother's and father's
mouths; I looked at their ink drawing of poor people snagging at their
neighbor's flotage with long flood hooks and pushing the girl babies on
down the river. And I had to get out of hating range. I read in an anthropology book that Chinese say, "Girls are necessary too"; I have never heard the
Chinese I know make this concession. Perhaps it was a saying in another
village. I refuse to shy my way any more through our Chinatown, which
tasks me with the old sayings and the stories.

The swordswoman and I are not so dissimilar. May my people under- 47
stand the resemblance soon so I can return to them. What we have in
common are the words at our backs. The ideographs for *revenge* are "report
a crime" and "report to five families." The reporting is the vengeance—not
the beheading, not the gutting, but the words. And I have so many words—
"chink" words and "gook" words too—that they do not fit on my skin.

Using the Dictionary

A. Check the following as needed: 1. *emigrant* (5)   2. *masculinity*
(16)   3. *compensate* (26)   4. *opulent* (34)   5. *disperse* (38)   6. *commune*
(40)   7. *khaki* (44)   8. *guru* (45)   9. *mystic* (45)   10. *medium* (45)   11. *martial* (45)   12. *tong* (46)   13. *concession* (46)   14. *ideograph* (47)

B. An **allusion** is a brief mention that calls to mind a familiar story or a familiar
situation. What images or associations come to mind when the author mentions Joan
of Arc (26)? What does the author allude to when she says, "Even now China wraps
double binds around my feet" (26)?

The Writer's Agenda

In this intensely personal and emotional account, Kingston registers, and comes to
terms with, deep-seated grievances. How does she make them real? How does she
cope with them?

1. What is the common strand in her earliest experiences as a child? (What
does she do to make them real?) How does she react—how does she deal with what
happens to her?

2. Does she shift her focus in recounting her experiences at work? Is there a connecting thread between her experiences in the family and at work?

3. How does Kingston deal with the fate of her relatives in China? What is her tone? What is her reaction?

4. How does Kingston draw on the world of fairy-tale and legend? What glimpses do we get of the world of traditional Chinese legend and custom? What is the role of fantasy and daydream in this essay?

5. Kingston makes frequent telling, damning use of what people say. What are striking examples?

6. Kingston takes her readers into her confidence with exceptionally candid, open expression of hostile and confused feelings. What are striking examples?

7. What is the author's last word? How does her conclusion return to earlier concerns of the essay? How is her perspective as an adult different from her perspective as a child?

For Discussion or Writing

8. How do you react as you read Kingston's essay? Do you get involved? How? Why or why not?

9. How extreme or unique are the traditional attitudes towards girls described in this essay? Are there parallels in other ethnic or cultural traditions that you know?

10. Are sexism and racism related? Do they spring from common roots? Or do they differ in their causes and effects?

11. If you had an opportunity to express a grievance of long standing, what would you choose? How would you enlist the sympathy of your readers?

12. Do you know another culture well enough through experience or study to serve as a guide to the outsider? Provide an insider's introduction to an ethnic, cultural, or religious tradition you know well.

BACKGROUND: E.B. White (1899–1985) worked for many years for *The New Yorker*, a magazine that from its beginnings in the twenties has published many of this country's most admired contemporary writers. In the years between 1938 and 1943, White wrote a series of **informal essays** that appeared as a monthly feature in *Harper's* and that became classics of their kind. Many of these essays start with an account of everyday happenings but lead to more general thoughts or reflections. Part of a tradition going back to the eighteenth century, these informal essays have a light touch and a leisurely pace but nevertheless often lead into a serious discussion of human life, of our relationship to nature or to society. Many of the readers White wrote for lived, as he did, in a large modern city but longed for a simpler existence closer to the permanent rhythms of nature. Many of his best-remembered essays report on his experiences as a part-time farmer in Maine, helping sheep with the births of their lambs, helping hens raise their chicks, listening to the thoughts and worries of people living in the countryside. White said about his intended audience that many people living in a world of war and violence find a positive value in memories of simple, peaceful pursuits. For these people, he wrote the following widely reprinted masterpiece of nostalgic reflection.

E. B. White

Once More to the Lake

GUIDE TO READING: This essay is a classic record of a writer's journey in search of the past. On the surface, it is the story of a week's camping trip to a lake remembered from childhood days. But the true purpose of the author is to relive bygone events, to revisit places long remembered, to recapture the mood of childhood summers when "the sun shone endlessly, day after day." What is he looking for? What does he find?

One summer, along about 1904, my father rented a camp on a lake in Maine and took us all there for the month of August. We all got ringworm from some kittens and had to rub Pond's Extract on our arms and legs night and morning, and my father rolled over in a canoe with all his clothes on; but outside of that the vacation was a success and from then on none of us ever thought there was any place in the world like that lake in Maine. We returned summer after summer—always on August 1st for one month. I have since become a salt-water man, but sometimes in summer there are days when the restlessness of the tides and the fearful cold of the sea water and the incessant wind which blows across the afternoon and into the evening make me wish for the placidity of a lake in the woods. A few weeks ago this feeling got so strong I bought myself a couple of bass hooks and a spinner and returned to the lake where we used to go, for a week's fishing and to revisit old haunts.

I took along my son, who had never had any fresh water up his nose ₂ and who had seen lily pads only from train windows. On the journey over to the lake I began to wonder what it would be like. I wondered how time would have marred this unique, this holy spot—the coves and streams, the hills that the sun set behind, the camps and the paths behind the camps. I was sure that the tarred road would have found it out and I wondered in what other ways it would be desolated. It is strange how much you can remember about places like that once you allow your mind to return into the grooves which lead back. You remember one thing, and that suddenly reminds you of another thing. I guess I remembered clearest of all the early mornings, when the lake was cool and motionless, remembered how the bedroom smelled of the lumber it was made of and of the wet woods whose scent entered through the screen. The partitions in the camp were thin and did not extend clear to the top of the rooms, and as I was always the first up I would dress softly so as not to wake the others, and sneak out into the sweet outdoors and start out in the canoe, keeping close along the shore in the long shadows of the pines. I remembered being very careful never to rub my paddle against the gunwale for fear of disturbing the stillness of the cathedral.

The lake had never been what you would call a wild lake. There were ₃ cottages sprinkled around the shores, and it was in farming country although the shores of the lake were quite heavily wooded. Some of the cottages were owned by nearby farmers, and you would live at the shore and eat your meals at the farmhouse. That's what our family did. But although it wasn't wild, it was a fairly large and undisturbed lake and there were places in it which, to a child at least, seemed infinitely remote and primeval.

I was right about the tar: it led to within half a mile of the shore. But ₄ when I got back there, with my boy, and we settled into a camp near a farmhouse and into the kind of summertime I had known, I could tell that it was going to be pretty much the same as it had been before—I knew it, lying in bed the first morning, smelling the bedroom, and hearing the boy sneak quietly out and go off along the shore in a boat. I began to sustain the illusion that he was I, and therefore, by simple transposition, that I was my father. This sensation persisted, kept cropping up all the time we were there. It was not an entirely new feeling, but in this setting it grew much stronger. I seemed to be living a dual existence. I would be in the middle of some simple act, I would be picking up a bait box or laying down a table fork, or I would be saying something, and suddenly it would be not I but my father who was saying the words or making the gesture. It gave me a creepy sensation.

We went fishing the first morning. I felt the same damp moss covering ₅ the worms in the bait can, and saw the dragonfly alight on the tip of my rod as it hovered a few inches from the surface of the water. It was the arrival of this fly that convinced me beyond any doubt that everything was as it always had been, that the years were a mirage and there had been no years. The small waves were the same, chucking the rowboat under the chin as we fished at anchor, and the boat was the same boat, the same color green and the ribs broken in the same places, and under the floor-boards the same fresh-water leaving and débris—the dead helgramite, the wisps of moss, the rusty discarded fishhook, the dried blood from yesterday's catch. We stared silently at the tips of our rods, at the dragonflies that came and went. I lowered the tip of mine into the water, tentatively, pensively dislodging the fly, which darted two feet away, poised, darted two feet back, and came to rest again a little farther up the rod. There had been no years between the ducking of this dragonfly and the other one—the one that was part of memory. I looked at the boy, who was silently watching his fly, and it was my hands that held his rod, my eyes watching. I felt dizzy and didn't know which rod I was at the end of.

We caught two bass, hauling them in briskly as though they were ₆ mackerel, pulling them over the side of the boat in a businesslike manner without any landing net, and stunning them with a blow on the back of the head. When we got back for a swim before lunch, the lake was exactly where we had left it, the same number of inches from the dock, and there was only the merest suggestion of a breeze. This seemed an utterly enchanted sea, this lake you could leave to its own devices for a few hours and come back to, and find that it had not stirred, this constant and trustworthy body of water. In the shallows, the dark, water-soaked sticks and twigs, smooth and old, were undulating in clusters on the bottom against the clean ribbed sand, and the track of the mussel was plain. A school of minnows swam by, each minnow with its small individual shadow, doubling the attendance, so clear and sharp in the sunlight. Some of the other campers were in swimming, along the shore, one of them with a cake of soap, and the water felt thin and clear and unsubstantial. Over the years there had been this person with the cake of soap, this cultist, and here he was. There had been no years.

Up to the farmhouse to dinner through the teeming, dusty field, the ₇ road under our sneakers was only a two-track road. The middle track was missing, the one with the marks of the hooves and the splotches of dried, flaky manure. There had always been three tracks to choose from in choosing which track to walk in; now the choice was narrowed down to two. For a moment I missed terribly the middle alternative. But the way led past the tennis court, and something about the way it lay there in the sun reassured me; the tape had loosened along the backline, the alleys were green with plantains and other weeds, and the net (installed in June and removed in September) sagged in the dry noon, and the whole place steamed with midday heat and hunger and emptiness. There was a choice of pie for dessert, and one was blueberry and one was apple, and the waitresses were the same country girls, there having been no passage of time, only the illusion of it as in a dropped curtain—the waitresses were still fifteen; their hair had been washed, that was the only difference—they had been to the movies and seen the pretty girls with the clean hair.

Summertime, oh summertime, pattern of life indelible, the fade-proof ₈ lake, the woods unshatterable, the pasture with the sweetfern and the juniper forever and ever, summer without end; this was the background, and the life along the shore was the design, the cottages with their innocent and tranquil design, their tiny docks with the flagpole and the American flag floating against the white clouds in the blue sky, the little paths over the roots of the trees leading from camp to camp and the paths leading back to the outhouses and the can of lime for sprinkling, and at the souvenir counters at the store the miniature birch-bark canoes and the post cards that showed things looking a little better than they looked. This was the American family at play, escaping the city heat, wondering whether the newcomers in the camp at the head of the cove were "common" or "nice," wondering whether it was true that the people who drove up for Sunday dinner at the farmhouse were turned away because there wasn't enough chicken.

It seemed to me, as I kept remembering all this, that those times and ₉ those summers had been infinitely precious and worth saving. There had been jollity and peace and goodness. The arriving (at the beginning of August) had been so big a business in itself, at the railway station the farm wagon drawn up, the first smell of the pine-laden air, the first glimpse of the smiling farmer, and the great importance of the trunks and your father's enormous authority in such matters, and the feel of the wagon under you for the long ten-mile haul, and at the top of the last long hill catching the first view of the lake after eleven months of not seeing this cherished body of water. The shouts and cries of the other campers when they saw you, and the trunks to be unpacked, to give up their rich burden. (Arriving was less exciting nowadays, when you sneaked up in your car and parked it under a tree near the camp and took out the bags and in five minutes it was all over, no fuss, no loud wonderful fuss about trunks.)

Peace and goodness and jollity. The only thing that was wrong now, ₁₀ really, was the sound of the place, an unfamiliar nervous sound of the outboard motors. This was the note that jarred, the one thing that would sometimes break the illusion and set the years moving. In those other summertimes all motors were inboard; and when they were at a little distance, the noise they made was a sedative, an ingredient of summer sleep. They were one-cylinder and two-cylinder engines, and some were make-and-break and some were jump-spark, but they all made a sleepy sound across the lake. The one-lungers throbbed and fluttered, and the twin-cylinder ones purred and purred, and that was a quiet sound too. But now the campers all had the outboards. In the daytime, in the hot mornings, these motors made a petulant, irritable sound; at night, in the still evening when the afterglow lit the water, they whined about one's ears like mosquitoes. My boy loved our rented outboard, and his great desire was to achieve singlehanded mastery over it, and authority, and he soon learned the trick of choking it a little (but not too much), and the adjustment of the needle valve. Watching him I would remember the things you could do with the old one-cylinder engine with the heavy flywheel, how you could have it eating out of your hand if you got really close to it spiritually. Motor boats in those days didn't have clutches, and you would make a landing by shutting off the motor at the proper time and coasting in with a dead rudder. But there was a way of reversing them, if you learned the trick, by cutting the switch and putting it on again exactly on the final dying revolution of the flywheel, so that it would kick back against compression and begin reversing. Approaching a dock in a strong following breeze, it was difficult to slow up sufficiently by the ordinary coasting method, and if a boy felt he had complete mastery over his motor, he was tempted to keep it running beyond its time and then reverse it a few feet from the dock. It took a cool nerve, because if you threw the switch a twentieth of a second too soon you would catch the flywheel when it still had speed enough to go up past center, and the boat would leap ahead, charging bull-fashion at the dock.

We had a good week at the camp. The bass were biting well and the sun shone endlessly, day after day. We would be tired at night and lie down in the accumulated heat of the little bedrooms after the long hot day and the breeze would stir almost imperceptibly outside and the smell of the swamp drift in through the rusty screens. Sleep would come easily and in the morning the red squirrel would be on the roof, tapping out his gay routine. I kept remembering everything, lying in bed in the mornings—the small steamboat that had a long rounded stern like the lip of a Ubangi, and how quietly she ran on the moonlight sails, when the older boys played their mandolins and the girls sang and we ate doughnuts dipped in sugar, and how sweet the music was on the water in the shining night, and what it had felt like to think about girls then. After breakfast we would go up to the store and the things were in the same place—the minnows in a bottle, the plugs and spinners disarranged and pawed over by the youngsters from the boys' camp, the fig newtons and the Beeman's gum. Outside, the road was tarred and cars stood in front of the store. Inside, all was just as it had always been, except there was more Coca Cola and not so much Moxie and root beer and birch beer and sarsaparilla. We would walk out with a bottle of pop apiece and sometimes the pop would backfire up our noses and hurt. We explored the streams, quietly, where the turtles slid off the sunny logs and dug their way into the soft bottom; and we lay on the town wharf and fed worms to the tame bass. Everywhere we went I had trouble making out which was I, the one walking at my side, the one walking in my pants.

One afternoon while we were there at that lake a thunderstorm came up. It was like the revival of an old melodrama that I had seen long ago with childish awe. The second-act climax of the drama of the electrical disturbance over a lake in America had not changed in any important respect. This was the big scene, still the big scene. The whole thing was so familiar, the first feeling of oppression and heat and a general air around camp of not wanting to go very far away. In mid-afternoon (it was all the same) a curious darkening of the sky, and a lull in everything that had made life tick; and then the way the boats suddenly swung the other way at their moorings with the coming of a breeze out of the new quarter, and the premonitory rumble. Then the kettle drum, then the snare, then the bass drum and cymbals, then crackling light against the dark, and the gods grinning and licking their chops in the hills. Afterward the calm, the rain steadily rustling in the calm lake, the return of light and hope and spirits, and the campers running out in joy and relief to go swimming in the rain, their bright cries perpetuating the deathless joke about how they were getting simply drenched, and the children screaming with delight at the new sensation of bathing in the rain, and the joke about getting drenched linking the generations in a strong indestructible chain. And the comedian who waded in carrying an umbrella.

When the others went swimming my son said he was going in too. He pulled his dripping trunks from the line where they had hung all through the shower, and wrung them out. Languidly, and with no thought of going in, I watched him, his hard little body, skinny and bare, saw him wince slightly as he pulled up around his vitals the small, soggy, icy garment. As he buckled the swollen belt suddenly my groin felt the chill of death. ₁₃

Using the Dictionary

A. White calls things by their right names. Which of the following do you need to check in your dictionary, and what help does it provide?   1. *spinner* (1)   2. *gunwale* (2)   3. *helgramite* (5)   4. *mussel* (6)   5. *plantain* (7)   6. *sweetfern* (8)   8. *flywheel* (10)   9. *snare* (12)   10. *cymbals* (12)

B. The unity of mood in this essay is reflected in a network of **synonyms** and related terms. Check the following words as necessary. Explain how they cluster around or relate to the central theme of this essay.   11. *placidity* (1)   12. *remote* (3)   13. *primeval* (3)   14. *pensive* (5)   15. *indelible* (8)   16. *tranquil* (8)   17. *sedative* (10)   18. *perpetuate* (12)   19. *indestructible* (12)   20. *languid* (13)

The Writer's Agenda

Study the way this classic **informal essay** maintains a light or humorous tone while yet conveying ideas and feelings that are basic to the author's outlook on life.

1. What humorous details in the introductory paragraph help set the **informal tone** of the essay? Point out humorous touches or amusing details later in the essay that help the author maintain an informal, understated tone.

2. What passages in this essay are most clearly nostalgic memories of the *distant past*? Point out striking concrete details that help make these scenes real for the reader.

3. The author at first fears that "time would have marred" the lake of his childhood memories. What are some of the things that have *changed*?

4. The high points of this essay occur where *past and present* blend—where the author discovers that "everything was as it had always been." Quote several passages restating the same central idea. Describe key passages that support this main idea: the fishing, the farmhouse dinner, the thunderstorm. Point out details that make them real and that help create the prevailing mood.

5. How does the presence of his *son* help the author bridge the gulf between the present and the past? What is the significance of the ending? (Defend your interpretation.)

6. White frequently uses **figurative language**—imaginative comparisons that not only create vivid pictures in our minds but at the same time bring into play the right attitudes and emotions. Many of these comparisons are **metaphors**: They describe one thing as if it were the other to which it is being compared. (In the early morning calm of the cool and motionless lake, White is afraid that the noise of a paddle would disturb "the stillness of the *cathedral*." Later, the small waves are "*chucking* the rowboat *under the chin*.") Find all uses of figurative language in the passage describing the thunderstorm (paragraph 12). Pay special attention to *sustained* metaphors—comparisons followed up through several related details.

For Discussion or Writing

7. When people look back to their childhood, their prevailing mood may be nostalgia, regret, resentment, bitterness. What is yours?

8. What do you think the experience described in this essay was like for the son? Tell the story of the trip from the point of view of White's son.

9. A high point of White's essay is the thunderstorm on a summer afternoon. Write your own description of a similar age-old natural event running its course—a blizzard, the first big rainstorm of a rainy season, a hurricane, or the like.

10. Write an informal essay about a place, person, or event from the past whose memory continues to play a role in your thoughts or in your life.

11. One test of a classic is that it often makes a time and a place come to life unforgettably for its audience, sometimes making the setting seem more real than the readers' memories of their own past. Write an essay in which you write as an imaginary visitor to one such well-remembered setting from your own reading.

BACKGROUND: Jonathan Swift (1667–1745), the author of *Gulliver's Travels*, is one of the great masters of satire in world literature. He aimed his biting wit at targets including religious fanaticism, political corruption, and war. Swift was born of English parents in Dublin, Ireland, at a time when Ireland was under English rule. Much of the wealth produced by Irish tenant farmers went to "absentee landlords." Religious divisions aggravated political conflicts: The Irish, then as now, were predominantly Catholic ("Papists," or followers of the Pope, in the language of the time). Their British rulers were Protestant, with the Church of England as the established or official state church. (Swift calls it "Episcopal," that is, guided by bishops.) Members of a third major religious group, the more extreme or more radical Protestants (dissenters or Puritans), were, like Catholics, barred from public office. As a young man, Swift was active in party politics in England, eventually siding with the Tories, traditionally the strongest supporters of the British monarchy and of the Church of England. He made a living as a clergyman and became Dean of St. Patrick's Cathedral in Dublin after his return to Ireland. In his famous "Modest Proposal" (1729), he aimed his slashing satire at the oppression and exploitation of the Irish under English rule. His mission as a writer was to bring out in his readers their buried sense of decency, to sharpen their blunted fellow feeling for suffering humanity, and to inspire in them contempt for callousness and greed.

Jonathan Swift

A Modest Proposal

GUIDE TO READING: Swift is a master of verbal **irony**. He often achieves his comic effects by saying the opposite of what he thinks—and wants us as the audience to think. As you read the essay, pay special attention to the difference between what he means and what he says. Where is he serious? Where is he mock-serious or ironic?

It is a melancholy object to those who walk through this great town or travel in the country, when they see the streets, the roads, and cabin doors crowded with beggars of the female sex, followed by three, four, or six children, all in rags and importuning every passenger for an alms. These mothers, instead of being able to work for their honest livelihood, are forced to employ all their time in strolling to beg sustenance for their helpless infants, who, as they grow up, either turn thieves for want of work, or leave their dear native country to fight for the Pretender in Spain,[1] or sell themselves to the Barbadoes.[2]

I think it is agreed by all parties that this prodigious number of

---

[1] [The people of England had forced the last Stuart king, James II, from the British throne because of his pro-Catholic leanings. A son of James II was still a threat to the current monarch as a "Pretender" to the throne, claiming it as his rightful inheritance in alliance with such Catholic powers as Spain and with strong support from Irish Catholics.]

[2] [Many poor Irish were emigrating to Barbados and other British colonies in the West Indies.]

children in the arms, or on the backs, or at the heels of their mothers, and frequently of their fathers, is in the present deplorable state of the kingdom a very great additional grievance; and therefore whoever could find out a fair, cheap, and easy method of making these children sound, useful members of the commonwealth would deserve so well of the public as to have his statue set up for a preserver of the nation.

But my intention is very far from being confined to provide only for the children of professed beggars; it is of a much greater extent, and shall take in the whole number of infants at a certain age who are born of parents in effect as little able to support them as those who demand our charity in the streets.   3

As to my own part, having turned my thoughts for many years upon this important subject, and maturely weighed the several schemes of other projectors, I have always found them grossly mistaken in their computation. It is true, a child just dropped from its dam may be supported by her milk for a solar year, with little other nourishment; at most not above the value of two shillings, which the mother may certainly get, or the value in scraps, by her lawful occupation of begging; and it is exactly at one year old that I propose to provide for them in such a manner as instead of being a charge upon their parents or the parish, or wanting food and raiment for the rest of their lives, they shall on the contrary contribute to the feeding, and partly to the clothing, of many thousands.   4

There is likewise another great advantage in my scheme, that it will prevent those voluntary abortions, and that horrid practice of women murdering their bastard children, alas, too frequent among us, sacrificing the poor innocent babes, I doubt, more to avoid the expense than the shame, which would move tears and pity in the most savage and inhuman breast.   5

The number of souls in this kingdom being usually reckoned one million and a half, of these I calculate there may be about two hundred thousand couples whose wives are breeders; from which number I subtract thirty thousand couples who are able to maintain their own children, although I apprehend there cannot be so many under the present distresses of the kingdom; but this being granted, there will remain an hundred and seventy thousand breeders. I again subtract fifty thousand for those women who miscarry, or whose children die by accident or disease within the year. There only remain an hundred and twenty thousand children of poor parents annually born. The question therefore is how this number shall be reared and provided for, which, as I have already said, under the present situation of affairs, is utterly impossible by all the methods hitherto proposed. For we can neither employ them in handicraft or agriculture; we neither build houses (I mean in the country) nor cultivate land. They can very seldom pick up a livelihood by stealing till they arrive at six years old, except where they are of towardly parts,[3] although I confess they learn the   6

[3][especially promising]

rudiments much earlier, during which time they can however be looked upon only as probationers, as I have been informed by a principal gentleman in the county of Cavan, who protested to me that he never knew above one or two instances under the age of six, even in a part of the kingdom so renowned for the quickest proficiency in that art.

I am assured by our merchants that a boy or girl before twelve years old is no salable commodity; and even when they come to this age they will not yield above three pounds, or three pounds and half a crown at most on the Exchange; which cannot turn to account either to the parents or the kingdom, the charge of nutriment and rags having been at least four times that value. 7

I shall now therefore humbly propose my own thoughts, which I hope will not be liable to the least objection. 8

I have been assured by a very knowing American of my acquaintance in London, that a young healthy child well nursed is at a year old a most delicious, nourishing, and wholesome food, whether stewed, roasted, baked, or boiled; and I make no doubt that it will equally serve in a fricassee or a ragout.[4] 9

I do therefore humbly offer it to public consideration that of the hundred and twenty thousand children, already computed, twenty thousand may be reserved for breed, whereof only one fourth part to be males, which is more than we allow to sheep, black cattle, or swine; and my reason is that these children are seldom the fruits of marriage, a circumstance not much regarded by our savages, therefore one male will be sufficient to serve four females. That the remaining hundred thousand may at a year old be offered in sale to the persons of quality and fortune through the kingdom, always advising the mother to let them suck plentifully in the last month, so as to render them plump and fat for a good table. A child will make two dishes at an entertainment for friends; and when the family dines alone, the fore or hind quarter will make a reasonable dish, and seasoned with a little pepper or salt will be very good boiled on the fourth day, especially in winter. 10

I have reckoned upon a medium that a child just born will weigh twelve pounds, and in a solar year if tolerably nursed increaseth to twenty-eight pounds. 11

I grant this food will be somewhat dear, and therefore very proper for landlords, who, as they have already devoured most of the parents, seem to have the best title to the children. 12

Infant's flesh will be in season throughout the year, but more plentiful in March, and a little before and after. For we are told by a grave author, an eminent French physician, that fish being a prolific diet, there are more children born in Roman Catholic countries about nine months after Lent 13

[4][French names for kinds of meat stew]

than at any other season; therefore, reckoning a year after Lent, the markets will be more glutted than usual, because the number of popish infants is at least three to one in this kingdom; and therefore it will have one other collateral advantage, by lessening the number of Papists among us.

I have already computed the charge of nursing a beggar's child (in which list I reckon all cottagers, laborers, and four fifths of the farmers) to be about two shillings per annum, rags included; and I believe no gentleman would repine to give ten shillings for the carcass of a good fat child, which, as I have said, will make four dishes of excellent nutritive meat, when he hath only some particular friend or his own family to dine with him. Thus the squire will learn to be a good landlord and grow popular among the tenants; the mother will have eight shillings net profit, and be fit for work till she produces another child. 14

Those who are more thrifty (as I must confess the times require) may flay the carcass; the skin of which artificially dressed will make admirable gloves for ladies and summer boots for fine gentlemen. 15

As to our city of Dublin, shambles may be appointed for this purpose in the most convenient parts of it, and butchers we may be assured will not be wanting; although I rather recommend buying the children alive and dressing them hot from the knife as we do roasting pigs. 16

A very worthy person, a true lover of his country, and whose virtues I highly esteem, was lately pleased in discoursing on this matter to offer a refinement upon my scheme. He said that many gentlemen of this kingdom, having of late destroyed their deer, he conceived that the want of venison might be well supplied by the bodies of young lads and maidens, not exceeding fourteen years of age nor under twelve, so great a number of both sexes in every county being now ready to starve for want of work and service; and these to be disposed of by their parents, if alive, or otherwise by their nearest relations. But with due deference to so excellent a friend and so deserving a patriot, I cannot be altogether in his sentiments; for as to the males, my American acquaintance assured me from frequent experience that their flesh was generally tough and lean, like that of our schoolboys, by continual exercise, and their taste disagreeable; and to fatten them would not answer the charge. Then as to the females, it would, I think with humble submission, be a loss to the public, because they soon would become breeders themselves: and besides, it is not improbable that some scrupulous people might be apt to censure such a practice (although indeed very injustly) as a little bordering upon cruelty; which, I confess, hath always been with me the strongest objection against any project, how well soever intended. 17

But in order to justify my friend, he confessed that this expedient was put into his head by the famous Psalmanazar,[5] a native of the island 18

[5] [a French imposter claiming to be from Formosa, now Taiwan]

Formosa, who came from thence to London above twenty years ago, and in conversation told my friend that in his country when any young person happened to be put to death, the executioner sold the carcass to persons of quality as a prime dainty; and that in his time the body of a plump girl of fifteen, who was crucified for an attempt to poison the emperor, was sold to his Imperial Majesty's prime minister of state, and other great mandarins of the court, in joints from the gibbet, at four hundred crowns. Neither indeed can I deny that if the same use were made of several plump young girls in this town, who without one single groat to their fortunes cannot stir abroad without a chair, and appear at the playhouse and assemblies in foreign fineries which they never will pay for, the kingdom would not be the worse.

Some persons of a desponding spirit are in great concern about that [19] vast number of poor people who are aged, diseased, or maimed, and I have been desired to employ my thoughts what course may be taken to ease the nation of so grievous an encumbrance. But I am not in the least pain upon that matter, because it is very well known that they are every day dying and rotting by cold and famine, and filth and vermin, as fast as can be reasonably expected. And as to the younger laborers, they are now in almost as hopeful a condition. They cannot get work, and consequently pine away for want of nourishment to a degree that if at any time they are accidentally hired to common labor, they have not strength to perform it; and thus the country and themselves are happily delivered from the evils to come.

I have too long digressed, and therefore shall return to my subject. I [20] think the advantages by the proposal which I have made are obvious and many, as well as of the highest importance.

For first, as I have already observed, it would greatly lessen the [21] number of Papists, with whom we are yearly overrun, being the principal breeders of the nation as well as our most dangerous enemies; and who stay at home on purpose to deliver the kingdom to the Pretender, hoping to take their advantage by the absence of so many good Protestants, who have chosen rather to leave their country than stay at home and pay tithes against their conscience to an Episcopal curate.

Secondly, the poorer tenants will have something valuable of their [22] own, which by law may be made liable to distress,[6] and help to pay their landlord's rent, their corn and cattle being already seized and money a thing unknown.

Thirdly, whereas the maintenance of an hundred thousand children, [23] from two years old and upwards, cannot be computed at less then ten shillings a piece per annum, the nation's stock will be thereby increased fifty thousand pounds per annum, besides the profit of a new dish introduced to the tables of all gentlemen of fortune in the kingdom who have any refine-

---

[6][seizure of property to pay off debts]

ment in taste. And the money will circulate amoung ourselves, the goods being entirely of our own growth and manufacture.

Fourthly, the constant breeders, besides the gain of eight shillings 24 sterling per annum by the sale of their children, will be rid of the charge of maintaining them after the first year.

Fifthly, this food would likewise bring great custom to taverns, where 25 the vintners will certainly be so prudent as to procure the best receipts for dressing it to perfection, and consequently have their houses frequented by all the fine gentlemen, who justly value themselves upon their knowledge in good eating; and a skillful cook, who understands how to oblige his guests, will contrive to make it as expensive as they please.

Sixthly, this would be a great inducement to marriage, which all wise 26 nations have either encouraged by rewards or enforced by laws and penalties. It would increase the care and tenderness of mothers toward their children, when they were sure of a settlement for life to the poor babes, provided in some sort by the public, to their annual profit instead of expense. We should see an honest emulation among the married women, which of them could bring the fattest child to the market. Men would become as fond of their wives during the time of their pregnancy as they are now of their mares in foal, their cows in calf, or sows when they are ready to farrow; nor offer to beat or kick them (as is too frequently a practice) for fear of a miscarriage.

Many other advantages might be enumerated. For instance, the addi- 27 tion of some thousand carcasses in our exportation of barreled beef, the propagation of swine's flesh, and improvement in the art of making good bacon, so much wanted among us by the great destruction of pigs, too frequent at our tables, which are no way comparable in taste or magnificence to a well-grown, fat yearling child, which roasted whole will make a considerable figure at a lord mayor's feast or any other public entertainment. But this and many others I omit, being studious of brevity.

Supposing that one thousand families in this city would be constant 28 customers for infants' flesh, besides others who might have it at merry meetings, particularly weddings and christenings, I compute that Dublin would take off annually about twenty thousand carcasses, and the rest of the kingdom (where probably they will be sold somewhat cheaper) the remaining eighty thousand.

I can think of no one objection that will possibly be raised against this 29 proposal, unless it should be urged that the number of people will be thereby much lessened in the kingdom. This I freely own, and it was indeed one principal design in offering it to the world. I desire the reader will observe, that I calculate my remedy for this one individual kingdom of Ireland and for no other reason that ever was, is, or I think ever can be upon earth. Therefore let no man talk to me of other expedients: of taxing our absentees at five shillings a pound; of using neither clothes nor household furniture except what is of our own growth and manufacture; of utterly rejecting the materials and instruments that promote foreign luxury; of curing the expensiveness of pride, vanity, idleness, and gaming in our women; of introducing a vein of parsimony, prudence, and temperance; of learning to love our country, in the want of which we differ even from Laplanders and the inhabitants of Topinamboo;[7] of quitting our animosities and factions, nor acting any longer like the Jews, who were murdering one another at the very moment their city was taken;[8] of being a little cautious not to sell our country and conscience for nothing; of teaching landlords to have at least one degree of mercy toward their tenants; lastly, of putting a spirit of honesty, industry, and skill into our shopkeepers, who, if a resolution could now be taken to buy only our native goods, would immediately unite to cheat and exact upon us in the price, the measure, and the goodness, nor could ever yet be brought to make one fair proposal of just dealing, though often and earnestly invited to it.

Therefore I repeat, let no man talk to me of these and the like 30 expedients, till he hath at least some glimpse of hope that there will ever be some hearty and sincere attempt to put them in practice.

But as to myself, having been wearied out for many years with offering 31 vain, idle, visionary thoughts, and at length utterly despairing of success, I fortunately fell upon this proposal, which, as it is wholly new, so it hath something solid and real, of no expense and little trouble, full in our own power, and whereby we can incur no danger in disobliging England. For this kind of commodity will not bear exportation, the flesh being too tender a consistence to admit a long continuance in salt, although perhaps I could name a country which would be glad to eat up our whole nation without it.

After all, I am not so violently bent upon my own opinion as to reject 32 any offer proposed by wise men, which shall be found equally innocent, cheap, easy, and effectual. But before something of that kind shall be advanced in contradiction to my scheme, and offering a better, I desire the author or authors will be pleased maturely to consider two points: First, as things now stand, how they will be able to find food and raiment for an hundred thousand useless mouths and backs. And secondly, there being a round million of creatures in human figure throughout this kingdom, whose sole subsistence put into a common stock would leave them in debt two millions of pounds sterling, adding those who are beggars by profession to the bulk of farmers, cottagers, and laborers, with their wives and children who are beggars in effect; I desire those politicians who dislike my overture, and may perhaps be so bold to attempt an answer, that they will first ask the parents of these mortals whether they would not at this day think it a great happiness to have been sold for food at a year old in the manner I prescribe,

---

[7][a place in the Brazilian jungle]

[8][When the Romans captured and destroyed Jerusalem in A.D. 70, the Jews were fighting among themselves.]

and thereby have avoided such a perpetual scene of misfortunes as they have since gone through by the oppression of landlords, the impossibility of paying rent without money or trade, the want of common sustenance, with neither house nor clothes to cover them from the inclemencies of the weather, and the most inevitable prospect of entailing the like or greater miseries upon their breed forever.

I profess, in the sincerity of my heart, that I have not the least personal ₃₃ interest in endeavoring to promote this necessary work, having no other motive than the public good of my country, by advancing our trade, providing for infants, relieving the poor, and giving some pleasure to the rich. I have no children by which I can propose to get a single penny; the youngest being nine years old, and my wife past childbearing.

Using the Dictionary

Swift's modern readers encounter words and meanings that are no longer in frequent or common use. Check in your dictionary each of the words italicized in the following phrases. Find the meaning that fits the context.   1. *professed* beggars (3)   2. schemes of other *projectors* (4)   3. *wanting* food (4)   4. food and *raiment* (4)   5. I *apprehend* there cannot be many (6)   6. *protested* he knew too few instances (6)   7. *a prolific* diet (13)   8. *popish* infants (13)   9. *repine* to give ten shillings (14)   10. skin *artificially* dressed (15)   11. *shambles* for butchers (16)   12. a prime *dainty* (18)   13. *mandarins* of the court (18)   14. a single *groat* (18)   15. stirring abroad without a *chair* (18)   16. an Episcopal *curate* (21)   17. talk of *expedients* (29)   18. animosities and *factions* (29)   19. will not *bear* exportation (31) 20. pounds *sterling* (32)

The Writer's Agenda

Satire employs exaggeration and ridicule to hold things that are objectionable up to scorn. But a satirist like Swift does not merely make us laugh at what is contemptible. His aim is to make his audience see clearly what is wrong and to point the way toward change for the better.

1. Swift sets out to shock, by an outrageous imaginary scheme, those who are too callous to be shocked by *horrible realities.* In the opening paragraphs, he makes us see what these horrible realities are. What do we learn in the first six or seven paragraphs about conditions in Ireland?

2. Much satire owes its comic effect to its *extreme exaggeration* of a basic truth. According to Swift, who is really "devouring" Ireland? Where does he say so?

3. Satirists are sometimes accused of criticizing shortcomings but offering little positive advice. Explain and discuss the *positive proposals* that Swift pretends to reject toward the end of his essay.

4. Throughout his mock-serious discussion of his "proposal," Swift never lets his audience lose sight of the *basic theme* of poverty and neglect. What are some

striking details that he adds as he continues beyond the picture that he has painted at the beginning? How does he summarize his indictment at the end?

5. In a famous essay, the English philosopher Bertrand Russell discussed our tendency to *glorify* the oppressed—to see in them virtues that are lacking in their exploiters. Does Swift glorify the Irish? Or does he criticize them? If so, where and how?

For Discussion or Writing

6. Who do you think is the major audience for whom Swift intended his satire—the oppressed Irish? their English exploiters? a combination of both?

7. In his satirical writings, Swift often uses a coarse outspokenness and a slashing, cruel humor that are not for the squeamish. Do you think many readers would be offended by the gruesome or grotesque details of this essay?

8. Can you think of a clear and present evil about which the audience of the modern mass media has become too complacent or fatalistic? What would it take to break through the crust of complacency or apathy? Write your own modest proposal on a topic like the following. Make sure your audience understands your ironic or satirical intent.
- how to rid a city of transients
- how to reduce juvenile delinquency
- how to lower the dropout rate
- how to end prostitution
- how to combat anti-American feeling abroad
- how to combat crime in the cities
- how to end the arms race
- how to combat unemployment

9. Eighteenth-century writers were fond of the pointed saying (or **aphorism**) that would be remembered and quoted by others. Study the following examples. Use several of them as *model sentences*. For each, write a very similar sentence on a topic of your own choice. Follow the structure of the original as closely as you can.

a. All looks yellow to the jaundiced eye. (Alexander Pope)
   IMITATION: All tastes sour to people with vinegar in their disposition.
b. To err is human; to forgive, divine. (Alexander Pope)
c. An honest man's the noblest work of God. (Alexander Pope)
d. We have just religion enough to make us hate, but not enough to make us love one another. (Jonathan Swift)
e. When a true genius appears in the world, you may know him by this sign, that the dunces are all in confederacy against him. (Jonathan Swift)
f. The stoical scheme of supplying our wants by lopping off our desires is like cutting off our feet when we want shoes. (Jonathan Swift)
g. No one ever yet became great by imitation. (Samuel Johnson)

BACKGROUND: George Orwell (1903–50) was a British socialist who had observed British imperialism at first hand in India and Burma and who had fought against fascism in Spain. (See the introduction to "Shooting an Elephant" for biographical details.) In *Homage to Catalonia* (1938), he documented the betrayal of the Spanish working classes by both the Western democracies and Stalinist Russia. He became one of the great critics of the rival totalitarian movements that in the thirties and forties were stringing barbed wire across most of Europe. In his novel *1984* (published in 1949), he predicted a totalitarian society of the future where Big Brother told everyone what to think and what to say; where records of undesirable people disappeared down the memory hole; and where history was constantly being rewritten to follow the zigzags of the party line. Telescreen and print were dominated by doublespeak, with the headquarters of the secret police called the Ministry of Love and the war department called the Ministry of Peace. Orwell's heroes were the lone individuals, struggling to reserve a corner of their lives for their own honest needs, who still found a way to express their own honest feelings. Although banned by school boards playing Big Brother, *1984* is still one of the most widely read books of our time. In 1948, Orwell had published "Politics and the English Language," an essay that developed a theme central to his nightmare vision of the future: the manipulation and debasement of language in contemporary politics.

George Orwell

Politics and the
English Language

GUIDE TO READING: Orwell's central assumption in this essay is that style is more than just "a matter of style." How we talk affects how we think, and how we think affects how we act. Study carefully the abuses of language that Orwell analyzes in this essay and the examples he provides for each.

Most people who bother with the matter at all would admit that the English language is in a bad way, but it is generally assumed that we cannot by conscious action do anything about it. Our civilization is decadent and our language—so the argument runs—must inevitably share in the general collapse. It follows that any struggle against the abuse of language is a sentimental archaism, like preferring candles to electric light or hansom cabs to aeroplanes. Underneath this lies the half-conscious belief that language is a natural growth and not an instrument which we shape for our own purposes.

Now, it is clear that the decline of a language must ultimately have political and economic causes: it is not due simply to the bad influence of this or that individual writer. But an effect can become a cause, reinforcing the original cause and producing the same effect in an intensified form, and so on indefinitely. A man may take to drink because he feels himself to be a failure, and then fail all the more completely because he drinks. It is rather the same thing that is happening to the English language. It becomes ugly and inaccurate because our thoughts are foolish, but the slovenliness of our language makes it easier for us to have foolish thoughts. The point is that the process is reversible. Modern English, especially written English, is full of bad habits which spread by imitation and which can be avoided if one is willing to take the necessary trouble. If one gets rid of these habits one can think more clearly, and to think clearly is a necessary first step towards political regeneration: so that the fight against bad English is not frivolous and is not the exclusive concern of professional writers. I will come back to this presently, and I hope that by that time the meaning of what I have said here will have become clearer. Meanwhile, here are five specimens of the English language as it is now habitually written.

These five passages have not been picked out because they are especially bad—I could have quoted far worse if I had chosen—but because they illustrate various of the mental vices from which we now suffer. They are a little below the average, but are fairly representative samples. I number them so that I can refer back to them when necessary: 3

(1) I am not, indeed, sure whether it is not true to say that the Milton who once seemed not unlike a seventeenth-century Shelley had not become, out of an experience ever more bitter in each year, more alien [*sic*] to the founder of that Jesuit sect which nothing could induce him to tolerate.

Professor Harold Laski*
(Essay in *Freedom of Expression*).

(2) Above all, we cannot play ducks and drakes with a native battery of idioms which prescribes such egregious collocations of vocables as the Basic *put up with* for *tolerate* or *put at a loss* for *bewilder*.

Professor Lancelot Hogben (*Interglossa*).

(3) On the one side we have the free personality: by definition it is not neurotic, for it has neither conflict nor dream. Its desires, such as they are, are transparent, for they are just what institutional approval keeps in the forefront of consciousness; another institutional pattern would alter their number and intensity, there is little in them that is natural, irreducible, or culturally dangerous. But *on the other side*, the social bond itself is nothing but the mutual reflection of these self-secure integrities. Recall the definition of love. Is not this the very picture of a small academic? Where is there a place in this hall of mirrors for either personality or fraternity?

Essay on psychology in *Politics* (New York).

---

*[Harold Laski (1893–1950) was a leading British socialist. John Milton was a militant English Protestant likened in this passage to the founder of the Jesuit society and archenemy of the Protestant Reformation.]

(4) All the "best people" from the gentlemen's clubs, and all the frantic fascist captains, united in common hatred of Socialism and bestial horror of the rising tide of the mass revolutionary movement, have turned to acts of provocation, to foul incendiarism, to medieval legends of poisoned wells, to legalize their own destruction of proletarian organizations, and rouse the agitated petty-bourgeoisie to chauvinistic fervor on behalf of the fight against the revolutionary way out of the crisis.

Communist pamphlet.

(5) If a new spirit is to be infused into this old country, there is one thorny and contentious reform which must be tackled, and that is the humanization and galvanization of the B.B.C. Timidity here will bespeak canker and atrophy of the soul. The heart of Britain may be sound and of strong beat, for instance, but the British lion's roar at present is like that of Bottom in Shakespeare's *Midsummer Night's Dream*—as gentle as any sucking dove. A virile new Britain cannot continue indefinitely to be traduced in the eyes, or rather ears, of the world by the effete languors of Langham Place, brazenly masquerading as "standard English." When the Voice of Britain is heard at nine o'clock, better far and infinitely less ludicrous to hear aitches honestly dropped than the present priggish, inflated, inhibited, school-ma'amish arch braying of blameless bashful mewing maidens!

Letter in *Tribune*.

Each of these passages has faults of its own, but, quite apart from avoidable ugliness, two qualities are common to all of them. The first is staleness of imagery; the other is lack of precision. The writer either has a meaning and cannot express it, or he inadvertently says something else, or he is almost indifferent as to whether his words mean anything or not. This mixture of vagueness and sheer incompetence is the most marked characteristic of modern English prose, and especially of any kind of political writing. As soon as certain topics are raised, the concrete melts into the abstract and no one seems able to think of turns of speech that are not hackneyed: prose consists less and less of *words* chosen for the sake of their meaning, and more and more of *phrases* tacked together like the sections of a prefabricated hen-house. I list below, with notes and examples, various of the tricks by means of which the work of prose-construction is habitually dodged:

DYING METAPHORS. A newly invented metaphor assists thought by evoking a visual image, while on the other hand a metaphor which is technically "dead" (e.g. *iron resolution*) has in effect reverted to being an ordinary word and can generally be used without loss of vividness. But in between these two classes there is a huge dump of worn-out metaphors which have lost all evocative power and are merely used because they save people the trouble of inventing phrases for themselves. Examples are: *Ring the changes on, take up the cudgels for, toe the line, ride roughshod over, stand shoulder to shoulder with, play into the hands of, no axe to grind, grist to the mill, fishing in troubled waters, on the order of the day, Achilles' heel, swan song, hotbed.* Many of these are used without knowledge of their meaning (what is a "rift," for instance?), and incompatible metaphors are frequently mixed, a sure sign that the writer is not interested in what he is saying. Some metaphors now current have been twisted out of their original meaning without those who use them even being aware of the fact. For example, *toe the line* is sometimes written *tow the line.* Another example is *the hammer and the anvil,* now always used with the implication that the anvil gets the worse of it. In real life it is always the anvil that breaks the hammer, never the other way about: a writer who stopped to think what he was saying would be aware of this, and would avoid perverting the original phrase.

OPERATORS OR VERBAL FALSE LIMBS. These save the trouble of 6 picking out appropriate verbs and nouns, and at the same time pad each sentence with extra syllables which give it an appearance of symmetry. Characteristic phrases are *render inoperative, militate against, make contact with, be subjected to, give rise to, give grounds for, have the effect of, play a leading part (role) in, make itself felt, take effect, exhibit a tendency to, serve the purpose of,* etc., etc. The keynote is the elimination of simple verbs. Instead of being a single word, such as *break, stop, spoil, mend, kill,* a verb becomes a *phrase,* made up of a noun or adjective tacked on to some general-purpose verb such as *prove, serve, form, play, render.* In addition, the passive voice is wherever possible used in preference to the active, and noun constructions are used instead of gerunds (*by examination of* instead of *by examining*). The range of verbs is further cut down by means of the *-ize* and *de-* formations, and the banal statements are given an appearance of profundity by means of the *not un-* formation. Simple conjuctions and prepositions are replaced by such phrases as *with respect to, having regard to, the fact that, by dint of, in view of, in the interests of, on the hypothesis that;* and the ends of sentences are saved by anticlimax by such resounding common-places as *greatly to be desired, cannot be left out of account, a development to be expected in the near future, deserving of serious consideration, brought to a satisfactory conclusion* and so on and so forth.

PRETENTIOUS DICTION. Words like *phenomenon, element, indi-* 7 *vidual* (as noun), *objective, categorical, effective, virtual, basic, primary, promote, constitute, exhibit, exploit, utilize, eliminate, liquidate,* are used to dress up simple statement and give an air of scientific impartiality to biased judgments. Adjectives like *epoch-making, epic, historic, unforget-table, triumphant, age-old, inevitable, inexorable, veritable,* are used to dignify the sordid processes of international politics, while writing that aims at glorifying war usually takes on an archaic color, its characteristic words being: *realm, throne, chariot, mailed fist, trident, sword, shield, buckler, banner, jackboot, clarion.* Foreign words and expressions such as *cul de sac, ancien régime, deus ex machina, mutatis mutandis, status quo, gleichschaltung, weltanschauung,* are used to give an air of culture and elegance. Except for the useful abbreviations *i.e.*, *e.g.*, and *etc.*, there is no real need for any of the hundreds of foreign phrases now current in English. Bad writers, and especially scientific, political and sociological writers, are nearly always haunted by the notion that Latin or Greek words are grander than Saxon ones, and unnecessary words like *expedite*, *ameliorate*, *predict*, *extraneous*, *deracinated*, *clandestine*, *subaqueous* and hundreds of others constantly gain ground from their Anglo-Saxon opposite numbers.[1] The jargon peculiar to Marxist writing (*hyena*, *hangman*, *cannibal*, *petty bourgeois*, *these gentry*, *lackey*, *flunkey*, *mad dog*, *White Guard*, etc.) consists largely of words and phrases translated from Russian, German or French; but the normal way of coining a new word is to use a Latin or Greek root with the appropriate affix and, where necessary, the *-ize* formation. It is often easier to make up words of this kind (*deregionalize*, *impermissible*, *extramarital*, *non-fragmentary* and so forth) than to think up the English words that will cover one's meaning. The result, in general, is an increase in slovenliness and vagueness.

MEANINGLESS WORDS. In certain kinds of writing, particularly in art criticism and literary criticism, it is normal to come across long passages which are almost completely lacking in meaning.[2] Words like *romantic*, *plastic*, *values*, *human*, *dead*, *sentimental*, *natural*, *vitality*, as used in art criticism, are strictly meaningless, in the sense that they not only do not point to any discoverable object, but are hardly ever expected to do so by the reader. When one critic writes, "The outstanding feature of Mr. X's work is its living quality," while another writes, "The immediately striking thing about Mr. X's work is its peculiar deadness," the reader accepts this as a simple difference of opinion. If words like *black* and *white* were involved, instead of the jargon words *dead* and *living*, he would see at once that language was being used in an improper way. Many political words are similarly abused. The word *Fascism* has now no meaning except in so far as it signifies "something not desirable." The words *democracy*, *socialism*, *freedom*, *patriotic*, *realistic*, *justice*, have each of them several different meanings which cannot be reconciled with one another. In the case of a word like *democracy*, not only is there no agreed definition, but the attempt to make one is resisted from all sides. It is almost universally felt that when we call a country democratic we are praising it: consequently the defenders of every kind of régime claim that it is a democracy, and fear that they might

[1]An interesting illustration of this is the way in which the English flower names which were in use till very recently are being ousted by Greek ones, *snapdragon* becoming *antirrhinum*, *forget-me-not* becoming *myosotis*, etc. It is hard to see any practical reason for this change of fashion: it is probably due to an instinctive turning-away from the more homely word and a vague feeling that the Greek is scientific. [author's note]

[2]Example: "Comfort's catholicity of perception and image, strangely Whitmanesque in range, almost the exact opposite in aesthetic compulsion, continues to evoke that trembling atmospheric accumulative hinting at a cruel, an inexorably serene timelessness. . . . Wrey Gardiner scores by aiming at simple bull's-eyes with precision. Only they are not so simple, and through this contented sadness runs more than the surface bittersweet of resignation." (*Poetry Quarterly*.) [author's note]

have to stop using the word if it were tied down to any one meaning. Words of this kind are often used in a consciously dishonest way. That is, the person who uses them has his own private definition, but allows his hearer to think he means something quite different. Statements like *Marshal Pétain was a true patriot, The Soviet Press is the freest in the world, The Catholic Church is opposed to persecution*, are almost always made with intent to deceive. Other words used in variable meanings, in most cases more or less dishonestly, are: *class, totalitarian, science, progressive, reactionary, bourgeois, equality.*

Now that I have made this catalogue of swindles and perversions, let 9 me give another example of the kind of writing that they lead to. This time it must of its nature be an imaginary one. I am going to translate a passage of good English into modern English of the worst sort. Here is a well-known verse from *Ecclesiastes*:

> I returned and saw under the sun, that the race is not to the swift, nor the battle to the strong, neither yet bread to the wise, nor yet riches to men of understanding, nor yet favour to men of skill; but time and chance happeneth to them all.

Here it is in modern English:

10

> Objective consideration of contemporary phenomena compels the conclusion that success or failure in competitive activities exhibits no tendency to be commensurate with innate capacity, but that a considerable element of the unpredictable must invariably be taken into account.

This is a parody, but not a very gross one. Exhibit (3), above, for 11 instance, contains several patches of the same kind of English. It will be seen that I have not made a full translation. The beginning and ending of the sentence follow the original meaning fairly closely, but in the middle the concrete illustrations—race, battle, bread—dissolve into the vague phrase "success or failure in competitive activities." This had to be so, because no modern writer of the kind I am discussing—no one capable of using phrases like "objective consideration of contemporary phenomena"—would ever tabulate his thoughts in that precise and detailed way. The whole tendency of modern prose is away from concreteness. Now analyze these two sentences a little more closely. The first contains forty-nine words but only sixty syllables, and all its words are those of everyday life. The second contains thirty-eight words of ninety syllables: eighteen of its words are from Latin roots, and one from Greek. The first sentence contains six vivid images, and only one phrase ("time and chance") that could be called vague. The second contains not a single fresh, arresting phrase, and in spite of its ninety syllables it gives only a shortened version of the meaning contained in the first. Yet without a doubt it is the second kind of sentence that is gaining ground in modern English. I do not want to exaggerate. This kind of writing is not yet universal, and outcrops of simplicity will occur here and there in the worst-written page. Still, if you or I were told to write a few lines on the uncertainty of human fortunes, we should probably come much nearer to my imaginary sentence than to the one from *Ecclesiastes*.

As I have tried to show, modern writing at its worst does not consist in picking out words for the sake of their meaning and inventing images in order to make the meaning clearer. It consists in gumming together long strips of words which have already been set in order by someone else, and making the results presentable by sheer humbug. The attraction of this way of writing is that it is easy. It is easier—even quicker, once you have the habit—to say *In my opinion it is not an unjustifiable assumption that* than to say *I think*. If you use ready-made phrases, you not only don't have to hunt about for words; you also don't have to bother with the rhythms of your sentences, since these phrases are generally so arranged as to be more or less euphonious. When you are composing in a hurry—when you are dictating to a stenographer, for instance, or making a public speech—it is natural to fall into a pretentious, Latinized style. Tags like *a consideration which we should do well to bear in mind* or *a conclusion to which all of us would readily assent* will save many a sentence from coming down with a bump. By using stale metaphors, similes and idioms, you save much mental effort, at the cost of leaving your meaning vague, not only for your reader but for yourself. This is the significance of mixed metaphors. The sole aim of a metaphor is to call up a visual image. When these images clash—as in *The Fascist octopus has sung its swan song, the jackboot is thrown into the melting pot*—it can be taken as certain that the writer is not seeing a mental image of the objects he is naming; in other words he is not really thinking. Look again at the examples I gave at the beginning of this essay. Professor Laski (1) uses five negatives in fifty-three words. One of these is superfluous, making nonsense of the whole passage, and in addition there is the slip *alien* for *akin*, making further nonsense, and several avoidable pieces of clumsiness which increase the general vagueness. Professor Hogben (2) plays ducks and drakes with a battery which is able to write prescriptions, and, while disapproving of the everyday phrase *put up with*, is unwilling to look *egregious* up in the dictionary and see what it means; (3), if one takes an uncharitable attitude towards it, is simply meaningless: probably one could work out its intended meaning by reading the whole of the article in which it occurs. In (4), the writer knows more or less what he wants to say, but an accumulation of stale phrases chokes him, like tea leaves blocking a sink. In (5), words and meaning have almost parted company. People who write in this manner usually have a general emotional meaning—they dislike one thing and want to express solidarity with another—but they are not interested in the detail of what they are saying. A scrupulous writer, in every sentence that he writes, will ask himself at least four questions, thus: What am I trying to say? What words will express it? What image or idiom will make it clearer? Is this image fresh enough to have an effect? And he will probably ask himself two more: Could I put it more shortly? Have I said anything that is avoidably ugly? But you are not obliged to go to all this trouble. You can shirk it by simply throwing your mind open and letting the ready-made phrases come crowding in. They will construct your sentences for you—even think your thoughts for you, to a certain extent—and at need they will perform the important service of partially concealing your meaning even from yourself. It is at this point that the special connection between politics and the debasement of language becomes clear.

In our time it is broadly true that political writing is bad writing. Where 13 it is not true, it will generally be found that the writer is some kind of rebel, expressing his private opinions and not a "party line." Orthodoxy, of whatever color, seems to demand a lifeless, imitative style. The political dialects to be found in pamphlets, leading articles, manifestos, White Papers and the speeches of undersecretaries do, of course, vary from party to party, but they are all alike in that one almost never finds in them a fresh, vivid, home-made turn of speech. When one watches some tired hack on the platform mechanically repeating the familiar phrases—*bestial atrocities, iron heel, bloodstained tyranny, free peoples of the world, stand shoulder to shoulder*—one often has a curious feeling that one is not watching a live human being but some kind of dummy: a feeling which suddenly becomes stronger at moments when the light catches the speaker's spectacles and turns them into blank discs which seem to have no eyes behind them. And this is not altogether fanciful. A speaker who uses that kind of phraseology has gone some distance towards turning himself into a machine. The appropriate noises are coming out of his larynx, but his brain is not involved as it would be if he were choosing his words for himself. If the speech he is making is one that he is accustomed to make over and over again, he may be almost unconscious of what he is saying, as one is when one utters the responses in church. And this reduced state of consciousness, if not indispensable, is at any rate favorable to political conformity.

In our time, political speech and writing are largely the defense of the 14 indefensible. Things like the continuance of British rule in India, the Russian purges and deportations, the dropping of the atom bombs on Japan, can indeed be defended, but only by arguments which are too brutal for most people to face, and which do not square with the professed aims of political parties. Thus political language has to consist largely of euphemism, question-begging and sheer cloudy vagueness. Defenseless villages are bombarded from the air, the inhabitants driven out into the countryside, the cattle machine-gunned, the huts set on fire with incendiary bullets: this is called *pacification*. Millions of peasants are robbed of their farms and sent trudging along the roads with no more than they can carry: this is called *transfer of population* or *rectification of frontiers*. People are imprisoned for years without trial, or shot in the back of the neck or sent to die of scurvy in Arctic lumber camps; this is called *elimination of unreliable elements*. Such phraseology is needed if one wants to name things without calling up mental pictures of them. Consider for instance some comfortable English professor defending Russian totalitarianism. He cannot say outright, "I believe in killing off your opponents when you can get good results by doing so." Probably, he will say something like this:

"While freely conceding that the Soviet regime exhibits certain features which the humanitarian may be inclined to deplore, we must, I think, agree that a certain curtailment of the right to political opposition is an unavoidable concomitant of transitional periods, and that the rigors which the Russian people have been called upon to undergo have been amply justified in the sphere of concrete achievement." 15

The inflated style is itself a kind of euphemism. A mass of Latin words 16 falls upon the facts like soft snow, blurring the outlines and covering up all the details. The great enemy of clear language is insincerity. When there is a gap between one's real and one's declared aims, one turns as it were instinctively to long words and exhausted idioms, like a cuttlefish squirting out ink. In our age there is no such thing as "keeping out of politics." All issues are political issues, and politics itself is a mass of lies, evasions, folly, hatred and schizophrenia. When the general atmosphere is bad, language must suffer. I should expect to find—this is a guess which I have not sufficient knowledge to verify—that the German, Russian and Italian languages have all deteriorated in the last ten or fifteen years, as a result of dictatorship.

But if thought corrupts language, language can also corrupt thought. A 17 bad usage can spread by tradition and imitation, even among people who should and do know better. The debased language that I have been discussing is in some ways very convenient. Phrases like *a not unjustifiable assumption, leaves much to be desired, would serve no good purpose, a consideration which we should do well to bear in mind*, are a continuous temptation, a packet of aspirins always at one's elbow. Look back through this essay, and for certain you will find that I have again and again committed the very faults I am protesting against. By this morning's post I have received a pamphlet dealing with conditions in Germany. The author tells me that he "felt impelled" to write it. I open it at random, and here is almost the first sentence that I see: "[The Allies] have an opportunity not only of achieving a radical transformation of Germany's social and political structure in such a way as to avoid a nationalistic reaction in Germany itself, but at the same time of laying the foundations of a cooperative and unified Europe." You see, he "feels impelled" to write—feels, presumably, that he has something new to say—and yet his words, like cavalry horses answering the bugle, group themselves automatically into the familiar dreary pattern. This invasion of one's mind by ready-made phrases (*lay the foundations, achieve a radical transformation*) can only be prevented if one is constantly on guard against them, and every such phrase anaesthetizes a portion of one's brain.

I said earlier that the decadence of our language is probably curable. [18] Those who deny this would argue, if they produced an argument at all, that language merely reflects existing social conditions, and that we cannot influence its development by any direct tinkering with words and constructions. So far as the general tone or spirit of a language goes, this may be true, but it is not true in detail. Silly words and expressions have often disappeared, not through any evolutionary process but owing to the conscious action of a minority. Two recent examples were *explore every avenue* and *leave no stone unturned*, which were killed by the jeers of a few journalists. There is a long list of flyblown metaphors which could similarly be got rid of if enough people would interest themselves in the job; and it should also be possible to laugh the *not un-* formation out of existence,[3] to reduce the amount of Latin and Greek in the average sentence, to drive out foreign phrases and strayed scientific words, and, in general, to make pretentiousness unfashionable. But all these are minor points. The defense of the English language implies more than this, and perhaps it is best to start by saying what it does *not* imply.

To begin with it has nothing to do with archaism, with the salvaging of [19] obsolete words and turns of speech, or with the setting up of a "standard English" which must never be departed from. On the contrary, it is especially concerned with the scrapping of every word or idiom which has outworn its usefulness. It has nothing to do with correct grammar and syntax, which are of no importance so long as one makes one's meaning clear, or with the avoidance of Americanisms, or with having what is called a "good prose style." On the other hand it is not concerned with fake simplicity and the attempt to make written English colloquial. Nor does it even imply in every case preferring the Saxon word to the Latin one, though it does imply using the fewest and shortest words that will cover one's meaning. What is above all needed is to let the meaning choose the word, and not the other way about. In prose, the worst thing one can do with words is to surrender to them. When you think of a concrete object, you think wordlessly and then, if you want to describe the thing you have been visualizing you probably hunt about till you find the exact words that seem to fit it. When you think of something abstract you are more inclined to use words from the start, and unless you make a conscious effort to prevent it, the existing dialect will come rushing in and do the job for you, at the expense of blurring or even changing your meaning. Probably it is better to put off using words as long as possible and get one's meaning as clear as one can through pictures or sensations. Afterwards one can choose—not simply *accept*—the phrases

---

[3]One can cure oneself of the *not un-* formation by memorizing this sentence: *A not unblack dog was chasing a not unsmall rabbit across a not ungreen field.* [author's note]

that will best cover the meaning, and then switch round and decide what impression one's words are likely to make on another person. This last effort of the mind cuts out all stale or mixed images, all prefabricated phrases, needless repetitions, and humbug and vagueness generally. But one can often be in doubt about the effect of a word or a phrase, and one needs rules that one can rely on when instinct fails. I think the following rules will cover most cases:

(i) Never use a metaphor, simile or other figure of speech which you are used to seeing in print.
(ii) Never use a long word where a short one will do.
(iii) If it is possible to cut a word out, always cut it out.
(iv) Never use the passive where you can use the active.
(v) Never use a foreign phrase, a scientific word or a jargon word if you can think of any everyday English equivalent.
(vi) Break any of these rules sooner than say anything outright barbarous.

These rules sound elementary, and so they are, but they demand a deep change of attitude in anyone who has grown used to writing in the style now fashionable. One could keep all of them and still write bad English, but one could not write the kind of stuff that I quoted in those five specimens at the beginning of this article.

I have not here been considering the literary use of language, but merely language as an instrument for expressing and not for concealing or preventing thought. Stuart Chase* and others have come near to claiming that all abstract words are meaningless, and have used this as a pretext for advocating a kind of political quietism. Since you don't know what Fascism is, how can you struggle against Fascism? One need not swallow such absurdities as this, but one ought to recognize that the present political chaos is connected with the decay of language, and that one can probably bring about some improvement by starting at the verbal end. If you simplify your English, you are freed from the worst follies of orthodoxy. You cannot speak any of the necessary dialects, and when you make a stupid remark its stupidity will be obvious, even to yourself. Political language—and with variations this is true of all political parties, from Conservatives to Anarchists—is designed to make lies sound truthful and murder respectable, and to give an appearance of solidity to pure wind. One cannot change this all in a moment, but one can at least change one's own habits, and from time to time one can even, if one jeers loudly enough, send some worn-out and useless phrase—some *jackboot, Achilles' heel, hotbed, melting pot, acid test, veritable inferno* or other lump of verbal refuse—into the dustbin where it belongs.

---

*[Stuart Chase, author of *Tyranny of Words* (1938), was a leading popularizer of the semantics movement, which fought propaganda, gobbledygook, and premature abstraction.]

Using the Dictionary

Orwell says that bad writers often use pretentious words taken over from Latin and Greek or borrowed from other languages. For each of the following examples, find a simpler word derived from Old English or Anglo-Saxon: 1. *egregious* (3) 2. *collocation* (3) 3. *vocable* (3) 4. *expedite* (7) 5. *ameliorate* (7) 6. *predict* (7) 7. *extraneous* (7) 8. *deracinated* (7) 9. *clandestine* (7) 10. *subaqueous* (7). What is the meaning of the following foreign expressions? 11. *ancien régime* (7) 12. *deus ex machina* (7) 13. *mutatis mutandis* (7) 14. *gleichschaltung* (7) 15. *weltanschauung* (7)

The Writer's Agenda

Orwell's commitment to honesty in speech and writing often causes him to write **inductively**. He often presents the facts or the evidence first and then goes on to generalize. Answer the following questions about the conclusions he draws from the evidence he presents in this essay.

1. Orwell sets his essay in motion by taking on a familiar or widely shared *assumption*. What is it? How does he deal with it?

2. One of the two major faults of prose style that Orwell attacks is "staleness of imagery." (What is the other?) Find the different discussions of *figurative language* in this essay. How does Orwell define the basic function of metaphor? How does he distinguish among fresh, dead, and worn-out metaphors? What are his objections to mixed metaphors? Find examples of Orwell's own use of fresh, vivid figurative language.

3. Describe and illustrate the different kinds of verbal padding and *inflated diction* attacked in this essay. What, according to the author, is their purpose? What is their result?

4. What abuses of language does Orwell analyze under the headings of "meaningless words"?

5. Orwell's analysis of common defects of prose style leads up to his indictment of political speech and writing as "largely the defense of the indefensible." What examples does he use to back up this charge? (According to the author, what is the role of euphemisms in the language of politics?)

6. What *misunderstanding* does Orwell try to prevent at the beginning of his concluding paragraph? (What are some possible misunderstandings that he tried to clear up earlier?) How does his conclusion restate and summarize the key ideas of his essay?

For Discussion or Writing

7. Where do you think Orwell's ideal reader would stand politically? Support your answer.

8. Orwell attacked the trite, cliché-ridden quality of the political language of

his time. Examine an example of current political language for ready-made phrases or prefabricated expressions. For example, choose an editorial, campaign speech, inaugural speech, or transcript of a press conference.

9. Study the use of euphemisms in current political discussions of subjects that make for bad news, such as unemployment, defense spending, or political oppression in countries allied with the United States.

10. Orwell attacks "meaningless terms" that have come to serve for hypocritical self-congratulation or ignorant abuse. Choose one of the following examples: *fascism, democracy, freedom, justice, equality, Americanism.* Prepare an extended definition designed to give the term an honest meaning.

11. An updated list of words frequently abused in political discussion might include *subversive, progressive, reactionary, bourgeois, terrorist, militaristic, exploitation.* Choose one or more of these and discuss uses and abuses.

STUDENT MODEL 13

FOR READING: Study the following short selection as a possible model for writing of your own. How do you react to it overall? What makes it interesting or effective? Answer the following more specific questions:

1. (PURPOSE) What was the writer trying to do?
2. (AUDIENCE) What kind of reader would make a good reader for this selection?
3. (SOURCES) Where did the writer turn for material?
4. (THESIS) Does the selection have a central idea or unifying thesis?
5. (STRUCTURE) What is the author's overall plan or strategy?
6. (STYLE) What makes the piece effective or memorable (for instance, striking details, memorable phrases)?
7. (REVISION) What do you think the writer could or should have done differently?

D. Cossina

A Good Neighbor

Love your neighbor. Simple as that. For the old man there weren't any qualifications. Walking home from the store, pockets filled with hard licorice candy for the ghetto children who lived between Bigliari Market and home, he knew everybody by name, everybody's heartache, everybody's joy. He brought home the news when Mrs. Garcia's baby died and took her one of Momma's embroidered dresser scarves to wrap the body in. He found out

from the mailman the Green boy was coming home—safe from Vietnam—
and used that as an excuse to open the last bottle of Granma's apricot
brandy: "Never saw a n——r so happy to have his boy home."

I remember listening, out of sight of the grown-ups, high in the avo- 2
cado tree where nobody knew to find me (and I always learned something
even if I didn't really understand what it was I was learning). Momma didn't
want Granpa to say such things as "nigger"—"it wasn't right"—didn't want
him bringing people home, people not our kind, Black, Mexican...poor.
"God knows how often they bathe, just like him to invite home some filthy
prune picker with dirt under his fingernails, trackin' mud all over my
good rugs."

Tonio said "n——r" once, talking about the boy who'd beat him at 3
basketball and Momma slapped him for talking like trash...what was he
doing playing ball with a "Negro" anyway?

I almost didn't have a birthday party one year because I'd invited Sara 4
Green and Annie Garcia, but the old man put his foot down, said it was his
house, said all God's children could eat at his table, said "Hell, we've got
enough ice cream to feed half of Orange County" so what was she complain-
ing for?

When the old man got too tired ("too old to take care of himself") he 5
went to stay in the back bedroom at Uncle Sal's. It got so he was as gray as
the inside bark of the avocado tree and had less and less to say every day. It
was like his world had become black and white, just light and shadows like
on the TV Momma gave him. But, the next winter, when he died, all the color
came back. The colors of the old neighborhood—between Illinois Street
and Bigliari Market—filled the church: the Green boy brought his children.
Old Mrs. Garcia needed a cane, hardly made it down the aisle but she did;
she was determined to say goodbye personally. When old Fred, the
shoeshine man, put a pine branch between the old man's hands, even
Momma cried.

I wonder now—years later—about what the old man taught me, 6
about the things I learned before I knew what I know. Granpa said "n——r"
and Momma didn't, but Granpa loved everybody and Momma only loved us.
Granpa wasn't afraid of anything, and Momma was afraid we'd say the
wrong thing, not wear clean underwear, talk with our mouths full. I wonder
if it's the old man inside of me who makes it important that my children will
grow up in a multi-ethnic neighborhood, who makes me believe that we're
citizens of the same world—neighbors.

FOR WRITING Write a personal essay in which you express a strong personal feeling
such as affection, nostalgia, resentment, love, anger. Guard against mere labels and
mere sentimentality—try to act out or dramatize what you feel. Feel free to appeal
to your reader's imagination or sense of humor.

ADDITIONAL WRITING TOPICS 13

Imaginative Essays

Write an essay in which you allow your imagination free rein, or an essay which brings your sense of humor into play. Some possibilities:

1. Write about life in twenty-first-century America after scientists, teenagers, health enthusiasts, the elderly, feminists, or other group have taken over the country.

2. Write about American education after it has been reconstructed on free enterprise principles.

3. Write about how your relatives and friends would have lived and behaved as members of a prehistoric tribe.

4. Write a script for a short film that acts out daydreams or wishes.

5. Write an imaginary interview in which a major historical figure meets a modern counselor or psychiatrist.

6. Write an imaginary letter in which an outstanding early American reports on a visit to modern America.

7. Write a State of the Union address that you would deliver if you had been elected president.

8. Write a letter of dismissal that you might write if you had suddenly acquired the power to hire and fire the chief executive of General Motors, a major television network, or another large corporation.

9. Write a eulogy, epitaph, or obituary you would like to see published about yourself at the end of a full, long life.

10. Write a parody or satirical imitation of a committee meeting, official reception, Barbara Walters or Dick Cavett interview, or the like.

INDEX

abstract vs. concrete, 475
ad hominem attack, 329
allusions, 307, 417, 485
"Americans at Work: Three Portraits," 219–23
analogy, 142, 343
  clarifying, 14
Anderson, Veda, 319–20
Angelou, Maya, **28–32**, 474
"Ant City and Human Society," 364–66
antithesis, 477
antithetical comparison, 349
aphorism, 502
"Appeal of the Androgynous Man, The" 194–97
areas for writing, 355-517
argument, 244–84
  and audience, 245
  and benefits for the writer, 245
  and cause and effect, 246–50
  and eliminating alternatives, 249
  and oversimplification, 247
  and post hoc fallacy, 248
  and purpose, 244–45
  and scapegoating, 248
  and scientific terms, 274
Ashe, Arthur, 104–05
  on professional writers and amateurs, 106–07
Asimov, Isaac, 360, 361, **374–78**
  on writing to inform, 379–81
audience, 2–3
  and argument, 245
  and classification, 204
  and comparison and contrast, 171
  and definition, 287
  and experience, 19
  and observation, 61
  and persuasion, 323–24
  and process, 137
  and science writing, 357–58
  and taking a stand, 97
  and writer, 339–40
autobiography, 22

Baldwin, James, 9, 474

"Barbarity of Boxing, The," 332–34
Barney, Maureen, **130–31, 131–32**
"Beeper for Violence, A," 409–11
benefits for the writer
  of argument, 245
  of classification, 205
  of comparison and contrast, 171
  of definition, 287
  of experience, 20
  of imaginative writing, 473
  and media and popular culture, 294
  of observation, 61
  of persuasion, 324
  of process, 138
  of science writing, 358
  of taking a stand, 98
  of writing about history, 424
  of writing to evaluate, 394
Bettelheim, Bruno, 396
Birnbach, Lisa, 400
"Black Athlete Looks at Education, A," 104–05
block quotation, 426
Bogan, Patrick, 326
"Born Among the Born-Again," 34–38
"Born to Run," 117–21
Bouslaugh, Sandra, 240–42
Bova, Ben, 362–63
Brody, Jane, 213–16
Brown, Harold O.J., 293
Burciaga, Cecilia Preciado, 326
"Bureaucrats," 161–65
Burress, Lee, 103

Carson, Rachel, 368–72
case history, 328
cause and effect, 244–84
  analysis of, 246–50
  eliminating alternatives, 249
  panacea, 248
  post hoc fallacy, 248
  scapegoating, 248
  challenging opposition, 328–29
Chapelle, Dickie, 295

Chisholm, Shirley, 100, 325
chronological order, 65
classic essays, 472–517
  and audience, 472–73
  and benefits for the writer, 473
  and purpose, 472
classification, 204–42
  and audience, 204–05
  and benefits for the writer, 205
  and categories, 207–08
  and detail, 209
  and division, 206–11
  and examples, 209
  and purpose, 204
  and transition, 210
"Competitive Edge: Japanese and Americans, The," 182–86
comparison
  antithetical, 349
  and audience, 171
  and benefits for the writer, 171
  and contrast, 170–202, 292–93
  and explanation, 172–73
  imaginative, 8–9
  parallel order, 174–75
  and persuasion, 326–27
  point-by-point, 173–74
  and purpose, 170
  and revision, 198–200
  and transitional signals, 175–76
concession, 13
conclusion, 12, 14, 448
concrete language, 8
concrete words, 66
connotations, 407, 474
connotative language, 267, 367
contrast, 82
  and audience, 171
  and benefits for the writer, 171
  and comparison, 170–202, 292–93
  parallel-order, 174–75
  and persuasion, 327
  point-by-point, 173–74
  and purpose, 170
  and revision, 198–200

and transitional signals,
175–76
Corliss, Richard, 397
Cossina, D., 515–16
Curie, Marie, 7, 177

"Day in the Life, A," 94–95
definition, 286–321
and allusions, 307
and audience, 287
and benefits for the writer,
287
extended, 288
formal, 288
and inductive pattern, 292
and purpose, 286
writing to define, 288–94
denotations, 474
De Santis, Marie, 144–46
description, and space, 65
detail, 22, 63, 64, 139, 209
DeVoto, Bernard, 475
Didion, Joan, 8, 63, **161–65**,
400–01, 475
"Different Drummer, A,"
178–80
Dillard, Annie, 64, 66, **72–75**,
359
direct quotation, 426–27
division, and classification,
206–11
documentation
documented paper, 425
of sources, 429–32
"Does America Still Exist?"
314–17
dominant impression, 64, 90
dramatizing, 23, 326–27

Edelson, Ed, 382–87
on using the word
processor, 389
Ehrlich, Gretel, 8, **84–90**
on writing and revising,
92–93
eliminating alternatives, 249
ellipsis, 426
emphasis, 7–8, 325
emphatic repetition, 349
"Erotica and Pornography,"
188–92
evaluative writing, 395–99
standards of, 396–97
exaggeration, 501
experience, personal, 18
extended definition, 288
extended metaphor, 349
extension, 13

Fallows, James, 289
"Family Out of Favor," 276–80
"Fifth Chinese Daughter,"
49–56

figurative language, 349, 475,
493
Finnegan, Sally, 350–51
formal definition, 288
formal writing, 90, 398, 399
Franklin, Benjamin, 474
Friedrich, Otto, 291–92
"Friends, Good Friends—and
Such Good Friends," 226–30

Gelhaus, Anne, 420–21
"Getting MADD," 350–51
Gilder, Joshua, 419–20
"Good Move, A," 129–32
"Good Neighbor, A," 515–16
Goodman, Ellen, 13–14, 172,
219–21, 221–22, 477
Gross, Amy, 194–97
on writing and revising,
198–200
"Growing Up Liberal," 469–70

Hamill, Pete, 328, 329
Harbaugh, William H., 432
Hardin, Garrett, 261–66
Harsham, Richard, 409–11
Hart, Jeffrey, 428
Heinemann, Larry, 433–36
on the process of writing,
438–39
historical terms, 90, 293
historical writing, 423–70
and audience, 424
and benefits for the writer,
424
block quotation, 426
conclusion, 448
direct quotation, 426–27
documented paper, 425
ellipsis, 426
and purpose, 423–24
summary and paraphrase,
427
and thesis, 448
and tone, 437
using and documenting
sources, 425–29
Hoberman, J., 177
Howard, Jane, 301–07
Howarth, William L., 154–55
Hughes, Langston, 425
"Humanity's Better Moments,"
460–67
Huxley, Aldous, 295

"I Have a Dream," 345–48
imaginative comparisons, 8
"In Search of the Good
Family," 301–07
"In Search of Our Mothers'
Gardens," 450–58
inductive pattern, 292, 514
informal essays, 487, 492

informal tone, 398–99, 492
and slang, 399
"Institution Is Not a Dirty
Word," 336–38
introduction, 10, 13
irony, 166, 477

Jacoby, Susan, 108–10
on point of view, 112–13
Jenkinson, Edward B., 103
Johnson, Samuel, 502

Kael, Pauline, 395–96
Kauffmann, Stanley, 396–97,
405–07
Keen, Sam, **222–23**, 246
Keillor, Garrison, 34–38
on story-telling, 39–40
Kettler, Robert R., 296
King, Martin Luther, Jr., 7,
345–48
Kingston, Maxine Hong,
480–85
Kupfer, Fern, 336–38
on writer and audience,
339–40

"L-Mode, R-Mode," 200–01
LaGuardia, Dolores, 390–91
"Land Rush," 156–59
language
concrete, 8
figurative, 349
formal, 399
informal, 399
"Last of the Wild Salmon,"
144–46
Leonard, George, 117–21
Lerner, Neal, 58
Lessard, Susannah, 297–98
on choosing and developing
a topic, 299–300
Lewis, Carolyn, 178–80
Lieberman, Stanley J., 329
"Lifeboat Ethics," 261–66
Lindsay, Robert, 142–43
"Looking Spring in the Eye,"
72–75
Lunt, Mina, 200–01

McBurnie, Diane, 68
McCabe, Charles, 114–15
McCarthy, Mary, 474
McLaughlin, Karen, 282–84
McPhee, John, 23, **148–53**
working methods of, 154–55
Mannes, Marya, 9, **233–38**,
397, 477
material
finding, 4–5
organizing, 5–7
Mead, Margaret, 123–28

media and popular culture,
  393–422
  and audience, 394
  and benefits for the writer,
    394
  and purpose, 393–94
  and tone, 398–99, 407
Mednick, Judy, 427
message, 3–4
metaphor, 153, 475, 493
  extended, 349
  mixed, 476
  sustained, 349
Meyer, Peter, 156–59
Michaels, Leonard, 22–23,
  69–70
Mithers, Carol Lynn, 8
mixed metaphors, 476
"Modest Proposal, A," 494–501
Momaday, N. Scott, 77–82
mood, 298
"Muggers and Morals," 114–15
Mumford, Lewis, 477

Nader, Ralph, 293–94, **309–11**
narration, 25
Neill, A.S., 12
"New Kind of Patriotism, A,"
  309–11
"New Options, New Attitudes,"
  240–42
"New York, New York," 69–70
Novak, Michael, 276–80
"Nuclear Fusion," 374–78
Nyad, Diana, 251

objective writing, 359
observation, 18, 61–95
  and audience, 61–62
  and benefits to the writer, 62
  and chronological order, 65
  and concrete words, 66
  and detail, 63, 64
  and dominant impression,
    90
  and formal writing, 90
  and purpose, 61
  and related terms, 90
  and revision, 92–93
  and spatial order, 65
  and thesis, 65
"Once More to the Lake,"
  487–92
"Oranges," 148–53
order
  chronological, 65
  spatial, 65
organizing material, 5–7
Ortego, Philip D., 250, 325
Orwell, George, **41–47**, 474,
  477, **503–13**
Ouchi, William, 182–86
"Our War Against Nature,"
  368–72

oversimplification, 247

Paine, Thomas, 177
panacea, 248
paradox, 82, 318
parallel order, 174
parallel structure, 477
paraphrase, 427
patterns for writing, 23,
  135–352
  inductive, 292
personal experience, 17, 19–60
  and attitudes, 24
  and audience, 19
  and autobiography, 22
  and benefits for the writer,
    20
  and detail, 22
  and dramatizing, 23
  and feelings, 24
  and narration, 25
  and patterns, 23
  and purpose, 19–20
  and story-telling, 39–40
  and synonyms, 32
persuasion, 323–52
  ad hominem attacks, 329
  and analogy, 343
  antithetical comparisons,
    349
  and audience, 323–24
  and benefits for the writer,
    324
  case history, 328
  challenging opposition,
    328–29
  and comparison, 326–27
  and contrast, 327
  and dramatizing, 326–27
  and emphasis, 325
  and emphatic repetition, 349
  and extended metaphor, 349
  and figurative language, 349
  and purpose, 323
  and statistics, 326
  strategies of, 325–29
  and transition, 343
Piro, Vincent, 26–7
point-by-point comparison, 173
points of view, 18, 97–132
  and audience, 97–98
  and benefits for the writer,
    98
  and examples, 100–01
  and introduction, 100
  and organization, 101–02
  and purpose, 97
  and revision, 129–32
  and selecting an issue, 99
  and thesis, 99–102
  and topic sentence, 103
  and transitional expressions,
    129
"Politics and the English
  Language," 503–13

Pollifrone, Joe, 94
Pope, Alexander, 177, 502
"Pornography and the First
  Amendment," 108–10
"Portraying Rape: Realism and
  Ratings," 420–22
post hoc fallacy, 248
preview, 11
process, 137–169
  and analogy, 142
  and audience, 137–38
  and benefits for the writer,
    138
  and comparison, 142
  and details, 139
  and explanation, 139–40
  and metaphor, 153
  and preview, 140–41
  and purpose, 137, 139
  and technical terms, 142
  and transitions, 141–42, 153
purpose, 2
  and argument, 244
  and classification, 204
  and comparison and
    contrast, 170
  and definition, 286
  and experience, 19
  of imaginative writing, 472
  and media and popular
    culture, 393–94
  and persuasion, 323
  and process, 137
  and science writing, 357
  and taking a stand, 97
  of writing about history,
    423–24
  of writing to evaluate,
    393–94

quotation, block, 426

Raines, Howell, 331
"Real Conservatism, The,"
  297–98
related terms, 90
repetition, emphatic, 349
"Return of Rambo, The,"
  405–07
"Reversing Discrimination,"
  319–20
revision, 92–93, 129–32,
  198–200
"Right Stuff, The," 413–17
Rivera, Edward, 24
Rodriguez, Richard, 314–17
Roiphe, Anne, 24
Romano, Vincent, 398
Rooney, Andy, 402–04
Russell, Catherine A., 167–68

Sagan, Carl, 269–74
Sanders, Marion K., 330–31

satire, 341
scapegoating, 248
Schell, Jonathan, 440–47
science writing, 357–91
  and audience, 357–58
  and benefits for the writer,
    358
  objective writing, 359
  and purpose, 357
  and technical terms, 361–62
scientific terms, 274
sentence style, 9
Shaw, George Bernard, 295,
  476
Sheehan, Susan, 66
"Shooting an Elephant," 41–47
shortcut thinking, 248
simile, 76, 475
slang, 399
"Smart Computers—Now
  They Speak Our Language,"
  382–87
sources, using and
  documenting, 425–29
space, 65
"Sports, Anyone?" 58–59
Steinem, Gloria, 188–92
"Step Forward in the Car,
  Please," 28–32
step-by-step process, 360–61
"Stress: The Combat Zone,"
  282–84
Strum, J., 469–70
style, 474–78
  abstract vs. concrete, 475
  and allusions, 485
  and antithesis, 477
  and aphorisms, 502
  and connotation, 474
  and denotation, 474
  and exaggeration, 501
  and figurative language, 475,
    493
  and informal essays, 487
  and informal tone, 492
  and irony, 477

  and metaphor, 475, 493
  and parallel structure, 477
  and simile, 475
  and word play, 477
summary and paraphrase, 427
supporting testimony, 13
sustained metaphor, 349
Swift, Jonathan, 7, **494–501**,
  502
synonyms, 32, 492

Taliaferro, Frances, 207
"Talking to Apes," 390–91
Taylor, Stuart, Jr., 327
technical terms, 361
"Television: The Splitting
  Image," 233–38
terms
  historical, 90
  related, 90
  technical, 361
"There's One Born Every
  Mihute," 402–04
thesis, 4, 10–11, 13, 65, 99–103,
  307, 448
Thomas, Lewis, 141, 142,
  364–66
Thoreau, Henry David, 9, 474,
  476, 479
"Three Kinds of Fatigue,"
  213–16
title, 9–10
Tobias, Sheila, 252–57
  on math anxiety and writing
    anxiety, 259–60
Toffler, Alvin, 143
tone, 398–99, 407, 437, 492
topic, choosing and
  developing, 299–300
topic sentence, 103, 246
"Tour of Duty," 433–36
transitional expressions, 129,
  175
transitions, 11–12, 153, 246, 343
"Tree-Cutting, Country Style,"
  167–68

Trimmer, Joseph F., 296
Tuchman, Barbara, 460–67
Twain, Mark, 9, 476, 478

Ulibarri, Sabine R., 10

Vietmeyer, Noel, 172–73, 173
Viorst, Judith, 226–30
  on the influence of reading,
    231–32
Vonnegut, Kurt, Jr., 341–43

Walker, Alice, 450–58
"War Preparers Anonymous,"
  341–43
"Warming of the World, The,"
  269–74
"Way to Rainy Mountain, The,"
  77
"We Are What We Do," 13–14
"We Need Taboos on Sex at
  Work," 123–28
"What Happened at
  Hiroshima," 440–47
White, E.B., 477, **487–92**
"Who's Afraid of Math, and
  Why?" 252–57
"Wide Open Spaces," 84–90
Will, George F., 8, 295, **332–34**
  on fact and fiction, 419–20
"Woman Warrior, The," 480–85
Wong, Jade Snow, 49–56, 174
word play, 477
word processor, use of, 389
words
  concrete, 66
  connotative, 367
writing
  formal, 90
  inductive, 514
  informative, 379–81

ACKNOWLEDGMENTS

Interviews with the editors of *Essay 2* appear in this volume with permission of Arthur Ashe, Isaac Asimov, Ed Edelson, Gretel Ehrlich, Amy Gross, Larry Heinemann, Susan Jacoby, Fern Kupfer, Susannah Lessard, and Sheila Tobias.

Veda Anderson, "Reversing Discrimination," is a student editorial from the *Spartan Daily*, Spring 1986.

Maya Angelou, "Step Forward in the Car, Please," is from Maya Angelou, *I Know Why the Caged Bird Sings.* Copyright © 1969 by Maya Angelou. Reprinted with permission of Random House, Inc.

Arthur Ashe, "A Black Athlete Looks at Education," is from *The New York Times.* Copyright © 1977 by The New York Times Company. Reprinted with permission of The New York Times Company.

Isaac Asimov, "Nuclear Fusion," is from *Parade*, February 18, 1979. Reprinted with permission of Parade Publications, Inc. and Isaac Asimov.

Jane Brody, "Three Kinds of Fatigue," is from *The New York Times*, January 23, 1980. Copyright © 1980 by The New York Times Company. Reprinted with permission of The New York Times Company.

Rachel Carson, "Our War Against Nature," is from Rachel Carson, *Silent Spring.* Copyright © 1962 by Rachel Carson. Reprinted with permission of Houghton Mifflin Company.

Marie De Santis, "Last of the Wild Salmon," is adapted from Marie De Santis, *California Currents*, 1985, Chapters 15, 16, and 19. The adaptation originally appeared in the *San Francisco Chronicle*, This World section, July 21, 1985. It is reprinted here with permission of the publisher of *California Currents*, Presidio Press, 31 Pamaron Way, Novato, CA 94947.

Joan Didion, "Bureaucrats," is from Joan Didion, *The White Album.* Copyright © 1979 by Joan Didion. Reprinted with permission of Simon & Schuster, Inc.

Annie Dillard, "Looking Spring in the Eye," is from Annie Dillard, *Pilgrim at Tinker Creek*, pages 117–122. Copyright © 1974 by Annie Dillard. Reprinted with permission of Harper & Row, Publishers, Inc.

Ed Edelson, "Smart Computers—Now They Speak Our Language," is from *Popular Science*, May 1962. © 1982 Times Mirror Magazines, Inc. Reprinted with permission of *Popular Science*.

Gretel Ehrlich, "Wide Open Spaces," is abridged from Gretel Ehrlich, "Wyoming: The Solace of Open Spaces." Copyright © 1981 by The Atlantic Monthly Company, Boston, MA. Reprinted with permission of Gretel Ehrlich.

Sally Finnegan, "Getting MADD," is a student editorial from the *Spartan Daily*, Spring 1986.

Otto Friedrich, "Going Crazy," contains excerpts from an article in *Harper's*, June 1975. The magazine article is an excerpt from the book *Going Crazy* (NY: Simon & Schuster, 1976). The excerpts are reprinted here with permission of Otto Friedrich.

Anne Gelhaus, "Portraying Rape: Realism and Ratings," is a student editorial from the *Spartan Daily*, December 3, 1985.

Joshua Gilder, "Tom Wolfe on Fact and Fiction," is from an interview in Joshua Gilder, "Tom Wolfe," *Saturday Review*, April 1981. © 1981 Saturday Review Magazine. Reprinted with permission of *Saturday Review.*

Ellen Goodman, "We Are What We Do," is from the *Boston Globe*, 1984. © 1984 The Boston Globe Newspaper/Washington Post Writers Group. Reprinted with permission of The Washington Post Company. "The Company Man" and "Super-workingmom or Superdrudge?" are from Ellen Goodman, *Close to Home.* Copyright © 1979 by The Washington Post Company. Reprinted with permission of Simon & Schuster, Inc.

Amy Gross, "The Appeal of the Androgynous Man," is from *Mademoiselle*, May 1976. Copyright © 1976 by The Condé Nast Publications, Inc. Reprinted with permission of Amy Gross.

Garrett Hardin, "Lifeboat Ethics," is from Garrett Hardin, "Lifeboat Ethics: The Case Against Helping the Poor," *Psychology Today*, September 1974. Copyright © 1974 American Psychological Association. Reprinted with permission of *Psychology Today* Magazine.

Richard Harsham, "A Beeper for Violence," is from Richard Harsham, "A Warning Tone for TV Violence," *San Francisco Chronicle*, November 30, 1985, page 32. Reprinted with permission of Richard Harsham.

Larry Heinemann, "Tour of Duty," is from Larry Heinemann, "Just Don't Fit," *Harper's*, April 1985. Copyright © 1985 by Larry Heinemann. Reprinted with permission of Larry Heinemann through his agent, the Ellen Levine Literary Agency, Inc.

Jane Howard, "In Search of the Good Family," is from Jane Howard, "All Happy Clans Are Alike," *Atlantic*, May 1978. Copyright © 1978 by Jane Howard. Reprinted with permission of The Sterling Lord Agency, Inc.

William L. Howarth, "An Editor on McPhee's

Working Methods," is an excerpt from William L. Howarth's Introduction to *The John McPhee Reader.* Copyright © 1977 by Farrar, Straus & Giroux, Inc. Reprinted with permission of Farrar, Straus & Giroux, Inc.

Susan Jacoby, "Pornography and the First Amendment," is from Susan Jacoby, "Notes from a Free-Speech Junkie," *The Possible She.* Copyright © 1973, 1974, 1976, 1977, 1978, 1979 by Susan Jacoby. Reprinted with permission of Farrar, Straus & Giroux, Inc.

Stanley Kauffman, "The Return of Rambo," is from *The New Republic,* July 1, 1985. © 1985 The New Republic, Inc. Reprinted with permission of *The New Republic.*

Sam Keen, "A New Breed," is from Sam Keen, "Lovers vs. Workers," *Quest,* September 15, 1981. Reprinted with permission of Sam Keen.

Garrison Keillor, "Born Among the Born-Again," is from Garrison Keillor, *Lake Wobegon Days,* pages 101–104, 109–110. Copyright © Garrison Keillor 1985. Reprinted with permission of Viking Penguin, Inc. "Garrison Keillor on Story-Telling" contains excerpts from two interviews: "I'm Starting to Believe Lake Wobegon Exists," *USA Today,* October 4, 1985, copyright 1985 *USA Today,* and reprinted with permission of *USA Today;* "Lonesome Whistle Blowing," *Time,* November 4, 1985, copyright 1985 Time Inc., and reprinted with permission of *Time.*

Martin Luther King, Jr., "I Have a Dream," copyright © 1963 by Martin Luther King, Jr. Reprinted with permission of agent Joan Daves.

Maxine Hong Kingston, "The Woman Warrior," is from Maxine Hong Kingston, *The Woman Warrior: Memoirs of a Girlhood Among Ghosts,* pages 45–53. Copyright © 1975, 1986 by Maxine Hong Kingston. Reprinted with permission of Alfred A. Knopf, Inc.

Fern Kupfer, "Institution Is Not a Dirty Word," is condensed from *Newsweek,* December 13, 1982. Copyright © 1982 by Newsweek, Inc. All rights reserved. Reprinted with permission of Newsweek, Inc.

George Leonard, "Born to Run," from *Esquire,* May 1985. Copyright © 1985 George Leonard. Reprinted with permission of The Sterling Lord Agency, Inc.

Susannah Lessard, "The Real Conservatism," is from Susannah Lessard, "Civility, Community, Humor: The Conservatism We Need," *The Washington Monthly,* July/August 1973. Copyright 1973 by The Washington Monthly Company, 2712 Ontario Road, N.W., Washington, D.C. 20009. Reprinted with permission of The Washington Monthly Company.

Carolyn Lewis, "A Different Drummer," is condensed from Carolyn Lewis, "My Unprodigal Sons," *Newsweek,* May 10, 1982. Copyright 1982 by Newsweek, Inc. All rights reserved. Reprinted with permission of Newsweek, Inc.

Charles McCabe, "Muggers and Morals," is from the *San Francisco Chronicle,* September 1981. ©

1981 *San Francisco Chronicle.* Reprinted with permission of the San Francisco Chronicle.

John McPhee, "Oranges," is an excerpt adapted from John McPhee, *Oranges,* pages 126–136. Copyright © 1966, 1967 by John McPhee. Reprinted with permission of Farrar, Straus & Giroux, Inc.

Marya Mannes, "Television: The Splitting Image," is from the *Saturday Review,* November 14, 1970. Copyright © 1971 by Marya Mannes. Reprinted with permission of the author's agent, David J. Blow.

Margaret Mead, "We Need Taboos on Sex at Work," is from *Redbook,* April 1978. Reprinted with permission of Rhoda Metraux and Mary Catherine Bateson.

Peter Meyer, "Land Rush," is from *Harper's,* January 1979. Copyright © 1978 by Harper's Magazine. All rights reserved. Reprinted with permission of Harper's Magazine.

Leonard Michaels, "New York, New York," is from Leonard Michaels, "The Visit," *The New York Times,* October 26, 1975. Copyright © 1975 by The New York Times Company. Reprinted with permission of The New York Times Company.

N. Scott Momaday, "The Way to Rainy Mountain," is from N. Scott Momaday, *The Way to Rainy Mountain.* © 1969 by the University of New Mexico Press. First published in *The Reporter,* January 26, 1967. Reprinted with permission of the University of New Mexico Press.

Ralph Nader, "A New Kind of Patriotism," is from Ralph Nader, "We Need a New Kind of Patriotism," *Life,* July 9, 1971, page 4. © 1971 Time Inc. Reprinted with permission of Life Picture Service.

Michael Novak, "The Family Out of Favor," is from *Harper's,* April 1976. Copyright © 1976 by Harper's Magazine. All rights reserved. Reprinted with permission of Harper's Magazine.

George Orwell, "Shooting an Elephant" and "Politics and the English Language," are from George Orwell, *Shooting an Elephant and Other Essays.* "Shooting an Elephant," copyright © 1950 by Sonia Brownell Orwell, renewed 1978 by Sonia Pitt-Rivers. "Politics and the English Language," copyright 1946 by Sonia Brownell Orwell, renewed 1974 by Sonia Orwell. Reprinted with permission of Harcourt Brace Jovanovich, Inc. and A. M. Heath & Company Limited, agents for the estate of the late Sonia Brownell Orwell and Martin Secker & Warburg Ltd.

William Ouchi, "The Competitive Edge: Japanese and Americans," is from William Ouchi, *Theory Z,* pages 47–51, 64–66. © 1981 Addison-Wesley Publishing Company, Inc., Reading, MA. Reprinted with permission of Addison-Wesley Publishing Company, Inc.

Richard Rodriguez, "Does America Still Exist?" is from *Harper's,* March 1984. Copyright © 1984 by Richard Rodriguez. Reprinted with permission of Georges Borchardt, Inc., agents for the author.